REINVENTING
IDENTITIES

STUDIES IN LANGUAGE AND GENDER
Mary Bucholtz, *General Editor*

Advisory Board
Penelope Eckert, Stanford University
Kira Hall, Yale University
Janet Holmes, Victoria University of Wellington, New Zealand
Miyako Inoue, Stanford University
Don Kulick, University of Stockholm
Sally McConnell-Ginet, Cornell University
Marcyliena Morgan, University of California, Los Angeles/Harvard University
Deborah Tannen, Georgetown University
Ana Celia Zentella, Hunter College, City University of New York

Reinventing Identities: The Gendered Self in Discourse
    Edited by Mary Bucholtz, A. C. Liang, and Laurel A. Sutton

REINVENTING IDENTITIES

The Gendered Self in Discourse

Edited by

Mary Bucholtz

A. C. Liang

Laurel A. Sutton

New York   Oxford

OXFORD UNIVERSITY PRESS

1999

Oxford University Press

Oxford   New York
Athens   Auckland   Bangkok   Bogotá   Buenos Aires   Calcutta
Cape Town   Chennai   Dar es Salaam   Delhi   Florence   Hong Kong   Istanbul
Karachi   Kuala Lumpur   Madrid   Melbourne   Mexico City   Mumbai
Nairobi   Paris   São Paulo   Singapore   Taipei   Tokyo   Toronto   Warsaw

and associated companies in
Berlin   Ibadan

Copyright © 1999 by Oxford University Press

Published by Oxford University Press, Inc.
198 Madison Avenue, New York, New York 10016

Oxford is a registered trademark of Oxford University Press, Inc.

Library of Congress Cataloging-in-Publication Data
Reinventing identities : the gendered self in discourse
/ edited by Mary Bucholtz, A. C. Liang, and Laurel A. Sutton.
p.   cm. — (Studies in Language and Gender : 1)
Includes bibliographical references and index.
ISBN 0-19-512629-7; ISBN 0-19-512630-0 (pbk.)
1. Language and languages—Sex differences.   2. Gender identity.
I. Bucholtz, Mary, 1966– .   II. Liang, A. C.   III. Sutton, Laurel A.
IV. Series.
P120.S48R47   1999
306.44—dc21   98-50041

9 8 7 6 5 4 3 2 1

Printed in the United States of America
on acid-free paper

To the memory of D. Letticia Galindo (1952–1998),
whose pioneering work has helped
to reinvent language and gender studies

SERIES FOREWORD

In the past decade, the subfield of linguistics known as language and gender studies has undergone an intellectual renaissance. From its original concern with sexist language in the 1970s to the 1980s' debate over "difference" and "dominance" models, language and gender research in the 1990s has developed its links to feminist and social theory and expanded its scope to include the interaction of gender with race, ethnicity, sexuality, social class, nationality, and other dimensions of social identity. This new body of work builds on the foundations of earlier research while integrating key insights of recent theory.

Such research has interdisciplinary relevance: current scholarship addresses a wide audience, offering insights not only to linguists but also to researchers in anthropology, sociology, ethnic studies, gender studies, and related disciplines. Yet, despite the topic's enduring interdisciplinary interest and the outpouring of important new scholarship, there has never been a series devoted to language and gender research until now.

Oxford's series Studies in Language and Gender fills this gap by offering a broad-based interdisciplinary forum for the best new scholarship in the field. The mandate of the series is to encourage innovative work on language and gender, a goal that may be achieved through the revisitation of familiar topics from fresh vantage points, through the introduction of new avenues of research, or through new theoretical or methodological frameworks. This emphasis ensures that the rejuvenated field of language and gender will continue to be replenished with original research. The series is also interdisciplinary in its scope: volumes may be authored by scholars in such disciplines as anthropology, sociology, literary studies, education, psychology, ethnic studies, and women's studies, as well as linguistics.

As the inaugural volume of Studies in Language and Gender, *Reinventing Identities* offers a broad vision of what the field of language and gender studies will look like in the new millennium. *Reinventing Identities* is as wide-ranging as gender it-self, which takes on new and surprising forms in new contexts. The volume emerges from what might be called the "third wave" of language and gender scholarship. The goal of this new approach is to understand the diversity of gendered experiences as they play out in a variety of situations. Third-wave language and gender research makes explicit its connections to feminist theory; of particular significance are those constructionist perpectives that emphasize how gender identities and ideologies are achieved in discourse. But this approach does not examine language to the exclusion of other social practices, such as physical self-presentation, gesture and movement, and activities. Such details are crucial for arriving at specific, local forms of gender, in contrast to approaches that aim for a general description of "women's use of lan-guage." *Reinventing Identities* counters this well-intentioned but reductive strategy with a series of studies of gender on the ground, formed under conditions of commu-nity and contact, shaped moment by moment through the details of discourse.

The fluidity of gender illustrated by the chapters of this volume suggests an al-ternative to more totalizing frameworks, an alternative that respects the variety of gendered selves that discourse makes possible. *Reinventing Identities* attends to myriad cultural forms of gender: within the U.S. context, chapters focus variously on African Americans, Latinos, Native Americans, and European Americans; on a more global scale, contributors examine discursive gender relations in local contexts in Europe and Africa, as well as in North America. And via the influence of the emer-gent field of queer linguistics, *Reinventing Identities* includes a sizable number of studies of sexuality as well as gender, the first volume of its kind to have substantial representation of both fields of inquiry.

A contextually and theoretically rich collection of studies of the gendering, ungendering, and regendering of language, *Reinventing Identities* is an important contribution to the field's current reinvention of itself. The volume invites scholars and students alike to rethink what it means to study the intersection of language and gender and where that intersection is located. The answers offered in its many chap-ters are as diverse, diffuse, and dispersed as the gendered selves who populate these pages. This undoing of a single unified tale of language and gender is the first step to envisioning new forms of feminist scholarship within linguistics.

—Mary Bucholtz,
Series Editor

The *Reinventing Identities* Web site, featuring additional data, graphics, and audio and video clips from the studies in this book, can be found at http://www-english.tamu.edu/pers/fac/bucholtz/oslg/re-id

CONTENTS

CONTRIBUTORS

Rusty Barrett
  Department of Linguistics,
  University of Texas, Austin
Mary Bucholtz
  Department of English,
  Texas A&M University
Lisa Capps
  Department of Psychology,
  University of California, Berkeley
Jennifer Coates
  Department of English,
  Roehampton Institute, London
Colleen Cotter
  Department of Linguistics,
  Georgetown University
Rebecca J. Dobkins
  Department of Sociology and
  Anthropology, Willamette University
Marjorie Harness Goodwin
  Department of Anthropology,
  University of California,
  Los Angeles
Caitlin Hines
  Department of English,
  San Francisco State University
William Leap
  Department of Anthropology,
  American University
A. C. Liang
  Department of Linguistics,
  University of California, Berkeley
Anna Livia
  Department of French,
  University of Illinois, Urbana-
  Champaign

Norma Mendoza-Denton
  Department of Anthropology,
  University of Arizona
Marcyliena Morgan
  Department of Anthropology,
  University of California,
  Los Angeles
  Graduate School of Education,
  Harvard University
Marjorie Faulstich Orellana
  School of Education and Social
  Policy, 3Northwestern University
Patricia E. Sawin
  Department of Anthropology,
  University of North Carolina,
  Chapel Hill
Laurel A. Sutton
  Department of Linguistics,
  University of California, Berkeley
Deborah Tannen
  Department of Linguistics,
  Georgetown University
Sara Trechter
  Department of English,
  California State University, Chico
Keith Walters
  Department of Linguistics,
  University of Texas, Austin
Kathleen M. Wood
  Department of English,
  Gallaudet University

REINVENTING
IDENTITIES

Bad Examples

Transgression and Progress in Language and Gender Studies

Reinventing language and gender scholarship

For much of its existence, language and gender research has had an uneasy relationship with feminist theory. Following an initial flurry of interest in linguistic approaches at the beginning of the second wave of feminism in the late 1960s and early 1970s, feminist theory retained its concern with language but soon found less inspiration in linguistics than in surrounding disciplines such as philosophy and literary criticism. At the material level, this tension has been manifest in the disproportionately low representation of linguists, broadly defined, in women's studies programs, conferences, and journals. At the intellectual level, the divide between the two enterprises has been evident until very recently in each field's relative lack of influence on the development of the other.

The reasons for this absence of communication are complex. In part it can be attributed to the scientific urge of much linguistic research, a paradigm that has been called into question by numerous feminist scholars (Harding 1991; Longino 1990). Moreover, working within the discipline of linguistics, which especially in the United States has been much slower than the other social sciences to shift its focus from the "science" to the "social" aspect of its intellectual mandate, feminist linguists have been cautious about the use of politically progressive theory in our scholarship. Some of the problem can also be ascribed to the small size of linguistics as a discipline and the resultant difficulty of forming a critical mass of influential feminist work, as our counterparts in sociology, sociocultural anthropology, and literary studies are more easily able to do. For their part, feminist theorists have often framed their concerns in such broad terms that language and gender scholars, with our attention to the fine details of language, have had difficulty seeing ourselves in contemporary discussions.

But recent changes in the shape of both fields augur the possibility of productive new interactions between language and gender on the one hand and feminist theory on the other. The rapid expansion of the subfield of discourse analysis within linguistics and the extension of its theoretical and methodological insights to many other disciplines have raised the profile of linguistics within the academy and have provided the conditions in which other branches of linguistics can finally get a new hearing within feminist scholarship. Most crucially, the fundamental observation of discourse analysis, that speakers' identities emerge from discourse, is highly compatible with the social-constructivist bent of much current feminist research. Conversely, feminist theory's vital interest in identity, which is now viewed as a local production rather than an enduring category, addresses a central yet largely unexamined dimension of language and gender research. With the advent of discursive approaches to identity and with the more contextual analyses of both language and identity that they enable, it may now be possible for language and gender scholars and feminist theorists to pool our resources in a shared intellectual enterprise.

Thus despite the current boom in language and gender scholarship, this volume is both timely and necessary: timely because it builds on existing work and necessary because, although its methods derive from linguistics, its theoretical question is taken from feminist theory.[1] To reinvent identity within language and gender research is to do nothing less than reinvent the field itself. In making the first steps toward a new alliance with feminist theory, the authors in this volume often exceed the boundaries of what is considered the core of language and gender scholarship. By investigating new sites by means of new methods and theories, as well as by casting a new eye on traditional research problems, the contributors to *Reinventing Identities* transgress—and thereby transcend—the limitations of business as usual both within linguistics as a whole and in the small corner of the discipline inhabited by language and gender.

Language and the identity crisis in feminist theory

If language and gender scholars are to explore the question of identity, we must enter into dialogue with feminist theorists, for the problem of contemporary feminism is the question of identity. Earlier varieties of feminism either finessed the question (by assuming the universality of the experience of white Western heterosexual women of the middle class) or reduced it to an ontological first principle (by taking an essential difference between women and men as axiomatic). More recent scholarship, however, has engaged the issue fully, recognizing that gender identity is at once more specific than most 1970s feminism realized and more fluid than much 1980s feminism allowed. Debates continue but on different terms: Where previously to dissent from the predominant feminist position was to assert that identity was, in fact, a problem (see hooks 1981; Hull, Scott, & Smith 1982), currently the disagreement lies in how to characterize the *kind* of problem that identity is (cf. Weir 1996). Indeed, as illustrated by two of the most important books in feminist theory in the past decade, Gloria Anzaldúa's edited collection *Making Face, Making Soul / Haciendo Caras* and Judith Butler's *Gender Trouble*, both published in 1990, despite considerable theoretical differences most contemporary feminist scholars agree that identity is far less static than previously thought:

> "Making faces" is my metaphor for constructing one's identity. . . . In our self-reflectivity and in our active participation with the issues that confront us, whether it be through writing, front-line activism, or individual self-development, we are also uncovering the inter-faces, the very spaces and places where our multiple-surfaced, colored, racially gendered bodies intersect and interconnect. (Anzaldúa 1990:xvi)

> Just as bodily surfaces are enacted *as* the natural, so these surfaces can become the site of a dissonant and denaturalized performance that reveals the performative status of the natural itself. . . . As the effects of a subtle and politically enforced performativity, gender is an "act," as it were, that is open to splittings, self-parody, self-criticism, and those hyperbolic exhibitions of "the natural" that, in their very exaggeration, reveal its fundamentally phantasmatic status. (Butler 1990:146–147)

Both Anzaldúa and Butler view identity as a construct. In this regard their theories mesh with the insights of recent language and gender scholarship. They differ, however, in the role they assign to the body. For Anzaldúa, gender and other aspects of identity are inextricably interconnected, so that bodies are not simply racial *and* gendered but "racia*lly* gendered." (See also Morgan, chapter 1, and Orellana, chapter 3, this volume.) Butler, on the other hand, views the body as the stage on which gender is performed, where elements of the self, rather than being uncovered, as Anzaldúa proposes, are projected and made to seem natural and, at times, unnatural. Such debates over the body have historically been remote from the concerns of language and gender researchers, but we would do well to attend to the discussions that have developed from the two positions staked out by Anzaldúa and Butler. This is so not only because feminist linguists are becoming aware of the importance of the body in language-based studies (see, for example, Goodwin, chapter 20, and Walters, chapter 10, this volume) but also because both theories, like most current strands of feminism, are predicated, as we will see, on the centrality of language. However, although bodies have come to matter in feminist theory—not only in the broad theoretical sense envisioned by French feminists such as Luce Irigaray (1985a, b) but also in the details of color, age, and so on—feminism has not yet accorded the same attention to the details of language. Hence feminist theory's current interest in the embodiment of language requires a fuller consideration of language itself, a task that language and gender researchers are well positioned to carry out. To avoid replaying the backlash against linguistics in the past, however, it is necessary to understand the history of linguistic analysis within feminism.

The linguistic focus of much recent feminist theory has its roots in feminism's second wave. At that time, scholarship on the language used by, to, and about women was part of the feminist project of documenting the dailiness of gender oppression (see discussion in Thorne, Kramarae, & Henley 1983). Most influential were studies of how language itself was implicated in women's subjugation through pejorative referring terms (Lakoff 1975; Schulz 1975; Stanley 1977) and overgeneralized male forms such as the use of the masculine pronoun as generic (Bodine 1975; Dubois &

Crouch 1987), as well as through power imbalances in cross-sex interactions (Fishman 1983; West & Zimmerman 1983). In the picture painted by such research, all women were oppressed by the overriding force of language. By making language visible and subjecting it to political analysis, language and gender scholarship furthered the feminist aim of uncovering the workings of male dominance everywhere in society. Though belittled or ignored by the scholars' own nonfeminist colleagues, this work had a profound impact on feminists in all disciplines.

However, opposition to research within this paradigm soon emerged within feminist circles as well. In the face of critiques, especially by women of color, feminist theory has moved away from an exclusive focus on the undifferentiated category of 'woman' and toward a recognition of the diversity of identities that such a vast cover term obscures. Formerly central issues of language have become less relevant in this context, but the new analytical frameworks pose new linguistic questions. Previously, feminist researchers, both within and outside the field of language and gender, framed the problem in terms of how language affects gender. The question now becomes how language *effects* gender. Thus where women were once cast as victims of the masculine power of language, they are now viewed instead as active language users in their own right. Yet the issue of power has not been set aside; rather, instead of invoking an invisible and omnipotent patriarchy as the source of power whereby women are interrupted and silenced, researchers have begun to examine the disruptions of this hegemonic system, the moments when women's voices interrupt the dominant discourse and subversive identities break through (cf. Dobkins, chapter 9, and Sutton, chapter 8, this volume). In acknowledging the complexity of women's identities, then, current feminist theorists also acknowledge the complexity of women's relationship to language.

During the period of rapid change wrought by feminists of color, the specificity of women's bodies became increasingly important in feminist theory. Likewise, as queer theory developed, the female body as the subject of feminism itself was called into doubt, and the field of gender theory emerged. This complexity is evident in the work of both Anzaldúa and Butler. The subjects of Anzaldúa's variety of feminism are women of color, who face both sexism and racism as well as other forms of power. The multiple identity positions they occupy offer multiple voices with which to speak: "When we come into possession of a voice, we sometimes have to choose with which voice (the voice of the dyke, the Chicana, the professor, the master), in which voice (first person, third, vernacular, formal) or in which language (Black English, Tex-Mex, Spanish, academese) to speak and write in" (Anzaldúa 1990:xxiii). In keeping with the theoretical emphasis of much multicultural feminism, Anzaldúa's view of language highlights the multifaceted nature of the self. No aspect of identity has priority and no language linked to these identities is privileged over any other. In fact, by legitimating such "impure" linguistic varieties as "Tex-Mex" (that is, Spanish-English codeswitching; see also Anzaldúa 1987) on par with prestigious forms such as "academese," Anzaldúa implicitly challenges the cultural hierarchy in which certain languages and the identities that they render are valued over others. Choosing such a voice is an act of rebellion against the power of linguistic ideology. She thus clearly separates herself from earlier feminist preoccupations: agency, choice, and voice here replace passivity, oppression, and silence.

Butler, too, considers how language mediates between the individual and wider cultural hegemonies: "Language is not an *exterior medium or instrument* into which I pour a self and from which I glean a reflection of that self. . . . Indeed to understand identity as a *practice*, and as a signifying practice, is to understand culturally intelligible subjects as the resulting effects of a rule-bound discourse that inserts itself in the pervasive and mundane signifying acts of linguistic life" (Butler 1990:143–145). Butler suggests that selfhood is manufactured through language. Identity is not a category at all for her; instead it is a semiotic activity whereby individuals are made to make cultural "sense." Yet there is space for dissent in this framework: Those who resist the dictates of the culture by troubling its categories highlight the constructed nature of these divisions.[2]

In this volume, some scholars implicitly align themselves with Anzaldúa and note the multiplicity of selves available to speakers (see, e.g., Barrett, chapter 16; Coates, chapter 6; Cotter, chapter 19; and Orellana, chapter 3), as well as the multiplicity of identities within what is often wrongly seen as a monolithic social category (Goodwin, chapter 20; Mendoza-Denton, chapter 14; Morgan, chapter 1; Sawin, chapter 12). Other researchers focus, as Butler (1990) does, on the hegemonic linguistic forces against which women and girls struggle and to which they sometimes capitulate (Capps, chapter 4; Dobkins, chapter 9; Hines, chapter 7; Livia, chapter 17) and on the linguistic practices, filtered through cultural ideologies, through which gender identities, both "culturally intelligible" and otherwise, are produced (Leap, chapter 13; Tannen, chapter 11; Trechter, chapter 5; Walters, chapter 10). Still others bring the two paradigms together by underscoring the interaction between fluid identities and rigid social structures (Bucholtz, chapter 18; Liang, chapter 15; Sutton, chapter 8; Wood, chapter 2). All these authors take intellectual risks—methodological, theoretical, and political—to advance the field of language and gender. In so doing they follow a time-honored tradition in language and gender studies of challenging the boundaries of permissible, respectable research. The past decades of scholarship provide numerous such "bad examples" for our contemplation: daring studies of the relationship between language and gender that were often criticized or misunderstood in their own day or that, though set aside too soon, have made crucial contributions to the present state of the field.[3] Like much of this previous work, the present studies are especially notable for their use of feminist and other social theory and their far-sighted analyses of identity. Also significant is their recognition of identity as a practice rather than a category, an actively constructed performance rather than a pre-existing role; their concern with identities that deviate from the traditional focus of scholarship; and their consideration of the balance between individual agency and structural inequality.

Bad habits: Identities in practice and performance

Much language and gender research in the past two decades has subscribed to the social-scientific premise that identity is a category that individuals inhabit. Analyses compared the linguistic behavior of women and men (usually in cross-sex interaction) as aggregates and did not discuss within-group differences. Membership in such groups, as well as in lesser-discussed groups based on race, ethnicity, or class, was viewed as self-evident. Meanwhile, locally defined groupings based on ongoing activities and concerns were rarely given scholarly attention; if they were, members were assigned to large-scale categories of gender, race, ethnicity, and class. During the same period, feminist theory was undergoing the above-described transformation initiated by the work of women of color, and it abandoned the category model of identity. Consequently, language and gender studies, which had in the 1970s been central to the feminist project, separated from other feminist research.

Not surprisingly, then, Penelope Eckert and Sally McConnell-Ginet's (1992) introduction of the community-of-practice model quickly revolutionized language and gender research. Although formulated in terms of community, the theory is easily applied to identity as well, for it shifts the focus from groups as undifferentiated categories to complex configurations of individuals acting in part together and in part separately. This new focus on individuals is part of a wider urge in sociolinguistics and language and gender (Johnstone 1996; Johnstone & Bean 1997). In this volume, for example, Keith Walters (chapter 10) revisits cross-sex interaction in a way that highlights the situated, embodied experiences of the individual speakers, and Norma Mendoza-Denton (chapter 14) and Patricia Sawin (chapter 12) each, in different ways, demonstrate how individual and cultural specificities interact in language use.

Eckert and McConnell-Ginet's emphasis on action as the basis of community renewed an interest in local, activity-based identities.[4] Participants in such activities assume a variety of roles and identities whose relevance varies from moment to moment. In this volume Colleen Cotter (chapter 19) and Deborah Tannen (chapter 11) both show how in workplace communities of practice, an understudied arena in language and gender studies compared to private contexts, "the difference that difference makes" is specific to speaker, situation, and other factors.

The display of the self in public settings also suggests another practice-based aspect of identity: performance. Widely used (though with a narrower definition) in linguistic anthropology (e.g., Bauman 1977; Briggs 1988; Hymes 1981) before it came to be popularized in gender theory (Parker & Sedgwick 1995), the concept of performance in current language and gender research highlights the fact that membership in particular communities and the identities they authorize is achieved rather than assigned: As Kathleen Wood (chapter 2) demonstrates, coherent lesbian or Deaf identities arise through participation in community practices that stand partly in opposition to hegemonic ideologies of heterosexuality and the hearing world. Such violation of biased cultural norms may lead to the misclassification of speakers as deviant or deficient: Marjorie Goodwin (chapter 20) argues that when girls play *with* the rules rather than *by* the rules in hopscotch games, researchers may fail to see that girls' games have any rules at all, when in fact girls' creative adaptation of preexisting structures allows them to project a range of local interactional identities.

A practice-based analysis thus forces scholars to reassess apparent inadequacies of speakers; one of the great strengths of the community-of-practice model, especially as originally articulated by education theorists Jean Lave and Etienne Wenger (1991), is that "marginal" members—novices, learners, and so forth—move to the center of analysis. In this dynamic framework, *practice* takes on a double meaning, suggesting both habitual social action and rehearsal for later social action—that is, for performance. Jennifer Coates (chapter 6) and William Leap (chapter 13) both invoke the second sense of *practice* in their discussions of linguistic, gender, and sexual socialization of adolescents. For Coates, adolescent girls' friendship talk provides a "backstage" (in Goffman's 1959 sense) in which to "try on" identities; Leap shows how gay adolescents start their "gender careers" by exploring gay resources in books, films, and other media.

Perhaps most important, the focus on practice in recent work reminds linguists that language is only one social activity among many and that it takes much of its meaning (both social and referential) from the other practices that surround it. Many contributors to this volume, recognizing the importance of such contextualizing information, provide images and rich descriptions of the words and activities of language users. Attention to such practices is often dismissed as "not linguistics," but like Goodwin's hopscotch players, the contributors to *Reinventing Identities* insist that breaking the rules is part of the game.

Bad girls: Transgressive identities

As the new focus on the margins of community membership may imply, another way that innovative language and gender researchers have set a "bad example" in their research is by using "bad examples" of speakers and linguistic phenomena. Much of the scholarship in language and gender has been what might be called "good-girl research": studies of "good" (that is, normatively female—white, straight, middle-class) women being "good" (that is, normatively feminine). Such research has been a necessary starting point. Yet this definition of what counts as a "good" example excludes many groups and practices. In fact, as Marjorie Orellana's research suggests, how girls use language to experiment with "badness" is itself a crucial question for feminist linguists. Being "good" is not a natural attribute but one constructed through the interplay of language and social expectation. "Bad" girls and women may pose problems for neat theories and hence be eliminated from research as atypical. What research does exist often succumbs to the urge to pathologize or exoticize such speakers. Conversely, speakers who conform precisely to cultural stereotypes of femininity, such as the drag queens in Rusty Barrett's study (chapter 16), are nevertheless almost entirely overlooked in language and gender research, not because of their anomalous femininity but because of their anomalous femaleness (but for examples of the growing scholarship on language and gender transgression, see Gaudio 1997; Hall & O'Donovan 1996; Kulick 1996). Barrett's chapter demonstrates the limitations of traditional definitions of the speech community as the locus of language and identity, for as developed in sociolinguistics by William Labov (1972a, b), membership in the speech community is a measure of cultural and linguistic authenticity as determined by gender, class, ethnicity, and other social factors. The artifice of many linguistic performances and practices cannot be accounted for in the Labovian framework. My study (chapter 18) of the shopping channel as an artificial community that constructs its own authenticity from consumers' linguistic practices indicates that authenticity is itself a production, not an objective measure of community membership and identity.

To display a transgressive identity is to risk not only exclusion but also retribution. Thus as A. C. Liang (chapter 15) shows, gay and lesbian speakers whose identities may put them in danger develop self-protective linguistic practices that allow them to reveal their identities only to those who are likely to be sympathetic. In a world where simply *being* can count as being bad, identities are often constructed in opposition to dominant cultural ideologies.

Bad subjects: The politics of gender identity

Such resistant identities recall Louis Althusser's famous declaration regarding the "bad subjects" of the state: "the 'bad subjects' . . . on occasion provoke the intervention of one of the detachments of the (repressive) State apparatus. But the vast majority of (good) subjects work all right 'all by themselves,' i.e. by ideology . . ." (1971:181). In the battle between the bad subjects and the forces of hegemony, language is a double-edged sword. Numerous social theorists have recognized the close relation between language and systems of power (see, e.g., Bourdieu 1991; Foucault 1980). Caitlin Hines (chapter 7) shows how this relationship plays out in the English lexicon, and Sara Trechter (chapter 5) reveals its workings in the verbal system of the Lakhota language. These analyses of gender ideology improve on earlier work: Hines demonstrates both the details of sexism in the linguistic system and the details of the linguistic system in sexism, and Trechter shows how the system is used in practice.

Practice-based research must also recognize the dynamism of language and thus the possibility of changing structural biases. Anna Livia (chapter 17) recounts the history of one widely debated attempt at feminist linguistic engineering. Women's agency, as exemplified by Livia, is in fact a central component of new research on the power of cultural ideologies in women's lives. Whereas earlier work portrayed women as passive victims of male power and privilege, recent scholarship also recognizes women's active contributions even in situations of extreme power imbalance. At times, women's struggle for autonomy and self-definition in interaction with men may only result in greater disempowerment, as Lisa Capps (chapter 4) shows. At other times, women's efforts are more successful, although they may be forced to rely on the linguistic tools of their oppressors to insist on their own identities—Rebecca Dobkins's study (chapter 9) of Native American women's letters to federal officials offers an illustration of this situation. Yet women may find alternative discursive forms, even, as Laurel Sutton describes in her work (chapter 8) on underground zines and online publications, reshaping male-dominated discourse domains to accommodate their expressions of resistant selves.

As women change the shape of cultural discourse, the contours of intellectual discourse are changing as well. Earlier critiques concerning the homogeneity of feminist theory have also had effects in language and gender scholarship. Thus the present volume features work on Latinas by Goodwin, Mendoza-Denton, and Orellana; on African Americans by Barrett and Morgan; on Native Americans by Dobkins and Trechter; and on non-Western women by Walters, as well as on lesbians and gay men by Barrett, Leap, Liang, and Wood. Many chapters in this book also contribute implicitly or explicitly to the recent project to interrogate previously invisible hegemonic categories such as whiteness, masculinity, heterosexuality, and the middle class (see the chapters by Barrett, Bucholtz, Wood, and others). New approaches to power in language and gender scholarship likewise require that linguists recognize their own complicity in the reproduction of inequities based on gender, race, class, and other factors. Marcyliena Morgan (chapter 1) describes the social and cultural censure that many African Americans level against the act of "breaking bad," or pretending to a level of knowledge that one does not in fact have. Unlike the other forms of researcher "badness" delineated above, "breaking bad" cannot be recuperated for feminist use, for it results in acts of scholarly negligence and harm ranging from wrongful omission to misrepresentation to out-and-out inaccuracies. Both Morgan and Sara Trechter point out instances in which linguists represent dominated social groups as exotic "others" who are portrayed as fundamentally different from the normative, dominant group. Their work reminds language and gender scholars that reflexivity must always be a part of research and that as we move further from the confines of "good-girl" research we have an increasingly heavy obligation to describe speakers and the worlds in which they move without the distorting effects of our own cultural and intellectual ideologies about how such speakers "should" or "must" be. Considering how linguistics itself has contributed to the promotion of such ideologies will help ensure that as we strive to be "bad examples," we do not produce bad research.

Overview of the volume

Taking seriously the diverse resources available to language users for identity construction, the chapters of *Reinventing Identities* draw on a variety of linguistic forms and contexts. Thus the authors examine every linguistic level, from phonetics and phonology to discourse phenomena, from lexical and semantic issues to broader pragmatic processes. In the realm of discourse, contributors turn to conversation, narrative, and activity-based language use, as well as to written language and media representations of the social world, recognizing that the practices associated with all such linguistic arenas may be conscious attempts to subvert social norms or the result of the speaker's effort to synthesize public displays and private imaginings of the self. The authors also consider a range of identities, from the most locally and interactionally grounded participant roles to the broadest transhistorical stereotypes, from identities rooted in race, ethnicity, sexuality, and class to those based on membership in social groups and communities of practice to those associated with large-scale social categories and imagined communities produced by industrialization, technology, and nationalism. This recognition of the multiple manifestations of the self in linguistic practice allows contributors to *Reinventing Identities* to avoid the narrowness of earlier analyses and to explore dimensions of identity hitherto uninvestigated in the field of language and gender.

The volume is divided into four parts, which describe the ways that identities, both chosen and imposed, are created, shaped, and altered across times, places, speakers, and contexts. The first part, "Identity as Invention," locates the originary moment in the construction of a variety of gendered identities. Next, "Identity as Ideology" explores the manifold ways that larger social forces may impose and perpetuate identities through language use. "Identity as Ingenuity" addresses the creative strategies that speakers employ in response to hegemonic expectations. Finally, "Identity as Improvisation" examines the emergence of new identities that rework traditional formulations of selfhood while engaging language in innovative ways.

Identity as invention

The chapters in part I make visible the often invisible process of identity construction through language use, thereby challenging the essentialist notion that gender identities are inevitable, natural, and fixed. All the chapters share the insight that identities, far from being given in advance for individuals to step into, emerge over time through discursive and other social practices. Nor is identity construction an exclusively individual act; instead, social selves are produced in interaction, through processes of contestation and collaboration.

The section opens with Marcyliena Morgan's overview of research on African American women's speech. African American linguistic practice holds a central place in the consolidation of sociolinguistics as a discipline, and Morgan points out that this situation has led to the generalization of models of African American identity that were first developed in research on lower-class vernacular-speaking urban adolescent male gang members. The speech of those who fall outside these parameters—especially female and middle-class African Americans—has been marginalized in research on the grounds that it is less authentic. Morgan corrects the biases of prior research by focusing on the language use of African American girls and women at different life stages. She shows that speech events such as signifying, instigating, and reading dialect have different degrees of social salience for children, teenagers, and adults, each of whom may enact them in different ways and for different purposes. These speech events are united, however, by their role in the interactive construction of "face" as part of a speaker's social identity and as part of a specifically African American cultural identity. Morgan's attention to the temporal dimension highlights the fact that identities are not static or universal across members of a group but are shaped over time through dialogic processes among speakers.

The creation of a shared cultural identity is also central to the work of Kathleen Wood (chapter 2) on Deaf and hearing lesbians' tellings of coming-out stories on the Internet, in writing, and in American Sign Language. Contrary to theories of lesbian identity that posit a priori commonalities among lesbians, Wood argues that the lesbians in her study actively create their on-line community through shared linguistic practices. Although such stories vary widely in their structure and content, they have in common their engagement with ideologies of normative heterosexuality, to which they respond. Wood's findings thus force a revision of frameworks that assert that local communities are structurally self-contained entities. Additionally, her research suggests that lesbian identity may intersect with other dimensions of the self such as Deafness. Like Morgan's findings for African American speakers, Wood's study indicates that culturally recognized speech events may be used to construct social identities. Moreover, the identities produced in coming-out stories may vary according to the resources available in the communicative medium and are therefore closely bound to the circumstances of narrative production.

Wood's insight that narrative content and communicative medium work together to create identity is supported by Marjorie Faulstich Orellana's research (chapter 3) on the written narratives of Latina and Latino children from low-income families in a Los Angeles classroom. Orellana examined the in-class production of student-authored books over the course of many months and found that children often wrote themselves into their stories as a way of trying on possible identities. Many of these fictive identities—such as superheroes, racing champions, and so on—projected students into positions that challenged the constraints of racism and poverty, but most storylines reproduced gendered expectations about who and what students could be. Girls often wrote stories that emphasized the importance of being good, whereas naughtiness was much more prominent in boys' stories about themselves. Such ideological restrictions were even more pronounced when students cast one another in their stories—for example, boys often placed girls in supportive or passive roles. Orellana concludes that students' imaginative writing is closely tied to the realities and possibilities of their lives, and although free-writing classes like the one she studied may have some liberatory potential, for many students, especially working-class girls of color, storytelling is an activity fraught with issues of power and inequality.

The recognition that identities may be simultaneously chosen and imposed through language use, a recognition that is fundamental to Orellana's research, is also central to Lisa Capps's work (chapter 4). Likewise, both authors demonstrate that seemingly cognitive or psychological phenomena are deeply social in their origins and effects. Whereas Orellana's work complicates cognitive theories of literacy, the tendency for theorists to root identities in naturalized and asocial explanations such as biology or psychology is dramatically challenged by Capps's research. Capps examines the interactional construction of agoraphobia, a condition in which an individual fears and avoids places and situations she perceives as dangerous. Many researchers who study this syndrome, which disproportionately affects women, attribute it solely to the sufferer's psychological makeup, but Capps demonstrates that women who have been diagnosed as agoraphobic are also socially constructed as irrational through interaction with family members. Based on a long-term case study of an agoraphobic woman and her family, Capps shows that the ordinary narratives that family members tell at the dinner table are important sites for the discursive linking of agoraphobia and irrationality. The responses of the woman's husband, as recipient of her stories, are particularly crucial in this process, which unfolds over a series of interactions. Yet the woman herself is not merely a passive victim of her husband; indeed, Capps traces a complex pattern in which the woman asserts her rationality through specific discourse strategies, but these very strategies trigger responses from her husband that insist on her irrationality; thus mental illness is here revealed to be a joint construction that has much of its source in family dynamics. Like Morgan and Wood, Capps identifies the temporal component of this pattern, but here discourse is a resource not for shared identities but for the distancing and differentiation of self and other.

Social differentiation is also at issue in Sara Trechter's investigation (chapter 5) of the creation of "women's language" and "men's language" as distinct categories in the Native American language Lakhota. Trechter's focus on language ideology at the cultural level complements Capps's analysis of how identities come to be imposed in the most intimate setting, that of the family. Like Capps, Trechter shows that a category often thought of as natural is instead historically contingent. Although some linguists present "women's language" and "men's language" as direct and exclusive expressions of gender identity, they are in fact cultural products that index a variety of social and interactional meanings. Trechter also makes clear through an examination of gendered final particles in the Lakhota verb system that although speakers may choose not to use the "appropriate" gendered form in a particular context, the cultural ideology that maps linguistic difference to gender difference is always available for observers to render anomalous speakers "culturally intelligible." Through observers' metalinguistic commentaries, interactional resources gradually come to be linked to gender.

Identity as ideology

The authors writing in part II take as their common theme the role of ideology in the construction of identity—not merely how speakers conform to an accepted or imposed ideology, but how they rebel against or subvert a powerful system of beliefs. As the authors show, ideological systems themselves exist as cultural constructs, subject to processes of change and revision by individuals and groups. Identity thus acknowledges ideology as one of the many elements in its framework.

Jennifer Coates (chapter 6) examines the ways in which gender beliefs and practices are manifested in the conversations of teenage girls. The years between childhood and adulthood are crucial in the individual's exploration of identity; it is here that society's messages and pressures may come to dominate a young woman's sense of herself. Using data collected over a 3-year period in a friendship group of four British girls, Coates documents the changes in discourse type and topic that reveal the process of gender construction. She shows how the girls' sense of their femininity is at times contradictory and precarious; they experiment with a range of discourse styles and subject positions but become increasingly restricted to more serious genres, avoiding the playful discourse of their early adolescence. Central to their new, adolescent discourse is what Coates terms "consciousness-raising / self-disclosure," a form of support for one another that positions the girls as victims of external forces (including their own bodies). But this period of girls' diminished sense of personal agency is temporary, serving them in later adolescence as a marker of the difficulties of moving from the freedom of girlhood to the constraints of womanhood.

Coates shows that one of the greatest pressures facing girls as they grow up is the set of cultural ideologies concerning women. Caitlin Hines explores one such ideology in her work (chapter 7) on the "woman as dessert" metaphor that pervades English. This metaphor is not merely a linguistic phenomenon but a larger cultural construct, for it has nonlinguistic reflexes, for example, in visual representations of women. Her research thus provides a much-needed analysis of the gender-based ideology inherent in the construction of an entire range of "woman as object" metaphors and opens the way for further examination of the place of gendered subtexts in long-established linguistic conventions. Hines uses a cognitive framework to establish the implications of women's imposed identity as sweet, possessable objects. Searching through many types and realizations of this image, she provides a thorough deconstruction of its history, form, and use. She finds that multiple linguistic levels from phonology to semantics work together to construct a coherent metaphorical system that has been a social resource for the representation of women over hundreds of years and can continue to be extended indefinitely. Her data show how a single ideologically created identity, once fixed in the language, permeates the discourse of speakers far removed from its source.

The channels of transmission of cultural ideology are the main focus of Laurel Sutton's work (chapter 8) on the status of popular media in language and gender studies. Contrary to traditional and mainstream linguistic practices of using only "authentic" data—that is, spontaneous spoken discourse—to establish patterns of language use, Sutton calls for the inclusion of all forms of expression in the analytic corpus, a move that has been initiated primarily by researchers of language and gender and other politically motivated scholars. She advocates, in particular, greater attention to often ephemeral forms of individually produced media that rely on new technologies for their production and circulation, such as feminist zines (self-published, low-circulation magazines) and on-line journals. Given the extent to which the mass media shape identity, especially for young women (such as those studied by Coates), the existence of such alternative media offers the possibility of forming an identity that is consciously resistant to prevailing cultural expectations. However, as Sutton notes, the publicizing of private selves in such media also opens their authors up to attack from apologists for the dominant culture. Such media—and their representations of alternative selves—therefore disappear quickly unless researchers make the effort to rescue them for study.

Another example of the recovery of dissenting voices comes from Rebecca Dobkins (chapter 9), who looks at letters written between Native American mothers and European American boarding-school officials in the early twentieth century. Letters were the only form of communication permitted these parents in their struggle to retain control over their children's place in their families and their children's larger identities as Native Americans. From Indian women's one-down position as racial and cultural minorities in a white society, identity was not negotiable, for Indian culture faced potential eradication daily at the hands of governmental policies of assimilation and cultural destruction. The Indian mothers' acts of resistance, made manifest in their letters, reveal the structure and mechanics of the official school authority, as well as the ruptures within it. The women who wrote these letters variously manage and challenge the language of the dominant culture. They thus recognize their roles both inside (as good American parents who, in their children's interest, cede their power to the government) and outside (as good Native American parents who reassert their cultural ties by bringing their children home) the government-imposed ideology of the time.

Finally, Keith Walters (chapter 10) looks at a contemporary case of gender and culture negotiation in Tunisia. Walters, like Hines, examines how the words used by speakers reflect cultural assumptions about identity and the roles women and men must fill. Here, the added dimension of religious ideology and the complexity of language choice raise important questions about the difference between imagined and practiced beliefs about gender. Walters considers the evidence of a sociolinguistic interview conducted between a female interviewer and a male interviewee. The two speakers shared a common cultural background and were of the same age, but the interviewer was of a higher educational and social status than the man she interviewed. Their interaction was already anomalous by the standards of this small-town Tunisian Muslim community of the 1980s, because free conversational exchange between unrelated women and men is not usually permitted. The speakers used linguistic resources to stake claims about their own identities and ideologies of gender and equality, which quickly came into conflict and were symbolized through the use of codeswitching and variant pronunciations of the crucial word 'woman'. Walters shows that in this encounter the two speakers use language to create their own embodiment as gendered, classed, and otherwise categorized individuals. Their struggle thus emblemizes the disjunction between ideologies of identity imposed by both researchers and cultural members and the way disparate elements of the self play out in interaction at moments of cultural shift.

Identity as ingenuity

Whereas the second part of *Reinventing Identities* treats the role of ideological forces in the construction of identity, part III locates identity at the intersection between culturally imposed and personal meanings. The chapters in this section explore how language serves as a vehicle for speakers' creative responses even as their linguistic behavior reflects the stability of existing social categories.

Part III begins with Deborah Tannen's analysis of two same-sex hierarchical office interactions. The chapter underscores the point that gender in particular and identity in general are the outcome of negotiation, by which speakers contest and give way to the social forces that shape and constitute identity. The complexity of the relationship between gender and power is highlighted through the concept of framing, that is, through analysis of the moment-by-moment alignments taken up by participants in interaction. Within this theoretical framework, small talk in work settings is seen to instantiate the negotiations between connection and status among participants. Higher-status participants have the power to frame the interaction, whereas lower-status participants are limited to contesting or acceding to the frame. The ways in which this negotiation takes place are, Tannen argues, borrowing a term from Erving Goffman, "sex-class-linked"—that is, linked to the class of women and the class of men. Whether constituted in gender difference or power imbalance, identity is therefore best understood as a matter of display, emerging through the course of interaction, not intrinsic to a particular individual. By bringing together two widely invoked theoretical approaches to gender and language—cultural difference and dominance—Tannen offers a balanced reconceptualization of gender identity.

Tannen articulates the phenomenon of gender as a performed display by which individuals, although constrained by the contingencies of interaction, nevertheless pick and choose from among an inventory of practices. Her implicit critique of essentialist conceptions of social categories is shared by Patricia Sawin (chapter 12), who raises several fundamental methodological and theoretical issues for the study of "women's narrative." Sawin observes that prevailing narrative models fail to account for the structure of the stories told by an elderly Appalachian woman who is the subject of her study. The discrepancy between data and theory prompts her to rethink the widespread concept of "women's narrative." She notes that this concept is an overextension and reification of theoretical models originally posited for a circumscribed set of social groups, primarily white middle-class women in the United States and England. In light of her findings, she theorizes identity and narrative as the result of a combination of interactional needs and existing social structures. According to Sawin, the study of women's stories of self as a means of identity construction requires more than the analysis of isolated narratives. Instead, narrative is better seen as the implementation of communicative strategies developed both in accordance with and in opposition to dominant social structures and discourses.

Tannen and Sawin are primarily concerned with critiquing the theoretical implications of traditional understandings of identity. By contrast, William Leap and the remaining authors in this part examine the creation of identity from the point of view of the agent and how she or he works within and against cultural ideologies of identity in order to construct a consciously chosen identity. In his examination of the gay male coming-out experience in chapter 13, Leap considers American gay identity as the outcome of a struggle to verbalize unnameable feelings. The transition between culturally dictated heterosexual reproductive roles and personally created gay identity, he suggests, takes place via a process of gay socialization akin to language acquisition through which speakers learn culture-specific text-building strategies. Leap's emphasis on gay identity as acquisition and process rather than as static essentialism calls attention to the socially constructed aspects of homosexuality. "Coming into gayness" is thus not a status achieved through biology or by the coming-out act alone but rather is an ongoing practice of learning and performing the many dimensions of a shared cultural identity.

Like Leap, Norma Mendoza-Denton (chapter 14) is also concerned with the processes by which individuals arrive at their individual and group identities. On the basis of the play-by-play interaction of a group of Latina teenagers, she shows how scholars who approach girls' and women's talk as cooperative miss the intricate strategies that speakers employ to align and disalign with one another at a variety of levels. The Latina speakers use turn-initial *no* as a discourse marker that signals these ongoing affiliation processes, which are based in part on shared Latina identity, on regional and class background, and on social attitudes and beliefs. At the same time, alignments may be disrupted by speakers' different pragmatic assumptions that may be remedied only by explicit metalinguistic work. Mendoza-Denton's research suggests that neither interaction-based nor category-based approaches alone are adequate for the understanding of identity in this context; instead, researchers must consider as well speakers' linguistic and pragmatic systems, their social backgrounds, their relationships to one another, and their individual beliefs and opinions.

A. C. Liang shares Mendoza-Denton's concern with the role of pragmatics in the production of identity. In chapter 15, she demonstrates how people can exploit the inherent ambiguity in language to create an equivocal identity. Examining the potential of Gricean pragmatics as a framework for the study of gender and sexuality, Liang assesses the adequacy of the Cooperative Principle of conversation against real-world examples, focusing in particular on the relationship between homosexuals and heterosexuals. She argues that H. P. Grice's (1975) notion of cooperativeness is dependent on power relations, and she questions the necessity of his assumption of common purposes or mutually accepted directions for the exchange of information. Given the risk to their physical and mental well-being if they elect to come out to their interlocutors, lesbians and gays may choose to employ communicative strategies from which their covert meanings, although misleadingly worded for straight listeners, can be properly inferred only if listeners disabuse themselves of the default assumption of heterosexuality. These creative strategies of simultaneous masking and display of sexual identity allow lesbian and gay speakers to protect themselves from the dangers of homophobia while locating themselves in solidarity with listeners who are familiar with these strategies. The ambiguous selves that lesbian and gay speakers project in this way exemplify the limitations of either universal pragmatic or categorical sociolinguistic models of identity.

Identity as improvisation

The process of identity creation and consolidation is not a one-time event. New social arrangements provide the means to shape new identities. As the chapters in part IV of *Reinventing Identities* demonstrate, resources as diverse as barroom entertainment, science fiction, mass media technology, and children's games are employed by speakers and writers in ways that cannot be predicted in advance. Through the innovative reworking of previously formulated structures, language users go beyond deterministic frameworks of identity, arguing through their actions that identity is instead a continuous creative practice.

Like Liang's, Rusty Barrett's research (chapter 16) reveals how speakers at once work within and subvert dominant ideologies in their construction of identity. His chapter opens part IV with a critique of the concept of identity in theories of sexuality, gender, and race. Based on an ethnographic study of African American drag queens' performances in a gay bar, Barrett's work argues against privileging a particular aspect of the performers' complex identities. As he demonstrates, race, gender, class, and sexuality become salient at different moments during drag performances. Barrett counters feminist charges that drag queens want to be women and the claims of some African Americans that black gay men want to be white; he shows that African American drag queens use the features of a stereotyped "white middle-class women's language" to challenge racism and homophobia. However, Barrett does not embrace the position of queer theorists, influenced by J. L. Austin's (1962) concept of the performative utterance, that drag is a celebratory performative assertion of the dissolution of gender categories. He notes that misogyny underlies some drag queens' routines, a fact that calls into question the usefulness for radical politics of the performative theory of identity.

Anna Livia's study (chapter 17) of nongendered pronoun systems in feminist fiction shares with Barrett's work a concern with how language users play with gender categories for political purposes. Livia notes that epicene (or common-gender) pronoun systems were frequently proposed as part of feminist activist efforts in the 1970s, yet such systems never enjoyed any currency even in feminist communities, although they occur in several futuristic and utopian feminist novels of the 1970s. Livia argues that epicene systems are meaningful only in juxtaposition to gender-based systems, and she shows how authors use both to contrast their utopias to sexist realities. She traces the development of several strategies that authors use to decouple gender and reference, including generic feminine, generic masculine, and invented nongendered forms. Livia's research contextualizes and recovers a moment in radical feminist linguistic history that is too often dismissed as mere "Whorfianism." Her study enjoins practitioners of text linguistics to take more seriously the political effects of fiction.

The fictional worlds explored in Livia's research find their counterpart in the virtual communities of television that are the subject of chapter 18. In this chapter I examine a relatively uninvestigated arena of media discourse: the shopping channel, a network that combines elements of advertising, talk-show discourse, and private conversation. I argue that the shopping channel, which targets primarily lower-middle-class women, uses a variety of visual and discursive strategies to create a fictive community in which middle-class identities are displayed by telehosts and linked to the purchase of the network's products. Although viewers may jointly construct the shopping-channel community and their identities within it through on-the-air conversations with the network host, the prevailing discourse, which furthers the channel's capitalist agenda, rests on gender and class ideologies. Callers' nonstandard language becomes another commodity that hosts use to construct their own positions of authority and middle-class identity and to position callers as authentic and enthusiastic endorsers of the network's products. Yet the power relations thus instantiated are destabilized by the demands of capitalism, so that viewers also derive a measure of discursive and economic power from the shopping channel, though always on the terms of the network itself.

Colleen Cotter (chapter 19) likewise investigates the complex power dynamics of media discourse, demonstrating in her study of Irish-language radio that the media can be a positive cultural and linguistic resource rather than a global homogenizing force. In so doing, she challenges the viewpoint held by many linguists that the media are a key component in the demise of endangered languages. After describing how the media are employed as a way of promoting Irish-language use and national identity in a late-twentieth-century discourse domain, Cotter examines the place of gender in Ireland's language revival effort at both the microlinguistic and the macrolinguistic levels. She observes that Irish-language use on the air is not dramatically different for women, who have a central place in all aspects of production at the radio station she studied. In fact, in an interaction between a female interviewer and interviewee, "gendered discourse" does not surface at all, for both participants are fulfilling nongendered roles appropriate to the media setting. This production of communicative competence in the media realm promotes competence in Irish as well. The result for women, who have traditionally been at the forefront of language retention efforts worldwide but in private roles, is that they occupy more publicly visible positions within the historically circumscribed contexts of media, language preservation, and gender.

Marjorie Harness Goodwin (chapter 20) closes the book with a discussion of how identities are shaped not through language alone but through entire activity systems. Goodwin's research, like that in all the chapters in this section, demonstrates that established discursive conventions may be employed in unexpected ways and with unanticipated effects. Her investigation of Latina girls' interactional practices while playing hopscotch revises earlier understandings of gender and ethnicity. As she points out, girls' games have often been theorized as cooperative activities with undeveloped rule systems that promote loose and nonhierarchical social structures. Moreover, Latinas are frequently stereotyped as noncompetitive and submissive. But Goodwin finds that the Latina girls she studied are fully capable of competitive and self-promoting behavior which, far from deviating from a normatively cooperative game structure, is built into the very fabric of play. Attempts to cheat and resultant efforts to identify and challenge rule violators pervade the hopscotch games Goodwin observed. Her detailed examination of how identities are linguistically built within situated activities offers an alternative framework for understanding gender and other dimensions of identity. The embodied activity that Goodwin considers introduces space, as well as time, to the study of linguistic practice, and the purposeful temporary identities that are constructed and reconstructed from moment to moment in social action are shown to have significance for speakers' more lasting identities based on age and friendship networks.

Goodwin's chapter thus brings together the central themes of *Reinventing Identities*: that language users' identities are not essential to their natures but are produced through contingent social interactions; that these identities are inflected by ideologies of gender and other social constructs; that speakers, writers, and signers respond to these ideologies through practices that sometimes challenge and sometimes reproduce dominant beliefs; and that as new social resources become available, language users enact and produce new identities, themselves temporary and historical, that assign new meanings to gender.

Conclusion

If the 1970s were the decade of discovery in language and gender research and the 1980s were a period of critique and correction of earlier work, the 1990s have turned out to be a transformative decade in which researchers have both revisited familiar territory with new tools and set forth into unexplored areas. We are in a period of "rethinking" the basic precepts and concepts of language and gender research (Bergvall, Bing, & Freed 1996; Taylor 1997). Like feminism itself, now undergoing a third wave of scholarship and activism, the field of language and gender has become an increasingly recognized academic enterprise while still maintaining the clarity of perspective that comes from being situated at the intersection of traditional disciplinary boundaries.

A rapprochement between feminist linguistics and feminist theory now seems more possible than at any time since the 1970s. Linguistics can offer a theoretically grounded view of language in practice, performance, and ideology, which is vital to present theorizing. Conversely, the interpretive turn in language and gender research and scholars' increasing willingness to look to feminist, as well as linguistic, theory have resulted in a new trend toward theoretically informed scholarship that addresses issues of fundamental concern to feminists in other fields. Most significant in this regard is the fact that the discipline has shifted away from a comparative framework in which discovering differences in the linguistic behavior of women and men as groups is the central research goal toward an approach rooted in the details of context, concerned with locally meaningful social groupings rather than global gender divisions and attentive to individual variation within, as well as across, gender categories.

In her historical discussion of feminism and pronoun politics, Anna Livia reminds those who would trivialize the efforts of the radical-feminist linguistic activists of the 1970s and 1980s that "one had to go there to get here." In other words, we cannot simply denounce research rooted in now-unfashionable theories, for these and other "bad examples" have ushered in entirely new theoretical paradigms. The shape of language and gender scholarship is tied, perhaps more than we sometimes acknowledge, to the shape of feminist theory. Mindful of our discipline's history, then, we must look to feminist theory, past and present, to get our bearings as we move into a new era of research. It is my hope that in the current period of change this volume will contribute to the growing urge toward theory in language and gender scholarship and inspire future researchers to transgress the existing boundaries that separate "good" and "bad" research in the investigation of the linguistic production of identity.

NOTES

My thanks to Caitlin Hines, A. C. Liang, Deborah Tannen, and Keith Walters for offering numerous useful suggestions on earlier versions of this introduction and to Jon McCammond for ongoing discussions about the issues explored here. I am also grateful to Kathryn Galyon for her skillful copyediting of this essay. Thanks are due as well to Peter Ohlin and Cynthia Garver of Oxford University Press and to Elaine Kehoe for ably shepherding the huge and complex manuscript of *Reinventing Identities* through the publication process.

1. Recent collections include those edited by Victoria Bergvall, Janet Bing, and Alice Freed (1996); Jennifer Coates (1997); Kira Hall and Mary Bucholtz (1995); Sally Johnson and Ulrike Meinhof (1996); Anna Livia and Kira Hall (1997); Sara Mills (1995); Sue Wilkinson and Celia Kitzinger (1995); and Ruth Wodak (1997). These are in addition to numerous journal articles, monographs, and textbooks that have recently been published or are in process.

2. There are, however, important differences in the details of these theories. Butler's skepticism about the universal category of the subject and the power of individuals in the face of hegemonic ideologies leads her to formulate her position in less active language than does Anzaldúa. (It has been a cause for dismay among many feminists that in Butler's writings language [which here "inserts itself in . . . linguistic life"] is often more agentive than individual subjects ["the resulting effects of . . . discourse" (1990:145)]. Yet her theory of drag also offers the possibility of speakers' active resistance to normative cultural discourse) Furthermore, where Butler maintains that language constructs the self (via cultural discourse), Anzaldúa implies that identities may exist prior to the language with which they are projected and displayed.

3. For details, see for example Marcyliena Morgan's (this volume) discussion of Claudia Mitchell-Kernan (1971); Bucholtz and Hall's (1995) rereading of Robin Lakoff (1975); Sara Trechter's (chapter 5, this volume) analysis of the work of Mary Haas (1944); and Caitlin Hines's (chapter 7) and Anna Livia's (chapter 17, both this volume) separate treatments of several "Whorfian" language and gender researchers. See also Patricia Nichols's pioneering sociolinguistic work on black women's language (e.g., Nichols 1978, 1983), which the field's patriarch, William Labov, did not cite until 1990, after Penelope Eckert (1989) discussed it

in an influential critique of his view of women's language. (My thanks to Keith Walters for this example.)

4. Not only has Eckert and McConnell-Ginet's essay inspired research within the model, but it also has provided a theoretical framework through which to understand work already being done. Thus their theory, like most others, is part invention and part discovery. Their work is a valuable example of how language and gender scholars can produce, as well as use, feminist theory in their work. It is also important to note that Eckert and McConnell-Ginet's concept of *practice* differs from Butler's. For Butler, practices are culturally imposed ideological structures that assign subjecthood; for Eckert and McConnell-Ginet, they are the activities taken up by participants in local communities, possibly in complicity with and possibly in resistance to cultural ideologies of identity.

REFERENCES

Althusser, Louis (1971). Ideology and ideological state apparatuses. In Althusser, *Lenin and philosophy and other essays*. Trans. Ben Brewster. New York: Monthly Review Press, 127–186.

Anzaldúa, Gloria (1987). *Borderlands / La frontera: The new mestiza*. San Francisco: Spinsters/ Aunt Lute.

——— (ed.) (1990). *Making face, making soul / Haciendo caras*. San Francisco: Aunt Lute.

Austin, J. L. (1962). *How to do things with words*. Cambridge, MA: Harvard University Press.

Bauman, Richard (1977). *Verbal art as performance*. Prospect Heights, IL: Waveland Press.

Bergvall, Victoria L., Janet M. Bing, & Alice F. Freed (eds.) (1996). *Rethinking language and gender research: Theory and practice*. London: Longman.

Bodine, Ann (1975). Androcentrism in prescriptive grammar: Singular "they," sex-indefinite "he," and "he or she." *Language in Society* 4:129–146.

Bourdieu, Pierre (1991). *Language and symbolic power*. Ed. John B. Thompson. Trans. Gino Raymon & Matthew Adamson. Cambridge, MA: Harvard University Press.

Briggs, Charles L. (1988). *Competence in performance: The creativity of tradition in Mexicano verbal art*. Philadelphia: University of Pennsylvania Press.

Bucholtz, Mary, & Kira Hall (1995). Introduction: Twenty years after *Language and Woman's Place*. In Kira Hall & Mary Bucholtz (eds.), *Gender articulated: Language and the socially constructed self*. New York: Routledge, 1–22.

Butler, Judith (1990). *Gender trouble: Feminism and the subversion of identity*. New York: Routledge.

Coates, Jennifer (ed.) (1997). *Language and gender: A reader*. Oxford: Blackwell.

Dubois, Betty Lou, & Isabel Crouch (1987). Linguistic disruption: He/she, s/he, he or she, he-she. In Joyce Penfield (ed.), *Women and language in transition*. Albany: SUNY Press, 28–36.

Eckert, Penelope (1989). The whole woman: Sex and gender differences in variation. *Language Variation and Change* 1:245–267.

Eckert, Penelope, & Sally McConnell-Ginet (1992). Think practically and look locally: Language and gender as community-based practice. *Annual Review of Anthropology* 21:461–490.

Fishman, Pamela (1983). Interaction: The work women do. In Barrie Thorne, Cheris Kramarae, & Nancy Henley (eds.), *Language, gender, and society*. Cambridge, MA: Newbury House, 103–118.

Foucault, Michel (1980). *Language, counter-memory, practice*. Ed. Donald F. Bouchard, trans. Donald F. Bouchard & Sherry Simon. Ithaca, NY: Cornell University Press.

Gaudio, Rudolf P. (1997). Not talking straight in Hausa. In Anna Livia & Kira Hall (eds.), *Queerly phrased: Language, gender, and sexuality*. New York: Oxford University Press, 416–429.

Goffman, Erving (1959). *The presentation of self in everyday life*. Garden City, NY: Doubleday.

Grice, H. Paul (1975). Logic and conversation. In Peter Cole & Jerry L. Morgan (eds.), *Syntax and semantics*. Vol. 3: *Speech acts*. New York: Academic Press, 41–58.

Haas, Mary (1944). Men's and women's speech in Koasati. *Language* 20:142–149.

Hall, Kira, & Veronica O'Donovan (1996). Shifting gender positions among Hindi-speaking hijras. In Victoria L. Bergvall, Janet M. Bing, & Alice F. Freed (eds.), *Rethinking language and gender research: Theory and practice*. London: Longman, 228–266.

Harding, Sandra G. (1991). *Whose science? Whose knowledge?: Thinking from women's lives*. Ithaca, NY: Cornell University Press.

hooks, bell (1981). *Ain't I a woman? Black women and feminism*. Boston: South End Press.

Hull, Gloria T., Patricia Bell Scott, & Barbara Smith (eds.) (1982). *But some of us are brave*. New York: Feminist Press.

Hymes, Dell (1981). Breakthrough into performance. In Hymes, *"In vain I tried to tell you": Essays in Native American ethnopoetics*. Philadelphia: University of Pennsylvania Press, 79–141. (Original work published 1975)

Irigaray, Luce (1985a). *Speculum of the other woman*. Trans. Gillian C. Gill. Ithaca, NY: Cornell University Press.

——— (1985b). *This sex which is not one*. Trans. Catherine Porter with Carolyn Burke. Ithaca, NY: Cornell University Press.

Johnson, Sally, & Ulrike Meinhof (eds.) (1996). *Language and masculinity*. London: Blackwell.

Johnstone, Barbara (1996). *The linguistic individual: Self-expression in language and linguistics*. New York: Oxford University Press.

Johnstone, Barbara, & Judith Mattson Bean (1997). Self-expression and linguistic variation. *Language in Society* 26:221–246.

Kulick, Don (1996). Gender in the speech of Brazilian transvestite prostitutes. Paper presented at the annual meeting of the American Association for Applied Linguistics, Chicago.

Labov, William (1972a). *Language in the inner city: Studies in the Black English Vernacular*. Philadelphia: University of Pennsylvania Press.

——— (1972b). *Sociolinguistic patterns*. Philadelphia: University of Pennsylvania Press.

——— (1990). The intersection of sex and social class in the course of linguistic change. *Language Variation and Change* 2:205–254.

Lakoff, Robin (1975). *Language and woman's place*. New York: Harper & Row.

Lave, Jean, & Etienne Wenger (1991). *Situated learning: Legitimate peripheral participation*. Cambridge: Cambridge University Press.

Livia, Anna, & Kira Hall (eds.) (1997). *Queerly phrased: Language, gender, and sexuality*. New York: Oxford University Press.

Longino, Helen E. (1990). *Science as social knowledge: Values and objectivity in scientific inquiry*. Princeton: Princeton University Press.

Mills, Sara (ed.) (1995). *Language and gender: Interdisciplinary perspectives*. London: Longman.

Mitchell-Kernan, Claudia (1971). *Language behavior in a black urban community*. Berkeley, CA: Language Behavior Research Laboratory.

Nichols, Patricia C. (1978). Black women in the rural South: Conservative and innovative. *International Journal of the Sociology of Language* 17:45–54.

——— (1983). Linguistic options and choices for Black women in the rural South. In Barrie Thorne, Cheris Kramarae, & Nancy Henley (eds.), *Language, gender, and society*. Cambridge, MA: Newbury House, 54–68.

Parker, Andrew, & Eve Kosofsky Sedgwick (eds.) (1995). *Performativity and performance*. New York: Routledge.

Penelope Stanley, Julia (1977). Paradigmatic woman: The prostitute. In David L. Shores & Carol P. Hines (eds.), *Papers in language variation: The SAMLA-ADS collection*. University: University of Alabama Press, 303–321.

Schulz, Muriel (1975). The semantic derogation of women. In Barrie Thorne & Nancy Henley (eds.), *Language and sex: Difference and dominance*. Rowley, MA: Newbury House, 64–75.

Taylor, Anita (ed.) (1997). *Women and Language*, 20(1). Rethinking gender. [Special issue].

Thorne, Barrie, Cheris Kramarae, & Nancy Henley (1983). Language, gender and society: Opening a second decade of research. In Thorne, Kramarae, & Henley (eds.), *Language, gender, and society*. Cambridge, MA: Newbury House, 7–24.

Weir, Allison (1996). Sacrificial logics: *Feminist theory and the critique of identity*. New York: Routledge.

West, Candace, & Don H. Zimmerman (1983). Small insults: A study of interruptions in cross-sex conversations between unacquainted persons. In Barrie Thorne, Cheris Kramarae, & Nancy Henley (eds.), *Language, gender, and society*. Cambridge, MA: Newbury House, 103–118.

Wilkinson, Sue, & Celia Kitzinger (eds.) (1995). *Feminism and discourse: Psychological perspectives*. London: Sage.

Wodak, Ruth (ed.) (1997). *Gender and discourse*. New York: Sage.

Part I

. . . .

IDENTITY
AS INVENTION

. . . .

No Woman No Cry

Claiming African American Women's Place

My work requires me to think about how free I can be as an African-American woman writer in my genderized, sexualized, wholly racialized world. To think about (and wrestle with) the full implications of my situation leads me to consider what happens when other writers work in a highly and historically racialized society. For them, as for me, imagining is not merely looking or looking at; nor is it taking oneself intact into the other. It is, for the purposes of the work, *becoming*.

My project rises from delight, not disappointment. It rises from what I know about the ways writers transform aspects of their social grounding into aspects of language, and the ways they tell other stories, fight secret wars, limn out all sorts of debates blanketed in their text. And rises from my certainty that writers always know, at some level, that they do this.

(Morrison 1992:4)

oni Morrison wrote the above passage to explain her need to enter the volatile terrain of criticism concerning African presence in U.S. literature. My analogous purpose, as an African American female linguist, concerns the racialized, sexualized, and genderized context of linguistic research. Any exploration of how language constitutes, instantiates, and constructs the social world is fraught with assumptions about race, class, gender, and sexuality that are conventionally accepted under the rubric of "knowledge," "findings," and "objectivity." Under the guise of science we, especially women, people of color, and women of color, are silenced or adroitly handled—as in *manhandled*—especially in work on the language of African Americans and the marginalization of women within such work.

This discussion, like Morrison's, rises from delight rather than disappointment. The issue is not to bemoan the past but to participate in and agitate for a present and future that are socially inclusive and intellectually productive. Because language is a social act, research on language constitutes social and cultural production that is influenced by issues of race, sexuality, class, and power. Thus the marginalization of women in African American language research is not about gender exclusively. One way to begin is to examine the representation of African American women's language use while pondering the challenges Black women face daily. Perhaps the most significant challenge, and one that biases all scholarly research, concerns how

African American women are viewed in relation to others, especially Black men and White women—how their identities are assigned as part of a system of dichotomies rather than discovered as something much more complex.

The exclusion and marginalization of Black women is not limited to scholarly research. In the legal system too, according to Kimberle Crenshaw (1992), race, class, and gender consistently intertwine in African American women's lives. She argues that Black women experience *intersectionality* in most legal decisions concerning race or gender. For example, Black women who sue employers for sexual harassment can seldom include White female workers in their suits. Similarly, they are challenged when they attempt to include Black men in racial discrimination cases involving Black women. Consequently, African American women's issues are hypermarginalized and are considered typical neither of all women's issues (because the women who face them are Black) nor of Black issues (because the Blacks who face them are women). It is not surprising, then, that all linguists—whether they include, marginalize, or fetishize Black women—always, at some level, take a position on this situation. The position taken here is that African American women participate in the development of language norms, the introduction of innovations, and the use of all varieties of African American English (AAE).[1] Moreover, their contribution is most apparent in cultural settings in which they are social actors—in places, that is, where identity is central.

The issue of African American women's identity, and women's identity in general, is shrouded in postmodernist discussions that are seldom based on the choices and challenges of everyday life. In fact, ethnographic and linguistic descriptions are often summarily dismissed as essentialist if they do not apply to all cultures and to all issues of globalization. Yet within postmodernist theorizing women continue to be essentialized. Stuart Hall both critiques and continues this practice when he applauds feminists' rejection of the Cartesian and the sociological subject: "Feminism challenged the notion that men and women were part of the same identity—'Mankind'—replacing it with the question of sexual difference" (1995:611). Although this description may suit Western academic feminism, it does not begin to address the complex ways women throughout the world (and in the West itself) experience and theorize their identity as women. Moreover, African American women's identity exists in relation to White women's identity, perhaps more so than to (Black) male identity. Black women are presented as problematic with respect both to feminist issues and to patriarchal ideals of White womanhood. The majority of Black women, after all, are workers who also have authority at home, a reality still unrecognized in White feminist political agendas. Thus Judith Butler's admonition, "Reading identities as they're situated and formed in relation to one another means moving beyond the heuristic requirement of identity itself" (1995:446), is appropriate, especially given American feminists' defining moments of gender and race in the Black community during the mid-1990s: the Clarence Thomas Senate hearing and O. J. Simpson's murder trial. Both cases heightened awareness that race and gender are not interchangeable concepts for Black women but rather fused. These events are significant not because they illustrate a racial split within feminism but because they forced all U.S. women to consider the difficulty of juggling issues of racial and sexual discrimination in reality rather than in theory. Notwithstanding the resulting acrimony, White feminists and feminists of color have a great deal in common. As bell hooks (1990, 1992), Kamala Visweswaran (1994), Dorinne Kondo (1997), and others challenge, feminist theory must be situated at home, a place we have been before but never really experienced. To explore this place is crucial, for the intersections of these factors greatly affect linguistic analysis in general and descriptions of language use among African Americans, women, and African American women in particular.

The following discussion is a description and reanalysis of African American women's language and cultural practice across generations. The interviews are based on long-term ethnographic fieldwork with Black women in the United States and other parts of the English-speaking African diaspora. With few exceptions, women who have been socialized within African American culture are familiar with three central interactional events: children's he-said-she-said interactions; teenagers' and young adults' instigating; and adult women's conversational signifying. These occur among each generation as part of a process of social face and identity construction. Previous study of these practices as unrelated to other cultural activities missed girls' significance in the description of the African American community (Goodwin 1990 is an exception) and the importance of social face among women.

The vernacular as male and poor

The concept of the vernacular is central to sociolinguistic study of African American language. Sociolinguistics uses quantitative methods to analyze linguistic variables: that is, structural items that occur frequently in conversation and whose frequency of occurrence is highly stratified according to age, class, and other factors (Labov 1972:8). Thus a study of the vernacular, the ordinary language of a people, implies analytic focus on everyday activities and social actors. Yet many descriptions of African American speech have been based on data from adolescent boys in research interviews (cf. Morgan 1994a; Mufwene 1992).

Until recently, the description of vernacular or AAE speakers effectively marginalized African Americans who did not fit the stated criteria, such as "black youth from 8 to 19 years old who participate in the street culture of inner cities" (Labov 1972:xiii). In particular, linguists too often view language varieties of adolescent male gangs as authentic or core AAE, as when William Labov contrasts his core (gang) group with the "lames," young Black men who accept parental influence, attend school regularly, pursue the advantages of the dominant culture, are inactive because of poor health, or are mentally or morally defective: that is, punks (1972:259). This description of vernacular culture constructed "authentic" African American membership, identity, and language as male, adolescent, insular, and trifling. Everyone else is a "lame." Since lames do not participate in core culture, do not use AAE features in the same ways, and speak another version of AE (Spears 1988), researchers do not view them as culturally African American. Moreover, where the Black community is seen as vernacular-speaking by definition, most studies consider Whites to be speakers of Standard English (cf. Morgan 1994b, c). Labov (1998) addresses these issues by distinguishing between American varieties under the headings of *General English* (*GE*), *Other American Dialects* (*OAD*), *African American* (*AA*), and *African American Vernacular English* (*AAVE*).

The confusion about African American vernacular language, especially its association with males, can also be seen in cultural criticism. Mary Helen Washington (1987) argues that Janie, in Zora Neale Hurston's novel *Their Eyes Were Watching God* (1937), uses folk language (dialect) to symbolize the limit of her power but that the Reverend John Pearson's use of folk language in Hurston's *Jonah's Gourd Vine* ([1934] 1990) leads to liberation. Washington condemns Hurston's differential treatment of her characters, but she equates dialect with maleness, concluding that it is limiting for the woman and liberating for the man. However, the vernacular is the likely variety for both characters.

When scholarly notions of the vernacular define everyday speech as male speech, women are not integral to generalized definitions and descriptions of speakers. It is not always clear whether women are even included in sociolinguistic data analysis. Still more alarming, the definition of the vernacular reifies stereotypes of African American culture: young men with nothing to do, doing nothing, talking trash, and going nowhere (Duneier 1992). Yet if we reclaim the general definition of the vernacular as core culture, as John Gwaltney (1981) does, and include women, men, and children along with adolescent boys, the vernacular becomes representative of "regular" speech, and women's voices can be heard. That is, core culture is not a question of an authentic subject but of one who lives within the social norms and cultural practices of a multiclass, intergenerational, and gendered African American culture.

Language and gender

Though often excluded or marginalized in language studies (cf. Eckert & McConnell-Ginet 1992; Henley 1995), African American women are occasionally mentioned. For example, Roger Abrahams (1970) remarks, with no explanation, that African American women refused to participate in his Philadelphia folklore project. He later describes them as not participating in verbal play and as "restrained in their talk, less loud, less public, and much less abandoned" compared with men (1974:242). Finally, in his examination of the representation of women's speech styles in literature, he suggests that women may have the same expressive acuity as men (Abrahams 1975).

Other reports of African American women's language use, while scarce, comment on their linguistic conservatism; their role as the "real" target and often the audience, observer, and supporter of male signifying games; and their willing collaboration in street encounters (e.g., Abrahams 1962; Kochman 1972; Labov 1972; Wolfram 1969). Claudia Mitchell-Kernan (1971) produced one of the few early works that did not describe urban African American women in relation to men and as aggressive, domineering, and emasculating. Her rich ethnography demonstrated that women participate in conversational signifying and employ other linguistic practices similar to those of men. Yet Mitchell-Kernan's work has been criticized because of her gender—she is reprovingly described as "a young attractive Black woman"—and her "middle-class" status (Kochman 1973:969, 970). In a vindication of Mitchell-Kernan's work, Henry Louis Gates Jr. (1988) relied heavily, point for point, on her description of signifying as a foundation for his theory of African American discourse. It is also important to remember that before the late 1980s and the implosion of the margins into the center of academic inquiry (Kondo 1997) with critical work by feminist and minority scholars, numerous works by women, natives, and Others were summarily dismissed as too personal and subjective (Visweswaran 1994).

Fortunately, the scholarship on women's language use in their communities is growing. Current research critiques the prevailing literature on African American women's and girls' speech (e.g., Ball 1992; Etter-Lewis 1991, 1993; Etter-Lewis & Foster 1996; Foster 1995; Goodwin 1980, 1982, 1985, 1988, 1990; Morgan 1989, 1991, 1993). Similarly, much of John Rickford's work, as well as his collaborations with colleagues (Rickford 1986; Rickford, Ball, Blake, Jackson, & Martin 1991; Rickford & McNair-Knox 1993) on variation and style-shifting in AAE, is based on long-term interviews with a young female community participant. Yet women and girls are still often compared with their male counterparts, which clouds both commonalities and gender differences. A vivid example can be found in the confusion over the significance of a cool social face.

Face to face: Staying cool

One important aspect of African American culture that equally affects women and men is the maintenance of the speaker's social face, an impression formed of a person based on her or his self-presentation (Goffman 1967). Perhaps the most widespread African American cultural concept that both critiques and symbolizes social face is the notion of being *cool*—current and trendsetting, calm, detached, yet in control (cf. Major 1994; Smitherman 1994). Gwaltney pays tribute to this cultural value in describing one of his community contributors, Nancy White: "She is the exemplar par excellence of the highest status that core black culture can accord—that of the cool, dealing individual" (1981:143).

A cool face is the ability to enact subtle symbolic cultural practices with eloquence, skill, wit, patience, and precise timing. Although some commentators have tied cool social face to racism or male coping skills (Abrahams 1962; George 1992; Grier & Cobbs 1968; Horton 1972; Kunjufu 1986; Majors & Billson 1992), coolness is mainly a cultural practice (cf. Gwaltney 1981; Smitherman 1977) used by both genders and having counterparts in all parts of Africa and the African diaspora (Alleyne 1980, 1989; Yankah 1991a, b).[2] It contrasts with *fools* or *acting a fool*—an insult that both denigrates and dismisses a person as a cultural member, as Mabel Lincoln, another woman in Gwaltney's study, describes: "To black people like me, a fool is funny—you know, people who love to break bad [i.e., to suddenly behave as though one is knowledgeable or an authority], people you can't tell anything to, folks that will take a shotgun to a roach. . . . But most of us try to be cool. That is what we respect the most in ourselves and look for in other people. That means being a person of sober, quiet judgment" (Gwaltney 1981:68–69).

Being cool is especially important in interaction, because discourse requires that all participants (including hearers) constantly assess and address potential meanings within and across contexts. A cool social stance is multiply constructed through social context and contrastive use of AAE and AE. As a symbolic "good" with exchange value, coolness can be used to accrue linguistic and pragmatic capital. Individuals can "lose their cool" or social face in interactions in which they are culturally challenged (for example, by not knowing current lexical terms or meanings) or in which the dominant culture (the police, the legal system, the school, and so on) claims not to understand a particular form of interaction, such as indirection. A third interviewee of Gwaltney's, Mrs. Briar, describes herself as a little girl learning how to be cool and the penalty to one's social face resulting from acting a fool.

> I was five when I learned not to lose my cool when the trucks backfired. I remember the day it happened. I had asked my father for something and he had said no. But when the trucks came by and backfired, I just sat there like nothing had happened. He said, "Girl, let me shake your hand!" and he gave me money and I felt just as tall as he was. My brother Harry, who is three years older than I am, without even looking at me said, "No cool." Then everybody teased him for running off at the mouth without knowing what he was talking about and he felt bad, I think. . . . We don't like to show out, but if you guess wrong, you might be, well, you might be out there all by your lonesome. (Gwaltney 1981:192)

This passage shows the role of explicit socialization practices in teaching children the importance of coolness. African American children also learn how to be cool through language play and play language, especially the ritual games of signifying and instigating.

Children's language play

Although African American children play numerous language games (Goodwin 1990), the one that has received the most scholarly attention is signifying, a verbal game of indirection also known regionally as *sounding, the dozens, joning, snapping, busting, capping, bagging,* and *ranking* (Abrahams 1962; Garner 1983; Gates 1988; Kochman 1972; Labov 1972; Mitchell-Kernan 1972, 1973; Percelay, Monteria, & Dweck 1994; Smitherman 1977). Mitchell-Kernan describes signifying as "the recognition and attribution of some implicit content or function which is obscured by the surface content or function" (1972:317–318). It is a form of play for adolescent boys in particular, and it can serve indirect functions in adult interaction, as in conversational signifying. Many have suggested that signifying started as an outlet for racial oppression (e.g., Abrahams 1962; Dollard [1939] 1973; Kochman 1972; Percelay et al. 1994) because one must maintain one's cool in order to play. However, verbal coolness is a culturally constructed form of social face, and its obvious function as an outlet is probably an added bonus for youth who must learn both the cultural rules of the Black community and the political reality of being Black in America.

The notion of play in signifying differentiates the real from the serious (Abrahams 1970, 1976; Goffman 1974; Kochman 1983, 1986) by placing socially or culturally significant topics (e.g., personal details, including one's mother, relatives, sexuality, physical appearance, class, and economic status, as well as cultural common ground such as political figures) in implausible contexts. Plausibility is partially determined by cultural values. Thus a signifying episode that places one's mother in a possible context such as being unemployed or pregnant could be considered an insult and lead to physical confrontation. Conversely, the notion of a police officer who "serves and protects" the Black community would be considered implausible and hence could be a resource for signification. Once the implausible or unreal state is established, cultural signs interact with context through irony, sarcasm, wit, and humor in order to play with the serious signifier. For example, one commonly heard signifying turn is "You're so ugly, you went into a haunted house and came out with a job application." If the sign fits the context (that is, if you *are* ugly), the interaction is considered an insult rather than play.

As verbal play, signifying or snapping is mainly performed by adolescent boys, although it also occurs among adult women and men involved in competitive activities such as sports or stock trading. Signifying may occur as routine play among boys, and losing one's cool within the parameters of the game is an indication that the player has lost. Winners and losers are determined by the onlookers. If a player loses, he may redeem himself during the next day's play. Thus his social face as a cool-headed individual can be retrieved. In contrast, girls' language activities have more inherent risks because they are not bounded as play. For example, a girl who talks about another girl behind her back risks being labeled an instigator, and unlike her male peer who plays signifying games, she cannot redeem herself during the next day's play. She must undergo an elaborate waiting game and reconciliation session before reestablishing herself among her peers.

Girls' verbal activities focus on the content of previous and future interactions. Goodwin's (1980, 1990, 1992) analysis of he-said-she-said disputes among African American girls illustrates the elaborate lengths to which participants are willing to go in order to determine who said what behind someone's back. The role or motive of the instigator is not generally investigated by the offended party (Goodwin 1992), who works to maintain or reestablish her social face by telling narratives projecting her own future action in response to instigating stories.[3] This response is expected; as Goodwin (1992:187) explains, "The goal of the instigator's storytelling is to elicit a statement from the offended party which leads to her confronting the offending party." Younger girls maintain social face by demonstrating that if someone is suspected of talking about another girl behind her back, the offended party will investigate the action rather than the intention of the instigator and then confront her, sometimes physically.

As girls get older, however, they shift their focus to include the intentions of the instigator and other participants and whether these correspond to the offended party's interpretations. Consequently, talk increases among all participants. Moreover, talking about someone behind her back takes on a new seriousness: The activity is not simply gossip but rumor. In the African American speech community, when a rumor achieves widespread audience discussion and assessment, it is often treated as truth, even when it is not believed to be factual (cf. Turner 1993). And because a rumor also signals a loss of social face, its target must defend her honor. By the time girls have become teenagers, they have a significantly different focus on the instigator in he-said-she-said events. Young African American women treat talking behind another's back with the same seriousness as a capital offense. Before the alleged offending party is confronted, the accused party must prove that the intermediary who reported the offense is not simply an instigator. When the offending party is ultimately confronted, she may avoid physical confrontation if she admits to starting the rumor and apologizes or if she convinces the offended party that her intentions were misunderstood. Often the offending party admits to making the incriminating remark but does not apologize, or she refuses to admit that she said anything, although others report that she did. In both cases, some sort of directed confrontation is possible.

Instigating events are therefore about participants and occurrences of talk, as well as about what was allegedly said by whom. For teenagers, the event is designed to expose and either acquit or convict the instigator and the offending party. Days or weeks may elapse as statements are denied or confirmed and analyzed by witnesses. The offended party's aim is to determine who started the rumor. In the process, friendships are tested, conversational roles are assessed, and all parties become invested in identifying the alleged perpetrator of the offending speech event. As with young children, the person reported to be the source of the statement is the last person contacted.

The following story told by Zinzi, a 20-year-old college student, describes an instigating episode initiated by Sheila against Zinzi when both girls were in high school. Zinzi told this story in an undergraduate class after reading Goodwin's (1990) book detailing he-said-she-said interactions. She introduced the episode amid joking from classmates (who had similar stories) that the instigator had told the truth; Zinzi then adopted a defensive posture, her head and eyes slowly rolling, and told the story.[4]

(1)

1	Zinzi:	. . . And then so she thought that she was close enough to Tyrone and so
2		Tyrone wouldn't tell me. BUT? Tyrone being the BEST friend that he
3		is, he's just like, "You know? Sheila is spreading ru?mors about you.
4		I don't know if anybody else? told? you, but you know, she saying that
5		you and Barry been DOing things and duh?duhduh.dahdah.dah?" And I
6		was just like (2) "Oh? she di:d? huh?" And then so I decided (2) just
7		instead of going up in her face—'cause I didn't like her anyway—
8		instead of going up in her face, that I'd go and ask my OTHer friends
9		and things like that. So I went and asked them, and they were like,
10		"Yeah, yeah, ((high-pitched, soft voice)) she did tell me about that but I
11		didn't believe her." And I'm like—Uh huh, yeah, right! That's how
12		come you didn't TELL me, because you didn't BELIEVE her. Yeah (2)
13		okay And so an?yway, when I went and confro:nted? her. And then I
14		just got the satisfac?tion out of it (2) because all it took was like a
15		little? confrontation and
16	Morgan:	What did you say?

17	Zinzi:	Well I, I asked her?—well not ACTually ASked her—but I accused?
18		her? and I was like "Oh, so I heard that you been telling ru?mors about
19		Barry and I." And then she? (2) didn't deny? it. And she was just like
20		"It DID? happen." And I'm like "How do you know it happened then?"
21		So, at first? we were talking? lo:w? and then got kind? of lou::d and
22		the:n? since this was like in front of the church? house. And then it
23		was like, okay (2) let's just take this ELSEwhere. And you KNOW
24		how when HIGH school kids get—just like (2) when you TAKE stuff
25		elsewhere and then EVERYBODY! FOLLOWS. And then it's like (2)
26		ALRIGHT (2) now I'm going to have to fight her 'cause EVERYbody
27		else is over here too. And then so she was still talking her little
28		SMACK LIP? (2) and things like that. And you know (2) everybody
29		was like "Yes you DI::D say that (2) and I HEARD IT" and she was
30		like "Yeah I DI::D say it because it IS TRUE?" And I'm just like
31		"You DON'T know NOTHING about NOTHING and
32		dah?dahdahdahdah? And then so—((suck teeth)) that was it (2) when
33		she just got up in my face. And I could just (2) SMELL her breath?
34		and FEEL her spit? and it was just like ((claps)) tat! And it was on
35		((laughs)).
36	Morgan:	Wait a minute. No! You fought?
37	Zinzi:	Of course. ((laughs)) Like, what did you WANT me to DO?: "Well
38		that's okay you can? go ahead and tell rumors about me? Go right
39		ahead" ((in a hypercorrect, high-pitched voice)). No!

In contrast to boys' signifying episodes, girls' instigating often leads to physical confrontations, which are not viewed as a loss of face or coolness but as a logical last resort. Zinzi confirms this in lines 7 and 8, where she reports deciding to ask her friends what Sheila said "instead of going up in her face."[5] Zinzi's story is different from those reported by Goodwin in one major respect: The basic three stages Goodwin (1990, 1992) describes—(1) offense, (2) instigating, (3) confrontation—have been expanded to include interrogation of "so-called" friends and punishment of the offender.[6]

The social order is clearly in jeopardy as Zinzi canvasses her friends for their role in Sheila's conversations in lines 9 through 11. She determines who her "real" friends are and whether Tyrone's report is true by interrogating friends and bystanders. Zinzi then finds out exactly how her friends responded to Sheila. During this time, all parties focus on past, present, and possible conversations with and about Sheila.

Once she has established the truth, Zinzi searches for, finds, and confronts the instigator. Sheila accepts responsibility for what she says (lines 19–20 and 29–30), Zinzi denies that it is true, and eventually she strikes Sheila. She explains her physical attack on Sheila by defending her right to protect herself against unfounded rumors.

Although all of these children's language activities are fraught with confrontations and accusations, they also illustrate the construction of social role and relationship through indirectness, cultural symbols, and audience coconstruction and collaboration. Participants desperately maintain a social face and the respect that it entails. This is true for both female and male children and adolescents, although girls, through their elaborate procedures, are much more active in maintaining social and cultural rules. Children are invested in and aware of the multilayered nature of such activities, especially how speaker intent and meaning are constructed and validated.

Signifying and instigating also occur in adult conversations, though in slightly different forms. Adults maintain and often expand the level of complexity common in childhood but have a very different attitude about how to play with available language styles and varieties.

Adult interaction: Reading dialect

A competent adult speaker already knows what children eventually learn through signifying and instigating routines: that audience and hearers are equal partners in interpreting talk. The Black expression "Know when you're playing" (also Gwaltney 1981:x) highlights the importance of audiences in constructing meaning in conversation. *Play* refers to the speaker's intentionality, as well as to whether she or he tells the truth and understands the consequences of what is said. This is an important characteristic of adult interaction, because in African American culture intentionality is considered not a psychological state but a collaborative social construct (cf. Duranti 1993).

The coconstruction of meaning and intention is tied to both language and culture in adult interaction. Unlike children, adults exploit the linguistic and pragmatic resources of both AAE and AE to constitute, construct, and sometimes expose social relations and cultural knowledge and norms.

An example of this process involves a practice I term *reading dialect* (Morgan 1994a), which should be understood in terms of the more general African American interpretive practice of *reading*, a form of directed discourse in which a speaker unambiguously denigrates another to her or his face (Goffman 1967).[7] Although one may self-report having read another person without witnesses (for example, in telling a story, the narrator may simply report, "I READ her!"), reading is legitimately accomplished only in the presence of other witnesses who corroborate that it occurred.[8]

Reading is directed, often accusatory, speech. When a target is read, her or his social face is attacked for inappropriate or offensive statements or for what the reader perceives as the speaker's false representation of her or his beliefs, personal values, and so forth. One may be read for acting out class privileges, failing to greet friends, or misrepresenting one's beliefs (Morgan 1996). The point is not the reader's correctness but the willingness to jeopardize her or his own social face by disclosing, regardless of setting or context, the target's perceived attempt to camouflage personal beliefs, attitudes, and so on.[9]

Reading dialect, a subgenre of reading, occurs when members of the African American community contrast or otherwise highlight obvious features of AAE and AE to make a point. The point is not necessarily negative, but the grammatical contrast indicates a challenge to someone's social face. These lexical and grammatical structures are well known in the community and are often the focus of verbal play, humor, and irony. For example, to stress a point a member might say, "It's not simply that I am cool. I be cool. In fact, I BEEN cool (a very long time)." In the African

American community, not only the two dialects of AAE and AE but also varieties within those dialects are regularly read by interlocutors.

Reading dialect often highlights the social-face contrast of being cool versus acting a fool in that the reader challenges the target's discourse. This challenge is also in defense of the reader, who does not want to be taken for a fool and thereby incur damage to her or his social face. Discussions between the reader and the target often involve clarification, agreement, and disagreement, ending with social face intact and opposing statements from the target and the reader: The target states that the reader's interpretation is wrong and the reader states that it is correct.

African American women in (inter)action

As African American girls grow into women, their everyday conversations often involve the expression and defense of social face. Active participation in discourse is often based on extent of personal involvement in the events being discussed. If all major participants are not present, especially when another's speech may be reported, the event is only minimally discussed, even when participants are close friends or relatives. The origins of this practice lie in the importance adult women attach to the audience's right to determine intentionality, even when information is delivered behind the speaker's back. Women learned the crucial role of the audience when, as teenagers, they went to elaborate lengths to determine what someone said and how others responded to rumors. These interrogations are filled with accusations, and people must prove their friendship. Within women's interactions, however, the main discourse focus is not whether someone instigates or backstabs but rather whether the intentionality assessments made by the audience are reasonable considering the context and whether the original speaker had the opportunity to address these assessments. Thus, instead of focusing on who said something negative about another, as preadolescent girls do, or on who intended to start a confrontation, as teenagers do, women focus on a speaker's right to be present to represent her own experience. This right is fiercely protected, for it provides the conditions for the more fundamental right that women and men should be allowed to interpret their own experiences. Yet adult women's social face is even more delicately constructed because it is continually challenged and tested by the audience.

Women operate with two dialogic styles, "behind your back" and "to your face," as represented by the statement "I wouldn't say anything behind your back that I wouldn't say to your face," which is often used to challenge someone's social face and can halt he-said-she-said or instigating attempts. A woman who makes such a statement is viewed as standing up for what she believes in and says, irrespective of the costs. Not surprisingly, then, interactions about people who are not present are considered tactless and divisive. Therefore, talking about someone behind her back does not mean that the speaker says something derogatory but that the teller's intentionality or actual words do not have the benefit of coauthorship, and as a result the interaction may be misunderstood. The "behind your back / in your face" dichotomy stipulates that intentionality is socially constructed and anyone who subverts this construction intends to deprive others of their discourse rights.

The following conversational segment is illustrative. Participants include three related women who grew up together: Ruby (a jazz musician, age 78), who does not speak in this segment; Baby Ruby (a retired prison guard, age 63); and Judy (a retired data-entry worker, age 63). Ruby and Judy are sisters and Baby Ruby is their niece. Baby Ruby is not happy that she is still called by her childhood name, and she is not happy that Ruby and Judy are her aunts, a fact she laments to anyone who will listen. Also present are Judy's six daughters (including me). Other than my attempts at questioning, no daughters participate in the conversation, because for African American women and girls, mere presence during a conversation does not authorize participation. Girls have two expressions for uninvited conversational participants: "This is an A and B conversation so C your way out" and "You're all in the Kool-Aid and don't even know the flavor."

(2)   "Auntism"
       1   Morgan: NUMBER ONE uh—the First! question is:
       2   (.)
       3   now: in terms of growing up: right. you two were born
       4   (.)
       5   same year? right
       6   (.)
       7   Baby Ruby: =Six months apart and I'm in [I'm
       8   Judy: [And she NEVER let me forget it.=
       9   Morgan: =((laughs))
      10   (.)
      11   Baby Ruby: Right
      12   (.)
      13   Baby Ruby: [But I
      14   Judy: [She's SIX months older than I am
      15   (.)
      16   Baby Ruby: But that's the aunt.
      17   (.)
      18   Judy: And I AM her aunt.
      19   (.)
      20   Baby Ruby: And I:: don't like it.
      21   (.)
      22   Judy: And I:: don't care=
      23   Morgan: =((laughs))
      24   (.)
      25   Judy: I am STILL the aunt
      26   (.)
      27   Morgan: NOW: you have to understand we never knew::
      28   (.)
      29   that—you were her—she's your aunt
      30   (.)
      31   Baby Ruby: [YOU—you's
      32   Morgan: [WE WERE AL:WAYS:! confused?

33		(.)
34		Yeah we—we were like what's the reLA:tionship
35		(.)
36	Baby Ruby:	((gazes at Morgan)) You're KIDDIN?
37		(.)
38	Baby Ruby:	That's my DAD'S si:ster ((nods head toward Judy))
39		(.)
40		Ain't THAT disGUSTin?
41		(.)
42	Judy:	Your bad what?
43		(.)
44	Baby Ruby:	[My DA::D'S sister
45	Morgan:	[My DA::D'S sister
46		(.)
47	Judy:	Right.
48		(.)
49	Judy:	I AM her fa:ther's sister ((winks at granddaughter/camera))
50		(.)
51	Judy:	My dad- father- And uh:: she- I don't know why: you all didn't know
52		it because she AL:ways sa::id: that I'm
53		[six months ol:der than you
54	Baby Ruby:	[I SURE DID!
55		(.)
56	Morgan:	Well YEAH- But you- Yeah- I'm six months older than you:: than you
57		doesn't mean:: [that
58	Baby Ruby:	[AH—DO—AND YOUR AUNTISM DOESN'T
59		GO ANYWHERE
60	Judy:	[And she'd always call me (?)
61		(.)
62	Judy:	She [A:Lways said it
63	Baby Ruby:	[CAUSE I'M THE OLDEST
64		(.)
65	Baby Ruby:	So your auntism: is: like nothing?

In "Auntism," Judy and Baby Ruby offer competing perspectives on their relationship. In the process, they talk "in each other's faces" about each other, using hearers (Judy's daughters) to mimic talking about someone behind her back.

Lines 1 through 14 initiate an interactional sequence in which Baby Ruby and Judy respond to my question about their being the same age, which for them is also a kinship question. This interaction quickly becomes a competition over who will tell the story: Judy overlaps Baby Ruby (line 8) and completes Baby Ruby's point while overlapping with Baby Ruby again in line 14. Beginning in line 16, Baby Ruby and Judy argue about their kinship, addressing each other and their daughters and granddaughters, who function as mock receivers and overhearers. Judy and Baby

Ruby do not use direct eye contact with each other, although they do manage a few sideways glances.

Baby Ruby and Judy signify on each other by reading dialect and using mock receivers. In particular, Baby Ruby signifies through reading dialect in line 16 when she invokes the unambiguous AAE usage of the demonstrative pronoun *that* to refer to an animate entity, namely Judy, in order to convey a negative reading. In AAE *that* is frequently used to emphasize that a person is the target of signifying. In these contexts *that* is marked negatively because many members of the African American community, especially older members, interpret use of an inanimate term in reference to a Black person as insulting, regardless of the speaker's race. *That* bears additional significance because many older African Americans were raised in the South, where white supremacists referred to Black adults as children or objects.

Baby Ruby directs her statement about Judy, *But that's the aunt*, to me (the mock receiver). Judy signifies back by also directing her comment to me and by reading dialect with the first-person Standard English noncontracted copula *AM* spoken loudly in line 18. *AM* is spoken as part of loud-talking, because it is noticeably louder than preceding and following utterances (cf. Mitchell-Kernan 1972). It thus marks the claim made in Standard English as authoritative: Judy *is* the aunt.

This turn also begins a series of contrasting parallel statements that are conjoined by *and* (lines 18–22), which are part of signifying because their rhythmic similarity highlights their contrasting lexical and grammatical relations. Line 16 begins the assessment dispute over the nature of the technical definition of *aunt* and the term's associated social norms. In line 20 Baby Ruby offers her subjective negative assessment of Judy's being her aunt. Judy responds with a parallel structure in line 22, a negative comment regarding Baby Ruby's statement, and in line 25 she mirrors line 18, with the adverb *still* highlighting the fact that although Baby Ruby doesn't like it, Judy will always be the aunt. However, the dispute over who has the right to define their relationship has not ended.

Although Judy's topic change interrupts the signifying episode (line 51), Baby Ruby has not finished asserting her right to define the relationship. In line 58, she further diminishes Judy's status by recasting Judy's repeated assertion—*I AM her aunt*; *I am STILL the aunt*—as "YOUR AUNTISM." She changes the quality of the noun *aunt* by adding the suffix *-ism*, which denotes the attitude, role, and responsibilities of being an aunt (cf. Quirk et al. 1972). Thus Baby Ruby replaces Judy's formal definition of their relationship with her notion that Judy never had the duties, responsibilities, role, and therefore status of an aunt. Baby Ruby successfully closes the signifying sequence with the statement in line 65: *So your auntism: is: like nothing?*.

Judy and Baby Ruby signify by using the lexical, grammatical, prosodic, and interactional resources available to members of the African American community. Signifying in this interaction concerns how speakers assert and contest the unequal aunt/niece relationship and simultaneously negotiate the solidarity of age-based friendship. Judy and Baby Ruby recognize when they are the intended targets and verbally collaborate in signifying through a turn-for-turn matching of comparable resources. The skills they developed as children are used both to tease and to confirm, mediate, and constitute familial and personal relationships. Judy signifies that she is the aunt, but Baby Ruby signifies that Judy is much more her friend and peer and the "auntism is like nothing."

Conclusion

This illustration of how African American girls, young women, and adults grow and function as core social actors in their communities demonstrates that they are part of rather than peripheral to vernacular culture.[10] Moreover, their identity as African Americans is tied to the construction of a cool social face, which they maintain and protect through language games such as he-said-she-said, instigating, and conversational signifying.

When the great reggae artist Bob Marley sang "No Woman, No Cry," he included the chorus and mantra "Everything's gonna be alright." He was not singing about the mistakes of the past but about how we must take lessons from the past. In our case, these lessons lead us to reanalyze the research that has defined the field and to conduct new research that includes women as social actors. To understand the African American speech community and women's role in it is possible only when scholars are self-aware. We must realize what we say about others, as well as ourselves, when we privilege some groups and marginalize others. And we must provide a sincere and exhausting critique when authors, analysts, and activists keep making the same mistakes.

NOTES

Since the original writing of this chapter, two publications on similar topics have been published (Morgan 1996, 1998), but the theoretical arguments presented here are new.

1. I use *African American English* (*AAE*) to refer to the language varieties of U.S. residents of African descent. *AAE* acknowledges speakers' African descent and connects U.S. speakers with those in the African diaspora, especially the English-speaking diaspora in the Americas. *American English* (*AE*) refers to varieties of U.S. English without regard to social or cultural markedness or class, region, gender, or age. These varieties include *standard*, *network*, and *mainstream*, as well as *working-class, Southern, Brooklyn*, and so on.

2. African American coolness is similar to the Akan notion of dry speech as clear, precise, witty, and full of integrity. This contrasts with Akan wet or uncool speech, which is viewed as immature, dull, and slurred (cf. Yankah 1991a:47–54). See Morgan (1998) for a detailed discussion of this subject.

3. Such self-construction through narrative is found in other discourse communities as well; see the chapters by Lisa Capps, Marjorie Orellana, Patricia Sawin, and Kathleen Wood in this volume.

4. In the transcript, CAPITAL LETTERS indicate some form of emphasis, signaled by changes in pitch or amplitude. A period (.) indicates a fall in tone, not necessarily the end of a sentence, whereas a comma (,) indicates a continuing intonation, not necessarily between clauses of sentences. Colons (:) indicate that the preceding sound is lengthened. A question mark (?) indicates a rising intonation, not necessarily a question, and an exclamation point (!) indicates an animated tone, not necessarily an exclamation. Dashes and hyphens (-) indicate a cutoff or interruption of sound. Overlapping utterances are marked with a single left

bracket ([). A period within parentheses (.) indicates a one-second pause. Numbers in parentheses (2) are timed pauses in seconds. Double parentheses are transcriber comments.

5. This expression means 'confront' or 'fight'.

6. Although this is a reported story, I have other recordings of teenagers engaged in actual instigating. I have also helped mediate the preconfrontation stage of these episodes, but with only minor success.

7. This form of directed discourse is also called *throwing shade*.

8. Some people use the term *reading* to mean 'telling someone off', but in the absence of an audience this claim cannot be confirmed.

9. In recent examples of directed discourse in hip hop, artists "diss" opponents who fail to "come correct," "represent," or "give props." It is especially severe because audiences wait for artists to do battle. Such interactions can be found between artists Tim Dog and Dr. Dre, Dr. Dre and Eazy E, Kool Moe Dee and LL Cool J, and MC Lyte and Antoinette, among others.

10. Whereas African American women's discourse skills originate in their childhood language practices, Jennifer Coates (chapter 6, this volume), by contrast, finds a disjunction between younger white British girls' playful discourse style and their more disempowered style as they grow older.

REFERENCES

Abrahams, Roger (1962). Playing the dozens. *Journal of American Folklore* 75:209–218.

———— (1970). *Deep down in the jungle*. Chicago: Aldine.

———— (1974). Black talking on the streets. In Richard Bauman & Joel Sherzer (eds.), *Explorations in the ethnography of speaking*. Cambridge: Cambridge University Press, 240–262.

———— (1975). Negotiating respect: Patterns of presentation among black women. *Journal of American Folklore* 88:58–80.

———— (1976). *Talking black*. Rowley, MA: Newbury House.

Alleyne, Mervyn (1980). *Comparative Afro-American: An historical-comparative study of English-based Afro-American dialects of the New World*. Ann Arbor, MI: Karoma Press.

———— (1989). *Roots of Jamaican culture*. London: Pluto Press.

Ball, Arnetha F. (1992). The discourse of power and solidarity: Language features of African American females and a male program leader in a neighborhood-based youth dance program. In Kira Hall, Mary Bucholtz, & Birch Moonwomon (eds.), *Locating power: Proceedings of the Second Berkeley Women and Language Conference*. Berkeley, CA: Berkeley Women and Language Group, 23–35.

Butler, Judith (1995). Collected and fractured: Response to *Identities*. In Anthony Appiah & Henry Louis Gates Jr. (eds.), *Identities*. Chicago: University of Chicago Press, 439–447.

Crenshaw, Kimberle (1992). Whose story is it anyway?: Feminist and antiracist appropriations of Anita Hill. In Toni Morrison (ed.), *Race-ing justice, en-gendering power: Essays on Anita Hill and Clarence Thomas, and the construction of social reality*. New York: Pantheon, 402–440.

Dollard, John (1973). The dozens: Dialectic of insult. In Alan Dundes (ed.), *Mother wit from the laughing barrel*. Jackson: University of Mississippi Press, 277–294. (Original work published 1939)

Duneier, Mitchell (1992). *Slim's table: Race, respectability, and masculinity*. Chicago: University of Chicago Press.

Duranti, Alessandro (1993). Truth and intentionality: An ethnographic critique. *Cultural Anthropology* 8(2):214–245.

Eckert, Penelope, & Sally McConnell-Ginet (1992). Think practically and look locally: Language and gender as community-based practice. *Annual Review of Anthropology* 21:461–490.

Etter-Lewis, Gwendolyn (1991). Standing up and speaking out: African American women's narrative legacy. *Discourse and Society* 2:425–437.

—— (1993). *My soul is my own: Oral narratives of African American women in the professions.* London: Routledge.

Etter-Lewis, Gwendolyn, & Michèle Foster (eds.) (1996). *Unrelated kin: Race and gender in women's personal narratives.* London: Routledge.

Foster, Michèle (1995). Are you with me?: Power and solidarity in the discourse of African American women. In Kira Hall & Mary Bucholtz (eds.), *Gender articulated: Language and the socially constructed self.* New York: Routledge, 329–350.

Garner, Thurmon (1983). Playing the dozens: Folklore as strategies for living. *Quarterly Journal of Speech* 69:47–57.

Gates, Henry Louis Jr. (1988). *The signifying monkey: A theory of African-American literary criticism.* Oxford: Oxford University Press.

George, Nelson (1992). *Buppies, b-boys, baps, and bohos: Notes on post-soul Black culture.* New York: HarperCollins.

Goffman, Erving (1967). *Interaction ritual: Essays on face-to-face behavior.* New York: Anchor Books.

—— (1974). *Frame analysis.* New York: Harper & Row.

Goodwin, Marjorie Harness (1980). He-said-she-said: Formal cultural procedures for the construction of a gossip dispute activity. *American Ethnologist* 7:674–695.

—— (1982). "Instigating": Storytelling as a social process. *American Ethnologist* 9:76–96.

—— (1985). The serious side of jump rope: Conversational practices and social organization in the frame of play. *Journal of American Folklore* 98:315–330.

—— (1988). Cooperation and competition across girls' play activities. In Sue Fisher & Alexandra Dundas Todd (eds.), *Gender and discourse: The power of talk.* Norwood, NJ: Ablex, 55–94.

—— (1990). *He-said-she-said: Talk as social organization among black children.* Bloomington: Indiana University Press.

—— (1992). Orchestrating participation in events. In Kira Hall, Mary Bucholtz, & Birch Moonwomon (eds.), *Locating power: Proceedings of the Second Berkeley Women and Language Conference.* Berkeley, CA: Berkeley Women and Language Group, 182–196.

Grier, William, & Price Cobbs (1968). *Black rage.* New York: Bantam.

Gwaltney, John (1981). *Drylongso: A self-portrait of black America.* New York: Vintage.

Hall, Stuart (1995). The question of cultural identity. In Stuart Hall, David Held, Don Hubert, & Kenneth W. Thompson (eds.), *Modernity: An introduction to modern societies.* Oxford: Blackwell, 596–631.

Henley, Nancy M. (1995). Ethnicity and gender issues in language. In Hope Landrine (ed.), *Bringing cultural diversity into feminist psychology: Theory, research, practice.* Washington, DC: American Psychological Association, 361–395.

hooks, bell (1990). *Yearning: Race, gender, and cultural politics.* Boston: South End Press.

—— (1992). *Black looks: Race and representation.* Boston: South End Press.

Horton, John (1972). Time and cool people. In Thomas Kochman (ed.), *Rappin' and stylin' out: Communication in urban black America.* Urbana: University of Illinois Press, 19–31.

Hurston, Zora Neale (1990). *Jonah's gourd vine.* New York: Harper. (Original work published 1934)

—— (1937). *Their eyes were watching God.* Philadelphia: Lippincott.

Kochman, Thomas (1972). Toward an ethnography of Black American speech behavior. In Thomas Kochman (ed.), *Rappin' and stylin' out: Communication in urban black America.* Urbana: University of Illinois Press, 241–264.

—— (1973). Review of *Language behavior in a black urban community* by Claudia Mitchell-Kernan. *Language* 49(4):967–983.

―――― (1983). The boundary between play and nonplay in Black verbal dueling. *Language in Society* 12(3):329–337.

―――― (1986). Strategic ambiguity in Black speech genres: Cross-cultural interference in participant-observation research. *Text* 6(2):153–170.

Kondo, Dorinne (1997). A*bout face: Performing race in fashion and theater*. London: Routledge.

Kunjufu, Jawanza (1986). *Countering the conspiracy to destroy Black boys*. 2 vols. Chicago: African American Images.

Labov, William (1972). *Language in the inner city: Studies in the Black English Vernacular*. Philadelphia: University of Pennsylvania Press.

―――― (1998). Co-existent systems in African-American Vernacular English. In Salikoko Mufwene, John Rickford, Guy Bailey, & John Baugh (eds.), *African-American English: Structure, history, use*. London: Routledge, 110–153.

Major, Clarence (1994). *Juba to jive: A dictionary of African-American slang*. New York: Penguin.

Majors, Richard, & Janet Mancini Billson (1992). Cool pose: *The dilemmas of black manhood in America*. New York: Lexington.

Mitchell-Kernan, Claudia (1971). *Language behavior in a black urban community*. Berkeley: University of California Language Behavior Laboratory.

―――― (1972). Signifying, loud-talking, and marking. In Thomas Kochman (ed.), *Rappin' and stylin' out: Communication in urban black America*. Urbana: University of Illinois Press, 315–335.

―――― (1973). Signifying. In Alan Dundes (ed.), *Mother wit from the laughing barrel*. Jackson: University of Mississippi Press, 310–328.

Morgan, Marcyliena (1989). From down South to up South: The language behavior of three generations of Black women residing in Chicago. Ph.D. diss., University of Pennsylvania.

―――― (1991). Indirectness and interpretation in African American women's discourse. *Pragmatics* 1(4):421–452.

―――― (1993). The Africanness of counterlanguage among Afro-Americans. In Salikoko Mufwene (ed.), *Africanisms in Afro-American language varieties*. Athens: University of Georgia Press, 423–435.

―――― (1994a). The African American speech community: Reality and sociolinguistics. In Marcyliena Morgan (ed.), *The social construction of reality in creole situations*. Los Angeles: Center for African American Studies Press, 121–150.

―――― (1994b). Theories and politics in African American English. *Annual Review of Anthropology* 23:325–345.

―――― (1996). Conversational signifying: Grammar and indirectness among African American women. In Elinor Ochs, Emanuel Schegloff, & Sandra Thompson (eds.), *Interaction and grammar*. Cambridge: Cambridge University Press, 405–433.

―――― (1998). More than a mood or an attitude: Discourse and verbal genres in African American culture. In Salikoko Mufwene, John Rickford, Guy Bailey, & John Baugh (eds.), *African-American English: Structure, history, use*. London: Routledge, 251–281.

Morrison, Toni (1992). *Playing in the dark: Whiteness and the literary imagination*. Cambridge: Harvard University Press.

Mufwene, Salikoko (1992). Ideology and facts on African American English. *Pragmatics* 2(2):141–166.

Percelay, James, Ivey Monteria, & Stephan Dweck (1994). *Snaps*. New York: Quill.

Quirk, Randolph, et al. (1972). *A grammar of contemporary English*. London: Longman.

Rickford, John (1986). The need for new approaches to social class analysis in sociolinguistics. *Language and Communication* 6(3):215–221.

Rickford, John, Arnetha Ball, Renee Blake, Raina Jackson, & Nomi Martin (1991). Rappin on the copula coffin: Theoretical and methodological issues in the analysis of copula variation in African American vernacular. *Language Variation and Change* 3(1):103–132.

Rickford, John, & Faye McNair-Knox (1993). Addressee- and topic-influenced style shift: A quantitative sociolinguistic study. In Douglas Biber & Edward Finegan (eds.), *Sociolinguistic perspectives on register*. Oxford: Oxford University Press, 235–276.

Smitherman, Geneva (1977). *Talkin and testifyin: The language of Black America*. Boston: Houghton Mifflin.

——— (1994). *Black talk: Words and phrases from the hood to the amen corner*. New York: Houghton Mifflin.

Spears, Arthur (1988). Black American English. In Johnnetta B. Cole (ed.), *Anthropology for the nineties: Introductory readings*. New York: Free Press, 96–113.

Turner, Patricia (1993). I heard it through the grapevine: Rumor in African-American culture. Berkeley: University of California Press.

Visweswaran, Kamala (1994). *Fictions of feminist ethnography*. Minneapolis: University of Minnesota Press.

Washington, Mary Helen (1987). *Invented lives: Narratives of black women 1860–1960*. New York: Doubleday.

Wolfram, Walter (1969). *A sociolinguistic description of Detroit Negro speech*. Washington, DC: Center for Applied Linguistics.

Yankah, Kwesi (1991a). Oratory in Akan society. *Discourse and Society* 2(1):47–64.

——— (1991b). Power and the circuit of formal talk. *Journal of Folklore Research* 28(1):1–22.

· ·

Coherent Identities amid
Heterosexist Ideologies

Deaf and Hearing Lesbian
Coming-Out Stories

he last decade has seen a rise in antihomophobia legislation and a com-
ercial production of positive images of queer lifestyles in the media, on
prime-time television, and in Hollywood.[1] Tempering this apparent acceptance is the reality that many queers still commonly experience both
family rejection and public acts of hatred. In this social context, how and where do
queers resist heterosexist boundaries and realize coherent identities as lesbians and gay
men? One site is the life stories they tell, where identities are discursively created amid
prevailing ideologies. Like other life stories about counterhegemonic living, the life
stories of queers are oftentimes stories of a movement away from a social mainstream
to life on the perimeter—stories of self-transformation about recognizing and revealing gender and attraction differences. These coming-out stories have been variously
examined in the literature of anthropology and sociolinguistics (cf. Deby 1996; Gaudio
1996; Liang 1997; Wood 1997), providing us with a theoretical backdrop for the study
of their structures. Julia Penelope and Susan Wolfe, in a widely read collection of lesbians' stories, explain that "coming out involves revealing one's identity to oneself,
family members, colleagues, and communities. Coming out stories characterize the
journey's two levels: the external events of becoming a lesbian, and the internal processes that accompany these events" (1989:10). In this chapter, I will examine the structures of coming-out stories of Deaf and hearing lesbians in order to show how coherent lesbian identities are realized, a narrative task that requires such women to contend
with hegemonic notions of gender, attraction, and sexuality.[2]

Coherence and identity in life stories and personal narratives

Social constructionists in anthropology, social psychology, rhetoric, and linguistics
have discussed the impact of social structures such as gender, sexual orientation, race,

class, linguistic background, and literacy ability on the discursive production of identity (e.g., Bakhtin 1981, 1986; Bruner 1990; Foucault 1982; Gergen 1992; Shotter 1993). This paradigm has little room for the rigid, monolithic view of identity taken by many linguistic variationists in which a specific linguistic form indexes a single identity category. Researchers from various fields have analyzed the discursive production of identities and cultures in autobiography (Bruner 1990; Rosen 1988), personal narrative (Labov 1972), oral history (Hymes 1981), language use (Kannapell 1989), and life stories (Linde 1993). Barbara Johnstone claims that narrative "structures our sense of self and our interactions with others, our sense of place and community" (1990:5). Others (Polanyi 1985; Polkinghorne 1991; Rosen 1988; Schank & Abelson 1995) support this tie between narrative and identity, showing that personal and social identity cannot be separated from stories of community and that stories cannot be separated from the social being. Yet little beyond the structural level is known of the narrative resources that create and display textual selves in social context.

One resource for the narrative construction of selves is *coherence*. Researchers who integrate frame theory into their analyses of talk argue that local and societal context is central to the production and analysis of coherent discourse (cf. Ribeiro 1993, 1994; Schiffrin 1994; Tannen 1985). In examining how lesbians realize identities through stories, then, we must go below the surface to the narratives' underlying logic or coherence by examining their local (interactional) and global (ideological) contexts. The coherence of stories—that is, the logic invoked by their interactional and ideological context—is created by inferences, shared assumptions, and subsequent presuppositions that underlie the discourses of a community.

In her discussion of the systems of coherence indexed in life stories, Charlotte Linde notes, "There is a limited number of coherence systems that can be present in a given culture at a given time, since one's addressee must at least recognize if not share any coherence system one chooses to use" (1993:165). Jerome Bruner (1990) likewise points out that personal narratives are simultaneously a recounting of significant events and a justification for life choices. Like all self-transformation stories, coming-out stories are rhetorical attempts to justify one's life, to realize acceptable selves by creating coherent identities. For a life story to be coherent, the justification of one's choices or experiences must be recognizable and acceptable. The coming-out stories that follow are successful in that they access ideologies and associated narrative patterns that are common and familiar within a general heterosexist context, while invoking local, interactional forms.

Lesbians telling coming-out stories

For five years, I have been a member of a national electronic-mail distribution list of a group of Deaf and hearing lesbian friends. We created this list in order to stay in touch with one another on a daily basis. Over the last two years, I have urged my friends, "Send me your coming-out stories." Although my original request was for electronic-mail stories, some women wrote them on paper or told them in American Sign Language (ASL).

My analysis of these stories supports what other researchers have suggested: Identity is not an immutable, monolithic realization. Following Elinor Ochs, I argue that the relation of language to identity is not "a straightforward mapping of linguistic form to social meaning"; rather, identity is "constituted and mediated by the relation of language to stances, social acts, social activities, and other social constructs" (Ochs 1992:336–337). Likewise, this analysis argues against essentializing the coming-out story or suggesting that it is very different in form from any other self-transformation story. Coming-out stories, like all self-transformation stories, reveal the tellers' identities as the result of their struggles with the ideologies surrounding their transformation.

What distinguishes lesbian coming-out stories from other transformation stories is that heterosexist ideologies comprise the most salient pool of coherence resources from which a woman constructs herself as sexual, gendered, attractive, and attracted. Lesbian self-transformation stories are stories of resistance about women loving women amid sexism and homophobia, facts that both constrain and provide resources for the realization of lesbian identities. Such stories trace the transformation from lifestyles grounded in dominant ideologies to lifestyles that question these ideologies. In order for this narrative transformation to be coherent, narrative logic must adhere to the sociolinguistic conventions of other stories whose coherence systems are bound to dominant ideologies. Lesbians must therefore tell coming-out stories that index the pool of acceptable (that is, coherent) narrative selves, selves that are recognized as either conforming to or resisting heterosexist ideologies.

Interactional and ideological resources and constraints

Johnstone claims that "it is more enlightening to think of factors such as gender, ethnicity, and audience as resources that speakers use to create unique voices than as determinants of how they will talk" (1996:56). Johnstone's focus on the creativity of the individual, on circumstances as identity resources, is on target, but it also attributes an undue amount of volition to the user and obscures the fact that these resources are both bountiful and restrictive. For this reason I use the term *resources and constraints* rather than simply *resources* for such factors.

Lesbian identities are created at the narrative intersection of dominant heterosexist ideologies and lesbians' counterhegemonic stories of gender, attraction, and sexuality. The narrative stances that lesbians take toward hegemony reveal their identities. By *narrative stance*, I refer to the intertextual relationship of the narrative self to the possible selves promoted by dominant ideologies.

Heidi Hamilton calls for "a relatively more linguistic definition of intertextuality" (1996:64). She notes that Nikolaus Coupland has cautioned her to include in her analysis not only real-life experiences but also those that are "wholly fictional," for they likewise participate in the formation of stereotypes. In the spirit of Coupland's advice, I argue here for a more integrative view of intertextuality. I suggest that there are at least two levels of resources and constraints that function intertextually and contribute to the coherence of identities: (1) the local or interactional level that indexes, in a specific speech act, tellers' membership within a community of practice (Eckert & McConnell-Ginet 1992); and (2) the societal level, which includes ideologies and prior discourses, real or imagined, in which certain archetypes, stereotypes, and prototypes are invoked.

Roger Schank and Robert Abelson describe narrative prototypes, which they call "skeletons," as follows: "Instead of telling all the details of a situation, we can index it as 'betrayal' or 'undermining my confidence' or 'ordering me around' or 'being inconsiderate.' Such prototypic stories need not be negative, of course. We have 'heroism' stories and 'defense of our nation' stories, and 'always there when I need you' stories as well. . . . Authors construct their own reality by finding the events that fit the skeleton convenient for them to believe" (1995:51–52). What are the underlying story-prototype resources that lesbians index when they tell their coming-out stories and realize their identities? What narrative "skeletons" do they invoke? How do these skeletons promote the coherent realization of identities?

Again, narrative skeletons are not necessarily benign resources. In fact, for many lesbians, especially for some very butch lesbians, narrating a lesbian life can be a painful, unpleasant task of reconciling oneself with what one "should" be. A butch lesbian must come to terms with the way she looks, walks, talks, and dresses and must narrate a story with the omnipresent realization that mainstream society, in its mass-media acceptance of lesbians, would prefer that she live at the lipstick-lesbian end of the spectrum and both narrate and live a more palatable life. From this perspective, ideologies of gender, attractiveness, and attraction in mainstream U.S. culture are less resources than constraints that force a lesbian to resist or risk being pulled to the hegemonic, heterosexist center.

Ideologies and cultural models provide life-story tellers with the tools to evoke the acceptable selves of a community of practice. In his examination of how fraternity men create powerful identities, Scott Kiesling (1996) considers how individual speakers create identities by invoking the models or roles that the fraternity's culture makes available. Michael Agar suggests in his discussion of "languaculture," however, that conversationalists do more than reproduce or conegotiate an immutable set of stereotypes, cultural models, or social facts. Once speakers have mastered the language and culture of a community of practice, they can begin to see languaculture as a set of resources (as opposed to constraints) through which they "can create, improvise, criticize, or struggle against, as you please" (Agar 1994:236). Likewise, although lesbians telling coming-out stories are constrained by the boundaries of narrative skeletons and acceptable selves (which index dominant and counterhegemonic ideologies), these constraints provide them with the opportunity to resist and to create themselves coherently yet uniquely.

Analyzing lesbian coming-out stories

When lesbians tell coming-out stories to a lesbian linguist who intends to make their stories public by analyzing their identity creation, they are engaging in a unique rhetorical occasion. In the nuances of this lesbian-to-lesbian interview occasion, we see how the local interactive situation (in this case a sociolinguistic interview) and the larger ideological context together provide the resources and constraints for each lesbian to realize her identity. The logic invoked in the interactive frames of the story and their accompanying schemata contribute to the story's coherence and point to the underlying narrative archetypes, skeletons, presuppositions, and stances toward ideologies, which in turn reveal identities.

Frames

Deborah Tannen (1993) discusses "the power of expectation" in each of the levels of frames that come into play in narrative discourse and demonstrates how these expectations are revealed in surface-level linguistic features. In this study, the coming-out stories trigger at least four kinds of interactive frames that contribute to the making of coherent, recognizable, and acceptable lesbian identities. The first is what Tannen calls the *storytelling frame*, the rules that tellers invoke as they attempt to tell a story according to the social rules of that task. That is, in this culture, stories often have a beginning, a middle, and an end, with a central point. Tellers adhere to this frame or transgress it in some way, but the frame, embedded unconsciously in individuals and in society, is always invoked. As Tannen points out, "there are a number of ways in which subjects reveal that they have expectations about how to tell a story" (1993:25), as when the teller says she is having trouble knowing what to include in the story or how to end it (Wood 1994, 1997). It is quite common for life-story tellers to have trouble closing the storytelling frame because the topic of a life story, a life still being lived, is not over. It is particularly difficult for a lesbian to close a story about coming out, for it is embedded in a heterosexist culture that forces her to deal with countless experiences of coming out, from those with intimates such as colleagues, friends, and families to those with strangers such as real estate agents and talkative airline seatmates.

A second interactive frame is the *performance frame*. The difference between a story that is told versus one that is performed is that form is foregrounded in the latter. As Richard Bauman explains:

> All framing, . . . including performance, is accomplished through the employment of culturally conventionalized metacommunication. In empirical terms, this means that each speech community will make use of a structured set of distinctive communicative means from among its resources in culturally conventionalized and culture-specific ways to key the performance frame, such that all communication that takes place within that frame is to be understood as performance within that community. (1978:16)

He lists some of the "communicative means" that index a performed story: special codes, figurative language, parallelism, special paralinguistic features, special formulae, appeals to tradition, and disclaimers of performance. Some of the tellers on the e-mail list are professional storytellers, and others assume a tale-teller role on the list. These storytellers clearly invoke a performance frame when they write or sign their stories.

Another frame is the *addresser/addressee frame*, in which certain forms index the addressee's discourse role or social identity. According to Isolda Carranza (1996), in this interactive phenomenon of dialogic text construction, the text shows traces of how it is continuously affected by the addressee's behavior. Texts are also shaped by the immediate communicative situation. For example, someone who tells a life story in a crowded and noisy coffee shop may raise her voice or cut the story short because of the physical strain of the communication situation. Likewise, stories told on e-mail contain evidence that the teller is aware of an *e-mail frame* (a type of *genre frame*) and the protocol involved, ratified or not. Although little research addresses the telling of stories via electronic mail, Sara Kiesler, Jane Siegel, and Timothy McGuire (1984) suggest that social-psychological factors (time and information-processing pressures, absence of regulating feedback, lack of status and position cues, social anonymity, and computing norms and etiquette) influence these transmissions, forcing special forms to take the place of, for example, backchanneling cues.

The last frame of expectation is the *event frame*, within which narrators describe real-world events and their role within them. Roy Baumeister and Leonard Newman note that "The ease of making a story is partly because there is an element of story narrative inherent in the events themselves as they happen. Stories are not just constructed after the fact as an aid to memory or explanation. Participants in events are aware of plans, goals, conflicts, links between actions, resolutions, and other narrative elements during (and sometimes even before) the episode" (1995:99). Other researchers refer to event frames as *event scripts*, *narrative prototypes*, or *skeletons*. These are the seemingly standardized versions of a real-life event indexed in surface features. For example, some lesbian coming-out stories index one of the following narrative skeletons:

Woman is raised in a heterosexual environment.

Woman behaves and looks like a heterosexual.

Woman is exposed to a lesbian lifestyle.

Woman switches to behaving like a homosexual.

Woman is raised in heterosexual environment.

Woman does not behave or look like a heterosexual.

Woman experiences social pressure to conform.

Woman continues living as she always has.

And regardless of structure, all lesbian coming-out narrative skeletons have an accompanying overlay of the real-world, often burdensome, event of self-disclosure. As Mary Elliott puts it,

What [coming-out] narratives elide, or mention only briefly and then recoil from (as an issue and experience), is the act of giving away the secret, that terrifying crossing of the abyss. One after another, these narratives present a minute glimpse of the dread, panic, confusion, and uncertainty of the actual moment of disclosure and then, as if mimetically reproducing the performance of the coming-out act itself as an uncomfortable (always) or even shameful (sometimes) but necessary ordeal, move on as quickly as possible and without comment to lengthy pedagogical, ethical, and sociological defenses of the coming-out process. (1996:694)

The event of coming out in a heterosexist society necessarily subverts ideologies of how we are to be women, how we are to be attractive and attracted, and how we are to behave sexually. By examining the various narrative frames in coming-out stories we can see how lesbians orient themselves to dominant ideologies, revealing their unique identities.

Ideologies

If identities are socially constructed via language and surrounding ideologies, then ideologies are the nucleus around which people orient themselves in order to reveal recognizable and acceptable identities. Gunther Kress and Robert Hodge define ideology as "a systematic body of ideas, organized from a particular point of view." They argue that "since normal perception works by constant feedback, the gap between the real world and the socially constructed world is constantly being reduced, so that what we do 'see' tends to become what we can say" (1993:5–6). What are the selves that dominant ideologies of gender, attraction, and sexuality allow us to "see" and say?

Lesbian coming-out stories are inevitably embedded in heterosexist ideologies, which tellers manage both to invoke and to transgress (cf. Liang, chapter 15, this volume). As Dorothy Holland and Naomi Quinn observe, "Among alternative versions of what is legitimate and what is inevitable, a given ideology is most compelling if its rightness engages the sense one has of one's own personal uprightness and worthiness, or if its inevitability engages the view one has of one's own inherent needs and capacities. These matters lie at the heart of our understanding of ourselves and our place in life" (1987:13). These all-pervasive abstract beliefs about what is right and legitimate, and thus most appropriate, pervade the discourses of the community; both mainstream and marginalized members of a society are constrained by dominant ideologies, and the identities of both groups are realized in relation to hegemony. That is, lesbians are able to see themselves through the same ideological lens through which homophobes see them.

While working on this chapter, I discovered that the homosexual "recovery group" Exodus was meeting on my campus for a three-day workshop, "Healing Homosexuality." The materials Exodus distributed conveniently indexed several heterosexist ideologies, which emanated from an overarching ideology that although homosexuality may be an inborn orientation, to act on it (that is, to have sexual relationships with members of the same sex) is a sexual sin. In one brochure Sy Rogers of the Church of Our Savior, a major ministry of homosexual conversion, discusses whether homosexuality is a sin or a gift: "As for Jesus, he did not specifically mention homosexuality. But then, he never mentioned incest, rape or bestiality for that matter. . . . Jesus showed mercy to those guilty of violating moral law—such as the woman caught in adultery. Yet He also commanded her to obey God with this second chance, and leave her life of sexual sin." Although the Exodus group represents a small segment of the heterosexist population, it clearly indexes mainstream ideologies.

Another useful source of information about heterosexist ideologies is the media, as shown by Shari Kendall's (1996) study of news stories concerning Salt

Lake City's 1996 ban of student gay groups in high schools. Kendall suggests that the heterosexist ideologies she locates emanate from the overarching ideology *Homosexuality is not natural and "not natural" is not good*:[3]

1. Homosexuality can be promoted.
2. Homosexuality is a decision.
3. There is no such thing as a homosexual, just an adoption of behaviors that make someone different.
4. Gay men and lesbians are rebellious children who don't know any better.
5. A homosexual lifestyle is different from a nonhomosexual lifestyle.
6. Homosexuality is a choice.
7. Homosexuality is not innate.
8. Homosexuality is sick.
9. All homosexuals are men.

For example, Kendall found that the textual presupposition that queers are less than human (that is, "unnatural") underlies the following excerpt from the *Salt Lake Tribune* (Feb. 3, 1996):

> As for [State Senator Charles Stewart], he says he has gotten nothing but support for his stance. While he has no anti-gay bills planned this session, he thinks other legislators might. And if some Utahns don't agree with him, Stewart makes no apologies.
> "It is a divisive issue for the whole society," he says. "It is drawing a line in the sand of what is civil and what is bestial. What is a human being and what is an animal."

Of course, one can argue that the articles and op-ed pieces Kendall examined are atypical of the U.S. mainstream and that this homophobic ideology is not culturally dominant. However, if this senator enjoys, at the very least, the support of those who elected him, and if this support enables him to proceed along a hegemonic trajectory, receiving privileged access to the media and an opportunity to declare what it means to be normal in this society, then Kendall's list of presuppositions does indeed represent a common sentiment within a heterosexist environment.

In such an environment, gay men's and lesbians' lives are sites of hegemonic resistance. So too are their life stories and the identities they create in telling them. In fact, there would be no need for a "coming-out" story in a society where queer lifestyles enjoyed the mainstream support that heterosexuality does in the United States today. The tellers of these stories therefore narrate from a vantage point of resistance, which allows them to access possible selves beyond the confines of heterosexual society.

Coming-out stories and the invention of identities

I collected the data for this study between 1994 and 1996. Table 2.1 is a summary of the profiles of the participants and the form in which I received their stories. Each woman did what all life-story tellers do: She created identity through frames amid surrounding

Table 2.1. Study participants and story formats, by communication mode and language choice

Storyteller	Deaf or hearing	Communication mode	Language used
Cindy	Deaf	E-mail	English
Barbara	Deaf	E-mail	English
Kim	Hearing	E-mail	English
Maria	Deaf	E-mail	English
Ellen	Deaf	Videotaped	ASL
Jennifer	Deaf	Handwritten	English

ideologies. One of the most important tasks the tellers accomplish is to establish their place within a community of practice, in this case, a geographically dispersed group of Deaf and hearing lesbians. Another important task is to orient themselves to dominant heterosexist ideologies, an act which is itself the realization of identity.

Cindy's e-mail story

On the day I sent my e-mail message requesting coming-out stories to the list, Cindy quickly responded with two messages constituting her fourteen-line coming-out story.[4] Cindy told me about her gay uncle who had had a nervous breakdown and had come out to his sister, Cindy's mother. He told Cindy that her mother had already guessed that Cindy too was gay. Cindy then delivered "all kind of book and information" to her mother under the guise of supporting her uncle, but eventually she came out to her. At this point in the narrative, Cindy tells me, in an embedded coming-out story, what she told her mother. It is the tale of her marriage, four children, grandchildren, and divorce. She ends by reporting that she is with her second and permanent "woman," "for good."

Cindy narrates within an e-mail frame, invoking the protocol of the list. The following unratified rules have emerged on the list over time:

1. Be brief. Limit posting to one screen.
2. Send without editing. Leave grammatical and mechanical errors in.
3. Don't capitalize if you don't want to.
4. Use "TTY" forms.
5. Use ASL-English contact forms.
6. Use humor whenever possible.

Cindy's orientation to the e-mail frame can be seen in her conformity to these rules. For example, she uses *I* six times in two lines, capitalizing it only twice. She uses *woman* instead of *women* for the plural form at one point and does not adhere to the subject/verb agreement rules of Standard English. These forms could be second-language errors, since Cindy is a native speaker of ASL, or the result of quick, unedited typing. In any case, they contribute to the realization of Cindy's lesbian identity on e-mail: Her adherence to the list protocol aligns her with the lesbian members in this community of practice and indexes a larger disregard for the conventions of standard written English.

Cindy, like many Deaf people who communicate on the phone with a teletype communication device (TTY), has transferred TTY conventions to electronic-mail communication. For example, she twice uses the abbreviation *abt* for *about*. Cindy thereby marks herself both as a member of the list, which expects such stylistic transfer, and as a regular TTY user and thus part of the larger Deaf community.

Other aspects of the e-mail frame in Cindy's story relate not to the protocol for posting to the list but to the limitations of the mode of communication itself. For example, *Me dont know how to tell my story abt my coming out hmm it started with my uncle who is gay and have been for years.* The form *hmm* is a conversational placeholding marker, something that would likely occur in a face-to-face conversation. Here it substitutes for the intimacy of unmediated interaction. Cindy also invokes the storytelling frame: Her statement *me dont know how to tell my story* indicates her awareness of the special demands of story construction.

Cindy thus uses sociolinguistic resources provided by e-mail and storytelling frames. But how is Cindy-as-lesbian realized in relation to dominant ideologies? She begins her story with, *My mom ask me why i became gay I told her i was crazy abt women ever since i was a kids but thought I can t have that so i got marry and had four great kids and grandchildren.* Cindy's mother's question indexes a presupposition that Cindy was not born gay, that her *homosexuality is not innate* (item 7 on the above list of homophobic ideologies). But Cindy's initial response indexes a presupposition that *homosexuality is innate, or at least can occur in very early childhood.* The immediacy of Cindy's response points to her current stance toward her sexuality and her orientation to dominant ideologies.

Cindy tells her mother, "but i thought I can t have that so i got marry . . . ," a comment that indexes the presupposition that *lesbianism is a set of behaviors* (item 3 in the preceding list). Cindy in the narrative assumed she could "choose" to adopt heterosexuality if she wanted to, by living like a straight woman. Cindy the narrator hence draws on several narrative presuppositions and engages in a dialogue with the underlying ideologies, thereby indexing a particular narrative skeleton.

The skeletons I present here are intended to represent not summaries of the coming-out stories but rather the underlying coherence model that the tellers apparently invoke in order to "make sense of their own lives" (Schank & Abelson 1995:59). Indexing established cultural models or narrative skeletons is an ongoing part of realizing a lesbian identity. "Baby dykes" (women new to lesbian communities of practice) may be more uncomfortable telling coming-out stories because they have not learned the skeletons for creating acceptable selves. (The issue of socialization into queer communities of practice is explored in greater detail by William Leap [chapter 13, this volume].)

Cindy's coming-out story skeleton is as follows:

Lesbian is raised as heterosexual.

Lesbian feels attracted to women.

Lesbian decides to ignore lesbian attractions and behave as a heterosexual.

Lesbian acknowledges being attracted to women and lives as a lesbian.

The above skeleton represents a model for the life events indexed by Cindy's coming-out story. But it is through Cindy's narrative stance to these events, her orientation to the underlying ideologies, that we come to know Cindy as a lesbian we can recognize and accept. The trajectory of her coming out is familiar and coherent.

By invoking the e-mail and storytelling frames, Cindy is able to maneuver around at least two underlying ideologies: (1) homosexuality is not innate, and (2) homosexuality is a set of behaviors. She indexes a skeleton in which her identity as a lesbian clearly transgresses these dominant heterosexist ideologies. This transgression reveals Cindy as lesbian.

Barbara's e-mail story

Barbara, also Deaf, sent a twenty-three-line story which chronicles her sense that she was always a lesbian even when she attempted to date boys in high school. Barbara's narrative skeleton is identical to Cindy's. Queers and heterosexuals alike can recognize the narrative self in such a skeleton because it represents an acceptable coherence pattern for indexing the narrative trajectory, the movement of the self within the story world.

Also like Cindy, Barbara uses several linguistic forms that indicate her adherence to list protocol. Her story is shorter than many of the others, and although she uses capital letters, she does not edit for spelling and grammar. She also follows one of the unratified list rules ("Use humor"): *but never felt so comfortable always panorid at the end of dating with men like do i have to kiss, then petting or necking ugh!!!!! haha.* Additionally, her use of the paralinguistic marker *haha,* which signals intended humor, reflects the rule "Use 'TTY' forms," for paralinguistic markers are very common in TTY communications.

Barbara's story also conforms to the list rule to use ASL-English contact forms. This raises wider narrative questions: If linguistic forms contribute to the coherence of this story, what happens if the life-story teller is bilingual? And how are contact forms used to realize coherent identities? These data suggest that bilinguals have a wider range of language-form resources with which to signify identity. Barbara employs a type of linguistic borrowing that is common in TTY and e-mail conversations among ASL-English bilinguals: she uses *wow* to portray her elation at the large number of women on campus when she arrived as a new freshman (*I always prefer to be hanging around girls that time so when I came to Gallaudet wow more women there ha and still hanging around girls too*). The English exclamation form *wow* is often lexicalized in ASL, fingerspelled rapidly in the air *W-O-W*, usually with both hands near the forehead. This form was perhaps first borrowed into ASL, then lexicalized (becoming a single sign), then borrowed back into English via TTY and e-mail communications, as in Barbara's story. She uses a similar form a little later in her narrative: *I did try to be hanging arund men to get married and have kids . . . . eeekkkk no way.* The form *eeekkkk* here is also lexicalized, signed with one hand holding the sign for *E* near the mouth and forcefully moving away into the sign for *K*.

These features are embedded in the narrative skeleton. Barbara indexes heterosexist ideologies when she explains how she tried to conform to heterosexual dating rituals: "and did try go out with boys but never felt so comfortable always panorid at the end of dating with men like do I have to kiss, then petting or necking ugh!!!!!! haha so I have to get lots of drink to ignore my feelings for men to relax . . . . no fun!!!!!! ha so for society's sake I did try to be hanging arund men to get married and have kids . . . . eeekkkk no way." Here again we see the ideology located by Kendall and indexed by Cindy: the belief that if one acts heterosexual, one can, in fact, *be* heterosexual. Barbara evokes—and rejects—this ideology in asserting that she tried to act straight, but it didn't work. Barbara thus manages a coherent lesbian identity, recognizable because of her orientation to dominant ideologies. We recognize Barbara as lesbian (that is, her story is coherent) because she indexes a larger, almost commonsensical theme that if one tries something that doesn't work out, then one should move on.

Kim's e-mail story

Kim sent the most distinctive e-mail story, a three-line narrative embedded in a longer message. After explaining that she was afraid to risk composing the long version of her coming-out story because of technical problems with her computer, she wrote:

> so i'll give you the short version:
> girl meets girl, girl falls in love with girl,
> girlz ride into the sunset to (town name), girlz live happily ever after.

In composing her coming-out story as a synopsis, Kim invokes the storytelling frame, specifically the love-story archetype. But by using this frame and then substituting *girl* in the place of *boy*, Kim transgresses the archetype, which draws on a heterosexist ideology present in fairy tales: Girls meet boys and live happily ever after (cf. Orellana, chapter 3, this volume). Her story works because, as Linde (1993) suggests, we recognize (but do not share) the system of coherence it invokes. This transgressed archetype produces Kim's identity as a lesbian in a heterosexist society. Her narrative skeleton is a slight variation of Cindy's and Barbara's:

> Lesbian meets lesbian and falls in love.
>
> Lesbian lives as a lesbian.

Maria's e-mail story

Maria's story bears very little resemblance to Cindy's, Barbara's, or Kim's, except that it shares the same skeleton as Cindy's and Barbara's. Maria narrates that she always knew she was attracted to women and ended up entering a Roman Catholic convent, where she met the first woman she ever fell in love with. Her story is a description of her family and the women she has loved. Maria's story is clearly more *written* than the others, which may be a result of Maria's identity as a professional writer.

Although Maria is a member of the distribution list, she does not adhere to its rules. In fact, the only rule she follows is the elimination of capital letters; she uses not a single one in her ninety-line story. Moreover, she begins her story without either invoking a storytelling frame or expressing difficulty with the task (such as *I don't know where to start* or *I'm not sure what you want*): "i've known since i was old enough to know my own name that i like girls especially. it's just the way i am. and growing up in north dakota in the 40s and 50s, there was never any mention of words like 'lesbian.' i was well into college before i ever ran across the notion." She narrates her days in the convent, her departure, her marriage and eventual divorce, and her relationships with nuns still in the convent. The unusual structure of her story is also evident in the words she uses when she describes one such relationship: "during all of this time, i'd ask her periodically to leave the convent and live with me. and she would always refuse. after a while, it began to *rankle*. her second crop of novices arrived, and among them was a wonderful young woman with whom i promptly, though much against my better judgment, fell in love. she left to go back home and finish her masters, and i was *bereft*." This formal register—constituted in part by words like *rankle* and *bereft*—is highly marked on the list, indicating that Maria may not be specifically invoking the e-mail frame and is instead marking her text as a performance.

Maria's lesbian identity is realized as she indirectly addresses ideologies of the origin of lesbianism: *I've known since i was old enough to know my own name that i liked girls especially. it's just the way i am.* Maria's use of the adverbial absolutive particle *just* responds to something that was never asked, as if someone has asked Maria to explain why she is a lesbian or how she became one. This may be the relationship between all personal narrative and public ideologies: responding to that which may not have been uttered but is all-pervasive. Maria addresses (actually transgresses) the ideology *Homosexuality is not innate* but does not make overt reference to any other ideologies and does not argue for her identity, implying that the *just* should end that part of the dialogue. Maria creates her identity in her coming-out story by evoking a recognizable lesbian narrative skeleton and by enlisting formal linguistic forms, which mark her as a writer-lesbian.

Ellen's ASL story

A similar invocation of these two identities—lesbian and professional teller of tales— is achieved very differently when different linguistic resources are available. Ellen, a Deaf lesbian who grew up in a large urban community, is a professional storyteller. In a videotaped interview with me, she narrated several events in her life, including early adolescence when she was oftentimes mistaken for a boy. She explains in one narrative sequence that when she was about 12 years old a screaming woman who mistook her for a boy pushed her out of a women's rest room. A policeman rushed up to Ellen, questioned her, groped her crotch, and demanded that she pull down her pants to prove she was a girl. How did Ellen coherently realize this frightened-young-butch identity?

Because ASL is a visuospatial language, the teller can allow the audience to shape the text. The active role of the audience is central to the effectiveness of Ellen's narrative. In ASL, the narrator has at least two choices for representing the complicating action of a story. She may narratively distance herself by using a placeholder or classifier sign for herself to show the action that happened to the protagonist of the story (herself). The signing space of this type of narrative is removed, literally occurring further out from the body with narrative/spatial trajectories emanating from this point in the signing space. Or she may take on the role of her past self (and the characters in her story), imitating countenance, body position, and action.

Ellen used the second technique for this part of the story. First, in a form of direct discourse, Ellen "became" her young self, a lesbian who was publicly harassed because of her gender-bent appearance. In this same narrative, through the use of role shifting (Padden 1986), another common feature of ASL narrative, Ellen also became the policeman who groped her. And because I was the audience with whom she maintained eye contact, when she "was" the policeman, the direction of the policeman's grope was toward me. In a sense, I briefly became "Ellen the young dyke" and felt the violation of that grope. I could see Ellen at that age in a way that no spoken version would have given me access to. A few minutes later, she explained that in order to avoid harassment, she began using the men's rest room instead.

The performative aspects of Ellen's story recall Maria's creatively written narrative. Ellen clearly invoked a performance frame, setting up the camera and handling the remote control. She began her story by emerging from a coat closet and looking directly into the camera, signing, "Should I come out now?" Splicing her story by turning the camera on and off, she taped herself going back into the closet before emerging again and beginning her story. After nearly an hour and a half of taping, and after her story was clearly finished and we had moved on to other topics, she jumped up, explaining that she had to "close the story." She positioned herself near the closet, turned on the camera, and walked backward into the closet from where she began the story, thus providing parallel closure. Here she invoked the performance frame, something she is accustomed to doing in her professional life, and created a lesbian identity by using the figurative language of the expression *coming out of the closet.*

Thus far I have focused on how the storytellers deal with prevalent ideologies about attraction. In this section of Ellen's coming-out story, however, the ideologies she confronts concern appearance: She was harassed because she did not look like a girl. We can presume the narrative coda, *from then on, I used the men's room,* to be a statement about her coming of age in a heterosexist society that dictates how gender should be realized. Again, this coda represents Ellen's transgression of hegemonic notions and allows us to understand her lesbian identity. Ellen's is the only coming-out story I received that embodies the following "butch" skeleton, but it is a common storyline:

Lesbian is raised as heterosexual.

Lesbian rebels early, becoming a butch.

Lesbian acknowledges her attraction to women.

Lesbian faces social disapproval.

Lesbian continues to live a butch existence.

Jennifer's handwritten English story

In her exploration of the intersection of Deaf and lesbian identities in the life story of a 28-year-old lesbian, Tina Neumann (1997) found that the coming-out-as-a-lesbian process was similar to the coming-out-as-Deaf process. Because of heterosexism, most lesbians go through a self-transformation process from a heterosexual childhood into a lesbian community or lesbian consciousness. Likewise, because approximately 90 percent of Deaf people are born into hearing families, realizing a Deaf identity requires a parallel self-transformation—from a hearing-based childhood and family to a Deaf-centered one. In Deaf lesbians' coming-out stories, it is not uncommon for both event frames, coming out as Deaf and coming out as lesbian, to be invoked and to create narrative coherence.

We can see this dual "coming out" in Jennifer's coming-out story. Jennifer begins with a narrative about realizing, after several dates with her male high school peers, that she was a lesbian. She also explains coming to terms with "becoming deaf in '69 and then Deaf in '77." She describes how she manages this intersection of "comings out": "Long before 1984 I knew I liked the company of womon. When I double-dated w/ my boyfriends I was always more interested in what the womon had to say. (They also tried to enunciate a lot clearer & that helped w/ lipreading. Sure I knew signs but all my boyfriends except 2 were non-Deaf and signing-impaired. But that's another story for another time.)" In these lines, Jennifer invokes both event frames, coming out as lesbian and as Deaf.

Like Maria's e-mail story, Jennifer's story does not make use of any of the typical e-mail frame devices. Her story has no TTY abbreviations and no ASL or contact forms, nor does she invoke an interactive frame. Her story has no title and no reference to me, the person who asked her to write it. Instead, she begins the story as follows: "When I'm asked how or when did I 'come out' I get this reaction where I freeze and there is this panorama of dates and places and people. Each and every one of those dates and places and people I spoke to about my sexual & cultural identity as a 'New Dyke on the Block' are equally very much a part of the 'process' of my coming out." Jennifer, like Maria, realizes her identity through the use of a more formal register, invoking special forms such as *New Dyke on the Block* and *womon*, and *I was by the flood of newly sensual emotions aroused by this* later in the narrative.

In addition to the English forms she uses to realize her Deaf and lesbian identities, Jennifer also invokes dominant heterosexist ideologies. In a later section, she explains that she wrote coming-out letters to family members and got varying responses: *At one other point I got a letter from my aunt telling me that my being a lesbian was "just a stage" in my life?!* The final punctuation is in boldface, which indicates a textual dialogue with the heterosexist ideology that Jennifer's aunt invoked, as if Jennifer were saying to the audience, "What?! Yes, she really did say that!" Although Kendall (1996) does not mention the ideology of homosexuality as "just a phase," it is a common assumption, related to the ideology that "gay men and lesbians are rebellious children who don't know any better" (item 4 in the preceding list). Jennifer creates herself as lesbian by narratively butting up against this assumption and covertly transgressing it.

Jennifer's coming-out story, embedded in the political peace movements of the last few decades, shows how life stories can have both major and minor narrative skeletons. It also represents how women of minority groups necessarily deal with a kind of coming out concerning their status in the dominant culture. Jennifer tells a coming-out story that includes every facet of her identity: She is Deaf, she is politically active, and she is a lesbian. In this way, Jennifer reveals an identity that is linked to her acceptance of her deafness and to her political coming of age during the late 1970s and early 1980s. Her story invokes a not-uncommon coming-out skeleton:

Lesbian is raised as heterosexual and hearing.

Lesbian is attracted to girls.

Lesbian accepts her deafness and lives in the Deaf-World.[5]

Lesbian acknowledges her attraction to women.

Lesbian lives as a lesbian.

Conclusion

I have shown how women in a single community draw on local and social systems of coherence to create their identities in coming-out stories. This analysis suggests that identity is both locally situated and embedded within the larger ideological context. As Deborah Schiffrin puts it, "who we are is, at least partially, a product of where we are and who we are with, both in interactional and story worlds" (1996:198).

I have shown how frames are used to appeal to locally constructed norms for realizing identity. We have seen how lesbians' coming-out stories invoke certain narrative skeletons, which reveal the lesbian-coming-out-story schemata and prototypes. And finally, these data have shown how identities are necessarily created within the ideological context in which they exist. Paradoxically, although lesbian identities exist outside of heterosexist ideologies, it is by means of such ideologies that they are recognizable and acceptable. In order to realize identities, lesbians at once draw upon and transgress ideologies as resources for coherence.

NOTES

I am grateful to Shari E. Kendall and the students in her course "Women, Men, and Language" at Georgetown University (spring 1997). In their analysis of heterosexual undergraduates' dating-and-attraction stories, they concluded that heterosexuals also construct gendered identities that support or resist hegemonic notions of what it means to be a woman or man and what it means to be attractive and attracted. Their comments steered me to the conclusions I make here about lesbians' coming-out stories, which, I would argue, are the queer analogue to the Georgetown students' dating stories. Thanks also to Jules NelsonHill, Carol Monigan, Kendra Smith, MJ Bienvenu, Shari Kendall, Keller Magenau, Galey Modan, and E. Lynn Jacobowitz.

1. I use the term *queer* to include lesbians, gay men, bisexuals, and transsexuals.

2. *Deaf* (capital D)—as opposed to *deaf* (lowercase d)—represents those deaf people politically and culturally aligned with the "Deaf-World." The term "Deaf-World" is recog-

nized by Harlan Lane, Robert Hoffmeister, and Ben Bahan (1996), who explain that it is the name members of the ASL-signing Deaf community call themselves.

3. It is interesting to note that the homophobic logic surrounding the arguments against gays and lesbians is strikingly similar to that of the Exodus group literature.

4. Due to length restrictions, full transcripts of the stories are not provided.

5. See note 2.

REFERENCES

Agar, Michael (1994). *Language shock: Understanding the culture of conversation.* New York: Morrow.

Bakhtin, Mikhail M. (1981). *The dialogic imagination.* Ed. Michael Holquist. Trans. Caryl Emerson & Michael Holquist. Austin: University of Texas Press.

———— (1986). *Speech genres and other late essays.* Ed. Caryl Emerson & Michael Holquist. Trans. Vern W. McGee. Austin: University of Texas Press.

Bauman, Richard (1978). *Verbal art as performance.* Rowley, MA: Newbury House.

Baumeister, Roy F., & Leonard S. Newman (1995). The primacy of stories, the primacy of roles, and the polarizing effects of interpretive motives: Some propositions about narratives. In Robert S. Wyer, Jr. (ed.), *Knowledge and memory: The real story.* Hillsdale, NJ: Erlbaum, 97–108.

Bruner, Jerome (1990). *Acts of meaning.* Cambridge, MA: Harvard University Press.

Carranza, Isolda (1996). Argumentation and ideological outlook in storytelling. Ph.D. diss., Georgetown University.

Deby, Jeff (1996). Looking into coming out: Why tell a coming-out story? Paper presented at the annual meeting of the Georgetown Linguistics Society, Washington, DC.

Eckert, Penelope, & Sally McConnell-Ginet (1992). Communities of practice: Where language, gender, and power all live. In Kira Hall, Mary Bucholtz, & Birch Moonwomon (eds.), *Locating power: Proceedings of the Second Berkeley Women and Language Conference.* Berkeley, CA: Berkeley Women and Language Group, 89–99.

Elliott, Mary (1996). Coming out in the classroom: A return to the hard place. *College English* 58(6):693–708.

Foucault, Michel (1982). The subject and power. *Critical Inquiry* 8:777–795.

Gaudio, Rudolf P. (1996). Out in the open without coming out: Queer narratives from Nigerian Hausaland. Paper presented at the annual meeting of the Georgetown Linguistics Society, Washington, DC.

Gergen, Mary (1992). Life stories: Pieces of a dream. In George Rosenwald & Richard Ochberg (eds.), *Storied lives.* New Haven, CT: Yale University Press, 127–144.

Hamilton, Heidi (1996). Intratextuality, intertextuality, and the construction of identity as patient in Alzheimer's disease. *Text* 16(1):61–90.

Holland, Dorothy, & Naomi Quinn (1987). Culture and cognition. In Holland & Quinn (eds.), *Cultural models in language and thought.* New York: Cambridge University Press, 3–40.

Hymes, Dell (1981). *"In vain I tried to tell you": Essays in Native American ethnopoetics.* Philadelphia: University of Pennsylvania Press.

Johnstone, Barbara (1990). *Stories, community, and place: Narratives from Middle America.* Bloomington: Indiana University Press.

———— (1996). *The linguistic individual.* New York: Oxford University Press.

Kannapell, Barbara (1989). An examination of Deaf college students' attitudes toward ASL and English. In Ceil Lucas (ed.), *The sociolinguistics of the Deaf community.* New York: Academic Press, 191–210.

Kendall, Shari E. (1996). Conflicting ideologies in the news coverage of Salt Lake City's ban on gay and lesbian clubs in public schools. Paper presented at the annual meeting of the Georgetown Linguistics Society, Washington, DC.

Kiesler, Sara, Jane Siegel, & Timothy W. McGuire (1984). Social psychological aspects of computer-mediated communication. *American Psychologist* 39(10):1123–1134.

Kiesling, Scott (1996). Language, gender, and power in fraternity men's discourse. Ph.D. diss., Georgetown University.

Kress, Gunther, & Robert Hodge (1993). *Language as ideology.* New York: Routledge.

Labov, William (1972). *Language in the inner city.* Philadelphia: University of Pennsylvania Press.

Lane, Harlan, Robert Hoffmeister, & Ben Bahan (1996). *A journey into the Deaf-World.* San Diego: Dawn Sign Press.

Liang, A. C. (1997). Creating coherence in coming-out stories. In Anna Livia & Kira Hall (eds.), *Queerly phrased.* New York: Oxford University Press, 287–309.

Linde, Charlotte (1993). *Life stories: The creation of coherence.* New York: Oxford University Press.

Neumann, Tina (1997). Deaf identity, lesbian identity: Intersections in a life narrative. In Anna Livia & Kira Hall (eds.), *Queerly phrased.* New York: Oxford University Press, 274–286.

Ochs, Elinor (1992). Indexing gender. In Alessandro Duranti & Charles Goodwin (eds.), *Rethinking context.* New York: Cambridge University Press, 335–358.

Padden, Carol (1986). Verbs and role-shifting in ASL. In Carol Padden (ed.), *Proceedings of the Fourth National Symposium on Sign Language Research and Teaching.* Silver Spring, MD: National Association of the Deaf, 44–57.

Penelope, Julia, & Susan Wolfe (1989). *The original coming out stories.* Freedom, CA: Crossing Press.

Polanyi, Livia (1985). *Telling the American story: A structural and cultural analysis of conversational storytelling.* Norwood, NJ: Ablex.

Polkinghorne, Donald E. (1991). Narrative and self-concept. *Journal of Narrative and Life History* 1(2/3):135–153.

Ribeiro, Bianca Telles (1993). Framing in psychotic discourse. In Deborah Tannen (ed.), *Framing in discourse.* New York: Oxford University Press, 77–112.

———— (1994). *Coherence in psychotic discourse.* New York: Oxford University Press.

Rosen, Harold (1988). The autobiographical impulse. In Deborah Tannen (ed.), *Linguistics in context: Connecting observation and understanding.* Norwood, NJ: Ablex, 69–88.

Schiffrin, Deborah (1994). *Approaches to discourse.* Cambridge: Blackwell.

———— (1996). Narrative as self-portrait: Sociolinguistic constructions of identity. *Language in Society* 25:167–203.

Schank, Roger C., & Robert P. Abelson (1995). Knowledge and memory: The real story. In Robert S. Wyer (ed.), *Knowledge and memory: The real story.* Hillsdale, NJ: Erlbaum, 1–86.

Shotter, John (1993). *Conversational realities.* London: Sage.

Tannen, Deborah (1985). Frames and schemas in interaction. *Quaderni di Semantica* 6:326–335.

———— (1993). What's in a frame? Surface evidence for underlying expectations. In Deborah Tannen (ed.), *Framing in discourse.* New York: Oxford University Press, 14–56.

Wood, Kathleen (1994). Life stories as artifacts of a culture: Lesbian coming-out stories. In Mary Bucholtz, A. C. Liang, Laurel A. Sutton, & Caitlin Hines (eds.), *Cultural performances: Proceedings of the Third Berkeley Women and Language Conference.* Berkeley, CA: Berkeley Women and Language Group, 777–786.

———— (1997). Iconicity in lesbian coming-out stories. In Anna Livia & Kira Hall (eds.), *Queerly phrased.* New York: Oxford University Press, 257–273.

3   MARJORIE FAULSTICH ORELLANA

Good Guys and "Bad" Girls

Identity Construction by Latina and Latino Student Writers

lassroom writing workshops—spaces created within school environments
for students to write, revise, and "publish" texts—have received considerable attention from literacy researchers over the last decade (see, for example, Atwell 1987; Calkins 1986; Graves 1983). Yet only a few researchers have explored the social negotiations that take place within free writing
environments (Dyson 1989, 1993; Lensmire 1994; Phinney 1994) and their gendered
dimensions, where stereotypes may be reproduced, reinforced, and implicitly sanctioned in children's texts (Gilbert 1993; Kamler 1994; MacGillivray & Martínez
1998). With few exceptions (e.g., Brooke 1991), most studies of school writing processes focus on cognitive processes and give little attention to students' uses of language to explore selves or construct social identities.

The children I observed in a writing workshop environment during two overlapping school years were involved in much more than the acquisition of literacy. In
this chapter, I examine how these Latina and Latino primary-school children experimented with a range of social identities and made sense of what it means to be a girl
or a boy, rich or poor, brown or white, good, bad, beautiful, or smart, through the
characters they created in their stories. I view language and literacy as important tools
that the children used for the invention of possible selves and examine the written
products—more than 300 stories produced over a 13-month period—for the insights
they provide into the inventors.

Inventing identities through language and literacy

A growing body of work, to which writers in this volume contribute, examines the
construction of identity through language practices and the linguistic presentation of

64

self as a member of particular social groups. Language is examined as an integral part of "doing" membership in these groups, something continually invented and reinvented in interaction with others (Barrett, chapter 16, this volume; Cook-Gumperz 1995; Gal 1995).

This new approach emphasizes human agency, highlighting choices that people make in adopting particular language forms and assuming membership in discourse communities. Yet researchers recognize that the freedom to invent identities is constrained by social forces. Bronwyn Davies (1993) explores the gendered discourses that frame children's talk about texts that they read and write, including variations in the construction of "femininity" in the talk of girls from different socioeconomic groups. Jennifer Coates (chapter 6, this volume) examines the range of discourses that a group of white middle-class teenage girls take up; through their talk they "do" both friendship and femininity. Lisa Capps (chapter 4, this volume) illustrates how language is used by family members to frame an agoraphobic woman within a discourse of irrationality, thus collectively constructing and maintaining her identity as that of an unstable person.

Much of this recent work on language as invention of self focuses on language used in live communicative contexts: Identity is performed, and jointly constructed, through choices about language forms. But narratives—oral or written, with the distinction between oral and written language practices more dubious than generally believed (see Shuman 1986)—provide another space in which identities can be constructed. Pam Gilbert argues that narratives "have a functional role in our culture: we live a good deal of our lives on the power of various stories, and it is through stories that we position ourselves in relation to others, and are ourselves positioned by the stories of our culture" (1992:186). Likewise, Capps (this volume) notes that in narratives we can see theories about emotions, self, and others, and about how past lived experiences are organized in "present, future, and imagined realms."

Gendered literacy

In a move away from strictly cognitive frameworks, some literacy researchers have begun to explore constructions of gender through both reading (Christian-Smith 1993; Davies 1989, 1993; Walkerdine 1990) and writing (Gilbert 1993; Kamler 1994; Phinney 1994). Judith Solsken (1993), for example, traces the experiences of four white middle-class children in relation to literacy over a period of three years, at home and school, highlighting children's unfolding processes of identity construction through the choices they make about reading and writing. Davies (1993) illustrates problems children face when they attempt to subvert traditional gendered narratives.

As with much of the work on gender in general, research on gendered aspects of literacy has typically been conducted using white middle-class subjects or assuming a white middle-class norm. Researchers often call for attention to intersections of gender, class, race, and ethnicity but rarely explore them in practice. In this chapter, I examine gendered and classed aspects of the identities that Latina and Latino working-class youth invent for themselves in their stories. I consider how the children position themselves through their characters within social discourses and how the discourses that are available to them are shaped by the social contexts in which they work.

Participants and setting

The site of my study, Carol Lyons's mixed-age classroom, was located in a Latino working-class community just outside a large metropolitan area.[1] Most of the children were immigrants or the children of immigrants from various regions of Mexico; a smaller number were recent immigrants from Central or South America. All of the students were fluent speakers of Spanish. Spanish predominated in most classroom talk, and all but a few of the books that the students used were written in Spanish. Carol was not a native Spanish speaker, but she was fluent in the language and used it in both her professional and personal life on a daily basis. Carol had taught in the school district for 10 years and was widely regarded as an excellent teacher within a child-centered, holistic tradition of instruction.

Approximately 10 students in each of Grades 1, 2, and 3 were in the classroom in the first year of my study. The mixture of ages partially shaped the topics and content of students' books and the power dynamics that were established in authorship teams; where possible, I attend to these in the discussion that follows. All the second- and third-graders remained with Carol for the second year of the study, when the classroom was redesignated as a third- and fourth-grade combination; only the first-graders dropped out, to be replaced by eight additional third- and fourth-graders. In all, twenty-three boys and sixteen girls were in the room for some period of time during the 2 years, although there were never more than thirty-five total at any one time.

Methods

This study, part of a larger ethnographic project, centered around understanding how the children invented identities in their written compositions. I engaged in participant observation several days each week for 13 months (across two overlapping school years) during the period devoted to the writing workshop and conducted eight follow-up visits over the subsequent 4 months. I compiled notes on 149 stories that were written during the first school year and 152 books from the second year and used these for analyses of topics, content, form, and structure. The notes included summaries of the story plots and verbatim excerpts from each text, as well as salient aspects of illustrations, design, and authorship.

In addition, I talked informally with the students during every observation period and with Carol as demands on her time allowed. Carol and I met for two semiformal audiotaped interviews in her classroom and for extended conversations at her home and by telephone. Carol also read and commented on drafts of this work.

Inventing stories—Processes and practices

Students wrote drafts for their stories during a reading/writing block in which they could choose from a variety of literacy activities. Writing and publishing books was the most popular activity, and a very social one, as the children actively sought out writing partners, sat together, and talked freely as they wrote. Like the kindergarteners in Margaret Phinney's (1994) study and the preschool children who were observed drawing pictures by Amy Kyratzis (1994), these elementary-school children used the writing workshop as a space for the negotiation of friendship groups and as an index of classroom popularity. Five or six of the oldest boys and one of the oldest girls participated in a large number of authorship teams. The three youngest boys almost always worked alone and the youngest girls worked alone or with each other as partners.

There were very few mixed-sex authorship teams. In the first year, only three of the eighty-seven multiply authored books were written by mixed-sex teams; in the second year, only nine out of seventy-five. I witnessed few overt forms of "border-work" (Thorne 1993)—social processes such as teasing that occur when gender-segregating norms are violated—but implicit rules seemed to keep girls and boys from writing together. This, in turn, may have led to more overt gender stereotyping in the content and characters represented in the stories.

After drafts had been prepared, students met with peers and the teacher to offer ideas for revising or developing the text. In these conferences, Carol frequently emphasized the fact that all suggestions were "just ideas" and that each student author could decide whether or not to incorporate them into the stories. She generally limited her comments in order to open up more space for peer feedback. Nevertheless, she challenged students when they wrote about themes that reinforced gender or other stereotypes.

After the writing conferences, students finished their stories and gave them to Carol for final editing and typing. The authors then pasted the typed text into premade booklets, illustrated them, and bound them in cardboard binders. The finished books were displayed in the classroom library and became the most popular reading material in the room. Excerpts of typical books are shown in figure 3.1.

Most students did not verbalize how they came up with ideas for their stories. When I asked, most told me that they did not know or that they "got it from their heads." In general, however, peers' books appeared to exert a strong intertextual influence on new narratives. As new topics were introduced, they were picked up by others and played out in related texts over time.

Overall, the students seemed more focused on the social than the literary aspects of the stories, and they negotiated the friendships that appeared in the stories much as they negotiated their own friendships in class. In their conversations with me and in letters that they wrote to their friends as part of the classroom mail system (another device Carol used to encourage literacy), many students mentioned the activity of coauthoring books as an index of friendship. This situation lends insight into why gender-segregated worlds appeared in so many texts, as discussed in a subsequent section. It also gives greater weight to my claim that students projected important aspects of themselves and their own desires through these texts; in students' books, the line between their actual and fictional lives often blurred.

Inventing characters—Talk and text

The degree to which the authors' lives melded with those of their characters is revealed by looking at the language forms they used to talk about texts and to position

Los niños se fueron a la casa y
encontraron $100 en la casa.

Los niños se fueron a la tienda y
compraron los trajes.

En la noche los niños salieron vestidos
de ninjas. Era el día de Halloween y los
niños fueron a pedir dulces.

Figure 3.1. Sample pages from a student text

characters in their stories. They would invite friends onto authorship teams by asking, "Do you want to be in my story?" When writing, students would usually introduce characters using the third person, but after a few lines, they would frequently slip into the use of the first person and begin to speak *in* the voice of the characters rather than *for* them. One team wrote, for example: "Once upon a time there were three boys named Carlos, Marcos, and Fernando. They wanted to enter a car race. And so we asked our parents for permission. They told us we couldn't go." I was present when Carol attempted to call the class's attention to this inconsistency in perspective, and I sensed that the group did not understand Carol's concern. They seemed more interested in establishing the connection between their characters and themselves rather than signaling authorial distance from their characters. This quick shift in point of view is perhaps the most obvious example of how the children truly invented—and reinvented—themselves through their stories.

The children also used language forms in ways that revealed their deeply gendered identification with the characters they created. When girls and boys did write stories together, they were extremely careful to distinguish between the language forms used for female and male characters in ways not required in the Spanish language. For example, Katia, Jesús, and Marco wrote a draft for a book called "Dos vampiros y una vampira" (Two male vampires and a female vampire), and Ofelia transformed "Los tres cochinitos" (The three little pigs) to "Dos cochinitas y un cochino" (Two little female pigs and a male pig). The children could have written about three generic vampires or pigs, leaving the gender ambiguous (or subsuming the feminine within the masculine, as is the rule in Spanish). Their careful language distinction may indicate personal identification with the characters and concern that they themselves be tagged with the proper gender label.

I have argued elsewhere (Orellana 1995) that because the Spanish language is gender-marked, gendered dimensions of literacy in Spanish-dominated classrooms may be more evident (though not necessarily more prevalent) than they are in other language settings. But when biases are more overt, they are more readily challenged. The girls' literary practices described here can be seen as efforts to subvert linguistic patriarchy by writing themselves into the language. The authors call attention to linguistic forms that promote masculinist readings of texts, and they push readers to recognize that the characters in their stories are *not* the "generic" male. These efforts are not unlike those made by professional feminist writers to avoid masculinist biases in their novels (Livia 1994; chapter 17, this volume).

Social relations within textual worlds

The authors' intense identification with their characters suggests that the worlds they sketch in their stories and the characters they personify are intimately connected with their own identities and social worlds—both the actual and the possible, both the real and the invented—or at least with the identities and worlds with which they are willing to be associated on paper. The tensions that appear in the stories may illuminate the children's struggles to seek space for themselves in the world, to try on potential identities and explore the implications of various choices.

Gender-separate worlds

Perhaps the most salient aspect of the children's stories was the extent to which they represented gender segregation. Girls were often completely absent from the boys' stories. Only one story written by a boy had a female lead character, and in only seven books were girls present as supporting characters. Women were somewhat more visible, appearing in a total of thirty-six of the boys' books, but mostly as mothers (who merely accompanied fathers in most of the texts); men appeared in fifty-two books in a range of positions, less than half of the time as fathers.

Although girls favored girls or women for the lead figures (usually fashioning them as minimally fictionalized versions of themselves), they occasionally gave boys or men a central position in their writing. In the first year of the study, girls wrote two stories that centered around a single man and one that featured two boys in the lead, as well as four books with both a girl and a boy or several girls and boys as the central characters. In the second year, they wrote nineteen stories that revolved centrally around men or with male leading characters and two additional stories about mixed-gender groups. The girls also portrayed men or boys in supporting roles in sixty-eight stories.

The fact that gender-separate worlds appear in most of the children's stories could suggest that the children value such segregation. However, although I did see some areas of clear gender separation in the children's work and play environments, I saw many other spaces in which the children mixed freely, both in the classroom and on the playground. In a sense, the children (the boys more than the girls) endorsed and sustained a *discourse* of gender segregation even as they disrupted or only partially maintained such segregation in practice.

Support for this claim can be found in the literal—pictorial—representation of female and male characters, in which the influence of wider social discourses of gender is also apparent (figures 3.2 and 3.3). When women were featured in illustrations, they often appeared wearing princess-like dresses, with large, heart-shaped bosoms; in more than half of the colored illustrations they were blond with blue eyes. Boys and men were rarely represented as blond in either boys' or girls' illustrations, but in a number of the books they were clearly featured with blue or green eyes. Yet all of the students in the classroom had dark hair and eyes. This suggests that even as the authors identify closely with their characters, they sometimes construct images of themselves that are bound up with dominant racial discourses. However, as Rusty Barrett (chapter 16, this volume) notes, "the appropriation of aspects of dominant culture need not necessarily indicate acceptance of its dominating force" and can instead represent a form of resistance. In playing with a range of images for themselves, the children challenge stereotyped notions of what Latinos "should" look or be like. At the same time, these images seemed informed by a narrow range of possible gender positions.

Thematic tensions

In major themes that run through their stories, the students in Carol's classroom played with their portrayal of their own gendered and classed identities. In many texts, the children describe characters who are gendered in very particular ways and who stand

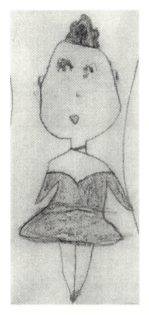

Figure 3.2. Representations of women and girls in texts

at the extremes of particular dichotomies—as rich or poor, smart or dumb, blond or dark-haired, and good or bad. The authors present these characters in different lights and make assorted judgments on their fates. In doing so, they pick up dominant discourses about gender and class that exist in the world around them and that exert influence on their developing notions of self. At the same time, they also contest, disrupt, and refigure those differences in the worlds they create on paper.

Love and romance

Love, romance, and jealousy were central themes in many of the girls' stories and were a peripheral aspect of others. During the first school year, when the students

Figure 3.3. Representations of
men and boys in texts

were in Grades 1 to 3, six stories by female authors revolved centrally around romance. For example, first-graders Janet and Mirna wrote about a female duck who
ignored her mother's advice to find a rich man, instead following her heart, which
led her to marry a poor male duck and have five babies. Four second- and third-grade
girls joined forces to write a story about butterflies who fell in love and got married.
These girls did not adopt Carol's conference suggestion that they consider alternative endings to the story, but they did seem to see through the illusion of living "happily ever after" when they remarked to Carol that caring for babies was hard and
often frustrating work.

The complex role of teachers in conferencing on such stories bears exploration.
In suggesting alternatives to the "and-they-lived-happily-ever-after" ending, Carol

aimed to expand the range of possibilities that the girls saw for themselves as projected through their characters. She always reminded her students that they could choose to accept or reject the suggestions that were made, but she consciously pushed students to explore options they had not considered. As she told me in our conversations, she wanted her students to critically examine the world and not to "accept all this unfairness in life." Yet this feminist challenge may echo institutional efforts to control young Latinas' sexuality and reproductive choices (Houghton 1995). Given that Latinas are effectively written out of dominant cultural narratives of romance, the girls' positioning can also be seen as a form of subversion of traditional norms.

By contrast with the prevalence of romance in the girls' stories, only one story that dealt centrally with romance was written by a boy. Mario, a first-grader, wrote about a personified blue (male) car who married a pink female car (*un carro muchacha*); together they had purple baby cars. Mario was the same boy who wrote the only male-authored story to feature a female protagonist. In that story he wrote about a female elephant whose parents didn't love her because she was ugly; when she was not accepted in a ballet class, the elephant then joined a circus, where she taught ballet to the other animals. Mario may have been able to write against the grain because he was one of the youngest boys in the classroom who worked largely independently and hence never adopted the "hegemonic" forms of masculinity (Connell 1987) established by the older boys.

In the next school year, when the children were in Grades 3 and 4 (with the first-graders moving to second grade in a different classroom), fewer stories followed a love-marriage-babies formula. Two third-graders, Wendy and Mirna, wrote a book about a rose that fell in love with a carnation from Mexico; the flowers then had two babies—a rose and a carnation. Olivia, another third-grader, wrote a story about two mermaid friends who at first did not have boyfriends ("because they didn't want them," as she explained), but then found two handsome boys, fell in love, got married, and had babies. But in general, the girls' treatment of romance was more complex in the second year. Carie and Elsa, both fourth-graders, wrote about impossible love when they retold the story of a man who fell in love with a ghost; Katia, a third-grader, later reworked this idea, introducing a woman who fell in love with a male ghost but then stopped loving him when she realized he was a ghost, leaving the man pining away for her (and wanting to kill her). Several other stories evinced the influence of Spanish television *novelas*, either explicitly or implicitly following the themes of jealousy and betrayal that are central to that genre.[2]

Two books by fourth-grader Rosa hint at the tensions some girls may feel between operating within a discourse of love and romance and an alternative "good girl/good student" discourse. Love and romance may represent a sanctioned cultural pathway for girls, but they receive conflicting messages about when and how they are to embark on it, such that in certain times and places for girls to operate within a discourse of love and romance is to position themselves as "bad." This may be especially true for Latinas, who are often stereotyped in good/bad binaries, and for girls within the context of schooling, where being "good" generally requires a denial of one's sexuality. In the initial draft of her story, Rosa wrote about a girl who watched too many soap operas, talked about them incessantly in school, kissed a boy while under their influence, and performed miserably as a student until her teacher talked to her mother. At that point the girl stopped watching *novelas* and became a model student. In a later version of the story, however, Rosa describes a girl who displays her resistance both to school and to being a "good girl"; she resists by watching television *novelas*, which deal centrally with love and romance and which position her within a highly gendered discourse. This leads to her failure to succeed in school and in life. The tensions here resonate with those described by Jean Anyon (1983) in her analysis of working-class girls' resistance to school and the ways that such resistance locks girls into traditional gendered and classed roles in life.

Rosa displayed this same tension in the corpus of her writing. She wrote detailed accounts of love triangles, jealousy, and passion in her two versions of the story, but she was also the first in the class to write a story railing against the actions of a serial rapist who was at large in the town at the time. She additionally wrote a series of stories and journal entries about strong women in her life: her mother (whom she referred to as *la mamá valiente* or 'the brave mother'), her teacher, the principal, and myself. In none of these writings did she describe women in relation to men; however, beauty and goodness were the chief traits highlighted in each. In these works, Rosa seems to oscillate between playing out romantic fantasies and protesting against the harsh realities of women's experiences.

Good Guys, Bad Guys . . .

As may be evident in Rosa's stories about love and romance, a second major tension that ran through the children's writing centered around what it meant to be good or bad. This tension became gendered because goodness and badness were inscribed differently for girls and for boys, and the children seemed to use the stories to play out different ways of being gendered and to consider the implications that followed from each.

Most of the lead characters in the girls' stories from the first phase appear to be "good girls"; they are obedient, submissive, passive, thoughtful, cheerful, kind, and peaceful. They either stay at home or go to a few places with friends, live happily with their families, and contemplate beauty in the surrounding world. They live, immobile, in homes that have few problems and that seem detached from the world around them, existing in a sort of idyllic social vacuum. When conflicts do arise, as in Denora and Noemí's story about a beautiful house that gets broken in a fight, people come back together to patch things up. Problems are resolved and the protagonists can live happily ever after.

Such stories contrast with those of the boys. In the boys' first stories, there are a few images of "good boys," who appear as compliant, hard workers and obedient children, but more often the boys assume much more powerfully good roles, when they become "Good Guys" who fight the forces of evil. Good Guys represent a rather different construction than good boys, in that they are bold, powerful, authoritative figures, while *good boys* suggests an image of quiet, respectful children who do as they are told. In these stories, however, the Good Guys get to get in on some really "bad" action; the theme seemed to allow the boys to be both good and very powerful through character traits that were not as accessible to girls. Many of these books also allowed the boys some vicarious participation in the deeds of the Bad Guys without having to become bad themselves; the authors used their own names for the heroes in the stories and set up the Bad Guys as "Others" but often provided elaborate details of the Bad Guys' dark deeds, and they sometimes wrote avidly about war even as they made their characters resolve their conflicts by waging peace. This may have allowed them to please two different audiences: their peers, who were as intrigued by war and "badness" as they were, and their teacher, who overtly promoted peace.

It is worth noting that the characters who were transformed into superheroes were often explicitly constructed as *poor* boys, and when they became superheroes they specifically used their powers to help the poor. Through these superhero characters, the boys may have found a way to assume power in a world that typically denies it to working-class children and to rectify some of the inequalities they sensed in the world around them. Boys from lower-class communities may feel their lack of formal social power more keenly than girls because public power is generally framed as masculine.

In other stories, the boys did not transform themselves into superbeings in order to play out powerful roles; they found other means to achieve similar ends. For example, fourth-grader Fernando wrote about a poor boy who overcomes great odds by studying hard, earning a scholarship to Yale, and joining the army. There he assumes a powerful position but uses his power to stop the war.

Although none of the girls ventured into the realm of superhero stories, several female authors did experiment with more active heroine-like roles in books produced during the second year of the study. For example, Carie, Vicky, and Elsa joined together to write "Las tres detectivas" (The three female detectives), a story in which the authors are the only detectives who are able to capture an international thief. In "Las angelitas" (The little angels), Carie takes this interest in powerful roles to new heights; she assumes an almost omnipotent role as a poor girl who gets killed but then unmasks the devil, defeats him in a fight, and liberates God himself. In the end, Carie celebrates with her friends because God is happy with them.

Rosa also experimented with at least one powerful role for herself, along with the strong characters she gave other women in the biographical sketches she wrote. In "Las tres mosqueteras" (The three musketeers), Rosa, Elsa, and a third female character (named for the teacher) ride on three horses (named for three of the most "popular" boys in the classroom) and go out to save the king's son at his request. The story ends before we find out if their mission is successful, however, and the authors never produced the promised continuation.[3]

Of all the girls in the room, it is not surprising that Rosa and Carie were the ones who experimented most with powerful portraits of women and girls in their writing. They were two of the most outspoken students in the room and held their own in public spaces that were largely dominated by boys, such as classroom meetings in which students presented their grievances (Orellana 1996). Other students in the classroom also often followed Rosa's and Carie's leads. Nevertheless, these girls experienced tension about their positions in the classroom and in their texts. Rosa and her coauthors, after all, left open the question of whether or not they save the prince at the end of their story. If they opted to save him, they would frame themselves as powerful but would play into a traditional gendered story line (albeit in a reversal of roles). Opting not to save him could be read either as a feminist decision or as evidence of "feminine" weakness. The decision not to choose may be the most radical one these girls could make under circumstances set up for them by societal expectations. Similarly, although Carie defeats the devil in "Las angelitas," she frames this act as done to make God happy (which could be construed either as a very powerful act or as father-pleasing), and she did not protest when her male coauthors assigned her the role of cheerleader in a story about a football team.

Through their stories, the children in this classroom seem to acknowledge that there are very different options for being good open to girls and boys, with different implications in terms of power, prestige, and influence on the world. The fact that a few of the girls did write adventure stories in which they present themselves as heroines suggests that there is some room for girls to cross this gender-marked border and some motivation for them to do so. Conversely, there were no instances of boys taking up a theme that had been established by the girls.

. . . and the lure of being bad

This interest in "goodness" in the early girls' stories was not matched in the boys' stories. The boys seemed as fascinated by "badness" as they were by "Good Guyness," and they wrote a number of books whose main characters were constructed as bad boys. Some of their earliest narratives on this theme took on moralistic tones, ending with the boys rectifying their ways or meeting their just fate (as in Fernando's account of a man who takes drugs, becomes an addict and a thief, and ends up in jail). Other stories, however, clearly suggest the boys' temptation to be "bad" and to display themselves in socially taboo ways. Two books were written about the *super pedoros* (super farters), in which boys who fart have a series of adventures but ultimately die in a fire started from their own fumes; and another was written about the *super traviesos* (super menaces)—twin boys who engage in a series of mischief.

In the second phase of the study, the boys experimented with ever bolder characters. In Fernie and Robby's "Los alrevezados" (The mixed-up ones), the bad boys come from another planet, steal things on Earth, laugh at others, live on the street, and eventually die from their own stench. In Carlos's "El super travieso" (The super menace), a boy who fights both in the United States and in Mexico gets kicked around the world (literally) as a consequence of his bad behavior. In Robby, Julio, and David's story about three boys who fight in school and get suspended, only one of the boys (the "little angel") is sorry for his deeds; the other boys seem confident in the power of their badness. Robby and Julio also wrote "Los super gordos" (The super fat ones) and "Los super tontos" (The super dumb ones), stories in which the authors seem to delight in having the characters engage in socially taboo activities such as farting, saying bad words, and defecating on the seats of an airplane. Later, Carlos, Robby, Jorge, and Fernie joined forces to produce a story that plays with taboo subjects in an especially provocative way: In "Los cuatro draculas" (The four Draculas), the spirit of the mother of four vampire boys appears on the scene, farting and calling to her sons as the character La Llorona does in the classical Latin American folktale. The boys order their mother to make underwear soup (*sopa de chonis*) for them to eat.

It is worth noting that in this story, the boys selected a female student in the class, Sarai, to play the less-than-flattering part of the mother who farts (and who abandons her children by dying). This situation raises the question, also raised by Timothy Lensmire (1994), of how writing workshop environments may allow authors to position their classmates in oppressive ways. The authors do not name one of themselves as the father in the story, perhaps because they are not willing to be associated in a textual marriage and subsequent pregnancies with Sarai. Although they do not name themselves as the children, the fact that there are four vampires and four authors is suggestive of their identification with that role.

By the third month of the second school year, however, it was not only the boys who were experimenting with having their main characters do really "bad" things. Three girls (Denora, Noemí, and Elsa) wrote about boys who engage in such socially unacceptable behavior as throwing the baby Jesus on the floor in a Christmas pageant and putting screws on each other's chairs. Still, in these texts the authors distance themselves from the characters and present clear consequences to the boys for their badness. In the first story, the "bad" boy does not receive any gifts from Santa Claus; during the same time frame, Denora wrote another book in which a "good" girl gets many presents for Christmas.

Seven other girls, however, took the theme of "badness" and made it their own. In different groupings over a period of several months, they produced at least five stories in which they themselves were featured being "bad," in several cases engaging in taboo behavior that rivaled that portrayed by the boys. For example, Vicky and Sarai wrote about girls who rob a store to get stickers after they fight over the stickers they have bought. Carie, Elsa, Sarai, and Mirna wrote about three girls who steal money, rob a store, and play with meat in a meat shop. Sarai, Laura, and Mirna wrote about girls who fight with each other and break each other's things. Sarai, Mirna, Wendy, Elsa, Carie, and Cindy joined forces to write about two girls who try to strangle each other, make jokes about bodily functions, and destroy things in their house.

Sarai was an author of each of these stories and seemed to be a principal force behind their more provocative aspects. When she was engaged with Laura and Mirna in writing "Las niñas traviesas," she seemed to delight in narrating to me: "Then she (the sister) is gonna kick her butt, and then she (the other sister) is gonna kick *her* butt. Like that." In general, Sarai presented herself as outgoing, confident, bold, and friendly. The other girls were quiet, soft-spoken students who projected an image of prototypically good girls: They rarely spoke publicly in class, they did their work diligently, and they never broke the classroom rules. Yet Mirna and Wendy by themselves wrote a fifth story about mischievous girls, in which they portrayed a struggle over what it means to be good or bad: They appeared as girls who destroy their mother's things until she sends them away to obedience school. When they return they are "good"—they clean the house (while their mother cooks and then watches television). Then, however, the girls watch a show on television about two mischievous girls and once again become "bad" and destroy the house; they remain "bad"— and powerful in their destructive forces—at the end of the book.

Intersections of poverty, wealth, power, and gender

As indicated in my previous discussion of story themes, references to poverty and wealth were prominent in the children's stories. The boys, in particular, wrote about winning money in car races and boxing matches; they wrote about poor boys who are transformed into superheroes who become rich; and they made frequent references to *los pobres* (the poor). By using this term, or by presenting themselves as poor boys who escape poverty, the boys distance themselves from poverty even as they identify with it; treat it as a condition that can be overcome by those who are strong, smart, or talented; and help to construct an image of those who remain in poverty as nameless, faceless "Others."

Just as in their treatment of goodness and badness, the children represented poverty and wealth as dichotomous, with transformations between the two possible but with little room for middle positions. The constructions of poverty, wealth, and power are in many ways bound up with constructions of goodness and badness, which are in turn interwoven with constructions of gender, so much so that it is difficult to separate the threads of these themes in my discussion. Yet in the interrelationships between the dimensions of poverty/wealth, goodness/badness, and gender displayed in the children's writing, the most important insights into their understanding of social identities may be gained.

For example, in only one story is a bad child specifically designated as rich, yet in more than a few stories good persons are, and other poor boys become both good and rich when they assume super power. Many of the bad children in the stories project an image of poverty, as indicated by homelessness. This portrayal suggests that the children may see poverty as a sort of punishment for being bad; the poor whom they see around them (and of which group, statistically at least, they are part) somehow deserve their fate. This interpretation is supported by the fact that in the single story in which a rich boy is "bad"—Fernando, David, and Walter's "El saborrión, el enojón, y el presumido" (The glutton, the mad one, and the presumptuous one)—the rich boy dies and loses all his money to the other boys in the story, who are poor, good, and not presumptuous, and so are apparently rewarded for their goodness. This story line has important implications for the boys' self-images—they seem to present themselves as good and powerful only when they deny or escape their current social-class positions.

The girls did not seem as concerned with issues of poverty and wealth as did the boys; they generally dealt only peripherally with the theme, with a few exceptions. Denora, Noemí, and Elsa wrote a story about a poor, homeless girl who entered a singing contest and won three million dollars. The girl didn't know what to do with so much money; she bought a house, grew up, got married, and "vivió muy feliz" (lived very happily). Later, the same girls wrote a fictionalized biography of the popular singer Gloria Trévil, who really did get rich by singing. In one other story, Denora and Noemí wrote about eight orphaned rich girls who are poisoned on Halloween, but the girls' wealth is only an incidental part of the story line.

Summary and conclusions

The students in this classroom can be seen inventing social identities through their narrative writing, where they write the word, the world, and their very selves. They write themselves into a range of possible existences and create multiple identities for themselves, even as their freedom to create is constrained by the realms of what they view as possible fictional lives. Some of the identities that students invent for themselves in their stories correspond closely with some of their actual behaviors in the world, and some do not. Some aspects of their identities are directly represented in print, and others are transformed, modified, denied, or erased. And some of the personas that individuals assume in different stories contradict each other: They may be Good Guys in one story and bad boys in the next; they may be girls whose main dream is to marry a handsome man in one story and musketeers going on heroic missions in the next. Yet such contradictions are inherent in the multiplicity of beings that all of us are or at times dare to be.

The "free-writing" process that was cultivated in this classroom allowed room for the invention of multiple identities in ways that are not open to students in more traditional classrooms, where writing topics are assigned or strict regulations are placed on what students can write about. Writing workshops such as this one may provide one of the only legitimate academic arenas in which students beyond the preschool age are able to play: to experiment with a range of characters and stories and try on a number of possible social identities. The stories became a place where the children could be rich, or powerful, or really good, or really bad. They could push the limits of social regulation, as when they wrote about taboo topics without any censure by their teacher. In doing so, they could at times cross borders such as those defined by gender. For the girls, the opportunity to be bad may be especially significant, given the strong pressures that are typically exerted on girls to be good and the ways in which their construction as good girls can repress other aspects of their identities, as Valerie Walkerdine (1990) suggests.

Yet in general the students did not voluntarily cross gendered borders in their writing, and when they did, their crossings were not equilateral. Both girls and boys created largely gender-separate worlds in their texts and generally inscribed their characters within supposedly gender-appropriate roles, but girls were more likely to move into territory that was defined by boys than vice versa. Several girls joined boys' groupings and took up topics that had been established by the boys, whereas only one boy, Mario, explored more overtly "feminine" topics such as love, romance, and ballet lessons. Thus, as the work of Gilbert (1992) and others would suggest, the "freedom" of this free-writing environment may be illusory; the fantasy worlds that the children created on paper were largely influenced by the social worlds that they saw around them and by the social discourses that regulate action in that world and define the range of possible identities that the children could safely try on.

The forms of border-crossing seen in the stories also deserve consideration. I found myself asking what it means for girls to break out of the strictures of the "good girl" mold by choosing to be bad. From a feminist perspective, is it necessarily "bad" to be "good"? Similarly, what does it mean when boys from low-income communities display in their writing their internalization of a work-ethic ideology which suggests that anyone who works hard enough or is smart enough can get rich? There are dangers in romanticizing resistance or in seeing all forms of subversion as liberatory. As Paul Willis (1977) and Jean Anyon (1983) demonstrate, working-class adolescents' resistance to the regulatory forces of school may help lock them into deeply gendered working-class lives, and resistance may serve to reproduce and reinforce the given social order. At the same time, as outsiders to these intimate processes of identity construction, we should be equally careful not to see children's expression of gendered and classed identities—even seemingly stereotypical ones—as evidence of their submission to the given order or as a sign that resistance is "really" reproduction. It may be a sign of both or of neither.

For researchers and theoreticians, the issue becomes one of how to interpret the identities that children invent for themselves within existing discursive—and structural—power relations. For teachers and activists, the question is how to respond to children's narratives in order to open up the widest range of possibilities to all students, how to encourage acts of subversion without reinforcing mere reactions and without imposing new limitations on the identities children are allowed to invent. The struggle is one of seeing, and helping our students to see, the complex mechanisms that maintain class and gender divisions in society while still exploring how to pursue our own dreams, invent our own futures, and write our own lives into existence in the world.

I would suggest that the best answer lies in seeing that no one is locked into a single position on either end of a system of binary opposites. We can all be both good and bad, both strong and weak, both students and lovers. We can speak from different positions simultaneously or choose where and when we want to fit into a particular set of discursive—and human—relations. We can invent ourselves again and again, in different ways in various places and times, and in doing this we can help challenge the forces that limit the realms of our real and invented worlds.

NOTES

Thanks to the teacher and students for sharing their classroom, ideas, and writing with me; thanks also to the editors of this volume, Laurie MacGillivray, and Barrie Thorne for thoughtful feedback on earlier drafts.

1. Pseudonyms have been used for the teacher, the students, and the school. In this chapter I refer to the teacher by her first name because that was her preferred form of address; however, most students called her "Miss Lyons" or "maestra" (teacher).

2. Spanish television *novelas*, while reminiscent of English-language soap operas, represent a distinct genre with their own historical and cultural traditions and should not be equated with their U.S. counterparts. A full discussion of this genre is beyond the scope of this chapter, however, as is an adequate discussion of the complexities of romantic genres and their reception. See Mary Bucholtz (chapter 18, this volume), Linda Christian-Smith (1990, 1993), Janice Radway (1984), Laurel Sutton (chapter 8, this volume), and Carol Thurston (1987) for discussions of "feminine" genres and their readings.

3. The lack of closure in this and other stories written by the students in this room merits investigation. On the one hand, it may represent the easiest way out of the uncertainty of how to end stories. This may be particularly important when any such decision would have moralistic overtones or would require the authors to make a statement about what they believe is proper, right, and good. By leaving the story inconclusive, the onus of the moral decision is removed from the authors and shared with the audience. At the same time, given the authors' close identification with the characters in their stories, the lack of closure may be motivated by an attitude such as that described by Kathleen Wood (1994:777) in her analysis of lesbian coming-out stories: Like the narrators in Wood's study, the children may not have "one fixed and rigid understanding of their lives"—or the lives of their characters—and so

they leave the audience with a sense that there is more but that they themselves may not be privy to that part of their characters' lives.

REFERENCES

Anyon, Jean (1983). Intersections of gender and class: Accommodation and resistance by working class and affluent females to contradictory sex-role ideologies. In Stephen Walker & Len Barton (eds.), *Gender, class, and education*. New York: Falmer Press, 19–38.

Atwell, Nancie (1987). *In the middle: Writing, reading, and learning with adolescents*. Upper Montclair, NH: Boynton/Cook.

Brooke, Robert E. (1991). *Writing and sense of self: Identity negotiation in writing workshops*. Urbana, IL: National Council of Teachers of English.

Calkins, Lucy McCormick (1986). *The art of teaching writing*. Portsmouth, NH: Heinemann.

Christian-Smith, Linda K. (1990). *Becoming a woman through romance*. New York: Routledge.

———— (ed.) (1993). *Texts of desire: Essays on fiction, femininity, and schooling*. Washington, DC: Falmer Press.

Connell, Robert W. (1987). *Gender and power*. Stanford, CA: Stanford University Press.

Cook-Gumperz, Jenny (1995). Reproducing the discourse of mothering: How gendered talk makes gendered lives. In Kira Hall & Mary Bucholtz (eds.), *Gender articulated: Language and the socially constructed self*. New York: Routledge, 401–419.

Davies, Bronwyn (1989). *Frogs and snails and feminist tales: Preschool children and gender*. Boston: Allen & Unwin.

———— (1993). *Shards of glass*. Cresskill, NJ: Hampton Press.

Dyson, Anne Haas (1989). *Multiple worlds of child writers: Friends learning to write*. New York: Teachers College Press.

———— (1993). *Social worlds of children learning to write in an urban primary school*. New York: Teachers College Press.

Gal, Susan (1995). Language, gender, and power: An anthropological view. In Kira Hall & Mary Bucholtz (eds.), *Gender articulated: Language and the socially constructed self*. New York: Routledge, 169–182.

Graves, Donald (1983). *Writing: Teachers and children at work*. Exeter, NH: Heinemann.

Gilbert, Pam (1992). Narrative as gendered social practice: In search of different story lines for language research. *Linguistics and Education* 5:211–218.

———— (1993). (Sub)versions: Using sexist language practices to explore critical literacy. *Australian Journal of Language and Literacy* 16(4):323–332.

Houghton, Cathryn (1995). Managing the body of labor: The treatment of reproduction and sexuality in a therapeutic institution. In Kira Hall & Mary Bucholtz (eds.). *Gender articulated: Language and the socially constructed self*. New York: Routledge, 121–142.

Kamler, Barbara (1994). Gender and genre in early writing. *Linguistics and Education* 6:153–182.

Kyratzis, Amy (1994). Tactical uses of narratives in nursery school same-sex groups. In Mary Bucholtz, A. C. Liang, Laurel A. Sutton, & Caitlin Hines (eds.), *Cultural performances: Proceedings of the Third Berkeley Women and Language Conference*. Berkeley, CA: Berkeley Women and Language Group, 389–398.

Lensmire, Timothy (1994). *When children write: Critical revisions of the writing workshop*. New York: Teachers College Press.

Livia, Anna (1994). The riddle of the Sphinx: Creating genderless characters in French. In Mary Bucholtz, A. C. Liang, Laurel A. Sutton, and Caitlin Hines (eds.), *Cultural performances: Proceedings of the Third Berkeley Women and Language Conference*. Berkeley, CA: Berkeley Women and Language Group, 421–433.

MacGillivray, Laurie, & Ana M. Martínez (1998). Princesses who commit suicide: Primary children writing within and against stereotypes. *Journal of Literacy Research* 30(10):53–84.

Orellana, Marjorie Faulstich (1995). Literacy as a gendered social practice: Tasks, texts, talk, and take-up. *Reading Research Quarterly* 30(4):674–708.

——— (1996). Negotiating power through language in classroom meetings. *Linguistics and Education* 8:335–365.

Phinney, Margaret Yatesvitch (1994). Gender, status, writing, and the resolution of kindergarten girls' social tensions. *Linguistics and Education* 6:311–330.

Radway, Jane (1984). *Reading the romance.* Chapel Hill: University of North Carolina Press.

Shuman, Amy (1986). *Storytelling rights: The uses of oral and written texts by urban adolescents.* New York: Cambridge University Press.

Solsken, Judith W. (1993). *Literacy, gender, and work in families and in school.* Norwood, NJ: Ablex.

Thorne, Barrie (1993). *Gender play: Girls and boys in school.* New Brunswick, NJ: Rutgers University Press.

Thurston, Carol (1987). *The romance revolution: Erotic novels for women and the quest for a new sexual identity.* Urbana: University of Illinois Press.

Walkerdine, Valerie (1990). *Schoolgirl fictions.* New York: Verso.

Willis, Paul E. (1977). *Learning to labour: How working class kids get working class jobs.* Farnborough, England: Saxon House.

Wood, Kathleen (1994). Life stories as artifacts of a culture: Lesbian coming-out stories. In Mary Bucholtz, A. C. Liang, Laurel A. Sutton, & Caitlin Hines (eds.), *Cultural performances: Proceedings of the Third Berkeley Women and Language Conference.* Berkeley, CA: Berkeley Women and Language Group, 777–786.

4   LISA CAPPS

. . . .

Constructing the Irrational Woman

Narrative Interaction and Agoraphobic Identity

T his chapter illuminates the construction of irrationality through analysis of family interaction involving a woman ("Meg") who identifies herself and is identified by clinicians and those around her as agoraphobic. In Meg's words:[1]

> I was diagnosed [with agoraphobia] two years ago . . . and now I identify myself first and foremost as agoraphobic. Fear is <u>constantly</u> in my mind. . . . I feel "less than" other people, kind of crazy somehow. And I know my kids and my husband, who's the world's <u>nicest</u>, most <u>normal</u> guy, <u>must</u> think of me as irrational. I'm somebody who's afraid to do most EVERYthing that normal people do without thinking twice. Just thinking about normal, everyday things . . . can send me into a panic.

Irrationality is widely considered to be a central characteristic of agoraphobia, which is most commonly diagnosed in women. Although genetics clearly contributes to the development of the disorder (e.g., Weissman 1993), environmental factors also play a significant role. Various theories have been proposed, the majority of which conceptualize the problem as existing within the mind of the individual. Further, researchers—even those examining hypotheses concerning the interpersonal dimensions of agoraphobia—typically employ measures designed to identify traits that constitute the "agoraphobic personality." Indeed, Meg's self-portrait is emblematic of this point of view as she identifies herself as "agoraphobic," "less than," "irrational," and "crazy" and differentiates herself from "normal" people.

This study offers an alternative view of psychopathology in general and agoraphobia in particular, a perspective grounded in the notion that psychological disorders are interactional achievements that cannot be divorced from a particular sociohistorical environment (Bateson 1972; Sass 1992; Szasz 1974). From this point of view identities are not static, individual entities. Rather they are dynamic, collaborative constructions that emerge moment by moment over the course of social interaction. Thus understanding agoraphobia requires examining interactions between people as they unfold over time and locating these interactions within a particular sociocultural context.

As described in the American Psychiatric Association's (1995) *Diagnostic and Statistical Manual of Mental Disorders* (DSM-IV), individuals with agoraphobia suffer irrational fear of being in a place or situation where it may be difficult to escape or to obtain help in the event of a panic attack or other potentially incapacitating or extremely embarrassing symptoms. A principal feature of agoraphobia is avoidance in response to this fear. Agoraphobic persons often describe feeling trapped by an ever-present threat of panic and their belief that they cannot risk leaving safe havens such as their homes. Although the term *agoraphobia* means 'fear of open spaces', the disorder is perhaps more appropriately described as a fear of being anyplace where one might feel alone and vulnerable to fear and panic.

Initial reports suggested that agoraphobia is extremely rare, a conclusion that is likely due in part to agoraphobic persons' reluctance to travel to therapy sites. In fact, the disorder is more prevalent than previously suspected. The most recent epidemiological study of psychiatric disorders in the United States conducted in-home interviews of 15,490 individuals from five metropolitan areas, 4 percent of whom reported having suffered from agoraphobia during the previous year (Eaton, Dryman, & Weissman 1991).[2] Although the disorder is more common in urban than rural areas, its prevalence appears to be similar throughout industrialized countries, across ethnic groups, and across age groups between 18 and 64 years. The epidemiological study found that agoraphobia is more than twice as prevalent among women as among men. Though compelling, this ratio is considerably lower than those found in earlier investigations of agoraphobia, which reported that up to 95 percent of sufferers are women (Marks & Herst 1970).

In the clinical literature, agoraphobia is consistently referred to as a "woman's syndrome" (e.g., Foa, Steketee, & Young 1984). Discussion of the association between agoraphobia and women has focused not only on prevalence rates but also on the similarity between symptoms of agoraphobia and stereotypical female gender roles. Conventional gender identities, after all, are not inborn; they are socialized. Moreover, language is central to the socialization process, in that expert members of society use language to socialize children and novices into particular identities, roles, and worldviews, the expression of which involves using language in certain ways (Ochs 1988; Ochs & Schieffelin 1984; Schieffelin 1990). A considerable body of research, for example, suggests that women are socialized into indecisive, indirect, and deferential communicative styles relative to the more direct, authoritative styles of men (Lakoff 1990). From a feminist perspective, such patterns of communication both reflect and constitute women's status as powerless. Enactment of conventional female roles, whether by women or men, is also often considered pathological. Indeed, neurotic symptoms have been conceptualized as an extreme form of indirect communication (Breuer & Freud 1957; Szasz 1974). Building on the premise that the powerless have more incentive than the powerful to use indirect strategies, feminist and critical theorists have concluded that the association between conventionalized feminine actions and stances and insanity or irrationality is a means of social control (e.g., Chesler 1972; Foucault 1965; Lakoff & Coyne 1993; Wenegrat 1995).

With respect to agoraphobia, feminist theorists propose that traditional ideologies of femininity are "phobogenic," such that women are socialized into dependent, unassertive, and accommodating behaviors that are characteristic of the disorder (Fodor 1974; Wolfe 1984). Surprisingly, however, studies designed to empirically evaluate these socially situated conceptualizations of agoraphobia have relied on static, individualized measures that look *through* language, not *at* language in social interaction (Capps & Ochs 1995a, b). For example, to test the sex-role theory of agoraphobia, researchers have administered personality inventories, including masculinity-femininity scales, to individual sufferers. Results generally suggest that both women and men with agoraphobia rate lower on indices of masculinity (such as assertiveness and independence) than does a normative sample (Chambless & Mason 1986; Kleiner & Marshall 1987). Although consistent with the sex-role theory, this methodological approach locates the problem within individuals' personalities and does little to illuminate relevant sociocultural processes.

Similarly, it has been proposed that people with agoraphobia wish to escape a close relationship but fear independence (e.g., Goldstein & Chambless 1978; Hafner 1982). Because the disorder confines sufferers to their homes, agoraphobia negates the first option and thus eliminates the conflictual situation. Many have dismissed this theory based on results of standardized questionnaires administered to persons with agoraphobia and their spouses which suggest that such couples experience no more marital distress than normal controls and that spouses of persons with agoraphobia show normative levels of psychopathology. These findings have led some researchers to claim that "agoraphobia derives from the individual patient's psychological make-up rather than the marriage or the husband, since the problem lies not in the marriage, nor in the husband, but within the patient herself" (Symonds 1973, as quoted in Arrindell & Emmelkamp 1986:600). Rendering agoraphobia an intrapsychic disorder, this statement makes explicit an ideology that is implicit both in the DSM-IV, which diagnoses disturbances in individuals, and in research that relies on individualized measures.[3]

In contrast to such assumptions, the following analysis is grounded in the notion that understanding psychological dispositions requires closely examining social interactions between people rather than the decontextualized responses of isolated individuals. The basic tenets of the present study are that people verbally attempt to establish their emotions, actions, and identities moment by moment during social interaction and that narrative provides a powerful resource for doing so (e.g., Bruner 1990; Heath 1983; Miller, Potts, Fung, Hoogstra, & Mintz 1990; Ochs 1993; Schieffelin 1990). In narrating, interlocutors attempt to construct themselves from a particular point of view, both as protagonists acting and feeling in the past and as narrators acting and feeling in the present. Narrators describe a setting in which a protagonist encounters a problematic event of some kind and relate ensuing psychological and behavioral responses and consequences. By forging causal connections between emotions and events, narratives build theories about experiences (Bruner 1986; Feldman 1989; Ochs, Taylor, Rudolph, & Smith 1992; White 1980). Further, a single telling can build conflicting theories about an experience or highlight conflicting dimensions of a protagonist's or narrator's identity (Capps & Ochs 1995a, b). Narrative interactions create opportunities for negotiating identities and worldviews, for resisting, challenging, and perpetuating the status quo. In this sense, narrative theories not only shape understandings of past events but also organize lived experience in present, future, and imagined realms (M. H. Goodwin 1991; Ochs 1993).

Narratives told in the course of social interaction are jointly produced by copresent interlocutors; that is, emergent narratives are interactional achievements (C. Goodwin 1981; C. Goodwin & M. H. Goodwin 1992; Jacoby & Ochs 1995). For this reason, individuals' attempts to construct a particular evaluative perspective in narratives require ratification from others. Conarrators also construct the identities of participants by shaping their roles as protagonists acting in the past and narrators acting in the present. Copresent interlocutors influence the unfolding of storytelling sequences through their gaze patterns, body orientation, and verbal contributions to the storytelling. In these ways, cotellers simultaneously display varying degrees of alignment with the initial teller's evaluation of the narrated events. In so doing they validate or repudiate the teller's legitimacy as narrator.

Storytelling interactions provide a medium for the construction of irrationality in that being "rational" involves having the authority to reframe experience in a way that is ratified by others, whereas being "irrational" involves failing to receive such ratification from legitimate others. The pain and isolation that accompanies mental illness is partly attributable to loss of the authority to reframe events and experiences in ways that will be ratified and loss of confidence in one's ability to regain this authority. This is particularly true of people suffering from agoraphobia, for whom familiar, seemingly innocuous territory away from home keys the threat of panic and helplessness. Meg articulates this predicament in the passage quoted at the beginning of this chapter: "Just thinking about normal, everyday things . . . can send me into a panic."

The construction of rationality and authority through storytelling is tied to the distribution of narrative roles. Elinor Ochs and Carolyn Taylor's (1992a, b, 1995) analyses of storytelling during family dinners have shown that members assume particular narrative roles and that these roles discursively arrange protagonists and interlocutors in relationships of power. Specifically, mothers in their study tended to introduce narratives, the majority of which featured themselves and their children as protagonists, whereas fathers most often served as primary recipients of the stories. By directing children to tell fathers about an incident in their day or by initiating narratives about their own personal experience, mothers nominate their children and themselves as protagonists whose actions are accessible to other interlocutors, particularly fathers, to review and sanction. Similarly, those who feel themselves to be irrational are likely to seek validation from others for the way they frame or make sense of their experiences. One way of doing so is by initiating stories about their own experiences so that they might be ratified by "rational" others. The act of designating a particular cointerlocutor as preferred responder constructs this recipient as rational and places her or him in a position to ratify the teller's explanation of a particular set of events.

The present study illuminates how family storytelling interactions construct the irrational woman by examining (1) the distribution of narrative roles (i.e., protagonist, initial teller, primary recipient) among members of a family in which the mother (Meg) has been diagnosed with agoraphobia; (2) other family members' contributions (e.g., gaze patterns, body orientation, and verbal contributions) to stories that Meg initiates about her own disturbing encounters and to stories in which Meg is not the narrative protagonist or principal teller; and (3) how narrative interactions might fuel the perpetuation of "irrational" panicky thoughts and feelings associated with past or hypothetical events, which in turn may perpetuate Meg's identity as agoraphobic.

Methodology

Data collection

Participants. The present study focuses on narrative interactions between members of a middle-class European American family (the "Logan" family), including a mother/wife ("Meg," age 36); father/husband ("William," age 38), daughter ("Beth," age 11) and son ("Sean," age 6). Meg was initially diagnosed with agoraphobia by a clinician in her community. Her symptoms increased over the subsequent 2 years, at which time Meg started a self-help group for persons with agoraphobia. As a graduate student in clinical psychology, I approached members of the group to recruit participation in a dissertation project on the psychological adjustment of children of agoraphobic parents (Capps 1996; Capps, Sigman, Sena, Henker, & Whalen 1996). When Meg expressed interest in the study, I evaluated the appropriateness of her participation by confirming her diagnosis of agoraphobia using the Anxiety Disorders Interview Schedule, or ADIS (DiNardo, O'Brien, Barlow, Waddell, & Blanchard 1983). After participating in the dissertation study, however, both Meg and her daughter Beth expressed concern that the methods used did not capture Meg's experience. Meg and the other members of her family then agreed to embark on the present discourse-analytic venture.

Corpus. The database for this study was collected as part of an in-depth ethnographic and discourse study carried out on the construction and socialization of agoraphobia in a single family (Capps & Ochs 1995a, b). Data collection consisted of (1) 36 months of participant observation of family life, including video and audio recordings of Logan family dinner interactions and leisure activities; and (2) audio-recorded, loosely structured interviews with Meg, alone and together with Beth.

Data analysis

In this study *narrative* is defined as a socially organized conventional telling of temporally ordered events in one's life from a particular evaluative perspective (Goffman 1959; Labov & Waletzky 1968). Seventeen narratives were gleaned from videotaped observations of dinner interactions, which served as the basis for determining the distribution of narrative roles. Subsequent analyses of family interactions focus on three stories in particular, which were selected in order to investigate how the irrational woman is coconstructed through storytelling interactions that involve family members in different roles. The three stories closely examined here are also thematically related in that each features a pit bull terrier, a notoriously ferocious dog: the first pit bull story is initiated and principally told by Meg, and the narrative centers on her own anxious experience; the second is initiated and principally told by Meg's

husband William and provokes anxiety in Meg in her role as coteller; and the third
story is initiated and principally told by Meg and centers on another female protagonist's distress.

Narrative roles

Examination of the stories reveals that the roles family members assume in narrative
activity shape the identities that emerge. Although narratives are collaboratively constructed by all copresent interlocutors (Duranti 1986; Goodwin & Duranti 1992), family members assume different roles in the telling. Storytelling interactions organize
protagonists and tellers in relations of power, which shape the identities that emerge.
The recurrent arrangement Ochs and Taylor (1992a) identified in their study of family
dinner activity establishes the father's position as "'panopticon'—the all-seeing eye of
power" (Ochs & Taylor 1992a:329), a term taken from Michel Foucault (1979). As
applied to narrative structure, the concept of the panopticon suggests that storytelling
lays out the lives of protagonists for surveillance by those in control. Analysis of the
seventeen narratives in the present corpus suggests that distribution of narrative roles
in the Logan family is consistent with this pattern, as shown in Table 4.1.

Table 4.1 demonstrates that the majority of stories are initiated by Meg, center
on Meg's or the children's experiences, and are directed to William, establishing his
power as inspector. Further, the majority of narratives Meg initiates (80%) center on
her own distressing or otherwise unnerving experiences. By routinely narrating her
anxiety-provoking experiences in this way, Meg establishes William in a position to
(de)legitimize her emotions and actions as protagonist in the narrated scenario, as
well as her present concern over this circumstance. Meg, perhaps like others who
feel themselves to be "irrational," appears to seek validation (especially from "the
world's *nicest*, most *normal* guy") for her framing of events and experiences, particularly those that remain unresolved. In the process, William obtains the authority
to confer or withhold a judgment that Meg's feelings and behavior are rational, and
his identity as "the world's nicest, most normal guy" is instantiated. Analyses of
conarration in the Logan family illuminate these dynamics.

Table 4.1. Distribution of narrative roles during Logan family
dinnertime interaction

Member	Initial teller	Primary recipient	Principal protagonist[a]
William	4 (23.5%)	14 (82%)	1 (6%)
Meg	10 (59%)	2 (12%)	7 (41%)
Beth	3 (17.5%)	3 (17%)	1 (6%)
Sean	0	0	4 (24%)

[a]Percentages do not add to 100 because two stories (12%) did not involve any family
member as principal protagonist.

Coconstructing irrationality in tales of distressing experience

The first of Meg's stories that will be considered here (Pit Bull Story #1) involves her unexpected encounter with two menacing pit bull dogs while paying a visit to her father-in-law (excerpts 1a and 1b). In the telling Meg makes her actions, thoughts, and emotions accessible to other interlocutors, particularly to William, the primary recipient.

Enduring mental activity

Meg builds her narrative around her mental activity. She emphasizes her psychological responses to the presence of the dogs by routinely using mental verb constructions that highlight not only the content but also the very fact of her thoughts and emotions. These constructions convey the sense that she continues to feel distressed, in part by concern about the appropriateness of her anxiety. Similarly, Meg's subsequent narrative contributions (that is, her responses to responses) seek validation both of the content of her past reaction and of her ongoing emotional preoccupation with the encounter with the dogs.

(1a) Pit Bull Story #1—Excerpt
      M = Meg (Mother) W = William (Father) B = Beth, age 11 S = Sean, age 6
      S: *looking at William*
      W: [Well you don't- *((looking down at food))*
      M: [*Turns body and gaze toward William*
          And your dad the whole time was=
      W: = [dare trust em
            [*looking down, leans away from Meg, toward Sean*
      M: kind of saying good boy good boy
          and you know how your <u>da:d</u> is
          (.2)
          [He can make any animal (.)
          [*Beth looks at Meg*
      B: tame=
      M: =his friend.
          [But I couldn't help but wonder
          [*looks down at food, body oriented toward William*
          what would happen [**if**
                   [*William does brisk vertical head nods still looking down,*
                   leaning away from Meg
          (.2) [you ↑know
             [*Meg looks up at William*
          (.4)
          Meg scratches top of head, then looks down at food
      W: They'd be in big trouble
      M: If he really did get into your dad's yard

(1b)   Pit Bull Story #1—Excerpt

    M: **I got to thinking** (.5) these [aren't <u>PETS</u>
          [*looking down at food*   [*looks up at William, does horizontal head shake*
          [*William looking at Meg*
          (.6)
          [↑No↓body would treat a   [↑<u>pet</u> like that
          [*William looks down at food* [*Meg eyeflash at William*
          [They're [strictly there to chew up [↑any↓body
          [*William looks up from food at Beth*
             [*Meg looks up at William*
                   [*William eyeflash at Meg, turns to Sean*
         [who might come into their ya:rd
         [*Sean wipes his mouth with his arm*
    W: [Sure they are
          [*William looks at Sean*
          [*Meg looks at Sean*
    M: **Wh-what [if that thing gets ↑<u>loo:se</u> and ↑<u>ki:lls</u> <u>somebody</u>**
          [*Meg looks at William, who continues looking at Sean*

When Meg uses forms such as *But I couldn't help but wonder what would happen if
. . .* and *I got to thinking . . .* , she is reporting not only *what* she is thinking and feeling but also *that* she is thinking and feeling. Mental verbs bring into focus Meg's
consciousness of engaging in the activities of thinking and feeling and invite assurance that mental activity of this sort would be expected of a rational, normal person.

In telling the story, Meg associates her thoughts and feelings with a particular
past event: encountering the pit bulls. Yet the excerpts presented here also give the
impression that her absorption with these thoughts and emotions continues through
the moment of the telling; she remains distressed over the threat of the dogs. Meg
constructs the objects of her thoughts and feelings in the present tense, depicting them
as current, enduring concerns rather than issues contained in the past. She asks, for
example, "what *would* happen . . ." rather than "what *would have* happened" and
"what if that thing *gets* loose" rather than "what if that thing *got* loose." Through
repeated use of these mental verb constructions, Meg indexes for her interlocutors
that the predicament has not been resolved but continues to plague her present and
imagined experience. In this way, Meg opens herself to others' assessments of the
reasonableness of her past and present anxious worldview.

Soliciting validation

Meg not only opens herself to others' assessments of her thoughts and feelings but
delivers the narrative in a way that actively elicits feedback on her thinking, in that
utterances containing mental verb constructions are characteristically delivered with
hesitations that solicit responsiveness (C. Goodwin 1981; Sacks, Schegloff, &
Jefferson 1978). This behavior is not unique to Meg but is characteristic of women's
speech styles more generally (see, e.g., Schiffrin 1987; Lakoff 1990; Tannen 1993;
Watzlawick, Beavin, & Jackson 1967). Meg most actively solicits feedback from her

husband—her body and eye gaze frequently orient toward him, requesting his participation as the preferred responder (C. Goodwin 1981, 1986)—both for the content of her thoughts and for being legitimately preoccupied at this point in the story. In these excerpts, however, William's validation of Meg is weak at best.

In excerpt (1a), for example, Meg presents statements conveying her thinking (*wondering*) about the pit bulls. Although William responds with brisk vertical head nods, his gaze remains fixed on his food, his body oriented away from Meg. After a short gap (0.2 seconds), Meg, who is looking at William, solicits additional feedback from him by asking, "you know?" William withholds feedback through a lengthier gap (0.4 seconds). In response to his silence—which signals disagreement or nonalignment (Davidson 1984; Pomerantz 1978)—Meg, still gazing at William, intensifies her display of confusion and request for input from him by scratching the top of her head. She then looks down at her food, at which point William says, "they'd be in big trouble." Here William does provide feedback, but in so doing empathizes not with Meg's past and ongoing distress over the situation but with his parents' predicament.

Similarly, in excerpt (1b), Meg presents four different statements conveying her thinking about pit bulls. Although William stares at Meg as she begins to relate her thoughts, he does not provide verbal feedback after her first predicate (*these aren't PETS*) nor after she looks straight at him and intensifies her message by shaking her head horizontally nor after a subsequent 0.6-second pause (which is a lengthy conversational invitation to take the floor). William continues to withhold substantive response during Meg's second thought (↑*No*↓*body would treat a* ↑*pet like that*), even though she flashes a glance at him. This prolonged lack of responsiveness can be taken as a strong sign of nonalignment. As Meg goes on to express a third thought (*They're strictly there to chew up* ↑*any*↓*body who might come into their ya:rd*), William looks up not at her but at his daughter Beth. He then glances at Meg momentarily en route to fixing his gaze on his son Sean. At this point, William finally responds verbally (*Sure they are*), but all the while his gaze remains fixed on Sean, signaling that his attention is divided and he is only partly available to her. Furthermore, this assessment is "downgraded" in that it does not match the intensity of Meg's portrayal. As Anita Pomerantz (1984) has pointed out, such responses undermine rather than ratify the assertion at hand. Continuing her bid for ratification, Meg goes on to express her fourth and most potent thought as a direct question to William, who is the object of her gaze; William, however, remains focused on Sean and never responds verbally or otherwise acknowledges the question.

Escalating bids for responsiveness

This conversational dynamic between Meg and William may perpetuate Meg's panicky thoughts and feelings associated with past or hypothetical events, which in turn may maintain her identity as an irrational agoraphobic. In response to silence or low-affiliative, downgraded responses, tellers typically escalate the intensity of both the narrative situation and their bids for alignment from conarrators (Pomerantz 1984). Indeed, these excerpts illuminate how William's low-affiliative responses lead Meg to increase the frequency of her bids for responsiveness. In so doing, she also describes her experience in progressively more self-threatening and anxious terms. Meg intensifies the dangerousness of the situation and attempts to increase the relevance of the threat to other interlocutors by expanding its scope to include those copresent and by rendering the dogs a present-tense menace. For example, in (1a), through the use of a hypothetical scenario, she casts the dogs as an enduring danger to *anyone* who visits William's parents, rather than confining the threat to *her* past experience: *I couldn't help but wonder what would happen if . . . If he really did get into your dad's yard.* Similarly, in (1b) Meg describes the dogs as creatures who exist for the sole purpose of mauling "anybody" in the vicinity. Finally, Meg asks her half-attending husband to ponder with her the possibility that the one particularly threatening pit bull, described emphatically as a *thing*, could "get ↑<u>loo:se</u>" and "↑<u>ki:ll some-body</u>." As is the case in (1a), these constructions increase the scope of the threat to include not just Meg but "anybody" and "somebody" and not only in the past but also in the present.

This progression can be viewed as an attempt to engage William's participation by drawing him into the realm of the story. Indeed, good storytellers often attempt to involve interlocutors by dramatizing past events as if they are taking place in the here and now (Buhler [1934] 1990; Schiffrin 1981; Wolfson 1979). However, for Meg, it seems that these experiences are so vivid and pressing that they force their way into her current consciousness—rather than narratively controlling the past, Meg is herself controlled by it.[4] These rhetorical strategies can also be brought to bear in discussing the coconstruction of irrationality. By casting the scenario with "anyone" and "some-one" as protagonists (rather than herself), Meg entreats her interlocutors to put them-selves in her shoes. At the same time, she constructs her actions and emotions as what would be expected of "anybody"; she attempts to fill her shoes with rational feet. In so doing, she attempts to legitimize her psychological responses as protagonist and her voice as narrator, but to no avail. Rather than constructing Meg as being like anyone or even someone else, the progressive escalation in this storytelling interaction seems to have the opposite outcome: It renders her *unlike* others in her midst.

Meg's unratified attempts attest to the fact that she alone cannot construct her-self as a rational woman—nor can any individual. Similarly, neither William nor anyone else can single-handedly confer irrationality. Social identities are an interac-tional achievement. Indeed, William's role as the "panoptical" primary recipient is also a collaborative construction by family members. Thus only through recurrent participation in such interactions are Meg's experiences and interpretations cocon-structed as "irrational" and "abnormal," thereby constituting and perpetuating her agoraphobic identity.

Coconstructing irrationality through alternative narrative roles

Meg's identity as irrational is also coconstructed through family storytelling inter-actions that she does not initiate and that do not center on her distressing encounters as a protagonist. One such storytelling, again involving pit bulls, took place a few weeks after the first within the context of a discussion about the death of the Logan family's dog and whether or not to get another one. In (2a), William reports having seen an advertisement for part pit bull / rottweiler / German shepherd puppies and proposes that they adopt one as a family pet:

(2a)   Pit Bull Story #2
      W: I got to tell you what they were *ad*vertising in Compton-
            on Compton Boulevard on the way home
            ((looking straight ahead at Beth))
      S: [*looks up at William*
      B: [*looks up at William*
      M: [What
            [*looks up at William*
      B: *looks at Meg, and then at William*
      W: We could ha:ve (.) a:: pit bull [and shepherd
                            [*Meg jerks backward, away from William*
            and part rott[weiler puppy
                        [*Beth gets up from chair, looks out window*
            HA HA HA ha ha
      M: [Oh yea:h
            [*looks down at plate*
      B: A pit bull [shepherd and ↓[rottweiler
                       [*walks out of the room, into the kitchen*
      M: [Who needs a gun with a dog like that *((solemn tone))*

Narratives have a family history

Narrative interactions are constructed within the context of developing individual and collective histories. They are not isolated units but build on each other. In varying ways and degrees, each storytelling shapes those that precede and follow. Although stories may be related by theme, genre, or participant structure, each telling contributes to the ongoing construction of participants' identities (see also Wood, chapter 2, this volume).

The second pit bull storytelling harks back to the first both thematically and interactionally. William's contributions to this story explicitly counter Meg's previous assessment of pit bulls and thus her authority to make valid, rational assessments. When William delivers his report he invokes and undermines Meg's prior evaluation of pit bulls as menaces to society by making light of the situation she deemed lethal. Moreover, in suggesting that they take such a dog into their home, William proposes that they enact the worst-case scenarios in Meg's prior account: In the first pit bull story (excerpts 1a, 1b), Meg posits a most-dreaded scenario in which the pit bull escapes and enters the family yard. In addition, William's suggestion that they adopt the pit bull mix as a pet explicitly opposes Meg's previously expressed thoughts: *I got to thinking (.5) these aren't* PETS. William's proposal thus directly refutes the legitimacy of Meg's narrative appraisal of the pit bulls she encountered outside her father-in-law's yard.

Bridging past and present narrative roles

The second pit bull storytelling resembles the first in that both render Meg as having irrational thoughts and feelings about the dogs. In doing the telling as a joke, William constructs Meg as having been irrational or abnormal for being mired in anxious thinking about the dogs. In contrast to William's jocular tone, Meg's solemn assessment of the situation (*Who needs a gun with a dog like that*) reinforces this construction, affirming her ongoing concern about pit bulls. Further, the generalized form of her comment (*Who*) harks back to previous failed attempts to construct herself as rational or normal by aligning herself and her assessments with those of generic others.

The third pit bull story is immediately touched off by the second. Following William's lead, Meg herself jokingly relates an incident in which a neighbor's mother-in-law unwittingly locks herself in the backyard with a pit bull. In this sequence (2b) Meg constructs an account of a ridiculous if not irrational female protagonist whose distress over the pit bull is laughable:

(2b)   Pit Bull Story #3—Excerpt
    M: [Joe and Charlotte have a pit bull
        [*looking at William*
        (.4)

        .
        .
        .

        He said his mother-in-law got <u>locked out</u>
        They have a ↑house (.2) they have a-
        the door to the backyard locks automatically when it closes be(h)hind you
        And and *((laughingly))* she went out in the backyard
        She was visiting them and they didn't know that (.3) she was back-
        in the backyard with the pit <u>bull</u>
        And all of a sudden she yells CHARLOTTE, CHARLOTTE OPEN THIS DOOR
        hee hee he he he *((laughs covering mouth with hand))*
    B: [WHAT
        [*looking at Meg*
    M: Joe's mother-in-law got locked out in the backyard
        with their pit <u>bull</u> and he said it would <u>eat</u> anybody
    B: SS-ss- HA ha ha
    M: [She didn't know
        [*looks down at plate*
    B: Oh really *((laughingly))*
    M: And they had the door that would
    W: [I'd be afraid to have it- to have that dog around the <u>kids</u>
        [*looks at Meg*
    B: What <u>dog</u> *((looks at William))*
    S: [Pit bull *((looks at Beth))*
    W: [The pit <u>bull</u> *((looks at Beth))*

B: [Oh. Across the ↑street
    [*looking at William*
M: No=
W: =No
B: OH
M: Any-
W: Joe and Charlotte's=
M: =Any pit bull actually *((looking down at plate))*

This third story is thematically linked to the first and second storytelling inter-actions. In this narrative, Meg locates their neighbor Joe's mother-in-law in the place in which she initially imagined herself and most feared being: in the yard of an un-leashed pit bull. At the same time, Meg locates Joe's mother-in-law in the position she herself occupied in the course of William's joke-telling, which cast her distress as laughable.

In telling a joke, Meg appears to be attempting to align with "normal" (that is, rational) William's lighthearted stance toward the situation. But paralleling the pro-gression in the second pit bull storytelling, by the end Meg's rendering of the sce-nario is menacing, not laughable. As occurred over the course of the first and second storytellings, Meg's anxiety over the dogs becomes apparent as she portrays the pit bull as threatening not just to the protagonist but to everyone. For example, when she reiterates her account (following Beth's *WHAT*), Meg describes the pit bull as threatening, saying, "it would *eat* anybody." This portrayal converges with her de-piction of the pit bulls in the first story—as animals that are "there to chew up ↑any↓body who might come into their ya:rd." Similarly, as in the first storytelling, Meg's anxiety as coteller seems to escalate as her focus shifts from the particular pit bull in Joe and Charlotte's backyard to "any pit bull." Rather than being confined to a particular dog in a particular yard, the scope of the threat includes a multitude of dogs in any imaginable setting. The narrated circumstance is not contained in the past but pervades present and imagined time and space. As in the first and second stories, Meg seems unable to distance herself from her fear. Moreover, she is unsuc-cessful in her attempts to enlist family members' support for her position. Thus par-ticipation in these narrative interactions yields the outcome Meg most fears: being alone and experiencing inescapable, irrational fear of imminent danger.

In the third pit bull story, this shift in tone is constructed in part by William's comment, *I'd be afraid to have it- to have that dog around the* kids. His remark seems to push Meg further into the expanding gulf of anxiety that envelops and overwhelms the particulars of this story. William's comment, however, frames the scenario as threatening to "the *kids*." This response does not validate the protagonist's—and by extension, Meg's—fears. Rather, William aligns himself with the protectors, the adults. This pattern is reminiscent of the first story, in which William responds to Meg's concern about what would happen if the pit bulls entered her father-in-law's yard—her location as protagonist in the story—by identifying with his parents' pre-dicament: *They'd be in big trouble.* In such interactions William constructs fear of pit bulls as valid with respect to children and the elderly but not to people like him-self. William thereby implies that he is not afraid for the female protagonists (the mother-in-law, Meg) and to some extent that their fear is irrational and illegitimate. William further differentiates himself (and other normal people) from this irrational lot by restricting the scope of the threat to the initial story setting.

Implications

The present analysis of storytelling interactions in the Logan family suggests that members routinely assume narrative roles that construct Meg's agoraphobic identity: Meg frequently addresses stories—particularly stories of her own distressing encounters—to William, establishing him in a position to evaluate her rationality both as a protagonist acting, thinking, and feeling in the past and as a narrator acting, thinking, and feeling in the present. Meg's attempts to contextualize narrated attitudes and behaviors are rarely ratified by her husband ("the most normal guy in the world"). This dynamic propels an escalating cycle in which Meg senses herself to be irrational (that is, unlike normal others in her midst) and attempts to secure ratification for her distress by widening the scope of her narrated anxiety, which often leads William to withdraw further.

Why is it that William does not enter deeply or for a sustained time into her narrative recollections and speculations? One possibility might be that he wishes to curtail panic. Interlocutors listening to Meg's accounts of her past anxieties may withhold feedback for an extended period of the narrative, perhaps to avoid validating her fears or aligning themselves with her anxiety. When Meg recounts prior anxious scenarios for her family, she brings her past anxieties into present collective consciousness. Members of her family, particularly William, may display only minimal responsiveness to such recountings to discourage Meg from continuing this process and perhaps from involving their children in experiencing the same fears. In other words, William's minimal displays of involvement may be attempts to shut down narrative emotionality before it gets out of hand and develops into full-blown panic, sweeping the family into submission. However, displays of minimal or no responsiveness by the primary recipient of the narrative—her spouse—lead to escalation, not curtailment, of expressed anxiety. For Meg, a persistent outcome of such interactions is a perception of herself as "less than," "crazy," "irrational," and otherwise abnormal, leading her to avoid places outside the home in which she fears experiencing such sensations and to identify herself "first and foremost as agoraphobic."

Countering the view that psychopathology exists in the isolated minds of individuals, investigation of storytelling interactions in this family suggests that disorders are constructed in interaction. In contrast to decontextualized research measures that categorize individuals according to self-reported traits, analysis of *how* people use language, gesture, and body orientation to negotiate the meaning of events illuminates identities and worldviews in the making. Studies of face-to-face interaction capture rather than mask complexities and undermine rather than perpetuate stereotypes (see also Goodwin, chapter 20, and Morgan, chapter 1, both this volume). This approach demonstrates that individuals do not simply "play out" preexisting roles and that identities are interactional achievements involving acts of resistance and unintended outcomes, achievements that cannot be divorced from a particular sociohistorical context. Analysis of language in interaction locates convergences between ideologies of gender and of mental illness and illuminates how different speakers respond to these ideologies through practices that challenge and reproduce dominant beliefs. Finally, analysis of language in interaction reveals opportunities for reconfiguring identities and for assigning new meanings to gender.

NOTES

1. See J. Maxwell Atkinson and John Heritage (1984) for transcription conventions.

2. This percentage is considerably higher than those found in previous investigations conducted in the United States, England, Germany, and Switzerland, which reported prevalence rates of agoraphobia ranging from 0.6 percent to 3.6 percent. The higher percentage reported in the epidemiological study is attributable to the fact that participants were asked about symptoms over the past year rather than at the time of the interview, as was the case in the other studies.

3. The statement also reveals the way in which research methodologies may perpetuate cultural biases, in this case a heterocentric view: Because most studies of agoraphobic persons' close relationships have involved agoraphobic women and their husbands, such work has promoted the belief that agoraphobia is a married women's syndrome. Yet according to epidemiological surveys, this is not the case (Eaton, Dryman, & Weissman 1991).

4. See Capps and Ochs (1995a, b) for further discussion of grammatical forms through which Meg's anxious past experiences overwhelm her present experience.

REFERENCES

American Psychiatric Association (1995). *Diagnostic and statistical manual of mental disorders.* (4th ed.) Washington, DC: American Psychiatric Association.

Arrindell, Willem A., & Paul M. G. Emmelkamp (1986). Marital adjustment, intimacy, and needs in female agoraphobics and their partners: A controlled study. *British Journal of Psychiatry* 149:592–602.

Atkinson, J. Maxwell, & John Heritage (eds.) (1984). *Structures of social action.* Cambridge: Cambridge University Press.

Bateson, Gregory (1972). *Steps to an ecology of mind.* New York: Ballantine Books.

Breuer, Josef, & Sigmund Freud (1957). *Studies on hysteria.* Trans. James Strachey & Anna Freud. New York: Basic Books.

Bruner, Jerome (1986). *Actual minds, possible worlds.* Cambridge, MA: Harvard University Press.

——— (1990). *Acts of meaning.* Cambridge, MA: Harvard University Press.

Buhler, Karl (1990). *Sprachtheorie: Die darstellungsfunktion der sprache.* Jena: Gustav Fischer. (Original work published 1934)

Capps, Lisa (1996). The psychological adjustment of children of agoraphobic parents. Ph.D. diss., University of California, Los Angeles.

Capps, Lisa, & Elinor Ochs (1995a). *Constructing panic: The discourse of agoraphobia.* Cambridge, MA: Harvard University Press.

——— (1995b). Out of place: Narrative insights into agoraphobia. *Discourse Processes* 19(3):407–440.

Capps, Lisa, Marian Sigman, Rhonda Sena, Barbara Henker, & Carol Whalen (1996). Fear, anxiety, and perceived control in children of agoraphobic parents. *Journal of Child Psychology and Psychiatry* 37(4):445–452.

Chambless, Dianne L., & Jeanne Mason (1986). Sex, sex-role stereotyping and agoraphobia. *Behaviour Research and Therapy* 24(2):231–235.

Chesler, Phyllis (1972). *Women and madness*. New York: Avon.

Davidson, Judy (1984). Subsequent versions of invitations, offers, requests, and proposals dealing with potential or actual rejection. In J. Maxwell Atkinson & John Heritage (eds.), *Structures of social action*. Cambridge: Cambridge University Press, 102–128.

DiNardo, Peter A., Gerald T. O'Brien, David H. Barlow, Maria T. Waddell, & Edward B. Blanchard (1983). Reliability of DSM-III anxiety disorder categories using a new structured interview. *Archives of General Psychiatry* 40:1070–1074.

Duranti, Alessandro (1986). The audience as co-author: Introduction. *Text* 6(3):239–247.

Eaton, William W., Amy Dryman, & Myrna M. Weissman (1991). Panic and phobia. In Lee Robins & Darrel A. Regier (eds.), *Psychiatric disorders in America: The American Epidemiological Catchment Area Study*. New York: Free Press, 155–179.

Feldman, Carol F. (1989). Monologue as problem-solving narrative. In Katherine Nelson (ed.), *Narratives from the crib*. Cambridge, MA: Harvard University Press, 98–122.

Foa, Edna B., Gail Steketee, & Mark C. Young (1984). Agoraphobia: Phenomenological aspects, associated characteristics, and theoretical considerations. *Clinical Psychology Review* 4:431–457.

Fodor, Iris (1974). The phobic syndrome in women: Implications for treatment. In Violet Franks & Vasanti Burtle (eds.), *Women in therapy*. New York: Brunner/Mazel, 132–168.

Foucault, Michel (1965). *Madness and civilization*. New York: Vintage.

———— (1979). *Discipline and punish: The birth of the prison*. New York: Random House.

Goffman, Erving (1959). *The presentation of self in everyday life*. Garden City, NY: Doubleday.

Goldstein, Alan J., & Dianne L. Chambless (1978). A reanalysis of agoraphobia. *Behavior Therapy* 9:47–59.

Goodwin, Charles (1981). *Conversational organization: Interaction between speakers and hearers*. New York: Academic Press.

———— (1986). Audience diversity, participation and interpretation. *Text* 6(3):283–316.

Goodwin, Charles, & Alessandro Duranti (1992). Rethinking context: An introduction. In Alessandro Duranti & Charles Goodwin (eds.), *Rethinking context*. Cambridge: Cambridge University Press, 1–42.

Goodwin, Charles, & Marjorie Harness Goodwin (1992). Assessments and the construction of context. In Alessandro Duranti & Charles Goodwin (eds.), *Rethinking context*. Cambridge: Cambridge University Press, 147–190.

Goodwin, Marjorie Harness (1991). Retellings, pretellings and hypothetical stories. In Lea Laitinen, Pirkko Nuolijarvi, & Mirja Saari (eds.), *Leikkauspiste*. Helsinki: Suomalaisen Kirjallisuuden Seura, 43–58.

Hafner, R. Julian (1982). The marital context of the agoraphobic syndrome. In Dianne L. Chambless & Alan J. Goldstein (eds.), *Agoraphobia: Multiple perspectives on theory and treatment*. New York: Wiley, 143–170.

Heath, Shirley Brice (1983). *Ways with words: Language, life, and work in communities and classrooms*. Cambridge: Cambridge University Press.

Jacoby, Sally, & Elinor Ochs (1995). Co-construction: An introduction. *Research on Language and Social Interaction* 28(3):171–183.

Kleiner, Liliana, & W. L. Marshall (1987). The role of interpersonal problems in the development of agoraphobia with panic attacks. *Journal of Anxiety Disorders* 1:313–323.

Labov, William, & Joshua Waletzky (1968). Narrative analysis. In William Labov, Paul Cohen, Clarence Robins, & John Lewis (eds.), *A study of the non-standard English of Negro and Puerto Rican speakers in New York City*. New York: Columbia University, 286–338.

Lakoff, Robin (1990). *Talking power: The politics of language in daily life*. New York: Basic Books.

Lakoff, Robin, & James Coyne (1993). *Father knows best: The use and abuse of power in Freud's case of Dora*. New York: Teachers College Press.

Marks, Isaac M., & E. R. Herst (1970). A survey of 1,200 agoraphobics in Britain. *Social Psychiatry* 5:16–24.

Miller, Peggy J., Randolph Potts, Heidi Fung, Lisa Hoogstra, & Judy Mintz (1990). Narrative practices and the social construction of self in childhood. *American Ethnologist* 17:292–311.

Ochs, Elinor (1988). *Culture and language development: Language acquisition and language socialization in a Samoan village*. Cambridge: Cambridge University Press.

——— (1993). Stories that step into the future. In Douglas Biber & Edward Finegan (eds.), *Sociolinguistic perspectives on register*. Oxford: Oxford University Press, 106–135.

Ochs, Elinor, & Bambi Schieffelin (1984). Language acquisition and socialization: Three developmental stories. In Richard A. Schweder & Robert A. LeVine (eds.), *Culture theory: Essays on mind, self, and emotion*. Cambridge: Cambridge University Press, 276–320.

Ochs, Elinor, & Carolyn Taylor (1992a). Family narrative as political activity. *Discourse and Society* 3(3):301–340.

——— (1992b). Mothers' role in the everyday reconstruction of "Father knows best." In Kira Hall, Mary Bucholtz, & Birch Moonwomon (eds.), *Locating power: Proceedings of the Second Berkeley Women and Language Conference*. Berkeley, CA: Berkeley Women and Language Group, 447–462.

——— (1995). The "Father knows best" dynamic in dinnertime narratives. In Kira Hall & Mary Bucholtz (eds.), *Gender articulated: Language and the socially constructed self*. New York: Routledge, 97–120.

Ochs, Elinor, Carolyn Taylor, Dina Rudolph, & Ruth Smith (1992). Story-telling as a theory-building activity. *Discourse Processes* 15(1):37–72.

Pomerantz, Anita (1978). Compliment responses: Notes on the co-operation of multiple constraints. In Jim Schenkein (ed.), *Studies in the organization of conversational interaction*. New York: Academic Press, 79–112.

——— (1984). Agreeing and disagreeing with assessments: Some features of preferred/dispreferred turn shapes. In J. Maxwell Atkinson & John Heritage (eds.), *Structures of social action*. Cambridge: Cambridge University Press, 57–101.

Sacks, Harvey, Emanuel Schegloff, & Gail Jefferson (1978). A simplest systematics for the organization of turn taking in conversation. In Jim Schenkein (ed.), *Studies in the organization of conversational interaction*. New York: Academic Press, 7–55.

Sass, Louis (1992). *The paradoxes of delusion*. Ithaca, NY: Cornell University Press.

Schieffelin, Bambi (1990). *The give and take of everyday life: Language socialization of Kaluli children*. Cambridge: Cambridge University Press.

Schiffrin, Deborah (1981). Tense variation in narrative. *Language* 57(1):45–62.

——— (1987). *Discourse markers*. Cambridge: Cambridge University Press.

Szasz, Thomas S. (1974). *The myth of mental illness*. New York: HarperCollins.

Tannen, Deborah (1993). The relativity of linguistic strategies: Rethinking power and solidarity in gender and dominance. In Deborah Tannen (ed.), *Gender and conversational interaction*. New York: Oxford University Press, 165–188.

Watzlawick, Paul, Janet Beavin, & Don Jackson (1967). *Pragmatics and human communication: A study of interactional patterns, pathologies, and paradoxes*. New York: Norton.

Weissman, Myrna (1993). Family genetic studies of panic disorder. *Journal of Psychiatric Research* 27(1):69–78.

Wenegrat, Brant (1995). *Illness and power: Women's mental disorders and the battle between the sexes*. New York: New York University Press.

White, Hayden (1980). The value of narrativity in the representation of reality. In W. J. T. Mitchell (ed.), *On narrative*. Chicago: University of Chicago Press, 1–23.

Wolfe, Barry E. (1984). Gender imperatives, separation anxiety, and agoraphobia in women. *Integrative Psychiatry* 2(2):57–61.

Wolfson, Nessa (1979). The conversational historical present alternation. *Language* 55(19):168–182.

· ·

Contextualizing the Exotic Few

Gender Dichotomies in Lakhota

The characteristics between male and female language are very peculiar. I think, before assuming the origin of the language as due to admixture of tribes, it might be well to consider whether the mannerism of speech of different social groups may not be a sufficient explanation. Take, for instance, our students' slang, which is only used in conversation in college, but which the students readily drop when talking to other people.

—Letter from Franz Boas to Edward Sapir concerning gendered language in Yana, August 28, 1907

Historically, the field of gender and language has been discursively framed in terms of oppositions: women's and men's speech (Haas 1944), exclusive and preferential gender (Bodine 1975), community and contest (Johnstone 1993). Recent feminist theory has questioned the biocultural presuppositions that underlie gender oppositions, locating the deconstruction of gender firmly in social interaction, where simple oppositions are difficult to maintain. Nevertheless, as Janet Bing and Victoria Bergvall (1996) have noted, language and gender researchers have sometimes been content to refine their contestation of dichotomous thinking in social terms rather than rid the field of such constructs entirely. Typically, academics no longer speak in terms of the first pseudodichotomy listed above, women's and men's language, but they sometimes focus on differential strategies that women and men practice as members of supposedly separate communities. Inevitably, *any* dichotomous framing either obscures or assimilates the diverse identities of those who cannot be recognized within that frame. Marcyliena Morgan (chapter 1, this volume) points out, for instance, that the way sociolinguists have cast the dichotomy for speakers of African American English has left out vital populations. In sociolinguists' effort to see the difference between European American and African American speakers, the class and gender diversity of both populations is ignored.

One might say that the ability to name difference at all is a first step in the recognition of diversity and therefore of the other as separate from self. However, Judith

Butler (1997) does not support such one-sided naming in her analysis of hate speech, arguing that it is through a dialogic process of addressing (or even name-calling) that subjectivity and agency are achieved. Moreover, Butler argues that adroit response to insistent categorization can subvert the meanings of an oft-repeated appellation. The appropriate comeback is not always at hand or easy to assert within sociohistorical confines of racism, sexism, or homophobia, but many of the chapters in this volume offer strategies to confront an unacceptable appellation. Caitlin Hines, for example, exposes the historical and ideological roots of the "woman as dessert" metaphor to weaken its deceptive force. And Morgan, Marjorie Goodwin, and Norma Mendoza-Denton engage in dialogue with the limiting categories of prior scholarship by contextually foregrounding the actual voices and emergent identities of African American women and Latina girls, respectively.

In this chapter, I explore the nature of gendered language in Lakhota in response to previous researchers' claims that some Native American languages such as Lakhota code gender rigidly through grammar or phonology (Bodine 1975; Haas 1944; Sapir 1949). I employ two strategic responses to earlier work. To understand the linguistic resources that Lakhota speakers draw on to establish gendered identities, I accentuate the various positions expressed in local contexts and emphasize how cultural scripts become associated with gendered behavior in specific interactions. The ways in which Lakhota speakers assert their gender through speech acts cannot stand without an ideological corollary, however. The Lakhota also speak about and frame their own gendered language use. Like the analyses of linguists, this metapragmatic talk is usually characterized by binaries. Rather than deny the existence of gender abstractions by further pointing to contextual and interactional fact, my second strategy is to expose the roots of native gender constructs in contextualized language by probing how their insistent force is silently invoked even as speakers confront them.

The context of gender and language in Native America

The association of phonological and morphological gendered differences with Native American languages is largely the result of two brief articles published by Mary Haas (1944) and her mentor, Edward Sapir (1949).[1] In six pages, Sapir outlined morphological and pronunciation differences in man-to-man speech in Yana society. Haas's seven-page article, "Men's and Women's Speech in Koasati," detailed the phonological variation present in Oklahoma Koasati, wherein speakers systematically pronounced verbs differently depending on their sexual categorization as female or male. Haas's major focus was interesting phonological derivations, which she illustrated through verbal paradigms. She also cited several unrelated languages—Thai, Chukchee, Biloxi (Siouan), Tunica, and Yana—to show that the supposedly rare phenomenon of distinctive women's and men's speech was not really so unusual. Two years later Regina Flannery (1946) published a three-page account of a similar pronunciation distinction in Atsina (Gros Ventre), an Arapaho dialect spoken in Montana. Like those before her she focused on linguistic rather than social contexts. Brief examples of the gender paradigms emphasized in these languages are given in (1).

(1) "Exclusively" gendered forms in Native American languages[2]

    a. Koasati (Kimball 1987)

        female   *male*

        alóhlq   alólo:ʃ   'He can drive.'

        Ákpq   ákpo:ʃ   'I do not eat.'

        Ocintq   ocínto:ʃ   'You can come.'

    b. Atsina/Gros Ventre (Flannery 1946)

        female   *male*

        [k] or [ky] [c]

        ikénibik   icénibic   'his gum'

    c. Yana (Sapir 1929)

        female   *male*

        ya   yana   'person'

        nisat^h nisat^{h}i   'it is said he goes'

        p^{h}at^h p^{h}adi   'place'

The Native American gender articles must be understood within the social and academic context in which they were produced. Coercive government policies mandating linguistic and social assimilation of Native Americans had already had a debilitating effect on Native American linguistic communities (see Dobkins, chapter 9, this volume). Anticipating the imminent death of Native American languages, linguistic anthropologists' stated purpose was to gather as much cross-linguistic information as possible before it was too late. Detailed social analysis of language use was difficult when the researcher was still struggling with basic grammar and lexicon. Consequently, the brief gender articles should be taken as contributions to a linguistic data pool rather than sociolinguistic analyses of gender. Of course, at the time of Boas and Sapir's correspondence in the early part of the twentieth century, anthropological linguists were already aware of sentence-final particles that gendered the identity of the speaker or addressee in the Siouan languages (such as Lakhota) and in many of the languages mentioned by Haas. Nonetheless, Haas's work was an important early development in the field of gender and language. She published her analysis of Koasati and a typology of speaker-addressee gender indicators in the journal *Language*, making the data available to linguists working outside of the (Native) Americanist tradition and to subsequent language and gender researchers.[3]

Haas's groundbreaking work is still influential, but perhaps not in the way she would have intended as a descriptive linguist who worked closely with Native Americans. Koasati (Muskogean), Yana (Hokan), and Atsina (Algonquian) are still cited in the literature and introductory linguistic textbooks as possessing exclusively gendered speech in which there is an isomorphic relationship between a form and the sex of the speaker or addressee (Bodine 1975; Bonvillain 1993; Finegan 1999; O'Grady, Dobrovolsky, & Aronoff 1997). These "gender-exclusive" languages are typically juxtaposed to those that are "gender-preferential" (or variable). And writers often exoticize them by contrasting the socially "dramatic" gender distinctions in Koasati with the distinctions in English (Finegan 1999:407). The languages "in which men and women *always* use linguistic alternatives appropriate to their own gender"

are invariably those cited in Haas's (1944) article (Bonvillain 1993:215; my emphasis). The brief treatment of language and gender in the textbook *Contemporary Linguistics* most clearly exemplifies this appropriation, and so I will quote it at length:

> Gender-exclusive differentiation refers to the *radically* different speech varieties used
> by men and women in particular societies. In these societies, a woman or man may, except
> in *special* circumstances, *not be allowed to speak the variety of the other gender.* . . . A
> society in which this is the norm is typically one in which the roles assigned the genders
> are *rigid*, and in which there is *little social change.*
>
> Gender-variable differentiation is *much more common* in the languages of the world
> than is gender exclusivity. This phenomenon is reflected in the *relative* frequency with
> which men and women use the same lexical items or other linguistic features. (O'Grady
> et al. 1997:518–519; my emphases)[4]

Combined with the authors' placement of Koasati examples under the "exclusive"
heading and English examples under the "variable" heading, it is not difficult to read
this social reworking of Haas's text as a manifestation of linguistic exoticism along
the following lines: People who have gendered linguistic forms are radically different from European Americans; they are people who actively restrict the speech of
others in their rigid societies, whereas *we* have the choice to prefer certain linguistic
variables over others in our free, modern society.[5]

Although a few Native American languages are reported over and over as possessing gender-exclusive systems, there is considerable doubt that this has ever been
the case, and it is more than likely that gender-exclusive systems do not exist in these
languages. Even Haas observed that the Koasati take on the voices of other genders
when quoting and in folktales. She also maintained that younger women were switching to the "male" forms. Regina Flannery (1946) reported that when men use women's
speech in Atsina they are regarded as effeminate, which clearly implies that some
men must have been using "women's" forms. Perhaps these are the "special circumstances" William O'Grady and his colleagues refer to above, where deviant gender
behavior is allowed or restricted by a society.

Yet masking all difference between people under the gender binary is problematic for the reasons mentioned above and in light of recent language and gender research and queer linguistic theory (Bergvall, Bing, & Freed 1996; Hall & Bucholtz
1995; Livia & Hall 1997). For instance, Rusty Barrett's discussion (chapter 16, this
volume) of African American drag queens illustrates that taking on the pronunciation styles of another in the context of a performance does not always signify only
one meaning, and it may in fact signify that gender is not binary. Native American
men's use of "women's language" may be similarly polysemous. Without sociocultural detail it is impossible to know in what contexts, or even if, effeminacy is a cultural taboo for male speakers in different Native American cultures. Many Native
American peoples such as the Lakhota and the Dineh (Navajo) traditionally recognize more than two genders.[6] Finally, even if crossing an imaginary gender line is a
cultural taboo, such linguistic crossing may have a healthy linguistic existence. Kira
Hall and Veronica O'Donovan (1996) have shown in their analysis of the referential
language of *hijras* (male eunuchs) in India that referring to the self or other *hijras*

with both female and male gendered forms is systemic and contextually meaningful. Given these perspectives, one might be tempted to regard the idea of gender-exclusive linguistic features as dubious.

In fact, several researchers have been puzzled on finding that the speakers they worked with had no clear notion of "women's" or "men's" ways of speaking. The Koasati people whom Geoffrey Kimball (1987) consulted did not use "male" forms of speech at all, even though Haas stated that women (and men) of the younger generation were adopting the "male" pronunciation. Kimball (1987, 1990) also discovered examples of women in the early part of this century using the "male" indicative/imperative -ʃ marker (which Haas described as a phonological rather than morphological phenomenon). One of these women was a famous doctor, and the other was the daughter and wife of a chief. In a move reminiscent of William O'Barr and Beryl Atkins's (1980) reanalysis of Robin Lakoff's (1975) women's language as powerless language, Kimball reinterpreted the use of the Koasati -ʃ as an indication of status or respect rather than gender. In the most recent account of gender in Atsina, Allan Taylor (1982) discovered that some men, if they display different styles at all, use "female" pronunciation features when speaking to children or outsiders, employing what they perceive to be an "easier" style of pronunciation in order to communicate. Taylor speculates that because Atsina children are traditionally cared for by women, they first learn the "female" pronunciation through caretaker language. Subsequently, some male children adopt "male" pronunciation, given enough exposure and overt socialization. Finally, there is doubt about the function of male-to-male speech in Yana, for Herbert Luthin (1991) found that men sometimes used "male" speech when speaking to women in formal contexts. Luthin concluded that Sapir's gender differences were in fact register differences.

Although there has been some debate over Kimball's reanalysis of the -ʃ in Koasati as a status marker (see Saville-Troike 1988), the doubts expressed concerning the validity or completeness of previous work have not reached the ears of the linguistic community as a whole. Just as anthropological linguists were aware of gendered language associations at the beginning of the twentieth century, Americanists now are aware that these associations lack definition, but that in most cases nothing can be done. A thorough sociolinguistic (re)analysis requires speakers who can interact in different social situations or records that provide different genres of texts to ascertain if linguistic differences correlate more nearly with register, gender, or both.

A reexamination of the kind of gender-categorizing systems that occur in Koasati (fewer than 200 speakers), Atsina (fewer than 10 speakers), or Yana (no speakers) would be impossible for several reasons, all of which concern the loss of available speakers and consequently the sociolinguistic contexts of their daily interaction. To begin with, in languages that are becoming obsolescent, the use of phonological, lexical, and grammatical indicators of distinct social categories is often lost through acculturation because the society no longer retains social autonomy. It is also difficult to ascertain the extent to which dialect variation plays a role as researchers question the validity of gendered speech accounts of the past. Claims for the existence of gendered forms vary a great deal from dialect to dialect, which may cause misinterpretation in languages for which there is little dialect information from an earlier period. Kimball (1990) and Muriel Saville-Troike (1988), for instance, disagree about gendered speech in Koasati partially because they worked with speakers in different locations. Furthermore, speakers who acquire dying languages often do so under restricted circumstances. For example, men may learn gendered forms from female speakers, such as grandmothers, who use primarily the female forms. With so few speakers it is difficult to ascertain if gender usage is related to conversational context, register, or status of participants when because of sheer lack of numbers, there are increasingly few contexts in which native speakers of the language converse. Finally, examination of the historical records reveals little, for much of the elicited speech was in the form of traditional literature or historical narrative in which speech was often idealized according to stereotypical norms. Complete reliance on records is therefore inadvisable.

The Lakhota context

Of all the Native American languages that have traditionally been cited as having "exclusive" gender, Lakhota is one of the few that still has a significant number of speakers. It is difficult to judge the actual number, but Dale Kinkade (1991) estimates that there are approximately 15,000 speakers of the five Siouan dialects remaining in Canada and the United States. Lakhota is one of these dialects. According to native speakers and linguists, Lakhota possesses morphological indicators of the sex of the speaker, which typically affix to the last verb in a sentence (Boas & Deloria 1941; Rood & Taylor 1997). Not only is gender still viable in Lakhota, but the historical records are numerous and particularly good because native speaker and linguist Ella Deloria had the foresight to write down conversations in which she took part, giving minute descriptions of participant relationships and overall context. In this study, I have drawn on both Deloria's sources and my own recordings of contemporary conversations in order to account for the relationship between stereotypical representations of gendered speech and its actual function.

The Deloria texts

The Deloria texts are a rich collection of different genres, including impromptu conversations, autobiographical accounts, historical narratives, folktales, aphorisms, puns, political speeches, and songs. Deloria could not tape-record speakers. In some cases, she transcribed the Lakhota simultaneously if the speaker was able to hold her or his train of thought while she typed (Deloria 1937?). But because of fieldwork constraints, she usually had to recall the "voice," the personal style and individuality of the narrator, after she returned home. Although she was meticulous about capturing dialect and individual variation, she did not indicate the "slips"—false starts or silent pauses that exist in informal speech. She did try to capture each individual's pitch, intonation, and voice quality, such as whispering, however (1937b:349). Whether as a native speaker Deloria regarded the use of morphology appropriate to the other sex as a "slip" we shall never know. In any case, her ethnographically detailed descriptions provide an invaluable source of contextual sociolinguistic information. Deloria's native perspective combined with her excellent skills as a linguist give life to her texts in ways that outsiders with primarily scientific linguistic goals could not.

Fieldwork context

To supplement the textual data and to understand more about the social-interactional use of gender particles in Lakhota, I conducted fieldwork at Pine Ridge Indian Reservation in 1993. I initially chose this site for the purpose of comparison; Deloria had collected most of her texts in and around Pine Ridge. The current and historical sociopolitical exigencies at Pine Ridge, however, affected my fieldwork and data dramatically (as illustrated later in example 5). Shannon County, South Dakota, the location of Pine Ridge Indian Reservation, is the poorest county in the United States: The per capita income ($3,417) is the lowest in the nation, and unemployment is approximately 80 percent (Carlson 1997:8). Inhabitants liken their home to a "Third-World country in the middle of the United States" and to "the inner city." It is therefore ironic that Pine Ridge has a history of being overrun every summer by people eager to delve into the Lakhota way of life, such as anthropologists. Likewise, Europeans and Americans wanting to live like "real" Indians as they quest for spiritual enlightenment have recently joined the seekers of the authentic Native American "experience" (Powers 1994). Although imitation may be seen as a form of flattery where all other things are equal, many Pine Ridge residents regard the summer influx as an attempt to steal their culture, religion, and language. I will not detail my problematic position as a European American linguist in the continuing colonialization of Lakhota culture as outlined here; needless to say, it is precarious (see Trechter 1998).

Finding consultants, taping, and translating conversations were accomplished with the help of Eli James, an Oglala/Sichangu Sioux, and his network of family relations and friends. All the consultants were between the ages of 40 and 80, largely because older people were more certain of their abilities to conduct conversations in Lakhota. The conversations ranged from short snatches of speech (unrecorded but transcribed) to 20-minute interchanges to 2-hour "chewing-the-fat" conversations around the kitchen table. All the participants were aware that they were being recorded and knew that I was generally interested in gender and language.

Gender in Lakhota

Lakhota speakers who were unaware of my interest in gender have often told me that women and men end their sentences in Lakhota differently. My Pine Ridge "permission to record" agreement contained a statement alluding to my interest in gendered speech styles. On reading this agreement, potential consultants directly addressed what they perceived to be my research question. Their explanation took the form of metapragmatic judgments or maxims about appropriate speech, which were the same as those offered in previous conversations: "Men say *yo* and women say *ye*" or "Men say *lo* and women say *le*." Such maxims are significant to linguistically gendered identity. Through overt ideology, they allude to possibilities of gendering talk while simultaneously restricting participation through the citation of opposite and complementary speech behaviors. The specific forms cited in these maxims are particularly interesting for two reasons: first, the forms associate gender directly with speech acts, and second, even in stereotypic representations of actual speech such as folktales, the maxims do not hold true.

Although certain interjections are gendered, Lakhota speakers associate gender most often with illocutionary or affective force. These sentence-final indicators of speech acts enable the speaker to take a stance or highlight her or his presence in relation to some proposition.

(2a)   osní?
        'It's cold.'

(2b)   osní ye_a
        'It's cold <u>assertion</u>.'

For instance, in explaining to me the differences of meaning between (2a) and (2b), James emphasized that there is no propositional difference. He went on to clarify through the following example: "In the morning, my stepfather might say '*osní?*'— it's cold. It's often cold here in the winter. Maybe he heard the weatherman. Maybe he's been outside. But when he comes in the room (demonstrating, touching finger to mouth and holding it up), he says, 'Ah, *osní ye*.'"

In James's hypothetical example, the speaker indicates through the use of *ye* that he is the immediate source of the proposition "It is cold"; the use of an illocutionary force marker therefore subtly focuses the speaker in relation to his speech act. Hence, the fact that some speech acts are more or less evocative of gendered selves is in no way remarkable if we see that indicating the presence of the speaker's identity leads to her or his contextual embodiment. Characterization of the speaker's identity through forms which emphasize her or his bodily presence, affect, stance, or authority occurs in many languages of the world, such as Japanese (Ochs 1992) and the Muskogean languages (Karen Booker, personal communication). Butler (1997:152) likewise argues that speech acts imply the body because in performance the body is "the rhetorical instrument of expression." In Lakhota overt speech-act markers instantiate the "presence of the body" in relation to an expressed proposition. They therefore implicate gendered readings.

Keith Walters (chapter 10, this volume) questions whether it is in such contextual embodiment that a person's multiple identities necessarily converge, but speakers' reliance on gender as the defining category that underlies Lakhota speech acts assumes such convergence. Linguists' and native speakers' emphasis on performative differences in the way women and men create and characterize a single gendered identity erases much of the subtlety of the act as described by Walters and leads to the binary oppositions summarized in table 5.1.[7] However, in a cross-genre examination of the different speech acts, in which I focused on the performative act rather than privileging the sex as the category of analysis, a very different picture emerged

Table 5.1. Lakhota clitics, by gender and speech act

Illocutionary/Affective force	*Women*	*Men*
Formal question	hųwe (obsolete)	hųwo
Imperative	ye$_a$	yo
Opinion/emphasis	le (archaic), ye$_a$	lo
Emphatic statement	kʃto	
Entreaty	na	ye$_e$
Surprise/opinion	mą	wą

(Trechter, forthcoming). A summary of these results is given in table 5.2. The gendered forms are no longer complementary and exclusionary in the same ways. Only three forms are used "exclusively" by men (*lo, yo, hųwo*) in the Deloria texts, and two are used "exclusively" by women (*na, mą*). In fact, Ella Deloria (1937a:118) astutely noted that "*Ye* is feminine, only in a negative sense. A man adds *lo*, to *ye*; a woman does not say *lo*, but stops with *ye*. Both say *ye*." Although this refocusing shows us that there are no complementary binary oppositions in Lakhota, it nevertheless supports native speakers' metapragmatic judgments that certain forms are exclusively gendered. In the remainder of this chapter, I demonstrate how claims of exclusive gender may be accurate in terms of prototypical categories of usage but that in actual speech events speakers manipulate context and their roles within it by choosing which gendered clitics to use and whether to use them at all.

We can further our understanding of the gender deixis system in Lakhota by adapting the notions of *frame* and *framework* from William Hanks's work on spatial deixis into the social realm. For Hanks, a frame "denote[s] a set of lexical items whose members correspond to different parts of a . . . conceptual whole" (1993:128). Any model of the gender system in Lakhota represents the prototypical associations of meaning and use for some hypothetical context. In this sense, it is a schematic frame. For example, to understand the speech act behind *ye$_a$* and *yo*, one must at least understand that they work within a cultural frame of gender and as imperatives in distinc-

Table 5.2. Lakhota clitics, revised

Illocutionary force	*Women*	*Men*	*Both*	*More used by women*	*More used by men*
Formal question		hųwo			
Imperative		yo			
Opinion/Emphasis		lo	ye$_a$		
Entreaty	na		ye$_e$		
Emphatic statement			kʃto		
Surprise/Opinion	mą				wą

tion from each other, ye_a typically being used for a woman's imperative and *yo* a man's. A framework, by contrast, is "the immediate social field of space and time perception, orientation, and participant engagement in acts of reference" (1993:127). A frame therefore contains structural aspects of meaning, which are conventional and fairly fixed, but a framework deals with a specific instance of language use. The framework is a local, variable production in space and time and contains the participants' orientation with respect to the social setting and the particular meanings they are constructing. Within specific frameworks, the meaning produced by using gendered performatives constructs a speaker with respect to the speech event.[8]

The gendered particles of Lakhota display variability of usage that depends on a number of factors: age, gender, personality, and authority. I shall first illustrate how underlying meanings of these gendered forms emerge from stereotypical contexts in which the meaning of the stance of the participant is fairly standard. Although these contexts represent stereotypic meanings, they are nevertheless frameworks because they orient a speaker to a speech event. Second, I will demonstrate how the prototypical associations of the meaning of a gendered particle vary from the norm in nonstereotypical frameworks while still retaining the underlying meanings.

Stereotypic meanings in context

Stereotypic speech is well represented in folktales, in which the speaker attributes gendered speech to a character in the narrative to illustrate her or his role in the plot. Because the gendered morphology is indicative of affect as well as illocutionary force, these markers function to represent the "voices" and therefore the characters in a story. In effect, they function to establish the heteroglossia of any discourse (Bakhtin 1981). For instance, *le*, which is conventionally associated with the speech of a woman, also carries a sort of maternal or nurturant quality in its prototypical usage when a woman is speaking to children or someone she cares for, as in examples (3) and (4). In example (3), the woman is portrayed as overly concerned for her husband's welfare. To represent her as sweet-talking him, the narrator uses *le* (with falling intonation) to express her position of exaggerated womanly concern. Example (4) emphasizes a grandmother's concern and relief on finding her twin grandsons safe after a *tʰipi* (dwelling) fire. Here the use of *le* and the diminutive form *-la* on the verb indicate the characters' connection and the speaker's regard for the naughty twins.

(3)   wanítukʰa ye*le*.
       'How tired you must be f.' (Deloria 1937b)

(4)   Hinú, uʃka micʰikʃi tohįni oʃótamakitʔapila tkʰa ye*lé*?
       'Well, did my poor little sons almost choke to death from the smoke f?' (Deloria 1932)

In contrast, *lo*, conventionally associated with a man's statement or opinion, implies a certain degree of masculine authority, especially when used by an elder male delivering a final opinion. The speech in (5) contains a large number of such statements.

The 80-year-old speaker, Luke, in this example had returned to his home to find me outside recording a story that his son (Pete) was telling. After asking his daughter (Mary) and James if I was Lakhota, and establishing that I was in fact *waʃicu* 'white' and a linguist, he began to talk very pointedly to me. This excerpt is directed toward me as the addressee, but Luke is responding as well to another conversation with outsiders that he has just arrived from. After setting up this context, he begins by imitating a white speaker's obnoxious question in English in a high-pitched voice.

(5) *Modern authoritative male speech.*

    1 Luke: . . . "We lo:ve your culture; why don't you practice it?" Hiyá, ųkiye
                 ųkitʰawapi cʰa
    2   íyųtokʰapiʃni ye ló. Ho hé, Ho hé, yąké kį he é ye ló.
    3 Mary: Ohątú ųlakʰótapi cʰá [į:
    4 Luke: Takú] á:taya yeye hayápi waʃte maʔų we ló.
    5   Há ki le ną we ki lena lakʰóta (speaker pinches the skin of his forearm
                 and holds it up).
                 (James and Mary begin to carry on another conversation
                 simultaneously.)
    6   Ną niʃ a:taya lakʰota. háyapi ną lená kʰo lakʰóta ną. owį tʰąkįkiyą nu
                 eyaʃ ( )
    7   ną háyapi cʰa oníyakįkte. Hecʰana waníʃicukte ló.
    8   Ho hé nakų osų uyakiye eyaʃ waníʃicukte ló.
    9   ųkiʃiyéye tagni ųku ʃni, eyaʃ lakʰota owe ki lé į: há ki lé ikʰówayake.
    10   Ho hená yąke ki, hena é yeló.
    11   Ho cʰaʃ lé táku ilúkca.

    1 Luke: . . . "We lo:ve your culture; why don't you practice it?" No, we have
                 ours, so
    2   we don't care m. That's how things are m.
    3 Mary: As it is we are Lakhota, [(verbal pause)
    4 Luke: Whatever] good clothes I have are on me m.
    5   This skin and this blood are Lakhota.
    6   and you everything you have is Lakhota, clothes and also these big big
                 earrings you wear.[9] But . . .
    7   and your clothes will tell on you. You will still be white m.
    8   You can also grow your hair, but you will still be white m.
    9   You and I here, we can wear nothing, but being Lakhota, this blood
                 (verbal pause) this skin is attached.
    10   Those of you sitting here, this is the way it is m.
    11   No matter what you think.

This monologue is fascinating, as well as uncomfortable, for me on a number of levels, but I will focus primarily on Luke's use of authoritative speech. Addressing me as a wannabe, he emphatically states in line 2 that those who are real Indians do not have to care about outward manifestations of culture. His use of *lo* twice in the same line serves to establish his certainty of this truth. He authoritatively asserts his poverty in line 4 in contradistinction to whites' wealth; real Lakhotas are above caring about material goods. In lines (4) through (8) Luke discusses outward signs of culture in detail: clothes, earrings, and hair. Comparing them to the authentic way of being Lakhota, through skin and blood, he reflects on his body as an authoritative embodiment. In this short speech, Luke establishes authority by signifying "I am real and you are not" and through the male performatives. The particular performative that he chooses (*lo*) consequently creates and restates his identity as an authoritative Lakhota man.

Lakhota speakers demonstrate that they are aware of these stereotypic meanings because they flout them or sometimes choose to undermine them in other ways. Because the use of *lo* suggests an authoritative stance, when men are not acting particularly authoritative but feel somewhat constrained to express their masculinity, they may modify their pronunciation of *lo* a bit. Ella Deloria (ca. 1937:306) notes one such instance in her interview of the man in example (6).

(6)   Oglálata tʰoká wahí kʔu̯há̯ wóixa wa̯zígzi awákʰipʰa kʔéyaʃ iyúhaxci̯ wóixaʃni.
      ʔ Wóyuʃʔiyaye nakú slolwáye <u>lo</u>. Yu̯kʰá̯ wa̯zí léчʰetu̯.

      'When I first came among the Oglala, laughable experiences were mine but not
      everything was funny. I also knew fear <u>m</u>. And one such time was as follows'.

Unlike the male authoritative speaker of (5), the man in example (6) is relating stories about himself in which he was truly frightened but kept his calm or in which he appeared weak or silly to himself and others but ultimately proved his strength of character. Even in the introduction to these stories, his "swallowed" use of *lo* reflects a narrative construction of a different authoritative self, as Deloria describes: "When the ending *lo* is used simply as a closing to statements by a man who isn't trying to be authoritative, he sometimes 'swallows' it instead of accenting it for emphasis. This informant does so constantly, except where he is quoting" (ca. 1937:306).

Of course, other contextual and interactive considerations affect the extent to which a speaker highlights the self in relation to an assertion. In examples (7) and (8), a man in his 50s (George) is speaking to his nephew (Eli James) at the kitchen table. Eli has asked him about the religious affiliation of their ancestors, ostensibly to ascertain to what extent they practiced Sioux religion. Also present are Anna (George's wife), who is preparing some meat for the Sundance, and me, sewing. George accounts for past religious practices and ultimately expresses his personal opinion regarding the stance the family should take with respect to Sioux religion and Christianity. Because he is expressing his own opinion, this might be viewed as a classic opportunity to use the male opinion marker *lo*, but he does not. It would be unusual for this quiet and unassuming man, who does not speak at great length, to use an authoritative male opinion clitic like *lo*. In fact he goes so far as to conclude most of his opinionated statements with verbs or morphology that serve as hedges. In (7), he uses *awábleze* 'I understand', *nacʰece* 'probably', and *ʃece* 'maybe' to modify the force of his statements, and in (8) he sums up with *kecʰami* 'I think' and *hecʰu̯pisʔe* 'like' or 'something like that'.

The context here is multifaceted. Unlike Luke in (5), George has no immediate need to reiterate or establish Lakhota male authority with respect to his addressee. He offers his opinion, but it is hedged as he creates and reiterates his diffidence. Hesitation is also entirely appropriate to the topic of religious choice in Lakhota society. Lakhota people place value on individual understanding of religious experience, and consequently authoritative opinions about which religion to choose have little place (Demallie & Parks 1987). Finally, after George engages in a brief verbal confrontation with Anna over the topic, they jokingly decide that they should not be fighting in front of the tape recorder. Whether the presence of the tape recorder and of Anna, who might possibly disagree with any authoritative assertions about religion, affected George's verbal presentation of self I cannot say, but he was aware of both.

(7) a. hecʰ ųpi sʔe ( ) eya <u>awábleze</u>.
   'In like manner they did ( ) <u>I understand</u>.'
  b. ki hé é <u>nacʰece</u>
   '<u>Probably</u> this is theirs.'
  c. kaʔúʃiʔcʔiya ųpi yapi <u>ʃece</u>
   'They humbled themselves to go there <u>maybe</u>.'

(8) Ho, héchiya tąhą ị: tokʰiʃ miʃʔeyą lé imáyalųye ki. Hel ị: lakʰota wocʰekiye ųnaʒįkta <u>kecʰąmi</u>? eyaʃ <u>hecʰųpisʔe</u> ị: . . .

   'There (refers to preceding monologue) from just a careless question. In <u>my understanding</u>, you and I should stand with Lakhota prayer/ritual or do <u>something like they did</u> (verbal pause)'.

People also flout the implied meanings of the gender clitics, especially in a joking context or relationship. Joking is the typical style of communication between Lakhota people who share an in-law type relationship. Thus by using *le* in example (9), the woman, who is in a joking, in-law relationship with Vine Deloria Sr., exploits maternal concern to show irony as she supposedly doubts his speaking ability. In addition, he is older than she, and for these reasons an interpretation of the clitic as expressing real maternal concern and nurturance would be unlikely. A similar effect is achieved in example (10) as the speaker insults herself but makes it a joke by using the emphatic female form *-kʃto*. Interestingly, the emphatic often occurs in either the context of gossip or joking between women. Ella Deloria often describes it as "chummy or confidential." Once again, a form associated with gender has other underlying connotations.

(9) ʃiké, ehąni eʃaʃ wąʒí owáwa ną yuhá yewákʰiyelaʃni. tókʰeʃkʰe yuhélhel nąʒikte <u>lé</u>!
   'Poor thing, why didn't I write a speech to take along! How pitifully he will grope about for something to say <u>f</u>!' (Deloria 1956:19)

(10) cʰa le hokʃí-ųzektepi eyápi ki hémacʰa <u>kiʃto</u>!
   'I am the sort that is called rectum-killed <u>emphatic</u>!' (Deloria ca. 1937:46)

For the forms discussed abo^ve (*lo, le, kʃto*), the stereotypic connotations that operate in identifying the speaker associate authoritative identities with men and confidential, chummy speaking with women. This parallels Elinor Ochs's claim that phonological or morphological indicators of gender are constitutive in that "linguistic features may index social meanings, stances, social acts, social activities, which in turn helps to constitute gender meanings" (1992:341). According to Ochs, the use of the particle *ze* (male) in Japanese coarsely intensifies an utterance, whereas *wa* (female) gently intensifies it. The speakers' associations of a certain affective quality with a specific gender leads them to use these particles differently in the production of local meanings. Although the functioning of such stereotypes is an important clue to the linguistic gendering of identities, I fear that by mentioning them in the context of Lakhota I may contribute to a new brand of Native American linguistic exoticism by implying that forms associated with women carry no authority and that therefore women in Lakhota society are without an authoritative voice unless they appropriate that of men's speech. This is simply not true. According to Bea Medicine (1987), Native American women have long held the ability to speak in the same spheres as men, and according to Marla Powers (1986), it is the very quality of their maternity (that is, their ability to remain unmoved by public opinion, just as when dealing with children) that permits them to succeed in such areas as the law.

Nonstereotypic meanings: Quoting and appropriation

Several researchers have sought to show how the appropriation or rejection of different gendered linguistic stereotypes or tropes are used to create queer languages (Barrett, chapter 16, this volume; Queen 1997). Often citing Butler (1993) as a source, these researchers examine how the repetition of a trope in a new context simultaneously undermines and reinforces its stereotypic meanings. Underlying this approach is the notion that no speech act is absolutely original, but that each speaker "calls on" voices or ways of speaking that she or he has heard before (see Silverstein & Urban 1996). The construction of linguistic stereotypes (consciously or unconsciously) therefore enables a speaker to categorize and manipulate a multiplicity of voices into (in)appropriate cultural scripts. Lakhota speakers, for instance, readily fit their metapragmatic judgments of appropriateness into a fixed frame as regards gender of speaker, but they are easily able to recognize nontypical examples and contexts, strategically recontextualize speech, and adapt the gendered form for the new context based on conventional interpretations. Thus they are free to construct identities while they are constrained by having to deal with the omnipresent cultural scripts.

An obvious example of such recontextualization is quotation. In example (11), Anna is ostensibly quoting a man secondhand; she has never heard him say the words she is quoting. She demonstrates her distance from the original speech event by using the second quotative *keye* at the end of the sentence. She also represents the speaker, a holy man, as using *lo* when he finishes a description of the proper procedure for ritually killing a dog. In this particular instance, we cannot be sure as listeners if Anna is using *lo* merely to show that a man is speaking, because indicating a speaker's gender is one way that various voices in a story are kept straight. In other words, she may just be invoking the binary frame "Men say *lo*. . . ." Yet the representation of the holy man's use of *lo* comes at a strategic point in Anna's story. She appeals indirectly to his authoritative stance because his position as an authority for cultural practices helps her make her point in the overarching narrative. She has been arguing that the youth of today do not follow the proper rituals for the Sundance. None of the addressees present assumed that Anna was using *lo* in her primary voice and therefore indicating her identity as a male or directly implying her authority. Typically, the gendered position of the original speaker does not attach to the current speaker. So although Anna is appealing to the holy man's male authoritative position as support and thereby lending herself some authority, the gendering of a quotation does not result in gendering of her identity.

(11)   oyate nilakʰotapikta hécina taku eyápikte ki hená ecʰąl ecʰanąpi ye*lo* eyá keye
       ' "If you want to be Lakhota people, these things they say, you will do *m*.," he said,
       it is said.'

Not all citations of other voices are as clear as Anna's quotation. In example (12), Arthur arrived home to find his 3-year-old nephew playing on the front stoop. He indicates his pleasure and surprise through the falling intonation on *le*. (Imagine an adult saying to a 2-year-old, "Well, look who's here," in a form of English caretaker language, and you will get the flavor of this quotation.) An older man speaking to a child can take on affective qualities such as nurturance by appropriating a woman's voice. Women are perceived as more experienced in dealing with children, and therefore children are thought more likely to relate to women's ways of speaking. In effect, the speaker here is manipulating prototypical meanings of nurturance and affection by quoting a typical nurturing script.

(12)   Wąlewą hiyu we*le*.
       'Oh *m*., look who's come *f*.'

Yet the meaning of *le* in (12) is ambiguous. Is it a sort of deictic projection—a shift from the speaker's place, time, social status, or gender to that of an implied other, or is the speaker constructing himself as a nurturer? Neither of these possibilities necessarily excludes the other. However, the latter option carries more weight considering Arthur's constant attention to his nephew.

Finally, appropriations have stereotypic meanings associated with them even though they are supposedly atypical in use. A common interpretation of a man using the forms framed as female is that he is gay, of a woman using the "male" forms that she is a lesbian. As I stated earlier, potential consultants often volunteered their account of gendered speech when reading my permission forms. Pete, the brother of Mary from example (5), had just cited such an opposition when Mary, who is a judge, immediately pointed out her own exceptional status in this paradigm by asserting, "Yeah, well, I say *yo* and *yelo*, but I'm not gay." Arthur also described another woman who routinely used the "male" gendered morphology as a "dyke" or a "woman with balls." When Arthur asked his sister to consider this woman's identity, she asserted that the woman was a "tomboy," because of her boyish occupations as a child and her current job as a police officer. Arthur's sister considered that the police officer could not be a lesbian because she had had children.

Regrettably, I have no instances of these women cross-using gendered morphology, but the way that cross-use is spoken about is revealing. Although these two women who hold positions of public authority may use male-gendered morphology to express authoritative stances, Mary at least indicates that she cannot express this authority without taking on the ideological frame of gendered use in Lakhota. The dichotomous frame implies that anyone who uses *lo* must be a man and therefore have the expected sexual proclivities of a man—desire for women. These associations of a speaker's language as an indicator of her or his sexual preference are a clear representation of how the meanings of a frame are present in local productions even as speakers seek to undermine them. However, such ideologies did not apparently bother Mary. She is defiant as she identifies herself as performing outside the frame. She is able to confront the insistent ideology overtly and, in her account, in practice.

Conclusion

I have tried to present data here that are both typical and atypical according to the ideological frame of gendering language in Lakhota. A Lakhota speaker would likely say that the data are so contextual at times as to be a partial misrepresentation, for local productions by necessity often deviate from stereotypical cultural scripts as speakers try to express their selves. In fact, a student of Lakhota told me at a conference that she had shown the title of one of my papers, which emphasized the exceptions, "Men Say *Yele* and Women Say *Yelo*" (Trechter 1994), to a Lakhota teacher. His response was, "Only if his grandmother raised him." In his opinion, most men, if they had had the proper exposure to male speakers and cultural scripts when growing up, would not regularly use the female-gendered forms if they could help it. Interestingly, Arthur made the same sort of observation about the speech of Mary and the police officer, noting that both of them grew up interacting mostly with men, which had probably affected their language. In the context of a threatened language like Lakhota, I fear that the ideological frame for dichotomously gendering language will gain force as the opportunity for acquiring a variety of cultural scripts is limited (for the converse situation see Cotter, chapter 19, this volume). Speakers who have fewer opportunities to hear the social nuances of the language in different contexts will be forced to rely more heavily on overt maxims.

When native speakers make these sorts of judgments about their languages or are engaged in elicitation tasks with linguists, they are presenting frames and sometimes stereotypic frameworks of usage, and thus the gender of the speaker or hearer is viewed as exclusive. I have demonstrated, however, that as speakers use language in a variety of interactive contexts or frameworks, they create subtle nuances that to them are not always the most salient features of their interaction but that nevertheless are important to meaning. I would argue that this is true for any language, so that to restrict a description of gendered speech to an idealization, though interesting, misses the highly important facet of performance, of gender as something both implemented and created through interaction.

NOTES

Portions of this chapter first appeared in Trechter (1995). I am grateful to a number of people who contributed to this work. Mary Bucholtz, Kira Hall, Amy Dahlstrom, and Bob Rankin provided constructive critique of different drafts, and Herb Lewis gave me the Boas quote in the epigraph. The American Philosophical Society supported field research, and California State University, Chico, supported archival work at the American Philosophical Society. I thank Eli James and other Pine Ridge inhabitants, who facilitated the fieldwork in innumerable ways and who never let me forget the continuing oppression of Lakhota people. Except for James's, all of the speakers' names have been changed.

1. See Ann Bodine (1975) for a detailed summary of the early history of gender and language.
2. Transcription key for non-IPA symbols:

ą į ų	nasal vowels	C$^?$	ejective consonant
ʃ	voiceless alveopalatal fricative	( )	pause
ʒ	voiced alveopalatal fricative	ye$_a$	assertion
c	voiceless alveopalatal affricate	ye$_e$	entreaty
C^h	aspirated consonant	[ ]	overlap

3. To highlight the significance of this accomplishment, it is well to note that for over 50 years (until the publication of Macaulay & Brice 1997) there had never been another research article on the topic of gender and language published in *Language*.
4. Examples of the variable features that are provided in the textbook are politeness, use of hyperbolic words such as *cute*, and verbal hedges. These are presumably taken from Robin Lakoff (1975).
5. Keith Walters (1995) observes a similar process of "othering" in introductory sociolinguistics textbooks' treatment of African American English; he notes that this instructional tendency invites European American students to imagine themselves as the possessors of a "correct" and "normal" variety of English.
6. Lakhota culture has a traditional category of hermaphrodites and cross-gendered men, called *wį-kte* 'woman-potential'. There is an effort either to reclaim the term *wįkte* or to promote a more encompassing pan-Indian term—*two spirit*, devised by "gay" Native Americans of North America. Cross-gendered Native Americans consider the anthropological term *berdache* extremely insulting because of its connotations of prostitution and because it was imposed from outside.
7. The form *-ye* becomes *-we* following a high back vowel.
8. Hanks's concept of *frame* originates in the work of Erving Goffman (1974). For a different application of Goffman's work, see Deborah Tannen (chapter 11, this volume).
9. I was dressed in jeans, tennis shoes, a white shirt, and Hopi earrings.

REFERENCES

Bakhtin, Mikhail (1981). *The dialogic imagination.* Ed. Michael Holquist. Trans. Caryl Emerson & Michael Holquist. Austin: University of Texas Press.
Bergvall, Victoria L., Janet M. Bing & Alice F. Freed (eds.) (1996). *Rethinking language and gender research.* London: Longman.
Bing, Janet M., & Victoria L. Bergvall (1996). The question of questions: Beyond binary think-

ing. In Victoria L. Bergvall, Janet M. Bing, & Alice F. Freed (eds.), *Rethinking language and gender research*. London: Longman, 1–30.

Boas, Franz, & Ella Deloria (1941). *Dakota grammar: Memoirs of the National Academy of Sciences* (2nd ser.) 23.

Bodine, Anne (1975). Sex differentiation in language. In Barrie Thorne & Nancy Henley (eds.), *Language and sex: Difference and dominance*. Rowley, MA: Newbury House, 130–151.

Bonvillain, Nancy (1993). *Language, culture and communication*. Englewood Cliffs, NJ: Prentice Hall.

Butler, Judith (1993). *Bodies that matter: On the discursive limits of "sex."* New York: Routledge.

——— (1997). *Excitable speech: The politics of the performative*. New York: Routledge.

Carlson, Peter (1997). The unfashionable. *Washington Post Magazine* (February 23):6–11, 20–24.

Deloria, Ella. (1932). *Dakota texts*. New York: Stechert.

——— (1937a). *Dakota song texts*. Boas Collection, MS 30 (x8a.14). Philadelphia: American Philosophical Society.

——— (1937b). *Dakota tales in colloquial style*. Boas Collection, MS 30 (x8a.6). Philadelphia: American Philosophical Society.

——— (ca. 1937). *Dakota autobiographies*. Boas Collection, MS 30 (x8a.4). Philadelphia: American Philosophical Society.

——— (1937?). *Old Dakota texts*. Boas Collection, MS 30 (x8a.21). Philadelphia: American Philosophical Society.

——— (1956). Short Dakota texts, including conversations. *International Journal of American Linguistics* 20:17–21.

Demallie, Ray, & Douglas Parks (eds.) (1987). *Sioux Indian religion*. Norman: University of Oklahoma Press.

Finegan, Edward (1999). *Language: Its structure and use*. 3rd ed. Fort Worth, TX: Harcourt Brace.

Flannery, Regina (1946). Men's and women's speech in Gros Ventre. *International Journal of American Linguistics* 12:133–135.

Goffman, Erving (1974). *Frame analysis*. New York: Harper & Row.

Haas, Mary (1944). Men's and women's speech in Koasati. *Language* 20:142–149.

Hall, Kira, & Mary Bucholtz (eds.) (1995). *Gender articulated: Language and the socially constructed self*. Routledge: New York.

Hall, Kira, & Veronica O'Donovan (1996). Shifting gender positions among Hindi-speaking hijras. In Victoria L. Bergvall, Janet M. Bing, & Alice F. Freed (eds.), *Rethinking language and gender research*. London: Longman, 228–266.

Hanks, William (1993). Metalanguage and pragmatics of deixis. In John Lucy (ed.), *Reflexive language*. Cambridge: Cambridge University Press, 127–157.

Johnstone, Barbara (1993). Community and contest: Midwestern men and women creating their worlds in conversational story telling. In Deborah Tannen (ed.), *Gender and conversational interaction*. New York: Oxford University Press, 62–80.

Kimball, Geoffrey (1987). Men's and women's speech in Koasati: A reappraisal. *International Journal of American Linguistics* 53:30–38.

——— (1990). A further note on Koasati men's speech. *International Journal of American Linguistics* 56:158–162.

Kinkade, M. Dale (1991). The decline of languages in Canada. In Robert H. Robins & Eugenius Uhlenbeck (eds.), *Endangered languages*. Oxford: Berg, 157–176.

Lakoff, Robin (1975). *Language and woman's place*. New York: Harper & Row.

Livia, Anna, & Kira Hall (eds.) (1997). *Queerly phrased: Language, gender, and sexuality*. New York: Oxford University Press.

Luthin, Herbert (1991). Restoring the voice in Yanan traditional narrative. Ph.D. diss., University of California, Berkeley.

Macaulay, Monica, & Colleen Brice (1997). Don't touch my projectile: Gender bias and stereo-typing in syntactic examples. *Language* 73(4):798–825.

Medicine, Bea (1987). The role of American Indian women in cultural continuity and transition. In Joyce Penfield (ed.), *Women and language in transition*. Albany: SUNY Press, 159–166.

O'Barr, William, & Beryl Atkins (1980). "Women's language" or "powerless language"? In Sally McConnell-Ginet, Ruth Borker, & Nellie Furman (eds.), *Women and language in literature and society*. New York: Praeger, 93–110.

Ochs, Elinor (1992). Indexing gender. In Alessandro Duranti & Charles Goodwin (eds.), *Rethinking context*. Cambridge: Cambridge University Press, 335–358.

O'Grady, William, Michael Dobrovolsky, & Mark Aronoff (eds.) (1997). *Contemporary linguistics*. 3rd ed. New York: St. Martin's Press.

Powers, Marla (1986). *Oglala women: Myth, ritual, and reality*. Chicago: University of Chicago Press.

Powers, William (1994). Playing with culture: The serious side of humor. *American Anthropologist* 96:705–710.

Queen, Robin (1997). I don't speak Spritch. In Anna Livia & Kira Hall (eds.), *Queerly phrased: Language, gender, and sexuality*. New York: Oxford University Press, 233–256.

Rood, David, & Allan Taylor (1997). A Lakhota sketch. In William Sturtevant & Ives Goddard (eds.), *Handbook of North American Indians*. Vol. 17. Washington, DC: Smithsonian Institution.

Sapir, Edward (1949). Male and female forms of speech in Yana. In *Selected writings of Edward Sapir*. Ed. David Mandelbaum. Berkeley: University of California Press, 206–212.

Saville-Troike, Muriel (1988). A note on men's and women's speech in Koasati. *International Journal of American Linguistics* 54:241–242.

Silverstein, Michael, & Greg Urban (eds.) (1996). *Natural histories of discourse*. Chicago: University of Chicago Press.

Taylor, Allan (1982). "Male" and "female" speech in Gros Ventre. *Anthropological Linguistics* 24:301–307.

Trechter (Sistrunk), Sara (1994). Men say *yele* and women say *yelo*. In Jule Gomez de Garcia & David Rood (eds.), *Proceedings of the Fourteenth Siouan-Caddoan Linguistics Conference*. Boulder: University of Colorado, 217–228.

——— (1995). Categorical gender myths in Native America. *Issues in Applied Linguistics* 6:5–22.

——— (1998). Balancing academic and gender roles in the field. Paper presented at the annual meeting of the Linguistic Society of America, New York.

——— (forthcoming). *Gendered voices in Lakhota*. New York: Oxford University Press.

Walters, Keith (1995). Contesting representations of African American language. In Risako Ide, Rebecca Parker, & Yukako Sunaoshi (eds.), *SALSA 3: Proceedings of the Third Annual Symposium about Language and Society—Austin (Texas Linguistic Forum* 36). Austin: University of Texas, Department of Linguistics, 137–151.

Part II

. . . .

IDENTITY
AS IDEOLOGY

. . . .

Changing Femininities

The Talk of Teenage Girls

esearch in the area of language and gender is no longer restricted to the margins of academe, and publications are appearing at an exponential rate (see, for example, recent collections such as Bergvall, Bing, & Freed 1996; Hall & Bucholtz 1995; Johnson & Meinhof 1997; Mills 1995; Tannen 1993). Yet there is little research that focuses on developmental aspects of language use in relation to gender. We know very little about the ways in which children become gendered speakers.[1]

In this chapter I shall ask the question: When do girls start to talk like women? I shall make the assumption that "talking like a woman" is something speakers learn to do, not something we are born with. I shall also assume that we now have a reasonably clear idea of the speaking practices of women (see, in particular, Coates 1996; Holmes 1995) and that girls do not share these practices. Girls' talk has been studied in a variety of cultures and from a variety of perspectives (see Eckert 1993; Eder 1993; Goodwin 1990), but these studies are synchronic. They present us with a snapshot of girls' speaking practices but do not help us to answer the question of how—and when—these practices are modified in the direction of the adult norm.[2]

My aim in this chapter is to analyze girls' talk to explore the ways in which teenage girls negotiate their identity during adolescence as they move from girlhood to womanhood. I shall take the position that discourses are "practices that systematically form the objects of which they speak" (Foucault 1972:49). I will argue that one of the chief things that is being done in the talk of teenage girls is the construction of gendered subjectivity: in the girls' case, the construction of femininity. In contemporary Western society, performing femininity normally entails performing heterosexuality, the "compulsory heterosexuality" discussed by Adrienne Rich (1980).[3] I will show how girls' sense of their femininity is at times contradictory and precarious; they experiment with a range of discourse styles and subject positions.[4] I will also attempt to show how "doing femininity" changes as girls get older, as they move from a more childlike identity to a more womanlike identity.

The data

The data drawn on in this chapter come from transcriptions of the talk of four friends: Harriet, Jenny, Laura, and Vanessa. They are white, middle-class girls who live in North London and have known each other since they were very young. Harriet and Jenny met at play school when they were four; Jenny and Laura knew each other through their families throughout their childhood; Vanessa, Jenny, and Harriet were at primary school together. But they only became a friendship group at age 11, when they were all placed in the same tutor group at a North London coeducational comprehensive school. I recorded them from the time they were 12 until they were 15. They agreed to turn on a tape recorder when they were together, and they were free to delete any portions of their talk that they did not want me to hear. They contacted me each time they had filled a 90-minute audiotape.[5]

The girls tended to record themselves at weekends, when they had time to amuse themselves and were less constrained by homework. They recorded themselves in their own homes, with Harriet's home being the preferred venue.[6] This group of friends was a very stable one, surviving throughout secondary school and acquiring a new member—Leah—when they were 15 (Leah is not involved in any of the conversations discussed in this chapter). However, it should be noted that two members of the group, Harriet and Jenny, were also best friends, although as they explained to me in a subsequent interview, this was left implicit rather than openly declared while the girls were in their early teens.

Postfeminism?

This chapter challenges the notion that we live in a postfeminist era, that women's struggles are over. On the contrary, the talk of these teenage girls shows them moving from a more carefree to a more problematic phase in which they struggle, more or less consciously, with dominant norms of femininity. Their apparent conformity to adult norms of feminine behavior is facilitated in part by their adoption of others' voices. At the age of 12, they play with a wide range of voices; the intertextuality that is characteristic of their talk seems to offer them freedom to explore different identities. As they get older, however, the continuing intertextuality found in their talk seems to constrain rather than liberate them.

Whether the girls are typical of their generation is a question this chapter cannot answer, given the limitations of the database. Certainly, they represent a particular class (the middle class) and a particular race (white) in a particular country (England). It is likely that the talk of girls from working-class backgrounds and from other racial and ethnic groups will differ in a variety of ways.[7] But given that these girls come from a relatively privileged background, it is surely striking that they appear to have difficulty maintaining more agentive identities and to be internalizing patriarchal values that undermine them as developing women.[8] We must explain how and why girls in relatively powerful positions, materially speaking, at times acquiesce to their own discursive powerlessness.

Discoursal range

The girls' talk often occurs against the background of some activity: flipping through old copies of *Just 17* (a teenage magazine); looking at a Body Shop catalogue; eating pizza; lying on the floor doing gymnastics; making friendship bracelets. One interesting finding is that at the beginning (when they were only 12) it took them months to fill a 90-minute audiotape: The tape would contain several separate conversations, recorded on different occasions. By the time they were 14 and 15, they filled a 90-minute tape at one session, and the tape ran out before they finished talking. These later tapes are, in this respect, like those made for me by adult participants in my research on all-female talk (see Coates 1989, 1991, 1994b, 1996).

The girls talk about a huge range of topics in the conversations I have on tape, the inevitable topics of female adolescence in the late twentieth century in Britain: pop stars, *Neighbours* (a TV soap opera), cosmetics, blackheads, school, boys, shopping, clothes, and pets, to mention just a few. On the earlier tapes they also have ridiculous quasi-philosophical debates on subjects such as "Would you rather be a rabbit or a goldfish?" and "Would you prefer a big face with tiny features or a skinny face with big features?" Such debates do not appear in the later tapes: by the time the girls are 14 and 15 their talk has become much more focused on the personal.

I want to start by looking at the range of discourses that appear in the girls' talk. Discourses were initially identified by content alone, then later examined for linguistic characteristics. Examples (1) through (7) come from the early tapes made when the girls were 12 and 13.[9]

(1) Factual/Scientific
J: did you know that the testicles produce thirty billion sperm in each month?

(2) Pseudo-scientific

- -
L: my skin/ instead of having normal oily skin like any ord- ordinary teenager/ <LAUGHTER>
- -

L: er my skin is so dry/ ⌜yesterday I I I-
J: ⌞% I've got % ⌜well look at me .   I've got oil-
H: ⌞maybe you wash it too much/

- -

L: ⌜it's combination/
J: I've got oil here/ ⌞oily here/   combination/ I've got combination skin/
- -

(3) Maternal
H: I know somebody who's just had a baby/ it's about two days old/ really sweet/

(4) Repressive
- -
L: Harriet don't stand over me with your skirt on/ %bloody hell% [. . .] <u>Harriet</u> <SHRIEKS>
- -

H: <u>I can't help it</u> <WHINY VOICE>
J: ((it's only some)) knickers Laura/ don't be so prudish/
- -

(5)   Romantic love
      (a)
- -
V: who do you think's the most good looking out of Bros? [. . .]
- -
J: sometimes I reckon one of the twins/
V: I don't/ I think Craig's the best looking/
- -
      (b)   [sings] "I may not be perfect but I'm all yours"
      (c)   [sings] "Love changes everything"

(6)   Liberal
- -
J: and the sound you can- kind of buzzing sound- it's this vibrator thing of Mum of erm
- -
J: Harriet's Mum/ and if you put it round your chin-
L: you're vibrating Harriet's Mum/ God/
- -
J: if you put it on your chin-   oh god/ . oh come here Vaness/
L: <LAUGHTER>   it's a massager/
- -
J: ⌈on your bone it feels really funny/ well what would happen on
V: no/ <WAILS> [. .] ⌊it makes my teeth crunch/
- -
J: on on your elbow?/ . not much/ <LAUGHS>
- -

(7)   Resistant/Feminist
- -
J: [reading from old copy of Just 17] have you got a boyfriend? what's wrong with you? this
- -
J: looks quite interesting/ [. . .]
H: I haven't got a boyfriend/ nothing's wrong with me I don't think/
- -

This wide range of discourses is still apparent in the later tapes, made when the girls were 14 and 15. The main difference is that a new discourse has been added to their repertoire, a discourse I shall call *consciousness raising* (CR) or *self-disclosure*. This is a discourse characterized by the expression of information of a highly personal nature. It is a subjective discourse, in contrast with others in the girls' repertoire. In other words, although other discourses may touch on topics such as bodies or boyfriends, they do not involve intimate self-disclosure. The new discourse makes the girls vulnerable in a way the others do not. Not surprisingly, then, it is also characterized by reciprocity: sections of conversation where it appears normally involve two or more girls in mirroring self-disclosure.[10] I use the label *consciousness raising* with the deliberate aim of calling attention to the similarity between this mode of talk and its antecedents in the consciousness raising of the Women's Liberation Movement, particularly in the 1950s and 1960s, when women would meet in groups for the express purpose of talking about our personal experience, to become empow-

Table 6.1. Discoursal range of friendship group, by age

Ages 12–13	Ages 14–15
factual/scientific	factual/scientific
pseudoscientific	pseudoscientific
maternal	maternal
repressive	repressive
romantic love	romantic love
liberal	liberal
resistant/feminist	resistant/feminist
.	.
.	.
.	.
	CR/self-disclosure

ered through an understanding that our experience was not unique but was shared by other women under patriarchy (see Sutton, chapter 8, this volume, for public uses of CR discourse). It is noteworthy that the girls have mothers who were themselves teenagers in the 1950s and 1960s, and although I am not saying that mothers have explicitly taught their daughters a particular way of talking, it is certainly the case that these girls, like many others of their generation, are growing up in households in which feminism is as routinely accepted as wholemeal bread.

Table 6.1 represents in tabular form the contrast between the discoursal range of the girls at two different ages. The discourses found in the girls' talk at 14 and 15 years of age is illustrated in examples (8) through (12).

(8) Factual/Scientific
(a)

- -
V: Laura, what's a jock strap?
L: it's a jo- it's what men use- it's their like their equivalent
- -
L: to a bra/ and they hold their dick up with it/
- -
(b) [*talking about periods*]
- -
J: I feel bloated . round "the abdominal regions" or whatever you say/
- -

(9) Repressive/Patriarchal
(a)

- -
L: why's he always teasing Polly?
H: cos ⌈ she's got big tits/
V: ⌊ ((xx)) she's got big tits/
- -

(b)

- -

```
J:              oh Harriet/         ⌈they're not fat/ .
V:                                  ⌊don't be so horrible/              ah!
H:   ((x)) fat thighs/                            they are/
```

- -

J: mine are skinny as a pencil/ . ugh!

- -

(c)

L: I don't want to bitch about this but I I just sort of think she's a bit of a um a little bit of a flirt

(10)   Liberal

V: [*talking about her mother and brother*] oh ((xx)) walking about/ pinning up his trousers/ and he was going "Don't ((xx)) my dick"/ <LAUGHS> and then he said "Don't prick my dick" or something/ and Mum said "Don't you mean your willy?"/ <H LAUGHS> and he went- and he went "My prick"/ and your Mum went- my Mum said "Don't prick your prick"/ <LAUGH> "((xx)) your prick"/ and they were going on and on/ I was going "Mum"/ <LAUGHTER>

H: oh no how embarrassing/

(11)   Resistant/Feminist

J: [*talking about boys harassing them by twanging bra straps*] remember in the first year/ [. . .] and I- and I just turned round and said "I don't wear a bra"/ and they went - <LAUGHS> "So - er er er" like this/ and he got really flustered/

(12)   CR/self-disclosure

(a)   why is it always that in school that your knickers start going up your bum?

(b)

- -

J: well, when I started fancying him in the SEcond year/ I fancied him ever since then/

- -

```
L:   yeah/ I [s]- I knew that/ sort of/
J:                         yeah you sort of guessed/ [. . .]
```

- -

```
J:   and then/ the real sort of clincher was ((still xx))            and I suddenly-
V:                                          <pp LAUGHS>
```

- -

```
J:   because I suddenly sort of fancying- you know people say love's  ⌈blind/ I think I
V:                                                                    ⌊oh but d'you
```

- -

```
J:   thought he was perfect apart from the ⌈((obvious things))/ and I just suddenly have seen
L:                                         │yeah
V:   think-                                ⌊mhm
```

- -

```
J:   how awful he is and horrible/      <PEAL OF LOUD LAUGHTER = release of tension>
L:                            ⌈yeah/
V:                            ⌊yeah/          <MATCHING LAUGH>
H:                             yeah/     <LOW CHUCKLE>
```

- -

The range of discourses occurring in the girls' talk positions them in a variety of different ways, not all consistent with each other. Even in these short extracts, we can see instances in which the discourses come into conflict. For example, in (4) Jenny challenges Laura's repressive discourse, accusing her of being "prudish"; in example (7), Harriet resists the heterosocial pressures of the magazine article; and in example (11), Jenny recounts an incident in which she challenged the boys who were sexually harassing her. These examples are not surprising: after all, there is no single unified way of doing femininity, of being a woman. Different discourses give these girls access to different femininities. More mainstream discourses position them in more conventional ways, whereas more radical or subversive discourses offer them alternative ways of being, alternative ways of doing femininity. They are unwittingly involved in the ceaseless struggle to define gender (Weedon 1987).

Intertextuality

As the examples given demonstrate, such talk between friends is immensely complex: It is far more heterogeneous than, for example, language occurring in the public domain in such contexts as the law courts or Parliament or even the school classroom. And what makes it even more complex and heterogeneous is its intertextuality. These texts are a very clear example of what Mikhail Bakhtin is talking about when he says: "our speech . . . is filled with others' words, varying degrees of otherness and varying degrees of 'our-own-ness,' varying degrees of awareness and detachment. These words of others carry with them their own expression, their own evaluative tone, which we assimilate, rework and reaccentuate" (1986:89). The intertextuality in the girls' talk is often "manifest," that is, other texts are explicitly marked by being introduced by words like *he says* or *she goes* or by being performed in a noticeably different voice.

Voices

Intertextuality has already been illustrated in examples (5), in which the girls sing pop songs; (7), in which Jenny reads from a copy of *Just 17*; and (10), in which we hear the voices of Vanessa's mother and brother. Further examples are given in (13) through (16).

(13)

H:	<LAUGHS> with grandpa it's so funny/ you know when you see sport on television
H:	like you're- you're supporting a team/
L:	[oorghhh] <SHOUTS - PSEUDO MALE VOICE>
others:	<LAUGHTER>
H:	if one team is losing you know/ if his team is losing it's "Oh you silly asses/ excuse
H:	my language/ Oh you silly asses"/

(14)

L: he thinks he's god's gift, man, god's gift to women/ . as Kylie says in
Neighbours/ she goes "god's sake, you think you're god's gift to women"/

(15)

```
- - - - - - - - - - - - - - - - - - - - - - - - - - - - - - - - - - - - - -
V:   Monica's so weird/ .                              Monica's sometimes kind of hyper hyper/
J:                         pardon? <LAUGHTER>
- - - - - - - - - - - - - - - - - - - - - - - - - - - - - - - - - - - - - -
V:                                              no and <LAUGHTER> sometimes kind of
J:   and sometimes kind of lowper lowper/
- - - - - - - - - - - - - - - - - - - - - - - - - - - - - - - - - - - - - -
V:   "We should care for the animals of this world" you know/
- - - - - - - - - - - - - - - - - - - - - - - - - - - - - - - - - - - - - -
```

(16)

```
J:   [sings] Safeway- everything you want from a store but it costs- it's going to cost a lot
     more/
```

In example (13), Harriet "does" her grandfather's voice, adopting a markedly old-fashioned "posh" accent. In (14), Laura adopts the voice of a character in the soap opera *Neighbours*. In (15), Vanessa uses a different voice to represent the weirdness of their school friend Monica. And example (16), like the examples given in (5), is sung rather than spoken; this one is a (corrupted) advertising jingle for a supermarket chain.

We have already seen how discourses can conflict with one another. The girls frequently subvert the voices they use, particularly where they have marked these as "other" by adopting another voice. Jenny subverts the advertising jingle given in (16) by altering the words to give a message that is certainly not what the supermarket wants the public to think. And it is Jenny again whose wordplay in example (15) (*hyper hyper/lowper lowper*) undermines what Vanessa is saying.

Maternal voice

The maternal voice is omnipresent in these texts: the girls refer to and compare their mothers a phenomenal number of times, particularly in the earlier tapes. (As the next section suggests, the maternal voice is to some extent displaced by boys' voices as the girls reach their mid-teens.) Fathers are referred to infrequently. When the girls compare their mothers, they cannot be said to be competing in the normally accepted sense of the word: There is a sense of amused rivalry at times, but it is essentially playful. The girls' references to their mothers seem to do a great deal of work: they allow them the solidarity of confirming that their mothers are of the same type, and they permit the girls to express a kind of proud affection for these odd, non-teenage beings. There is a tension between a perception of their mothers as women, that is, as the kind of human being they themselves will become, and a strong sense of them as occupants of a particular role, the mother, to whom they relate as daughters.

Examples (17) through (19) give some idea of the ways in which mothers' voices are represented in the girls' talk. Example (17) is from a conversation recorded when the girls were 12; examples (18) and (19) are from recordings at age 13.

(17)

```
- - - - - - - - - - - - - - - - - - - - - - - - - - - - - - - - - - - - - -
V:   here's Mum: "oh all the fashions are f- are for short hair and clean bodies aren't
- - - - - - - - - - - - - - - - - - - - - - - - - - - - - - - - - - - - - -
```

```
V:   they?"/                            Mum/
J:           <LAUGHS> who said that?/
- - - - - - - - - - - - - - - - - - - - - - - - - - - - - - - - - - -
J:   clean bodies/ you wouldn't like a dirty body would you?/
- - - - - - - - - - - - - - - - - - - - - - - - - - - - - - - - - - -
```

(18)
- -
```
H:   you said like seven times in that sentence/
J:                            <LAUGHS>
L:                            sorry/ I say like all the time/
- - - - - - - - - - - - - - - - - - - - - - - - - - - - - - - - - - -
V:   my mum alway- my mum's always saying "Don't say that"/
- - - - - - - - - - - - - - - - - - - - - - - - - - - - - - - - - - -
```

(19)
- -
```
L:   my Mum gets . sss- SO angry when people sniff/ <LAUGHTER>
- - - - - - - - - - - - - - - - - - - - - - - - - - - - - - - - - - -
J:   it's ((so)) . the same with . erm- ⌈no . your Mum it's the hiccups/
H:                                     ⌊MY Mum . my Mum goes neurotic ((xx)) if
- - - - - - - - - - - - - - - - - - - - - - - - - - - - - - - - - - -
H:   you sniff/
V:           my Mum doesn't mind so much/ but she says "blow your nose/ blow your
- - - - - - - - - - - - - - - - - - - - - - - - - - - - - - - - - - -
V:   nose/ %blow your ⌈nose%/ <LAUGHS>
L:                   ⌊oh my Mum goes "for God's sake blow your nose"<SHOUTS>
- - - - - - - - - - - - - - - - - - - - - - - - - - - - - - - - - - -
```
<LAUGHTER>
- -

The girls quote their mothers explicitly and then defend their opinions, or they say things in their own voices that show how they have internalized the maternal voice. So in (17) Jenny says *you wouldn't like a dirty body would you?* in support of the position voiced by Vanessa's mother. They are also eager to match one another's claims about their mothers, so after Laura has stated her mother's aversion to sniffing, in (19), Harriet makes a matching statement, and Vanessa brings in her mother's voice: *Blow your nose!*; using the same phrase, Laura contrasts her impatient, outraged mother with Vanessa's more quiet resigned one. Where the mothers' voices appear, they are nearly always presented in a positive light.

Example (20) is an exception. Here, Jenny tells a story about her mother's lack of sympathy for her menstrual cramps.

(20)
> J: she was saying "You're pathetic/ you're- there's nothing wrong with you/ you don't want to go into school"/ and I just got out of the bath/ and I put my shirt on when I was still wet / and I said "I don't care/ I'm just going to go into school" . . . . "Oh Jenny don't go."

In this example, Jenny self-discloses about a painful episode at home. The support she expects (and receives) from her friends is implicitly contrasted with the mother's failure to support her at this particular time. The fact that such examples are rare would suggest that the girls' view of their mothers is positive; only on occasions when their mother fails to support them—and when they therefore need to gain support from each other—do they seem to be prepared to voice criticism or report events that undercut the positive image of the mother.

Boys' voices

The mothers' voices are present throughout the girls' recorded conversations between the ages of 12 and 15. But what is striking about the later conversations is the growing prominence of boys' voices. When the girls were younger, the male voices were those of fathers, brothers, and grandfathers, or of pop stars and characters from soap operas. At age 14 and older, it is real boys they talk about and whose voices we hear in the texts. Examples of boys' voices in the girls' talk are given in (21) through (23).

(21)

> she jumped out/ and she couldn't get back in/ <LAUGHS> and all the boys were standing and going "What are you doing out there, man?"/

(22)

> and Keith's sort of going "oh you're too fucking proud to talk to, you're too fucking proud to talk to me"/ ((what do you expect?))/ if they're bloody- ((if)) they bloody swear at us/

(23)

> I was in the library/ and we were- we were just sitting down and . . . . [Gerald] just went jumping round the book table and going "HEY"/ <LAUGHTER> ((xx)) like really strange thing going "You like me now?"/ <MIMICS ASIAN ACCENT>

The use of taboo words like *fucking* is restricted to contexts such as (22), in which Laura has adopted a male voice. Swearing is rare in the girls' talk, apart from relatively innocuous terms like *bloody* in fixed collocations such as *bloody hell* (see example 4). And in (23), the use of stylized Asian English only occurs in a context such as this, in which one of the girls is mimicking a boy. For these girls the playful use of stylized Asian English is clearly gender-marked.[11] In other words, the girls demonstrate an awareness of some of the features that accomplish youthful masculinity, but they do not adopt them for their own use. This contrasts with their use of their mothers' voices: The evidence of these texts is that the girls do adopt their mothers' views and style of talking.

Three examples in detail

I turn now to three more extended extracts, to give some idea of how these discourses interact, how the different voices are done, how the talk varies in terms of specific linguistic features, and how it changes as the girls get older.

The first extract comes from a tape recording made when the girls were 12 years old; they are in Harriet's bedroom, looking at old photographs.

(24) Text A: Aunts, babies, and testicles
[*Harriet shows photos of her two aunts*]

- -
```
1  H:        Mary=                           ((xx))
   V:  so that's aunt-=Mary and that's aunt Jane/    ((xAnn)) aunt Ann/
```
- -
```
2  J:  I've got a great aunt Mary/
   V:                         mm mm <TRUMPETING> everyone seems to have a
```
- -
```
3  H:                              I have/
   J:                                    well I've got a great great aunt
   L:              haven't even got a great aunt/
   V:  great aunt Mary/
```
- -
```
4  J:  Mary/ <LAUGHS> no she's a [step great great aunt Mary/
   V:                            [do you know anyone who's pregnant?/
```
- -
```
5  H:                                    [yeah I  [do/
   J:                                    [no/     [no I'm not/ <LAUGHS>
   L:                                    [no/
   V:  everyone seems to be pregnant at the moment/
```
- -
```
6  H:  I know somebody who's just had a baby/ it's about two days old/
```
- -
```
7  H:  really sweet/
   ?:              oh! <MOCK MATERNAL>
   V:              Harriet you always know people who've just had babies
```
- -
```
8  J:          did you know that-
   V:  and things/              ((Harriet said))
```
- -
```
9  H:  [babies are dropping out everywhere/
   J:  [did you know that the testicles produce thirty billion sperm in each month?
```
- -
```
10 H:  yeah/ [you know-            [you know that ((xxxx))
   L:        [did you know <LOUD>  [(((xxxxxxxxxxxxxxxxxx)) did you know that the
```
- -
```
11 L:  testicles - produce erm oh a thousand every second and six million every hour?
```
- -
```
12 V:  what- what do they do all their life? <LAUGHTER>
```
- -

In this extract several different discourses are present, among which we can mention the following: a familial discourse that positions the girls as feminine subjects, "doing" family concerns (staves 1–4); a maternal discourse, which has already appeared in Example (3) (staves 5–7); and a factual/scientific discourse (which starts at stave 8). Vanessa subverts Harriet's maternal discourse in staves 7 through 8, and she also subverts Laura's factual/scientific discourse in stave 12.

Linguistically, several features of this passage are worthy of comment:

1. Topic change is rapid.
2. Speech is tied to ongoing activity: (a) looking at photos; (b) the *did you know* questions arise from reading *Just 17* and a Fact Book.

3. Turn-taking patterns are anarchic: The girls are all eager to talk, and they interrupt each other in order to grab the floor (see interruptions in staves 4, 9, 10).
4. Information-seeking questions are used to move the conversation along or switch topic.
5. Backchannel support is absent: Forms like *yes* and *yeah* occur only after direct questions.
6. Utterances are unmitigated (in other words, there is a total absence of hedging devices), and disagreement is openly expressed.

The second extract comes from a conversation recorded when the girls were 13 years old. They are all at Harriet's house and are just finishing a meal.

(25) Text B: South African grapefruit juice
1 H: [*reading blurb on Safeways juice carton*] "Del Monte" <DELIBERATE VOICE>
- -
2 H: "man from-" oh yeah . I'll go and ask my Mum then <LEAVES ROOM>
- -
3 J: what's Mum gonna- . ((I mean)) what's Harriet gonna do?
   V: ask her if it comes from
- -
4 J: ⌈Del Monte <DELIBERATELY>
   V: South Africa probably=   ⌊it probably does/
   L: =what does?   what?
- -
5 H: Laura - Laura . Del Monte is South African/
   V: "Del Monte he say Yes" <SING-SONG>
   L: it is?
- -
6 H: ((xxx get))   no it is South African/
   V: you've got South African grapefruit juice/ <SHOUTS>
- -
7 H: Mum said ⌈it was/
   J: ⌈   ⌈well . she might not be wrong- might be wrong/
   L: ⌊let's hope you never have ⌊it again/
- -
8 J: . ((xx say))
   V: my Mum says she doesn't feel strongly about that/
- -
9 H: she should feel strongly/ cos
   V: she doesn't/
   L: she doesn't or she does?   huh/ <TUTTING NOISE>
- -
10 H: cos the white people exploit the black people/ to work in factories/
- -
11 H: so they can produce that/
   J: erm-
   V: well she doesn't/   I asked her if she's going
- -
12 H: what?
   J: ⌈my Mum says . that Safeways is a lot more expensive/   my Mum says
   V: ⌊to go ((xx))
- -

```
- - - - - - - - - - - - - - - - - - - - - - - - - - - - - - - - - - - - -
13  H:                                    I know/ . so?
    J:  that Safeways is a lot more expensive/            you always used to say that it
- - - - - - - - - - - - - - - - - - - - - - - - - - - - - - - - - - - - -
14  H:                                              ⌈not THAT much more
    J:  wasn't when I said "it's much more expensive"/ and you ⌊said
- - - - - - - - - - - - - - - - - - - - - - - - - - - - - - - - - - - - -
15  H:  expensive/ like . three p more expensive or something/          %no%
    V:                                              not ten p/
- - - - - - - - - - - - - - - - - - - - - - - - - - - - - - - - - - - - -
16  H:                                              ⌈yeah/
    J:  even if it's three p "the three ps mount up"/
    V:                              <LAUGHS> ⌊((so to speak))/
- - - - - - - - - - - - - - - - - - - - - - - - - - - - - - - - - - - - -
```

At the discursive level, we can observe an apolitical discourse, voiced by Vanessa (and Vanessa's mother); this discourse is opposed by an antiracist discourse, voiced by Harriet (staves 1–11). In the second part of the passage (staves 12–16), Jenny's "good housekeeping" discourse is contested by Harriet.

A great deal is going on intertextually in this extract. In staves 1, 2, and 5 we hear snatches of jingles advertising Del Monte products. In staves 8 and 9, we hear Vanessa's mother's views on buying South African produce. In staves 12 and 13, Jenny's mother's voice is heard, while in stave 14 Jenny performs herself, reproducing her mother's words. Finally, in stave 16, Jenny defuses the conflict between herself and Harriet by adopting a mock-serious voice that makes a joke of her statement: *the three ps mount up.*

At the linguistic level, the following patterns can be observed:

1. Topic change is less frenetic.
2. Speech is tied in with activity again (the talk here arises from Harriet's reading of the grapefruit juice carton).
3. Turn-taking is adversarial: There are examples of interruption in staves 7, 12, and 14, and in both staves 12 and 14 next speaker seizes the turn and stops current speaker from finishing.
4. Backchannel support is absent.
5. Hedges are absent and conflict is unmitigated: (a) Vanessa and Harriet argue about the ethics of buying South African produce; (b) Jenny and Harriet argue about whether or not Safeways is an expensive place to shop—note Harriet's extremely confrontational challenge in stave 13: *I know—so?*

The third extract, Text C, from a conversation recorded when the girls were 14 years old, is longer: One topic (about periods) is sustained over several minutes of talk. The full text is given in the appendix to this chapter.

We can pick out three dominant discourses in Text C: first, a medical/factual discourse that is characterized by lexis associated with backaches, headaches, hysteria, and PMT (premenstrual tension); second, a discourse of consciousness raising and self-disclosure; and third, a repressive (or patriarchal) discourse. At the intertextual level, we can observe Jenny "doing" her Mum in stave 8 (*is that you coming up to your periods then?*); Jenny and Harriet reenacting themselves in staves

23 and 24; Jenny adopting Justin's voice in stave 30 (*Jenny looks like she's about to burst into tears*); and finally Vanessa saying *oh dear!* in a baby voice that signals mock concern.

The linguistic strategies used by the girls have changed dramatically from the earlier conversations. The main characteristics of their talk in this extract are as follows:

1. One topic is sustained over several minutes (this topic begins before the start of the extract).
2. Speech is not tied to activity; talk is the sole focus.
3. Turn-taking patterns have changed noticeably: There is considerable overlap, but it is nearly always supportive rather than interruptive (e.g., staves 4, 12, 21, 27, 29).
4. There is frequent use of minimal responses (e.g., staves 2, 4, 11, 15, 26, 28).
5. Hedges are used, especially *really, just, sort of* (e.g., staves 12, 13, 20, 25, 27, 28).

Finally, I want to return to the discursive patterns manifest in the talk of the 14-year-old girls. The three dominant discourses in this extract—a medical discourse, a discourse of consciousness raising and self-disclosure, and a repressive (or patriarchal) discourse—are intertwined. In order to illustrate this intertwining, I shall examine in detail two brief extracts from the "Periods" text. The first extract focuses on backache (appendix, staves 1–5). This passage shows very clearly the way the three discourses are intertwined. The CR discourse manifests itself through patterns of agreement. First, there is a chain of agreement in relation to backache: Jenny initiates this (*my back is connected with my periods*), and the theme is taken up by Vanessa (*I get really bad back . . . ache*) and then by Laura (*so do I/ I get . . . backaches/*). A second chain of agreement revolves around the subject of hot water bottles: Vanessa initiates this (*hot water bottles help*), and her statement is echoed by Harriet and Jenny (*hot water bottles help*) and then by Laura (*help so much*). This pattern of agreement can be termed *reciprocal self-disclosure*. Other key features of the CR discourse here are lexical repetition, collaborative overlap, and the frequent use of well-placed minimal responses.

At the same time, the girls' choice of lexis such as *bad back* and *backache* positions them within a medical discourse in which periods are understood in a frame of ailments or ill health, with *back rest* and *hot water bottles* coming from a lexical set pertaining to possible cures. A third, repressive, discourse is realized in part through syntax. The girls represent themselves as affected rather than as agents (*hot water bottles help me*); the proposition *x helps me* presupposes *I need help*. Verbs are stative: *is*; *get*. The only agentive verb in this short excerpt occurs in conjunction with the negated modal *can't*, where *can't* means *not able/not possible*: *I can't go . . .* is thus a statement of powerlessness.

Another short extract from later in the same text shows again how the three discourses interact. This passage focuses on premenstrual tension (appendix, staves 21–25). It is part of a lengthier chain of mutual self-disclosure on the subject of mood swings. The three discourses are again simultaneously present. The lexis associated with PMT is part of a medical discourse. The CR discourse expressing solidarity and sisterhood is realized through overlapping turns, expressions of agreement, and the joint construction of text (Jenny and Harriet share in constructing the utterance *so whenever I'm on my period I say to Harriet um "Right I might be horrible to you but don't take any notice"*). Again, they jointly represent themselves as affected rather than as agents through their choice of stative verbs—*was, had, got*—and through the use of negative lexis such as *horrible* and *bitch*. This is the repressive discourse. Thus the girls are simultaneously positioned as sisters, in a feminist sense, and as oppressed.

Friendship and femininity

Now that we have looked at a few extracts in greater detail, we can try to summarize what is going on in the girls' talk. The two main things that are being "done" are friendship and femininity, and these are interlinked in complex ways.

Doing friendship changes as the girls get older. When they are 12 years old, one of the key ways they accomplish friendship is by playing with language. They flip in and out of subject positions, singing snatches of pop songs, chanting advertising slogans, mimicking the voices of mothers, friends, and teachers. They also subvert the discourses they use in a variety of ways. They treat topics like colored balls to be tossed around and then discarded. And as their laughter testifies, they are having fun doing this. The ludic aspect of the girls' talk is constitutive of friendship: flipping from subject position to subject position constitutes doing friendship for the girls at this age.

But clearly they are also accomplishing femininity. As we have seen, the variety of discourses that appear in these conversations position the girls as different kinds of feminine subjects, some of them in direct conflict with one another. This is possible because what has been recorded is backstage talk, to use Erving Goffman's (1959) term. Among the functions of the backstage are that "the performer can relax" and that "the team can run through its performance" (Goffman 1959:115). This allows a degree of experimentation which would be too risky in other contexts.

But as the girls get older, their talk changes. They experiment less, and certain discourses become more prominent: doing friendship now means supporting new ways of doing femininity. It is not that they shift to a completely new set of discourses: as examples 8 through 12 show, there is much that is consistent with the earlier talk. But as the girls reach ages 14 and 15, the new discourse that I have called *CR/self-disclosure* emerges as significant, and the ludic aspect of their talk decreases. Life is much more serious: They are struggling with changes in their world and look to each other for support, support that is expressed in the form of matching self-disclosure rather than in more playful ways.

When I first started work on this material, I focused on linguistic features such as minimal responses, turn-taking patterns, and epistemic modality. I was amazed at how much the 12-year-olds' talk differed from the talk of adult female friends in my corpus. I was equally amazed at the way the girls changed over the years, beginning to talk more like adult female speakers. I have to confess that in my excitement about what was going on at the microlinguistic level I imagined that anything I wrote on the girls' talk would be a sort of triumphalist narrative, showing how they developed from being relatively anarchic, egocentric conversationalists to being more cooperative, sisterly coparticipants in talk.

138 IDENTITY AS IDEOLOGY

As I have worked on this chapter, I have realized that such a claim would mis-represent the data. Although I want to argue that the girls have become more so-phisticated as language users, I also want to assert that this is much less important than what is going on at the discursive level. There seems to me to be a significant difference between the girls' talk when they are young and when they are older. The conversations I recorded when the girls were 12 and 13 demonstrate convinc-ingly that they are social agents "capable of resistance and innovations produced out of the clash between contradictory subject positions and practices" (Weedon 1987:125). At this age not only are they shaped by the discourses but they also resist and subvert them.

By contrast, less evidence of the girls' agency appears in the later conversations. I was initially fooled by their growing use of the discourse of consciousness raising, with its origins in the Women's Liberation Movement, into thinking they were part of a brave new feminist world. But if we look again at Extract C ("Periods"), we can see how they are positioned here as oppressed, as suffering, as at the mercy of their bodies. They talk about their bodies in a medicalized way that is overwhelmingly negative. Worse, they name themselves as "bad" (e.g., *I'm a bitch/ I'm really hor-rible/*). This later talk shows how well they have internalized the values of the Fa-ther, the values of patriarchy. I think we have to ask whether these young white middle-class girls—a privileged group, who will be the professional women of the next gen-eration—are in fact liberated. Or is it more accurate to say that, although they think they are speaking, they are in fact being spoken?

Conclusion

This chapter has looked at a particular group of girls at a particular, transitional, moment in their adolescence. The conversations recorded when they were younger (12 and 13 years old) are snapshots of them at the end of childhood, beginning to identify as teenagers but exploring their world and the discourses available to them in a playful and carefree way. The mood has changed in the conversations recorded in their mid-teens (ages 14 and 15): The girls seem less playful and, as I have dem-onstrated, are positioned by dominant discourses so that they present themselves as relatively powerless. But it would be wrong to end the chapter on this gloomy note. I interviewed Jenny and Harriet in their late teens, when they were about to leave home and go to university, and they both agreed that their mid-teens had been a low point, a point between childhood and womanhood when they felt they had lost con-trol of their lives.

What struck me in this long (90-minute) loosely structured interview was the girls' reflexivity. They were able to reflect on their teenage years—particularly the early years when they had recorded themselves for me—in a very clear way. I sug-gested to them that their talk had changed and that they had been very different when they were 12. They responded as follows:

Jenny: When you're twelve you don't really think about things like that do you, I mean
          you don't think about feeling.

Jen: That's right—so feelings is— that's something you've become more conscious of?

Jenny: Yeah.

Harriet: Definitely, also you see your experiences differently, I don't know, between— you experience diff- really differently things between the age of twelve and eighteen . . . you know, eleven downwards I can't really remember much about how I was feeling, whereas if you ask me how I was feeling when I was about sixteen I could probably tell you quite well.

Jenny and Harriet agreed that their talk had changed, but for them the significant difference is their new awareness of their feelings. They seemed to see the stage between 12 and 18 more constructively from their new vantage point. They agreed that they had felt negative at times during their mid-teens, but they now asserted the value of their friendships (both within the group and their particular best-friendship) and the significance of these friendships in their passage through their teens. Jenny, for example, said that friendship is important to her because it means "just having someone that you can just be yourself with . . . with Harriet and my older friends I feel completely I can be myself entirely."

Jenny's focus on "being myself entirely" brings us back to the question of identity. This chapter explores the changing identities of girls through close analysis of conversational data. I have argued that the girls' sense of their femininity is at times contradictory and precarious, and I have attempted to show how "doing femininity" changes as the girls get older. But the construction of identity does not stop at the age of 15 or 18. It is an ongoing and constantly contested process. Like all of us, these girls are involved in the struggle to define gender. As Chris Weedon puts it, "The nature of femininity and masculinity is one of the key sites of discursive struggle for the individual" (1987:98). But the evidence of the interview data shows that the outlook for young women like Jenny, Harriet, Laura, and Vanessa is not as bleak as might be suggested by their talk in their mid-teens. By the time they reach 18 they are much clearer about who they are and what they want and about the value of female friendship. In the long term, it is friendships like these that help us to resist particular versions of femininity and to prefer others, as well as to reconcile contradictory femininities. Although the evidence even from adult female speakers is far from unilaterally positive (see Coates 1996, 1997), it would seem that girls in their mid-teens have a particularly difficult time. Yet during this stage they learn new ways of talking and become aware of the importance of friendship, as they struggle to "be themselves."

APPENDIX

Text C: Periods

- -

1 J: my back- my back is connected with my periods/ and I

- -

2 J: ⌈(xx)) yeah/

L: ⌈((so do I)) I get-

V: ⌊so's mine/ I get really bad back[ei]- ⌊backache down there/

- -

3 J: ⌈((xxx))
   L: ⌊((get)) backaches- I can't go like that/ and I can't go like
- -
4 J: <QUIET LAUGH>   ⌈yeah
   L: that/ and I just ((xx)) a back rest/ |
   V: ⌊but . [ho] hot water bottles
- -
5 H: ⌈hot water bottles help me ⌈as well/
   J: ⌊hot water bottles help/ |
   L: ⌊help so much/ yeah it's lovely/
   V: help/
- -

.

- -
6 J: well whenever there's anything wrong with me/ whenever I'm feeling at all upset/
- -
7 J: or I've got a headache or something/ my Mum always thinks it's my period/
- -
8 J: she says "Is that you coming up to your periods then?"/
- -
9 H: <LOW LAUGH>   <LAUGH>
   J: and I say "No/ -   it's ((xx)) weeks away actually"/
- -
10 H: ⌈well
   L: ((sometimes I'm just sitting there)) ⌊like- I suddenly feel as if I'm going to cry
- -
11 H: ⌈I was lying in the bath-
   L: right/ |((xxx)) suddenly- it just suddenly your eyes like this/   if your face goes hot/
   ?:   ⌊yes   oh right/
- -
12 J: ⌈your eyes sting/
   L: and you- then it just goes ⌊((xx))/   they sudden- they just like comes
   ?: mhm/
- -
13 H: ⌈well what-
   J: your nose is-   it feels like your nose is just sort of . expanding/ |or something/
   L: ((like a heat wave))/   ⌊it sometimes
- -
14 L: happens in a lesson/ you're just sort of sitting there going- it goes "hwoom"
- -
15 H: ⌈well what happened to me was . it was
   J: I get that- ⌈I got that last time/ |((xxxxxxxxxxxxxxxx))
   L: ⌊yeah/ |
   V: ⌊((xxxx))
- -
16 H: one day this week/ and I was just SO hysterical/ and I was lying in the bath/ and I was
- -
17 H: sobbing- I sobbed s- constantly for half an hour/   and I was just getting so- and
   J: mhm/
- -
18 H: every time I dropped the soap or something ⌈in the bathwater/ I'd go "aaah"/
   ?:   ⌊yes I know I get so-
- -
19 H: I'd scream/ and I'd go like this/ and every time I dropped the top or something-
       and like
- -

20 H: everything seemed to be going wrong and everything/ it was horrible [. . . .] it was
   really

- -

21 H: horrible ⌈that day/
   L: ⌈do you get PMT? ((xx))
   V: ⌊but you know when I had ⌊that really bad . um premenstrual tension/

- -

22 H: <LAUGHS>   <LAUGHS> so I've noticed/
   J: yeah I'm a bitch/ <LAUGHS> I'm REally HORrible/

- -

23 H: no-   no but ⌈some-   "Right I might
   J: no but-   ⌊so whenever I'm on my period/ I say to Harriet um-

- -

24 H: be horrible to you but-   ⌈can you-   some of you move up ((xx))
   J: "Don't take ⌊any notice"/

- -

25 J: ⌈no but remember that time I had really really bad back pain/ . it was on a Friday/
   L: ⌊which ((xx)) which ((xx))

- -

26 H: yeah/
   J: and remember I cried after school/   I cried IN school as well and
   L: yeah I know/

- -

27 H: really?
   J: nobody noticed?   yeah/ ⌈yeah it was in SPACE*/ and I was just crying/ and I
   V: ⌊when was this?

- -

28 J: was sitting really upright/ . and I sort of just buried my head/ and I cried/   not for
   V: mhm/

- -

29 J: very long/ just sort of . ⌈a few tears/   I know/ and Jus- and I just looked
   V: ⌊I hate it when no one notices/

- -

30 J: up like this/ and and Justin said "Jenny looks like she's about to burst into tears"/

- -

31 J: <LAUGHS> like this/ and ((xxx)) he's the only person that noticed/
   V: oh dear/<BABY VOICE>

- -

*SPACE = Social, Personal, and Careers Education

NOTES

This chapter arose from a new phase of my work on the talk of women friends. It is a revised
version of a paper given at the Third Berkeley Women and Language Conference (Coates
1994a). I am very grateful to the editors of this volume for their helpful advice on how to
improve the chapter and for their patience during its revision.

   1. For a microdevelopmental study of gender and subjectivity, see Marjorie Orellana
(chapter 3, this volume).
   2. An exception in the specific area of grammatical variation is Edina Eisikovits's (1988)
study, which compared the talk of 13-year-olds and 16-year-olds in Sydney, Australia, and
which showed how girls' speech moved closer to standard norms as they got older, whereas
boys increased their use of nonstandard forms.

3. See Deborah Cameron (1997) for a discussion of the effects of compulsory hetero-sexuality on young men.

4. I use the term *discourse* both in the more linguistic sense of 'a way of speaking asso-ciated with a particular position or worldview' and in the broader sense of 'social practice' (Fairclough 1989, 1992; Lee 1992).

5. I cannot express too warmly my gratitude to Harriet, Jenny, Laura, and Vanessa for participating in this research and for allowing me to use transcripts of their speech in this chapter. They have seen a draft of it and are happy for it to be published. (Note: Their real names are used throughout, as they explicitly said that they did not want their names to be changed.)

6. One reason that most of the recordings were made at Harriet's house is that Harriet's mother was my initial contact with the group, and she would remind them to switch on the tape recorder when they came over to her house.

7. There is a dearth of research in this area. Penelope Eckert's (1997) findings reveal a suggestive pattern: She analyzed phonological variation in the speech of adolescents in De-troit and found that the Jock (more middle-class) girls were the most linguistically conserva-tive group, whereas the Burnout (more working-class) girls were the most advanced speakers with respect to new vernacular forms. Eckert argues that the girls' usage is more polarized than the boys' because the girls have to work harder at being "good" Jocks or "good" Burn-outs since, as females, they are marginalized in the linguistic "marketplace." See also Edina Eisikovits (1988), Suzanne Romaine (1984), and Joan Swann (1992) on the talk of children and adolescents.

8. The question of whether the issue is one of loss of self-esteem (see Brown & Gilligan 1992; Pipher 1994) or more of power and ideology (see Fairclough 1992; Weedon 1987) is one that deserves further exploration. Whereas these white middle-class girls become more interactionally constrained as they move into adolescence, for many African American and Latina girls language in interaction continues to be an important resource for personal agency (see, in this volume, Goodwin, chapter 20; Mendoza-Denton, chapter 14; Morgan, chapter 1).

9. The transcription conventions used for my data are as follows:

/	end of a tone group or chunk of talk
?	end of a chunk of talk with rising intonation
-	incomplete word or utterance
.	short pause
—	long pause
[	overlap between utterances
≡	absence of a discernible gap in utterances by two speakers
(( ))	doubt about accuracy of transcription
((*xxx*))	inaudible material
< >	clarificatory information about previous underlined material
CAPITALS	words or syllables uttered with emphasis
% %	words or phrases spoken very quietly
[ ]	phonetic transcription

10. Mirroring is a key structuring principle of the talk of adult women (Coates 1996).

11. See Ben Rampton (1995) for a detailed account of the practice of linguistic cross-ing in adolescent speech.

REFERENCES

Bakhtin, Mikhail (1986). *Speech genres and other late essays.* Ed. Caryl Emerson & Michael Holquist. Trans. Vern W. McGee. Austin: University of Texas Press.

Bergvall, Victoria, Janet Bing, & Alice Freed (eds.) (1996). *Rethinking language and gender research: Theory and practice.* London: Longman.

Brown, Lyn M., & Carol Gilligan (eds.) (1992). *Meeting at the crossroads: Women's psychology and girls' development.* Cambridge, MA: Harvard University Press.

Cameron, Deborah (1997). Performing gender identity: Young men's talk and the construction of heterosexual masculinity. In Sally Johnson & Ulrike Hanna Meinhof (eds.), *Language and masculinity.* Oxford: Blackwell, 47–64.

Coates, Jennifer (1989). Gossip revisited: An analysis of all-female discourse. In Jennifer Coates & Deborah Cameron (eds.), *Women in their speech communities.* London: Longman, 94–122.

——— (1991). Women's cooperative speech: A new kind of conversational duet? In Claus Uhlig & Rüdiger Zimmermann (eds.), *Proceedings of the Anglistentag 1990 Marburg.* Tübingen: Max Niemeyer Verlag, 296–311.

——— (1994a). Discourse, gender, and subjectivity: The talk of teenage girls. In Mary Bucholtz, A. C. Liang, Laurel A. Sutton, & Caitlin Hines (eds.), *Cultural performances: The proceedings of the Third Berkeley Women and Language Conference.* Berkeley, CA: Berkeley Women and Language Group, 116–132.

——— (1994b). No gap, lots of overlap: Turn-taking patterns in the talk of women friends. In David Graddol, Janet Maybin, & Barry Stierer (eds.), *Researching language and literacy in social context.* Clevedon, England: Multilingual Matters, 177–192.

——— (1996). Women talk: Conversation between women friends. Oxford: Blackwell.

——— (1997). Competing discourses of femininity. In Helga Kotthoff & Ruth Wodak (eds.), *Communicating gender in context.* Amsterdam: John Benjamins, 285–314.

Eckert, Penelope (1993). Cooperative competition in adolescent "girl talk." In Deborah Tannen (ed.), *Gender and conversational interaction.* Oxford: Oxford University Press, 32–61.

——— (1997). Gender and sociolinguistic variation. In Jennifer Coates (ed.), *Language and gender: A reader.* Oxford: Blackwell, 64–75.

Eder, Donna (1993). "Go get ya a French!": Romantic and sexual teasing among adolescent girls. In Deborah Tannen (ed.), *Gender and conversational interaction.* Oxford: Oxford University Press, 17–31.

Eisikovits, Edina (1988). Girl-talk/boy-talk: Sex differences in adolescent speech. In Peter Collins & David Blair (eds.), *Australian English.* Brisbane: University of Queensland Press, 35–54.

Fairclough, Norman (1989). *Language and power.* London: Longman.

——— (1992). *Discourse and social change.* Cambridge: Polity Press.

Foucault, Michel (1972). *The archaeology of knowledge and the discourse on language.* New York: Pantheon.

Goffman, Erving (1959). *The presentation of self in everyday life.* Harmondsworth, England: Penguin.

Goodwin, Marjorie Harness (1990). *He-said-she-said: Talk as social organization among black children.* Bloomington: Indiana University Press.

Hall, Kira, & Mary Bucholtz (eds.) (1995). *Gender articulated: Language and the socially constructed self.* London: Routledge.

Holmes, Janet (1995). *Women, men and politeness.* London: Longman.

Johnson, Sally, & Ulrike Hanna Meinhof (1997). *Language and masculinity.* Oxford: Blackwell.

Lee, David (1992). *Competing discourses: Perspective and ideology in language.* London: Longman.

Mills, Sara (ed.) (1995). *Language and gender: Interdisciplinary perspectives*. London: Longman.

Pipher, Mary Bray (1994). *Reviving Ophelia: Saving the selves of adolescent girls*. New York: Putnam.

Rampton, Ben (1995). *Crossing: Language and ethnicity among adolescents*. London: Longman.

Rich, Adrienne (1980). Compulsory heterosexuality and lesbian existence. *Signs* 5(4):631–660.

Romaine, Suzanne (1984). *The language of children and adolescents*. Oxford: Blackwell.

Swann, Joan (1992). *Girls, boys and language*. Oxford: Blackwell.

Tannen, Deborah (ed.) (1993). *Gender and conversational interaction*. Oxford: Oxford University Press.

Weedon, Chris (1987). *Post-structuralist theory and feminist practice*. Oxford: Blackwell.

Rebaking the Pie

The WOMAN AS DESSERT Metaphor

> . . . the question [is] how do feminists not only get women a piece of the pie, but rebake the whole pie.
> —Susan Faludi, *San Francisco Chronicle & Examiner*
> *Image Magazine*, Sept. 27, 1992, p. 12

A venerable approach in language and gender scholarship has been to analyze the ways in which sexism is built into a language (usually English). Muriel Schulz's classic article "The Semantic Derogation of Women" (1975) is one such careful deconstruction of linguistic chauvinism, using the tools of dictionary definitions and etymology. Despite much solid work, this entire line of inquiry was trivialized and branded as "radical feminism" based on the misunderstood and decontextualized claims of a few researchers in the 1970s (see especially Penelope 1990 (reprint of 1975 work); Todasco 1973; and, for a book-length articulation, Spender 1980). Language and gender studies moved on to the macro issues implied by sexist usage on the one hand, with gender seen as but one of many social variables speakers bring to the table (largely the concern of sociolinguistics), and to the micro issue of sexist usages in individual conversations on the other hand (exemplified by discourse analysis). Meanwhile, cognitive linguistics was establishing itself as a subfield dedicated to elucidating the interdependencies of thought and language, focusing mainly on the (ungendered) role of metaphors in constructing cognition. In this chapter I bring together these two disparate approaches, using each to illuminate the other.

There is a consistent, widespread, generally unconscious and undocumented metaphor in English equating women-as-sex-objects with desserts, manifested both in linguistic expressions (such as *cheesecake, cookie, tart,* and so on) and in customs (such as women jumping out of cakes). The presence of a virtual bakery of dessert terms for women considered sexually (see appendix to this chapter) is evidence of an underlying conceptual metaphor of WOMAN AS DESSERT—a metaphor that functions as what Claudine Herrmann has called "a micro-language filled with winks and allusions specifically aimed at [women]" ([1976] 1989:7) and that can have unexpected psycholinguistic side effects.

Background: Beyond objectification

It is unremarkable that the WOMAN AS DESSERT metaphor reduces women to the status of objects, with the attendant implications of powerlessness, inanimacy, and procurability; the metaphorical commodification and belittling of women is well known (e.g., *baby, bimbo, doll*—see R. Lakoff 1975; Penelope 1977; Schulz 1975; and, for how girls can internalize these beliefs, Coates, chapter 6, this volume). What is surprising is the degree to which the metaphor is extended: Women here are not just objects, but *sweet* (that is, compliant, smiling), and not just desserts, but *pieces* or *slices.*

I use a cognitive framework to tease apart linguistic and conceptual features of this metaphor and to pose questions such as "Why desserts?", "Why baked desserts?", and "Why *cupcake* but not **shortcake*?" I take as a point of departure Sally McConnell-Ginet's finding that natural languages "both encode and perpetuate speakers' beliefs and attitudes." McConnell-Ginet notes that "it is in part because the connections of language to thought and to social life are seldom explicitly recognized that language use can enter into the transmission and preservation of attitudes and values that are seldom explicitly articulated. . . . Many of the messages we convey and receive are 'loaded' with import beyond their overt content and perhaps beyond what the speaker intended" (1980:7). I show that these covert messages exploit available linguistic channels: semantics, syntax, the lexicon, and phonetics. This chapter is part of a larger work on the DESIRED WOMAN metaphor, wherein I also examine the functionally parallel semantic fields of SMALL ANIMALS/ GAME (*chick, filly, fox*) and FEMMES FATALES (*siren, tigress, vamp*), in each case finding unexpected phonosemantic or morphosemantic coherences that are correlated with ways of expressing diminution and derogation in English (Hines 1996b). Such iconicity between form and meaning is central to cognitive linguistics, which takes the position that metaphors are not "a matter of mere language [but] rather . . . a means of structuring our conceptual systems," in George Lakoff and Mark Johnson's (1980:145) formulation. I turn this around, showing that metaphors are not merely a matter of conceptual systems but can also be a means of structuring our language—and our identity.

Throughout, I use an "ecological" approach, in Richard Rhodes and John Lawler's sense of "reject[ing] monocausal explanations" (1981:1). My goal is to reveal the systematic linguistic patterning at work and thereby to question the assumed arbitrariness of the metaphorical sign, simultaneously bringing into awareness the social role that metaphors play in transmitting coded messages.

Evolution of the metaphor

Conceptual metaphors are not arbitrary; indeed, their insidious power hinges on the degree to which they "make sense." When a metaphor captures a felt truth, its compelling logic seduces us into accepting unstated conclusions. As Richard Lewontin cautions, "The price of metaphor is eternal vigilance" (quoted in Gentner & Grudin 1985:181).

I describe the evolution of the WOMAN AS DESSERT metaphor in figure 7.1. It begins harmlessly enough with the ubiquitous metaphor PEOPLE ARE OBJECTS, an example of which is the special case that George Lakoff, Jane Espenson, and Alan Schwartz have called PEOPLE ARE BUILDINGS, as in *Eyes are windows to the soul* (1991:192). This ungendered metaphor collides (and colludes) with the cultural stereotype "women are sweet" (as in the nursery rhyme "What are little girls made of?/Sugar and spice and everything nice . . .") and with another common metaphor, ACHIEVING A DESIRED OBJECT IS GETTING SOMETHING TO EAT (as in *She tasted victory*), yielding WOMEN ARE SWEET OBJECTS (in this case, DESSERTS). Notice that the sweetness predicated of women is itself metaphorical, referring to their supposed sweet nature rather than an actual flavor, as in this Jamaican English appreciative comment to a woman: "You don't have to sugar up your lips for me" = 'You don't have to make yourself more dessert-like, i.e., wear makeup' (metonymically and metaphorically represented here by lipstick, which is not usually literally sweet).[1]

As the folklorist Alan Dundes observes, there are many associations of women and food, from breastfeeding to clichés such as *Motherhood and apple pie*; *[A woman's place is] barefoot, pregnant, and in the kitchen*; and *The way to a man's heart is through his stomach*, all of which, he writes in ironic understatement, "tend to restrict the range of female activity" (1980:165). The DESSERT metaphor, however, goes further, implicitly trivializing women, first reducing them to their sexuality and

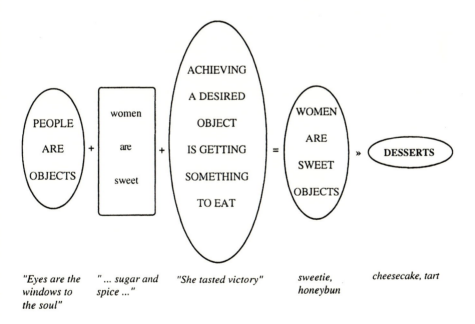

Figure 7.1. Evolution of the WOMAN AS DESSERT metaphor

then equating them with not just any edible objects but specifically peripheral food items: compare the clearly fanciful male *beefcake* with the readily available female *cheesecake*. As desserts, women can be bought and sold, eaten, elaborately decorated (as in the use of *frosting* to describe the makeup of beauty pageant contestants), admired for their outward appearance, dismissed as *sinful* and *decadent*—or, in the ultimate degradation, simply done without: desserts are optional/inessential, frivolous, perhaps even a waste of time.

Although many writers have commented on "the subconscious relating of sex and food" (Wentworth & Flexner 1975:xiii; see also Dillard 1977), there are few discussions of specific gender-related terms (notable exceptions are Rawson 1989 and Todasco 1973). I was thus pleasantly surprised to find Dundes's discussion of "the socially sanctioned saccharine quality of females [which] is confirmed later in life by such terms of endearment as sweetheart, honey bun(ch), sugar, sweetie pie, and the like . . . one can appreciate the large number of slang terms for the female or her genitalia which draw upon dessert metaphors" (1980:164). Dundes cites the "sugar and spice" nursery rhyme, as well as several other childhood verses supporting the stereotype of female sweetness; his discussion parallels parts of this chapter.[2] There is, however, a subtle but crucial distinction between mere toothsome objects, such as *sweetie* or *honeybun*, which can be used of either women or men, and actual items that could be ordered off a menu, such as *cheesecake* or *tart,* which are used only of women; it is this second set that I will examine in this chapter.[3]

Cupcakes and buttered buns

I began this research by collecting as many terms as possible. Because the semantic fields of eating and sex are highly taboo, especially in the subfields of desserts and women, I drew on a variety of sources, some decidedly beyond the academic pale, for citations of actual use, of metaphor "as she is spoke." I became something of a lexical detective as I sorted through slang dictionaries. For example, *cookie* is variously defined as

> A dear, a sweetheart, or an alluring young woman. (Jacobson 1993:54)
>
> A promiscuous female likely to be found in an American bar. (Holder 1989:221)
>
> An attractive young person of the opposite sex, esp. a young woman; . . . the vulva and vagina. (Lighter 1994:472)
>
> A girl or young woman, esp. an attractive, vivacious one; . . . the female genitalia. (Wentworth & Flexner 1975:120)
>
> The female genitals; cf. bun, cake. (Spears 1981:84)
>
> Female genitals. (Richter 1995:53)

To avoid basing my analysis on a term of dubious currency, I struck a balance between the vulgar (Grose [1796] 1992; the racy journal *Maledicta*) and the academic (Cameron 1992; Hughes 1991), with a smattering of items drawn from popular culture *(Glamour* and *Seventeen* magazines, television sitcoms, advertisements). As a final check, I sorted through 2 years' worth of elicited slang data from undergraduate students in an introductory linguistics class at the University of California at Berkeley.[4] All of this data collection resulted in a large and unwieldy set of terms (see the appendix to this chapter). It was obvious to me that *cupcakes* and *pumpkin* (*pies*) were conceptually more central to the metaphor than *buttered buns* and *sugar doughnuts*, but I wanted a way to capture that intuition, so I devised the following tests for metaphorical centrality:

1. It must have a nonmetaphorical sense—that is, it must refer both to a woman-considered-sexually and to an actual dessert, which rules out the fanciful *cutie pie*, *honeybun*(*ches*), *sweetie* (*pie*), and so forth and foods not primarily served as desserts, such as *muffin, pancake, tootsie roll*.
2. It must be multiply cited, which rules out *available jelly* [*roll*], *cream puff, fortune cookie*, and so forth.

Applying these tests to the complete list of collected terms yields the following set of central terms: (*piece of*) *cake, cheesecake, cookie, crumpet* [*Brit.*], *cupcake*, (*a tasty bit of*) *pastry*, (*cherry*) *pie, poundcake, pumpkin* (*pie, tart*), *punkin*, [*jam*] *tart, tartlet/-lette*. It is this group that will be analyzed herein. Some of these terms will seem more prototypical than others, and some readers may even object that a given term (such as *pastry*) is archaic in their dialect. This is probably inevitable: Slang is a hotly contested area of language, and one that is constantly in flux. However, I do have recent citations for all the central terms; for example: "From MTV tartlet to art-house pastry du jour. No wonder the adoring critics who droolingly dub her 'luminous' are so eager to gobble Liv Tyler up. You can almost sniff a just-from-the-oven freshness about her as she strides into the room" (*USA Today*, quoted in *The New Yorker*, July 15, 1996:84). The correlations detailed here are pervasive, and the overall pattern they form is not significantly altered by the removal of any single lexical item (for every *poundcake* there is a *cheesecake*; for every *pastry* a *tart*).

My conclusions are meant to apply only to Standard English, which largely means white, heterosexual, middle-class English. Not being fluent in other dialects, I find myself unable to account for the different connotations of, for example, *jelly-roll* 'one's lover, spouse; from the twenties to the forties, a term for the vagina' (Major 1994:256) and *sweet-potato-pie* 'term of endearment for either sex' (Major 1994:460), both from African American slang. Until very recently, slang dictionaries were almost exclusively compiled by straight white men for other straight white men; women, men of color, and gay men were not welcomed. As Cheris Kramarae and Paula Treichler point out, "whatever their intentions . . . dictionaries have functioned as linguistic legislators which perpetuate the stereotypes and prejudices of their writers and editors, who are almost exclusively male" (1990:8)—and, we might add, white and straight. Slang used by and about gay men in particular could be quite illuminating of the overlap between terms for women and terms used to disparage gay men as effeminate, such as *cream puff*, as well as of how identity is subversively reclaimed (see Leap, chapter 13, this volume). I hope to be able to include this exciting and largely uncharted area of research in future analyses.[5]

Semantic shifts: Pejoration and amelioration

Linguistic expressions based on the WOMAN AS DESSERT metaphor have undergone various semantic shifts, including pejoration, or the acquisition of negative evaluative senses, which has the effect of narrowing the range of meaning; and amelioration, or the acquisition of positive or neutral evaluative senses, which has the effect of broadening the range of meaning. Pejoration is the more common process, as Muriel Schulz notes: "Again and again in the history of the language, one finds that a perfectly innocent term designating a girl or woman may begin with totally neutral or even positive connotations, but that gradually it acquires negative implications, at first perhaps only slightly disparaging, but after a period of time becoming abusive and ending as a sexual slur" (1975:65).

An example of a term that has taken on pejorative connotations is *tart*, which in the nineteenth century was an affectionate term for a pleasant or attractive woman, as in this 1864 definition:

> *Tart,* a term of approval applied by the London lower orders to a young woman for whom some affection is felt. The expression is not generally employed by the young men, unless the female is in 'her best'. (Hotten's *Slang Dictionary*, quoted in the *Oxford English Dictionary* 1989)

This sense coexisted well into the twentieth century in Liverpudlian, Australian, and New Zealand dialects of English alongside its usual U. S. meaning, 'prostitute' (*Oxford English Dictionary* 1989; Rawson 1989:381; Wilkes 1990:326), to such an extent that George Orwell could write in 1931, "This word [*tart*] . . . seems absolutely interchangeable with 'girl', with no implication of 'prostitute'. People will speak of their daughter or sister as a tart" (quoted in the *Oxford English Dictionary* 1989).

Other expressions have undergone amelioration with resulting generalization: Consider the phrase *easy as pie*, a representative slang definition of which is the following:

> *Pie* A woman considered sexually. From the expression "as easy as pie," also reinforced by 'nice piece of pie,' which is euphemistic for 'nice piece of ass.' Cf. *cake, tart.* (Spears 1981:298)

Another example is a *piece of cake*, which might seem entirely unconnected to gender. Yet as Eric Partridge (1984:878) wrote of *piece*, "it has, in C.19–20, been usu. apprehended as elliptical for *piece of tail*; cf. *piece of mutton*. . . ." Compare also the list of terms in the appendix, especially *cut yourself a piece of poontang. Cake* by itself is slang for 'prostitute', making this reading doubly motivated (Spears 1981:61).

These two senses converge in *cherry pie*. Jane Mills writes:

> In the second half of the C19th *cherry* and *cherry pie* began to be used colloquially for an attractive young woman. By the mid-C20th *cherry pie* came to mean something easily obtainable . . . perhaps influenced by the notion that a young woman who was considered attractive was sexually promiscuous, i.e., a ripe fruit ready for picking and for

(male) consumption. This probably influenced the development of *cherry* as a euphemism for the hymen. (1989:46)

In addition to the cherry-as-hymen metaphor (which has been extended to mean 'mint' or 'virgin' in the case of restored cars and is applied contemptuously to a new military recruit, "one who has yet to be bloodied" [Mills 1989:46]), a woman can be called a *peach, plum,* or *(hot) tomato,* and a woman who sells sex for drugs, especially crack cocaine, is known as a *(straw)berry.* There are numerous fruit terms for breasts, such as *apples, casabas, cantaloupes, grapefruits, lemons* (especially used of small breasts), *melons,* and *watermelons* (large breasts), as well as *cherries, raspberries,* and *strawberries* for nipples, all of which accentuate the *ripe, fresh, juicy* quality of desirable women (compare *a wrinkled old prune* 'a woman past her sexual prime'). Extensions include *cherry orchard* (girls' dormitory), *cherry picker* (man who desires young girls), and *cherry splitter* (penis).

I am not claiming that speakers today intend or are even aware of these associations; people of both sexes call each other *honey pie* all the time with genuine affection. Nor am I claiming that every term that can be traced to the underlying metaphor of WOMAN AS DESSERT is hopelessly polluted with sexist overtones and must automatically be expunged from our speech; as Susan Ehrlich and Ruth King have shown, attempts at such linguistic cleansing have proven largely unsuccessful. Discussing the actual use of supposedly gender-neutral terms (for example, in job listings in the *Chronicle of Higher Education*), they write:

> Rather than ridding the language of a masculine generic . . . the introduction of neutral generic forms . . . has led to a gender-based distinction between forms such as *chairperson* or *chair* (used to designate females) vs. *chairman* (used to designate males). Thus both the title *Ms.* and these true generics are used in ways that maintain distinctions the terms were intended to eliminate—distinctions that are clearly important to the speech community. (1994:63)

Feminist linguists have eloquently addressed the "chicken-and-egg" question of the relationship between word and world. For example, Julia Penelope writes:

> English does more than hinder and hurt women: it proscribes the boundaries of the lives we might imagine and will ourselves to live. The many ways the language obstructs our ability to conceive of ourselves as agents in the world . . . go beyond mere hurt to emotional, intellectual, and physical immobility that keeps us men's easy prey . . . [women] ponder cosmetics while men plan "star wars" and their conquest of the cosmos. (1990:xiv)

On the other side of this debate, Deborah Cameron argues that it is not the words we should be changing but the minds of their users—"in the mouths of sexists, language can always be sexist" (1985:90)—while Muriel Schulz strives for a compromise position:

> I began with the acknowledgement that we cannot tell the extent to which any language influences the people who use it. This is certainly true for most of what we call language.

However, words which are highly charged with emotion, taboo, or distaste do not only reflect the culture which uses them. They teach and perpetuate the attitudes which created them. To make the name of God taboo is to perpetuate the mystery, power, and awesomeness of the divine . . . and to brand a class of persons as obscene is to taint them to the users of the language. . . . The semantic change . . . by which terms designating women routinely undergo pejoration, both reflects and perpetuates derogatory attitudes towards women. They should be abjured. (1975:73)

I am sympathetic to all of these views; my intention in writing this chapter is not to choose among them but instead to call attention to the process by which this derogation is accomplished through metaphor and to suggest that we examine the language we use as we would any tool, remembering that, in Roland Barthes's phrase, "language is never innocent; words have a second-order memory which mysteriously persists in the midst of new meanings" ([1953] 1968:16).[6]

Synchronic feature analysis

The desserts in terms of which women-as-sex-objects are habitually described can be analyzed on the basis of shared semantic, syntactic, lexical, and phonetic features. They are semantically isomorphic: firm on the outside, soft or juicy in the middle, and either able to be cut into more than one piece (*cheesecake, cherry pie, poundcake*) or conceptualized as one (snatched) serving of an implied batch (*cookie, crumpet, cupcake*). Terms such as **custard, *ice cream cone*, or **mousse* do not occur with this meaning; speakers "know" and adhere to the unstated rules governing well-formed expressions of the metaphor. (Compare the British *She's joined the Pudding Club* or the American *She has a bun in the oven*, meaning 'She's pregnant', that is, sexually undesirable or unavailable.) There are sometimes nonce coinages that do not meet these semantic criteria, such as *available jelly* [*roll*], *gooseberry pudding*, or *hot chocolate*—but the fact that these don't catch on gives implicit support for the "grammatical pull" of the underlying structure around which they orbit.

Of sweethearts, tarts, and stereotypes

Sweetheart originally referred to a sweet or sugar cake in the shape of a heart and was then applied metaphorically to a lover. It is of course now used not only without any suggestion of WOMAN AS DESSERT but also even to refer to a man (although never to refer to a dessert). Captain Francis Grose saw fit to include the expression in his *Classical Dictionary of the Vulgar Tongue*:

> SWEET HEART A term applicable to either the masculine or feminine gender, signifying a girl's lover, or a man's mistress. ([1796] 1992:332)

Notice the lexical asymmetry in the pairs *girl/man* and *lover/mistress*, which shows that just because a word is applicable to both women and men doesn't mean it carries the same connotations in actual use (a classic example of asymmetry is given by

Robin Lakoff with reference to the term *professional* [1975:30]). The sexual sense of *sweetheart* has been so thoroughly displaced over the past hundred years by the rhyming slang [*jam*] *tart* that many speakers of English, including sympathetic readers of this chapter, find it literally incredible that such a synchronically innocuous endearment could really be related to such a highly charged epithet. The evidence, however, is overwhelming (see, among others, Franklyn 1975:82; Holder 1989:178; Mills 1989:235; *Oxford English Dictionary* 1989, s.v. "sweetheart," "tart"; Wilkes 1990:326). *Sweetheart* is even listed as a synonym for *tart* by one source (Farmer & Henley [1890–1904] 1965(5):80). This shift in meaning is an example of what McConnell-Ginet has called "language use [which] can enter into the transmission and preservation of attitudes and values that are seldom explicitly articulated," even those "that have long since been rejected at a conscious level" (1980:7–8).

These attitudes include stereotypes of female promiscuity (as in *crumpet*), procurability (as in *piece of cake*), and the part/whole metonymy of referring to a woman by her genitals (as in *cherry pie*). Hugh Rawson notes, "the use of the same word for both [a woman and her genitalia] is common. Others with this double meaning include . . . *bit, bunny, . . . cookie, . . . piece, . . . snatch, . . . tail,* and *twat*" (1989:315; see also Sutton 1995). Peripheral terms that exploit this relationship include *pink taco, split apricot,* and *knish* (literally, Yiddish for 'dumpling', but slang for 'vagina' [Rosten 1992:276]).

A final semantic point worth savoring: Why fruits and baked goods? Why not, for instance, frozen desserts? (The only exception to this feature requirement is *crumpet*, which speakers seem to be treating as an essentially baked item that here happens to be modified [cooked on a griddle]; we do not find the otherwise parallel **scone* used of women.) A possible answer is suggested by Adrienne Lehrer: "The semantic distinction is that baking refers to the preparation of cakes . . . and other things which are sold in bakeries and prepared by professional bakers. Cooking refers to the preparation of most other kinds of food" (1969:41). This corresponds nicely with the inescapable conflation of WOMAN AS DESSERT and WOMAN AS PROSTITUTE: both kinds of *tart* can be sold in specialty shops, and both can be prepared by "professionals," in the sense that a pimp or madam grooms his or her girls. A tart or cookie purchased in a shop can be entirely consumed there with few or no dishes and utensils to clean up, just as a man can have sex with a prostitute in a brothel or a hotel and then return home with few or no domestic complications. The extensions *cakeshop* (Australian) and *tart shop* (British), meaning 'brothel', and *cake eater* (ladies' man) rely on this correspondence, which also complements the metaphors for lust described by George Lakoff: THE OBJECT OF LUST IS FOOD and LUST IS HEAT (1987:409–410). Such cross-domain structural coherence allows the perception of similarity, so that women as heated desserts can be easily seen as the objects of lust.

As has been well documented (R. Lakoff 1975; Penelope 1977; Schulz 1975), any word for a woman can, in the right context, mean 'prostitute' (from *abbess* and *actress* to *lady* and *woman*); it is as though any woman could, in the right context, be a prostitute (a recent example from popular culture is the movie *Indecent Proposal*, in which Robert Redford pays one million dollars to sleep with Demi Moore, playing Woody Harrelson's wife; the payment of the money to the husband/pimp rather than the wife underlines the metaphorical point).[7] As John Farmer and William Henley note in the entry for *tart* in their seven-volume *Slang and Its Analogues*, "The distinction between Woman, Wife, Concubine, Mistress, Harlot, and Bawd is very loosely observed, in literary and popular usage, both in English and French" ([1890–1904] 1965(5):77).

Formal promiscuity and syntactic depersonalization

Selectional restrictions further reinforce the stereotype of promiscuity: A *slice* or *piece* of the mass nouns *pie* or *cake* implies a remainder, and a single serving of a *cupcake* or a *tartlet* implies the batch. Put simply, desserts are made to be shared. Thus not only are women grammatically objectified, reduced to mere syntactic objects, but also they are depersonalized, robbed of their uniqueness: One piece of *cheesecake* or one *cookie* is very much like another. Some illustrations of this point: *Next time you make a pie, will you give me a piece?* is a Canadian expression for "a male hint to a girl that she should sexually co-operate with him" (Partridge 1986:215), and *Everybody in town has had a slice of her* is from a definition of *slice* in *Playboy's Book of Forbidden Words*, to which is added: "An intrigue with a married woman. . . . The origin is probably the old proverb that 'a slice off a cut loaf is not missed.' This may explain the odd imagery in piece, piece of ass, piece of tail" (Wilson 1972:266).

The confluence of violent slicing in one domain and sexual consumption in another is made more logically acceptable by the systematic coherence of metaphors for anger and lust in English, the most common example of which is the ambiguous word *mad* (and see Caputi 1991; Johnson 1987; G. Lakoff 1987). This syntactic depersonalization is compounded by the frequent use of the modifier *little*, as in *my little croissant*, *little honeydip*, and *little marzipan confection*, which blurs the line between diminution and derogation.

Lexical domain overlap

The use of words from the same lexical field to talk about both desserts and women-considered-sexually provides another link between the domains. A *cupcake* and a woman can each be described as *decadent, an indulgence, inviting, luscious, mouth-watering, seductive, sinful, tasty, voluptuous*, and so on. A classic eloquent expression of this mixture of lust and distrust is Alexandre Dumas's provocative introduction to his *Dictionary of Cuisine*, wherein he writes of "the appetite roused at the end of a meal when, after normal hunger has been satisfied by the main courses, and the guest is truly ready to rise without regret, a delicious dish holds him to the table with a final tempting of his sensuality" ([1873] 1958:13).

Similarly, the verb *to tart (up)*, meaning 'to make oneself more attractive', draws on both the literal and figurative senses of 'tart' and "clearly reflects a view that prostitutes—and possibly all women—deceive by dressing to give the impression of quality which does not underlie an attractive exterior" (Mills 1989:235).

Phonetic considerations

A final correspondence that merits further study is the shared phonetic shape of these metaphoric expressions. There is an overwhelming tendency for each of the central terms to begin each stressed syllable with one of the three possible English voiceless stops, /p/, /t/, or /k/ (as in *pumpkin* [*pie*], *tart*, *cookie*); terms such as **gingerbread*, **scone*, and **sherbet* do not occur with this meaning, and occurring terms that violate this sound-symbolic pattern either do not catch on (*?biscuit*, *?golden doughnut*, *?sweet-potato-pie*), are fanciful coinages (*baby cake(s)*, *cinnamon girl*, *sweet thing*), or are not typical dessert foods (*gum drop*, *lollipop*, *muffin*). The only exception is the somewhat syntactically odd *cheesecake*, which begins with the voiceless palato-alveolar affricate /č/—a common element in diminutives and pet names in what Yakov Malkiel calls "a wide variety of by no means closely related languages" (1990:159; see also de Reuse 1986); even the peripheral terms show an unusual preponderance of initial stops (*baby cake*, *biscuit*, *buttered bun*, [*love*] *cake*, *cream puff*, *croissant*, *cutie pie*, *dumpling*, etc.). There is also strong pressure to conform to the monolexemic prototype, so that *punkin* appears for *pumpkin pie* and *pastry* for *a tasty bit of pastry*. (These correspondences have been italicized in (1) in the appendix.)

Of course, dessert terms for women must be drawn from the preselected lexical set of all dessert terms, so it could be argued that these phonetic correspondences, if they say anything at all, say more about a linguistically encoded attitude toward sweet foods than toward women—if there were not other terms available that are *not* used. Consider the phonetically incorrect but semantically plausible set {**brownie*, **gingerbread*, **gingersnap*, **scone*, **shortbread*, **shortcake*}, for which I have not found a single citation to describe women-as-sex-objects.[8]

Although the phonetic pattern is inescapable, it is not as inexplicable as it first appears. One motivation may be the frequent association in English between syllable-initial voiceless stops (/p/, /t/, and /k/) and diminutive, trivial, or feminine things, as in the contrasting end-of-scale pairs /p/*uny* versus /b/*ig*, /t/*iny* versus /d/*eep*, /c/*ute* versus /gr/*eat*. Admittedly, the case is circumstantial, and counterexamples will be easy to find, since this is a tendency rather than an absolute rule. However, as John Lawler wrote of the contrasting assonance pair /br-/ and /pr-/, as in *broad* and *prude*, *bray* and *pray*, *brute* and *prig*: "What is fascinating about the social terms [beginning with /br-/] is that they are so diametrically opposed in register to the roles exemplified in [terms beginning with /pr-/] (both of which are one-dimensional categories). One is tempted to look at this as a sociosemantic version of Grimm's Law, with the devoicing of the stop cluster an iconic representation of "devoicing" of the social connotations of the role stereotypes" (1990:37). He notes that /br-/ words "tend to represent aspects of female cultural stereotypes that go back to our rustic Germanic origins. The image of a bride in braids, brewing broth and breeding brats, is hard to avoid"(1990:34). A near-minimal pair in the present data illustrating a similar point is the (voiced) male *beefcake* and the (voiceless) female *cheesecake*.

Interacting linguistic levels: Phonosemantics

It is tempting to dismiss these phonetic features as coincidental—dessert terms not used for women could already have been blocked at the semantic level (**hot fudge sundae*, **pudding*, and **souffle*, for example, are not usually subject to slicing into discrete pieces). However, it turns out that the interplay of linguistic levels motivates the use of *cake* but not the equally phonetically correct **custard*, which fails on semantic grounds, and of *cupcake* but not the morphologically comparable **shortcake*, which does not match the phonetic profile. In other words, matching either (but not both) the phonetic or semantic profile is a necessary but not sufficient criterion for central category membership: *Cream puff* and *cutie pie* fail the semantic test, while *angel food* and *muffin* fail phonetically. Fanciful extensions such as *chocolate bunny*, *love cake*, and *sugar dumpling* are not constrained by the phonetic pattern, whereas terms that name real desserts, such as *cupcake*, *(cherry) pie*, and *tart*, overwhelmingly are. (Appropriately, *sweetheart* belongs with the extensions, having transferred both its pejorative and dessert connotations to the phonetically correct rhyming slang, [*jam*] *tart*.) Particularly noteworthy is the nonappearance of the semantically ideal but phonetically bad **brown Betty*, **Charlotte*, **crepes Suzette*, and **madeleine*, desserts named after women. This distinction is paralleled by that between the edible and the appetizing, between *buttered bun* and *pumpkin (pie)*, as nicely illustrated by a suggestive entry in a seventeenth-century book of proverbs: "I love thee like pudding, if thou wert pie I'de eat thee" (Ray's *English Proverbs*, quoted in Browning 1982:384).

Lexical ambiguity and psycholinguistics

Because much sexism is encoded in language, forming part of the background, there is a great deal of plausible deniability available to speakers (as in the indignant retort that serves as the title of Deborah Tannen's 1986 bestseller on conversational style, *That's Not What I Meant!*). Psycholinguistics gives us a way of measuring what Roland Barthes termed the "second-order memory," or inheritance, of language, and studies have provided quantifiable evidence for this elusive phenomenon, demonstrating that all meanings of an ambiguous word are initially activated by a listener; Patrizia Tabossi writes that activation takes place "regardless of [the word's] context of occurrence . . . context intervenes in selecting the appropriate interpretation of the lexical item only subsequently" (1988:324; see her bibliography for numerous studies confirming these results). Further, Tabossi cites a lexical-decision experiment by W. Onifer and D. A. Swinney (1981) on sentences that bias dominant meanings of ambiguous words, which found that "neither dominance nor context affects the initial activation of a word, whose access is an autonomous subprocess of the process of language comprehension" (Tabossi 1988:325). With respect to this chapter, this means that calling a woman a *tart* summons images of an edible, sweet, possessable *object*—even though we may later reject that meaning in favor of the figurative sense of 'loose woman', not just in deliberate double-entendres such as (1) but even in sentences that seem contextually unambiguous, such as (2):

(1)   Boy, I'd like to get some of *that* tart for dessert! (Said as a waitress displays a dessert tray.)

(2)   Many people dismiss Madonna as a tart.

In other words, metaphoric expressions are loaded with implications, including some that work subliminally. As Robin Lakoff put it in the opening sentence of *Language and Woman's Place*, "Language uses us as much as we use language" (1975:1).

Conclusion

The WOMAN AS DESSERT metaphor is alive and well; witness the birth announcement I received for a child born February 2, 1998, "The bun is done"; the reference to political gadfly Arianna Huffington as "the Greek Pudding" (*New Yorker*, April 13, 1998:40); the press muffins of *Primary Colors* (Anonymous [Klein] 1996); and the description of actor Goldie Hawn's image "morph[ing] . . . overnight from puff pastry to clever cookie" (*Vanity Fair*, January 1997:118).

Idioms such as *piece of cake* and *easy as pie* are now "dead metaphors," and as such are unlikely to trigger unconscious associations, for all that they once carried double meanings (*piece*, *cake*, *easy*, and *pie*, of course, appearing alone, are subject to the same ambiguity as *tart* or *cookie*). Similarly, *sweetheart* is synchronically unambiguous: It bears no hint today of its dessert origins or former illicit connotations. I have traced the history of these expressions, as well as the more transparently objectionable *cheesecake*, *crumpet*, and *tart*, because I wanted to reveal the systematic pattern of the WOMAN AS DESSERT metaphor, which suggests, in Julia Penelope's phrase, "a paradigm of the definition of women in our culture" (1977:316). Awareness of the underlying cognitive metaphors by which thought and language are coconstructed at least brings this "metaphoric derogation of women" to a conscious level, an essential starting point if we are ever to begin rebaking the pie.

APPENDIX

Lexical Items

(1) WOMAN AS DESSERT
(*piece* of) cake
*cheese*cake (cf. *beefcake* 'sexy man')
cookie
*crump*et
*cup*cake
(a *tasty* bit of) *pastry* (du jour)
(*cherry*) *pie*
*pound*cake
pumpkin (*pie*, *tart*), *punkin*
[*jam*] *tart* ← sweetheart*
tartlet/*tart*lette

(2) ELABORATIONS; AS . . .
(a) . . . TOOTHSOME OBJECTS
angel cake
angel food
available jelly [roll]
baby cake(s)*
biscuit (*cookie* in Brit. usage)
brown sugar ('sexy black woman')
bunny cakes
buttered bun

chocolate bunny
cinnamon girl
cream puff
croissant
cutie pie
dumpling
fortune cookie ('sexy Asian woman')
golden doughnut
gooseberry pudding†
gum drop
honeybun(ches)* honeydip, honeypie*
hot chocolate ('sexy black woman')
hot tamale
jelly roll*
knish ('vagina' in Yiddish slang)
little honeydip
little marzipan confection
lollipop
love cake
meringue
muffin (cf. *studmuffin* 'sexy man')
pancake
pink taco
press muffin ('sexy female reporter')

pudding
sugar doughnut
sugar dumpling
sugar pie, sugar-pie-honey-bun
sugar plum
sweet chocolate ('sexy black woman')
sweetie (pie)*
sweet-potato-pie*
sweets, sweetness
sweetmeat
sweet thing/thang
tootsie roll

(b)   . . . FRUITS/SWEET SPREADS
apple
apples ('breasts')
banana ('sexy mulatto woman')
berry
cantaloupes ('breasts')
casabas ('breasts')
cherry, pop/lose one's cherry
cherrylets, cherries ('nipples')
fig, split fig
grapefruits ('breasts')
honey (pot)*
jam (pot)
jelly (bag)
kumquat
lemons ('breasts', esp. small ones)
melons ('breasts')
peach(es)
plum (cf. [wrinkled old] prune 'woman past her prime')
raspberries ('nipples')
split apricot
(straw)berry ('woman who sells sex for drugs', esp. crack)
strawberries ('nipples')
(hot) tomato
Venus's honeypot
Watermelons ('large breasts')

(c)   . . . MISCELLANEOUS
bit (on a fork, of jam)
bite
coffeehouse, coffee-shop
creamie
dish*

easy,* easy as pie
fancy piece
juicy ('sexually aroused woman')
just-from-the-oven freshness
morsel
next time you bake a pie, will you give me a piece?
piece (of cake, cut yourself a piece of poontang)
ripe (for the picking)
slice, everybody in town has had a slice of her
snack, snatch
treat

(3)   EXTENSIONS
baking muffins ('having sex with a woman')
be in the Pudding Club ('be pregnant')
cake eater ('ladies' man')
cakeshop ('brothel' [Australian])
cherry orchard ('girls' dorm')
cherry pipe ('sexually aroused woman'; rhyming slang for 'ripe')
cherry picker ('man who desires young girls')
cherry splitter ('penis')
cut the cake ('deflower a virgin')
frosting ('makeup')
have a bun in the oven ('be pregnant')
honey shots (revealing photos of female athletes or spectators)
hot roll with cream ('copulation')
gooseberry ranch† ('brothel')
muffin hunting ('looking for sex' [said of men])
shake a tart ('have sex with a woman')
sugar hill ('brothel')
sugar up one's lips ('wear makeup' [Jamaican English])
tart shop ('brothel' [Brit.])
tart up (verb) ('dress up, fancy up')

(4)   MEN AS TOOTHSOME OBJECTS
beefcake
chocolate twinkie ('black man's penis')
fruit loops ('gay man')
studmuffin

*Can sometimes be used of a man, but usually of a woman
†obsolete

NOTES

Earlier versions of this chapter were presented at the Third Berkeley Women and Language Conference and the First Conceptual Structure, Discourse, and Language Conference in San Diego and are published in the conference proceedings (Hines 1994, 1996a); I am grateful to those audiences for stimulating comments and questions. Thanks also to the many friends and colleagues who provided essential encouragement, references, and patience, among them Suzanne Fleischman, Thomas Scovel, Eve Sweetser, Mark Turner, Rachelle Waksler, and especially Julia Williams. The editors of this volume made wonderful suggestions for expanding and clarifying the original paper; thank you, Mary, Anita, and Laurel. Finally, this chapter could not have been written without the help of Sherry Hines, my mother and chief research assistant, who first gave me a reprint of Captain Francis Grose's *A Classical Dictionary of the Vulgar Tongue*, wherein I learned the history of *sweet heart*.

1. I am indebted to G. Lakoff and Johnson (1980), especially chapter 22, on "the creation of similarity," for the scaffolding on which this analysis is built, although the conclusions drawn herein are entirely my own.

2. In contrast, notice that food terms for men tend to be image-schematic metaphors for the penis ([*vienna*] *sausage, tube steak, wiener*), which, unlike nonfood terms (*dick, prick, wanker*) are not used metonymically to refer to a man (**he's a real (vienna) sausage/*tube steak/*wiener*—see Cameron 1992 for additional examples). These are semantically consistent with the stereotype of men as virile, central, and important. The one apparent exception is the curious coinage *chocolate twinkie* 'a black man's penis'; like *beefcake* and *studmuffin* for a sexy man, this compound subverts the metaphor it is supposedly built on by prefixing an actual dessert term with a modifier that destroys its credibility (although Twinkies are available at any convenience store, *chocolate twinkies* no longer exist outside this metaphor).

3. The only citation I could find in which a straight man is called a *tart* is in an article about Rod Stewart, where the fading rock star and sex symbol is called "the Hollywood tart, the definite parody, the saddest poseur" (*St. Petersburg Times*, May 10, 1996:D5). Promiscuous gay men are also sometimes called *tarts*. Another example of a gender-specific term is *tootsie roll*, which in this form is unambiguously female; clipped to *tootsie*, it may ostensibly be used of either sex (as in the name of the 1982 movie starring Dustin Hoffman in drag).

4. My thanks to Leanne Hinton for allowing me access to the Linguistics 55 data for the spring and fall semesters of 1993 and 1994 (an update to the data used in Sutton 1992).

5. For now, see James Valentine (1997) and Michael J. Sweet (1997).

6. For further discussion of feminist approaches to what is known as the Sapir-Whorf hypothesis, or "linguistic relativity," see Anna Livia (chapter 17, this volume). Both Edward Sapir and Benjamin Lee Whorf are highly readable; a good introduction is Whorf's essay "Science and Linguistics," with its well-known statement that

> We dissect nature along lines laid down by our native languages. The categories and types that we isolate from the world of phenomena we do not find there because they stare every observer in the face; on the contrary, the world is presented in a flux of impressions which has to be organized by our minds—and this means largely by the linguistic systems in our minds. We cut nature up, organize it into concepts, and ascribe significances as we do, largely because we are parties to an agreement to organize it in this way—an agreement that holds throughout our speech community and is codified in the patterns of our language. The agreement is, of course, an implicit and unstated one, *but its terms are absolutely obligatory*; we cannot talk at all except by subscribing to the organization and classification of data which the agreement decrees. . . . We are thus introduced to a new principle of rela-

tivity, which holds that all observers are not led by the same physical evidence to the same picture of the universe, unless their linguistic backgrounds are similar, or can in some way be calibrated. (1956:213–214)

7. This entailment makes people uncomfortable; for example, a male reader of an earlier version of this chapter protested that the DESSERT metaphor is not meant to apply to *all* women but merely to certain women, an objection that misses the fundamental insight that calling any woman a *tart* automatically places all women in the category of potential *tarts,* for no woman is an island.

8. In the wildly popular 1946 Frank Capra movie *It's a Wonderful Life,* Jimmy Stewart calls his little daughter *gingersnap* (not *cookie* or *cupcake*), which illustrates and reinforces this phonetic distinction.

REFERENCES

Dictionaries and Word Sources

Anonymous [Joe Klein] (1996). *Primary colors.* New York: Random House.

Browning, D. C. (1982). *The Everyman dictionary of quotation and proverbs.* London: Chancellor Press.

Cameron, Deborah (1992). Naming of parts: Gender, culture, and terms for the penis among American college students. *American Speech* 67(4):367–382.

Dillard, J. L. (1977). *Lexicon of Black English.* New York: Seabury Press.

Dumas, Alexandre (1958). *Dictionary of cuisine.* Trans., abridg., & ed. Louis Colman. New York: Avon. (Original work published 1873)

Farmer, John S., & William Ernest Henley (eds.) (1965). *Slang and its analogues.* 3 vols. New York: Kraus Reprint. (Original work published 1890–1904)

Franklyn, Julian (1975). *A dictionary of rhyming slang.* London: Routledge & Kegan Paul.

Grose, Francis (1992). *A classical dictionary of the vulgar tongue.* Ed. Eric Partridge. New York: Dorset Press. (Original work published 1796)

Holder, R. W. (1989). *The Faber dictionary of euphemisms.* Rev. ed. London: Faber & Faber.

Jacobson, John D. (1993). *Eatioms.* New York: Laurel.

Lighter, Jonathan Evan (ed.) (1994). *Random House historical dictionary of American slang.* Vol. 1. New York: Random House.

Major, Clarence (1994). *Juba to jive: The dictionary of African-American slang.* New York: Penguin.

Mills, Jane (1989). *Womanwords: A dictionary of words about women.* New York: Henry Holt.

Oxford English dictionary (1989). Ed. John A. Simpson & Edmund S. C. Weiner. 2nd ed. Oxford: Oxford University Press.

Partridge, Eric (1984). *Partridge's dictionary of slang and unconventional English.* Ed. Paul Beale. London: Routledge & Kegan Paul.

——— (ed.) (1986). *A dictionary of catch phrases.* New York: Stein & Day.

Rawson, Hugh (1989). *Wicked words.* New York: Crown.

Richter, Alan (1995). *Sexual slang.* New York: Harper & Row.

Rosten, Leo (1992). *The joys of Yinglish.* New York: Signet.

Spears, Richard A. (1981). *Slang and euphemism.* New York: Jonathan David.

Sutton, Laurel A. (1995). Bitches and skankly hobags: The place of women in contemporary slang. In Kira Hall & Mary Bucholtz (eds.), *Gender articulated: Language and the socially constructed self.* New York: Routledge, 279–296.

Todasco, Ruth (1973). *An intelligent woman's guide to dirty words.* Chicago: Loop Center YWCA.

Wentworth, Harold, & Stuart Berg Flexner (1975). *Dictionary of American slang.* 2nd supp. ed. New York: Thomas Y. Crowell.

Wilkes, G. A. (1990). *A dictionary of Australian colloquialisms.* Sydney, Australia: Sydney University Press.

Wilson, Robert A. (ed.) (1972). *Playboy's book of forbidden words.* Chicago: Playboy Press.

General

Barthes, Roland (1968). *Writing degree zero.* Trans. Annette Lavers & Colin Smith. New York: Hill & Wang. (Original work published 1953)

Cameron, Deborah (1985). *Feminism and linguistic theory.* London: Macmillan.

Caputi, Jane (1991). The metaphors of radiation, or, Why a beautiful woman is like a nuclear power plant. *Women's Studies International Forum* 14(5):423–442.

de Reuse, Willem (1986). The lexicalization of sound symbolism in Santiago del Estero Quechua. *International Journal of American Linguistics* 52(1):54–64.

Dundes, Alan (1980). The crowing hen and the Easter Bunny. In Dundes, *Interpreting folklore.* Bloomington: Indiana University Press, 160–175.

Ehrlich, Susan, & Ruth King (1994). Feminist meanings and the (de)politicization of the lexicon. *Language in Society* 23:59–76.

Gentner, Dedre, & Jonathan Grudin (1985). The evolution of mental metaphors in psychology: A ninety-year retrospective. *American Psychologist* 40:181–192.

Herrmann, Claudine (1989). *The tongue snatchers.* Trans. Nancy Kline. Lincoln: University of Nebraska Press. (Original work published 1976)

Hines, Caitlin (1994). "Let me call you sweetheart": The WOMAN AS DESSERT metaphor. In Mary Bucholtz, A. C. Liang, Laurel A. Sutton, & Caitlin Hines (eds.), *Cultural performances: Proceedings of the Third Berkeley Women and Language Conference.* Berkeley, CA: Berkeley Women and Language Group, 295–303.

——— (1996a). What's so easy about pie?: The lexicalization of a metaphor. In Adele Goldberg (ed.), *Conceptual structure, discourse, and language.* Stanford: Center for the Study of Language and Information, 189–200.

——— (1996b). Lexicalization and the metaphorical woman. Master's thesis, San Francisco State University.

Hughes, Geoffrey (1991). *Swearing: A social history of foul language, oaths, and profanity in English.* Oxford: Blackwell.

Johnson, Mark (1987). *The body in the mind.* Chicago: University of Chicago Press.

Kramarae, Cheris, & Paula A. Treichler (1990). *A feminist dictionary.* London: Pandora.

Lakoff, George (1987). *Women, fire, and dangerous things.* Chicago: University of Chicago Press.

Lakoff, George, Jane Espenson, & Alan Schwartz (1991). *Master metaphor list.* 2nd ed. Berkeley, CA: Cognitive Linguistics Group.

Lakoff, George, & Mark Johnson (1980). *Metaphors we live by.* Chicago: University of Chicago Press.

Lakoff, Robin (1975). *Language and woman's place.* New York: Harper & Row.

Lawler, John (1990). Women, men, and bristly things: The phonosemantics of the *BR-* assonance in English. *Michigan Working Papers in Linguistics* (Winter):27–38.

Lehrer, Adrienne (1969). Semantic cuisine. *Journal of Linguistics* 5(1):39–55.

Malkiel, Yakov (1990). *Diachronic problems in phonosymbolism.* Amsterdam: John Benjamins.

McConnell-Ginet, Sally (1980). Linguistics and the feminist challenge. In Sally McConnell-Ginet, Ruth Borker, & Nelly Furman (eds.), *Women and language in literature and society.* New York: Praeger, 3–25.

Onifer, W., & D. A. Swinney (1981). Accessing lexical ambiguities during sentence comprehension: Effects of frequency of meaning and contextual bias. *Memory and Cognition* 9:225–236.

Penelope Stanley, Julia (1977). Paradigmatic woman: The prostitute. In David L. Shores & Carol P. Hines (eds.), *Papers in language variation: The SAMLA-ADS collection.* University: University of Alabama Press, 303–321.

———— (1990). *Speaking freely: Unlearning the lies of the fathers' tongues.* London: Routledge.

Rhodes, Richard A., & John Lawler (1981). Athematic metaphors. In Carrie S. Masek, Roberta A. Hendrick, & Mary Frances Miller (eds.), *Papers from the Seventeenth Regional Meeting of the Chicago Linguistic Society.* Chicago: Chicago Linguistic Society.

Schulz, Muriel R. (1975). The semantic derogation of women. In Barrie Thorne & Nancy Henley (eds.), *Language and sex: Difference and dominance.* Rowley, MA: Newbury House, 64–75.

Spender, Dale (1980). *Man made language.* London: Routledge.

Sweet, Michael J. (1997). Talking about *feygelekh*: A queer male representation in Jewish American speech. In Anna Livia & Kira Hall (eds.), *Queerly phrased: Language, gender, and sexuality.* New York: Oxford University Press, 115–126.

Tabossi, Patrizia (1988). Accessing lexical ambiguity in different types of sentential contexts. *Journal of Memory and Language* 5(27):324–340.

Tannen, Deborah (1986). *That's not what I meant!* New York: Morrow.

Valentine, James (1997). Pots and pans: Identification of queer Japanese in terms of discrimination. In Anna Livia & Kira Hall (eds.), *Queerly phrased: Language, gender, and sexuality.* New York: Oxford University Press, 95–114.

Whorf, Benjamin Lee (1956). Science and linguistics. In John P. Carroll (ed.), *Language, thought, and reality: Selected writings of Benjamin Lee Whorf.* Cambridge, MA: MIT Press, 207–219. (Original work published 1940)

All Media Are Created Equal

Do-It-Yourself Identity in Alternative Publishing

I don't know, I think I would have to do this zine even if nobody read it, just to get this shit off my chest.
—Cristina, *Queen of the Thundercats* 2 (1995:1)

The medium is the message.
—Marshall McLuhan (1964:7)

In a world where weekly magazines provide the answers to life's questions, where movies provide role models and television is often a babysitter, the message of media is no longer optional. Identity—especially women's identity, which in Western culture is so often framed as "other" (cf. Morgan, chapter 1, and Sawin, chapter 12, this volume)—is a mosaic made up of bits and pieces of the self stolen from media that pervade every waking hour of our lives.

If the medium is the message, why has it taken linguists so long to receive it? Sociolinguistics has, until recently, relied almost exclusively on data collected in the traditional way: tape-recorded (or, more recently, videotaped) conversations and interviews with naive subjects. But this is certainly a narrow view of what linguists can and should use as data, a view bound by tradition and a lingering distrust of the popular press. Why is one channel of transmission more acceptable than another? Who determines what media are taken seriously in linguistics and in society?

Being taken seriously is a problem women still face. Despite some shifts toward greater representation (Cotter, chapter 19, this volume), women's voices are still the exception rather than the rule in mass-media outlets, and media targeted at women run heavily toward advice on dieting, cosmetics, sex, and shopping (Bucholtz, chapter 18, this volume). This kind of discourse is considered by the patriarchy to be lightweight, frivolous, and nonthreatening—and, until recently, it was thought to be unworthy of academic attention. If a woman finds that the only way to express "dangerous" thoughts that fall outside this realm is to put Selectric to paper (or the electronic equivalent) and publish it herself, who will hear her voice?

In this chapter, I call for the inclusion of new forms of expression in the analytic corpus, a move that has been initiated in large part by researchers of language and gender (e.g., Cameron 1995; Talbot 1995). Especially for young and marginalized members of a speech community, identity is largely shaped through images of themselves shown in movies, television, magazines, and music; in response, their voices may reproduce or subvert deeply ingrained stereotypes (Barrett, chapter 16; Coates, chapter 6; Hines, chapter 7, this volume). Exposure of the self through media is one path in the construction of an identity, and it is especially meaningful to those who see around them a dearth of examples on which to pattern their own narratives (cf. Leap, chapter 13, this volume). Creating a record of experience thrusts the creator into the public eye as she reveals her "self," a risky business even under the best of publishing conditions. To self-publish—which can mean performing every aspect of production literally by hand—is to leave every aspect of the self open to praise or ridicule.

I call attention to two types of emerging media in which authors control their creations completely: zines and on-line journals. These avenues of expression are often characterized by nonstandard vocabulary and spelling, haphazard narrative lines, unfinished thoughts, unanswered questions, and (in print) a jarring mix of hand-printed verse, cut-and-pasted newspaper headlines, defaced advertisements, and sometimes even confetti. Their authors' voices exist outside the mainstream, speaking to each other and to themselves. Through their words we may catch a glimpse of the future of identity.

New media and the masses

> i'm talking to, primarily, white, middle-class, teenage punx who have been exposed to feminism, healthy rebellion, etc. i want the cheerleaders at my old skool to be exposed to girl power. they need it b/c one of them had to run away from home last week b/c her brother was beating her and b/c they don't even know they experience sexism every day.
> —Zoë, *pixxiebitch* 5 (1995:3)

Linguistic analysis of written texts has its own tradition (e.g., Livia, chapter 17, this volume), and queer, feminist, and other politically progressive studies have been responsible for groundbreaking research on the language of movies, television, and mass media (e.g., Creekmur & Doty 1995; Faludi 1991; Hall, Hobson, Lowe, & Willis 1980). Yet, until very recently, there have been few studies in the field of language and gender written from a (socio)linguistic viewpoint that use nontraditional data—and specifically mass-media data.

Why is this the case? Clearly it is not lack of access nor indeed lack of data; it is certainly not because sociolinguistic theory has nothing to say about mass media.[1] Rather, it is because the types of media cited here—television, movies, magazines—simply are not a very good source of linguistically relevant data as that concept has been traditionally defined. They are, at best, a third- or fourth-generation copy of the kind of discourse that reveals cognitive processes, interaction strategies, and identity construction—the soul of classic sociolinguistic research on gender. Mainstream media are almost exclusively preplanned, committee-produced, and carefully packaged to please the greatest number of consumers. As a linguistic resource, it tells us much about how we are supposed to sound rather than how we actually do sound, a situation that is perfect for a deconstruction of patriarchal values but of very little use in analyzing idiolects.

The linguist must tread especially carefully when using mass-media data in language and gender research. The difficulty lies in separating the artifice of the author(s) from the art: that is, we should never mistake the reproduction for the original. An elegant (and very funny) example is Kira Hall and Beth Daniels's (1992) examination of portrayals of female psychoanalysts in films. On the whole, feminist scholars have accomplished this kind of dissection admirably, commenting on the crafted language of media as well as the intentions behind the language (see Caldas-Coulthard 1995; Patthey-Chavez & Youmans 1992; Talbot 1995). More interaction-based approaches are illustrated in this volume by the work of Mary Bucholtz on callers and hosts on the shopping channel and by Colleen Cotter on women in Irish-language radio. But in addition to established industries of print, film, and broadcasting, there is a new source of data: what are coming to be known as *alternative media.*

In the late twentieth century, control of generally accessible ("mainstream") media has become concentrated in the hands of a few powerful billion-dollar corporations. The content of network and most cable television is controlled almost entirely by its advertisers; storylines and characters are quickly changed or dropped if an advertiser threatens to pull commercial time. Book publishers measure success by the number of units sold, not by the critical acclaim accorded individual authors. Mainstream magazines, too, are virtual slaves to their advertising dollars, to the politics of their holding corporations, and to the corporate culture that produces them. Bound as they are by these constraints, mainstream media make it their business to appeal to everyone and offend no one.

In contrast, anything outside the mainstream could be considered "alternative." But these efforts require funding and organizational skills beyond the capacity of any single person: They are the product of the many, not the one, and are therefore too linguistically diluted to reveal much to the researcher of language and identity. (Even essays or columns written by a single person are usually edited and revised before publication.) This is the unique feature of alternative media: They represent the words and thoughts of an individual who is solely responsible for their expression. Whereas mass media concern themselves with constructing an implied reader as addressee in order to "assign assumed shared experiences and commonsense attitudes as givens to a mass audience" (Talbot 1995:146), the creator of alternative media produces what pleases her: She herself is the implied addressee, simultaneously constructing and observing her own identity, and her intended audience is women just like her: "Equally significant is the social position of those who speak out in this way: Like their punk rock predecessors of the 1970's, today's 'zine publishers are usually individuals who see little of their lives reflected in the pages of *Time* and *Newsweek.* The realm of modern-day 'zines exists as an arena for many marginalized populations, but perhaps for none more fittingly than feminists" (Richardson 1996:10). Whether they exist outside the mainstream by choice or by force, alternative subcultures—including class-, ethnicity-, gender-, and sexual orientation–based communities of practice (Eckert & McConnell-Ginet 1992)—cannot express themselves fully within mass media. Their values and priorities may be different; their thoughts and experiences certainly are, and the very words used to express them (profanity, slang, dysphemism) would not be palatable to the corporate culture of advertisers.[2]

This divide can be illustrated through a comparison of a mainstream on-line publication, News Corp.'s *iGuide*, and a woman-produced on-line alternative journal, *Words of the Tyrtle*. *iGuide* was conceived and produced as a magazine-like Web site, divided into special-interest sections (TV, music, movies, sports) that contain news, features, reviews, advertisements, and links to related sites (Krantz 1996). A team of editors assigns and approves the feature stories (a normal magazine operating procedure), which are then turned over to the technical staff for design and HTML coding. Any *iGuide* text that goes out on the Internet passes through many hands before it sees electronic print. In sharp contrast, the *Words of the Tyrtle* is "a web site one hundred percent created and maintained on a daily basis by one woman: Sage Lunsford." In addition to a daily journal, the author presents material similar to that in *iGuide*: book and movie reviews, essays, and real-world news she finds interesting; she has no editor and only occasionally allows others to read her writing before it is published at the Web site. The diary ("Coffee Shakes") is posted as it is first written, in the unmistakable voice of a single author:

> When I was very young, I used to write "About The Author" blurbs about myself in preparation for the day when I'd be famous. Well, okay, who am I kidding—not only when I was very young. All throughout elementary school, junior high, high school, and even college, I wrote them, on paper and in my head. I looked through my old writings in the hopes of finding one or two to quote here, but no luck. I remember what they were like, though. "Sage Lunsford lives in Northern California. She is in fifth grade and spends most of her time alone. She loves to read and sing and watch tv. Her favorite book is The Secret Garden. She owes everything to her fourth grade teacher, Ms. Randolph." Every time my life changed I'd rewrite it. Every time I moved, every time my father got a new girlfriend, every time I had a new crush or hated a teacher, or adored a teacher, I would rewrite it. I realized the other day that for the first time I can sit down and write an About The Author that people will actually read. Now if I can only figure out which page of my web site constitutes the back flyleaf. (March 20, 1997)

Lunsford is responsible for every aspect of her publishing, an independence that would not be possible without the autonomy of her own Web site.

Because most media companies not only create content but also have a hand in its distribution, alternative voices are also physically locked out of the public sphere: Hearst owns Eastern magazine distributors; Time Warner is a content company but also a cable company; News Corp. is a content company but also a satellite company. So alternative voices must completely circumvent the established distribution (as with pirate radio), rely totally on government intervention (as with public-access television), or work to curry the favor of bookstore conglomerates and distributors (as with zines).

Zines and Web-based journals are fast becoming outlets for the voices of many who would otherwise remain silenced. There are, of course, other alternative channels of expression equally rich in data, but these forms are usefully discussed together because they are complementary in many ways, with zines representing a history of low-tech, do-it-yourself publications and communication via computers at the far end of the spectrum of newness (in time and technology). Yet these two forms of alternative media have much in common, and they have both become an important discursive space for women as they create identities within and without mass-media culture.

Gender in the equation

> remember practicing for your first kiss on your pillow? now practice your first punch/
> kick/eye gouge on it. Do not let yourself become a victim.—Courtney, *No Means No
> Now* 2 (1995:4)

Historically, women's language has been part of the private rather than the public sphere; even today, women find it difficult to publish their writing in the mainstream media. Only relatively recently have women's voices been heard in public, and although they are still a small percentage in the media world, there are at least some female politicians, authors, and performers who speak for themselves and for other women. What were once the stories of individuals are now the stories of millions.

Why is this sharing through language so important for women? Perhaps simply because the alternative is a narrative and an identity created by men and filtered through mass media. For a population whose members have been denied autobiographies for so long, it is the chance, as Robin Lakoff puts it, to "make one's 'story' coherent again—to give oneself a meaningful history by making everything fit together for the first time" (1990:63). Lakoff here is speaking of therapy; women have been practicing this "talking cure" in private for hundreds of years, through letters and diaries, without receiving the respect and affirmation that come only from public discourse. To have a public history is to be taken seriously.

But in the mass media, the author's voice is filtered through the business that supports it. In the days before cheap copying and even cheaper Internet communication, self-publishing was an option only for those with significant disposable income. Now, with the advent of easy-to-use desktop publishing, the proliferation of copy shops (and access to copiers at the workplace), and virtually programming-free Web publishing, almost anyone can self-publish and self-distribute. To make a zine, an aspiring publisher does not even need to know how to type—all that is essential is the ability to number pages correctly and use a copier. Web publishing, to be sure, requires more technical knowledge, but it is a medium that can be mastered quickly, as the exponential growth of Web sites has shown. If the author has the commitment to do it herself, she can write, design, lay out, and download files, or copy and mail her unfiltered story to the world: Her history is now public. An individual woman's voice can be heard; we can read her words and begin to know who she is.

Form and function

My analysis is based not only on the content but also on the form of alternative media. Here I refer not to the physical form, such as xeroxed pages, inclusion of art, or use of color on a Web page (although, as we shall see, that is sometimes an important component), but to the type and style of the discourse used in zines and computer-mediated communication (CMC). I propose a set of genre features common to both channels of expression. Characteristic of the genre is its flouting of H. P. Grice's (1975) conversational maxims.

Just as in oral exchanges, violations of the maxims in written discourse occur all the time. Intentional violations in the form of indirectness are often ways of reinforcing friendship and group membership and come under the heading of *flouting*—a violation of a maxim that gives rise to conversational implicature. Indirectness might be used for politeness, or self-defense, or just playfulness, aesthetic pleasure, intimacy (wit, irony, etc.).

The types of discourse I examine fit well into the category 'monologue' or, perhaps more accurately, 'soliloquy'. An author using zines and CMC as her mode of expression positions herself both as a self-constructed character who reveals her thoughts to an intended audience and as part of that audience, so that she is indeed "talking to herself." Violations of the maxims occur in ways specific to this discourse mode:

> *Exclusive use of first-person pronoun:* Although the diary-like, confessional nature of zines and CMC implies honesty, the constant use of *I* is a reminder that the audience is reading a version of events and self that is constructed by the author. The addressee can never know whether each author really is sincere or truthful. This feature violates the maxim of Quality.

> *Use of nonstandard forms:* Slang, misspellings, ungrammatical forms, and so forth, are often intentionally used to emphasize rejection of expected norms in writing and publishing and to highlight individuality. The audience, however, may find such forms obscure or ambiguous and hence a violation of the maxim of Manner.

> *Blended formats:* Each "soliloquy" may combine stylistic elements of poetry, essay, criticism, or persuasive speech. This "format hopping," although representative of the author's self-exploration, may not allow full development of a contribution in any given format and thus violates the maxim of Quantity.

> *Noncohesive subject matter:* The stream-of-consciousness narrative style used by many zine and CMC authors allows them to move from topic to topic very quickly, much like a face-to-face conversation. The decision to include (seemingly) irrelevant subject matter without conventional organization violates the maxims of both Relation and Manner.

Each genre feature may occur alone or in combination with other features. The examples I will be dealing with here all exhibit at least one feature and a few exhibit all four features.

It is important to note that these maxim violations are examples of true flouting—that is, they are *intentional* violations, crafted to provoke a response from the assumed audience. The author is at once asserting her individuality (she refuses to be bound by the accepted rules of discourse) and creating a shared community with the reader through the use of indirect communication.

Low-tech voices, high-tech voices

> Women's magazines are anxiety-based. I mean, that's why we started BUST, because if you read Mademoiselle or Cosmo, all they tell you is all the things you have to do to make yourself attractive to men. When they say "indulge yourself" they don't mean "Go out, get drunk, and sleep with whoever you want," they mean "Spend the entire day in the bath and give yourself a pedicure." Like your whole thing is about someone else.
> —Celina Hex, *BUST* 6 (1995:55)

Zines

In the past few years, there has been an explosion of—and growing mainstream interest in—the independent publications called *zines*. They have been featured in the *New York Times* (Gross 1995), *Time* (Quittner 1995), *Ms.* (Austin 1993), *Rolling Stone* (Sherrill 1994), even the *Chronicle of Higher Education* (Shea 1993) and the *Wall Street Journal* (Muto 1995). Major bookstore chains now carry a selection of zines in their periodicals sections, and a number of books on the subject have been published (Friedman 1997; Gunderloy & Janice 1992; Rowe 1997).

Although zines may seem a uniquely late-twentieth-century product, this type of independent publication has a longer history:

> These idiosyncratic, self-published titles can be traced to the small literary magazines and artsy chapbooks of the 1940s and '50s—as well as political dissension expressed in Soviet samizdat publications—but the name "zine" comes from an abbreviation of the punk-era "fanzine" (itself a corruption of "magazine," which itself dates from post-war Hollywood). . . . By 1995, *Factsheet Five*'s R. Seth Friedman was estimating the zine universe between 20,000 and 50,000 titles. (Wice & Daly 1995)

Fanzines began to grow in number during the 1960s, when like-minded fans wanted to find ways to share and discuss the works of certain authors or genres (often science fiction or comics). The "do-it-yourself" aspect of zines was further reinforced by the antiestablishment punk ethic of the 1980s, which rejected anything, from magazines to toothpaste, that was seen as imposing the standards of the larger authoritarian society.[3]

When does a publication cross the line between zine and magazine? Should we use circulation as a unit of measurement? Number of pages? Quality of paper stock? Lack of advertising? To answer "all of the above" is to begin to draw a distinction, but it is perhaps the quality and level of self-revelation that are most significant. A zine has a point of view, a desire to share something, to invite the reader into an idiosyncratic little universe. They are "distinctly not mechanical, but spontaneous; not statistically impersonal, but intensely personal . . . they are unmanipulated from above" (Wertham 1973:35). Because self-publishing is rarely rewarding financially, the zine author has a much more personal stake in the content of the publication than, for example, Rupert Murdoch does in the *New York Post*. If the paper fails, Murdoch loses some money and possibly some degree of standing in the business world; if a handwritten, "intensely personal" xeroxed zine like *Cometbus* fails, then Aaron, its author, has lost part of his identity and his life narrative. Zine authors are willing to spend huge amounts of time and money, with little or no compensation, just to speak out:

> Zine publishers create their publications because of the psychological need to produce and consolidate a sense of identity for themselves, an impulse that operates simultaneously in the Lacanian registers of the Symbolic, Imaginary, and Real . . . the zine functions as an instance of the Lacanian Borromean knot through which human subjects experience a sense of substance and self-consistency—that is, identity. The heightened sense of identity produced by this function explains the great attraction of zine publishing for so many people. (Wright 1996:137–138)

For women, particularly adolescent women, zines may serve as one of the only public places to establish an identity, to make sense of their narrative. In many ways, zines closely resemble those forms of writing to which women were restricted for so long, journals and letters; now, however, the journal is public and the letters are open.[4] Here, a woman may speak about deeply personal (and therefore political) topics such as date rape, body image, oppressive school policies, drugs, and so on. She may choose to say as much or as little as she wishes; she can tell jokes or compose poetry or fill pages with cartoons, with no one but herself to please. Sometimes the results are vapid and self-indulgent, but more often they tell a vivid story.

Often, the writing in zines (especially "perzines," or personal zines) works as a therapy session. The author tries to report to the audience about herself and her place in the world, not as packaged goals to strive for but as she lives and feels them. The structure is most often that of a soliloquy, which may begin in one place and end up somewhere else entirely; one is struck by the constant self-examination, the need to explain thoughts and behaviors, the willingness to share almost anything with the invisible audience. (By positing an audience for her soliloquy, the author constructs herself as *having* an audience, even if it is only herself.) The frequent changes in style and format reflect different aspects of the self, varying according to topic or mood; identity is constructed line by line, as the author writes, reads what she has written, then writes again in response.

In example (1), the author, a teenage girl, writes about her vacillations between strength and insecurity:

(1)

> here i stand: a whole girl with her arms wrapped around her waist. i am complete within myself. i am best on my own. but once in a while, i find myself doubting what is mine & what is coming from me . . . i make myself aware of what i'm doing & sometimes i feel the strength in myself. i make myself aware of what i'm doing & sometimes i can't push it away . . . i want you to like me. i am so afraid you won't.—Zoë, *pixxiebitch* 5 (1995:4)

Zoë begins by creating an image of herself as a "whole girl" (and exemplifies this description with a solid black, featureless drawing; see figure 8.1), "complete within myself." Such phrases imply self-reliance and empowerment. Yet in the very next line Zoë confesses that she is unsure of "what is mine" and "what is coming from me," a statement that reflects her confusion about her identity, both her inner self (*what is mine*) and her public persona (*what is coming from me*). The inner/outer dichotomy continues as she establishes a "me/them" opposition: The intensely personal diary style identifies the reader as part of the "me" group for most of the page, until the last few lines, when Zoë suddenly addresses the reader, rendering the audience other than herself, and the monologue becomes a dialogue that can be resolved only by the reader (will we like Zoë or not?).

In this excerpt, Zoë's writing displays all of the genre features proposed earlier. She uses the first-person singular throughout, firmly establishing herself as the sole author; the reader is very much aware that she is seeing Zoë through Zoë's own eyes. Nonstandard forms include instances of alternate spellings (*skool, kool*), ellipses used

here i stand: a whole girl with her arms wrapped around her waist.

i am
complete
within
myself.

i am
best
on my
own.

but once in a while, i find myself doubting what is mine & what is coming from me...

what will they think?
am i kool enough for them?
i should change that, then it won't seem like...

my parents have always encouraged me to follow my dreams. i've grown up in a home that has always taught me i can do anything & anything i do will be good.

so why, inside, do i still want everyone to nod their heads? tell me it's good enough... i'm good enough. why do i want yr approval?

did skool do this to me? did i do this to myself? was i born with self-concious genes?

i make myself aware of what i'm doing & sometimes i feel the strength in myself. i make myself aware of what i'm doing & sometimes i can't push it away.

i want you to like me. i am so afraid you don't. i want to be loved by everyone... the assholes who laugh at me when i go past... i want you to like me. i am so afraid you won't.

Figure 8.1. Page from *pixxiebitch* 5 (1995.4)

instead of periods to end sentences (five uses in figure 8.1), and the hand printing itself, a mixture of upper- and lowercase letters. Zoë's narrative begins with an illustrated statement (*here i stand: a whole girl* . . .), which is supported with the statements *i am complete within myself* and *i am best on my own.* From this essay-like beginning, Zoë shifts into something more like poetry when she asks *what will they think?:* She sets off the lines by indenting them and spacing them as if they were the chorus to a song, or they could be from a private letter (*i want you to like me*). Although one could summarize the main thought of this excerpt as "Zoë wonders why she can both feel self-reliant and also crave others' approval," Zoë's prose bounces from affirmations of strength (*anything i do will be good*) to confessions of self-doubt (*tell me i'm good enough*) to analysis of root causes (*did skool do this to me?*) to a direct plea for approval (*i want you to like me*).

Note Zoë's constant self-evaluation (*am i kool enough for them?*; *i find myself doubting*; *i make myself aware of what i'm doing*) and her expressed need for a public confirmation of her identity (*i want you to like me. i am so afraid you won't*). The entire selection is written in the present tense, which lends an air of immediacy to the essay but also has the effect of putting it outside time: Zoë's *once in a while* becomes the moment at which the reader picks up *pixxiebitch*, a moment repeated each time the words are read, regardless of the "real" Zoë's thoughts. Her frequent use of the lowercase *i* (twelve uses in this small excerpt) may allow her to write faster (an important consideration for the author of a hand-printed zine) or it may serve, along with alternative spellings like *kool* and the quasi-oxymoronic title *pixxiebitch* itself, as examples of the unconventional discourse conventions of the alternative media (see also Wood, chapter 2, this volume).[5]

Sometimes the author struggles for a way to explain herself to the imagined reading audience. The focus of example (2) is the author's perception of silence in between the words of an oral narrative, silence which may exist only in her perception. By describing it, she brings it from the realm of the imagined into reality, verifying its existence for herself as part of the audience. In trying to explain her obsession with "gaps," Amy reveals her need to understand the patchwork nature of reality, of language, and of her own narrative:

(2)

> What I do listen to, very carefully, is the space between each word . . . I listen for the gaps. The gaps are what I love. I hear one. I sit perfectly still. I stop breathing. I want so bad to hear it completely, but I can't. I can only hear the tip of it. . . . I hear a gap and then I can't listen to anyone else's story anymore. I become sick with excitement over the question of why it is here. I can't listen to anything but the stories I tell myself about the answer.—Amy Fusselman, *bunnyrabbit* 6 (1996:3)

Here again the author uses the present tense to convey the habitual nature of her thoughts: Amy is always listening for "the gaps," not just when she wrote this selection but today and tomorrow and possibly forever. Her prose exactly reflects what she describes, the short sentences forcing the reader to come to a complete stop at the end of each thought: *I hear one. I sit perfectly still. I stop breathing.* Amy trusts her readers to believe that she can hear "the space between each word" and that there is a story about "why it is here." Amy constructs herself as honest enough to confess her imperfections as a listener, describing how the gaps in conversation compel her to listen to them. In using the phrase *I become sick with excitement*, Amy recognizes her behavior as out of the ordinary, yet she does not offer any explanation or defense: It simply exists, and the audience must accept her identity as given.

Like Zoë, Amy uses *I* often (fourteen uses in this excerpt), leaving no doubt that we are in her world. Amy's prose is much closer to the standard than Zoë's, with only one ungrammatical form (*I want so bad to hear it*) among the otherwise well-formed sentences. And although Amy writes about only one topic, the "gaps" between words, she does so by describing her reactions to those silences in styles that shift from essay (*What I do listen to, very carefully . . .*) to declamatory lines that could be part of a stage performance (*I hear one. I sit perfectly still. I stop breathing*) and finally to the last line, which approaches metaphysical poetry: *I can't listen to anything but the stories I tell myself about the answer.*

As example (2) shows, zines are also a forum for metadiscourse. This focus on the effects of form is also found in example (3), in which the author, Pagan Kennedy, describes how she first constructed and then deconstructed her zine-published self. Writing about who she was (or who she thought she was) and sharing that self with the public brought an awareness of the process of becoming and of how little control she really had:

(3)

> Pagan[2] [the author's alter ego] would narrate the tale of a woman who creates a literary character with her own name and face. At first, this woman's character lives only on paper; and then one day the woman realizes that she herself has turned into her own literary creation. . . . [Later,] the woman, chastened by circumstance, learns that she is not the author of her own experience. Nor is she the one who creates her own personality: rather, it is tragedy and chance that do that. And so she begins to search for a new way to move through the world, a humbler attitude that will allow her to make peace with all she cannot control. (Kennedy 1995:182–183)

Pagan, too, prefers the present tense, despite the linear nature of her narrative and its actual occurrence in the past; the effect of the switch into the present tense, like its use in the earlier examples, is to create not vividness (cf. Schiffrin 1981; Wolfson 1979) but timelessness. In this selection, the author becomes less like the author and more like the audience by referring to herself in the third person and further depersonalizing herself as *this woman*: Pagan becomes the reader, watching herself shed an old identity (*her own literary creation*) for the new, and the reader experiences Pagan's moment of revelation (*she is not the author of her own experience*) as if it were her own. Pagan's story thus becomes every woman's story, shaped by "tragedy and chance"; she does not hold herself up as a role model or portray herself as a victim (either characterization would be inevitable in mass media, if such a story could be told at all). Instead, she tells her story in order to begin her search for a "new way to move through the world."

In contrast to Zoë and Amy, Pagan deliberately avoids the use of the first-person pronoun *I*, although the entire selection is, in fact, about a construction of herself; by

removing the subjective narrator, Pagan is asserting the objective truth of her statements. Ultimately, though, the audience knows that it is Pagan herself who is writing this passage and that the use of third-person pronouns is merely a literary device.
Pagan's writing is more carefully crafted than either Zoë's or Amy's, closer to mainstream standards in its avoidance of nonstandard grammar and spelling. And although
the format resembles, on the surface, a straightforward plot summary such as one
might find in a book review, the reader is continuously aware that Pagan is writing
about her own journey of identity construction and reconstruction; thus example (3)
reads both as a piece of reportage and as anonymous self-confession. Is the subject
matter really Pagan, the woman setting down these words, or Pagan^2, the alter ego
who wrote the zines years ago, or "this woman," the literary character who came to
life? Perhaps it is all three simultaneously, and all three women are now aspects of
Pagan's "humbler attitude."

Such texts demonstrate that zines are all about the revelation of the self. Like
therapy, some zines may be short-lived, a flurry of words to fill a void and make
sense of the moment, whereas others may publish for years, uncovering new insights,
reconstructing memories, leaving evidence of a life. Frederic Wertham recognized
early on that "zines belong to the American cultural environment, that they exist and
continue to exist as genuine human voices outside of all mass manipulation"
(1973:35). For young women who do not find themselves in the images projected by
the mainstream media, building an alternative identity through words and sharing it
with others provides a way to go public with the private self.

Computer-mediated communication

> Zines were instrumental in effecting the shift to highly personalized culture (or the "micro-
> politics of identity") that now thrives on the Internet. The World Wide Web's home
> pages—the reigning playground of self-publishing and ego-gratification—may eventu-
> ally render the zine medium obsolete, or at least a nostalgic remnant of print culture.
> (Wice & Daly 1995)

Whereas zines owe their existence to the ubiquitous copy machine, another new medium has been built on the very short history of computer networks. CMC—whether it
takes the form of e-mail, newsgroup postings, mailing list discussions, or Web page
text—is a curious combination of familiar media in unfamiliar surroundings. In print
we are deprived of the extralinguistic code of face-to-face conversation, including gaze,
stance, and kinesics in general, and paralinguistic cues such as intonation, vocal mechanisms, and so on. CMC strips communication down further, ultimately reducing
everyone's words to eighty-character lines of the same Monaco font on a screen. Could
this be the most democratic form of communication yet invented?

The answer is both yes and no. In some ways CMC is inherently more democratic than face-to-face conversations: Physical intimidation is not implied, everyone can have a turn at speaking for as long as she or he likes, and participants need
not fear censorship. On the other hand, the Internet has brought together millions of
people who have very different interaction rituals, leading to constant verbal clashes,

and as with any other cultural artifact, CMC (and computer culture in general) remains highly gendered, with all the power imbalance that such a situation implies (see Cherny 1994; Cherny & Weise 1996; Hall 1996; Herring, Johnson, & DiBenedetto 1995). We are in great need of studies that explain how women use the Net; the majority of research that has been done on gender on the Internet, however, like the majority of research on language and gender in other contexts, focuses on private conversations rather than on more thoroughly public forms of expression. And ironically, the combative nature of relatively private discourse on the Net, such as discussions in user groups and chat rooms, has led some women to seek the relative discursive safety of more public, impersonal spaces such as the Web for exploration of the self (with varying success, as we will see).

There may have been a time when Net culture was more homogeneous and cultural values were shared by the few who regularly used computers to communicate with one another. Even though there has always been a division between those who used the Net for research and development ("scientists") and those who used it for their own ends or just for fun ("hackers"), the Net was, and continues to be in many ways, a masculine place. There have been many comparisons to the early days of the American West and the concept of "frontier justice," and Ed Krol (1992:35) claims that the two overriding premises of network ethics are "Individualism is honored and fostered" and "The network is good and must be protected." These two non-Gricean "maxims" reflect what is most valuable about the Net: that it allows one to explore individual interests and find like-minded friends without leaving one's desk and without the risk of societal persecution (not that electronic persecution does not occur). Anyone with $19.95 a month can design and put up a Web page that expresses her likes, dislikes, loves, and hates, with little or no fear of censorship.

Perhaps this is why so many authors find Web publishing the perfect medium for journals. An on-line journal provides a public forum for innermost thoughts and opinions, presented in a linear fashion that sustains the narrative thread of the "story." Women who have been permitted only to write for themselves can now compose their public history, filled not with historical events or momentous deeds but the details of everyday life and the struggle to reconcile the inner self with outer expectations. The real story is the construction of an identity through an individual voice (example 4):

(4)

> Someone wrote and asked if I leave things out of my offline diary that I'm embarrassed about, or ashamed to talk about. I don't, but it did get me thinking about something funny that I've started doing since I started keeping this journal back in June of last year. Speaking of which, it's almost been a year since Coffee Shakes began— gad, it feels like two months, at the most! The funny thing that I've started doing is to gradually change the way I behave and the choices I make. Like if I'm presented with a situation and a choice, and one option is fair but difficult and the other option's fun but not very fair, I'm less likely to go for the fun but not fair option because I think, "Hm . . . do I really want to write about how I made a selfish choice tomorrow in my journal?" Interesting.—Sage Lunsford, "Coffee Shakes," *Words of the Tyrtle* (April 1, 1996)

Like the print zine examples above, this on-line journal abounds in slang, idiosyncratic constructions, run-on sentences, and other spontaneous verbal play, exemplifying each of the genre features previously established. Here Sage adopts the interaction-oriented style characteristic of informal, non-information-oriented text genres (Biber 1988). In (4) she uses *I* thirteen times; she is clearly addressing the audience, acknowledging them in the first line with *someone wrote*. She then interrupts her story with the conversational phrase *speaking of which* and interrupts again by interjecting *gad*, a playful, self-consciously old-fashioned regionalism. Coming back to the topic, *the funny thing that I've started doing*, Sage introduces an example, *Like if I'm presented with a situation . . .* , which runs on to fifty-nine words and includes a direct self-quotation. She concludes this observation with a reflective *interesting*, as if she were responding to another's conversational turn. This further reinforces the author's position as part of the audience; as Zoë does, Sage examines her own thinking, but here comments on it in a way that distances herself from "Sage-as-author": *Interesting* is a third-person assessment of "Sage-as-author."

Like Pagan in example (3), Sage sees herself as a character in the narrative she is weaving; she has come to the point where she considers the audience's perceptions of her actions before she makes a decision. "Sage" is now not only the woman writing the journal but also a self-constructed identity that coexists with the flesh-and-blood woman. This character assumes different roles at different points in her discourse: At times Sage takes on the perspective of the audience, as when she notes in the agentless sentence that *it's almost been a year since Coffee Shakes began*, as if she were not the one creating journal entries every day; at times she engages in dialogue with herself, shown both in the self-quotation *"Hm . . . do I really want to write about how I made a selfish choice tomorrow in my journal?"* and finally in the metacomment *Interesting.* She is both the writer and the reader, and the readers, by their very existence, now help to shape her actions. The journal becomes the focal point in the interaction between author and audience.

The interactive quality of Sage's on-line journal is not limited to the discourse itself. Sage often customizes her journal entries with multimedia effects. Some of the text appears in a larger font size or in color; there are sound files of Sage reading parts of the journal entries; she sometimes includes drawings she has made, scanned photos, and video captures. Using the HTML coding available on Web pages, she can provide immediate hyperlinks to the Web sites she discusses or pointers to a photo gallery of the real people who populate her journal. The addition of graphics, stylized text, and sound transforms the text into a three-dimensional experience; like a visit to someone's bedroom, all the personal quirks are evident in the décor, a deliberate display of the self.

The advantage of the Web journal over the more ephemeral print zines is that all the material can be kept "alive," that is, open and accessible to browsers. The evolving real-time narrative can be traced from the original impulse to publish, through triumphs and crises, to the last-minute details of what the journalist thought as she stared out the window a few moments ago. Because the work is available at all times, it can be visited again and again, with perhaps something new published on each visit: The site grows according to the whim of the author, rather than ratings or sales. Like a zine, it is the vision of an individual.

However, like zines, Web journals tend to be short-lived, no longer maintained or updated as they outgrow their purpose of providing an outlet for the author's narrative. By opening her life to millions of people, the author also opens herself to harassment via e-mail or through direct tampering with her Web pages; although the abuse is one step removed from the physical (a threatening e-mail message is not the same as a rock through the window), it is nevertheless frightening. The self-publisher has no publishing house to hide behind. Sadly, Sage's *Words of the Tyrtle* was just such a casualty of time and harassment. The author took down the site in April of 1997, after almost 2 years on-line and over 400 journal entries. In a farewell letter to her faithful readers, she explained that the site's demise was due to a combination of hate mail from a few individuals and the huge time commitment necessary to keep the site running. Sage had to live her life and write about it as well, leaving her no private life and no energy to write about other things. At the time of its closing, *Words of the Tyrtle* had hundreds of regular readers, and its end was lamented loudly in many chat boards. This example suggests that women's struggles against the dominant ideologies projected by the mainstream media may meet with opposition even in alternative venues and that the opportunities for self-expression found in on-line journals (and zines) create their own burdens of responsibility. But when one Web journal dies, ten more spring up to take its place. Ultimately, the value of alternative media for women's exploration of identity should not be assessed by the permanence of women's written products, because such channels of communication are by their very nature fluid and temporary. More important is the opportunity these channels provide for women to construct narratives that will "give oneself a meaningful history," in Lakoff's (1990:63) words. Voices that were once locked in private diaries are free to explore, to question, and ultimately to share their constantly reconstructed identity with an audience.

Conclusion

> ... it was a news special. It was about whether or not there is actually a biological difference between boys and girls . . . I tryed [sic] really hard to see this from all sides, not just in my feminist way, but somehow the whole show alienated me, it was like, even though they had feminists talk, you didn't feel like they were being taken seriously. It was just this concept of we have an idea to excuse sexism so let's do it and whether or not it's true really has nothing to do with it in my opinion.—Katy, *The Jellybean* 15 (1995:9)

Alternative media do not exist entirely independently of mainstream media, for the authors of zines, on-line journals, and other noncorporate forms of communication are constantly mindful of the existence of dominant cultural images and ideologies as they create their texts. The conscious rejection of these systems is perhaps the fundamental contribution that alternative media make to women's identity construction. Maintaining a precarious existence at the edges of public discourse, zines and on-line journals provide a place in which women who do not see themselves in the mainstream can invent new ways of being: as authors, as actors, as reporters, but also as teenagers who won't shave their legs, girls who meet rape threats with violence, women who speak out angrily about sexism wherever they see it.

Likewise, media continue to grow and reinvent themselves in ways hardly imagined 10 years ago, while keeping language central. It is the linguist's responsibility, then, to take such forms of discourse seriously. And given the limited opportunities for women to express themselves through mass media, it is especially important for language and gender researchers to look to vehicles like zines and Web journals, where a world of alternative identities is being created through language.

NOTES

1. Allan Bell's theory of audience design (1990, 1991), which is based on his work on the media, is an exception that illustrates the truth of this claim.

2. Further proof of this division is apparent in the mainstream media's quest to regain the individual voice; since mass-media companies cannot produce it themselves, they must acquire it in the way they know best—by buying it.

3. An eloquent explanation of this belief and its lingering effects is given in *Cometbus* 31 (1994:62).

4. But like women's letters to public officials, such as those described by Rebecca Dobkins (chapter 9, this volume), zines also exhibit an urge toward public declarations of dissent and resistance.

5. The use of the term *bitch*, which usually has a misogynistic denotation, may also suggest rebellion against the gender expectations of the mainstream media. The juxtaposition of two contrary cultural positions for women to occupy—charming pixie and dangerous bitch—further underscores the extent to which being a "whole girl" is an achievement that takes place in active struggle with the dominant culture. For young women's appropriation of the term *bitch* and its recent history in youth culture, see Sutton (1995).

REFERENCES

Zines

bunnyrabbit, 51 MacDougal St., Box 319, New York, NY 10012. $2.00.
BUST, P.O. Box 319, Ansonia Station, New York, NY 10023. $3.00.
Cometbus, BBT, P.O. Box 4279, Berkeley, CA 94704. $2.50.
The Jellybean, 6234 Wynmoor Dr., Cicero, NY 13039. $1.50.
No Means No Now, 1780 Wrightstown Road, Newtown, PA 18940. $0.50.
pixxiebitch, RD1 Box 37B, Montrose, PA 18801. $1.00.
Queen of the Thundercats, 15–20 22nd Ave., Whitestone, NY 11357. $1.00.

On-line publications

iGuide, http://www.iguide.com

Books and articles

Austin, Bryn (1993). The irreverent (under)world of 'zines. *Ms.* 3(4):68.
Bell, Allan (1990). Audience and referee design in New Zealand media language. In Allan Bell & Janet Holmes (eds.), *New Zealand ways of speaking English*. Bristol, England: Multilingual Matters 165–194.
——— (1991). *The language of news media*. Oxford: Blackwell.
Biber, Douglas (1988). *Variation across speech and writing*. Cambridge: Cambridge University Press.

Caldas-Coulthard, Carmen Rosa (1995). Man in the news: The misrepresentation of women speaking in news-as-narrative-discourse. In Sara Mills (ed.), *Language and gender: Interdisciplinary perspectives*. London: Longman, 226–239.

Cameron, Deborah (1995). *Verbal hygiene*. London: Routledge.

Cherny, Lynn (1994). Gender differences in text-based virtual reality. In Mary Bucholtz, A. C. Liang, Laurel A. Sutton, & Caitlin Hines (eds.), *Cultural performances: Proceedings of the Third Berkeley Women and Language Conference*. Berkeley, CA: Berkeley Women and Language Group, 102–115.

Cherny, Lynn, & Elizabeth Reba Weise (eds.) (1996). *Wired women: Gender and new realities in cyberspace*. Seattle, WA: Seal Press.

Creekmur, Corey K., & Alexander Doty (eds.) (1995). *Out in culture: Gay, lesbian, and queer essays on popular culture*. Durham, NC: Duke University Press.

Eckert, Penelope, & Sally McConnell-Ginet (1992). Think practically and look locally: Language and gender as community-based practice. *Annual Review of Anthropology* 21:461–490.

Faludi, Susan (1991). *Backlash: The undeclared war against American women*. New York: Crown.

Friedman, R. Seth (ed.) (1997). *The Factsheet Five zine reader: Dispatches from the edge of the zine revolution*. New York: Crown.

Grice, H. P. (1975). Logic and conversation. In Peter Cole & Jerry Morgan (eds.), *Syntax and semantics*. Vol. 3: *Speech acts*. New York: Academic Press, 41–58.

Gross, David M. (1995). Zine dreams. *New York Times Magazine* (December 17):72–74.

Gunderloy, Mike, & Cari Goldberg Janice (1992). *The world of zines: A guide to the independent magazine revolution*. New York: Penguin Books.

Hall, Kira (1996). Cyberfeminism. In Susan Herring (ed.), *Computer-mediated communication: Linguistic, social and cross-cultural perspectives*. Amsterdam: John Benjamins, 147–170.

Hall, Kira, & Beth Daniels (1992). "It's rather like embracing a textbook": The linguistic representation of the female psychoanalyst in American film. In Kira Hall, Mary Bucholtz, & Birch Moonwomon (eds.), *Locating Power: Proceedings of the Second Berkeley Women and Language Conference*. Berkeley, CA: Berkeley Women and Language Group, 222–239.

Hall, Stuart, Dorothy Hobson, Andrew Lowe, & Paul Willis (eds.) (1980). *Culture, media, language*. London: Unwin Hyman.

Herring, Susan, Deborah A. Johnson, & Tamra DiBenedetto (1995). "This discussion is going too far!": Male resistance to female participation on the Internet. In Kira Hall & Mary Bucholtz (eds.), *Gender articulated: Language and the socially constructed self*. New York: Routledge, 67–96.

Kennedy, Pagan (1995). *'Zine*. New York: St. Martin's.

Krantz, Michael (1996). February rebirth for Delphi: News Corp./MCI online service working out final kinks for launch. *Mediaweek* (January 8):6–8.

Krol, Ed (1992). *The whole Internet user's guide and catalog*. Sebastopol, CA: O'Reilly.

Lakoff, Robin Tolmach (1990). *Talking power*. New York: Basic Books.

McLuhan, Marshall (1964). *Understanding media: The extensions of man*. New York: McGraw-Hill.

Muto, Sheila (1995). Zines of the times: Have an obsession? *Wall Street Journal* (September 1):A1–A2.

Patthey-Chavez, Genevieve, & Madeleine Youmans (1992). The social construction of sexual realities in hetersexual women's and men's erotic texts. In Kira Hall, Mary Bucholtz, & Birch Moonwomon (eds.), *Locating power: Proceedings of the Second Berkeley Women and Language Conference*. Berkeley, CA: Berkeley Women and Language Group, 501–514.

Quittner, Joshua (1995). Hot 'zines on the Web. *Time* 146(10):64.

Richardson, Angela (1996). Come on, join the conversation!: 'Zines as a medium for feminist dialogue and community building. *Feminist Collections* 17(3–4):10–13.

Rowe, Chip (1997). *The book of zines: Readings from the fringe*. New York: Owl Books.

Schiffrin, Deborah (1981). Tense variation in narrative. *Language* 57(1):45–62.

Shea, Christopher (1993). The zine scene. *The Chronicle of Higher Education* 40(11):A37–A38.

Sherrill, Stephen (1994). Behind the 'zines. *Rolling Stone* 689:73, 75, 100.

Sutton, Laurel (1995). Bitches and skankly hobags: The place of women in contemporary slang. In Kira Hall & Mary Bucholtz (eds.), *Gender articulated: Language and the socially constructed self*. New York: Routledge, 279–296.

Talbot, Mary (1995). A synthetic sisterhood: False friends in a teenage magazine. In Kira Hall & Mary Bucholtz (eds.), *Gender articulated: Language and the socially constructed self*. New York: Routledge, 143–165.

Wertham, Frederic (1973). *The world of fanzines: A special form of communication*. Carbondale: Southern Illinois University Press.

Wice, Nathaniel, & Steven Daly (1995). *Alt.culture: An a-to-z guide to the '90s: Underground, online, and over-the-counter*. New York: HarperCollins. http://www.pathfinder.com/altculture/entries/a/zines.html.

Wolfson, Nessa (1979). The conversational historical present alternation. *Language* 55(19):168–182.

Wright, Fred (1996). Identity consolidation in zines. *Journal for the Psychoanalysis of Culture and Society* 1(1):136–138.

Strong Language, Strong Actions

Native American Women Writing against Federal Authority

These old times have changed and [the Indians] should be taught in strong language and actions that the Government insists on their children going to some school and staying there.
                    —Superintendent Edward K. Miller (National Archives 1921a)

My life is very disagreeable without [my daughter] at home. I wish you would please send her home, with her father. I remain in great anxiety.
                    —Lola Phillips (National Archives 1918d)

The relationship between language and gender identity has only rarely been a focus of anthropological studies of Native Americans. Conversely, language and gender studies have been slow to incorporate research on Native American women. The picture of Native American women's lives and linguistic practices remains fragmentary, when visible at all, and needs much further development.[1]

The crisis facing Native American languages—almost all are endangered, with many on the brink of disappearing—makes consideration of gender even more crucial. In Lakhota, for example, language decline affects the linguistic expression of gender ideologies (Trechter, chapter 5, this volume). Language-revival efforts may be partly gendered in some settings (Hinton 1994) and not at all in others, despite women's participation in language maintenance (Cotter, chapter 19, this volume). Another linguistic product of colonialism and cultural assimilation, literacy, also may usher in new opportunities for women (Walters, chapter 10, this volume) or enforce disempowering gender roles while promoting the native language (Orellana, chapter 3, this volume). But the interaction of language and power is everywhere complex and unpredictable. The tools of state and corporate power may even be a part of women's (and men's) liberatory struggles against such interests (Sutton, chapter 8, this volume). In this chapter I examine how Native American women used literacy in similar struggles to resist the authority of federal officials.

"Strong language and actions," on both sides of the power equation, are my focus in analyzing correspondence in the period 1916–1922 between California Indian mothers and other female relatives and the superintendent of the Greenville Indian School, a federal boarding school operating from 1888 to 1922 in the Sierra Mountains of Plumas County, California.[2] Due to the personal nature of this correspondence, I use pseudonyms, except for school and other government officials whose names are already part of the public record.

I examined 77 student files concerning 118 individual pupils, 63 of them girls. Thirty-four files contained letters from 36 mothers and other female relatives, whereas 25 contained letters from 27 fathers and other male relatives. The fact that women wrote to school officials more often than did men raises questions that are difficult to answer from the archival documents alone. One explanation may be that Indian women were considered to have primary responsibility for children's welfare. Additionally, women's literacy rates may have been higher, although such rates are impossible to calculate, given the notorious inaccuracy of both the federal census and the Bureau of Indian Affairs in gathering data about California Indians (Commonwealth Club 1926).[3] Literacy levels were probably very low, for only a small percentage of California Indian youth attended public schools before the Indian Citizenship Act of 1924. Before that date, many public schools argued that they had no responsibility to fund Indian children's attendance because Indians were claimed not to be citizens and thus not taxpayers. However, by the 1910s and beyond, many California Indians had received some schooling, whether in reservation day schools, in off-reservation boarding schools such as Greenville, or through missionary efforts, as evidenced by the literary conventions employed in many of the letters, particularly salutations and closings. In addition, the files reveal that some nonliterate parents used an amanuensis, usually their reservation's official agent or "matron" willing to write to the school on the family's behalf. Because such letters may have been edited, I confine my sample to letters that appear, from handwriting and sentence structure, to have been written by the authors themselves.[4]

In focusing on the letters of Indian women rather than men, I am not arguing that women's correspondence is distinct or causally associated with gender identity. Nor am I suggesting that the women were acting out of gender consciousness. Although additional research into other boarding schools' records may reveal that female relatives were somewhat more active than men in communicating with school officials, the research is insufficient to reach such a conclusion. My goal is much more modest: to describe a heretofore completely ignored area of Native American women's history and to focus on those aspects of women's identities that are clearly at the forefront in these letters: their identities as mothers and as unwilling subjects of a paternalistic colonial government.

The data analysis is of course limited by the nature of the archival collections. The archival documents may not represent all the correspondence for a given school. In the case of Greenville, few student- or parent-authored documents exist for the years 1888–1915, probably due to fire damage at the school and inconsistent record keeping. And only literate parents' records have survived; we have access to others' responses indirectly, if at all. Though they constitute a nonrandom and perhaps non-representative sample, the letters offer valid qualitative data for exploring the relationship between gender, identity, and ideology: in this case, the conflict between California Indian women intent on maintaining family ties and cultural identity and federal officials intent on enforcing the government's policy of assimilation. And although all the documents must be understood as products of these coercive power relations, the native-authored documents, ironically preserved by federal institutions charged with quieting native voices, also allow us a rare look into students' and their families' views of the boarding-school experience.

I reject easy oppositions between school authority and parental and student resistance. Many boarding-school alumni remember their school days fondly if sometimes ambivalently: Many formed lifelong bonds with other students that they celebrate in annual alumni gatherings. K. Tsianina Lomawaima, in her oral history of the Chilocco Indian School in Oklahoma (1994), has made the critical point that students' sense of "Indian" identity was not just broken down but also formed, through complex interactions with peers and school staff. Lomawaima views the schools as "arenas for a reciprocating exercise of power . . . between school staff and students— in other words, as an interaction Indian students helped to create" (1993:227). The documents I examine here demonstrate that parents and tribal communities also played important roles in constituting boarding schools and in shaping the exercise of their authority.

My approach is informed by Lila Abu-Lughod's (1990) inversion of Foucault's proposition that "where there is power, there is resistance." She argues that resistance is a diagnostic of power and urges those endeavoring to understand "resistance," especially in its everyday forms (cf. Scott 1985), not merely to identify and celebrate its manifestations but to scrutinize them: "We should learn to read in various local and everyday resistances the existence of a range of specific strategies and structures of power" (1990:53). She cautions against romanticizing resistance, in part because doing so can obscure the complex workings of power relations. In the present context, the questions thus become: What can we identify as women's acts of resistance, and what do they reveal about the exercise of power by the boarding schools and the federal government?

Indian women's forms of resistance suggest that schools exercised power fundamentally through the separation of Indian families. Given that the boarding schools were mandated to assimilate the Indian child into the American mainstream, virtually any exertion of maternal or familial influence on Indian children can be read as resistance. For an Indian woman to maintain her identity as a mother under these conditions is therefore an act of rebellion. A range of resistant actions can be identified: first, those that were acceptable to boarding-school authorities but achieved the women's goal of reestablishing contact with their children; second, those intended to circumvent but not overturn authority; and third, outright refusals to cooperate with the routines of power. I scrutinize these strategies to see what they reveal about the mechanics of, as well as the weaknesses in, official school authority. However, I first want to explore briefly the history of federal Indian boarding schools and the ideology that informed them.

Federal Indian boarding schools and
the ideology of assimilation

The Greenville Indian School originated in the social reform movements led by white women in the late nineteenth century. Begun in 1888 by a white female settler as an open-air revival for the area's Indian population, by 1891 the school came under the sponsorship of the Women's National Indian Association (WNAI), a white interdenominational group founded in 1879 and one of the earliest "Indian rights" organizations. Supporting full assimilation of Indians, WNAI focused on seeking passage of the General Allotment Act of 1887 and on social welfare, education, and missionary work (Hertzberg 1988). Beginning in 1894, the federal government provided funds for the Greenville school's maintenance, and by 1899 WNAI had transferred the school to the federal government.[5] However, white women continued their involvement in the school: A mission sponsored by the Women's Home Missionary Society of the Methodist Episcopal Church was maintained adjacent to the school grounds and was, according to the school's annual report of 1916, "a big help in the religious training of the school children" (National Archives 1916a:4). Because one of the aims of the federal boarding schools was to Christianize Indian youth and eradicate native religions, the government welcomed the mission's presence. The school became a regional BIA agency in 1911, and the superintendent served as head of both the school and the agency.

Toward the end of the nineteenth century, after decades of policy aimed at removing or destroying Indian communities in the path of westward settlement, the federal government turned to education and individual property ownership as the central means of assimilation. The ideology that underpinned this policy was social evolutionism: Those cultures thought to be located on the lower levels of barbarism, such as the American Indians, could, with help, progress toward civilization. Progress was to be achieved through two vehicles designed to inculcate ideals of individualism, capitalism, and self-reliance. The first was the General Allotment Act of 1887, which provided for the allotment of individual parcels from tribal lands that were once communally held or, especially in California, from lands in the public domain. In theory, land ownership would lead Indians to adopt an agrarian, self-sufficient lifestyle and would erode the communal values that were thought to hinder Indian participation in white American society. The second was the Indian school system, comprising both reservation boarding and day schools and off-reservation boarding schools such as Greenville.

Beginning in the 1870s, the federal government promoted education as a central assimilation strategy. Greenville was an example of the nonreservation boarding school initially favored by the BIA to "prepare Indian youth for the duties, privileges and responsibilities of American citizenship" in institutions geographically and ideologically separated from traditional Indian communities (National Archives 1919a). The first federal boarding school, the Carlisle Indian Training and Industrial School in Pennsylvania, was opened in 1879 by Colonel Richard H. Pratt, who got his start in Indian education while supervising Indian prisoners at Fort Marion in Florida. Based on a military system, complete with uniforms, companies, and ranks, the schools were designed to transform Indian children via vocational training, moral instruction, physical discipline, and English-language learning. Native languages were strictly prohibited, and children were punished if caught speaking their tribal tongues. Although many continued to speak their native languages in secret and during visits home, the boarding schools had an overwhelmingly negative impact on the viability of American Indian languages by removing children from their primary language environments and by making parents and children feel their languages were inferior. As Leanne Hinton has put it, the schools "robbed a generation of the right to feel pride in their language and culture" and caused subsequent generations who grew up without learning their language of heritage to feel tremendous loss and a sense that "their ability to express their cultural identity has been denied them" (1994:174).

One purported aim of the schools was to make Indians self-reliant, and this self-reliance was deeply gendered and often class-specific: boys acquired manual skills needed for agriculture, forestry, or trades, and girls learned the skills necessary for domestic service and for establishing their own households according to a white middle-class model (Prucha 1984). The students worked about half of every day and performed nearly all the tasks necessary to keep the school operating; in concrete terms this meant, for example, that at Greenville students (mostly girls) washed 17,914 items of laundry by hand in the month of June 1916 (National Archives 1916b). Ironically, the agrarian world was fast disappearing, and the middle-class domestic ideal was unattainable for most graduates, whether they returned to their economically impoverished reservations or moved to more urbanized areas where employment was limited. More important than the practical worth of vocational training was its underlying racial ideology: that the civilizing influences such training offered could move Indians up the social evolutionary ladder. However, the very nature of the tasks reinforced Indians' subservient position and was never intended to move the students into the higher echelons of white society (Lomawaima 1993).

School attendance was compulsory because of legislation passed by Congress in 1891 to authorize the BIA to compel enrollment and in 1893 to withhold provisions such as food and clothing from Indian parents who refused to send their children to school (Adams 1995). Force was used in some cases but not all, and in the Greenville school, most children were enrolled with at least the appearance of parental consent (evidenced by parent signatures or marks denoting consent on student enrollment forms). Although some parents indeed refused to send their children to school, many willingly gave permission, for a number of complex reasons. Some families, suffering dire poverty, saw the schools as a welcome means of providing sustenance for their children. Often, a family's primary caregiver, incapacitated through illness or accident, was unable to provide for the children. Widows, widowers, and abandoned spouses, particularly women, often were unable to care adequately for their children alone and believed boarding school was a better option than placing their children in public custody. Finally, some parents genuinely wanted their children to gain the education and literacy the boarding schools promised, hoping that through these tools they would escape the problems of the reservation. In the letter that follows, a woman articulates some reasons why Indian parents felt compelled to send their children away to school, including the expense of having to pay for them to attend the local public schools, which often greeted Indian children with hostility. Her complaint about the "strict" application process refers to the regulation that Indian children must have at least one-fourth Indian "blood" and must lack access to free public schools in order to enroll in federal Indian schools.[6]

Marshall Cal

Nov 9, 1917

E.K. Miller

Dear Sir

just a fue lines to let you know that I am sending 3 application blanks and if they are not filled right it can't be healped as I had them filled out by three diferent parys [parties?]. I don't see why they are so stick [strict] as any body will know if we ware no Indans we would not try and send our chirlden there and if I could affort to send my childen to the pulice [public] school here I would not send them away from me so if this blank are not filled right it will make me much disaponted as I would like to send my girls to school all winter. . . .

from truly

Jennie Frank   (National Archives 1917)[7]

The Greenville Indian School, with an enrollment of about 80 to 100 students, was one of five Indian boarding schools in California by 1900. Its student body was linguistically diverse, with Yokuts, Mono, and Miwok children from as far south as the Tule River Reservation near Bakersfield and Maidu, Northern Paiute, and Achumawi children from Northern California. Many children arrived at school speaking their native tongue, although most also knew some English. Prior to European American contact, indigenous California was extraordinarily diverse linguistically, with over 100 different languages representing five major and various smaller language families (Hinton 1994). So children would not necessarily have understood one another's language; ironically, the boarding schools created intertribal communities unprecedented in Native California.

In accordance with federal policy, students were enrolled at Greenville for terms of 3 to 5 years and were not to return home unless parents paid the costs of round-trip transportation. Superintendents generally discouraged home visits, which threatened the assimilation process; at worst, students might not come back to school at all. Parents who wished to have their child return home for summer vacation had to deposit a sum equivalent to the round-trip transportation costs. This amount, in 1919 approximately thirty dollars, represented a substantial sum for most Indian families. A female teenage student, for instance, might expect to earn only about 45 dollars for an entire summer's worth of live-in domestic work on the school's "outing" program (National Archives 1921b). If the child did not return to school, the monies were forfeited to the government (National Archives 1918a). In a 1921 letter to the BIA agent of the Porterville district near the Tule River Reservation, Superintendent Edward Miller of the Greenville Indian School and Agency outlined the policy:

These old times have changed and [the Indians] should be taught in strong language and actions that the Government insists on their children going to some school and staying there.

We have had trouble with those old Indians under you because I have stood firm for getting expense money on students going home, according to regulations. In several cases students went home and never came back, I depositing to the credit of the Government those moneys held. I do not believe one singel students returned here as per their promise. . . . On this account you will find some critical sentiment [on the part of Indians] against this school. I am sorry for it, but rather than have a lot of Indians dictating to me what should and should not be done I will get oyt of the work. . . .

My idea is to hold children in school as long as I can, where they are progressing and in good health. I have transferred them direct to other larger [boarding] schools after they finish here, in some cases without the consent of the parents, or where parents, and guardians, objected, with the consent of the Office [the BIA office in Washington], after putting the matter up to it. (National Archives 1921a)

This letter clearly identifies the key area of contention between the school and the parents: controlling the education—and the bodies—of Indian children. Miller makes explicit the tools of this control, "strong language and actions," although he fails to recognize that the Indian community resisted his attempts at control through their own "strong language" of "critical sentiment" and their "strong actions" of keeping their children at home.

The letters reveal that control was not absolute but was negotiated between native communities and the schools. Two arenas of negotiation emerge: children's health and children's ability to return home.

California Indians' health care in the early twentieth century was considered "deplorable" even at the time, according to the state Board of Health in 1926, which reported high rates of infant mortality, tuberculosis, and trachoma, an eye disease (Commonwealth Club 1926). Because few county hospitals welcomed Indian patients, the meager health services at Greenville were often an improvement over what many children had available at home. Though the children may have had better access to health care, boarding schools were also prime breeding grounds for infectious diseases, particularly during the deadly worldwide flu epidemic of 1918–1919 (Jones 1978).

Much of the correspondence concerns children's health. The boarding school rarely released children to parents unless they were extremely ill or posed a threat to other children's health; children were sometimes sent home only to die soon after. As a result, few children actually died at Greenville according to the school's annual reports, although this was not the case at many larger schools across the country. It also appears that Superintendent Miller, at least, cared about the children's well-being and expended a great deal of energy on monitoring individual children's health.

The school's control over children's attendance was weaker than its control over their health care, although the administrators had official policy on their side and could discourage parents from bringing their children home during vacations. Children could simply never return to school after a vacation home or could run away from the school grounds, which, following the superintendent's orders, were not tightly guarded. Student escape was a common occurrence, the rate at times exceeding twenty a month in a school with an enrollment of only 100 (Jones 1978). However, most students quickly returned to campus, perhaps daunted by the journey to their homes hundreds of miles away or perhaps after the escape had served its purpose as an act of defiance. In any event, both children and their parents yearned to reunite at home, as evidenced by the numbers of runaways and the letters from family members. These arenas of negotiation are explored in the following sections.

Reuniting families

Mothers and female relatives often negotiated for their children to come home on vacations, sometimes questioning the regulations established by the school but eventually abiding by them. In the following letter, Jennie Frank, the aunt of two Greenville School girls who was cited above, suggests an alternative to the school's policy of requiring a round-trip deposit for students' trips home:

Marshall, Calif

June 7, 1918

Mr. Edgar Miller

Dear Sir

I will just drope you this fue lines to ask you if there is any chance of getting my girls home on the government expenc as Annie Frank wrote to her mother and told her that she could come home on the government expense but I don't see how that can be so that is the reason I am droping you this lines and fine out as I don't leve, on less it is in account of the war of corse if I could get the girls home paying one way I could make them pick berries and others fruits as there is lots of that work around Sebestopol as I am going out picking berries in two or thee week more so please let me know at once.

From your truly

Jennie Frank

Marshall Cal   (National Archives 1918b)

Jennie Frank at first takes an indirect tone: After the formulaic *I will just drope you this fue lines* she wonders "if there is any chance of getting my girls home on the government expenc." Her apparent pessimism (*I don't see how that can be*) masks her real project: to make her nieces' return home palatable to the superintendent.

   In Superintendent Miller's reply, he restates the policy that children cannot return home unless parents pay the round-trip fare in advance. Jennie Frank was unable to raise those funds in 1918; however, the correspondence reveals that by the following year, she apparently saved enough money, and the girls went home for summer vacation. Though working within terms set by the school, Jennie Frank reasserted familial ties by finding a way to bring her nieces home and by insisting on her right to do so.

More direct than Jennie Frank's approach is this letter to Superintendent Miller from Mrs. Bessie Ventura, mother of Louise, who entered school in 1918 at 7 years of age:

Madera Cal.

June 4th, 1919

Mr. E. K. Miller
Greenville Cal

Dear Sir!

I am writing in regard to my daughter Louise of coarse I want her home for the summer vacation. Mrs. L. told me she would not be able to bring her children home this year so am writing to find out how I will be able to get Louise home should I come after her and I would would like to know as I am very busy as I work out all the time, and I would like to have her home about the last of this month. I take it for granted that her health is good by the reports you send me. I there are no other children coming down this way I will try and come for Louise let me know soon please. I am

yours very sincerely

Bessie Ventura   (National Archives 1919b)

Mrs. Ventura's tone is confident, from the exclamation point following the salutation to her firmly worded statements and direct questions (*of coarse I want her home* . . . ; *should I come after her*). No less polite than Jennie Frank, Mrs. Ventura too works within the school's system to achieve her purpose. In fact, Superintendent Miller, in a letter to Mrs. Ventura dated June 11, 1919, restated school policy but went on to write that if "you send me fifteen dollars [I] will see that Louise gets home all right" (National Archives 1919c). Mrs. Ventura did so, and judging from the files' contents, Louise went home but returned to school, where she remained enrolled until 1922.

The women's success at reuniting their families, achieved within the regulations established by the BIA, makes clear that the boarding schools' power to separate families was not absolute. The school policy left open the means through which families could be reunited, but many families without adequate funds did not see their children for 3 to 5 years. And while the deposits were required as financial incentives to parents to return their children to school, they also pointed to a budgetary problem: The BIA provided inadequate funds to the schools for such transportation. The Greenville school's annual reports show that as a small outpost in the federal boarding-school system it was always underfunded. More broadly, Indian schools were tremendously costly and were attacked early on as wasteful drains on the federal budget (Adams 1995). Thus the power to keep Indian children from their families' influence was undermined not only by the families' determination but also by the schools' economic inability to consistently enforce separation. The BIA did provide funds to send children from reservations to distant boarding schools. However, by the late 1910s, the increasing problem of truant students was not easily remedied given the limits of the boarding schools' budgets and the pressure of parent and student resistance.

Circumventing authority

The second category of resistance, acts that attempt to circumvent school authority, is illustrated by letters from a National Archives file marked "The Thomas Girls." Mrs. Thomas first writes on September 27, 1916:

> Dear Mr. Miller:
>   I take the pleasure in droping you this few lines to ask you if you will send Myrtle home for a few weeks she wrote to me and she said she is not feeling well I will send you her fair so you can send her home she's got to be doctor by an indian doctor the sickness she's got can't be cure by a white doctor so I wish you would let me know wright away so I can send you the money she must come home because her father wants to have her doctored she will come back just as soon as she gets well she is bother with her head and when a child is that way they can't study much she was sick with the same sickness and we had an indian doctor and she got alwright we took her to a white doctor and he said he couldn't do any thing for her so I wish you would let me know wright away
>
> I remain as ever yours truely
>
> Mrs. A. Thomas
> PS please answer soon   (National Archives 1916c)

This letter is remarkable in several ways. Appearing in several variations in other writers' letters, the formulaic opening, *I take the pleasure in droping you this few lines*, and closing, *I remain as ever yours truly*, signal a familiarity with the letter-writing conventions of the day. There is no punctuation whatsoever throughout the letter and no evidence of an amanuensis, suggesting that Mrs. Thomas wrote it herself. The tone is also striking: urgency is conveyed through repetition (*I wish you would let me know wright away*) and the postscript, *please answer soon.*

Mrs. Thomas's letter was prompted by her daughter Myrtle's writing to say she was not well, and that letter, though not extant, must have been alarming enough for the mother to write requesting her release in these strong terms. Most compelling about Mrs. Thomas's letter is her insistence that an Indian doctor treat her daughter, an adamant assertion of her parental right to care for her child in culturally appropriate ways.

The superintendent replied on October 2, 1916:

> Dear Mrs. Thomas:
>   I have your letter in which you ask that Myrtle Thomas be allowed to go home.

I am sorry you ask this and am sorry that it is against the rules to allow her to go unless your agent, Mr. Shafer, makes the request. It is for some extraordinary reason that we allow students to leave the school after entering.

Myrtle has never been ill. She has no hospital record and her card shows that she is in good health. I can see no reason for her wanting to leave. In fact, nothing has ever been said to her matron or to me that would lead one to believe that she wanted to go home.

Under the circumstances I believe Myrtle is better off here with her sisters. I will talk with her and tell her what I told you in this letter. We will take good care of her and she will be cared for in every way. There is no use in worrying about her for she is in good health.

She has complained of dreaming some in the night time, but that is nothing to worry over at all. If there should anything get the matter with any of the girls you would hear from me.

I will send a copy of this letter to Miss Tibbetts and to Mr. Shafer and I am sure they will advise you to not worry and that it will be best for Myrtle to not think of coming home.

Very truly yours,

Superintendent [Edward K. Miller]   (National Archives 1916d)

What Superintendent Miller no doubt intended as words of assurance, *If there should anything get the matter with any of the girls you would hear from me*, must have confirmed Mrs. Thomas's worst fears, for to her, the superintendent unintentionally verified that something was definitely wrong with Myrtle: *She has complained of dreaming some in the night time*. For many California Indian people, dreams indicate health, illness, or power. Miller either did not realize the significance of dreams or did but chose to stress that dreams are "nothing to worry over at all." Hence, parents' concerns went unaddressed if the illness they feared their children had was unrecognized or ignored by the school administration. The above correspondence must have reinforced Mrs. Thomas's fear that her daughter's actual condition was being obscured. In a letter to Superintendent Miller dated July 28, 1919, Mrs. Thomas's husband asks that his daughter be allowed to come home because he believes her 3-year term to be over. Mr. Thomas takes a more direct, even confrontational, tone than his wife: "you must think I dont know how to read I read all the papers before I put my name on them and why is the reason she dont write home" (National Archives 1919f). This difference in tenor may be due less to gender than to the 3-year span between the letters, and hence the family's growing impatience. We do not know whether Myrtle was ever allowed to go home; the remaining letters in the file concern other matters. Although we cannot determine whether Mrs. Thomas's attempt to influence her daughter's health care was successful, this correspondence reveals conflicting cultural definitions of illness and the difficulty Indian parents faced in trying to maintain traditional modes of treatment.

Elsewhere, mothers and maternal relatives threaten action, such as visiting the school or going to other authorities, including Indian reservation agents and attorneys, to assist them.

Supt Indian School

Dear Sir

Just a line to you how is that some one of you cant write for my little girl to let me know how she is getting along. please ans this for her this time. if I dont get letter from her afeter 2 weeks Ill be down see what is wrong.

very truly yours

Mrs Winnie Duncan
Sacramento Cal   (National Archives n.d. a)

Although convention is still minimally followed (*Just a line to you*), the tone here has clearly crossed from polite request to ultimatum. The file gives no clue as to whether Mrs. Duncan did visit the school. The threats are even less mitigated in the next example, in which the students' mother makes clear in her last sentence that she has consulted with an attorney.

                                                                    Elko Nevada

                                                                    June 25, 1919

Supt Indian School
Greenville Cal

Dear Sir -

    Long time ago I write you send my children home I no hear from you. I want them home pretty bad.

    When you send them home you write Supt Indian School at Carson [a boarding school in Nevada] so he can send my two little girls home with them. He send them home but they too little to come alone.

    Lawyer tell me they have to stay only three years at your school - When I send them-

Yours truly

Alice Hanley   (National Archives 1919d)

Alice Hanley dispenses with polite preliminaries and uses imperatives unmitigated by any hedges (*you write Supt Indian School at Carson . . .*). Her final line (*- When I send them-*) emphasizes that she has kept her part of the bargain and the superintendent is now obliged to keep his. Apparently, Superintendent Miller took her seriously and consulted with a higher administrator, Colonel L. A. Dorrington, special agent at large for the BIA. Dorrington replied to Miller that "it is my opinion that our right to hold the children after expiration of contract is doubtful" and that the children had to be returned to their home, although he urged Miller to insist that the children be returned to Greenville or another school after the vacation was over (National Archives 1919e). Clearly, Alice Hanley's invocation of authority had sufficient impact on Miller that he too sought the advice of those with greater institutional power.

These examples suggest the range of women's actions and language to circumvent school regulations. They also show that one of the central ways boarding schools exercised power was by separating families. Women resisted this intervention by questioning the schools' authority and reasserting their own influence over their children's lives, even if only briefly.

Noncooperation with authority

At times Indian parents moved from "strong language," as in the above examples, to "strong actions." This shift is seen in a series of letters written by Lola Phillips and her husband Francisco about their daughter Philomena in 1918, during the great flu epidemic. From the Tule River Reservation Mr. Phillips inquired about their daughter's health; Superintendent Miller replied that she "seems to be getting along all right," although he also wrote that she had malaria just after getting over the flu! Her parents wired for Philomena to be sent home immediately; Superintendent Miller wrote back, saying, "We have no money to advance to her or for her fare. She is all right here, a little lonesome at times, but getting along nicely. She is a girl that will like it better as she gets more acquainted and talks more. . . . I will be unwilling to send her home unless Mr. Virtue [the Indian agent at the reservation] says so or her health is not good here" (National Archives 1918c). Miller's aim is not to comfort the parents but to assert the authority of the school, the hospital, and the Indian agent.

But Mr. and Mrs. Phillips did not accept this control over their daughter. After meeting with another Indian, Jose Varga, who had visited the school and brought back firsthand accounts of the child's condition, Lola Phillips wrote on November 7, 1918:

> Edgar K. Miller, Greenville, Cal
> We are informed that our daughter is sick at the Greenville School. Jose Varga, states that your clerk at the school told him that the girl was sick internally. My life is very disagreeable without her at home. I wish you would please send her home, with her father.
>
> I remain in great anxiety
>
> Lola Phillips   (National Archives 1918d)

This terse letter is devoid of the conventional opening and replaces the usual *Yours truly* with the rhetorically powerful *I remain in great anxiety.* The letter is also notable for its standard and formal language. Whether the force of Mrs. Phillips's letter or the pressure of Mr. Phillips's presence was the deciding factor, the superintendent capitulated. Superintendent Miller notes at the bottom of this letter: "Philomena left Sat. Nov. 9th with her father." There is no further correspondence in the file.

The intervention of the parents is all the more astonishing given that the journey between Tule River and Greenville is over 400 miles and in 1918 would have taken great effort. In the face of the school's refusal to send the child home, the Phillipses took matters into their own hands and retrieved her, a clear example of the third category of resistance, Indian noncooperation with school authority.

From the Greenville records, such open noncooperation was rare, although there are references to a few similar instances. Another form of noncooperation is more common: refusal to return the child to school after a vacation. The last document in several students' files is a memorandum indicating that this had occurred. The superintendent circulated to other Indian schools and to reservations a list of "truant students" who were not to "be enrolled at any other Government Indian School" (National Archives 1919g). Although this may not sound like a punishment, especially when parents did not want the child to return to school anyway, it often meant that she or he had little or no access to education. And although education was supposed to be compulsory for Indian children, the overcrowded government-run day and boarding schools lacked space for all who wanted to attend.

This third category of resistance is perhaps most prone to being romanticized. These acts of noncooperation also reveal how Indian children and families were caught up in the federal Indian educational system, even when they tried to remove themselves. Paradoxically, in choosing noncooperation, parents risked that their children might be denied any formal education, thus limiting access to the tools of literacy necessary to escape powerlessness and dependency. Indian women employ these tools in their letters to resist the federal government's authority and to assert their own identities as mothers and as Indians. Thus we should not focus on Indian women's discursive choices as reflections of their limited literacy; indeed, as we have seen, authors who use nonstandard spelling and punctuation often adhere to discursive convention, and some highly literate writers, such as Lola Phillips, choose to flout these conventions to rhetorical effect. Instead, the letters reveal that strong language alone is not enough: Equally important are Indian women's strong actions to preserve their families.

Conclusion

The Greenville Indian School burned down in December 1921 in a mysterious fire. Alumni, interviewed in the 1970s, were certain that the fire was set by disgruntled students (Jewell 1987). Over the years, students had set other fires; in 1920, for example, Superintendent Miller reported a fire in the girls' quarters, two small fires in the boys' bathing room, and a fire of undetermined origin in the boiler room (National Archives 1920). School matron A. Dietrich, in a 1919 or 1920 note to the superintendent, described her suspicions that two girls were involved in setting fires:

> Both of them were striking matches in the dormitory. I found a box of matches in Lucy's
> bed that she had taken from the kitchen when Mrs. Groves turned her back a minute.
> several times we had an oder of rags burning here in the building & making a panic among
> the children. these girls are so tricky & thieving & then lie out of it. . . . (National Archives, n.d. b).

After the 1921 fire, the BIA decided not to rebuild but to close the remote and costly Greenville Indian School. It sent children to other boarding schools within the region. The children were still under the control of the federal Indian education system, and decisions about their transfer were sometimes made without parental consultation:

Independence Cal

Jan 2, 1922

Dear sir

Mr. Miller

recived your letter last wekk—on Saturday evening—about your burned down. I am very sorry to hear about that—then I went to Mr. Parrot supt. office [the Indian agent] and heard he telegraph already and heard 4th grade are coming home and never heard they coming or not. because my boy—Arthur is 4th grade. That why I am wainting him to come home. Then I can send him school here. Till your school open again. I am worry abuot him all the time. Wil you please send him home with other boys, or lone if to late. send him in Bishop, please.

From yours truly

Mrs. Clara Simmons   (National Archives 1922a)

Mrs. Simmons's polite, even placating, tone (*Till your school open again*) is not reciprocated. In his reply, Superintendent Miller cuts off any negotiation:

January 6, 1922

Dear Madam:

I have your letter about ARTHUR going home and would advise you it came too late. We transferred him to the Chemawa, Oregon, School at his own request. He is there now. It is a fine school and he will have wonderful opportunities there to get a good education.

He was well and happy when he left here. He did not want to go home at all.

Sincerely yours,

Supt.   (National Archives 1922b)

One wonders how a fourth-grader could have requested to be transferred without parental knowledge to a school several hundred miles farther north from home. The desire to remain with his peers could have played a role, or the child may have protested and had no avenue to express his dissent. The student file does not reveal any further correspondence between the mother and the school.

Despite this level of ongoing intervention into the educations of Indian children, at the time Greenville Indian School closed, it was seen, like the larger federal boarding-school project, as an expensive failure. By the 1920s, the realization had been growing for years that the schools had failed to render the expected transformation: Most students who attended boarding schools did not graduate, and their return to their home reservations or communities often meant a return to their former "uncivilized" lifestyles (Adams 1995). Although boarding schools did not disappear entirely (indeed, a handful still operate today), they were never again advocated as the primary means of educating and transforming Indian children.

Underlying this national policy shift was the resistance of Indian students and families. As Superintendent Miller lamented in his 1921 letter, children's attendance was difficult to compel, and his personal complaint, "rather than have a lot of Indians dictating to me what should and should not be done I will get [out] of the work," reflected what happened in the BIA educational service. Boarding-school officials indeed got out or were put out of "the work," largely because many Indians refused, some overtly and some quietly, to undergo the transformation demanded of them.

As intimate documentary evidence of a chapter in Indian-white relations that has yet to be fully understood, particularly from the vantage point of Indian women, the letters discussed here illuminate a previously obscured intersection of culture, gender, and power. They indicate that the federal government's strategy of separating Indian children from their families was an effective means of interrupting parental and cultural influence on generations of Indian children. However, they also show that this power to separate was never absolute and was resisted by women acting both within and outside the regulations established by the schools. Thus the archival documents simultaneously give texture to the mechanisms of federal authority and give voice to the California Indian women who sought to weaken the tools of that authority, "strong language and actions," with corresponding tools of their own.

NOTES

I appreciate the support of the Sourisseau Academy of San Jose State University, which helped make this research possible. Thanks go to Kathleen O'Connor of the National Archives Pacific Sierra Region for her assistance, and to Leanne Hinton, Tsianina Lomawaima, and Judith Lowry for ongoing discussions about the impact of the federal Indian boarding schools. I especially thank the editors of this volume and Francesca Freccero for thoughtful suggestions on earlier drafts.

1. Linguistic dimensions of American Indian gender relations have been touched on by some of the contributors to *Women and Power in Native North America* (Klein & Ackerman 1995). For critiques of the continuing inaccurate and biased representation of women and girls of color in linguistics and related fields, see the chapters by Marjorie Goodwin, Norma Mendoza-Denton, and Marcyliena Morgan in this volume.

2. Until recently, this correspondence, found in student files in the National Archives (Pacific Sierra Region), has been unavailable for study because the Archives restricts access to personal documents for a 72-year period (approximately a lifespan), so that personal materials in government records are released after the subject's death. Many of the off-reservation federal boarding schools in operation from the 1880s to the 1920s have similar records being released for the first time in the 1990s.

Twenty-five federal Indian boarding schools were opened between 1879 and 1902; in addition, there were approximately 125 other on-reservation boarding schools and 154 day schools operated by the BIA in 1900 (Adams 1995:57–58). Among the few scholars working with native-authored correspondence in the boarding-school records are Genevieve Bell (1995) and Brenda Child (1998). David Wallace Adams's (1995) overview of federal Indian boarding schools between 1875 and 1928 draws on some student-authored accounts of their experiences. Other important scholarship dealing with the boarding-school experience includes that of K. Tsianina Lomawaima (1993, 1994), which draws on alumni oral history, and Clyde Ellis (1996), which utilizes personal memoirs and archival documents. Both Caitlin Hines and Sara Trechter (this volume) also use the evidence of historical data—albeit of a very different kind—to illuminate how language, gender, power, and identity interact.

3. Some notes as to terminology: At the turn of the century, what is now known as the Bureau of Indian Affairs was referred to as the *U.S. Indian Service* or informally as the *Indian Bureau*; in this chapter, for clarity, I will refer to it as the *BIA*. I also will refer to the indigenous people of North America using various terms, including *Native American, American Indian, Indian*, and *native*, reflecting the variety of terms these peoples are currently using to identify themselves.

4. The English spoken and written by many American Indians is structurally different from other varieties of American English; in some cases, it has been influenced by the tribal language, even among those who are monolingual English speakers (Leap 1993). However, nonstandard language is also present in the letters of the school officials, as can be seen in the examples given. The relationship of language and power is therefore not as straightforward as it first appears.

5. See William Allan Jones (1978) for the most complete history of the Greenville Indian School to date.

6. The enrollment application forms explained these regulations in specific detail; there were provisions to educate children with any Indian heritage if their parents resided on a reservation or if they would not otherwise have access to education. The form also quoted from the 1893 law empowering the Secretary of the Interior to "withhold rations, clothing, and other annuities from Indian parents or guardians who refuse or neglect to send or keep their children of proper school age in some school during a reasonable portion of the year" (National Archives 1918a).

7. The letters are here reproduced without grammatical or spelling corrections, and I have inserted an ellipsis when any text is omitted.

REFERENCES

Abu-Lughod, Lila (1990). The romance of resistance: Tracing transformations of power through Bedouin women's lives. *American Ethnologist* 17:41–55.

Adams, David Wallace (1995). *Education for extinction: American Indians and the boarding school experience, 1875–1928*. Lawrence: University Press of Kansas.

Bell, Genevieve (1995). Writing home, writing back: Exploring the documentary record of the Carlisle Indian School. Paper given at the annual meeting of the American Anthropological Association, Washington, DC.

Child, Brenda J. (1998). *Boarding school seasons: American Indian families, 1900–1940*. Lincoln: University of Nebraska Press.

Commonwealth Club (1926). *Indians in California*. San Francisco: Transactions of the Commonwealth Club.

Ellis, Clyde (1996). *To change them forever: Indian education at the Rainy Mountain Boarding School, 1893–1920*. Norman: University of Oklahoma Press.

Hertzberg, Hazel Whitman (1988). Indian Rights Movement, 1887–1973. In Wilcomb E. Washburn (ed.), *Handbook of North American Indians*, Vol. 4: *History of Indian-white relations*. Washington, DC: Smithsonian Institution Press, 305–323.

Hinton, Leanne (1994). *Flutes of fire: Essays on California Indian languages.* Berkeley, CA: Heyday Books.

Jewell, Donald P. (1987). *Indians of the Feather River: Tales and legends of the Concow Maidu of California.* Menlo Park, CA: Ballena Press.

Jones, William Allan (1978). The historical development of the Greenville Indian Industrial School: Greenville, Plumas County, California. M.A. thesis, California State University, Chico.

Klein, Laura F., & Lillian A. Ackerman (eds.) (1995). *Women and power in Native North America.* Norman: University of Oklahoma Press.

Leap, William L. (1993). *American Indian English.* Salt Lake City: University of Utah Press.

Lomawaima, K. Tsianina (1993). Domesticity in the federal Indian schools: The power of authority over mind and body. *American Ethnologist* 20:227–240.

—— (1994). *They called it Prairie Light: The story of Chilocco Indian School.* Lincoln: University of Nebraska Press.

National Archives, Pacific Sierra Region, San Bruno, CA (n.d., a). Letter from Mrs. Winnie Duncan to Supt. Edward K. Miller. RG [Record Group] 75, S [Series] 42, B [Box] 120, F [Folder] Duncan.

—— (n.d., b). Letter from A. Dietrich to Supt. Edward K. Miller. RG 75, S 42, B 121, F Lewis girls.

—— (1916a). Annual Report Greenville School and Agency. RG 75, S 31, B 110, F Annual Reports, Narrative and Statistical, 1916.

—— (1916b). Report of articles passing through the Greenville Indian School Laundry. RG 75, B 5, F Greenville Inspections.

—— (1916c) Letter from Mrs. A. Thomas to Supt. Edward K. Miller. Sept. 27. RG 75, S 42, B 122, F Thomas Girls.

—— (1916d). Letter from Supt. Edward K. Miller to Mrs. A. Thomas. Oct. 2. RG 75, S 42, B 122, F Thomas Girls.

—— (1917). Letter from Jennie Frank to Supt. Edward K. Miller. Nov. 9. RG 75, S 42, B 120, F Frank.

—— (1918a). Application for enrollment in a nonreservation school. RG 75, S 42, B 120, F Cumberland Children.

—— (1918b). Letter from Jennie Frank to Supt. Edward K. Miller. June 7. RG 75, S 42, B 120, F Frank.

—— (1918c). Letter from Supt. Edward K. Miller to Francisco Phillips. Nov. 2. RG 75, S 42, B 122, F Phillips.

—— (1918d). Letter from Lola Phillips to Supt. Edward K. Miller. Nov. 7. RG 75, S 42, B 122, F Phillips.

—— (1919a). Annual calendar of the Greenville Indian School. RG 75, S 30, B 86, F Calendars, 1913–1920.

—— (1919b). Letter from Bessie Ventura to Supt. Edward K. Miller. June 4. RG 75, S 42, B 122, F Ventura.

—— (1919c). Letter from Supt. Edward K. Miller to Bessie Ventura. June 11. RG 75, S 42, B 122, F Ventura.

—— (1919d). Letter from Alice Hanley to Supt. Edward K. Miller. June 25. RG 75, S 42, B 120, F Hanley.

—— (1919e). Letter from Col. L. A. Dorrington to Supt. Edward K. Miller. June 26. RG 75, S 42, B 120, F Hanley.

—— (1919f). Letter from Mr. Alec Thomas to Supt. Edward K. Miller. July 28. RG 75, S 42, B 122, F Thomas Girls.

—— (1919g). Truant students of the Greenville Indian School, Term 1919–1920. Dec. 1. RG 75, S 42, B 120, F Gunther.

———— (1920). Letter from Supt. Edward K. Miller to Commissioner of Indian Affairs. Nov. 29. RG 75, B 5, F Greenville Indian School, Miscellaneous #2.

———— (1921a). Letter from Supt. Edward K. Miller to Agent Joe Taylor. RG 75, S 42, B 120, F L. Chalmers.

———— (1921b). Letter from Geneva Browne to Homer Morrison. RG 75, S 42, B 120, F Hanley.

———— (1922a). Letter from Mrs. Clara Simmons to Supt. Edward K. Miller. Jan. 2. RG 75, S 42, B 120, F Rhodes.

———— (1922b). Letter from Supt. Edward K. Miller to Mrs. Clara Simmons. Jan. 6. RG 75, S 42, B 120, F Rhodes.

Prucha, Francis Paul (1984). *The great father: The United States government and the American Indian.* Abridged ed. Lincoln: University of Nebraska Press.

Scott, James C. (1985). *Weapons of the weak: Everyday forms of peasant resistance.* New Haven: Yale University Press.

"Opening the Door of Paradise a Cubit"

Educated Tunisian Women, Embodied Linguistic Practice, and Theories of Language and Gender

[In earlier centuries in Tunisia], a woman could in no way ask for divorce according to Islamic law. One of the rare occasions when the *Shari'a*, or Islamic law, consented was when the husband sodomized his wife. She had to go ask for justice from the *Qadi*, or judge in the Islamic court. Arriving before him, she squatted and arranged her shoes upside down [*à l'envers*], thereby indicating that her husband had entered her from behind [*à l'envers*].

—Largueche & Largueche 1992:64

Lived experience and theories of gender

When it comes to theorizing gender, students of language and culture, it seems, generally prefer simplistic social and linguistic categories and reductionist criteria for category membership. Much like Simone de Beauvoir (1953) in *The Second Sex*, Robin Lakoff (1975), in her groundbreaking work on language and gender, seemed to define women as Other, a departure from the norm, which could only be construed as male. Early work in quantitative sociolinguistics did no better. The embarrassment I feel when my students, the majority of whom are female, and I examine the interview questions used in William Labov's (1966) research on linguistic variation and change in the Lower East Side of New York City grows yearly; it is made only greater when we scrutinize the stimuli for subjective-reaction tests, including the following passage about Hungry Sam, a pet dog:

> We didn't know we cared so much for him until he was hurt.
> There's something strange about that—how I can remember everything he did: this thing, that thing, and the other thing. He used to carry three newspapers in his mouth at the same time. I suppose it's the same thing with most of us: your first dog is like your first girl. She's more trouble than she's worth, but you can't seem to forget her. (1966:597)

Although I can rejoice that sociolinguists today are increasingly aware of the problems of sex stereotyping in research stimuli, my students and I are still unable to interpret the "data": subjective responses by women and men to misogynist passages narrated by a heterosexual male narrator, likely of the working class, speaking for "most of us" but read by women of various classes, assumed by the analyst to have more standard speech than their male counterparts in each class cohort. What possible interpretations of the data might have been offered in the early 1960s, when they were gathered? What interpretations might be possible now? I do not feel capable of untangling all the issues relevant for Labov's well-defined questions about language variation and change (Weinreich, Labov, & Herzog 1968) as they relate to issues of sex. I feel even less able to evaluate these artifacts as the efforts of social science, including sociolinguistics, to understand language and gender.

Increased sensitivity to some of these issues may have eradicated misogynist reading passages, but it has certainly heralded no consensus on issues of sex and gender among sociolinguists. Aki Uchida's (1992) review outlines the continuing differences between those who subscribe to a no-fault "two cultures" model for understanding language and gender and those who believe that issues of power and differential access to it must be central to any understanding of gender and language. Even among orthodox variationists, there is little agreement. Although Penelope Eckert calls for a fundamental rethinking of the treatment of sex and gender in the quantitative paradigm, arguing that researchers have generally "fall[en] back on unanalyzed notions about gender to interpret whatever sex correlations emerge in the data and do not consider gender where there are no sex correlations" (1989:247), Labov's (1990) response is that the category of sex should be maintained in the name of comparability and possible replicability. Thus he responds characteristically to a question of social theory with a statistical solution: analyze sex × class interactions rather than simply analyzing by class and later by sex. Such a move represents impeccable logic if one shares with him and many variationists a particular set of assumptions about sex, gender, class, and social categories.

Yet the point is rarely made that quantitative work in sociolinguistics has always treated sex as a dichotomous variable, an objective category, when it is in fact little more than rarefied common sense (Geertz 1983), particularly since *sex* in sociolinguistic research has meant apparent or reported biological sex. One possible response to this problem, perhaps the most objective and "scientific," would be to require chromosomal analysis of those whose language sociolinguists analyze, but such a suggestion is risible: Such tests would simply yield more data to be correlated and likely misunderstood unless there were sound theories of the relationship between chromosomal structure, body morphology, and gender to help contextualize the meanings of such analyses. The problem, then, is not being more objective but finding ways to understand gender as part of lived experience, which influences language.

In this chapter, I offer one response to this challenge. Borrowing from the work of Pierre Bourdieu and Judith Butler, I first attempt to sketch some of the ways in which bodies might matter for sociolinguists, especially with regard to attitudes about language. Then I examine in detail part of a sociolinguistic interview between a young educated woman and a young less educated man in a small Tunisian town in terms of the relationship between what is said and how it is said, focusing particularly on issues of the body. As background for this latter examination, I discuss the sociolinguistic situation in Tunisia, examining the very different historical and contemporary situations of women and men with respect to access to linguistic resources. Following the analysis of the interview, I conclude by contextualizing it in terms of Malika Zamiti-Horchani's (1986) research on Tunisians' attitudes toward women and of the earlier discussion of the body in sociolinguistic research.

Bodies that matter

In an effort to escape biological essentialism, sociolinguists have, I fear, preferred to act as if individuals do not have bodies. We claim to wish to understand the social construction of language, sex, and gender, yet seem embarrassed by the fact that speech is necessarily embodied, ultimately theorizing as if bodies don't and can't matter (but see several chapters in this volume, including those by Goodwin and Wood, for wide-ranging explorations of embodied linguistic practice). The issues raised by thinking about language in terms of embodied practice are much more complex than merely naming the body as the site where "a bundle of social categories" (Bell 1984:168) is located. Indeed, as Butler notes, when writing about identity categories like 'queer', which are certainly related to Bell's social categories: "One might be tempted to say that identity categories are insufficient because every subject position is the site of converging relations of power that are not univocal. But such a formulation underestimates the radical challenge to the subject that such converging relations imply. For there is no self-identical subject who houses or bears these relations, no site at which such relations converge" (1993:229–230). In other words, a fruitful field for analysis should be the conflicts *between* embodied social or identity categories and the ways in which these categories fail to converge. As Butler's comments make clear, such categories cannot help but be imbued with power of varying sorts.

Bourdieu's (1977) notions of *habitus* and the bodily *hexis* may help us begin examining the body and its consequences for sociolinguistics. As John Thompson notes, Bourdieu sees the habitus as "a set of *dispositions* which incline agents to act and react in certain ways. The dispositions generate practices, perceptions, and attitudes which are 'regular' without being consciously co-ordinated or governed by any 'rule'" (1991:12; emphasis in original). One acquires these dispositions through the process of socialization—Thompson uses the term "inculcation" (12)—in the communities to which one belongs; hence, they reflect and are structured by the social conditions of acquisition. These dispositions, which as Bourdieu's work makes clear include everything from posture to style of speaking, eating, moving, and claiming public or private space, are "durable," "generative," and "transposable" to novel situations (13). At the same time, they are "pre-conscious and hence not readily amenable to conscious reflection and modification" (13). Thus these dispositions represent habits of being in one's body, ways of orienting one's physical and psychological self to the world. Bourdieu has distinguished between these dispositions—the habitus—and the bodily hexis, "a certain durable organization of one's body and of its deployment in the world" (13). In his work, he has attempted to use the notions of the habitus and the hexis to avoid some of the traps that frequently characterize social theorists' discussions of structure and agency. Especially significant for this discussion is his acknowledgment of and focus on the body itself as "the site of incorporated history" for the individual (13) with all of the conflicting experiences that have shaped the body and its dispositions for acting in the world.

Such a perspective helps justify Butler's contention that the social and identity categories that intersect in individual bodies can never really converge. It also permits us to ask about the specific ways in which bodies might matter from a sociolinguistic perspective, although I will acknowledge immediately the considerable slippage between issues of the body's morphology and its social construction. I do not think that I am able to draw a clear distinction between the two, nor am I sure that doing so is necessary. What is required is that sociolinguists acknowledge that the research "subjects" whose speech we study are embodied subjects and that each speaker's body, itself socially constructed, simultaneously permits and regulates the subject's patterns of language use in complex ways. Here, I wish to consider one relevant example of this phenomenon, the embodied nature of language attitudes.

As Kathryn Woolard has pointed out, language attitudes are visceral and hence necessarily embodied:

> In most people's experience, reactions to certain styles of speech, particularly stigmatized ones, can be visceral, and may conflict with more consciously and deliberately held evaluations of the people we hear. Even in less dramatic moments, we make surprisingly definite judgments about people's intellectual and moral quantities on the basis of the way they "sound" (Allport & Cantril 1934). These associative judgments are part of what Bourdieu (1977) calls our "habitus," in the sense that they are incorporated or literally embodied in our aural perceptions. (1989:89)

Thus these responses derive from our dispositions and are ultimately linked to our hexis, a fact whose importance should not be lightly dismissed. A possible conclusion from recent research on the enteric nervous system (Blakeslee 1996) is that visceral responses to language varieties learned through early socialization are in fact *physiologically* different from the reasoned responses that one might learn from formal training in linguistics or other disciplines. As Woolard implied, although training may permit us to use logic or reason to intervene consciously to prevent ourselves from acting on our initial feelings, the feelings themselves are very real, linked in complex ways to socialization and hence notions of normativity. In the analysis of the sociolinguistic interview that follows, I seek to demonstrate ways in which bodies matter in Tunisia in the construction of conflicting attitudes about language and about gender.

The sociolinguistic situation in Tunisia

Although over 98 percent of Tunisians are Arab Muslims of the Malaki rite, making Tunisia the most ethnically and religiously homogeneous of the countries in the Arab world, the linguistic situation there is quite complex. Characterized by a postdiglossic Arabic language continuum and postcolonial bilingualism involving Arabic and

French, it offers speakers many resources for creating identities while using language for referential and nonreferential purposes (Walters 1996b, in preparation). Except for a declining number of native speakers of Berber (less than 1 percent of the population) and any foreigners who might live there, children growing up in Tunisia learn as their first language a variety of Tunisian Arabic (TA) linked to their regional, social, and confessional background. Certainly from the time they are exposed to broadcast media, they hear other varieties of Arabic and other languages. All have early exposure to Classical Arabic (CA), the sacred language of the Islamic inheritance, because of the ubiquity of Qur'anic recitation, whether live, broadcast, or recorded (Nelson 1985). Daily news programs and some feature broadcasts expose them to Modern Standard Arabic (MSA), the contemporary version of CA. Television programs and movies on videocassette from other Arab countries generally employ the Arabic dialect of the country in which the program or movie is produced. Consequently, many educated Tunisians claim at least passive competence in Egyptian Arabic because Egypt has long produced the majority of syndicated television programs and movies. One local television channel broadcasts in French, and the children of those who are educated also hear French spoken, if only as part of codeswitched utterances. Satellite dishes now bring additional channels broadcasting in MSA, various dialects of Arabic, French, and other European languages.

On beginning school, children first learn to read and write MSA in order to be able to read Arabic as written today and in the past. In addition to being the only variety of Arabic legitimated for writing, MSA is the variety of Arabic used in nearly all public, formal settings—or at least the norm against which language used in such settings is evaluated. In fact, however, much of the extemporaneous language heard in formal settings, including schools, involves diglossic switching, or the practice of switching between varieties along the postdiglossic continuum, generally with TA as the matrix language.

Tunisian children also study French from early elementary school. Whereas earlier generations of Tunisians, especially those educated under the colonial system, used French as a medium of instruction for nearly all courses, it is now important as a subject of study. Because French is known to many Tunisians, because of the history of bilingual education in the country, and, most important, because Arabic and French index different identities, each of which is positively viewed by most educated Tunisians, one also finds a great deal of codeswitching (CS) between TA and French; most commonly, the switching is what Carol Myers-Scotton (1993:117–131) has termed "CS as unmarked choice." In other words, between bilingual peers, the expected behavior is to codeswitch intrasententially, with the extent and nature of switching indexing degree of education, degree of urbanity, and individual choice, as well as other sociodemographic variables such as gender. Within the context of Tunisia and the larger Arab world, such codeswitching enables the speakers simultaneously to mark their Tunisianness (because Arabs from other countries, even francophone Arabs, will engage in different patterns of codeswitching, using their native dialect as matrix) and their degree of education (because less educated Tunisians will not be able to codeswitch with ease).

As this description implies, distribution of these communicative resources is not equal across the speech community. In fact, report data taken from the 1984 census show clear differences in access to CA/MSA, French, and English, all varieties acquired through formal education, with respect to age of the speaker and her or his sex, as demonstrated in figure 10.1; other data in the census make clear that, as might be expected, region of birth, size of community in which one was born, and economic status of the family constitute other axes of differentiation. The data offer some indication of the sociolinguistic implications of colonialism, independence, and social and economic development as they interact with speaker sex. Thus, Tunisians 35 years of age or older in 1984 (those of school age at the time of independence) had far fewer educational opportunities than those born after 1950. The figure also demonstrates that, as in many postcolonial countries in which "universal" education has been a goal, opportunities for literacy and hence access to prestige varieties of language have been slower to reach females than males, although the government of independent Tunisia has done a far better job of educating girls and women than the French colonial government ever managed—or intended. Ultimately, these data help account for the fact that, in Korba, the town of 20,000 or so where I did fieldwork in the mid-1980s, no one could name a woman over 50 who could read or write, yet many of these women's daughters had received some education, a small minority of them even at the postsecondary level. They also pave the way for understanding why female and male bodies are perceived in very different ways when they, as speaking subjects, use CA/MSA, French, English, or some combination of these in addition to TA, which all Tunisians share.

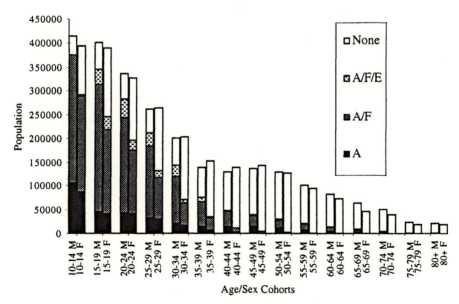

Figure 10.1. Languages read and written by Tunisians aged 10 and older, according to age cohort and sex. None = Illiterate (= speaker of TA only). A = CA/MSA. A/F = CA/MSA + French. A/F/E = CA/MSA + French + English. SOURCE: Institut National de la Statistique (1984:8, 85–90).

Zeineb and Brahim's interview and embodied difference

The interview discussed here was one of a corpus collected from 1985 to 1987 in Korba, a small town that has existed at least since the time of the Phoenicians. Though at the intersection of the main north-south coastal highway and the major road connecting Tunis with the eastern side of the northern coast, Korba is known as a conservative town. Leaders in the community have long discouraged the development of a tourist industry that would surely attract Europeans, who have very different notions from small-town Tunisians about appropriate displays of the female and male body at the beach. In contrast, most other seaside towns along the coast, especially those with beaches as wide as Korba's, have a well-developed (or overdeveloped) tourist sector, the country's major source of hard currency.

The corpus consists of interviews with twenty-six Korbans. Elsewhere, I have analyzed several of the sociolinguistic variables that occur in the local dialect, considering the variable of speaker sex as crucial in understanding the distribution of variants, one that does not always fit comfortably into Western predictions about linguistic variation and gender (Walters 1989, 1991). In the interview considered here, Zeineb, a student of modern languages at the University of Tunis, was the interviewer. Like most of her female classmates, she came home in public transportation nearly every weekend during the academic year. Like nearly all university students, she was unmarried. She spoke TA, MSA, French, and English. During high school, she had spent a year in the United States as an exchange student. Her family was fairly well off by local standards; they owned a traditional Arab house (in contrast to a European-style *villa*) and had a farm in the nearby countryside. Obviously, they had supported her desire to get an education and to have a life that had already been quite different from theirs, indeed one that would likely result in her moving from Korba to take up residence in a more urban, less traditional area.

The interviewee, Brahim, was 26 at the time of the interview. He, too, was single. He had received an eleventh-grade education, far more than most men his age. Because he did not finish high school, he could not qualify for a government-subsidized university education as Zeineb had. At the time of the interview, he worked in Tunis on the Metro Léger, part of the mass transit system, commuting daily; by the time my fieldwork was complete, he had quit his job in Tunis and opened a small grocery in Korba, a longtime dream. Brahim's family background was far more modest than Zeineb's, although his family also owned a traditional Arab house. Unlike Zeineb, he had never left the country. Not having completed his military service, he was ineligible for a passport, a fact that keeps many young Tunisian men from traveling abroad.

Both Zeineb and Brahim had come of age long after the country's independence in 1956. As natives of the same small town and members of the same generation, they shared a great deal of experience, having certainly witnessed much social change during their short lifetimes. Further, both had also spent a considerable amount of time in Tunis, though in different places and for very different reasons. Yet they differed in sex, level of education, and life chances, differences that had influenced the habitus of each and differences that each embodied in her or his hexis.

Among these differences were attitudes about the ways in which female and male bodies were regulated in public spaces in small-town Tunisia at that time, especially with regard to contact of any sort between women and men not related by blood or marriage. In fact, the interaction analyzed here violated local norms, which would have decreed that the protracted conversations between a woman and a man that constitute some sociolinguistic interviews should not occur, especially since Zeineb and Brahim, both unmarried, belonged to different social classes. This interview took place in a watch repair shop owned by a young single man of about the age of the interviewer and interviewee. The setting offered the balance between publicness and privateness necessary to permit the interview to happen and be recorded clearly without violating too many other social conventions.

The passage analyzed occurred not quite halfway through the 45-minute interview, accounting for nearly 10 minutes of the interaction. Brahim spoke in a declamatory style, taking the floor, talking at a rapid rate, and using an impassioned tone, neither waiting for nor receiving verbal backchannel cues. His was a manner of speaking I associate with much public discourse in the Arab world, almost uniquely a male genre, and with public debate on heated issues such as abortion or gay rights in our own: A speaker chooses a position from the predictable ones available and concedes little. There is great frankness and little apparent concern for the opinions, feelings, or face of others present who might hold very different opinions.

With respect to the variety of language employed, Brahim used TA almost exclusively. From time to time, elements from MSA or French—generally isolated lexical items or set expressions—were embedded. These embeddings were not randomly distributed but often seemed to serve some sort of rhetorical or discoursal function such as repeating an idea, quoting a source in support of an argument, or chunking the discourse into units (cf. Gumperz 1982). Items from MSA frequently clustered at the beginning of an extended turn at talk, an observation to which I return.

In characterizing Brahim's use of Arabic, a Tunisian working with me on the translation commented that he spoke like "someone mutilating the language." He often chose a word from MSA that did not quite fit the context, the sort of behavior a teacher of written composition would label "a persistent problem with diction." He sometimes did not finish utterances or ideas, nor did he "speak in paragraphs," as a more educated person might have. These behaviors would surely not have been lost on Zeineb because of her own education, her concentration on language and languages, and her experience interviewing a range of Korbans from various backgrounds. After she had completed all the interviews, I asked her some general questions about her impressions of them, including whether or not some speakers had, in her opinion, used French in an effort to show off, a pattern of behavior Tunisians are quite sensitive to and often speak about. (In my experience, they talk far less about the use of what I have termed diglossic switching; however, because educated speakers may borrow resources from CA/MSA and/or French and because TA is almost always the matrix language for switching, relative overuse of CA/MSA may co-occur with relative overuse of French and be coded as the latter.) Such sensitivity should not be surprising in a situation where codeswitching as unmarked choice occurs, because to codeswitch intrasententially is to claim peer status. Brahim was among those Zeineb named, although throughout his interview almost no French actually occurred. Hence, she likely perceived that with his very limited use of French, he was trying to behave as if he were her peer, a formulation she not surprisingly rejected.

The topic of the excerpt considered here remains among the most complex in Tunisian society, the role and status of women.[1] In fact, the real subject is much larger, touching on politics, religion, public and private life, and the family. Scholars of the Arab world, especially female and feminist scholars, have long reminded Westerners that the Arab world does not see the issue of women and their rights as an issue separate from issues of the family or even of men, a fact that is certainly true for that society and likely for our own more than we realize. One of the major topics in this excerpt is the control of the female body, mind, and life chances, a topic that looms large in discussions of contemporary Islam, including the work of Islamic feminists (e.g., Mernissi 1991), who for a variety of religious, cultural, and personal reasons respond to their faith's traditional marginalization of women in ways quite different from their Western sisters who are religious believers. It is not too much of an exaggeration to argue that the perspective espoused by Brahim—and many conservative Muslims, especially Muslim men—is one that is preoccupied (and many would claim obsessed) with limiting and controlling the female body, limiting its display in public contexts as well as its access to education. A corollary of limited education is limited access to prestigious linguistic varieties that might increase the likelihood that the female body would not only feel empowered to speak but also be able to make itself heard in public settings.

Given the nature of Brahim's views, the directness with which he stated them, and his frequent use of rhetorical questions using the second-person singular pronoun, I must contend that he was at least indirectly criticizing Zeineb's behavior. Certainly, her status as a university-educated woman (and perhaps her role as the interviewer) had little or no place in Brahim's ideological world, a perspective that Zeineb obviously rejected, as her comments in interviews with other young educated women and her decisions to attend university and not to wear the *hijêb*, or scarf emblematic of conservative Islamic dress, made unambiguously clear. Do any sociolinguistic manifestations of these differences occur during the interview? That is, does Zeineb perform embodied actions that contest Brahim's position? Certainly, she offered few verbal backchannel cues, except for laughter when Brahim offered an especially amusing hypothetical example. Rather, she offered silence, a not uncommon response by Tunisian women in similar situations or by Tunisians in general when deferring for whatever reason to an interlocutor whose comments threaten their face. There is, however, a more subtle battlefield on which this difference in perspective and values is played out, one involving the postdiglossic continuum and the political economy of language (Walters 1996b).

The postdiglossic continuum as resource

Generally, discussions of diglossia (Ferguson 1959), whether learned or popular, treat the phenomenon as a sort of deviancy, much as the continuing existence of social and regional dialects in English, described always as departures from the standard, is treated as deviant in most discussions of the linguistic situation in the United States. Diglossia obviously presents particular problems for nationist concerns (Fishman

1972) in the modern nation-state, especially universal literacy and education; yet it also provides language users with particular sorts of resources that do not exist in monoglossic communities. For example, Brahim often chose MSA lexical items in an effort to elevate his speech, but he sometimes failed to choose *le mot juste*, thus embodying an image quite different from the one he likely intended to project to Zeineb. In addition to lexical items that have no exact dialectal equivalent and that may be used when speaking the dialect or an elevated form of it, MSA frequently offers alternate realizations of lexical items that in fact exist in the dialect. In some cases, the differences in the two, the MSA and the dialectal, are questions of vowel quality. In other cases, however, the differences between the MSA and the dialectal variant are sharper, involving sounds that are not part of the phonemic inventory of the dialect. Not surprisingly, the use of one of the sounds associated uniquely with MSA marks the word (or stretch of speech) as classicized or elevated. The phrase for 'the woman', which recurred throughout this section of the interview, is one such case, as illustrated in figure 10.2.

The most elevated form, [(al).ˈma.ra.ʔa], includes the suffix [-a], a nominative case marker used only when speakers are reading aloud or making every possible effort to follow all the prescriptive rules of MSA. Generally, however, the word is realized by those speaking MSA extemporaneously as [(al).ˈma.ra.ʔ] with a word-final glottal stop, a sound not part of the phonemic inventory of uneducated speakers' TA. Lacking the glottal stop but still marked as elevated is the form [(al).ˈma.ra], in which neither vowel of the noun is reduced. In contrast, the corresponding dialectal form, [(l).mra:], is easily distinguished from the more elevated variants. Significantly, although these variants can be arranged along a single continuum relating to something we might term "formality," the variants are not distinguishable by the presence or absence of a single sound that might serve as a sociolinguistic variable. Rather, the differences relate to the co-occurrence of several phenomena—the presence or absence of the glottal stop, the realization of the definite article, vowel quality, prosodic template. Further, the variants do not represent interval data; they can be ranked along the diglossic continuum, but the distance between variants in terms of social evaluation is in no sense equal.

The battle of the glottal stop

Careful study of the transcript demonstrates that Zeineb and Brahim exploited this continuum in very different ways and to very different purposes as they spoke. Their differences in practice can be seen in (1), a list of tokens of 'woman' from the open-

CA/MSA	TA
[al.ˈma.ra.ʔa][al.ˈma.raʔ] [al.ˈma.ra]	[l.ˈmra:]

Figure 10.2. Some of the possible realizations of 'the woman' available to educated Tunisians when speaking Arabic. Periods represent syllable boundaries. In Arabic, because the definite article is a clitic, it combines with the noun to form a single phonological word. The definite article is /al/ for CA/MSA and TA, but is usually rendered [l] in the dialect.

ing lines of the 173-line transcript[2], along with the line number in which the token occurred:

(1)

> Zeineb: [ḷ.ma.raʔ t.tun.siy.ya] 'the Tunisian woman' (line 2)
> Brahim: [ḷ.ma.raʔ t.tun.siy.ya] 'the Tunisian woman' (3)
>   [mə.raʔ t.tunsiy.yə] 'Tunisian woman' (7–8)
>   [ḷ.mra:] 'the woman' (9)

When Zeineb posed the opening question about Brahim's opinion of the Tunisian woman (lines 1–2), when she asked for clarification (23, 38), and when she redirected the topic (97, 99–100), she used [(al).ma.raʔ], an elevated form, without exception.

Brahim's behavior contrasted sharply with Zeineb's. He used the form with the glottal stop, a classicized form, when repeating her topic (3, 98). Such a practice is common throughout this and other interviews, especially with educated speakers, who appear to repeat the topic of the interviewer's question as a floor-holding strategy in order to plan their response. As in other cases, Brahim repeated the relevant topic using Zeineb's exact words and even her phonological realization of this phrase. He likewise used the form with a glottal stop in his second use of the phrase 'the Tunisian woman' (7–8), although he used the form with a reduced vowel, [mə.raʔ t.tunsiy.yə] 'Tunisian woman'. As previously noted, MSA terms are often clustered near the beginning of a declamation or new topic. In this case, the form in lines 7 and 8 is classicized but simultaneously sliding toward the dialect. From line 9 on (except for the repetition of Zeineb's question in line 98), Brahim used only the TA form [ḷ.mra:] in each of the nine realizations of this term (9, 10, 12 [three times], 16, 30, and 34). Furthermore, part way through his discourse, Brahim shifted from talking about Tunisian women in general to discussing unmarried women, referred to as 'girls' in TA, regardless of their age.

Brahim's behavior is not idiosyncratic. In the interviews involving educated speakers, who are the only ones capable of exploiting the diglossic continuum to any degree, male speakers, whether educated or uneducated, consistently spoke about this topic using the dialectal form for 'woman', whereas educated women used a form that was somehow classicized; uneducated women used the TA variant [(ḷ.)ˈmra:]. Thus when the male interviewer spoke with male interviewees, both parties used [(ḷ.)ˈmra:] (with the exception of, e.g., quotations from the Qur'an). When the educated female interviewer spoke with educated female interviewees, both parties used [(al).ma.raʔ] or at least [(al).ˈma.ra], with no glottal stop but two distinct syllables, each of which contained an unreduced vowel. In cross-sex conversations, however, the variants used were almost always sex-exclusive except, as noted, for quotations. When asked about these practices at lectures I gave and in private discussions in Tunis during 1997–1998, many educated Tunisians of both sexes concurred that such patterns represent the behavioral norm.

Thus, when discussing this topic, educated women prefer formulating and enacting this word in MSA (or at least using a form that is influenced by MSA), the linguistic variety associated with serious matters, with education (and hence logic and reason), and with the Islamic religion. Certainly, these same women's mothers, who are generally illiterate, have no access to such resources. Hence, by using this variant (and others influenced by MSA) in such a context, educated women embody not only their knowledge of MSA but also the social changes of the past 4 decades and their hopes for a future different from the past. (When using the word 'woman' in everyday conversation—e.g., 'The woman who knocked has gone'—educated women use the dialect form as would all other Tunisians.) In contrast, men, including educated men, prefer formulating the topic using the dialectal term, thereby placing it in the discourse of everyday tradition, common sense, and a status quo that in fact hearkens to an imagined and idealized past.

Among Brahim's borrowings from MSA in this excerpt are five lexical items realized with the glottal stop. When using these words, many Tunisians, including highly educated ones, would nativize them and thus not use this sound. Hence, it cannot be argued that Brahim, because he was less educated than Zeineb, was uncomfortable using MSA lexical items containing the glottal stop. Rather, it appears that in rendering 'the woman', Brahim, like many men, had chosen not to use a glottal stop or to classicize the word in any way. Consequently, there appears to be a ritualized divergence or disaccommodation (Myers-Scotton 1985), which permits Zeineb's behavior to provide a metalinguistic commentary on Brahim's responses and the interaction itself. Embodied as it is, such commentary constitutes a clear counterdiscourse, a use of the resources at the speaker's disposal to interrupt and critique the discourse of Brahim and powerful segments of the society at large.

Further, when Zeineb redirected the topic (172–173), encouraging Brahim to discuss tourism by picking up on his earlier remarks, she asked about its [tɛʔ.θiːr] 'influence', using the glottal stop in her realization of the term, a realization Brahim "quoted" and used more or less consistently throughout his comments (in contrast to his behavior with 'woman'). I attribute no particular agency, conscious or preconscious, to Zeineb's realization of 'influence' at this point in the interview; however, her behavior was certainly within the bounds of the normal or expected for a highly educated person. By using the glottal stop and using it correctly and appropriately, she reminded Brahim of her relative place in Tunisian society—and his. Both "places" were defined by the nonconverging intersection of gender, education, class, and hence access to linguistic varieties and contexts for their acquisition and for mastery of their appropriate use. In this regard, Zeineb's behavior was literally the embodiment, the instantiation, of a world Brahim wished to reject and deny: a world in which an unveiled female body, as speaking subject, exploits the resources of symbolic and even economic capital associated with CA/MSA.

Conclusion: "Opening the door of paradise a cubit"

When Brahim began his comments on women in Tunisia, he complained that Tunisia's president at the time of independence, Habib Bourguiba, had "opened the door of paradise a cubit" for women, an idiom that translates roughly as 'he gave 'em an inch and they took a mile' and carries the same critique of excess as its English equivalent. In ways Brahim did not realize, he was correct in claiming that Tunisian women have taken great advantage of the opportunities offered them, often in ways not fore-seen by those who made these opportunities possible. Whether one evaluates and responds to this situation in a positive or negative way depends largely on one's own habitus and even hexis, the dispositions resulting from life experience and carried in the body.

I began this chapter with a passage recounting a highly unusual situation in which a Tunisian woman, who could not appear as a witness in court under traditional in-terpretations of the *Shari'a* law in centuries past, could appear to plead her own di-vorce case, but only under circumstances that the culture constructed as the most horrific possible: when she had been sodomized by her husband. The morphology of the body and its social construction mattered with respect to not only the sexual act involved but also the reporting of it. Not authorized to speak, the woman, almost surely illiterate, entered the court silently. She squatted before the judge in an em-bodied act of submission before the law, a male-dominated institution requiring the use of a variety of language (CA) that she did not command. Finally, she, the victim, had to commit a wordless act of apparently iconic significance, turning her shoes over so that the soles faced up. Even picturing in my mind such a sequence of events sends shivers through my body. (Had a man been unwillingly sodomized, I assume that he would not have sought redress by silently placing his shoes sole-up before a judge. He certainly could not have filed for a divorce because legal marriage and hence divorce in Tunisia, as well as in the anglophone West, assumed and assume heterosexuality. Further, the topic itself might have been unspeakable—even indi-rectly so, at least in courts of law. Surely, the meaning of the act would have been different because of the morphology of the bodies involved and the ways in which those morphologies and their meanings were socially constructed through action and language.)

In contrast, in the excerpt of the sociolinguistic interview examined in this chap-ter, the woman, a university student, pleaded a very different sort of case in a very different way. Although she spoke little, she was by no means silent. She was, after all, being paid to conduct interviews for a foreign researcher, using the linguistic and social skills she embodied, evidence of her life's experiences. Further, when she spoke, she did not hesitate to use the linguistic resources at her disposal in ways increas-ingly conventionalized for educated women in Tunisia, ways that were not available to the male interviewee, who had had less formal education than she. Her use of the classicized variants of 'the woman' contrasted markedly with the male interviewee's, each indexing a view of the world and life in Tunisia in clear conflict with the other's. There can be no real convergence between the view of the world narrated and per-formed by Brahim and the view of the world embodied by Zeineb. Clearly, the so-cial and identity categories relating to women and their lives constructed by Zeineb and Brahim through their linguistic practice and daily lives coexisted even in the small town of Korba, but they did not necessarily do so peaceably.

The research of Tunisian sociologist Malika Zamiti-Horchani (1986) has expli-cated the specific nature of some of these nonconverging views of Tunisian women and their rights. In her survey of 400 adult Tunisians conducted at about the time of the sociolinguistic interview examined here, nearly all younger women between 20 and 40 and many women over 40, even those who were illiterate, supported the notion of a "modern" Tunisian woman who is free to decide the outcome of her life and control her income. Older men, especially those over 40 who were educated town dwellers, as well as those who are uneducated, whether they lived in rural or more urban areas, and some older women over 40, especially those who had had no education, subscribed to what Zamiti-Horchani termed the "conservative" view, preferring the "traditional woman" who focuses on home and family, always under the supervision of her husband. A third group, comprising the majority of younger men, especially those with some education who dwelled in cities, and some older educated urban women and men, offered what Zamiti-Horchani termed "intermediate responses," which were "contradictory and reveal an ambivalent attitude" (1986:111). Brahim's views fell somewhere between the second and third positions Zamiti-Horchani outlined. During the discussion analyzed here, Brahim acknowledged that women should receive some education, but he was certainly not ready to deal with the consequences of their becoming educated. He, like many similarly situated men in Tunisia, would "endeavor, through a strategy of retrieval, to hi-jack the new by integrating it into the old" (Zamiti-Horchani 1986:119).

And while younger educated women may well be integrating the linguistic resources they now control into patterns of daily language use in Tunisia, they are simultaneously reconfiguring the social, sociolinguistic, and linguistic categories of variation there. Even in this situation, however, there is no convergence, at least not at the symbolic level. As noted, Zeineb, like many young educated women, used classicized variants of 'the woman' (and many other lexical items, though variably so), thereby embodying her education while simultaneously indexing the rights and obligation sets associated with CA/MSA—authority, logic and reason, seriousness, and Islam. Although Tunisian laws, written in CA/MSA and promulgated by a male president who holds near-complete power (Marzouki 1993), have enabled these women to engage in these practices, this same linguistic variety is very close to the one used by Brahim when he recited a Qur'anic sura about men having control over women. Just as the rights and obligations indexed by CA/MSA do not converge neatly, neither do the identity categories—'traditional woman' or 'modern woman'—that educated Tunisian women embody. The likelihood of any possible convergence diminishes greatly when one considers the many other identity or social categories that might intersect and that Zeineb embodied—university student, small-town native, religious believer but not "fundamentalist," someone who lived for a year in the United States as an exchange student, and myriad others—all within contexts where normativity is ever palpable.

We are thus left to ponder an issue raised by Butler: "To what extent do *regulatory practices* of gender formation and division constitute identity, the internal coherence of the subject, indeed, the self-identical status of the person? To what extent is 'identity' a normative ideal rather than a descriptive feature of experience?" (1990:16, emphasis in original). I offer no answer to Butler's question. The most appropriate answer would likely be to question the social and linguistic categories and the reductionist criteria for category membership we so frequently employ in the study of language and especially language and gender. Although these categories intersect in individual bodies, they do not and cannot converge, nor can they account for gender as lived experience, which cannot help but influence language use. To the extent that our answers prod us to admit these facts and to behave accordingly, we are well on the way to theorizing a very different sort of notion of the self and identity, of the body and embodied linguistic practice, from those on which we now rely.

A postscript from the field

Listening to this interview in Tunisia in 1998, I feel I must note that if Brahim continues to hold the opinions he expressed so openly a decade ago, he might well not express them in public today and certainly not during a taped interview. On November 7, 1987, a little over a year after the interview took place, Bourguiba, Tunisia's first and then only president since independence, was replaced in a bloodless coup by Zine El Abidine Ben Ali. In the decade since President Ben Ali's coming to power, Tunisia has changed in many ways. With even limited economic liberalization, Tunisia's middle class has grown into the largest and strongest in the Arab world, and the standard of living has risen greatly for nearly all Tunisians, even the rural poor. For his achievements, Ben Ali has been the recipient of numerous international awards, and Tunisia is to some extent regaining its position as one of the success stories of the developing world. This economic growth has come at the expense of what some Western commentators and Tunisian intellectuals characterize as infringements of human rights: Mosques are locked except at prayer time, women are prohibited from wearing the *hijêb* in the government workplace, and, according to many reports, numerous male fundamentalists were arrested, imprisoned, or worse after Ben Ali came to power. (Each of these actions, of course, controls or disciplines bodies, limiting their ability to participate in particular linguistic or larger symbolic economies.) Yet many Tunisians appear to accept willingly the government's dichotomous formulation of the country's alternatives: the bloody chaos of neighboring Algeria or the stability and economic growth with concomitant limitations on freedom of expression offered by the current powers.

During the decade since *le changement*, women's legal rights have been further cemented. No doubt partly as a response to fundamentalist tendencies among certain Muslims, concern for women's issues has become a trope of government discourse, and strides continue to be made in increasing school attendance by young girls, improving health care for women, and decreasing the rate of infant mortality. Yet, although nearly 90% of school-aged girls who were born between 1980 and 1984 attended school in 1994, girls in that age cohort were three times more likely to be illiterate than boys that age. This "feminization" of illiteracy contrasts with the situation for adults born 1914 or earlier, when well over 95% of the population was illiterate, but females and males had nearly equal chances of being so.

A recent television broadcast on March 21, 1998, Youth Day, demonstrates the complex situation in which young Tunisian women—and men—attempt to create identities for themselves. The announcers, one female, the other male, both in their early 30s, spoke Arabic, often switching from the dialect to MSA and back again, the norm for unscripted media discourse, as did those they interviewed. (Arabic/French codeswitching rarely occurs in media discourse in Tunisia.) In a semicircle on a stage behind the announcers sat couples, aged 20 or so, each wearing the "traditional" wedding garb of Tunisia's major geographical regions and cities. The styles of clothing date back at least to the turn of this century, and such outfits would have been worn by only the most economically privileged, a fact never mentioned and rarely noted in the frequent displays of such clothing. During the program, the couples wearing wedding garb sat stiffly, as is the custom at weddings even today, especially for brides. After interviewing each pair as representative of its particular region, the announcers introduced contemporary entertainment, choreographed dancing of the sort broadcast on Tunisian television each Saturday afternoon during the hit parade of Arab and Western popular songs, which includes MTV-style videos. The adolescent girls who danced to the English-language music wore silvery stretch halter tops and black pants; their bare midriffs echoed those of the young women dressed in traditional wedding wear of certain regions. The costumes of the boys, baggy black pants and shirts, differed sharply from those of the men in wedding dress. In traditional Tunisian culture and in *des spectacles folkloriques*, there are occasions when women and men dance as groups, but rarely at the same time. The complex continuities and discontinuities of such juxtapositions, jarring to my Western eyes, characterize daily life in all of Tunisia, having become naturalized. They remind social scientists of the ways in which gender, like language use, is practiced, enacted, displayed, regulated, and necessarily embodied within a social context that is grounded in history at both the personal and global levels.

NOTES

I gratefully acknowledge the support of numerous institutions that have made this research possible, including the United States Information Service, the United States Department of Education, the American Institute for Maghribi Studies, the Social Science Research Council, and the Graduate School, University Research Institute, and Center for Middle Eastern Studies of the University of Texas at Austin. Comments by Naima El-Arbi, Naima Boussofara, Elizabeth Fernea, Jonathan Tamez, and the editors of this volume on earlier drafts of this chapter have greatly improved its quality and my thinking about these issues. These data were discussed from a different perspective in Walters (1996a).

    1. Westerners are generally unaware that this topic has been the subject of great intellectual debate in the Arab world since at least the turn of the century. An earlier generation of feminists held the view that well-educated Arab men—Qasim Amin (1863–1908) in Egypt and Tahar Haddad (1899–1935) in Tunisia—and Western women, often the wives of colonial administrators, were the impetus for the struggle for women's rights in the Arab world (Raccagni 1983). The work of more recent scholars, Arab and non-Arab (e.g., Bakalti 1996; Baron 1994; Marzouki 1993), complicates such a reading of history.

    2. A copy of the translated transcript is available from the author, Department of Linguistics, University of Texas at Austin, Austin, TX 78712-1196 USA.

REFERENCES

Allport, Gordon W., & H. Cantrill (1934). Judging personality from voice. *Journal of Social Psychology* 5:37–55.

Bakalti, Souad (1996). *La Femme tunisienne au temps de la colonisation, 1881–1956.* Paris: L'Harmattan.

Baron, Beth (1994). *The women's awakening in Egypt: Culture, society, and the press.* New Haven: Yale University Press.

de Beauvoir, Simone (1953). *The second sex.* New York: Knopf.

Bell, Allan (1984). Language style as audience design. *Language in Society* 13:145–204.

Blakeslee, Sandra (1996). Complex and hidden brain in the gut makes cramps, butterflies, and valium. *New York Times* (23 January):B5, B10.

Bourdieu, Pierre (1977). *Outline of a theory of practice.* Cambridge: Cambridge University Press.

Butler, Judith (1990). *Gender trouble: Feminism and the subversion of identity.* New York: Routledge.

——— (1993). *Bodies that matter: On the discursive limits of "sex."* New York: Routledge.

Eckert, Penelope (1989). The whole woman: Sex and gender differences in variation. *Language Variation and Change* 3:245–269.

Ferguson, Charles (1959). Diglossia. *Word* 15:329–340.

Fishman, Joshua (1972). *Language and nationalism: Two integrative essays.* Rowley, MA: Newbury House.

Geertz, Clifford (1983). Common sense as a cultural system. In Geertz, *Local knowledge: Further essays in interpretive anthropology.* New York: Basic Books, 73–93.

Gumperz, John (1982). Conversational code-switching. In Gumperz, *Discourse strategies.* Cambridge: Cambridge University Press, 59–99.

Institut National de la Statistique (1984). *Recensement général de la population et de l'habitat, 30 mars 1984.* Vol. 4: *Caractèristiques educationnelles.* Tunis: Ministère du Plan, Republique Tunisienne.

Labov, William (1966). *The social stratification of English in New York City.* Washington, DC: Center for Applied Linguistics.

——— (1990). The intersection of sex and social class in the course of linguistic change. *Language Variation and Change* 2:205–251.

Lakoff, Robin (1975). *Language and woman's place.* New York: Harper & Row.

Largueche, Dalenda, & Abdelhamid Largueche (1992). *Marginales en terre d'Islam.* Tunis: Cérès Productions.

Marzouki, Ilhem (1993). *Le Mouvement des femmes en Tunisie au XXème siecle.* Tunis: Cérès Productions.

Mernissi, Fatima (1991). *The veil and the male elite: A feminist interpretation of women's rights in Islam.* Trans. Mary Jo Lakeland. Reading, MA: Addison-Wesley.

Myers-Scotton, Carol (1985). "What the heck, sir": Style shifting and lexical coloring as features of powerful language. In R. L. Street, Jr., & J. N. Cappella (eds.), *Sequence and pattern in communicative behaviour.* London: Edward Arnold, 102–119.

——— (1993). *Social motivations for codeswitching: Evidence from Africa.* Oxford: Oxford University Press.

Nelson, Kristina (1985). *The art of reciting the Qur'an.* Austin: University of Texas Press.

Raccagni, Michelle (1983). Origins of feminism in Egypt and Tunisia. Ph.D. diss., New York University.

Thompson, John B. (1991). Editor's introduction. In Pierre Bourdieu, *Language and symbolic power.* Cambridge, MA: Harvard University Press, 1–31.

Uchida, Aki (1992). When "difference" is "dominance": A critique of the "anti-power-based" cultural approach to sex differences. *Language in Society* 21:547–568.

Walters, Keith (1989). Social change and linguistic variation in Korba, a small Tunisian town. Ph.D. diss., University of Texas at Austin.

——— (1991). Women, men, and linguistic variation in the Arab world. In Bernard Comrie & Mushira Eid (eds.), *Perspectives on Arabic linguistics III.* Philadelphia: Benjamins, 199–229.

———— (1996a). Gender, quantitative sociolinguistics, and the linguistics of community. In Mary Bucholtz, A. C. Liang, Laurel A. Sutton, & Caitlin Hines (eds.), *Cultural performances: Proceedings of the Third Berkeley Women and Language Conference*. Berkeley, CA: Berkeley Women and Language Group, 757–776.

———— (1996b). Gender, identity, and the political economy of language: Anglophone wives in Tunisia. *Language in Society* 25:515–556.

———— (in preparation). *"Without Tunisian Arabic, we're not Tunisian": Identity and the changing political economy of language in Tunisia.*

Weinreich, Uriel, William Labov, & Marvin Herzog (1968). Empirical foundations for a theory of language change. In Winfred P. Lehmann & Yakov P. Malkiel (eds.), *Directions for historical linguistics*. Austin: University of Texas Press, 95–189.

Woolard, Kathryn A. (1989). *Doubletalk*. Stanford, CA: Stanford University Press.

Zamiti-Horchani, Malika (1986). Tunisian women, their rights, and their ideas about their rights. In Monique Gadant (ed.), *Women of the Mediterranean*. Trans. A. M. Berrett. London: Zed Books, 110–119.

Part III

· ·

IDENTITY
AS INGENUITY

The Display of (Gendered) Identities in Talk at Work

Over the course of my career analyzing interaction, I have found myself repeatedly returning to *framing* as the theoretical and methodological approach that sheds most light on what individuals are doing when they interact. In this chapter I suggest that the framing approach is also enlightening for understanding the relationship between language and gender. One of the chief crafters of the theoretical construct of framing, Erving Goffman (1974), wrote a key paper that has been overlooked by those concerned with language and gender: a 1977 essay entitled "The Arrangement Between the Sexes." Though not focused on language per se (the focus on language did not appear in Goffman's work until later, with the articles collected in *Forms of Talk* [1981]), the 1977 essay provides a theoretical framework that is strikingly consonant (prescient, you might say) with the notion of gendered identity as display that is the theme of this volume.

In this chapter, I suggest a theoretical approach that combines Goffman with my own earlier work, then illustrate with examples of workplace conversations between, on the one hand, two men, and, on the other, three women. In both cases, the conversants are of different ranks. When people talk to each other at work, the hierarchical relations among them are likely to be in focus: Talking to a boss is different from talking to a subordinate, and speakers are relatively aware of these alignments. The effect of hierarchical relations on communication in this setting has been a focus of my research. I have also been interested in how gender patterns interact with the influence of hierarchical relations; that, too, is a subject addressed here (see Tannen 1994c for my earlier explorations of these topics).

While focusing on speakers' relative status, I also illustrate a number of theoretical points that I have developed elsewhere (Tannen 1994b). First, I argue that linguistic strategies are both ambiguous and polysemous; with this in mind, I show how the strategies used by the speakers in these examples are used and interpreted, and I explore their relation to the speakers' genders. In the process, I attempt to bring together two theoretical frameworks and make the following points about them: (1) understanding language and gender is best approached through the concept of framing; and (2) framing is a way of simultaneously balancing the dimensions of status and connection.

Finally, I hope in this chapter to offer a corrective to two misconceptions that have surfaced in the literature. The first is that status and connection are mutually exclusive poles. My claim is that they both are at play at every moment of interaction; they dovetail and intertwine. The second misconception is that a "cultural-difference" approach to gender and language and a "dominance" approach are mutually exclusive and opposed to each other. My claim is that dominance relations and cultural influences of all types (gender-related as well as other influences, such as geographic region, ethnicity, class, age, sexual orientation, and profession) are at play at every moment of interaction; they too dovetail and intertwine.

Sex-class-linked framing

I have put the word *gendered* in parentheses in the title of this chapter to reflect my conviction that often it is preferable to look at ways of speaking that pattern by gender out of the corner of the eye rather than head-on. The reason I believe that this is the most productive way to look at gender is captured by Goffman's (1977) terminology. Unfortunately, however, this very terminology muddies the waters, because Goffman uses the term *identity* to mean the opposite of the sense in which it is used in this volume. For Goffman, *identity* refers to the notion against which he was arguing—one which would be roughly equivalent to what today is (sneeringly) referred to as "essentialized" notions of gender. Goffman's use of *identity* is more or less the noun corresponding to the adjective *identical*: the assumption that women and men behave in ways that are necessarily linked to their biological gender. It is like identity relations in formal logic.

In Goffman's terms, ways of talking that pattern by gender are not "sex-linked" but "sex-class-linked," where *class* refers not to social class but rather to set theory, as in "the class of women" and "the class of men":

> In referring to an attribute of gender, it is easy to speak of matters that are "sex-linked" (or "sex-correlated") in order to avoid the more cumbersome locution, "sex-class-linked." And, of course, it is very natural to speak of "the sexes," "cross-sex," "the other sex," and so forth. And so I shall. But this is a dangerous economy, especially so since such glossing fits perfectly with our cultural stereotypes. (1977:305)

In other words, you might say that "the class of women" and "the class of men" are social categories, whereas "women" and "men" are biological categories. Certain behaviors in certain cultures are more likely to be associated with the "class" of women or the "class" of men. This association is real, but it does not mean that every individual in the class will exhibit those behaviors. Associating the behaviors with every member of the class rather than with the class itself is, in Gregory Bateson's (1972) terms, an error of logical types. This difference in logical types is, I believe, what Goffman intends by distinguishing the concept *sex-linked* (which he rejects) from the concept *sex-class-linked* (which he supports). It is, in Goffman's elegant phrasing, a "dangerous economy" because the behavior comes to be thought of as an individual phenomenon, as if it were linked to a chromosome, rather than as a social phenomenon that links (in the minds of members of that culture) individuals who display those behaviors with that class. In current terminology, this error in thinking, about which Bateson wrote extensively, could be called "essentializing"— although I caution against the use of this term since it has, in recent years, devolved into a kind of academic name-calling (as Emily Nussbaum [1997:24] aptly and wittily put it: "that generic gender studies *j'accuse!*").

In a way, Goffman's distinction between *sex-linked* and *sex-class-linked* parallels the distinction commonly made today between *sex* and *gender*—the former being regarded as a biological phenomenon, the latter as a socially constructed one. It is wise, however, to bear in mind that this distinction, although compelling in the abstract, is problematic in the particular. As Stephen Jay Gould emphasizes, biology and environment are inextricably intertwined: "It's logically, mathematically, philosophically impossible to pull them apart" (quoted in Angier 1993:B1).

A similar point is made by Eleanor Maccoby, who notes that the practice of using the word *gender* to refer to culturally determined characteristics and the word *sex* for biologically determined ones serves to reinforce a false ideology that biological and cultural factors can be distinguished:

> Some writers attempt to distinguish the biological aspects of sex from the social aspects by using the terms *sex* for the one and *gender* for the other. This usage is not adopted here, on the assumption that the two factors interact in any psychological function that we might want to consider. Furthermore, uncovering the biological and social connections to behavior is a major research objective, not something to be assumed at the outset through the choice of terminology. (1988:755)

While bearing these cautions in mind, we can note that Goffman's distinction between *sex-linked* and *sex-class-linked* is roughly parallel to the biological versus cultural or sex versus gender distinction, since *sex-linked* refers to the assumption that a particular behavior is linked to every individual of a given sex, whereas *sex-class-linked* associates the behavior with the group identity—the "class" of women or the "class" of men as they are constructed in a given culture.

In another essay concerned with gender, Goffman introduces another set of terms to capture this distinction—and here is where the use of the term *identity* can be confusing to current readers. He explains that ways of talking and behaving that are associated with gender are a matter not of identity but of *display*. By this he means that the behavior is not a reflection of the individual's nature (identity) but rather of some performance that the individual is accomplishing (display):

> Instead of having to play out an act, the animal, in effect, provides a readily readable expression of his situation, specifically his intent, this taking the form of a "ritualization" of some portion of the act itself, and this indication (whether promise or threat) presumably allows for the negotiation of an efficient response from, and to, witnesses of the display. (1979:1)

In other words, *identity* here is like identity relations in philosophy: A = B, because they are, by nature, the same thing. *Display*, in contrast, refers to the symbolic nature of human interaction, the "ritualized" performance of behaviors that represent culturally recognizable situations, intentions, or activities. Interaction, then, is a "ceremony" made up of "rituals," which Goffman defines as "perfunctory, conventionalized acts through which one individual portrays his regard for another to that other" (1979:1). Herein lies Goffman's key notion of *face*—individuals' concern with how they come across to others.

Goffman goes on to explain that "emotionally motivated behaviors become formalized—in the sense of becoming simplified, exaggerated, and stereotyped," and consequently, more efficient. Again, an explanation of terms is needed. Goffman's use of the term *stereotyped* is not like the one most often encountered in common parlance—the tendency to attribute unfounded negative generalizations to individuals associated with a particular social group—but rather refers to the ceremonial nature of human interaction: Behaviors are "stereotyped" in that they become associated with culturally recognizable meanings. For example, crying comes to indicate feelings of sadness and laughter feelings of amusement. These conventions are culturally relative—witness the confusion created in cross-cultural communication between Westerners who regard laughter as a stereotyped expression of amusement and Asians who regard it, in some situations, as a stereotyped means of covering embarrassment or other social discomfort.

Crucially, Goffman continues, such displays "provide evidence of the actor's *alignment* in a gathering, the position he seems prepared to take up in what is about to happen in the social situation" (1979:1). He elaborates:

> Displays don't communicate in the narrow sense of the term; they don't enunciate something through a language of symbols openly established and used solely for that purpose. They provide evidence of the actor's alignment in the situation. And displays are important insofar as alignments are. (1979:1)

Alignment, then, is a type of framing: By talking in particular ways, speakers display their attitudes toward interlocutors, the situation, and the material being talked about. *Alignment* refers to what Bronwyn Davies and Rom Harré (1990) call *positioning*: how ways of speaking demonstrate and create the context and the relationships among speakers.

This is a radically different view of language than is common not only in language and gender research but also in the field of linguistics in general, in which language is seen as a code. As A. L. Becker (1995) argues, the "code" metaphor gives us an inert concept of language, much like the "conduit" metaphor for language that Michael Reddy (1979) has described. In contrast, Becker suggests we think of language as languag*ing*—a way of *doing* something. Framing, then, is one thing we do with language—displaying our alignments.

Our tendency to locate gender differences in the individual rather than in the relation among individuals in a group also reflects American ideology. In this spirit, Maccoby (1990) points out that when she and Carol Jacklin published their classic survey *The Psychology of Sex Differences* in 1974, they concluded that research had uncovered no significant sex differences. Looking back in 1990, however, Maccoby notes that this finding, besides reflecting the ideological climate of the times, emerged because the studies they had surveyed were looking for differences in individual abilities—for example, testing children for their mathematical skills. When subsequent research (their own and others') examined the behavior of girls and boys in interaction, highly significant patterns of difference became evident, such as the tendency of little boys to monopolize toys when they played with girls.

Even power itself tends to be conceptualized by Americans as inherent in an individual, in contrast to members of other cultures who tend to conceptualize it as a social phenomenon. Patricia Wetzel (1988) points out that the Japanese see power as a matter of connection—the individual's place in a hierarchical network. In other words, individuals don't "have" power as a personal attribute but rather gain it as a function of their relations to others. In my own framework (Tannen 1994b, c), I have pointed out that power and solidarity are intertwined: Having a wide network of friends on whom you can call enhances your power to get things done.

The most fruitful approaches to examining gender and language, then, do not try to link behavior directly to individuals of one sex or the other but rather begin by asking how interaction is framed—in Goffman's terms, what *alignments* speakers are taking up; in the terms of Davies and Harré (1990), how speakers are *positioning* themselves with respect to the situation—and then ask where women and men tend to fall in this pattern of framing. This captures the "performance" or "display" aspect of gendered patterns, which is, after all, the aspect that most truly reflects how verbal and other forms of behavior really work in interaction.

In one such study, Frances Smith (1993) compares the sermons of four women and ten men in a preaching lab at a Baptist seminary. She began by determining the various "footings" the preachers took in relation to the texts they were interpreting. In other words, she asked how they positioned themselves in relation to the material they were preaching about and the task they were performing. One footing she identified was a style in which speakers foregrounded their authority by putting themselves "on record" as interpreters of the text and by calling attention to the fact that they were in the position of authority, interpreting the text for the audience. To emphasize that the gender pattern is a tendency, not an absolute divide, Smith illustrates this "on-record" style with a sermon performed by a woman, Meg; however, she notes that Meg was the only woman who adopted this style, along with four men. For example, Meg posed a question and then said, "I've done a lot of thinking about that and I came up with several possible reasons." At another point Meg said, "I'd like to insert something here." Using a different style, another woman spoke as if she were telling a story to a group of children. She began, "A little boy grew up in a Samaritan village. He had a happy childhood and sometimes his parents would take him to the neighboring villages, to market, or occasionally they might even go to Galilee to the

226 IDENTITY AS INGENUITY

sea for a vacation." A third woman, rather than stepping outside the text to comment on it in her own voice, retold the story in a literary register. For example, she said, "The clarity of the directions that God gave him were as a stab in his heart." The fourth woman simply downplayed her authority by maintaining a "low-profile" stance.

By asking first what alignments the preachers took up in relation to their audiences and to the material about which they preached, and only then asking which alignments were adopted by the women and men in her study and what linguistic strategies were associated with those alignments, Smith arrived at a much fuller understanding of gender patterns than she would have if she had asked only what linguistic features appeared in the sermons preached by the women and men. The footings assumed by the women in her study—the ways they positioned themselves with respect to their audiences and their material—tended to background rather than foreground their authority.

In another exemplary study, Elisabeth Kuhn (1992) examines the classroom discourse of professors at American and German universities. She noticed that the American female professors she taped were more assertive in giving their students direct orders at the beginning of the term. This finding initially surprised her, but she eventually realized that it was because they spoke of "the requirements" of the course as if these were handed down directly from the institution and then told the students how they could fulfill them. For example, one female professor said, "We are going to talk about the requirements." Kuhn contrasts this with the male professors in her study, who also handed out lists of requirements in the form of syllabi but made it explicit that the syllabi represented decisions they personally had made. For example, one man said, "I have two midterms and a final. And I added this first midterm rather early to get you going on reading, uh, discussions, so that you will not fall behind." In Smith's terms, this professor put himself "on record" as the authority who authored the requirements. Thus an apparently unexpected verbal behavior—women's speaking more assertively than men—was explained by the alignments they were taking up in relation to the course requirements and the students they were addressing. Both Smith's and Kuhn's findings are consistent with Shari Kendall's (1993) observation that women often create and display their authority in ways that downplay rather than emphasize it.

The approach I am describing as related to framing is also found in Elinor Ochs's essay "Indexing Gender" (1992). Ochs argues that rather than seeing gender-related patterns of behavior as individuals' direct expressions of gender (or sex), we should regard such behavioral patterns as associated with identifiable stances that, in a given cultural context, become associated with being female or male.[1] I see this notion of *stances* as parallel to Goffman's concept of *the class of women* or *the class of men*.

Finally, I borrow Gregory Bateson's (1979) concept of *the corner of the eye* to capture the idea that some phenomena are understood best when they are not looked at directly but rather come into view when some other aspect of the world is the object of direct focus. This is the sense in which I am suggesting that the relation between gender and language may be best understood when the focus of attention is on framing.[2] Framing, which more closely captures participants' senses of what is going on in an interaction, also captures more closely the relationship between language and gender.

power	solidarity
hierarchy	equality
distance	closeness

Figure 11.1. A unidimensional model of status and connection

Status and connection

The second aspect of the theoretical framework I am proposing here is the notion of status and connection as intertwined, ambiguous, and polysemous rather than mutually exclusive and opposed to each other. I have developed this idea at length elsewhere (Tannen 1994b). The discussion in this section is condensed from that source.

In research and in conventional wisdom, Americans have had a tendency to conceptualize the relationship between status and connection as unidimensional and mutually exclusive. This can be illustrated in the form of a continuum with two opposite poles (see figure 11.1). This conceptualization underlies Americans' use of the terms *sisters* and *brothers* to indicate 'close and equal', so that "We are like sisters" or "They were like brothers" implies not only closeness but also "there are no status games here." In contrast, hierarchical relationships are assumed to preclude closeness. Thus in my own interviews and observations in work settings, I was frequently told that being friends with subordinates or superiors is either impossible or problematic.

I have suggested that what we are dealing with is really not a single dimension but a multidimensional grid (see figure 11.2). This grid illustrates that hierarchy/equality is one axis, and closeness/distance another.[3] Americans seem to conceptualize relationships along an axis that runs from the upper right to the lower left: from hi-

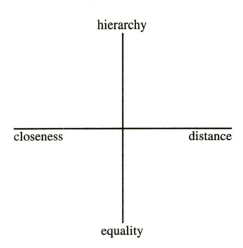

Figure 11.2. A multidimensional model of status and connection

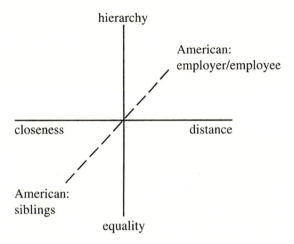

Figure 11.3. The American model of status and connection

erarchical and distant to equal and close. We put business relations in the upper right quadrant and family and close friendships in the lower left (figure 11.3). In contrast, Japanese, Chinese, and Javanese tend to conceptualize relationships along an axis that runs from the upper left to the lower right: from hierarchical and close to equal and distant. The archetype of a close, hierarchical relationship for members of these cultures is the mother-child (or grandparent-grandchild) constellation (figure 11.4).[4] The locus of equal relationships, in this schema, is not found in the intimate family context but rather at work, among colleagues of the same rank and seniority.

Complicating matters further, or perhaps reflecting the complex relations represented by these grids, linguistic strategies are both ambiguous and polysemous in exhibiting status and connection in interaction. In other words, a given utterance may

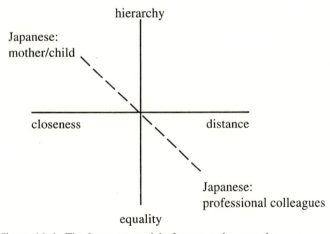

Figure 11.4. The Japanese model of status and connection

be intended or interpreted in terms of connection or of status (whence ambiguity), or it may reflect elements of both at the same time (whence polysemy).

Workplace examples

In this section I present two examples of workplace interaction—one among men and the other among women—in order to illustrate how the speakers balance status and connection and to suggest that their ways of speaking are sex-class-linked and best understood through a theory of framing.

The first example is from a conversation taped by Lena Gavruseva (1995).[5] The conversation, which took place in the office of a local newspaper, involved John, the editor-in-chief, and Dan, a recently hired writer. Dan was walking past John's office, spied him sitting at his desk with his door open, and stepped in to engage in friendly chat, which he initiated by asking, "What are you scowling at, John?" In response, John launched into a discourse about problems involving someone's computer (making it into an amusing anecdote about how the computer exploded), in the course of which he referred to Dan's computer in the following way:

John: You just have that little shitburner of an XT.

Soon after, John asked Dan, "How is your computer?" and the following conversation ensued:[6]

Dan: It sucks. I mean
John: Why?
Dan: I- 'Cause it doesn't
John: Why, it's slow?
Dan: No, it's not that.
        It's just like there are all sorts of keys
        that don't work and stuff.
John: What do you mean keys that don't work.
Dan: Like the caps lock doesn't work.
John: It can- You want it to?
Dan: No, it doesn't.
John: You want it to?
Dan: Okay.
John: All right. What else would you like?
Dan: um I don't know. It was just sort of-
John: No no no, come on.
Dan: Like I can't turn it off because
John: You would like-
        you'd like to be able to turn it off?
        Why? 'Cause it bothers you?
Dan: and it's it's frozen up on me
        like three times.

John: Yeah?
Dan: Yeah.
John: Like is there a pattern?
Dan: No, I mean maybe there is
         I haven't noticed it.
         I- I don't know.
         It hasn't done it for about a week or so,
         so don't worry.
         I'm just griping.
         I'm just griping.
         I've never-
         I've got no particular complaints
         because it- all I need to-
         I'm not I'm not one of these,
         I'm not a computer junkie
         so I don't really care.
John: So if you want your caps lock key to work
         there's no problem.
         I can come in and do that.
Dan: No, I don't really need a caps lock.
John: It'll take me twenty-five seconds.
Dan: I'd like to s-
         Okay I challenge you to do it.
         I think it's broken.
         I challenge you, John Ryan.
John: Yes, the John Ryan challenge?
         (2–second pause)
         You are a fool if you think
         you can challenge *me*, Mr. Computer!

In this interaction, connection-focused banter turned into a statusful (and stressful) interchange because of hierarchical relations. During playback, Dan told Gavruseva that he intended his remark *It sucks* in the spirit of what sociolinguists would call troubles talk—a ritual exchange of woes in the service of solidarity. In choosing the vulgar verb *sucks*, he took his cue from John's use of the term *shitburner*. Because Dan intended his remark in this spirit, he averred, he was taken aback when John treated his remark as a literal complaint and offered to fix his computer. Because of the paralinguistic and prosodic quality of John's offers—fast-paced and overbearing, from Dan's point of view—Dan became increasingly uncomfortable, a discomfort that peaked when John proclaimed that he could fix the problem in 25 seconds. It is also possible (although there is no way to know for sure) that John was putting Dan back in his place because he perceived Dan's use of profanity as cheeky or that he felt obligated, as the boss, to do something about a problem brought to his attention, regardless of the spirit in which it was mentioned. In any case, Dan told Gavruseva that he felt John was "showing him up" and putting him "on the spot." Gavruseva observes that John was framing Dan as a supplicant.

At this point, Dan restored balance by playfully challenging his boss, and the boss agreed to the shift in alignment by playing along. I suggest that in the excerpt that follows, Dan's reframing signaled to the boss that he had stepped over a line and that John tacitly agreed to redress the imbalance of power by bonding with Dan as two men who can talk indelicately and can align themselves in opposition to women.

Knowing that John had been suffering from an intestinal ailment, Dan shifted the topic to John's health. John's surprise at the topic shift (and frame shift) is evidenced in his initial response, *What's that?*:

Dan: How are you feeling today, John?
John: What's that?
Dan: How are you feeling? Are you still-
John: um Actually my guts started grinding
        and I thought, "Hey, it's back,"
        but I had like a heavy night last night.
        I mean I went to bed at six,
        and only came out to
        like piss and drink water,
        and eat a can of tuna fish.
        I mean it was bad.
        I get a gastro-intestinal thing
        at both ends.
        It was it was spewing.
        It was violent.
Dan: (laughing) Not simultaneously.
        Please tell me no.
John: No no no but it was intense.
        And it made me so glad
        that there was no girlfriend around,
        nobody could take care of me.
        There's only one fucking thing I hate
        it's being sick
        and somebody wants to take care of me . . .

With his query about John's health, Dan redirected the conversation away from talk that framed Dan as subordinate (both because he needed to report his problems to John and because John declared himself able to fix in 25 seconds a problem that Dan was unable to fix) in favor of a conversation that framed John as potentially one-down (a sufferer of embarrassing physical ailments). John went along with the reframing by recounting the symptoms of his intestinal distress. By talking explicitly about body functions gone awry, he seems to be positioning Dan as an equal—they are now two men who can talk openly about such topics, which they might not do if women were present. John then goes further toward aligning himself with Dan, man to man, by referring to how annoying women can be when a man is sick. Moreover, the very act of choosing the topic and having John accede to it reframes Dan as higher in status than he was in the preceding interchange. At the same time, how-

ever, as Gavruseva pointed out to me, John is still positioning himself as someone
who does not need help. In this example, then, Dan and John reflect and negotiate
their relative status while apparently engaging in office small talk.

Contrast this with the following segment that was taped by Janice Hornyak (in
preparation) in connection with her study of discourse in an all-woman office. Tina
had been telling a story when June, the mail clerk, entered the office to deliver the
mail. Tina stopped her narrative and invited June into the room, and into the interaction, by commenting on her clothing. The other women joined in:

June:	Hi:.
Tina:	Hey! Ah, we gotta see this getup.
	Come on in.
Heather:	C'mere June!
Tina:	She she she's uh ... that's cute.
Heather:	Lo:ve that beau:tiful blou:se!
Janice:	Hey, high fashion today.
Tina:	Cool.
June:	Hi ... I had the blouse /?/
	and didn't know what to wear it with.
	And I just took the tag off
	and /?/ said /?/
	I'm gonna wear it with a vest.
Tina:	And that hair too.
Janice:	Oh that's neat.
Heather:	Is that your Mom's?
[Tina laughs]	
June:	No I got this from uh /?/
Tina:	What is it?
June:	/It's from/ Stylo.
Tina:	I've heard of it.
June:	The one in Trader Plaza
	that has all that wild stuff.
Heather:	What'd you do to your hair?
June:	Added /?/.
	Judith said you just are bored,
	you have to do something.
[All laugh]	

At first glance, this too is an instance of office small talk, or what I have called *rap-
port talk* (Tannen 1990) to refer to conversational discourse in which the phatic function seems to override the informational. Nonetheless, relative status is a pervasive
influence on this interaction as well. The complimenting ritual is initiated by Tina,
who is the manager of the office and also the daughter of the company's owner. She
is the highest-status person in the interaction. June, the mail clerk (and also the in-
truder into the office), who is the object of the complimenting, is the lowest-status
person present. Complimenting June on her clothing was a resource by which Tina

could include her in the conversation, even though Tina did not want to include June in the interrupted narrative event, as she might have done if a status equal or friend had entered unexpectedly. In other words, complimenting June on her clothing was a conventionalized ritual that Tina could use as a resource to attend to her as a person, even as Tina failed to include June in the storytelling event that her arrival interrupted. Importantly, one could not imagine their alignment reversed: June would not likely have entered with the mail and called out to Tina regarding her clothing. As with John in the computer-fixing segment, in this interaction the highest-status person controlled the framing of the interaction.

The other two speakers' participation can be arrayed along the status dimension as well. Heather is next in status under Tina, and she follows Tina's lead with alacrity. Hers is the most extreme expressive intonation, in contrast to the subdued intonational contours used by June and by Janice, who is a temporary office worker (and the researcher). Thus Janice and June, who have the lowest status, are also the lowest-key in their paralinguistic contours.[7] Keeping a low profile paralinguistically is an element of demeanor that creates and reflects their lower status in this encounter. Furthermore, both of Janice's contributions are immediate ratifications of a superior's comments:

Heather: Lo:ve that beau:tiful blou:se!
Janice: Hey, high fashion today.

                . . .

Tina: And that hair too.
Janice: Oh that's neat.

Thus, at the same time that Janice is aligned with Heather and Tina as a complimenter of June's clothing, she is also positioning herself as subordinate, or at least not superior, to them insofar as her contributions are subdued echoes and ratifications of theirs rather than initiations of utterances that reframe the interaction.

In summary, these two examples illustrate parallel ways of balancing status and connection in interaction. The ways that the speakers created connection also reflected and created their relative status. Or, to reverse this statement, the ways that they negotiated their relative status also reflected and created connections among them. We are not dealing with an either/or choice: *Is status or connection at play?* Instead, we see that every moment of the interactions exhibited complex interrelations among the two dimensions.

Moving to the second main point of this chapter, the linguistic patterns exhibited in these examples, which negotiate both status and connection, are also sex-class-linked. It is not coincidental and haphazard that the first conversation is characterized by vulgarity; play challenge; displays of helping, expertise, and needing no help; and bonding against women and that it took place among men with no women present. Nor is it coincidental and haphazard that the second conversation is characterized by lengthy complimenting; focus on clothing and shopping; balancing of display and gaze; and expressive intonation and that it took place among women with no men present. Imagining these two conversations taking place among speakers of the other gender yields the stuff of comic theater or of sexual and gender transgression (in the latter regard, see Rusty Barrett, chapter 16, this volume). Patterns associated with gender are pervasive in the interactions, reflected on a range of levels including vo-cabulary, topic, intonation patterns, and the whole array of alignments that can be considered in the domain of framing.[8]

It is well to recall at this point that ways of conventionalizing the balance of hierarchy and connection are culturally relative. I have no intention of implying that the conversations presented in these examples would be typical in other cultures. Cultural relativity is particularly apt in connection with the element of spectatorship versus display that emerges in the second example. Margaret Mead (1977) notes that there are cultures in which higher social status is associated with display and lower status with spectatorship, as in the British assumption that adults speak whereas chil-dren should be seen and not heard. In other cultures these alignments may be reversed, as when American children are called upon to display their talents for onlooking adults ("Show Aunt Ann and Uncle Harry how you can say your ABCs"). This dynamic is evidenced in the women's conversation, in which the higher-status women take the role of spectators to the lower-status woman's display of her clothing. This is remi-niscent of an example discussed by Goffman (1981:124–125) in which President Nixon reframed journalist Helen Thomas as "domestic" and "sexual" rather than "professional" by interrupting a press conference to remark on her wearing pants, asking her to "turn around" so that he could appraise how well they suited her, and inquiring as to whether her husband approved of that mode of dress. Here, too, the discourse is sex-class-linked: It seems far less likely that the display of clothing had the sexual overtones in the all-women context that it clearly had in the press confer-ence, in which Thomas was asked to "pirouette" (in Goffman's terms) for a male president in front of an audience of male reporters and cameramen (who, we are told, roared with laughter at the president's wit).

Discussion

Dramatic evidence that gendered patterns of behavior are a matter of display, not identity, lies in the autobiographical writing of a woman with autism, Donna Wil-liams. In her books *Nobody Nowhere* (1992) and *Somebody Somewhere* (1994), Wil-liams explains that despite her inability to understand what people were saying and doing, she was able to function in the world by imitating others. She regarded her convincing performances not as expressions of her own self, whom she calls Donna, but as the creations of two imaginary personas that she calls her "characters" or "façades": one named Willie and the other named Carol. Williams explains that, until she was well into her 20s, she had lived in her own world of autism, which she calls "my world," yet managed to function in "the world" as "the characters I called Carol and Willie (my 'the world' façades) . . . " (1994:6). She maintained these outward personas, Williams writes, until "progressively, Donna was seen in smaller and smaller snapshots until there was no longer anything visible left of her" (10).

According to Williams, "Willie started life as a pair of green eyes under my bed when I was two years old" (1994:7); "Carol came along a year and a half after Willie" and was "based on a little girl I met only once in the park" (9). Although she gave them female and male names respectively, and Carol was based on a particular little girl, Williams never explicitly mentions the characters' sex and gives no reason to believe that she herself thought of them as quintessentially female and male. Yet her account of how they spoke and acted through her mouth and body reads like a caricature of stereotypically female and male styles. A small sampling of a much larger repertoire follows.

Willie went for interviews; Carol held down jobs. "Willie was the scholar. Carol was a repertoire of stored-up 'social' skits" (19–20). Willie was a speed reader who accumulated facts to impress people; Carol smiled, cocked her head, and filled the air with social chatter. Willie was strong, feared nothing, and was always in control. He appeared indifferent, responsible, and detached. Carol was "all that people wanted her to be: a smiling, social imp. . . . With language echoed from storybook records, TV commercials, and stored conversations, Carol could buy my way through life . . ." (9–10). Carol had a "cheery" facade (10). Willie seized upon key words and elaborated them (40). "As Carol," Williams explains, "I never had to understand anything that happened. I just had to look good" (89). When she determines to confront the world without invoking her characters, Williams panics: "Carol could have looked at him and laughed. Willie could have imparted his latest store of interesting information" (13). "Willie wasn't there to help me understand, depersonalize, and deny. Carol wasn't there to make me laugh and pretend nothing mattered" (69).

Carol, above all, smiled:

Smiling works wonders though—smile and people think you can do almost anything, you know. (1994:42)

Mockingly I put on a disturbing minute-long medley of action replays of Carol smiles, poses, and witty lines. (1994:47)

Carol is always ready to entertain with "quick jokes, clever lines and a smile— always the smile" (1994:55). Looking back on her earlier life, Williams focuses on the role of Carol's smiling in allowing others to exploit and abuse her:

I burned with the injustice of having been taught to put a smile on the face of hatred. I raged silently with the memory of how others justified what they'd done as long as I did as I was told and smiled, always smiled. (1994:56)

People could do the most atrocious things as long as they smiled peacefully at me. A smile always called for a smile and unintentionally I not only let them get away with murdering Carol again and again but my innocent smile seemed to tell them it was okay. (1994:111)

Goffman's comments on smiling provide an explanation for Williams's behavior in the role of Carol. He includes smiling (like the head-cocking in which Williams also engages as Carol) as a form of "ritualization of subordination" linked with the female sex class:

Smiles, it can be argued, often function as ritualistic mollifiers, signaling that nothing agonistic is intended or invited, that the meaning of the other's act has been understood and found acceptable, that, indeed, the other is approved and appreciated. Those who warily keep an eye on the movements of a potential aggressor may find themselves automatically smiling should their gaze be "caught" by its object, who in turn may find little cause to smile back. In addition, a responding smile (even more so an appreciative laugh) following very rapidly on the heels of a speaker's sally can imply that the respondent belongs, by knowledgeability, at least, to the speaker's circle. All of these smiles, then, seem more the offering of an inferior than superior. In any case, it appears that in cross-sexed encounters in American society, women smile more, and more expansively, than men. . . . (1979:48)

Norma Mendoza-Denton (1996) reports that the gang girls she studied refrained from smiling as part of their "macha" style. Bonnie McElhinny (1995) makes a similar observation concerning female police officers, who assume a demeanor they consider appropriate to their professional role—a role previously associated with the male sex class. Williams's ability to take on the personas of both Willie and Carol, as needed, supports Goffman's claim that gender is not a matter of identity—inherent modes of behavior that are "given off" helter-skelter—but of display: chosen from a range of possible behaviors and linking speakers to others of a sex class. That Williams was apparently unaware that in Willie and Carol she was performing male and female roles is evidence of the wider phenomenon that people are often unaware that their ways of speaking are sex-class-linked.

This unawareness makes our task as researchers all the more challenging. Barbara Johnstone (1995) discovered this attitude when she interviewed four prominent and successful Texas women who do a great deal of public speaking: a union leader; a former congresswoman; a journalist, writer, and musician; and an attorney. Johnstone notes that when she asked them where they thought their speaking styles came from, all four denied that their being female affected their ways of speaking, although they all readily acknowledged the influence of being Texan. The lawyer was typical in saying that her success as a litigator was unrelated to being female but simply reflected her being "herself": "People have told me that they think that I'm successful in the courtroom because I can identify with the jury, that the juries like me. And I haven't ever figured out why, except that I try to smile, and I try to just be myself. And I don't put on any airs" (1995:197).

Much could be said about this woman's ability to "identify" with the jury, her likability, her not putting on any airs, and the relation of all these patterns of behavior (and the language attitudes they reflect) to female sex-class-linked behavior. But what leapt out at me was her saying that she tries to smile. Her certainty that this behavior has nothing to do with her gender but just reflects her being "herself" should not impede our ability to understand the extent to which her way of being herself is sex-class-linked. Donna Williams's performance as Carol aside, a cursory glance at female and male news anchors and television news correspondents, or a random assortment of women and men in a social situation, will confirm that women tend to smile more than men. (One must never cease to emphasize that this is not to claim that every individual woman necessarily smiles often nor that every individual man does not; however, it is clearly the case that women are expected to smile more often than men are and that women are seen as severe and lacking in humor if they do not smile, whereas men who do not smile often are not likely to meet with negative reactions as a result.)

Johnstone's study provides evidence that individuals may not be aware that their styles are sex-class-linked; some may even take offense at the suggestion that they are. Others, however, may be aware of such linkage but nonetheless be reluctant to admit it. Mona Harrington (1994) describes a group of female attorneys who left large law firms to start their own. The women told Harrington that they believe they practice law differently than they were able to when working for large traditional firms. They said that they represent clients not by being as aggressive and confrontational as possible but by listening, observing, and "reading" opponents better. One pointed out that in taking depositions, she gets better results by adopting a "quiet, sympathetic approach" (1994:186), charming witnesses into forgetting that the attorney deposing them is their adversary, than by grilling witnesses and attacking them. Yet when interviewed by the press, these same women do not mention their different styles, not even to explain how well they work. Instead, they stress that they are "tough" litigators and seasoned veterans of traditionally contentious legal settings. The reason, they explained, was that if they told the truth about their styles, they would be dismissed as soft and weak. Their conclusion has been that they can't talk about it: "You have to just *be* it, and develop a reputation" (1994:187).

It is nothing new for linguists to recognize that speakers often cannot or will not accurately describe how they speak or why and that researchers must draw conclusions from observation, not self-report (although interviews with speakers may well provide further material for observation). Researchers in the field of language and gender need to be especially attuned to this dilemma. We want to describe and understand linguistic behavior that patterns by gender, and we want to listen to those we study, but speakers who exhibit gendered patterns may be unaware of the influence of gender on their styles and may resist acknowledging that influence even if they are aware of it. At the same time, we need to beware of a range of dangers that can follow from describing gendered patterns, even if those descriptions are accurate. For example, patterns can be misread as norms, and anyone who finds a behavior unappealing can hear its description as a slur. I believe that the theoretical construct of framing, or the sex-class-linked nature of the relationship between language and gender, can provide a solution to this dilemma.

Conclusion

I have attempted to show that understanding language and gender is best approached through the concept of framing, by which gendered patterns of behavior are seen as sex-class-linked rather than sex-linked, as a matter of display rather than of identity, in Goffman's terms. With reference to analysis of two examples of workplace discourse, I have shown that framing allows us to see how speakers simultaneously balance the dimensions of status and connection. Thus these dimensions are not mutually exclusive poles but rather are both at play in every moment of interaction.

Finally, by showing, first, the interrelation between status (that is, dominance) and connection, and, second, the role of culture in negotiating both, I have demonstrated that it is a misconception to regard a "cultural" approach to gender and language (such as that advanced in my own work, as well as the earlier work of Daniel Maltz and Ruth Borker [1982]) as opposed to and irreconcilable with a "dominance" approach (which sets out to show how gender-associated language patterns reflect the dominance of women by men). Rather, culturally mediated framing conventions provide unique ways of negotiating relationships along both the status dimension of hierarchy/equality and the connection dimension of distance/closeness—in sex-class-linked ways.

TRANSCRIPTION CONVENTIONS

Line breaks are intended to capture the rhythmic chunking that characterizes speech.

A hyphen indicates abrupt cutting off of breath, as in a false start.

<u>Underline</u> indicates emphatic stress.

Three spaced dots (. . .) indicate ellipsis. The speaker's turn did not end at this point.

Three unspaced dots (...) indicate pause of approximately a half second.

: indicates elongation of preceding vowel.

/?/ indicates inaudible utterance.

/Words/ in slashes indicate uncertain transcription.

NOTES

This chapter is a revised version of a paper originally presented at the Third Berkeley Women and Language Conference and published in the conference proceedings (Tannen 1994a). A somewhat different version is also included in the paperback edition of my book *Gender and Discourse* (Tannen 1994b).

1. Interestingly, this leaves open the question of whether women and men who speak in ways associated with the other gender may not be indexing the other gender. It seems clear that this is so when gay men refer to each other as *she* or *Miss*. But is it also the case when heterosexuals or lesbians and gay men who are not "out" speak in ways associated with the other gender? In this volume, William Leap (chapter 13) and A. C. Liang (chapter 15) provide two different starting points for investigating this question.

2. The corner-of-the-eye concept is further explored by Mary Catherine Bateson in her book *Peripheral Visions* (1994). For a related notion, see Mary Bucholtz's (chapter 18, this volume) advocacy of "quick-cut camerawork" as a metaphor for language and gender research methodology.

3. After developing this framework, I discovered that Peter Mühlhäusler and Rom Harré (1990) came up with a similar one.

4. For Javanese, see Clare Wolfowitz (1991); for Japanese, see Takeo Doi (1973); my source for Chinese has been Ron Scollon (personal communication).

5. Gavruseva taped the conversation in connection with a seminar I taught in the fall of 1993 at Georgetown University. The initial part of the analysis presented here, which illuminates the power relations between the two speakers, is taken from Gavruseva's term paper,

written for that seminar and later presented at the 1995 annual meeting of the Linguistic Society of America in New Orleans. Her analysis, however, did not extend to the second part of the conversation, beginning *How are you feeling today, John?* This section of analysis is my own interpretation of the conversation she taped and transcribed.

6. Dialogue is presented in lines representing breath groups rather than undifferentiated paragraphs because this more closely resembles the way in which spoken language is realized and perceived.

7. Although I am here focusing on hierarchical relations as the key variable, other influences on conversational style are, as always, operative. Hornyak points out that Heather is from the South, and her style of speaking calls that to mind for everyone who hears her (see Cynthia McLemore [1991] on Southern women's intonation). On the other hand, June is African American, and it is possible that her style would exhibit more paralinguistic variation if she were talking to peers (for other elements of African American women's conversational style, see Marcyliena Morgan, chapter 1, this volume).

8. Jennifer Coates (chapter 6, this volume) explores a similar range of linguistic dimensions in her work on British girls' friendship talk; she likewise finds that both status and connection are accomplished in the girls' conversations and that as they grow older these are achieved in what I am calling sex-class-linked ways. The negotiation of status and connection is also found in the interaction of the Latina girls studied by Norma Mendoza-Denton (chapter 14, this volume).

REFERENCES

Angier, Natalie (1993). An evolving celebrity. *New York Times* (February 11):B1.

Bateson, Gregory (1972). *Steps to an ecology of mind*. New York: Ballantine.

———— (1979). *Mind and nature*. New York: Ballantine.

Bateson, Mary Catherine (1994). *Peripheral visions*. New York: HarperCollins.

Becker, A.L. (1995). *Beyond translation: Essays toward a modern philology*. Ann Arbor: University of Michigan Press.

Davies, Bronwyn, & Rom Harré (1990). Positioning: Conversation and the production of selves. *Journal for the Theory of Social Behavior* 20(1):43–63.

Doi, Takeo (1973). *The anatomy of dependence*. Tokyo: Kodansha.

Gavruseva, Lena (1995). Constructing interactional asymmetry in employer-employee discourse. Paper presented at the annual meeting of the Linguistic Society of America, New Orleans.

Goffman, Erving (1974). *Frame analysis*. Boston: Northeastern University Press.

———— (1977). The arrangement between the sexes. *Theory and Society* 4(3):301–331.

———— (1979). *Gender advertisements*. New York: Harper & Row.

———— (1981). *Forms of talk*. Philadelphia: University of Pennsylvania Press.

Harrington, Mona (1994). *Women lawyers: Rewriting the rules*. New York: Knopf.

Hornyak, Janice (in preparation). Shifting between personal and professional frames in office discourse. Ph.D. diss., Georgetown University.

Johnstone, Barbara (1995). Sociolinguistic resources, individual identities, and public speech styles of Texas women. *Journal of Linguistic Anthropology* 5(2):183–202.

Kendall, Shari (1993). Constructing competence: Gender and mitigation at a radio network. Paper presented at the annual meeting of the American Association for Applied Linguistics, Baltimore.

Kuhn, Elisabeth D. (1992). Playing down authority while getting things done: Women professors get help from the institution. In Kira Hall, Mary Bucholtz, & Birch Moonwomon (eds.), *Locating power: Proceedings of the Second Berkeley Women and Language Conference*. Berkeley, CA: Berkeley Women and Language Group, 318–325.

Maccoby, Eleanor (1988). Gender as a social category. *Developmental Psychology* 24(6):755–765.

———— (1990). Gender and relationships: A developmental account. *American Psychologist* 45(4):513–520.

Maccoby, Eleanor E., & Carol N. Jacklin (1974). *The psychology of sex differences*. Stanford, CA: Stanford University Press.

Maltz, Daniel N., & Ruth A. Borker (1982). A cultural approach to male-female miscommunication. In John J. Gumperz (ed.), *Language and social identity*. Cambridge: Cambridge University Press, 196–216.

McElhinny, Bonnie (1995). Challenging hegemonic masculinities: Female and male police officers handling domestic violence. In Kira Hall & Mary Bucholtz (eds.), *Gender articulated: Language and the socially constructed self*. New York: Routledge, 217–244.

McLemore, Cynthia Ann (1991). The pragmatic interpretation of English intonation: Sorority speech. Ph.D. diss., University of Texas at Austin.

Mead, Margaret (1977). End linkage: A tool for cross-cultural analysis. In John Brockman (ed.), *About Bateson*. New York: Dutton, 171–231.

Mendoza-Denton, Norma (1996). "Muy macha": Gender and ideology in gang-girls' discourse about makeup. Paper presented at the annual meeting of the American Association for Applied Linguistics, Symposium on Gendered Discourse Communities, Chicago.

Mühlhäusler, Peter, & Rom Harré (1990). *Pronouns and people: The linguistic construction of social and personal identity*. Oxford: Basil Blackwell.

Nussbaum, Emily (1997). Inside publishing. *Lingua Franca* (December/January):22–24.

Ochs, Elinor (1992). Indexing gender. In Alessandro Duranti & Charles Goodwin (eds.), *Rethinking context: Language as an interactive phenomenon*. Cambridge: Cambridge University Press, 335–358.

Reddy, Michael (1979). The conduit metaphor: A case of frame conflict in our language about language. In Andrew Ortony (ed.), *Metaphor and thought*. Cambridge: Cambridge University Press, 284–324.

Smith, Frances Lee (1993). The pulpit and woman's place: Gender and the framing of the "exegetical self" in sermon performances. In Deborah Tannen (ed.), *Framing in discourse*. New York: Oxford University Press, 147–175.

Tannen, Deborah (1990). *You just don't understand: Women and men in conversation*. New York: Ballantine.

———— (1994a). The sex-class-linked framing of talk at work. In Mary Bucholtz, A. C. Liang, Laurel Sutton, & Caitlin Hines (eds.), *Cultural performances: Proceedings of the Third Berkeley Women and Language Conference*. Berkeley, CA: Berkeley Women and Language Group, 712–728.

———— (1994b). The relativity of linguistic strategies: Rethinking power and solidarity in gender and dominance. In Tannen, *Gender and discourse*. New York: Oxford University Press, 19–52.

———— (1994c). *Talking from 9 to 5: Women and men in the workplace—Language, sex, and power*. New York: Avon.

Wetzel, Patricia J. (1988). Are "powerless" communication strategies the Japanese norm? *Language in Society* 17:555–564.

Williams, Donna (1992). *Nobody nowhere: The extraordinary autobiography of an autistic*. New York: Times Books.

————(1994). *Somebody somewhere: Breaking free from the world of autism*. New York: Times Books.

Wolfowitz, Clare (1991). *Language style and social space: Stylistic choice in Suriname Javanese*. Urbana: University of Illinois Press.

Gender, Context, and the Narrative Construction of Identity

Rethinking Models of "Women's Narrative"

"Do women and men tell stories about their lives differently?" It now seems naive, if not reactionary, to formulate a question about personal narrative in such general terms. From the now-central antiessentialist perspective in feminism and queer theory we recognize that 'women' and 'men' are naturalized cultural categories, not biological givens. We cannot assume a commonality of needs, purposes, or identities within such broad groupings. To do so reifies the binary categorization and privileges the practices of the white, heterosexual, middle class (Fuss 1989; Mills 1990). A feminist poststructuralist perspective further reminds us that any individual's identity is multiple and constantly re-created as the speaker adopts subject positions in cultural discourses (Davies & Harré 1990; Hollway 1984; Moore 1994).

Still, for most of the two last decades the question of the differences between "women's" and "men's" narration seemed reasonable, and substantial research has been dedicated to demonstrating that women create distinctive forms of personal narrative. Rather than ignore this body of research while pursuing discourse-centered analyses, we should reexamine this foundational work for three reasons. First, these essays represent solid, empirical research, accurately characterizing personal narration by defined groups of women. Second, the models of "women's narrative" presented therein can present a stumbling block for researchers if they are taken as truly generalizable because students do not understand the historical circumstances of their production. Precisely because these works should be read, it is important to provide contextual reinterpretation. Third, the current poststructuralist, discourse-oriented approach to narrative self-construction focuses attention primarily on theme or semantics, asking, What discourses does the speaker place herself in and what positions does she take up? This approach consequently ignores other storytelling features applicable in gendered self-construction which the earlier works highlight, notably: (1) formal features, including narrative structure, paralinguistic features, degree of fixity or entextualization of the story, and the relation of story segment to surrounding conversation; (2) contextual aspects such as setting, time, and audience; and (3) social and communicative goals. In telling stories about themselves, women respond to and negotiate with a lived world of social and linguistic structures relating to gender. Our analyses of narrative self-construction must take account of the entire context.

I will first reexamine the foundational models of "women's narrative," considering their connection to the dominant feminist paradigm of the period in which they were created and the tacit image of female storytellers they encode. I will then contrast these models with stories I have collected from a North Carolina woman, demonstrating slippage between previously postulated form-function pairings but also using the models heuristically to suggest the range of resources available for the narrative construction of gendered identity. I argue that there are no formal or contextual features that belong exclusively to women conceived as a class and perhaps not even any necessary connections between particular narrative forms or techniques and certain goals of narration. Nevertheless, in creating a gender identity via narrative, the speaker works not only with thematically defined discourses but also with formal and contextual resources that range from story structure to paralinguistic features to discourse structure to the social constitution of the storytelling event. My approach parallels that of Deborah Cameron (1985) and Jennifer Coates (chapter 6, this volume) in arguing that personal-narrative research cannot conceptualize self-construction in purely semantic terms.

"Personal-experience narrative" and identity

The study of stories of personal experience burgeoned in the 1970s (Abrahams 1977; Bauman 1972; Labov & Waletzky 1967; Stahl 1977, 1983). The genre is a type of "narrative," that is, "a kind of discourse organized around the passage of time in some 'world' [in which] a time line is established, demarcated by discrete moments at which instantaneous occurrences (*events*) take place in the world created through the telling" (Polanyi 1985a:10). More specifically, a personal-experience narrative is a "story"—an "affirmative past time narrative which tell[s] about a series of events . . . which *did* take place at specific unique moments in a unique past time world" and is "told to make a point" (and which is thus differentiated from the unevaluated, pointless "reports," "generic narratives" that are "structured around indefinite past time events," and "plans" for as yet unrealized sequences of events) (Polanyi 1985a:10–11). And, of course, the stories that we call "personal-experience narratives" describe events the speaker claims to have witnessed or participated in, often as the central character (Stahl 1983).

Folklorists have tended to treat personal narratives as singly authored "act[s] of self-presentation" that are formally separable from the surrounding conversation, whereas linguists, conversational interactionists, and communication-studies scholars have emphasized the ways informal narratives are built up in multiperson talk (Langellier 1989:256). The assumption that personal narratives are intended to reveal the speaker's identity was encouraged both by the lingering dominance of the functional approach to folklore (see Bascom 1954) and by the influence of Erving Goffman's (1959) analysis of the "presentation of self" on the developing context-sensitive folkloristics. Consideration of the genre remains influenced by Sandra Dolby Stahl's (1977, 1983) theme-based paradigm, and this semantic emphasis has been reinforced by Bakhtinian and feminist poststructuralist theories about the constitution of the self in the course of social interaction, although with the significant refinements of viewing that self as nonunitary, changing, constantly re-formed and renegotiated (Bakhtin 1981; Hollway 1984).

Models of "women's personal narrative"

Analyses that came to be treated as general models of "women's personal narrative" developed concurrently with the concept of "personal-experience narrative" as a story told to express the speaker's identity. These feminist models challenged several widely held tenets about narrative: the expectation that a single narrator would hold the floor in telling a personal narrative; the assumption that the narrator's motivation was to present herself in a positive light; and the rigidity of the Labovian formal model of oral narrative as sequentially composed of abstract, orientation, complicating action, evaluation, resolution, and coda (Labov 1972:363). Between the early 1970s and the late 1980s, feminist scholars developed analyses of narration by certain groups of women that, though not so intended by the authors, were widely promulgated as ways that "women" tell stories.

According to these models, "women's personal narrative" displayed one or more of five qualities, each of which could be traced to either a kind of experience or a quality of character that women were assumed to share. Such narratives were said to be *collaborative*, like "kernel stories" in women's rap groups, in which several speakers share the floor and create a single point (Kalčik 1975:7), or corroborative telling in which speakers reinforce each other's points (Baldwin 1985:156) or mother-and-daughter storytelling in which interruptions and overlaps construct a collective description (Hall & Langellier 1988). Karen Baldwin depicted women's "visiting" (in contrast to men's more rigidly structured stories) as *interruptible*, sustainable in the face of children's demands on a woman's attention (1985:154). Susan Kalčik (1975) showed how women in consciousness-raising groups used supportive storytelling to help others make sense of conflicted lives, and Margaret Yocom described the stories told by women even in her conservative family as "*exemplum-like*, . . . provid[ing] support as they teach other women what is possible for them" (1985:50). Both Yocom and Baldwin emphasize women's tendency to tell *stories of habitual action* in contrast to men's evaluated, point-driven stories and women's frequent secondary role as correctors, who either do not crave the spotlight or cannot get it and so content themselves with verifying the details of the men's stories. Finally, Kalčik, Baldwin, and Gillian Bennett all celebrate the *nonlinearity* of women's narration, whether it produces rap-group sessions in which several women's experiences are brought together (Kalčik 1975) or accounts of habitual action with which women counter men's accounts of noteworthy singular events (Baldwin 1985:152–153) or women's narratives that repeatedly circle back over the same events, revealing more at each pass (Bennett 1989:174–175). This, then, was what I as a graduate student came to assume that "women's narrative" must be like. How and why did the models proposed by these researchers become a set of generalized rules for the way women tell stories about their lives?

We can point first to a discrepancy between explicit authorial claims and implicit scholarly practice. The authors professed to describe the narrative practice only of specified groups of women. Kalčik cautions, "No definitive statement about women's storytelling, interaction, or use of language is attempted except in terms of the . . . situation and narratives analyzed here" (1975:3). However, in the feminist climate of the early 1980s, in which scholars sought to define and celebrate "women's" expressive styles as distinct from "men's," accepted practice welcomed and reified these models as a corrective to the tendency to regard women as aberrant and inferior practitioners of forms, presumed to be the standard for all, in which men excelled.

This reification then seemed easy to accept intuitively, theoretically, and politically. Early feminist scholars called attention to observable aspects of informal narration not accounted for in the highly formalized Labovian paradigm. Because other women reading such analyses recognized aspects of their own narrative practice and because a touchstone of this phase of feminist scholarship was that most prefeminist work had generalized to both genders findings based only on men's practice, it made sense to assume that these new narrative qualities belonged particularly or even peculiarly to women. In several cases folklorists studying groups of women identified and innocently assigned only to women techniques that had been or were soon to be identified by linguists as non-gender-specific components of conversational narrative.[1] Only later did the overextension of models that felt right to white, middle-class heterosexuals spur corrections from women of color and lesbians (e.g., hooks 1992).

It was also appealing to generalize these analyses of particular women's storytelling because the models thus generated promoted images of women congruent with feminist scholars' developing sense of how they wanted to be perceived: in essence, as competent. Where folk models portrayed women as unable to tell a good story, Kalčik's analysis depicted women as skilled at crafting a type of narration that just happened to be different from the assumed universal but actually male model. The work of Kalčik and other feminist folklorists resonated with similar developments in other disciplines (e.g., Belenky, Clinchy, Goldberger, & Tarule 1986; Gilligan 1982).

However, we now see the revaluing of "feminine" traits as dangerously essentializing. Even if one acknowledges that women are culturally trained to have these qualities and that supposedly formative experiences (such as motherhood) are not universal, and even if one wishes to praise women for exhibiting formerly devalued qualities, to claim that there are "women's ways" of thinking or speaking leads almost inevitably to biological determinism. To appreciate the narrative models' appeal without being trapped by them, we must remember that at the time this promotion of "women's" unique qualities was perceived as a significant step forward.

Where, then, does the issue of "women's narrative," or rather, the influence of gender on narration, currently stand? Relatively few scholars have directly challenged the early models, although many express skepticism (Johnstone 1993; Langellier &

Peterson 1992; Linde 1993), and others have implicitly critiqued earlier analyses by demonstrating that girls' narrative play involves striving for dominance (formerly assigned to boys), as well as fostering intimacy (Goodwin 1990, 1992, 1993, chapter 20, this volume; Kyratzis 1994). In folklore during the late 1980s and early 1990s, feminist research turned away from the explicit question of gender influences on personal narrative. Neither of the two major 1990s collections of feminist folklore includes an article on personal narrative (Hollis, Pershing, & Young 1993; Radner 1993). Feminist folklorists who considered personal narrative did so mainly as a means to discuss some other issue (Borland 1991; Lawless 1991).

Resurgent interest in the way women construct and use narrative focuses on particular, contextualized, strategic use rather than pan-gender models (Berman 1994; Farr 1994; Liang 1994; Livesay 1994; McDonald 1994; Orellana, chapter 3, this volume; Wood, chapter 2, this volume). This work on narrative is part of a larger project to conceptualize the role of speaking and attendant linguistic, paralinguistic, discursive, and cultural resources in the creative constitution of identity, of which gender is one facet. The history I have offered of the development of models of "women's narrative" traces one of the routes scholars have taken to arrive at our current stance. The analysis that follows will provide an example of precisely how one woman in one cultural situation employs linguistic resources to construct narrative. This may contribute to the accumulation of theoretically and empirically grounded studies that might lead to a recognition of regularities between discourse and gender at a higher level of complexity.

A woman and her stories

I was motivated to reconsider the relationship between gender and personal narrative by my acquaintance with Bessie Eldreth. Eldreth was born in 1913 and has lived all but a few years of her life in Ashe and Watauga counties in the mountains of North Carolina. Until about 20 years ago Eldreth led a life similar to that of neighbors of her generation and class. She married at 16 and raised eleven children. Her life was harder than it might have been because her husband "didn't seem to let it bother him whether he really worked or whether he didn't" and because he was disabled in a sawmill accident early in their marriage. Consequently, Eldreth herself, in addition to raising her family and keeping her own house, has frequently labored on others' farms and households. From childhood she has been a devout Baptist and talks often about how her faith and church community have provided essential emotional support.

Eldreth's greatest love—after her family—has been singing. For most of her life, Eldreth was known only for singing around the house and performing solos in church. Over the past 2 decades, however, she has been invited not only to give demonstrations for school programs and workshops at nearby Appalachian State University but also to sing at concerts and folklife festivals as far away as New York City. Although long-distance travel and public performance is highly unusual for anyone in her community, it conforms to a cultural expectation that older women should be free to play a somewhat more public role and do what they like after a lifetime of sacrifice (Beaver 1986:104–105).

I met Eldreth in 1987, when she participated in the Smithsonian Institution's Festival of American Folklife in Washington, D.C. I approached her hoping to study her singing and experience as a singer. However, once Eldreth told me her repertoire of personal narratives, I realized it would be essential to take these into account to characterize her as a person and an artist.

I spent the summer of 1988 with Eldreth and made numerous visits in subsequent years. I accompanied her to church, to visits with neighbors, and to singing performances, talked with her family members, and tape-recorded more than 50 hours of informal interviews in which she sang and told stories about her life.[2]

A woman's narration that wasn't "women's narrative"

When I began to transcribe and analyze Eldreth's personal narratives, my first sense was that these were very much a *woman's* stories. She talks mostly about experiences she encountered while fulfilling female roles: preparing meals, caring for children, delivering babies. The form she chose, the way she told these stories, and, indeed, her choice to put examples of women's work forcefully and repeatedly before listeners, also impressed me as conditioned by her experiences as a woman of a particular age and class in a particular society.

Soon, however, I realized that Eldreth's stories bore little resemblance to the models promulgated for "women's personal narrative." Eldreth's personal narratives are definitely linear, and although they differ significantly from the Labovian model, they are not accounts of habitual action, nor do they circle repeatedly over the material. I never heard Eldreth collaborate with another teller. As linear, noncollaborative accounts, the stories were not easily sustainable across interruptions, and (in her one resemblance to the familiar models—see Baldwin 1985) Eldreth took pains to tell them only when she was safe from interruption. Finally, the stories seemed firmly directed at self-representation and not at serving as exempla for other women. My intuitive attempts to corroborate Eldreth's experiences by supportively "matching stories," as is common for women of my generation and class (see Allen 1989; Kalčik 1975; Tannen 1990), met with apparent incomprehension. Thus Eldreth had lived a "traditional" woman's life, focused on home, family, and church, yet this did not impel her to tell the kinds of stories that extant models predicted.

Bessie Eldreth's personal narratives: Description

Recognizing the lack of fit between Eldreth's personal narratives and models of "women's narrative" initially led me to the panicked conclusion that Eldreth was not narrating "as a woman" and that her practice undermined my feminist study of the influence of gender on informal narration. Calmer reflection, however, suggested that I was accepting the models too rigidly. I determined to investigate exactly what social and personal factors shaped Eldreth's narratives and exactly what effects these influences produced. My study suggests that slippage is common between form and function: There is no necessary connection between Eldreth's life experience and the way she tells stories; she could have chosen other formal solutions to achieve similar communicative goals. However, we can recognize connections between the situation in which Eldreth found herself defined by gender, local culture, religion, class, age, education, and personal experiences, the purposes for which she might want to tell personal narratives, and the story forms she developed.

I have recorded from Eldreth at least twenty stories of personal experience that she structures according to a consistent and distinctive formal pattern and inserts into conversation in consistent ways. Two texts will illustrate Eldreth's narrative style.

"As Good a Doctor"

1   I know one time . . . now I delivered the baby.
2   Marie Rash's on Three Top.
3   Now her sister was there with me, but she left, she wouldn't stay, she just took outside.
4   And I stayed right with her 'til that baby was borned.
5   And when Dr. Robison got there he said he didn't I couldn't understand why they sent after him, that they had as good a doctor there as they could've had.

(11-14-87)

"The Mean Horse"

1   I know one time I's setting there and, uh, well, I wasn't a-setting there, I's a-getting supper.
2   And my husband come in and he said, "I guess that horse has killed s—" I they had, May Rash's had a *mean* fighting horse.
3   And he said, "I guess that that horse has killed some of them young 'uns."
4   And I started out, and he said, "You ain't a-going out. It'll I that horse'll kill you."
5   Said that it had got out the gate.
6   Somebody'd left the gate open and it'd come out right down amongst, in that bottom, right amongst I I guess there's eight or ten children playing.
7   [Sighs.]
8   And I took out and I met that horse in the road and just screamed and throwed up my arms up over my head? and scared it.
9   And it took around me; it didn't try to h—I paw me or anything.
10   And took on down through the bottom, and I went up through that bottom just a-flying.
11   Well, all the children had made it safe and got to the house but Clyde.
12   And he was I he's about two.
13   Toddling along.
14   And I run up through there just as hard as I could go and grabbed that young 'un on my hip, and, young 'uns, now I'm a-telling you the truth—this looks unreasonable and I'm I I've never known how I done it—but I come over a garden fence that had about eight planks . . . on a fence.
15   I got over that fence with that young 'un in under my arm—I used my other hand, you know, to climb.

16 And as I fell on my knees in the garden I as I looked up that horse was a-
     standing on its hind feet on the other side of the garden fence.

17 It's after me.

18 It's a-trying I well, it'd killed me if it'd a got to me.   (6-24-88)

Eldreth's narrative style displays significant features at three distinguishable
levels: thematic, formal and contextual, and behavioral. Thematically, or in terms of
semantic structure, Eldreth's personal narratives tell one basic story: A person is in
trouble and needs help that another single human being can provide. A woman has
gone into labor, a child's life is threatened, a neighbor suffers an accident, an ailing
sister must feed her guests, Eldreth's mother needs a front porch, a church member
wants someone to sing her son's favorite song at his funeral, a friend is terminally ill
but lacks the faith essential to his soul's salvation. Eldreth herself then provides the
needed help: She delivers the baby, rescues the child, cooks the meal, comforts the
injured person, builds the porch, sings for the funeral, prays with the dying person.
Often the stories emphasize the incompetence of other helpers or Eldreth's peculiar
fitness for the task: The laboring woman's sister gets squeamish; Eldreth's husband
won't risk his life for their son; no one else knows the dead man's favorite song.
Even events that would seem amenable to another narrative interpretation conform
to this pattern in Eldreth's telling. The only story Eldreth tells about her 1986 performance in New York City for the series "The Roots of Country Music" stresses not
her musical accomplishment, not bewilderment in this first trip to a big city, but rather
the comfort she brought to lonely, alienated city folk who flocked to hug her after
the concert. Notably, Eldreth's actions are almost always mundane (cooking a meal,
visiting the sick, singing in church, even helping deliver a baby in an area with few
doctors) or expected (a mother should love her children as much as her life); she rarely
steps outside what her culture sees as "women's work," yet she is portrayed not just
as competent and compassionate but as unique, special, the only one who could do
what was needed.

   In formal terms, Eldreth's personal narratives are linear, recount discrete events,
and have evident points. They are not collaborative or circular, and although Eldreth
sometimes reports habitual action, such reports introduce the narration of specific,
single-time occurrences. Nevertheless, these stories differ significantly from the
Labovian model (Labov 1972; Labov & Waletzky 1967).[3] At this formal level
Eldreth's personal narratives display three distinctive features: (1) abruptness of the
beginning of the story proper and its emergence from conversation; (2) deemphasis
of her own actions in the central event clauses; and (3) use of reported speech in the
evaluation.

   I analyze formal and contextual features together because the formal structure
of a narrative includes its relation to the surrounding discourse. Exactly where the
narrative begins and the occasioning discussion ends is itself a matter of interpretation. In transcribing the Eldreth tapes, I have relied on a distinct shift of subject matter
or a discourse marker to delimit the beginning of the story proper. In both stories
quoted above, Eldreth begins the narration with the phrase *I know one time I . . .* ,
which indicates that she is about to give an example (*I know*), draws listeners into
the specific time of an event to be recounted (*one time*), and places Eldreth there as

the first character (*I*). By comparison with the Labovian model, Eldreth starts the story abruptly, plunging listeners directly into story time and deferring what Labov and Waletzky call the "orientation," the nonevent clauses that set the scene. In "As Good a Doctor" the abstract falls in the second half of line 1, *Now I delivered the baby*, and the entire orientation is accomplished in line 2, *Marie Rash's on Three Top*, whereas in "Mean Horse," lines 2 through 6 form the abstract, and Eldreth's self-interruption in line 2, *And my husband come in and he said, "I guess that horse has killed s—"* | *they had, May Rash's had a* mean *fighting horse*, constitutes the orientation.

Critics of Labov and Waletzky argue that the initial positioning of abstract and orientation are not natural features of conversational narrative but artifacts of the interview situation (Langellier 1989; Polanyi 1985b). In our interviews, however, Eldreth consistently introduced narratives without an abstract or orientation; she began the story action before describing characters or setting. In "As Good a Doctor," Eldreth responded to an explicit question with a generic narrative (Polanyi 1985a) that eventually led her to the story:

PS: Mary told me, I think, that you were a midwife //for a while?//
BE: //Yeah, yeah.//
PS: //Did you do that?//
BE: //Yeah.// I worked in baby cases. I always called it baby cases. Nearly every time someone in my community would . . . go in labor . . . dark or daylight or whatever, they'd call or they'd come after me. Weren't no phones then, but they'd just come after me. And here I'd go. And, young 'uns, a few times I have crawled footlogs, with a flashlight, you know, where there'd just be a narrow bridge and hold the flashlight in my hand, and crawl that because I was afraid to try to walk it and it so dark? And go to places. And, uh, let's see now . . . I delivered | I delivered | I've delivered the babies . . . by myself. I know one time . . . now I delivered the baby . . . Marie Rash's on Three Top.

The "Mean Horse" story emerged when I asked Eldreth about her ancestors. She quickly abandoned genealogy to narrate how her grandmother swam her horse across a flooded river, concluding, "But the young 'uns was all safe when they got | when she got home. But there's . . . I guess a mother'd risk things that . . . that a dad wouldn't." Eldreth then proceeded into the story of her analogous experience, *I know one time I's setting there.* . . .

Ordinarily, an orientation signals an impending story and constitutes an implicit request for permission to take the floor (Polanyi 1985b). By not beginning with an abstract and orientation, Eldreth denies interlocutors the opportunity to refuse to cede her the floor. Eldreth's first lines also place her in story time and identify her as the principal actor, whereas the orienting clauses she subsequently supplies, if placed first, might suggest that the laboring mother or the owner of the mean horse or her husband was the focal character.

The central event clauses are the backbone of a narrative. The second distinctive formal feature of Eldreth's narratives is the brevity of her accounts of what she actually did. The five-line "As Good a Doctor" has only two event clauses, line 3, about the sister who did not help, and line 4, about what Eldreth did. In "Mean Horse," Eldreth provides an uncharacteristically detailed description of her actions in lines 8 to 11 and 14 through the first half of 18, with embedded evaluation to heighten the listener's appreciation. In longer stories Eldreth devotes most of the event clauses to others' actions. In a twenty-five–line story about cooking Sunday dinner for her sick sister, for example, she devotes four lines to the phone call requesting her help and seven more to her sons' discussion about who will drive her to her sister's, then almost forgets to mention that she did what she promised. Except in rare cases, Eldreth constructs event clauses to name what she did (usually some kind of women's work) but not to provide actual description or details.

The most striking formal feature of Eldreth's personal narratives is that she almost always ends them with the reported speech of someone who positively evaluates her capacities and activities. In the story of Marie Rash's baby, the well-respected local physician who arrives after the birth insists that the expectant parents already "had as good a doctor there as they could've had" (line 5). The dinner story ends with the grateful sister praising Eldreth to a guest: "Now right here, I want to tell you something, now right here is a good Christian lady." In stories where no story-internal evaluator was present and Eldreth must provide the point-making evaluation herself, she typically finds a way to deflect attention from her own claim. In "Mean Horse," she stresses the horse's viciousness and refers only obliquely to her own heroism. To invoke again the connection between form and context, note that Eldreth told this story immediately after the one about her grandmother's endangering herself to take care of her children. Thus Eldreth's own experience is prefaced by the conclusion of the previous story, "I guess a mother'd risk things that a dad wouldn't," which serves as both evaluation and disclaimer.

Given that the formal structure of a narrative reflects the teller's decisions about how to conduct herself while narrating, the line between *formal features* and *behavioral features* is also blurry. I focus on the choices Eldreth makes, separate from the verbal organization of the story itself, about when, where, to whom, and how to tell her personal narratives.

Eldreth's storytelling approaches the "women's-narrative" models most closely in that she reserves stories for situations in which she has only one or two listeners. Although she used these personal narratives to introduce herself to me, she never tells them on stage during a singing performance or employs them to compete for the floor in large-group conversations. Eldreth similarly avoids "performing" her personal narratives in Bauman's sense of calling attention to the intrinsic qualities of the text, setting it apart from the "everyday" surround, presenting it to audience members for the enhancement of their experience, and inviting their evaluation of the teller's skill (Bauman 1984; Bauman & Briggs 1990). Eldreth is acquainted with men who do "perform" stories in this sense by varying voice volume and speed dramatically, taking on distinctive voices for different characters, dragging out or clipping words, gazing intently at listeners to command their attention, rolling their eyes, changing facial expression, or gesticulating. Eldreth, by contrast, maintains a conversational tone and neutral expression throughout her narration and makes her story merge as seamlessly as possible into the contextualizing conversation. The effect is to focus the listener's attention on the information conveyed rather than on the effectiveness of the story as story or on Eldreth's skill as a narrator.

In sum, Eldreth tells personal narratives that consistently present her as performing kind and valuable services for others. Formally and contextually, the narratives effect a smooth transition from the preceding conversation, describe almost cursorily the service Eldreth renders, and conclude with a positive evaluation of Eldreth's action via the reported comment of another character. Eldreth tells the stories to only a few listeners at a time, avoiding both the competition of large-group conversations and the performance expectations of narration on stage, and eschews paralinguistic features that would mark her narratives as performed primarily for entertainment or formal excellence.

Analysis: A form of narration for a particular woman's life and circumstances

Although each of Eldreth's stories holds intrinsic interest, their thematic, formal, and contextual regularity is noticeable. Why would she consistently tell stories with these qualities? I suggest that these personal narratives fulfill a particular social and communicative need traceable both to the general situation of women of Eldreth's age and race in small, conservatively Protestant, Southern mountain communities and to variations within this pattern in her own life.

During their middle years, when they have the greatest responsibility for children and for making a living, women and men in the Southern mountains have markedly divergent life experiences. Men experience an increase in respect and public exposure (in community or church affairs) that accompanies increasing responsibility, accomplishment, and skill. Women bear tremendous responsibility and are subject to never-ending demands on their labor, energy, and sympathy as they raise their children and provide for their husbands. Yet they are specifically denied access to public prominence (for example, by Baptist adherence to St. Paul's prohibition against women's teaching in church), and their children are too young to provide the appreciation and respect that improve women's old age (Beaver 1986). Many mountain women derive emotional support from their faith and church, but these years are predictably the hardest of a woman's life.

Ideally, women in this cultural system experience the consolation of conjugal love and increasing material security to carry them through these stressful years. Eldreth's friends speak about the good times they had with their husbands and young families. Eldreth, however, at her parents' urging, married a man whom she did not love and who proved indifferent to her happiness. Furthermore, Ed Eldreth worked only cursorily before a serious workplace accident and even less thereafter, which forced his wife to supply even more family support. Perhaps because of his own inability to provide for his family as a man was expected to, he was especially unwilling to see his wife get credit for her achievements. Later, when Bessie Eldreth started to get attention for her singing, her husband was jealous of her celebrity and tried to persuade her that performances conflicted with her duty to care for him.

I would therefore argue that Eldreth's storytelling responds to her need, as a gendered subject in a particular cultural situation, to hold up her accomplishments for public recognition and to evaluate them as praiseworthy. Toward the achievement of this goal, form, context, and narrative behavior react to cultural limitations on storytelling and talk, yet they also take advantage of cultural and linguistic resources available in the speech economy. Eldreth thus creates a narrative practice that makes the most of possibilities for gendered self-representation.

Thematically, Eldreth's stories highlight positive self-presentation. She rarely depicts herself in the personal narrator's other two common guises, as victimized or humorously mistaken (Abrahams 1977; Dégh 1985; Robinson 1981). Eldreth's self-presentation combines themes that Barbara Johnstone (1993) found divided between Midwestern women and men. Eldreth promotes community, as do the women in Johnstone's study, by thematizing her neighborliness, a strong value in the mountains (Beaver 1986; Johnstone 1993). However, unlike the Midwestern women, she does not solve problems with a group; even the laboring mother is not depicted as a cooperative actor in the birth drama. Eldreth portrays herself acting heroically alone and making up for others' inabilities, as do the Midwestern men, whose stories emphasize solo contest with external forces (Johnstone 1993).

Marjorie Faulstich Orellana (chapter 3, this volume) notes that women's and girls' self-presentation as "good" can be problematic, manifesting either self-approval and self-confidence or a self-limiting capitulation to hegemonic standards (see also Walkerdine 1990). Indeed, in ghost stories Eldreth tells, her self-alignment with "good" women reinforces repressive stereotypes of acceptable female behavior (Sawin 1993). In her personal narratives, however, Eldreth effectively negotiates with local standards to secure approbation for past deeds and inherent qualities (not only altruism, but also courage and skill as a singer, midwife, and carpenter) of which she is proud.

Eldreth's tendency formally to construct stories without orientation or abstract works together with her tendency behaviorally not to introduce the stories into large-scale conversations. She thus avoids negotiating with listeners for permission to narrate. This suggests that Eldreth anticipates that coconversationalists would deny her the floor, either because of who she is or because her experiences and stories would be assumed uninteresting. Given that Eldreth told all the recorded texts only to me when I was encouraging her to tell stories, this practice is presumably an artifact of past experience or a response to internalized expectations.

The other distinctive formal qualities of Eldreth's personal narratives—minimal event clauses and evaluation via reported speech—likewise respond to anticipated discouragements. Eldreth's tendency not to give details of the women's work she performs and her decision to employ the reported statement of another character to accomplish the final evaluation mute or camouflage her audacious claims for the value of her own actions. Other aspects foreground Eldreth's accomplishments, but she cannot be accused of bragging if she spends so little time on her supposedly central activities. As I have argued elsewhere (Sawin 1992), the reported-speech evaluation circumvents local prohibitions on self-praise by recontextualizing and emphasizing a kind of objectivized compliment that is characteristic in her community. The speakers whom Eldreth quotes may not actually have said the words she attributes to them (see Tannen 1989), but the remarks are plausible. This further conceals the extent to which Eldreth, as recontextualizer, controls the functional meaning of the "reported" remarks: "the speech of another, once enclosed in a context, is . . . always subject to certain semantic changes" (Bakhtin 1981:340).

These techniques not only disguise the extent of Eldreth's positive self-presentation but also contribute to the stories' import. By treating her activities as so everyday that they need not be described in detail and yet as worthy of explicit and repeated praise, Eldreth makes a quiet but radical claim for the value of women's labor. These stories provide precisely what Eldreth needs: They enable her to portray herself as heroic precisely because she fulfills a mature woman's ordinary duties. And while making a claim for her own value, Eldreth also argues implicitly for the need to revalue all women's repetitive, invisible work.

The reported evaluation likewise creates a cascade of effects. Eldreth's point is not simply to blow her own horn gratuitously. Constructing the reported statement as the final event clause while deemphasizing what she actually did depicts complimentary speech as the most story-worthy activity (Urban 1984). By repeating past examples of praise, Eldreth thanks and commends those who have praised her, encouraging them and others to continue the practice. As a poor woman married to a shiftless husband, Eldreth was the subject of considerable gossip. By treating positive talk about herself as an activity significant enough to be narrated, she promotes such speech to counter the pitying or denigrating talk she knows is also circulating.

Further, because the reported remark accomplishes the evaluation within story time, none of these narratives has a coda, a "state clause that extends beyond the time frame of the story world proper" and functions to return the verbal perspective to the present and to demonstrate how the effects of the reported action have influenced the character's subsequent life (Labov & Waletzky 1967; Polanyi 1985b:193).

There is consequently no *Bildungsroman* quality to the stories: Eldreth depicts herself as unchanging, as having always had the resourcefulness and altruism she repeatedly displays. Given that her society offers women none of the role alternatives or status changes available to men, she simply magnifies and reinstantiates qualities for which she can receive approbation because her society sees them as aspects of her "essential womanly nature." The behavioral aspects of Eldreth's narration—telling these stories only to small groups and avoiding both performance settings and qualities of presentation that would key a story as "performed" for an audience's enjoyment—might be seen as the retiring, self-effacing, noncompetitive behavior natural in an older woman. I would argue, however, that Eldreth acts strategically, though not consciously. Any intentional performance, any piling up of techniques to achieve an effect, is liable to be seen as a contrivance and a falsehood (Goffman 1959). In Eldreth's experience, the role of performer—an instrumental musician, for example—is strongly associated with disreputability (Bauman [1977] 1984). Furthermore, the highly performed narrative genres at which men in this culture excel—Jack tales and tall tales—though enjoyed, are seen as akin to lying. Eldreth herself desires the attention paid to performers and has developed means of retaining respectability while being recognized for her singing (Sawin 1993). With her personal narratives, however, the paramount concern is to present the account as true and the evaluation as credible. Eschewing any marks of performance reinforces listeners' impression of these narratives as truth—as events to be told about—rather than as fiction.

Finally, creating a private space for storytelling identifies the interaction as a type of women's talk prevalent in the South, in which hard truths about gender relations may be spoken because privacy is assured and the interlocutor may choose to encourage critical talk or to pass over controversial topics (Beverly Stoeltje, personal communication). With the story so framed, the listener can infer a much more trenchant criticism of male domination than is explicitly voiced in, for example, Eldreth's matter-of-fact report of the time she delivered a baby by herself and Dr. Robison showed up later, praised her, and collected the fee or in her comment reflecting on bravery by her grandmother and herself in the face of danger to their children: "I guess a mother'd risk things that a dad wouldn't." Over the past decade Eldreth has become increasingly explicit in criticizing her late husband and articulating her objections to marriage. I now recognize that she was telling me these things all along, but I was not yet culturally savvy enough to understand.

For much of her adult life, Bessie Eldreth, like many women of her generation in the Southern mountains, bore hardships and responsibilities equal to men's and yet was excluded from the recognition in which men find compensation. In response, she devised a means of relating her personal experiences that allowed her to repeat the little praise she had received and attract further approbation. Even in old age, when responsibilities have lightened and she receives much more explicit appreciation from her grown children, fellow church members, and public audiences, Eldreth continues to recount these firmly entextualized versions of who she is, what she has done, and how she has been appreciated. Her narrative form and practice reinforce her claims of truthfulness, mute and excuse any excess in calling attention to herself, and enable to her express her version of her own life and her criticisms of the gender roles that shaped it.

Conclusion: Contextualized personal narratives

What broader lessons might Eldreth's stories teach about the influence of gender on individuals' practice of narrating their own lives? I elaborate this analysis not to replace extant models of "women's narrative" with a new one but to suggest that we look at the issue differently, reconceptualizing any person's narrative as multiply contextualized narrative. Women's stories of self are not simply dictated by transcultural gender roles. Each teller develops narrative forms and narrating strategies that work with available symbolic and linguistic resources, within and against local social structures and discourses, and that respond to culturally, historically, and personally determined needs and lacks. Eldreth uses resources made available by her culture and negotiates with her immediate social situation to create a personally satisfying and socially acceptable self-presentation. Both the situation and her access to communicative resources are profoundly influenced by her gender, that is, by the expectations held about women in her community and by her particular historical and personal experiences as a woman. Thus she acts always "as a woman" to create and present her public persona, but the forms she employs must be seen as products of strategic situational negotiation, not as general models. I nevertheless believe that an ethnology of women's narrative built on comparative ethnography could be developed. My study of Eldreth's practice—along with the work of other scholars who have documented other narrators—may point to aspects of strategy, use, access, or even form that future feminist analyses might profitably investigate further. The goal of an ethnology of gender-specific narrative practice, however, must be—without seeking to reinscribe the essential category 'woman'—to trace the range of social gender structures and the range of women's rhetorical, self-defining responses to each structure, and only then to seek possible regularities in these pairings of structure and rhetoric.

TRANSCRIPTION CONVENTIONS

Each numbered line corresponds to an audible intonational unit.

.	falling intonation and brief pause at the end of a phrase
?	rising intonation whether or not the phrase is grammatically an interrogative
. . .	a pause, especially within a phrase when the sense carries across the temporal disjuncture
|	an abrupt break in sense or syntactic flow, as when the speaker repeats a word, corrects a phrase before she has completed it, or changes topic in midphrase
// //	overlapping speech

NOTES

I am grateful to Bessie Eldreth for sharing her personal narratives and to Beverly Stoeltje and Leslie Bloom for helping me to conceptualize the role of gender in Eldreth's stories. Other chapters in this volume analyze the historical situatedness of research on aspects of women's speaking (Cotter, chapter 19; Livia, chapter 17; Morgan, chapter 1; Walters, chapter 10). For foundational work in the effort to correct earlier overgeneralizations about gendered speech see Cameron (1985) and Hall, Bucholtz, & Moonwomon (1992).

1. Kalčik elaborated her model of women's "kernel stories" without benefit of Deborah Tannen's (1984) work on mixed-gender "story rounds"; Hall and Langellier described collaborative interruption as a women's form without considering Livia Polanyi's (1985b) discussion of story construction in conversation; and although in 1990 Bennett revised her 1989 claim that *and*-linked "supersentences" are a peculiarly female technique, she seems unaware of Deborah Schiffrin's (1987) work on phrase-initial *and* as a discourse marker in oral narrative regardless of the teller's gender.

2. From these tapes I have transcribed the narratives on which both my dissertation (Sawin 1993) and this study are based. Eldreth told all the recorded stories with only me for audience, but I believe she has recounted them to family members and neighbors in much the same form. The texts reflect the influence of their means of collection, as well as of earlier family interactions.

3. Despite the valid criticisms leveled against this model, I employ it heuristically both because Eldreth's narratives exhibit many of the features it predicts and because it represents the way many people *think* oral narratives are or should be told, even though Polanyi (1985b) and others demonstrate they often are not.

REFERENCES

Abrahams, Roger D. (1977). The most embarrassing thing that ever happened: Conversational stories in a theory of enactment. *Folklore Forum* 10(3):9–15.

Allen, Barbara (1989). Personal experience narratives: Use and meaning in interaction. In Elliott Oring (ed.), *Folk groups and folklore genres: A reader*. Logan: Utah State University Press, 236–243. (Original work published 1978)

Bakhtin, Mikhail M. (1981). *The dialogic imagination*. Ed. Michael Holquist. Trans. Caryl Emerson & Michael Holquist. Austin: University of Texas Press.

Baldwin, Karen (1985). "Woof!": A word on women's roles in family storytelling. In Rosan A. Jordan & Susan J. Kalčik (eds.), *Women's folklore, women's culture*. Philadelphia: University of Pennsylvania Press, 149–162.

Bascom, William (1954). Four functions of folklore. *Journal of American Folklore* 67:333–349.

Bauman, Richard (1972). The La Have Island general store: Sociability and verbal art in a Nova Scotia community. *Journal of American Folklore* 85:330–343.

———— (1984). *Verbal art as performance*. Prospect Heights, IL: Waveland Press. (Original work published 1977)

Bauman, Richard, & Charles L. Briggs (1990). Poetics and performance as critical perspectives on language and social life. *Annual Review of Anthropology* 19:59–88.

Beaver, Patricia Duane (1986). *Rural community in the Appalachian South*. Lexington: University Press of Kentucky.

Belenky, Mary Field, Blythe McVicker Clinchy, Nancy Rule Goldberger, & Jill Mattuck Tarule (1986). *Women's ways of knowing: The development of self, voice, and mind*. New York: Basic Books.

Bennett, Gillian (1989). "And I turned round to her and said . . . ": A preliminary analysis of shape and structure in women's storytelling. *Folklore* 100(2):167–183.

———— (1990). "And . . . ": Controlling the argument, controlling the audience. *Fabula* 31(3–4):208–216.

Berman, Laine (1994). Empowering the powerless: The repetition of experience in Javanese women's narratives. In Mary Bucholtz, A. C. Liang, Laurel A. Sutton, & Caitlin Hines (eds.), *Cultural performances: Proceedings of the Third Berkeley Women and Language Conference*. Berkeley, CA: Berkeley Women and Language Group, 28–36.

Borland, Katherine (1991). "That's not what I said": Interpretive conflict in oral narrative research. In Sherna Berger Gluck & Daphne Patai (eds.), *Women's words: The feminist practice of oral history*. New York: Routledge, 63–75.

Cameron, Deborah (1985). *Feminism and linguistic theory*. London: Macmillan.

Davies, Bronwyn, & Rom Harré (1990). Positioning: The discursive production of selves. *Journal for the Theory of Social Behavior* 20(1):43–63.

Dégh, Linda (1985). "When I was six we moved west . . . ": The theory of personal experience narrative. *New York Folklore* 11(1–4):99–108.

Farr, Marcia (1994). *Echando relajo:* Verbal art and gender among *Mexicanas* in Chicago. In Mary Bucholtz, A. C. Liang, Laurel A. Sutton, & Caitlin Hines (eds.), *Cultural performances: Proceedings of the Third Berkeley Women and Language Conference*. Berkeley, CA: Berkeley Women and Language Group, 168–186.

Fuss, Diana (1989). *Essentially speaking: Feminism, nature and difference*. New York: Routledge.

Gilligan, Carol (1982). *In a different voice: Psychological theory and women's development*. Cambridge, MA: Harvard University Press.

Goffman, Erving (1959). *The presentation of self in everyday life*. New York: Doubleday.

Goodwin, Marjorie Harness (1990). *He-said-she-said: Talk as social organization among black children*. Bloomington: Indiana University Press.

———— (1992). Orchestrating participation in events: Powerful talk among African American girls. In Kira Hall, Mary Bucholtz, & Birch Moonwomon (eds.), *Locative power: Proceedings of the Second Berkeley Woman and Language Conference.* Berkeley, CA: Berkeley Women and Language Group, 182–196.

———— (1993). Tactical uses of stories: Participation frameworks within boys' and girls' disputes. In Deborah Tannen (ed.), *Gender and conversational interaction.* Oxford: Oxford University Press, 110–143.

Hall, Deanna L., & Kristin M. Langellier (1988). Storytelling strategies in mother-daughter communication. In Anita Taylor & Barbara Bate (eds.), *Women communicating.* Norwood, NJ: Ablex, 107–126.

Hall, Kira, Mary Bucholtz, & Birch Moonwomon (eds.) (1992). *Locating power: Proceedings of the Second Berkeley Women and Language Conference.* Berkeley: Berkeley, CA: Berkeley Women and Language Group.

Hollis, Susan, Linda Pershing, & M. Jane Young (1993). *Feminist theory and the study of folklore.* Urbana: University of Illinois Press.

Hollway, Wendy (1984). Gender difference and the production of subjectivity. In Julian Henriques, Wendy Hollway, Cathy Urwin, Couze Venn, & Valerie Walkerdine (eds.), *Changing the subject: Psychology, social regulation and subjectivity.* London: Methuen, 227–263.

hooks, bell (1992). *Black looks: Race and representation.* Boston: South End Press.

Johnstone, Barbara (1993). Community and contest: Midwestern men and women creating their worlds in conversational storytelling. In Deborah Tannen (ed.), *Gender and conversational interaction.* Oxford: Oxford University Press, 62–80.

Kalčik, Susan (1975). " . . . like Ann's gynecologist or the time I was almost raped": Personal narratives in women's rap groups. In Claire R. Farrer (ed.), *Women and folklore: Images and genres.* Austin: University of Texas Press, 3–11. Reprint, Prospect Heights, IL: Waveland Press, 1986.

Kyratzis, Amy (1994). Tactical uses of narratives in nursery school same-sex groups. In Mary Bucholtz, A. C. Liang, Laurel A. Sutton, & Caitlin Hines (eds.), *Cultural performances: Proceedings of the Third Berkeley Women and Language Conference.* Berkeley, CA: Berkeley Women and Language Group, 389–398.

Labov, William (1972). The transformation of experience in narrative syntax. In Labov, *Language in the inner city: Studies in the Black English Vernacular.* Philadelphia: University of Pennsylvania Press, 354–405.

Labov, William, & Joshua Waletzky (1967). Narrative analysis: Oral versions of personal experience. In June Helm (ed.), *Essays on the verbal and visual arts.* Seattle: University of Washington Press, 12–44.

Langellier, Kristin M. (1989). Personal narratives: Perspectives on theory and research. *Text and Performance Quarterly* 9(4):243–276.

Langellier, Kristin M., & Eric E. Peterson (1992). Spinstorying: An analysis of women storytelling. In Elizabeth C. Fine & Jean Haskell Speer (eds.), *Performance, culture, and identity.* Westport, CT: Praeger, 157–179.

Lawless, Elaine (1991). Women's life stories and reciprocal ethnography as feminist and emergent. *Journal of Folklore Research* 28(1):35–60.

Liang, A. C. (1994). "Coming out" as transition and transcendence of the public/private dichotomy. In Mary Bucholtz, A. C. Liang, Laurel A. Sutton, & Caitlin Hines (eds.), *Cultural performances: Proceedings of the Third Berkeley Women and Language Conference.* Berkeley, CA: Berkeley Women and Language Group, 409–420.

Linde, Charlotte (1993). *Life stories: The creation of coherence.* New York: Oxford University Press.

Livesay, Jennifer (1994). "Without this group I'd be a total bitch": Discrimination, narrative, and Catholic identity in a women's home liturgy group. Paper presented at the Meeting of the American Folklore Society, Eugene, Oregon.

McDonald, Mary Anne (1994). "It's not nothing I like to talk about": Personal experience narratives of five African American women. Paper presented at the Meeting of the American Folklore Society, Eugene, Oregon.

Mills, Margaret (1990). Critical theory and the folklorists: Performances, interpretive authority, and gender. *Southern Folklore* 47(1):5–15.

Moore, Henrietta L. (1994). *A passion for difference*. Bloomington: Indiana University Press.

Polanyi, Livia (1985a). *Telling the American story: A structural and cultural analysis of conversational storytelling*. Norwood, NJ: Ablex.

——— (1985b). Conversational storytelling. In Teun A. van Dijk (ed.), *Handbook of discourse analysis*. Vol. 3: *Discourse and dialogue*. London: Academic Press, 183–201.

Radner, Joan Newlon (ed.) (1993). *Feminist messages: Coding in women's folk culture*. Urbana: University of Illinois Press.

Robinson, John A. (1981). Personal narratives reconsidered. *Journal of American Folklore* 93:58–85.

Sawin, Patricia E. (1992). "Right here is a good Christian lady": Reported speech in personal narratives. *Text and Performance Quarterly* 12(3):193–211.

——— (1993). Bessie Mae Eldreth: An Appalachian woman's performance of self. Ph.D. diss., Indiana University.

Schiffrin, Deborah (1987). *Discourse markers*. Cambridge: Cambridge University Press.

Stahl, Sandra Dolby (1977). The personal narrative as folklore. *Journal of Folklore Research* 14(1–2):9–30.

——— (1983). Personal experience stories. In Richard M. Dorson (ed.), *Handbook of American folklore*. Bloomington: Indiana University Press, 268–276.

Tannen, Deborah (1984). *Conversational style: Analyzing talk among friends*. Norwood, NJ: Ablex.

——— (1989). *Talking voices: Repetition, dialogue, and imagery in conversational discourse*. Cambridge: Cambridge University Press.

——— (1990). *You just don't understand: Women and men in conversation*. New York: William Morrow.

Urban, Greg (1984). Speech about speech in speech about action. *Journal of American Folklore* 97:310–328.

Walkerdine, Valerie (1990). *Schoolgirl fictions*. New York: Verso.

Yocom, Margaret R. (1985). Woman to woman: Fieldwork and the private sphere. In Rosan A. Jordan & Susan J. Kalčik (eds.), *Women's folklore, women's culture*. Philadelphia: University of Pennsylvania Press, 45–53.

. . . .

Language, Socialization, and Silence in Gay Adolescence

This chapter explores a component of the "coming-out" experience that remains largely overlooked in the literature on gay adolescence: How do gay teenagers go about acquiring the language of gay culture?[1] My discussion of this question builds on three assumptions: (1) that something called "gay culture" (as distinct from gay "lifestyle" or erotic interests) really exists; (2) that "gay culture" includes distinctive "ways of talking" within its inventory of symbolics and semiotics; and (3) that these "ways of talking" are sufficiently rich and complex to justify being termed gay *language*, rather than an argot, "secret code," or rhetorical style.[2]

By exploring the convergence of language, identity construction, and gay socialization, this chapter joins other recent studies exploring the close connections between language and culture that underlie, for example, recollections of childhood in a "lesbian living room" (Morgan & Wood 1995), dialogue between entertainer and audience at a black drag club (Barrett 1995; chapter 16, this volume), menu-planning for a lesbian seder (Moonwomon 1996), or the in-flight disclosure of gay identities between an airline passenger and an airline steward (Leap 1993). These studies show how participation in lesbian- and gay-centered text-making in different social settings builds familiarity with the rules of lesbian- and gay-centered grammar and discourse and with other cultural practices relevant to those domains. They also demonstrate how participation in such social moments assumes some degree of familiarity with lesbian- and gay-centered language and cultural practices. In the absence of such information, text-making becomes highly dependent on situated (rather than prediscursive) meanings, on negotiation and inference, on "double (that is, hearer- as well as speaker-based) subjectivity" (Goodwin 1989:12), and in some instances on conditions of risk (Leap 1996:72–73).

None of these processes is uniquely lesbian or gay in its basis, but all the same, text-making conducted on such terms has clear implications for lesbian and gay experience. Particularly vulnerable in this regard are young persons who are just beginning to lay claim to lesbian or gay identities and who turn to lesbian- and gay-centered text-making as a format for acting on those claims. Text-making in these cases ranges from the disclosure of same-sex desires to close friends or adult authority figures to the construction of silence as agemates use an individual's ambiguous sexuality as a focus for teasing and taunting. Overlapping with the construction of textual silence, of course, is the almost epidemic-like incidence of attempted suicide reported for American teenagers struggling to come to terms with their homosexuality.[3]

Understandably, when gay men look back on their adolescence, they often speak of this period of their gender career as a time of loneliness and isolation, conditions that one gay man summarized powerfully with the phrase "a vast desert of nothing" (Leap 1996:127).[4] But some gay men also describe this period as a time when they set out to make sense out of newly discovered feelings, emotions, and interests; when they assembled information that would help them better understand those discoveries; and when they tried to locate other individuals who might share (or understand or at least not dismiss) these concerns. And—of particular importance to this chapter—gay men talk about attempts to find a language through which they can describe, interpret, and account for the new directions now taking shape within their lives.

Some examples of such statements appear below. They were chosen from a larger set of texts I collected during a recent study of gay language socialization (reported, in part, in Leap 1994, 1996:125–139).[5] Each example describes a young man's attempts to make sense out of a male-centered sexual identity, even though the details of that identity were just beginning to be disclosed. And each example shows how language became a resource during this process.

Jim (a 22-year-old gay white man who was born in Buffalo, New York, and lived there until he started college in Washington, D.C.) told me:

> I was never sat down by my mom and dad and told the heterosexual version of the birds and the bees. Um, you know, when you get to the time where you are twelve, thirteen, or fourteen, you begin to be sexually aware, you really look, strive for sources of information.
>
> I started looking for information about homosexuality . . . and eventually I branched off into the *Encyclopaedia Britannica* we had in the house. I looked up in the index as far as sexual goes: penis, phallus, every single adjective, synonym of that. . . . I eventually went to the public library, school library and that wasn't easy because it was public and you had to build up your confidence. . . .
>
> I tried to do as much as possible, reading, whatever I thought might have gotten somewhere. For example, if I came across a column like for example Ann Landers might have mentioned it, I'd be her fan for a couple of months so maybe she'd bring it up again.

Sam (a 21-year-old gay white man who was born and raised in central Ohio and attended college in Washington, D.C.) told me:

> *Brothers* (a cable television sitcom) had an effeminate stereotyped gay man. That was a good example of how not to talk. I didn't believe gay people talked like that. *Consent-*

ing Adult related a view which I knew was true and was looking for: a normal guy can be gay. *Deathtrap*—my mom was disgusted by the kissing scene. I was distracted.

Wallace (a gay white man in his early 30s who grew up in the Washington, D.C. suburbs and is a professional actor with several companies in the Washington area) noted in an interview published in the *Washington Post* (Brown & Swisher 1994):

> I grew up in Maryland, right outside of D.C., and spent my childhood listening to *West Side Story* and *A Chorus Line*. Those cast albums and movie musicals on TV were sort of secret messages from a world we didn't experience in our suburban, private school upbringing. That saved us.

Robert (a 27-year-old gay white man who was born in northern Florida, finished graduate school in North Carolina, and is now on the faculty of a junior college in northern Virginia) told me:

> Later in high school, my junior year, I guess, people started calling me faggot. I don't know if it was a joke or what, but they called me that. A lot. Even my teammates, they'd toss me a towel and say, "Hey faggot, catch this," or someone'd say, "Hey faggot, the coach needs to talk to you."
> (Q: did you get angry? Did this upset you?)
> You know, it's funny. I didn't get mad at all. I was uncomfortable, but I was not mad. See, I knew by then that I was gay so—without even knowing it, they were right! They were telling the truth. I couldn't get mad at them for telling the truth.

Joe (a 24-year-old gay white man and a campus and community activist) told me:

> I have been gay since the womb: I started experimenting with sex when I was very young and when I found others doing the same thing I knew there was something to all of this—but I didn't know exactly what it was.
> (Q: So when did you come out?)
> You mean, telling anybody about all this experimentation? Not 'til I was a teenager. I met an older woman, middle-aged, who had lots of gay friends. She introduced me to some other, older gay men and they took me under their wing. That is how I learned the rest of it, the social thing, the networks.

Sam continues:

> (Q: Did you know or know about gay people in [your hometown] when you were in high school?)
> No, not at first, but by the time I ended ninth grade, I had learned about five people: one aged thirty-five, three older than that, and one my own age. He became my best friend in high school.
> (Q: How did you find these people?)
> Pure luck. . . . I wanted to find someone like me. Found him by pure luck. Met him in the eighth grade. I told him in the ninth grade. He told me he was bisexual in the tenth grade. Both of us were scared. Having been friends, we did not want to jeopardize each

other's secret. We talked a lot. No topic was safe. Though really, it was me doing the talking. He was the novice, someone for me to talk to.

Jim continues:

> I, later in my senior year, when I was seventeen or eighteen, I had an English teacher, too. It was real interesting, our relationship, because he was very pull-students-aside-and-get-into-their-lives kind of thing. I do not know for what reason, but he did that with me. He was very helpful in that he knew I was gay and kind of brought me out a bit more. I remember that, for some reason, he approached me, and said: How does your mother feel about this? And I said: Wow! And I told him, and the dam was lifted, and all the information I needed in my life was there, me seeking advice from him, that sort of thing.

Charting a path through the "desert of nothing"

Although life stories are subjective (and in some sense fictional) documents, they do provide a *detail* of gay experience that cannot be retrieved from statistical surveys or other broadly based forms of data-gathering.[6] And in the present case, many details in these narratives speak directly to the importance of language and language learning for gay socialization and for the construction of gay identity during adolescence.

The close connection between language, identity, and heteronormativity provides the background for the present discussion, and I begin my analysis with some general comments on this connection.

Heteronormativity versus the gay imaginary

By *heteronormativity*, I mean the principles of order and control that position heterosexuality as the cornerstone of the American sex/gender system and obligate the personal construction of sexuality and gender in terms of heterosexual norms. Heteronormativity assumes, for example, that there are two sexes and therefore two genders. Heteronormativity then requires that all discussions of gendered identity and opportunity be framed strictly in terms of this dichotomy, forcing gendered actors to be labelled as either 'woman' or 'man', regardless of the identification that the actors might give to themselves.

An abundance of institutions, "a pervasive cluster of forces" (Rich 1980:640), in Western society conspire to give heteronormativity its natural and normal façade. Importantly, however, while heteronormativity is certainly powerful and pervasive in late modern Western societies, it is not entirely totalizing. Alternative constructions of sexuality and gender are possible within this system, although particular alternatives do not always intersect smoothly with normative claims to authority. Hence the regulation of heteronormativity unfolds through distinctions between acceptable and unacceptable sexual/gendered identities and practices and through an ordering of the social worth of individuals on the basis of their allegiance to such distinctions.

In this way, heteronormativity co-occurs with, and profits from, the social presence of the *subaltern* (an "identity-in-differential" which is set apart from both the ideal and the elite [Spivak 1988:284]), the *queer* ("a unity . . . of shared dissent from the dominant organization of sex and gender" composed of lesbian, gay, and other lifestyles "whose icons are heavily associated by cultural outsiders with the culture of gay life, politics and practices" [Whittle 1994:27]); the *stigmatized* (persons who, through various means, must contend with a "spoiled identity" [Goffman 1963]), as well as other stances situated on the margins of late modern society.

Language holds a prominent place in the intersection of the heteronormative and the marginal. In English and other Western languages, conversation, narration, and other forms of text-making provide contexts within which heteronormative messages are produced and reproduced in everyday life. Morphemic and lexical contrasts, processes of reference and inference, and other structural details provide the framework through which heteronormative messages become inscribed in, remembered within, and retained beyond the textual moment.

Unavoidably, language keeps heteronormative stances in the foreground of daily activity and keeps alternative forms of reference in the background, the margins, and the shadows. Such arrangements ensure that normative assumptions become expectable, reasonable, and acceptable components of the local cultural inventory and that alternative stances remain less familiar, more mysterious, and less desirable.

But even while it imposes such limitations on social reference, language-based normativity does not always disrupt the workings of the personal imaginary. Individuals still construct their own sense of sexual/gendered possibilities and apply their own meanings to those constructions, even if they do not find referential support for these imagined constructions within normatively sanctioned sex/gender discourse. Hence the pervasive presence of silence within heteronormative domains, a silence that reflects an absence of articulation but not necessarily an absence of personal voice. And hence the delight in the discovery of labels, even when the points of reference are not intended to be complimentary or to have any positive implications.

By my reading of his statement cited above, this is the point of Robert's reactions to his peers' taunting and teasing in the high school locker room. Robert's teammates called him *faggot*, but rather than becoming angry at this name-calling, Robert diffuses the statements by acknowledging the truthfulness of their reference: He admits that he *was* gay, after all, and says that he could not be upset at his colleagues for telling the truth. We must not be sidetracked by Robert's seemingly naive rewriting of logical argument. Instead, we must consider how Robert's interpretation of these statements gives him a way of living through moments when he was the target of invective, moments when he had no alternative but either to "confirm" his manhood through a fistfight or some other form of competitive force, thereby directing the team's teasing toward the vanquished party, or simply to maintain his silence. As he told me in our interview, the latter seemed the more reasonable option for a young man growing up in a small Southern town.

Such choices are familiar parts of the gay adolescent social landscape; they are found not only in the narratives collected here but also in more overtly fictional work representing gay adolescent experience. Robert Reinhardt's character Billy in his novel *A History of Shadows* (1986), for example, would understand Robert's decision. Like Robert, in the novel Billy remembers thinking that he "was the only homo-sexual in the world." He continues:

> Well, that's not quite true. . . . But I felt I was the only homosexual. It's hard being some-thing for which one doesn't even have a name. And I didn't for a long time. I used to wonder, what am I? I saw the boys in my class and longed for them, but I couldn't figure out what the vague aching was, and I couldn't recognize it in others. I couldn't see that anyone looked at me with the same longing.
>
> I found out about sex in the streets. The first name I had for what I was, was "cocksucker." . . . (It) was an awful word the way they used it, but it meant that my con-dition was nameable. I knew I was awful, but I finally had a name for all those odd feel-ings. I wasn't nothing. I was awful, but I wasn't nothing. (Reinhardt 1986:25)

My condition was nameable. I finally had a name for those odd feelings. I wasn't nothing. Here, the relief in finding a label for "those odd feelings" outweighs the negative content surrounding this usage. And once again, rather than being over-whelmed by negative sentiment, Billy found a way to pull something useful from the statements and to disregard the remainder of the message. Wallace did the same thing, as he reports in the passage cited above, when he began to locate "secret mes-sages from a world we didn't experience" in cast albums and Broadway musicals. Sam did the same thing when he rejected the stereotyped homosexual's use of lan-guage on *Brothers* because he "didn't believe gay people talked like that." And Jim did the same thing when he searched through Ann Landers's columns for her occa-sional comments on homosexuality.

All of these narratives speak to a process that Julia Kristeva (1982) describes in some detail. Even though I may willingly subordinate myself to some object that "precedes and possesses me," an object over which I have no control, "sublimation" allows me to "dissolve [it] in the raptures of a bottomless memory."[7] Then, "as soon as I perceive [the now-sublimated object], as soon as I name it, the sublime triggers— as it has always triggered—a spree of perceptions and words that expands memory boundlessly. I then forget the point of departure and find myself removed to a sec-ondary universe, set off from the other where I 'am'—delight and loss" (1982:10–11). Kristeva's description speaks to a re-creation of awareness, a construction of a personal imaginary, that does not challenge the dominant and oppressive hetero-normativity but does enable individuals to make their own way in spite of hetero-sexual norms. For Robert and Billy, for Sam and Wallace and Jim, and for the other men contributing life stories to this chapter, the journey of self-discovery moves them through the "desert of nothing." Expressions of personal agency are central to this journey, and—as I will show below—familiarity with a gay-centered language is central to expressions of personal agency. But first, I must say more about personal agency.

Self-managed socialization

A striking feature in the life stories I have collected from gay men has been the con-sistent presence of the first-person active voice. That is, narrators position themselves as narrative agents, not merely as objects, in their stories. They describe personal struggles to take charge of their gay socialization and present the socialization process itself as a self-initiated, self-managed experience, even while they discuss the frustration and pain it causes.

It is tempting to view such claims as a consequence of the life-story genre: that is, stories that describe events in the speaker's own life are likely to position the speaker as the central character. But genre alone is an inadequate explanation for this component of textual design, because speakers can always adapt narratives to their own needs (see Sawin, chapter 12, this volume). If the events in these narratives reflect the tensions between social heteronormativity and the personal gay imaginary as they unfold in adolescent lives, then the pervasiveness of first-person reference must be part of this reflection and its presence must be explained in similar terms.

What then are the narrators telling me when they describe gay adolescence as a time of self-managed socialization? First, these references suggest that gay socialization is quite different from the socialization experiences that unfold elsewhere in the life course. The complex of institutional support that enables the transmission of heteronormative conventions and practices between and within generations (some of which are described in Coates, chapter 6, this volume) has very little parallel within gay adolescence, even with the expanding numbers of gay community centers, youth outreach programs, and religious support groups that have emerged in recent years. Understandably, then, statements like *I knew I was different but didn't have a word for it* and *I thought I was the only such person in the world* continue to assume an almost trope-like status in gay men's descriptions of their teenage years. Nothing like these statements appears in the ethnographic descriptions of normative language socialization (e.g., Heath 1983; Ochs 1988; Schieffelin 1990; Ward 1971) or in the comments on socialization experiences that these researchers have collected from members of the speech communities under study. The predominant socialization processes in those settings have to do with incorporating the individual into the social group, not with enabling individuals to claim space on its margin. Claiming space on the margin is, however, the predominant theme in gay men's socialization narratives, as the examples reviewed here have shown. Support for such efforts could come from external sources such as guidance from friends, family members, teachers, or other authority figures, but the narratives always describe such support as accidental and unplanned occurrences, as interventions over which the individual has no control. Sam refers to his relationship with a sympathetic agemate as "pure luck"; Jim "do[es]n't know for what reason" a high school teacher started asking him helpful questions about his sexuality. The point is that although external support is always possible in gay socialization, the availability of such support is in no sense reliable. This leaves only one resource to provide accessible guidance to the individual as he struggles to understand male-centered desire and gay-centered identity: the individual himself.

For this reason, I find it imperative to read the pervasive references to personal agency, to narrator-as-actor, in these life-story segments not as indications of "what I really did to learn about gay life" but as after-the-fact realization that "this (self-managed socialization) was the only way, at this point in my life, that I could have learned about gay experience." Such an analysis places the narrative's emphasis on first-person agency squarely within the narrative strategy that Arthur Kleinmann (1988:50) terms "retrospective narratization." This emphasis reflects the narrator's sense of "significance and validity in the creation of life story," not his "fidelity to historical circumstances" (51): In this case, it is the depiction of loneliness and emptiness combined with the discussions of self-managed socialization that gives these narratives their intended significance and validity.

Retrieving gay messages

Also important is the narrators' descriptions of the sources they consulted while conducting their individualized, personalized search for information about gay experience and about themselves: library books, magazines, newspaper columns, motion pictures, television sitcoms, talk shows, Broadway musicals, gay folklore, jokes, supportive responses from friends and strangers. As already discussed, even derogatory homophobic statements become useful resources in this process.

The particular items that narrators include in this inventory are not as important as the range and variety of materials. Perhaps no single source provided sufficient information to answer the narrators' questions, or the narrators were not satisfied with deriving information from only one source. Either way, the narratives suggest that seeking out information about gay experience is an important part of self-managed socialization.

But seeking out information assumes that the individual knows where to find appropriate sources or is willing to search sufficiently broadly until he stumbles across the right locations. Events in the narratives cited here position both of these practices within the gay socialization process, and they also imply that, once the searching begins, locating gay-relevant materials is not a difficult task. Indeed, as Alexander Doty (1993) argues, any text in today's mass culture contains (at least potentially) a queer message and hence contains information that could be relevant to gay socialization.

At the same time, Doty continues, "unless the text is *about* queers, it seems to me that the queerness of most mass culture texts is less an essential waiting-to-be-discovered property than the result of acts of production and reception" (1993:ix). It would be valuable to know more about the specifics of the reception process described in these narratives. It seems easy enough (as Jim explained) to scan the index of the *Encyclopaedia Britannica* "as far as sexual goes: penis, phallus, every single adjective, synonym of that." But Sam's rereading of the gay character on *Brothers* and Wallace's "queering" of *West Side Story* speak to a more complex interpretation of textual material. What are the clues, the cues, the signals, the signifiers that call forth gay-centered interpretation of such texts?

Answering these questions is similar to answering questions about the mechanics of *gaydar*, the recognition strategy which Michael Musto describes as "the art of spotting sisters [i.e., other gay men], no matter how concealed, invisible or pretending to be straight they are" (1993:120). Gay men who freely discuss using gaydar are not necessarily explicit regarding the criteria that guide their evaluation of "suspect gay" status; and, when described, such criteria differ greatly from one gay man to the next (see discussion in Leap 1996:49–66). It is likely that the interpretive processes relevant to queer reading in such encounters are closely linked to the processes that underlie location and retrieval of information about gay-centered culture and language during gay adolescence. If so, then interpretive skills that are central to self-managed socialization during gay adolescence continue to be valuable resources throughout the gender career.

Homophobia, rehearsal, and the language of the closet

Particularly important in regard to the movement from adolescence to adulthood are the ways in which a retrieval of gay-centered messages from written and other media texts provides *rehearsal* for encounters with gay-centered messages in social settings. Learning how to recognize and make sense out of gay-centered messages in seemingly heteronormative texts is one part of rehearsal. And so is building a personal repertoire of gay commentary by memorizing words, phrases, and sentences from novels, motion pictures, or plays with explicitly gay themes. *Boys in the Band* (Crowley 1968) and *Consenting Adult* (Hobson 1975) remain two popular sources for this purpose. Equally helpful, reported gay men in their 20s, were the dialogues from television soap operas; for gay men in their 40s, additional sources included memorable lines from the films of Bette Davis and the numerous anecdotes attributed to the private life of Tallulah Bankhead.

These sets of information gave gay adolescents opportunities to anticipate the linguistic skills (both of reception and of production—see the previous comment by Doty) that they would need in conversation with another gay, gay-friendly, or potentially gay-friendly individual. On some occasions, as Sam's discovery of "someone like me" suggests, being prepared for those conversations helped both parties secure a long-lasting friendship or led to other successful outcomes. Unfortunately, modeling real-life exchanges around media-derived images of gay communication and its social dynamics can also yield misleading expectations about a conversation and its effects. Often, the resulting (mis)communication leads to unpleasant consequences, as the following story (from Rhoads 1994) suggests.

Andrew (one of Rhoads's key informants) had sex with his best friend in junior high school, and he "found the experience eye-opening":

> "I thought, 'Oh wow, maybe this isn't so wrong.'" . . . He learned all his life that having sex with a man was wrong, but his experience seemed to tell him something different. "I thought it seemed like he enjoyed it and I enjoyed it. So it was something we shouldn't do? I was like, 'Oh this is great. There is someone else who feels like I do.'"
>
> The next day, Andrew's friend (the one with whom he had sex) spread it all over school that Andrew had sexually assaulted him. "It was horrendous; I mean it was my first real encounter with homophobia." (1994:74)

There was little Andrew could do to prevent his "friend" from spreading stories about sexual assault. To deny the charge would be a predictable reaction and would only draw greater attention to the event. Besides, to whom would Andrew voice his denial? Such events require more subtle responses on the part of the gay-accused: silence, secrecy, abjection, erasure, and disguise—each of which gains representation through a language of restraint, a language that parallels the restricted discussions of gay life and gay opportunity in public heteronormative discourse and that transfers those restrictions into the personal linguistic inventory.[8]

Silence, secrecy, disguise, privacy, and restraint are, of course, features that define the experience of "the closet" in Western tradition. Understandably, many gay theorists view "the closet" as a primary obstacle to gay self-determination and consider "coming out of the closet" as the culmination of the move from individuation to disclosure (Davies 1992:76ff.), "the most momentous act in the life of any lesbian or gay person" (Plummer 1995:82), and the primary rite of passage in contemporary gay experience (Rhoads 1994:7–8). The life stories that I have collected contain ample documentation of the damage created when the closet becomes the long-term anchor for a person's gay identity. At the same time, these stories also point out that the closet is not a site of gay denial. Certainly, being "in the closet" discourages explicit expressions of gay identity, but gay socialization is still possible within that enclosure—especially if the socialization process unfolds in personalized, self-managed terms. Closets have keyholes, closet doors have cracks, and closet walls are thin.

So although it is often appropriate to theorize the closet in terms of regulation and repression, it is also possible to theorize this construction as a simpler and less threatening form of gay experience, a subdued alternative to the more explicit demands of a public gay voice. The term *voice* is important here. If the closet is part of gay culture, then the closet, too, has a language—a language that privileges silence over speech, restraint over expression, concealment over cooperation, safety over risk (see also Liang, chapter 15, this volume). And for some gay adolescents, learning the language of the closet is as integral to gay self-managed socialization as are the gay messages in TV sitcoms and rock and roll lyrics, the negotiations of gay disclosure between good friends, or the other strategies that guide their journey through the "desert of nothing."

Language and survival

As my analysis of "the closet" suggests, interpreting gay adolescence in terms of self-managed socialization offers a somewhat different perspective on gay adolescence from that usually presented in the scholarly literature. Certainly, as Rhoads argues: "Adolescence is a stressful time for everyone. . . . For gay and bisexual men, this period of life is even more traumatic because in addition to the typical stressors such as leaving home, dating and thoughts of career, they must also come to term with their same-sex attractions" (1994:67). Yet the narratives that Rhoads discusses, like the life stories in Gilbert Herdt and Andrew Boxer's (1993) study of the Horizon Project in Chicago, the life stories in Jim Sears's *Growing Up Gay in the South* (1991), or the life-story segments I have discussed here, are not just narratives of trauma and frustration. They are also survivors' stories. They describe the narrators' efforts—to use Plummer's (1995:50) formulation—to "move from secrecy, suffering and an often felt sense of victimization toward a major change: therapy, survival, recovery or politics." These efforts may still be continuing at the time of narration, the move may be ongoing, but the narrative stance is consistently the same in these collections: Narrators may find homosexuality to be disruptive, painful, and isolating, yet they search out ways to define gay identity to their own satisfaction and to articulate it successfully with other components of adolescent experience.

Worth interrogating, then, are the reasons why other gay teenagers are not successful in such efforts at self-managed socialization and why still others do not underake such efforts in the first place. We can move this interrogation forward by recognizing that gay adolescents are not, in any categorical sense, neurotic, maladjusted, and self-destructive, but they are likely to become so when their search for information about gay experience and their other efforts toward self-discovery are devalued, thwarted, and ridiculed at every turn. We can ask, accordingly, whether our own institutions and communities provide teenagers with the opportunities, incentives, and resources on which self-managed socialization depends; we can ask what support each of us is providing to that end.

NOTES

This chapter builds on a discussion of gay English and language socialization that first appeared in Leap (1994) and that I develop further in Leap (1996). I presented versions of this work as an invited lecture at Pennsylvania State University's Lesbian/Gay Studies Series (February 1995) and in a session on lesbian and gay discourse held at the annual meeting of the American Association for Applied Linguistics (Long Beach, CA, March 1995). Mary Bucholtz gave a close reading to the chapter in preliminary draft, and her guidance helped immeasurably in the development of the final argument. My thanks, as well, to Liz Sheehan (American University), Tony D'Augeli (Penn State), Rick Arons (St. John's), and the other editors of this volume for their useful contributions to this project.

1. By the term *gay teenagers* I mean male teenagers who are in the process of discovering male-centered desire and constructing personal identity in response to those discoveries.
2. These assumptions are warranted by a number of works of scholarship: Ken Plummer (1995:91–95) traces the factors that prompted the emergence of gay culture in recent years; Gilbert Herdt and Andrew Boxer (1992:3–13, 1993:1–24) explore the ways in which an authentically gay culture provides a moral critique of contemporary U.S. society; Esther Newton (1993) employs historical perspectives to show how gay culture offers complex if often subtle sites for resistance to heteronormativity; Plummer assigns stories and storytelling a prominent place in gay culture; Birch Moonwomon's (1995) distinction between linguistic and societal discourses in such stories argues powerfully in favor of the existence of lesbian and gay language(s), as well as lesbian and gay texts; Leap (1995:xi–xvii, 1996:1–11 and introduction) offers additional arguments to that end.
3. Recent estimates suggest that gay teenagers are twice as likely to attempt suicide as are their heterosexual agemates and that as many as three out of every five gay teenagers give serious thought to suicide at least once during their adolescent years (Gibson 1989; Rhoads 1994:67–68).
4. The remainder of this chapter focuses on gay men's experiences with linguistic and cultural socialization during adolescence. How closely these experiences parallel the socialization experiences of lesbians remains to be determined.

5. The statements below come from a collection of quotations assembled for Leap (1996) and are reproduced here with permission of the University of Minnesota Press. Statements without a bibliographic citation come from interviews I conducted between 1989 and 1992 with self-identified European American and African American gay men aged 18 to 25 and 40 to 55. My lead-in questions for this discussion established my interest in learning about the respondent's experience with gay adolescence. I intentionally kept the focus of discussion open-ended and unstructured, so that I could hear how the respondent himself would talk about his "discovery" of a "gay self."

6. I recognize the limitations of using life-story narratives as a database for studies of gay socialization. Life stories are not factual documents but a form of fiction—that is, they are constructed, crafted texts; they emerge out of the respondent's subjective (re)framing and (re)claiming of a life experience; and, as retrospective narratives (Kleinmann 1988:50–51), their vision of "the past" is likely to be influenced by the politics of the present. But as I see it, the subjective, reflexive nature of these texts makes them especially valuable to the study of gay life as lived experience. In fact, just as telling these stories allows respondents to experiment with presentations of memory, listening to them allows the audience (in this case, the researcher) to coparticipate in those experiments, and by extension to coparticipate in the events that the respondents' narratives now reclaim. Ellen Lewin (1993, especially pages 9–11) reached similar conclusions when she examined the life-story narratives of lesbian mothers. So did Faye Ginsberg (1989, especially pages 141–145) when she studied abortion-rights controversies in Fargo, North Dakota. A particularly vivid example of researcher coparticipation in retold events is found in Kathleen Wood's (chapter 2, this volume) discussion of a lesbian coming-out story told in American Sign Language.

7. The wording here retains Kristeva's pronominal usage.

8. I want the term *language* in the phrase *language of restraint* to be read literally. Silence, abjection, and so on are not arbitrary components of conversational or narrative structure; their presence conforms to linguistic rules derived from the *grammar* (that is, the knowledge of language) that the gay adolescent brings into the speech event and from the *discourse practices* that actualize this knowledge within specific text-making settings. By referring here to a language of restraint, I position the textual occurrences of silence, abjection, and so on as products of a particular aggregation of linguistic knowledge and linguistic practices, some of which I have described in Leap (1996:24–48). Gay teenagers build familiarity with this aggregation of knowledge and practice, this "language," as a part of their experiences with gay socialization and their everyday encounters with heteronormative living; what happened to Andrew in the example cited here is telling in both regards.

REFERENCES

Barrett, Rusty (1995). Supermodels of the world unite: Political economy and the language of performance among African-American drag queens. In William Leap (ed.), *Beyond the lavender lexicon*. Newark: Gordon & Breach, 207–226.

Brown, Joe, & Kara Swisher (1994). Backstage: The one who fit the bill. *Washington Post* (August 6):C2.

Crowley, Matt (1968). *Boys in the band*. New York: Samuel French.

Davies, Peter (1992). The role of disclosure in coming out among gay men. In Ken Plummer (ed.), *Modern homosexualities*. New York: Routledge, 75–85.

Doty, Alexander (1993). *Making things perfectly queer: Interpreting mass culture*. Minneapolis: University of Minnesota Press.

Gibson, Paul (1989). Gay male and lesbian youth suicide. In M. R. Feinlieb (ed.), *Report of the Secretary's Task Force on Youth Suicide*. Washington, DC: U.S. Department of Health and Human Services, 110–142.

Ginsberg, Faye (1989). *Contested lives: The abortion debate in an American community*. Berkeley: University of California Press.

Goffman, Erving (1963). *Stigma: Notes on the management of spoiled identity*. Englewood Cliffs, NJ: Prentice Hall.

Goodwin, Joseph P. (1989). *More man than you'll ever be: Gay folklore and acculturation in Middle America*. Bloomington: Indiana University Press.

Heath, Shirley Brice (1983). *Ways with words: Language, life, and work in communities and classrooms*. Cambridge: Cambridge University Press.

Herdt, Gilbert, & Andrew Boxer (1992). Introduction: Culture, history and life course of gay men. In Gilbert Herdt (ed.), *Gay culture in America: Essays from the field*. Boston: Beacon Press, 1–27.

——— (1993). *Children of horizons: How gay and lesbian teens are leading a new way out of the closet*. Boston: Beacon Press.

Hobson, Laura Z. (1975). *Consenting adult*. Garden City, NY: Doubleday.

Kleinmann, Arthur (1988). *The illness narratives: Suffering, healing and the human condition*. New York: Basic Books.

Kristeva, Julia (1982). Approaching abjection. In Kristeva, *Powers of horror*. New York: Columbia University Press, 1–31.

Leap, William L. (1993). Gay men's English: Cooperative discourse in a language of risk. *New York Folklore* 19(1–2):45–70.

——— (1994). Learning gay culture in a "desert of nothing": Language as a resource in gender socialization [Special issue]. *High School Journal* 77(1–2):122–131. "The Gay Teenager."

——— (1995). Introduction. In William Leap (ed.), *Beyond the lavender lexicon*. Newark: Gordon & Breach, vii–xxix.

——— (1996). *Word's out: Gay English in America*. Minneapolis: University of Minnesota Press.

Lewin, Ellen (1993). *Lesbian mothers: Accounts of gender in American culture*. Ithaca: Cornell University Press.

Moonwomon, Birch (1995). Lesbian discourse, lesbian knowledge. In William Leap (ed.), *Beyond the lavender lexicon*. Newark: Gordon & Breach, 45–64.

——— (1996). Lesbian conversation as a site for ideological identity construction. Paper presented at the annual meeting of the American Association for Applied Linguistics, Chicago.

Morgan, Ruth, & Kathleen Wood (1995). Lesbians in the living room: Collusion, co-construction and co-narration in conversation. In William Leap (ed.), *Beyond the lavender lexicon*. Newark: Gordon & Breach, 235–248.

Musto, Michael (1993). Gaydar: Using that intuitive sixth sense. *Out* 12:120–124.

Newton, Esther (1993). *Cherry Grove, Fire Island*. Boston: Beacon Press.

Ochs, Elinor (1988). *Culture and language development: Language acquisition and language socialization in a Samoan village*. Cambridge: Cambridge University Press.

Plummer, Ken (1995). *Telling sexual stories: Power, change and social worlds*. London: Routledge.

Reinhardt, Robert C. (1986). *A history of shadows*. Boston: Alyson Press.

Rhoads, Richard (1994). *Coming out in college: The struggle for a queer identity*. Westport, CT: Bergin & Garvey.

Rich, Adrienne (1980). Compulsory heterosexuality and lesbian existence. *Signs* 5:631–660.

Schieffelin, Bambi (1990). *The give and take of everyday life: Language socialization of Kaluli children*. Cambridge: Cambridge University Press.

Sears, Jim (1991). *Growing up gay in the South: Race, gender and journeys of the spirit.* Binghamton, NY: Harrington Park Press.

Spivak, Gayatri Chakravorty (1988). Can the subaltern speak? In Cary Nelson & Lawrence Grossberg (eds.), *Marxism and the interpretation of culture.* Basingstoke, England: Macmillan, 271–313.

Ward, Martha (1971). *Them children: A study in language learning.* New York: Holt, Rinehart & Winston.

Whittle, Stephen (1994). Consuming differences: The collaboration of the gay body with the cultural state. In Stephen Whittle (ed.), *The margins of the city: Gay men's urban lives.* Brookfield, VT: Ashgate, 27–41.

. . . .

Turn-Initial *No*

Collaborative Opposition among Latina Adolescents

Traditional language and gender research has focused on investigating the correlations between gendered speech and pragmatic styles such as cooperativeness and interactional supportiveness. Some important exceptions to this trend (Eckert 1993; Modan 1994) have illustrated a complex relationship between gender and pragmatic style and between apparently cooperative or competitive surface structures and their actual effects in interaction. It is therefore crucial to examine speakers' own interactional categories, as well as speaker identities, in order to better understand apparently cooperative or conflictive language use.

The aim of the present study is to explore the relationship between stance-taking in conversation and the use of discourse markers with regard to the linguistic and social practices of a group of Spanish-speaking adolescent Latina girls living in Northern California. I define *linguistic stance taking* as a pragmatic function whereby the speaker's type and degree of commitment, or stance, on the propositions being expressed is reflected through linguistic means. Stance taking has been studied as an integral part of meaning making, where meaning making is construed as going beyond propositional meaning to include speaker's meaning. It is also central to the production of identity. On the local level, stances display interactional identities as speakers align or disalign with one another by expressing agreement or disagreement with one another's propositions. On the wider social level, stances reflect and construct aspects of social identity as speakers take up positions associated with particular social categories and groups. And *how* they take up these positions—the pragmatic systems they use—may also be closely tied to identity, for such systems are cultural in origin and may therefore index particular regional, class, or national identifications. Insofar as stances mark disaffiliation as well as affiliation, their investigation serves as yet another corrective to overgeneralized claims about women's and girls' interactional cooperativeness.

Stance taking is manifest in all areas of language. Metalinguistic and interpersonal uses of specific lexemes—stance adverbs such as *actually, roughly, exactly*—were investigated by Mava Jo Powell (1992). In phonetics, an example of a study of stance taking is the California Style Collective's (1993) study of a white California teenage girl's manipulation of the extreme variants in her vowel space for strategic purposes. Marjorie Goodwin (chapter 20, this volume) describes how gesture, intonation, and physical action are deployed in concert to embody stance in girls' conflictive evaluation of one another's turns at hopscotch. Studying conflict and its expression among girls and women has become an important avenue in linguistic and anthropological challenges (M. Goodwin 1990; chapter 20, this volume; Thorne 1993) to scholarly accounts of gendered behavior that polarize women as cooperative and men as conflictive and specifically link these discourse patterns to patterns of socialization and childhood interactions (Maltz & Borker 1982).

However, these newer and more careful studies go beyond simply maintaining that girls are in fact capable of engaging in conflict; they further demonstrate that cooperation and conflict are both at work in girls' and women's interactions. Such revisions of earlier work are important means of bringing previously overlooked groups, such as Latina children and adolescents, into focus and understanding their practices and identities. Thus in this volume Marjorie Goodwin debunks the myth of Latina submissiveness and Marjorie Faulstich Orellana (chapter 3) shows how Latina student writers construct brave and even "bad" selves through stories. In both cases the authors show how the poles of conflict and cooperation, "badness" and "goodness," mutually implicate each other in Latina girls' productions of interactional and social identity.

In a similar vein, this study explores how Latina adolescents interactionally exploit the polysemy of an apparent marker of negation. I examine how turn-initial *no* can have properties of strict semantic negation, mark oppositional stance, and contain elements of collaboration, all coexisting within the meaning of a single surface form. Although this form appears unambiguously oppositional and invites an interpretation of conflict, I will show by looking at the local context that in fact turn-initial *no* serves as a complex resource that modulates evaluation and stance in the girls' conversation about social class.

For this study I will focus specifically on the use of *no* where it is a discourse marker—that is, where it does not have strict semantic properties as a negative operator (see example (1)):

(1)

    A: Olga se junta a veces con nosotras, pero más con ellas.
          Olga hangs out with us sometimes, but more with the others.

    L: **No**, ps::, nomás, o sea, tú sabes, **no**?, a veces echa relajo por aquí, tú sabes como son las cosas, **no**?
          *No, ps::, just, o sea, you know, **no**?, sometimes she comes to have a good time over here, you know how things are, **no**?*

In this example, L uses a turn-initial *no* to provide further explanation of A's assertion. What follows A's assertion is a repetition and elaboration rather than a contradiction. Given this fact, why did L begin with what appears to be an overt negation? It is the conversational uses of this kind of discourse-marker *no* that I will consider. I will also touch on the role of other kinds of *no*, like the sentence-medial or sentence-final, question-intonational *no?* also illustrated in L's utterance. In the process I will demonstrate the stances that speakers assume and the identities that they display by virtue of their use of this socially meaningful discourse marker. Such identities, as I will show, have much less to do with gender or ethnicity alone than with the complex interplay of these categories with speakers' interactional, personal, and social histories (see also Sawin, chapter 12; Tannen, chapter 11, both this volume).

Discourse markers and social meaning

Although researchers have not reached a clear consensus as to the definition of *discourse marker*, most of the research in this rapidly expanding area treats discourse markers as signposts of discourse coherence (Fraser 1992; Schiffrin 1987) rather than as carriers of a social message. Also known under such aliases as *discourse connectives* and *conversational markers*, discourse markers have only recently been conceptualized as separate, patterned units of talk. Stephen Levinson suggests that the crucial features of discourse markers are that they "indicate the relationship between an utterance and the prior discourse" and that they "resist truth-conditional treatment" (1983:87). The conceptualization of discourse markers as primarily serving to indicate sequential relations between units of talk is one that has dominated the research since Levinson's original observation.

Deborah Schiffrin defines discourse markers as "sequentially dependent elements which bracket units of talk" (1987:31). These brackets can be initial, medial, or final in position, but they always serve to signal both anaphoric and cataphoric relations between the units of talk. By *sequential dependence* Schiffrin means that these units work with reference to the larger discourse coherence level and thus depend on sequencing of clauses for their meaning. The meaning of discourse markers (henceforth DMs) is consequently independent of the syntactic, semantic, and phonological levels of talk. For instance, devices like *well, now, but, right,* and *you know* do not signal syntactic relations, but they do provide information at the level of discourse content.

Bruce Fraser characterizes DMs by breaking down the various components of sentence meaning (figure 14.1). In this framework, basic pragmatic markers signal the speaker's basic illocutionary intention (for example, declarative and interrogative structures are basic pragmatic markers). Commentary pragmatic markers signal an entire separate message consisting of the speaker's comment on the utterance (such as sequential relations or speaker's attitude). Parallel pragmatic markers also signal a message separate from but concomitant with the basic message (for example, politeness).

In Fraser's framework DMs are lexical adjuncts, units syntactically and phonologically independent of the well-formed sentence, which are a type of commentary pragmatic marker. They function as a comment on how the sentence is to be interpreted by adding contextual coherence—tantamount to Schiffrin's sequential dependence—with respect to the surrounding discourse.

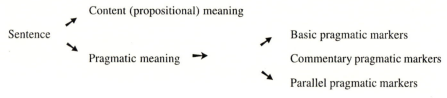

Figure 14.1. Types of discourse markers in sentence meaning. SOURCE: Fraser 1992:21

Fraser does not consider stanceful commentary pragmatic markers such as *frankly* to be DMs, whereas Schiffrin (1987) does, as her analysis of *I mean* shows. Both researchers, however, hold that DMs are incapable of carrying social meaning. The following analysis of *no* and other devices for stance taking and disagreement will attempt to show how interpersonal, stance-taking uses of DMs cannot be excluded from functional typologies, since in addition to bearing and deploying a variety of social meanings, they are also part of a continuum of sometimes multiple meanings for their homophones. Thus an instance of *no* can have overlapping meanings as a negative sentential operator, a postresponse request for response, a turn-initial collaborative marker, or a general signal of speakers' oppositional stance. Moreover, since the stance-taking functions of DMs are inevitably socially meaningful, they also provide insight into the moment-by-moment production of identity at multiple levels. In order to look at patterned uses of *no* in Latina adolescents' discourse, I will first introduce the discourse setting.

Research context: Sor Juana High School

My study emerges out of ethnographic fieldwork conducted for two years in a Northern California urban public high school, which I will call Sor Juana High School (SJHS). SJHS is located in a small urban setting, and like many other schools in the area, the majority of the students (62 percent) are students of color, and over half of that majority is Latino. Located in Santa Clara County, which has the fourth largest Hispanic population in the state of California (Camarillo 1985), SJHS has changed in the past 10 years from a predominantly white school serving one of the wealthiest communities in the Bay Area to a predominantly "minority" school that draws many of its students from nearby ethnic neighborhoods.

One of my main data-collection methods is participant observation. This involves participating in adolescent girls' single-sex and mixed-sex social networks and observing the organization of social structure and language use in their groups. In collaboration with the girls themselves, I have been mapping out their social networks and attempting to observe as many different networks as possible. In the following section, I summarize those networks at Sor Juana High School that are relevant to this chapter. I also provide a brief explanation of the high school's social situation, as understood both by the girls and by me.

The group of girls who are participants in the interaction I will analyze are representative of the diversity in the "minority" populations of many schools. These girls, who would be classified under one census category—the monolithic "Hispanic" category—come from many different countries, social-class backgrounds, and prior educational experiences. In order to better understand social organization in general it is necessary to know more about the participants than simply their age, country of origin, and gender. Although the teens in this interaction can all be classified as recent Latina immigrants, their backgrounds are crucially important in the unfolding of their interaction, in motivating their choices on everything from what kind of syntax to use to what floor-taking strategies are available and licensed. For the researcher of conversational and social organization, ethnographic background is essential in understanding how features of language that go beyond the purely propositional might enter into the construction of stance and social meaning. And for the scholar of language and gender, an ethnographic approach is vital in producing analyses of women's and girls' talk that are grounded in the specific practices of local communities (Eckert & McConnell-Ginet 1992) and thus reflective of the speakers', rather than the analyst's, view of the role of gender and other identities in daily life.

The interaction

Background

The interaction I analyze here consists of an unstructured conversation among five teenage high school girls who are best friends and me, a researcher in my mid-20s; I had known the girls for about a full school year at the time of the interview. In order to illuminate the social dynamics at play in the conversation, I will give a short description of each of the participants.

Three of the girls come from the central region of Mexico and are from middle-class backgrounds that have given them access to the prestigious Greater Mexico City dialect. Of these girls, one (Laura) is from Mexico City proper, and the other two (Andrea and Marisol, who are sisters) are from Puebla, an outlying city. Although they all use the phonology and syntax of the prestige dialect, they have very different attitudes toward class issues among Latinas/os in their high school. Laura and Marisol are central members of their group, which I call the Mexican Urban Middle Class (abbreviated MUMC throughout this chapter). Andrea, on the other hand, has multiple group memberships. She is part of MUMC but also part of the Mexican Rural Class (MRC) by virtue of her friendship networks and her developing views about social class (she repeatedly champions the working class over the middle class, as can be seen in this interview). In many ways she travels between groups: In the year after the interview her friendship networks came to be based more in the MRC than in the MUMC group. She has little tolerance for *fresas*, the upper-class end of the MUMC—the spoiled rich kids, as it were—who are the antithesis of the MRC. In this interaction, a large part of the argument centers around the status of *fresas* vis-à-vis *los de barrio* 'people from the barrio'.

Also in the conversation is Graciela, a girl who was born in Los Angeles but spent her formative childhood years in rural Michoacán (western Mexico), only to return to the United States at the age of 13, three years prior to the taping of this conversation. She is a dominant Spanish speaker and in the past adopted the identity of a *Sureña*, a Mexican-identified gang girl. At the time of the interview she had been trying to move out of the gang for a few months and had traveled from her former networks to a completely different part of the spectrum of the Spanish-speaking social world in the school: the MUMC. Graciela's participation in the interaction is very important, because she is peripheral in the group. There are two primary reasons for her peripherality: (1) She is an atypical member who does not share the urban-teen tastes and orientation of the others; and (2) she is a speaker of the Michoacán dialect of Spanish rather than a "standard" urban dialect. This latter feature distinguishes her in this conversation primarily by virtue of her pragmatics and underscores her social peripherality.

The fifth participant is Yadira, an adolescent from Perú who, despite her different nationality and background, is very similar to the MUMC girls. She lived in Lima, the capital of Perú, before coming to the United States, and in this respect shares in the broader Latin American urban teen style. Because in many instances Latin American urban dialects are closer to each other cross-nationally than to rural dialects within their own countries (Canfield 1981), Yadira's conversational style and pragmatics are actually more similar to the MUMC core patterns than are Graciela's, even though Graciela is from Mexico.

I am the last participant in the conversation. I am in some ways similar in background to the core MUMC girls, being an urban young person from Mexico City, but I am 10 years older and in many respects an adult figure. Although at the time I would socialize and interact with these girls on a daily basis, they also saw me as a kind of older sibling and would, in times of conflict, try to get me to take sides or settle disputes. It is in this role that I enter into the interaction toward the end of the transcript.

Analysis

For the purposes of economy of space and clarity of explanation, I will not reproduce the entire transcript of the conversation here but will instead ask the reader to review and refer to appendix 1 for transcription conventions and other notation and to appendix 2 for the complete transcript. In the analysis I will quote relevant parts of the transcript as necessary.

The segment of conversation begins with Graciela speaking simultaneously with Andrea in lines 1 and 2 (see example (2)). Andrea, the louder speaker, wins out, and Graciela gives up her attempt to get a turn. Although this interactional sequence may look like an uninteresting and common conversational occurrence, it begins a pattern for Graciela's participation in the interaction: Her bids for the floor are repeatedly ignored (see lines 4, 23, 25, 27, to be discussed later). Her unwillingness to fight for the floor in a conversation where everyone else does so through loudness and overlap coincides with her peripherality as a speaker of rural, nonstandard Spanish in a community of practice dominated by standard-Spanish, urban-teen pragmatics.

In line 2, Andrea puts forth her opinion about the relationship between people from the barrio and *fresas*: 'the atmosphere is better with people from the barrio'. She speaks loudly but with a modulated epistemic stance—the phrase *yo creo que* serves as a stance marker and signals a less-than-total degree of speaker commitment to the assertion

(Powell 1992; Traugott 1995). But why would Andrea modulate her epistemic stance if she feels so strongly about the issue? One answer is that several people who consider themselves *fresas* are among her interlocutors. Laura does, for instance, and she latches onto Andrea's utterance and disagrees with it (line 3):

(2)

   1 Graciela: [Yo- e:hh- ahh:]

   2 Andrea: [YO CREO QUE] HACEN MÁS AMBIENTE: UNOS DE BARRIO
                  que todos unos pinches fresas, me caen bien mal.=
                  I THINK THAT THE ATMOSPHERE IS BETTER WITH PEOPLE
                  FROM THE BARRIO than with a (expletive) bunch of fresas, they get
                  on my nerves.=

   3 Laura: =Bueno, > depende no? porque si estás e<n:: (.) >depende como te
              sientas tu a gusto<, no, porque si te sientes a gusto en la ↑onda de: (.)
              de con los de barrio, pus - se te [va-]=
              =Well, it depends no?, because if you're in (.) it depends where you
              feel comfortable no?, because if you feel comfortable with the, the
              barrio thing, then [you're-]

 ☞ L ✗ A

   4 Graciela: [Pero-]
                 [But-]

   5 Laura: =s'te va a hacer lo máximo.
              =then you'll think it's the best.

In disagreeing with Andrea, Laura points out tactfully and indirectly the relativity of her statement: *If* you are comfortable with people from the barrio *then* you will think it's great. There is a very strong inference here that if you are not comfortable with people from the barrio, if you are a lone *fresa* among those from the barrio, then you won't think it's great.

Laura's indirectness is key: She sets up a whole possible world of a solitary *fresa* who is uncomfortable in the barrio by actually saying the opposite and allowing her scenario to be inferred. This type of indirectness is accompanied by hedging—the use of contrastive DMs such as *bueno* and *depende*. Also present is *no?* in the capacity of a postresponse pursuit of response (as in Jefferson's [1980] analysis of the similar German particle *ne?*, also termed a request for feedback in Oliveira and Tavares's [1992] analysis of Brazilian Portuguese *né*). Interestingly enough, this postresponse pursuit of response can actually have no response because the speaker accelerates her rate of speech and leaves no room for the interlocutor to come in. What we might ordinarily otherwise call a tag question has undergone routinization and lexicalization and can now function as a DM, needing no response, with hardly a rising intonation left in it.

Following Laura's response, Marisol (Andrea's sister), aligns herself with Laura by making fun of people from the barrio. She does this by uttering the phrase 'I'm from the barrio' with a set of linguistic devices, intended to be comical, that subvert the meaning of the utterance: She uses creaky voice, a drastically lower pitch, and an exaggerated trilling gesture on the word *barrio* to take a stance in line 6 of example (3):

(3)
```
    6 Marisol:   ↓~Yo soy del ba:RRio:~=
                 ↓~I'm from the baRRio:~=

    ☞M → L
    7 Laura:                          =Aha:,=
                                      =Aha:,=

    ☞L ✓ M, L → M
```

In line 7 Laura utters a confirmation of Marisol's subtextual message. She has understood her and mutually aligns with her. This gesture from Marisol is a slight to her sister Andrea. Andrea does not respond to it right away; she must deal with Laura's challenge to her proposition, which is sequentially first in order. But we will see that she returns to her sister several turns later by denying her space on the conversational floor.

Let us now examine Andrea's response to Laura in line 8 (example 4):

(4)
```
    8 Andrea:                         =NO, ↓no, ↓no, ↑yo no digo que si están
    revueltos los dos, yo digo que- [(0.3) que (.) ve-]
                                      =NO, no, no, I'm not talking about when
    they're both together, I'm saying that- [(0.3) that (.) see-]
    ☞A ✗ L
```

Andrea begins with a series of *nos* that are clearly of the sentential negative-operator meaning. She returns to the possible world set up by Laura in line 3 and begins to say that this is not the scenario that she meant. 'I'm not talking about when they're both together' is the best evidence that we could have to confirm that Laura's inference-derived possible world was taken up: It was explicitly rejected. Andrea is about to give her own version of the scenario (with *fresas* considered separately from people from the barrio and independently evaluated) when Laura overlaps her. Laura forcefully takes the turn by means of a loud turn-initial *no* and displays her understanding by attempting to finish Andrea's sentence with an insertion of the noun phrase *cada quien* (line 9) that latches on to the *que* uttered by Andrea (line 8):

(5)
```
    9 Laura: [NO, pero, no, pus,] o sea, tu sabes, no, cada quien,=
             [NO, but, no, pus,] o sea, you know, no, each one,=
    ☞L ✗ A
```

Remarkably, Laura's syntactically and semantically noncontentious contribution to Andrea's sentence is preceded by a string of seven DMs, three of which are tokens of *no* and two of which are also oppositional in meaning (*pero* and *pus*). The others are *o sea*, which has been analyzed by Scott Schwenter (1996) as a marker of

politeness, and *tu sabes*, in this case analogous to *you know*, a DM analyzed by
Schiffrin (1987) as establishing a participation framework or ratifying listenership.
It is no accident that Laura's contentful contribution is delayed until it is free of overlap; the string of DMs here serve the function of holding her turn. After uttering the
collaborative noun phrase, Laura herself is reinterrupted by Andrea (example (6)):

(6)

    10   Andrea: =no, claro, propia onda=
                                                      =no, of course, own thing=

Andrea here displays her understanding of Laura's meaning, quickly latching after
the first noun phrase (*cada quien*) to finish the sentence that she already knows Laura
is helping her to construct: *Cada quien tiene su propia onda*. She takes the turn with
no and follows it immediately with the agreement DM *claro*. A simplified version of
Andrea and Laura's twice coconstructed sentence is as follows:

        . . . yo digo que   cada quien   (tiene su)   propia onda.
        Andrea   Laura   ellided   Andrea

    Even as we understand that the speakers agree on the emergent syntax and seman-
tics of this sentence under construction (cf. C. Goodwin 1979), it is striking that this
agreement takes place amid the lush flora of oppositional DMs. Their agreement and
coconstruction does not resemble the harmonious collaborations found in some of the
prior coconstruction literature (cf. C. Goodwin 1979, 1995). What functions, then, are
these oppositional DMs serving? Here I advance the proposal that, in this case, although
there is syntactic and semantic collaboration in the construction of the sentence, at a
pragmatic level there is conflict. Neither Laura nor Andrea allows the other to finish a
turn, and they repeatedly interrupt each other to contentiously display their understanding. In this case one can even construe coconstruction as hostile and the coconstructed
sentence as frustrating: None of the speakers can "get a word in edgewise."
    Both lines 9 and 10 (examples (5) and (6)), in which the instances of cocon-
struction occur, begin with a turn-initial phonologically independent *no*, which has
no trace of its strict semantic meaning as a negative sentential operator. What follows these turn-initial *no*s remains positive in polarity, and as seen in line 10 (example (6)), a marker of agreement can even occur: *claro*, 'of course'. I will call this
use of *no*, which bids for the floor and inserts an explanation, a *turn-initial collaborative expansion*. This phenomenon has also been documented for Italian by Carmen
Licari and Stefania Stame (1992), and there is strongly suggestive evidence for it in
Marjorie Goodwin (chapter 20, this volume) as well. A similar meaning is operative
in the use of the English construction *yeah but*, as in example (7), in which Nancy is
talking to Hyla about what her doctor said in reference to acne:

(7)

    Nancy: He says 't's all inside you it's 'n emotional thing'n,
                  *hhh e[:n,]
    Hyla: [Yeah] buh whatchu ea:t if you eat greasy foo:d=

Here Hyla is agreeing with Nancy and adding her own contributory explanation (greasy food) to Nancy's doctor's explanation of acne (that it is psychosomatic). It is possible that European American English speakers' preferences for agreement are satisfied with *yeah but* whereas other speakers may be following different rules and may perform the same function—turn-initial collaborative expansion—with a negative instead of a positive marker. I have also made some casual observations of this phenomenon among Jewish American speakers of English. In example (8) S is a Jewish American woman:

(8)

> A: Why don't you do it like this, it's better that way.
> S: No, yeah, you're right.

Immediately following the utterance I inquired as to its status with S, who informed me that it was common in her repertoire and *not* a repair. This may be related to collaborative disagreement among Jewish Americans (cf. Modan 1994; Schiffrin 1984). Such examples remind us that early claims about women's collaborative styles do not reflect the practices of all women.

One interesting consequence of the finding that turn-initial collaborative expansions have surface disagreement shapes in Spanish is that it requires an elaboration of one of the most important concepts in conversation analysis: the *agreement preference*, that is, that agreement is preferred and negation is dispreferred. Emanuel Schegloff, Gail Jefferson, and Harvey Sacks (1977) postulate that disagreement between parties in a conversation is strongly dispreferred. Conversation-analytic research has borne this prediction out for American and British speakers (Davidson 1984; Pomerantz 1984; Yaeger-Dror 1986, among many others) and has been shown to be an important dimension in patterning the behavior and distribution of such phenomena as request, invitation, repair, and assessment sequences.

I suggest that agreement preferences may be gradient rather than categorical and that different speech communities, speakers, or individual situations may have a weaker or a stronger form of this preference rule. A weak form of the rule would allow speakers to display agreement through what may look on the surface like an opposition marker, such as the turn-initial *no*, or to express conflict and disagreement through apparently collaborative strategies such as coconstructions. Based on these data, it is also possible that speakers with a weaker form of the preference rule would be more tolerant of overlap. The copatterning of these behaviors in additional communities would provide a confirmation of this hypothesis.

Resuming the analysis of the Latina girls' interaction, we find that after line 10 and with the end of the coconstructed segment, both Marisol and Laura try to take the floor. By this time, there has been so much careful posturing, hesitation, taking of negative stances, and use of DMs that very little is being said, and speakers are interrupting each other before any of them get to say anything. In line 13, Andrea erupts in a scream (example (9)):

(9)

> 11   Marisol: =Yo digo que[::
>   =*I say that[::*

12   Laura: =[O sea, [no creo que-]
             =[O sea, [I don't think that-]

13   Andrea: [GRITA]
              [SCREAM]

This scream is directed at no one in particular and releases enough tension that all participants laugh heartily. At this point (example (10), line 15), after pitch, volume, and tempo are reset to normal—a sort of cleaning of the conversational slate—Andrea returns to settle accounts with her sister, who slighted her in line 3 (example (2)). This is interesting in that it shows how speakers can keep track, even after several sentences, of unfinished conversational business. Andrea retroactively turns down her sister's prior bid for a turn (in line 11 of example (9)), and Marisol reacts with a denial and reassertion of her previous position (line 17 of example (10)). Note that in both of these instances *no* is turn-initial and phonologically separate, as in the collaborative uses in examples (5) and (6). In the first instance (line 15), *no* is clearly negative in its semantics: It is a denial of the previous speaker's assertion (that is, Andrea denies that Marisol has something to say) and also functions as a negative operator that has scope over the whole sentence, with a NEG marker on the verb as well:

(10)
   15   Andrea: [No:], ella no dice nada.= ((acerca de Marisol))
                [No:], she doesn't say anything.= ((about Marisol))

   ☞ A ⚡ M

   . . .

   17   Marisol: =[No, sí digo algo, no?=
                 =[No:, I do say something, no?=

   ☞ M ✗ A

In line 17, however, despite its similarity in morphological, phonological, and syntactic shape with line 15, the intonationally separate *no* is not a negative sentential operator, since it is immediately followed by a positive-polarity sentence over which it does not have scope (for an intonational-theoretic discussion of the status of DMs, see Hirschberg & Litman 1987). It is impossible in this case to assign a single meaning to *no*. From the example it is clear that it is both a negation of the previous speaker's assertion and a bid for the floor followed by the speaker's own assertion. Thus from the context, both interpretations are not only possible but necessary. Table 14.1 summarizes some of the possible uses for *no* as a DM as they emerge in the data. These show that the intonationally bound uses of *no* are those in which strict syntactic and semantic relations of scope are best preserved and that those that are intonationally free are the discourse-marking uses which do not necessarily preserve strict semantic relations. Thus we explain the absence of intonationally bound *no* at the end of a turn, because by virtue of its position it cannot have scope over the clause. One apparent exception to the lack of preservation of syntactic/semantic relations in the intonationally free DMs is that of the turn-initial, free *no*, which appears to pre-

Table 14.1. Positions and functions of *no*

No *position*	No *function*	
	Intonationally free	*Intonationally bound*
Turn-initial	Negation of prior assertion (Semantic NEG operator) Bid for the floor Turn-initial collaborative expansion	Semantic NEG operator
Medial	Postresponse pursuit of response/ Request for feedback	Semantic NEG operator
Final	Postresponse pursuit of response/ Request for feedback	

serve some of the semantics of the operator. The reason for this preservation is that, as a consequence of its function as an opposition to the previous speaker's statement, the intonationally free *no* will reverse the polarity of the matrix clause when it is a repetition or paraphrase of the previous speaker's statement.

For example, in the following triad of oppositions (repeated as example (11)) the first turn-initial *no* shifts the polarity from positive (line 11) to negative (line 13), and the second shifts it again from negative (line 13) to positive (line 15). The underlying proposition is "Marisol says something." Marisol advances the proposition as part of her turn, but her sister negates it and she reasserts it again:

(11)

    11   Marisol: =Yo digo que[::
                         =*I say that[::*

    . . .

    15   Andrea: [No:], ella no dice nada.= ((acerca de Marisol))
                         [No:], she doesn't say anything.= ((about Marisol))

  ☞ A ⸲< M

    . . .

    17   Marisol: =[No, sí digo algo, no?=
                         =[No:, I do say something, no?=

  ☞ M ✗ A

It is apparent that by line 19 the tension continues to escalate as Marisol threatens to terminate her participation in the conversation and later embodies a display of her conflict stance by slamming her papers three times on the desk (line 21). Laura in the meantime uses an oppositional DM (*pus*) in an attempt to redirect the conversation (example (12)):

(12)

    19   Marisol: =Para eso no hablar.=
                        =*In that case I won't talk.*

  ☞ M ⊰ A
    20   Laura: =Ay, pus.
                        =*Oh, come on.*

    21   Marisol: No, vaya, ((papeles contra el escritorio 3×))=
                        No, well, ((slaps paper on table 3×))=

As the two sisters argue between lines 15 and 21, they start almost all their utterances, whether positive or negative, with *no*. It is possible to conceptualize this as an example of format-tying, in which a speaker incorporates a feature (or more) of the previous speaker's discourse into her or his own speech to show simultaneous understanding and similar orientation (cf. M. Goodwin 1990). Here the sisters orient to each other's disagreement; through their use of turn-initial *no*, they display for each other their oppositional stance.

    At this point Graciela, the ex-*Sureña*, makes a bid for the floor. She does so in line 23 (example (13)) not by using a turn-initial *no* as the rest of the speakers did but by making an overt request for the floor in the form of a verb of locution. This type of bid is very different from what the Central Mexican dialect speakers are used to:

(13)

    23   Graciela: =Di:go[ohh::]
                        =*I say::*

So involved are the other speakers in the arguments and their mutual posturing that they do not listen to, or do not recognize, or in any case ignore, Graciela's bid for the floor, partly because its form is not transparent to them as such. She makes two more attempts (Example (14)):

(14)

    25   Graciela: **DII::G[OHH::=**
                        I S[AY:::

    26   All: [Hhhhn[hhh::]

    27   Graciela: =[Digo,] ((quedito))
                        =*[I say,] ((softly))*

After these bids are ignored and even Yadira (who has been silent until this time) manages to get a turn (line 28 of example (15)) through the characteristically loud

turn-beginning that we saw before, Graciela finally, exasperatedly, takes the floor
and explicitly complains to her friends for not letting her talk. It is significant that
she has had to resort to such an overt form, a metalinguistic complaint (with marked
pitch, intensity, and intonation) regarding the structuring of turns and the rules of
talk. The overtness of this criticism, along with the markedness of her use of an expletive, produces what is for this group a very long silence, during which all participants look at one another in surprise at her utterance:

(15)
    28 Yadira: SEGÚN LAS NOVELAS . . según mis novelas,=
                     ACCORDING TO THE SOAP OPERAS . . , according to my soap operas,=

    29 Graciela: =No dejan HA↑BLA:R, ↓fregado. ((quejándose))
                     =You're not letting me TALK, (expletive). ((plaintively—whining))

    ☞ G ✄ L,A,M,Y,N
    (1.0)

After this silence, Laura negotiates with Graciela over the status of her utterance
(example (16)). She does not understand why Graciela is upset, and she utters a lengthened and high-pitched request for clarification:

(16)
    30   Laura: O:::YY:: QUE:::::?

Graciela chooses not to take this up but instead suddenly turns to me, and in example
(17) asks me to leave the room with her, ostensibly to make photocopies. I do not
have a photocopy card, however, and I turn down her request:

(17)
    31 Graciela: Ve:n a copia:r. ((a Norma))
                     Come make some copies. ((to Norma))

    32 Norma: No puedo.
                     I can't.

Why does Graciela ask me to go away with her immediately following her aggravated complaint to her friends? It may be because throughout this conversation I have
not taken sides or because she is trying to get me to align with her and to display this
by leaving with her. On the other hand, she may also be trying to avoid disagreement. Based on her avoidance of overt disagreement shapes to take a turn or to provide expansions, I postulate that Graciela's tolerance for disagreement is much lower
than that of the other participants and that, having been forced to make a strong overt
disagreement, she is now trying to exit this sequence, to open up a closing (Schegloff
& Sacks 1973), in order to save face in front of her interlocutors.

    Yadira's better understanding of the MUMC conversational rules is evident when
she gives Graciela some very explicit metalinguistic advice (example (18)) designed

to address the problem raised by Graciela, as well as to explain to her why she was not being let into the conversation before:

(18)

    33   Yadira: Métete, Graciela:
                     Interrupt, Graciela:

    ☞ Y → G

It is interesting to note that this explanation does not come from a core member of the MUMC. Yadira, as a relative outsider from a different country's urban teen culture, is the one to articulate the shape of the preferred turns for the other relative outsider. In the next turn, syllable by syllable, all participants gradually join in a chanting chorus of Graciela's name, erupting in laughter and hugs in line 35 (example (19)):

(19)

    34   All except Graciela, joining in gradually: **GRA:-CI:-E:-LA::::**
    ☞ A,M,L,Y,N → G
    35   All including Graciela: HhhhhHhhhh:: ((hugging))

After they have all laughed and hugged and done their best to repair the conflict caused by Graciela's complaint, they move on to another conversational topic altogether.

What emerges from an overview of this interaction is how individual turn-taking behaviors directly correlate with central and peripheral social status in the group. Graciela appears to have a different system for turn-taking, with more highly preferred overt agreement and dispreferred overlaps. In fact, she seems to be observing the norms held as prototypical in Sacks, Schegloff, and Jefferson (1974). Unfortunately, it is also the case that in this group those norms are not the standard, and following them serves to reinforce her marginality: She has a very difficult time entering a conversation in progress.

This analysis reveals the multiple identities that girls bring to interaction. Their linguistic practices cannot be adequately explained merely by invoking global categories such as 'female' or 'Latina'. Instead, we must appeal to the variety of resources of which speakers avail themselves: friendship patterns, sibling relationships, regional and social-class backgrounds, and personal beliefs and opinions. It is only by recognizing the diversity of such resources—and of the speakers who use them—that we can come to understand their role in the formation of identity.

Conclusion

In this chapter I have attempted to show how conflict is managed in the conversation of a group of Spanish-speaking Latina adolescents. I have looked at opposition, collaboration, and stance enacted through the use of DMs, especially the different uses of *no,* as well as through other devices like overt complaints, denials of requests for the floor, and even paralinguistic banging on the table. This clustering of resources to show speakers' evolving orientations to and evaluations of their interlocutors and their actions are all components of what I call *stance*. I have given examples of oppositional coconstruction and also collaborative denials and have tried to expand conversation-analytic notions of preference by showing that what is highly dispreferred in one setting can be the norm in another.

A substantial body of research on adolescent girls' interactions reveals that neither a cooperative nor a conflictive paradigm is sufficient to capture the details of talk in context (cf. also Coates, chapter 6, this volume). Penelope Eckert (1993) has found a model of "cooperative competition" useful in her analysis of white teenage girls' conversations. Similarly, the present study points to the possibility of both collaborative opposition and what might be termed *conflictive corroboration* in the use of turn-initial *no* by Latina adolescents. The carefully calibrated alignments that speakers produce by means of this DM interact with other, more enduring facets of identity. Together they help to complete a picture of Latina adolescent girls' interactional practices in all their social complexity.

APPENDIX 1

Transcription conventions

In my transcript I follow standard conversation-analytic transcription procedures, pioneered by Gail Jefferson and widely adopted in the field:

Bold, *italics*, <u>underline</u>	Text in bold, italics, or underlining receives special emphasis.
:::	Colons indicate lengthening of segments.
(1.2)	Numbers in parentheses mark gaps—silences in seconds and tenths of seconds.
> <	The combination of "less than" and "more than" symbols indicates that the talk between them is compressed or rushed.
↑ ↓	Upward and downward arrows mark sharp intonation rises and falls or resettings of pitch register.
~talk~	Talk between tildes is spoken with creaky voice, or laryngealization.

The following punctuation symbols are used to mark intonation rather than as grammatical symbols:

.	A period indicates a falling contour.
?	A question mark indicates a rising contour.
,	A comma indicates a fall-rise.
-	A dash indicates a cutoff of the current sound.
[ ]	A left bracket marks the precise point at which an overlap begins. When the end of the overlap is itself overlapped, a right bracket defines the ends of the overlapped segments.

=	An equal sign indicates "latching," that is, when there is no interval between units of talk by the same or different speakers.
hh	Hearable aspiration counted in pulses; the more aspiration, the more *h*s. Also used for laughter. When the laughter has a vocalic quality, it is indicated by an approximate vowel. When nasal, it is indicated by an *n* as in *hnh*.
*hh	If the aspiration is inhalation, it bears a dot or asterisk before it.
(talk)	Transcriber doubt.
((comment))	Transcriber comment.

Other notation

As an aid in understanding the interaction, I have made a simple and preliminary attempt to mark some of the stance taking of the various speakers. After the relevant utterance, I use a pointer (☞) and the speaker's initial, along with the following symbols for four basic relationships:

✓ agrees with

→ aligns with

✗ disagrees with

✀ dissociates from

So for example:

☞ A ✓ Y = Andrea agrees with Yadira

APPENDIX 2

The transcript

1   Graciela: [Yo- e:hh- ahh:]
2   Andrea: [YO CREO QUE] HACEN MÁS AMBIENTE: UNOS DE BARRIO
que todos unos pinches fresas, me caen bien mal.=
*I THINK THAT THE ATMOSPHERE IS BETTER WITH PEOPLE
FROM THE BARRIO than with a (expletive) bunch of fresas, they get
on my nerves.=*
3   Laura: =Bueno, > de↑pende no? porque si estás e<n:: (.) >depende como te
sientas tu a gusto<, no, porque si te sientes a gusto en la ↑onda de: (.)
de con los de barrio, pus - se te [va-]=
*=Well, it depends no?, because if you're in (.) it depends where you
feel comfortable no?, because if you feel comfortable with the, the
barrio thing, then [you're-]*

☞ L ✗ A

4   Graciela: [Pero-]
[But-]

5   Laura: =s'te va a hacer lo máximo.
                  =*then you'll think it's the best.*

6   Marisol: ↓~Yo soy del ba:RRio:~ =
                  ↓~*I'm from the baRRio:~*=

☞ M → L
7   Laura: =Aha:,=
                                              =*Aha:,*=

☞ L ✓ M, L → M
8   Andrea: =<u>NO</u>, ↓no, ↓no, ↑yo no digo que si
                  están revueltos los dos, yo digo que- [(0.3) que (.) ve-]
                                              =*NO, no, no, I'm not talking about*
                  when they're both together, I'm saying that- [(0.3) that (.) see-]

☞ A ✗ L
9   Laura: [NO, pero, no, pus,] o sea, tu sabes, no, cada quien,=
                  [NO, but, no, pus,] o sea, you know, no, each one, =

☞ L ✗ A
10 Andrea: =no, claro, propia onda=
                                                           =*no, of course, own thing*

11 Marisol: = Yo digo que[::
                  = *I say that[::*

12 Laura: = [O sea, [no creo que-]
                  = *[O sea, [I don't think that-]*

13 Andrea: **[GRITA]**
                  [*SCREAM*]

14 Graciela, Andrea, Laura: Hhnhh Hhnhh .Hhnhh [Hhh Mmm:]

15 Andrea: [No:], ella no dice nada.= ((acerca de Marisol))
                  [No:], she doesn't say anything.= ((about Marisol))

☞ A ✄ M
16 Graciela: =[Hhhnh::

17 Marisol: =[No, sí digo algo, no?=
                  =*[No:, I do say something, no?*=

☞ M ✗ A
18 Andrea: =>Aha, aha, aha.<=

19 Marisol: =Para eso no hablar.=
                  =*In that case I won't talk.*

☞ M ✄ A
20 Laura: =Ay, pus.
                  =*Oh, come on.*

21 Marisol: No, vaya, ((papeles contra el escritorio 3×))=
                  No, well, ((slaps paper on table 3×))=

22 Laura: =Oye,=
                  =*Hey,*=

23 Graciela: =**Di:go[ohh::]**
                  = *I say::*

24 Laura: [No, de una vez,]
                  [No, let's have it right now,]

25 Graciela: **DII::G[OHH::=**
                I S[AY:::
26 All: [Hhhhn[hhh::]
27 Graciela: =[Digo,] ((quedito))
                = *[I say,] ((softly))*
28 Yadira: SEGÚN LAS NOVELAS . . según mis novelas,=
                ACCORDING TO THE SOAP OPERAS.., according to my soap operas,=
29 Graciela: =No dejan HA↑BLA:R, ↓fregado. ((quejándose))
                =You're not letting me TALK, (expletive). ((plaintively—whining))
☞ G ✂ L,A,M,Y,N
(1.0)
30 Laura: O:::YY:: QUE:::::?
31 Graciela: Ve:n a copia:r. ((a Norma))
                Come make some copies. ((to Norma))
32 Norma: No puedo.
                I can't.
33 Yadira: Métete, Graciela:
                Interrupt, Graciela:
☞ Y → G
34 All except Graciela, joining in gradually: **GRA:-CI:-E:-LA::::**
☞ A,M,L,Y,N → G
35 All including Graciela: HhhhhHhhhh:: ((hugging))

REFERENCES

California Style Collective (1993). Variation and personal/group style. Paper presented at the annual New Ways of Analyzing Variation Conference, Ottawa.

Camarillo, Albert (1985). *Chicanos in California: A history of Mexican Americans in California.* San Francisco: Boyd & Fraser.

Canfield, D. L. (1981). *Spanish pronunciation in the Americas.* Chicago: University of Chicago Press.

Davidson, Judy (1984). Subsequent versions of invitations, offers, requests, and proposals dealing with potential or actual rejection. In J. Maxwell Atkinson & John Heritage (eds.), *Structures of social action: Studies in conversation analysis.* Cambridge: Cambridge University Press, 102–128.

Eckert, Penelope (1993). Cooperative competition in adolescent "girl talk." In Deborah Tannen (ed.), *Gender and conversational interaction.* New York: Oxford University Press, 32–61.

Eckert, Penelope, & Sally McConnell-Ginet (1992). Communities of practice: Where language, gender, and power all live. In Kira Hall, Mary Bucholtz, & Birch Moonwomon (eds.), *Locating power: Proceedings of the Second Berkeley Women and Language Conference.* Berkeley, CA: Berkeley Women and Language Group, 89–99.

Fraser, Bruce (1992). Types of English discourse markers. *Acta Linguistica Hungarica* 38(1–4):19–33.

Goodwin, Charles (1979). The interactive construction of a sentence in natural conversation. In George Psathas (ed.), *Everyday language: Studies in ethnomethodology.* New York: Irvington, 97–121.

——— (1995). Co-construction in conversations with an aphasic man. Paper presented at the

Conversation Symposium, Linguistic Society of America Summer Institute, Albuquerque, New Mexico.

Goodwin, Marjorie Harness (1990). *He-said-she-said: Talk as social organization among black children.* Bloomington: Indiana University Press.

Hirschberg, Julia, & Diane Litman (1987). Now let's talk about "now": Identifying cue phrases intonationally. Paper presented at the annual meeting of the Association for Computational Linguistics, Stanford, California.

Jefferson, Gail (1980). The abominable "ne?": A working paper exploration of the post-response pursuit of response. (Occasional Paper No. 6). University of Manchester, Department of Sociology.

Levinson, Stephen (1983). *Pragmatics.* Cambridge: Cambridge University Press.

Licari, Carmen, & Stefania Stame (1992). The Italian morphemes *no* and *niente* as conversational markers. *Acta Linguistica Hungarica* 38(1–4):163–173.

Maltz, Daniel N., & Ruth A. Borker (1982). A cultural approach to male-female miscommunication. In John J. Gumperz (ed.), *Language and social identity.* Cambridge: Cambridge University Press, 196–216.

Modan, Gabriella (1994). Pulling apart is coming together: The use and meaning of opposition in the discourse of Jewish American women. In Mary Bucholtz, A. C. Liang, Laurel Sutton, & Caitlin Hines (eds.), *Cultural performances: Proceedings of the Third Berkeley Women and Language Conference.* Berkeley, CA: Berkeley Women and Language Group, 501–508.

Oliveira e Silva, Giselle M. de, & A. Tavares de Macedo (1992). Discourse markers in the spoken Portuguese of Rio de Janeiro. *Language Variation and Change* 4:235–249.

Pomerantz, Anita (1984). Agreeing and disagreeing with assessments: Some features of preferred/dispreferred turn shapes. In J. Maxwell Atkinson & John Heritage (eds.), *Structures of social action: Studies in conversation analysis.* Cambridge: Cambridge University Press, 57–101.

Powell, Mava Jo (1992). The systematic development of correlated interpersonal and metalinguistic meanings of stance adverbs. *Cognitive Linguistics* 3(1):75–100.

Sacks, Harvey, Emanuel Schegloff, & Gail Jefferson (1974). A simplest systematics for the organization of turn-taking for conversation. *Language* 50:696–735.

Schegloff, Emanuel, Gail Jefferson, & Harvey Sacks (1977). The preference for self-correction in the organization of repair in conversation. *Language* 53:361–382.

Schegloff, Emanuel, & Harvey Sacks (1973). Opening up closings. *Semiotica* 8:289–327.

Schiffrin, Deborah (1984). Jewish argument as sociability. *Language in Society* 13:311–335.

——— (1987). *Discourse markers.* Cambridge: Cambridge University Press.

Schwenter, Scott (1996). Some reflections on *O SEA*: A discourse marker in Spanish. *Journal of Pragmatics* 25(6):855–874.

Thorne, Barrie (1993). *Gender play: Girls and boys in school.* New Brunswick, NJ: Rutgers University Press.

Traugott, Elizabeth (1995). The development of discourse markers in English. Paper presented at the Discourse Markers Workshop, Stanford University.

Yaeger-Dror, Malcah (1986). Intonational prominence on negatives in English. *Language and Speech* 28(3):197–230.

15   A. C. LIANG

. . . .

Conversationally Implicating
Lesbian and Gay Identity

An anecdote

While S and her parents were sitting around the kitchen table, her mother reported that in a recent telephone conversation, S's aunt had asked when S was going to get married. S's mother said she had explained that S just hadn't found the right person yet, to which her aunt had replied that not being married was easier anyway. In response to this story, S's father remarked that if S found the right person, she didn't have to rule out marriage. This conversation continued despite the fact that S, who, unbeknownst to her parents, is lesbian, said nothing to indicate her agreement or disagreement. In the absence of S's protestations, S's parents could retain their assumptions regarding how a woman is defined in American culture. Had S elected to express her real feelings—for instance, if she had announced her intention to live with a woman or said that her definition of marriage was quite different from theirs—she might have, minimally, aroused her parents' embarrassment, or she might even have been thrown out of the house. But she chose not to speak, and they could define her sexual identity without feeling contradicted.[1]

The question of which selves are present in interaction depends on at least three overlapping elements: (1) what constitutes a culturally approved self; (2) the degree to which that self is acceptable to participants, including the speaker and the addressee; and (3) the relative power of each participant within and outside the interaction.[2] Culturally approved selves are those that make up a culture's inventory of acceptable identities and roles. For S's parents and aunt, as well as for most people in American culture, and probably the world, part of being a legitimate woman involves marriage to a man; lesbian relationships do not enter the picture. Contrastively, for S (and other lesbians), along with a growing number of heterosexuals, the notion of 'woman' includes acting on emotional and erotic attractions to women, establishing committed relationships with them, and so on. This expanded concept of 'woman' opens up the possibility of other nontraditional relationships and identities.

In interaction, culturally approved identities are revealed and displayed in accordance with culturally and individually determined expectations of appropriate self-presentations. In addition to global constraints, participants' expectations at the local, interactional level also exert limitations. To the extent that S anticipated a skirmish with her parents and consciously decided not to dispute their assumptions, she shared their comprehension of womanhood as both an insider and an outsider. So strong are normative expectations for a woman in American society that unless an individual indicates otherwise, her identity will be a matter for others, whether in interaction or society as a whole, to settle.[3] S's decision not to contest these expectations shows that self-presentation does not occur in a vacuum but is subject to the audience and their expectations and assumptions in relation to the speaker's own.

Finally, identities may be imposed by fiat. In this culture, parents may "define" or label their children until their level of autonomy makes such definition inappropriate and unwholesome.[4] Institutions may also impose identities on individuals: for instance, the medical system has the power to define individuals in terms of conceptions of illness (as homosexuality was viewed prior to 1975). And as a member of a culture, the individual herself works out a self-definition partly in terms of her understanding of culturally approved identities.

Grice's conversational logic

The Western cultural understanding of communication is to be as informative as necessary because knowledge is seen as beneficial (Sweetser 1987). In view of this understanding, H. P. Grice observed that when people are engaged in conversation, they often deviate from informational language use by failing to say what they mean, and yet they remain understandable. Grice (1975) attempted to supply an explanatory theory for how hearers arrive at the meanings conveyed by speakers apart from and beyond the literal meanings of their utterances. He termed his theoretical rubric *conversational logic*.

The mainstay of conversational logic (and indeed of any communicative behavior) is the Cooperative Principle (hereafter abbreviated CP). CP holds that people will make whatever efforts are necessary to calculate another person's intended meanings and to communicate their own meanings so that the hearer understands them. In Grice's words: "Make your conversational contribution such as is required, at the stage at which it occurs, by the accepted purpose or direction of the talk exchange in which you are engaged" (1975:45).

One instantiation of CP consists of the Maxims of Conversation, precepts of conversational behavior observed by interlocutors in accordance with their cultural understanding of language behavior as informative. The maxims include, briefly, injunctions against lying or exaggerating (the maxim of quality), against verbosity or indirectness (the maxim of manner), against offering superfluous or insufficient detail (the maxim of quantity), and against straying from the topic at hand (the maxim of relevance).

Usually, however, conversational contributions are indirect, often superfluous, not entirely truthful, and irrelevant. Expecting that such utterances comply with the maxims at some unspoken level, listeners will try to fill in the gap between the literal and intended meaning of an utterance. Grice termed the process of linking apparently uninformative utterances to their informative equivalents *conversational implicature*. Since conversational implicature is another way of conveying and interpreting the speaker's meaning, it is also a manifestation of CP.

Gender: A basic implicature

The presentation of self is one configuration of meanings among many others—including propositions, presuppositions, and entailments; illocutionary and perlocutionary forces; frames; and alignments. Yet among all these meanings, it is unique. In face-to-face interactions, information about gender (along with other social categories such as ethnicity), rather than being stated explicitly, is continually constructed through nonverbal (e.g., gestures, clothing), paralinguistic (e.g., vocal fundamental frequency, intonation), and linguistic signals (e.g., indirectness). A basic cultural implicature is therefore "I am a woman" or "I am a man," which itself evokes a whole set of presuppositions.[5] That there is no name for asserting that one is a woman or a man—as the term *coming out* exists for the assertion that one is lesbian or gay—implies that behavioral expectations associated with womanhood and manhood are normative and pervasive. Thus gender identity appears self-evident. In American and many other cultures, gender is dichotomous: Members of one gender are expected to be attracted to and form coupled relationships with members of the other gender. These assumptions together constitute a fundamental presupposition about gender in this culture, namely, the *heterosexual presumption*.

Gender identity is socially required information for interaction, as relative status among interlocutors is required among speakers of languages such as Japanese that grammatically encode such information. The discomfort aroused when the gender of one's interlocutor is indeterminable or when gender roles are transgressed reveals these categories as a sociocultural organizing principle.[6] Because gender is a category that is fundamental to people's beliefs about the world, anyone who questions the foundation of those beliefs is, in some sense, questioning her personal existence. My point here is not to embark on a discussion of the expression of gender per se—there are many excellent works that explore that theme[7]—but to note that because gender is often implied rather than stated explicitly, it can be categorized in Gricean pragmatic terms as implicature. And because the interpretation of implicature hinges crucially on shared culture-specific presuppositions (Matsumoto 1989; Ochs Keenan 1975), it is useful for the investigation of gender identity.

The problem of lesbian and gay self-presentation

Homosexuality has thus far not achieved the status of a culturally approved plotline (Polkinghorne 1987).[8] Consequently, lesbians and gays continually confront the issue of disclosing or concealing their lesbian and gay selves. In every interaction, they must decide whether to reveal their identity and then which strategies they will use to disclose or conceal it. Typically, the situations in which lesbians and gays find themselves fall into three broad categories, with different responses associated with each. In one scenario, self-disclosure would terminate the relationship between the speaker and addressee or, in the worst case, would endanger the speaker's well-being. The possibility of disclosure is overridden by considerations of survival (of the relationship or of the individual). Another scenario is one in which the addressee is clearly supportive of or indifferent to the speaker's identity as lesbian or gay. In these contexts, the speaker may self-disclose without compunction.

The present concern, however, revolves around the third possibility, in which the speaker is unclear as to the addressee's opinions regarding homosexuality. In this scenario, the speaker is required to consider factors such as her relationship with the addressee and her own socially and culturally shaped beliefs of what is or is not appropriate to disclose. Within American culture, where members value personal truth and sincerity, lesbians and gays are in a double bind. If they observe CP, then they are communicating in good faith because they are making their intentions known. But they are also revealing that they violate gender norms, in which case they risk ostracism, violence or abuse, and discrimination. However, if they fail to observe CP, and, for instance, lie about their sexuality, then they engage in questionable communicative behavior. They may feel guilty for lying or dissembling. Additionally, there is the potential for social sanctions if their nonobservance of CP is discovered later. Cultural norms force on some lesbians and gays a decision that heterosexuals do not have to contend with.

Managing lesbian and gay identity

A number of strategies have presented themselves in view of the dilemma faced by lesbians and gays. Erving Goffman offers three possible courses of action in this kind of "normative predicament" faced by members of stigmatized groups:

> One solution was for a category of persons to support a norm but be defined by themselves and others as not the relevant category to realize the norm and personally to put it into practice. A second solution was for the individual who cannot maintain an identity norm to alienate himself from the community which upholds the norm, or refrain from developing an attachment to the community in the first place.
>
> The processes detailed here constitute together a third main solution to the problem of unsustained norms. Through these processes the common ground of norms can be sustained far beyond the circle of those who fully realize them. . . . Passing and covering are involved, providing the student with a special application of the arts of impression management, the arts, basic in social life, through which the individual exerts strategic control over the image of himself and his products that others glean from him. (1963:129–130)

The first solution Goffman proposes may apply, for instance, to lesbians and gays who do not want to be lesbian or gay but who cannot manage to live a normal heterosexual lifestyle. CP is not in question because such individuals attempt to conform to the norm or at least express commitment to it by repudiating offending behaviors in themselves, as well as in others. The second solution is a form of opting out and includes such strategies as minimizing contact with others to reduce the risk of exposure and abstaining from asking about others' personal lives so as not to invite queries about their own. The third solution that Goffman describes, "passing or covering," may involve lying and, therefore, flagrant violation of CP. It also covers avoidance strategies, which are also violations of CP insofar as the speaker intends to withhold information from the hearer. Because avoidance strategies may also implicate the speaker's sexuality, they can be viewed as cooperative. Such strategies may be less problematic than others, such as outright lies, in terms of both the speaker's own sense of integrity and her need for self-protection. These strategies, in which the status of CP is ambiguous, will be examined next.

When CP is ambiguous

Ann Weiser (1975) identifies a set of strategies whereby cooperativeness is defined less by the speaker's informativeness than by the degree to which the speaker's intentions can be inferred. She proposes a pair of communicative strategies: *conversational devices* and *conversational stratagems*. Both are linguistic means of achieving one's interactional purpose. The former involve direct speech acts, indirect speech acts, and implicature, all of which entail the listener's recognition of the speaker's intention. Use of these strategies signifies the speaker's on-record expressed intention to achieve a given purpose; hence adherence to CP is operative. The latter involve strategies by which the speaker masks her intention to achieve a given purpose. She is not on record as having expressed her intention, and consequently the speaker covertly opts out of CP. For Weiser, then, CP involves not only an exchange of information but also a displayed orientation toward participants' shared goals, whereas nonobservance of CP involves a covert nonorientation toward those goals and this nonorientation appears to promote shared interests. Conversational devices are exemplified by the following dialogue between Jill, a straight woman, and Jack, a gay man:

(1)

Jill:	Jack, do you like guys?
Jack [who is gay]:	a. ∅
	b. Nice weather we're having.
	c. None of your business.
	d. What kinda question is that?

In (1), although all of the listed responses differ in degree of directness (responses a and b being the most indirect since they do not explicitly acknowledge the question and hence are most evasive), all are oriented to the question and all conversationally implicate or explicitly express the speaker's hesitance or refusal to answer the question. Silence (a) conversationally implicates reluctance to respond, as does a change of topic (b). Response (c) is an explicit refusal. And the metacommunicative remark in (d) brings the interaction to another level, but in doing so, it communicates the speaker's refusal to answer the question. Here, cooperation involves acknowledgment or orientation to the addressee's remark, although in Robin Tolmach Lakoff's (1995a) terms, (c) and (d) are in clear violation of politeness principles.

A conversational stratagem, on the other hand, may arise when a speaker is asked a question that she does not want to answer but is not willing to acknowledge this fact because any response she might undertake would be socially problematic (for example, communicating refusal to answer would implicate her lesbianism). She may therefore pretend that "a sudden thought may have struck, something demanding comment may have occurred in the environment, or the second speaker may not have heard that the first speaker said anything" (Weiser 1975:651). If the questioner believes the response had nothing to do with the question, she will not understand it as a refusal to answer. Furthermore, if she has posed a question with multiple possible interpretations, the speaker can avoid answering without being heard as having refused to respond by responding to an interpretation that the questioner did not intend:

(2)

Jill:	Jack, do you like guys?
Jack [who is gay]:	a. Oh no! I forgot to turn off the stove!
	b. Wow, did you taste how strong this cappuccino is?
	c. White rice only. I hate brown rice.
	d. Some of my best friends are guys.

The respondent employs, respectively, the "sudden-thought" device in (a), the "something-presently-demanding-comment" device in (b), the "mishearing" device in (c), and in (d) the "selection-by-reply" device (that is, responding to an unintended interpretation) (Weiser 1975:651).

Another way that a conversational stratagem may be achieved is via the construction of an image within which characteristics that might otherwise betray the individual's homosexuality may be reinterpreted as idiosyncrasies. In example (3), Jill, an unmarried woman in her late 30s, may construct an image that emphasizes experiences such as a childhood spent in many different countries, characteristics such as an unusual dialect, or abilities such as ambidexterity. Deviations from the expected life course for a woman would then be seen as another peculiarity about her and not an indicator of her homosexuality.

(3)

Jack [a naive heterosexual]:	Jill, why aren't you married yet?
Jill [a lesbian]:	I want to live alone.

Jill's response is interpreted within the context of her overall personality rather than in terms of her homosexuality. Her response is a stratagem because she is encouraging Jack to make the default assumption of heterosexuality.

The status of CP differs according to whether conversational devices or conversational stratagems are used. With conversational devices, one or more of the maxims may be violated, but because CP in some form is upheld, the speaker's meaning corresponds to what is conversationally implicated. In example (1), Jack observes CP to the extent that Jill can calculate an informative meaning even though Jack's response does not conform with the maxims. With conversational stratagems, the listener's ability to calculate the speaker's purpose is suppressed, as in example (2); thus the interlocutors do not share a "set of common purposes or at least a mutually accepted direction." However, the distinction between stratagems and devices is not clear-cut. The two strategies can be functionally identical such that stratagems too can be recognized by listeners as evasive. So the responses in example (2) may also generate implicatures. Consider the following:

> Joel runs a weekly church discussion group that focuses on minority issues. The group is small, he says, and the conversation is often intimate. Yet Joel has never revealed his own sexuality to anyone in it. "If I were asked directly, I might just say, 'Well, we're really not talking about our own orientations here.' Another possible response might be, 'I'm black, I'm a woman, I'm a Muslim, I'm gay, I'm very poor, I am *all* those things that are discriminated against.' " (Woods & Lucas 1993:143–144)

The first response given by Joel is both a conversational device and a conversational stratagem. It is an overt refusal to answer the question and is legitimate to the extent that the discussion is not focused on him personally. But it is also a way of deflecting attention from himself and so is evasive. The engendering of similar effects from the use of different strategies, known as pragmatic synonymy (Lakoff & Tannen 1979), consequently also renders adherence to CP ambiguous. The following excerpt shows how conversational stratagems may fail and end up being interpreted, correctly, as a desire not to respond.

> Dave remembers a typical conversation with Audrey, a woman from personnel. "She had a friend who was gay, very blatantly and openly gay, and I know him. One day Audrey came over and says, 'Oh, I didn't know you knew Victor.' Then she says, '*How* do you know Victor?' Luckily Victor and I lived in the same apartment building at the time, so I said, 'We live in the same apartment building and there are social functions; that's how I met him.' "
>
> The initial dodge seemed to satisfy Audrey's curiosity, but before long she raised the issue again, this time with a question about Dave's roommate (and lover) Kyle. "I guess Audrey put more and more together," Dave says. "I don't know *how* she found out, but last fall we were walking through the Reading Terminal Market and she asked if I was going to my parents' house or to Kyle's parents' house for Thanksgiving. And I said, 'Well, my parents invited Kyle, but we're going to his parents' house.' " As the conversation continued, Dave grew uncomfortable. Finally, when Audrey asked how long he and Kyle had "been together," Dave responded with an explicit dodge. "She started talking about how long she'd been with *her* boyfriend, so I finally said, 'Audrey, I'm not going to discuss relationships with you.' I just changed the subject." (Woods & Lucas 1993:142–143)

Whether the stratagem is successfully carried out depends on the hearer's willingness to recognize an implicature or to follow up on the point that was redirected when the conversational stratagem was interjected into the interaction. In the passage above, Dave initially uses a conversational stratagem, the "selection-by-reply" strategy, to respond to Audrey's query. He knows she is asking if he knows Victor because both he and Victor are gay. But because he and Victor both live in the same apartment building, he can exploit this fact and form a response to her query that does not reveal his sexual orientation. However, in a subsequent interaction, she initiates a line of questioning about Dave's relationship with his lover Kyle, which suggests that she was not persuaded by his original strategy. In response, Dave resorts to a conversational device in which he places himself on record as refusing to respond to her question, by which he may have implicated his sexuality. Thus the effectiveness of a conversational stratagem may be considered as much a construction of the hearer as it is of the speaker. (See Rusty Barrett [chapter 16, this volume] for how ethnicity, performed by out-group members, can succeed as a coconstruction of the audience based on the latter's stereotypes of the ethnic group in question.)

The tension between having to tell the truth about oneself and having to protect oneself puts some lesbians and gays in a communicatively awkward position. On the one hand, if they employ the strategy of conversational devices, they implicate their sexuality, which involves some degree of risk to their relationships or to their physical well-being (in the case of violence) or their mental well-being (in the case of verbal abuse). If, on the other hand, they successfully employ the strategy of conversational stratagems, they achieve their interactional purposes, such as avoiding having to answer an incriminating question, without conversationally implicating those purposes and without appearing to have opted out of CP. And yet, even in these instances, lesbians and gays often feel deceitful. A fourth solution to the "normative predicament" faced by lesbians and gays is gay implicature.

Gay implicature

A relationship is cooperative if mutually shared assumptions allow the speaker to conversationally implicate her meaning and the listener to infer it. Cooperative strategies range from close observation of the maxims to the generation of implicature through clear violation of the maxims to overt defiance of the maxims for reasons such as those enumerated in Lakoff (1995a)—to conform with politeness, aesthetics, and so on. Uncooperativeness comprises behavior that adheres neither to politeness principles (whether in observance of the maxims or not) nor to clarity-based communication (insofar as the hearer's ability to calculate the speaker's meaning is impeded). Weiser's (1975) conversational stratagems occupy a possible middle area, for the speaker only gives the impression of being cooperative, although, as mentioned, the conversational stratagem can also be coconstructed by speaker and hearer. Here the avoidance of a delicate subject preserves social relations for both self-protection (that is, self-defense) and other-protection (that is, politeness), though at the expense of cooperation at the level of the maxims.

Given that talk always has, to use William Labov and David Fanshel's (1977) term, immanent reference—that is, that ultimately we are always talking about ourselves—and given that interaction depends on mutual knowledge of the other's social status (Linde 1993; Matsumoto 1989), the lesbian (or gay) individual is culturally compelled to reveal her (or his) homosexuality or at least finds circumvention difficult. She is also constrained by cultural values or, more precisely, her perception of them as a member of the culture in what she can reveal about herself just in case her interlocutor is hostile to gays. Hence, she must invent conversational strategies that neither implicate her homosexuality, in order to protect herself, nor negate it, in order to conform to the requirement of social interaction that the information she provides about herself adhere more or less to the truth. Confronted with this dilemma of either risking possibly dangerous consequences by coming out or feeling hypocritical in having to lie, lesbians and gays have devised ways of communicating to circumvent it.[9] Although these ways of communicating seem to involve deceptive behaviors, often the information from which to draw the correct inferences is there for those who can bring the correct assumptions to bear in an interaction.

These communicative strategies comprise what I call *gay implicatures*. Their covert meanings—though misleadingly worded for "credulous," that is, straight, listeners—can be inferred only if listeners disabuse themselves of the default assumption of heterosexuality. These strategies are unlike Weiserís conversational stratagems in that listeners can and are expected to infer the speaker's sexuality from what she has conversationally implicated. This expectation is justified, for instance, by the fact that the speaker and hearer live in a place such as the San Francisco Bay Area, where lesbians and gays are publicly visible.[10] Thus, to the extent that lesbian and gay speakers implicate their sexuality, they adhere to CP. But because sucessful inference depends on being able to adduce the relevant assumptions, lesbians and gays also circumvent CP when listeners fail in this task. Consequently, just as speaker meanings are coconstructed over the course of interaction, so too is CP.

Examples

The following are examples of what a hearer needs to know in order to realize the presence of a gay implicature.

Genderless reference terms

The first and most common strategy is the use of genderless reference terms such as *they* or *spouse* in discussing intimate relationships:[11]

(4) *Scenario*:   A lesbian speaker is talking with a (presumably) naive heterosexual.
(a) Lesbian: Well the last person I was involved with was <blahblahblah>, they
                      <blahblahblah>.
(b) Lesbian: Well the last person I was involved with was <blahblahblah>.

This strategy generates a gay implicature because it supplies less information than necessary: Rather than *they*, why not say *he*? Because the speaker did not say *he*, the listener should draw the appropriate inference. In response (b), the speaker uses the relative clause to avoid the gendered pronoun, which should also trigger an implicature. The strength of the implicature in both responses (a) and (b) increases when the avoidance of the gendered pronoun persists over the course of several turns.

A related strategy for avoiding gendered pronouns is the repeated use of *the person*.

(4′)

> *Scenario*: Same as (4).
>
> Lesbian: I went out on a date with this person, and the person and I got along really well. I'm seeing them again next weekend, etc.

The strength of the heterosexual presumption (along with the speaker's failure to correct wrong assumptions of the gender of the individual being referred to) offsets the lack of cohesiveness entailed by repetition of the noun phrase *the person* (Halliday & Hasan 1977; cf. Livia, chapter 17, this volume). Once again, the audience's role in the coconstruction of identity is evident.

Slightly trickier, however, is the avoidance of gendered terms, even while the listener employs the wrong gendered pronoun. The following dialogue, reported by a lesbian narrator, A, takes place after the narrator's coworker, B, has described her plans to go dancing with a man she has been dating.

(5) *Scenario*: A lesbian speaker (A) is conversing with her naive heterosexual female co-worker (B), to whom she has not disclosed her sexuality.

> A: I'm looking forward to the weekend.
> B: You doing anything special?
> A: Well, I'm having a visitor.
> B: Ooh . . . *that* kind of visitor? Does he come in often?
> A: Actually, yes. . . .
> B: Is this someone special?
> A: I think so . . . we'll see.

To draw the implicature, the listener must note that the speaker avoids referring to the visitor with gendered pronouns. Thus the omission of expected information may also trigger gay implicature. However, Grice never discusses the issue of whether allowing the listener to draw the wrong implicature is an instance of uncooperative behavior. So although the lesbian speaker herself does not state anything to commit to the heterosexual presumption, and therefore may be said to be conveying a gay implicature, one can imagine B, on discovery of her lesbian co-worker's homosexuality, saying indignantly, "Why did you let me go on thinking that?" The possibility that B may feel deceived suggests that the lesbian speaker may not be observing CP.

"Not my type"

Another strategy involves narrowly construing queries concerning romantic interests, as in (6):

(6)   *Scenario*:   B, a naive heterosexual, is inquiring of a lesbian speaker, L, about her
                    availability.

> B: So, dating any men?
> L: No.
> B: Why not?
> L: I'm not interested in finding a man.
> B: Just haven't found a good enough man, eh?
> L: No, I'm just not interested in finding a man.

In this example, the statement *I'm not interested in finding a man* should be understood as conversationally implicating interest either in finding a woman or in finding no one at all. Stress can signal a difference in the meaning that is implicated.
Thus putting the stress on *find*, as in *I'm not interested in fínding a man*, leaves the
heterosexual presumption intact by rejecting the proposition in its entirety. If the
emphasis is placed on *man*, as in *I'm not interested in finding a mán*, contrastive stress
signals that the speaker is interested in finding something else, namely a woman. Gay
implicature appears to be generated when the stress is placed on *interested*, as in *I'm
not ínterested in finding a man*, because it leaves the crucial part of the proposition,
finding a man, neutral.

Other strategies

(7)   *Scenario*:   A naive heterosexual male (B), who is potentially interested in the
                    lesbian speaker, queries her about her availability. The lesbian speaker
                    (L) has been dating another lesbian, but she also has conflicts about being
                    lesbian, that is, she would rather be heterosexual.

> B: Have you been seeing anyone recently?
> L: (a) I haven't been seeing any men recently.
>   (b) I haven't been seeing anyone recently.

Finally, in (7), a lesbian was asked by a prospective male suitor, B, "Have you been
seeing anyone lately?" Although she uses a strategy categorizable as gay implicature,
her self-presentation is ambiguous. She could have lied and stated that she had not
been seeing anyone romantically. More subtly, she might have responded with either an elided form, *No, I haven't*, or a repetition of the proposition, *No, I haven't
been seeing anyone lately*, and be understood as having said she had not been seeing
anyone of the other sex, without implicating anything about the same sex. However,
such a response presupposes the default assumption of heterosexuality. Because she
could not honestly maintain that assumption, she could not give either negative response without opting out, unless she explicitly indicated that a maxim had just been
violated. In this sense, she did not lie. Yet neither did she tell the truth since she could
have replied with a version of an affirmative response. Hence, she replied, "I haven't
been seeing any men recently" with no contrastive stress placed on *any men*. By stat-
ing the obvious, that is, by violating the maxim of manner, she answered the suitor's

question without compromising her moral stance. Her statement that she had not been seeing any men lately should have triggered the less obvious unstated alternative, namely that she had been seeing a woman. Therefore, the listener should have concluded that she was lesbian. "So," she said, pursuing her reasoning to its conversationally logical conclusion, "I came out to him." He seemed satisfied with her reply, as evidenced by ensuing dates, while the speaker had maintained her commitment to cooperativeness, making what she termed her self-disclosure apparent (to anyone who listened closely).

Note that if she had given response (b), there would likely be no implicature. The reason for the difference is that response (b) acquires its function as gay implicature in relation to what was said previously. Contrasting with the suitor's use of *anyone*, the lesbian's use of *any men* in a sense defeats the implicature of *any men* in the former's use of *anyone* and triggers another, that is, gay, implicature. In response (b), however, there is no implicature generated by the suitor's *any men*, and hence, none in the repetition of the corresponding noun phrase by the lesbian.

Example (7) attests to how complex identity is, and how ambiguity itself can be polysemous. In examples (4) through (6), individuals implicated their unwillingness to enact a heterosexual identity, but they did not preclude false conclusions about their sexuality. If listeners maintained the expectation of heteronormativity, the lesbian or gay speaker did nothing overt to disabuse them of their erroneous conclusion. Their identities were in this sense ambiguous. However, in (7), the speaker employs gay implicature as a way of being different things to different people (e.g., arguably straight to her suitor and lesbian to the lesbian interlocutor to whom she reported the dialogue). If she had truly believed that she were or could be heterosexual, she could merely have stated that she had not been seeing *anyone* lately, which could have been interpreted as fully cooperative and informative. That is, her intention to be heterosexual would render such a statement, which would implicate not having seen someone of the other sex, as completely relevant and as providing just the information required by her interlocutor, even if she were exploiting the heterosexual presumption. She would thereby eliminate any possibility of gay implicature. Yet the fact that she did not do so and, further, the fact that she believed that she "came out" to the suitor suggest that her self-concept is lesbian. Thus her presentation of an ambiguous self was not merely a conscious strategy adopted out of self-defense or the need to perceive herself as a moral person. The speaker was, in addition, attempting to have it both ways by retaining the option of being either straight (by allowing the suitor to believe that she was available) or lesbian (by nonetheless implicating her homosexuality).

Ambiguity: Lesbian/gay identity and the Cooperative Principle

The selves presented by lesbians and gays who engage in the use of gay implicature implies noncommitment to, and thus has the quality of ambiguity in relation to, accepted (heterosexual-based) gender categories. A possible motivation for gay implicature is a model of the self by which the speaker tries, to the extent possible, to be honest and sincere in her interactions rather than one by which she attempts to do what is necessary to conform, even if it means violating CP.

Gay implicature is less socially problematic than other violations of interactional rules. Although words exist for other discursive acts of lesbian and gay self-presentation (e.g., *coming out, coming-out stories*), no such culturally recognized term exists for gay implicature even though it is a common form of discourse among lesbians and gays. Likewise, there are words for infractions against CP, such as *lie, fib, falsehood*, and those who commit them, such as *liar, perjurer, prevaricator* (cf. Verschueren 1979). But it is more difficult to think of words describing conversational behaviors that suppress the addressee's ability to calculate a speaker's intentions or even give the addressee the option of calculating them. The absence of any such terms for gay implicature suggests that the way the culture evalutes such strategies is open and indeed ambiguous. Inasmuch as such strategies are less accessible to naming and therefore to value judgments, the moral implications are less problematic than for maxim violations.[12] Thus it cannot be said that gay implicature (and conversational stratagems, which are pragmatically homonymous with utterances that give rise to implicatures) are overtly deceptive; moreover, the relevant information is in the message, and the speaker is acting out of self-defense. To this extent, then, speakers employing these strategies are "passing" by means of their ambiguous adherence to CP.

Because the strategies present an ambiguous self, and because the speaker does not seek confirmation for whether or not the audience has detected the speaker's ploy, the possibility exists that the audience is able to infer the speaker's sexuality. Goffman observes that those who are stigmatized and those who are normative may cooperate in the construction of "normativity" of the stigmatized.

> Also involved is a form of tacit cooperation between normals and the stigmatized: the deviator can afford to remain attached to the norm because others are careful to respect his secret, pass lightly over its disclosure, or disattend evidence which prevents a secret from being made of it; these others, in turn, can afford to extend this tactfulness because the stigmatized will voluntarily refrain from pushing claims for acceptance much past the point normals find comfortable. (Goffman 1963:129–130)

Consequently, what hearers are actually aware of and how much they actually cooperate when the speaker uses such strategies is not necessarily known. What is important is when the speaker's ambiguous self-presentation goes unchallenged. In such instances, it is not unreasonable to speculate that CP may be observed by both parties, whereby norms remain superficially intact even if the deviator is in (tentative) violation of them.

Conclusion

Identity is not constant but emerges from the interactional flow through which shared meanings are negotiated between the speaker, whose intentions to self-presentation are culturally and individually determined, and the addressee, whose expectations of possible and legitimate identities likewise combine personal and cultural beliefs. Depending on which assumptions are shared, certain implicatures, and hence identities, are more likely to be conveyed and inferred than others.

Gay implicature is one site where language, cultural beliefs, and identity intersect. By invoking this conversational strategy, lesbian and gay speakers can exploit addressees' cultural expectations of legitimate persons in order to present an ambiguous identity. Strategies such as conversational stratagems and gay implicature suggest that adherence to CP cannot be defined as the calculability of default implicatures. Adherence to CP, and thus the calculability of implicatures, also depends on other real-life considerations like relative social status, face, power relations, and politeness principles. As noted, conversational stratagems that are ostensibly CP violations can be ambiguous with utterances that give rise to implicatures; in such instances, whether the speaker has violated CP is as ambiguous as the stratagem itself. The status of CP, then, is not simply one of speaker adherence or nonadherence. In regard to gay implicature, the hearer's ability to calculate the speaker's intended meaning is a result of an ongoing and perhaps implicit process of negotiation between the speaker and hearer. Identity results from the interaction between the individual's perceived cultural expectations of what a "normal" human being is and her own subjective experiences in relation to those expectations. Cultural imperatives in the form of shared expectations of what is "natural" place individuals who cannot conform with them (or who conform more easily with negatively evaluated social categories) in psychologically difficult situations because the individual encounters a predicament through which, for example, her subjective experience of same-sex attraction prevents her from realizing the norm of heterosexuality. Thus cultural imperatives impose moral dilemmas that are not faced by "normative" individuals within the culture: Lesbians and gays must "decide" whether to present a self that conforms with or violates cultural expectations. A naive hearer may fail to calculate a gay implicature, and in some formulations of CP (such as Lakoff's), the speaker may be said to be uncooperative. Where the community as a whole has had exposure to lesbians and gays, the speaker's continued use of gay implicature over the course of an interaction may lead the hearer to make the correct inference. In this case, based on the hearer's success in decoding the speaker's intended meaning, the speaker observes CP without changing her intentions regarding the calculability of her homosexuality. Over the course of an interaction, gay implicature can implicate a noncommitment to the heterosexual presumption, which can eventually lead the hearer to infer the speaker's homosexuality.[13]

Finally, the status of lesbian or gay identity as a culturally acceptable identity can be assessed by the speaker's degree of adherence to the maxims in communicating her sexuality. In the act of coming out, for instance, the maxims are observed and there is no room for the audience to do any inferencing. Coming out presupposes that the audience subscribes to the normative model of gender and sexuality and that the most effective way to dislodge at least one component of this model, the heterosexual presumption, is through clarity-based communication. The distress that such directness causes to those who maintain the heterosexual presumption implies that the two underlying models of gender (that individuals are meant to be coupled with the other sex versus the absence of such a constraint on choice of mate) are unshared by speaker and audience; this cognitive mismatch is also evidenced in the numerous books that have been published and organizations that have been established whose main purpose is to deal with the consequences of this communicative act.

The emergence of gay implicature demonstrates that the status of lesbian and gay identities on a culture-wide level is changing. The mere possibility of decoding utterances that implicate the speaker's sexuality suggests that the heterosexual presumption has been disengaged from current cultural presuppositions regarding gender. If homosexuality were as taboo as, say, pedophilia, the odds would be very slight that the speaker would allow identification of these tendencies. Given the illicit status of pedophilia, he would lie, thereby committing a clear infraction against CP. Gay implicature, in contrast, perhaps indicates lesbians' and gays' hope that the heterosexual presumption is losing ground.

Lesbians and gays are in the peculiar position of being at the forefront of cultural change, depending on whether they decide to lie (thereby maintaining the status quo), to tell the truth (thereby forcing, at the risk of physical or psychological self-harm, another person to confront her conception of normality), or to convey their identity through gay implicature (thereby avoiding commitment to the old normative category and initiating a process of "training" in the new nonnormative lesbian or gay category). The flip side of this moral dilemma also offers "choices" between possible self-presentations. If lesbians and gays give the appearance of being heterosexual (by "passing" or even adopting all the external trappings of heterosexuality, including living a wholly heterosexual lifestyle) or of being ambiguously heterosexual and homosexual, in some sense (one exploited by antihomosexual political groups) identity is conscious and therefore voluntary. Yet this reasoning fails to differentiate between performed (social) identities and biographical (personal) identities, a disjunction that lesbians and gays, because of the absence of inherent identifying traits, make salient. The range of self-presentations available to lesbians and gays merely exemplifies the performed nature of all identities and social categories, whether or not they correspond to the individual's biographical self. Lesbians and gays who "pass" as straight perform an identity that is dissonant with who they actually experience themselves to be. Identities, both stated and implicated, are a result of linguistic decisions made over the course of an interaction, in which each individual's contribution reflects both the individual's intention and the local and global social constraints. This process of negotiation between individuals, intentions, and social and cultural forces illustrates the intimate connection between language and identity.

NOTES

I am grateful to Robin Tolmach Lakoff and Sara Gesuato for their assistance in elucidating the theoretical basis of this chapter. Pamela Morgan, Collin Baker, Mary Bucholtz, Susan Ervin-Tripp, and Michael Meacham have my thanks for providing ample and useful comments. I also wish to thank the unnamed individuals who contributed their stories. Any shortcomings are my own.

1. I thank Christopher Liang for this anecdote.
2. For ease of discussion, I consider the presentation of self from the perspective of the speaker, but the addressee also displays a self through her listening behaviors. Whether speak-

ing or silent, one cannot *not* communicate in social interaction (Bateson 1972); consequently, one cannot *not* present a self.

3. That identity hinges on power is illustrated by the question of how Jewishness is defined. Strictly speaking, according to Judaic law, only if the mother is Jewish do the offspring "count" as Jewish. Yet even those who do not themselves identify as Jewish recognize that Jewishness is contingent on who has the power to characterize those who are and those who are not. Were a right-wing white supremacist anti-Semitic group to seize control of the country, it is likely that anyone with Jewish blood would be defined as Jewish, regardless of the individual's own self-identifications or of what Judaic law states.

4. Some diseases with psychological components (cf. Bateson 1972 on schizophrenia) are viewed as a result of the ways families impose a role on a family member in order to ensure survival of the larger family unit. See also Lisa Capps (chapter 4, this volume).

5. In Robin Tolmach Lakoff's construal of Grice's conversational logic (the system of precepts or maxims adhered to by speakers and listeners in producing and interpreting utterances in conversation), "maxim-observant utterances do exactly and succinctly express pure semantic meaning; but they may not incorporate many of the pragmatic signals that orient participants to significant aspects of the message: discourse genre, deictic situation, seriousness, level of intimacy, mutuality of trust, delicacy of subject matter, and much more. Implicature provides that information, often as important in the full understanding of a communication as its explicit denotation" (1995b:191). To Lakoff's specification of the meanings covered by implicature, I would add culturally approved, situation-appropriate identities.

6. The discovery that Brandon Teena, a preoperative transgendered man living in Humboldt, Nebraska, was biologically female aroused the rage of two of his former acquaintances. In 1993, Teena was arrested on misdemeanor charges for check forgery. The information, including the fact that he was anatomically and legally female, was released by police to the local newspaper, the Falls City *Journal*. A week later, Teena was raped by two men who threatened to kill him if he went to the police. Although he reported the rape to the police and identified the two assailants, no charges were filed against them. Teena was subsequently hunted down by them and murdered, along with his female lover and another friend.

7. See, for example, the chapters by Rusty Barrett, Jennifer Coates, Marjorie Faulstich Orellana, Deborah Tannen, and Keith Walters in this volume and numerous contributions in Anna Livia and Kira Hall (1997).

8. Cf. also Mandy Aftel (1996), William Leap (chapter 13, this volume), Charlotte Linde (1993), Theodore Sarbin (1987), and Kathleen Wood (chapter 2, this volume) for other narrative-based conceptions of culture-specific identities.

9. Perhaps another factor compelling the use of gay implicature rather than bald-faced lies is lesbians' and gays' resentment of the double standard: When lesbians and gays merely state their sexual orientation, they are often viewed by heterosexuals as "flaunting" their lifestyles. Susan Ervin-Tripp (personal communication) has recounted the story of a heterosexual colleague who objected to a pink triangle sticker on the door of the office of a fellow academic who was lesbian. According to the colleague, the lesbian academic's sexuality was irrelevant to her capabilities as a researcher and teacher. (Presumably, this same colleague did not consider that wearing a wedding band was equally irrelevant to the qualifications of an academic.) Gay implicature enables lesbians and gays to thwart the proscription against "flaunting" it by refusing to commit to the heterosexual presumption, albeit covertly.

10. However, it is also the case that some naive heterosexuals will never get the implicature, no matter how many times it is repeated, whether due to willful blindness, lack of experience, or other factors.

11. Examples (4) through (7) were provided by members of several lesbian and gay electronic-mail lists. From a methodological and theoretical point of view, these data may be

problematic insofar as they may neither reflect what actually happened—that is, as self-reports, the examples are tantamount to being constructed examples—nor be representative of the behavior of lesbians and gays as a group. Nonetheless, the examples cited do indicate the extent to which the devices in question are consciously aimed toward the avoidance and transformation of a difficult social situation.

12. Regardless, behavior that is less accessible to naming and therefore to a value judgment is not necessarily unproblematic for the hearer. It is in fact convenient for the speaker that there are no ready-made names or value judgments to condemn the suppression of the hearer's ability to calculate the speaker's intention.

13. Sara Gesuato (personal communication) has given me the analogous example of the use of *signora* versus *signorina* in Italy. In recent years, it has become a law that all women over eighteen years of age can adopt the title *signora* whether or not they are in fact married. The title has become the Italian equivalent of the American English *Ms. Signorina* meanwhile retains the meaning of *Miss*. According to Gesuato, since the law has been effective for several years, her use of the title *signora* over *signorina* should convey to strangers that she is not willing to state her marital status (and that, furthermore, they should not inquire). The fact that some of her fellow Italians continue to ask about her marital status indicates that the law and its social significance for women have only partly been incorporated into Italians' collective consciousness.

REFERENCES

Aftel, Mandy (1996). *The story of your life: Becoming the author of your experience*. New York: Simon & Schuster.

Bateson, Gregory (1972). *Steps to an ecology of mind*. New York: Ballantine.

Goffman, Erving (1963). *Stigma: Notes on the management of spoiled identity*. Englewood Cliffs, NJ: Prentice Hall.

Grice, H. P. (1975). Logic and conversation. In Peter Cole & Jerry L. Morgan (eds.), *Syntax and semantics*. Vol. 3: *Speech acts*. New York: Academic Press, 41–58.

Halliday, Michael A. K., & Ruqaiya Hasan (1977). *Cohesion in English*. London: Longman.

Labov, William, & David Fanshel (1977). *Therapeutic discourse*. New York: Academic Press.

Lakoff, Robin Tolmach (1995a). Conversational implicature. In Jef Verschueren, Jan-Ola Östman, & Jan Blommaert (eds.), *Handbook of pragmatics*. Amsterdam: John Benjamins, 1–11.

——— (1995b). Conversational logic. In Jef Verschueren, Jan-Ola Östman, & Jan Blommaert (eds.), *Handbook of pragmatics*. Amsterdam: John Benjamins, 190–198.

Lakoff, Robin Tolmach, & Deborah Tannen (1979). Communicative strategies in conversation: The case of *Scenes from a Marriage*. In Christine Chiarello et al. (eds.), *Proceedings of the Tenth Meeting of the Berkeley Linguistics Society*. Berkeley, CA: Berkeley Linguistics Society, 581–592.

Liang, A. C. (1995). Gay implicature as straight delusion. Paper presented at the annual meeting of the American Association for Applied Linguistics, Long Beach, California.

Linde, Charlotte (1993). *Life stories: The creation of coherence*. Oxford: Oxford University Press.

Livia, Anna, & Kira Hall (eds.) (1997). *Queerly phrased: Language, gender, and sexuality*. New York: Oxford University Press.

Matsumoto, Yoshiko (1989). Reexamination of the universality of face: Politeness phenomena in Japanese. *Journal of Pragmatics* 14:237–261.

Ochs Keenan, Elinor (1975). The universality of conversational implicature. In Ralph Fasold & Roger Shuy (eds.), *Studies in language variation*. Washington, DC: Georgetown University Press, 255–268.

Polkinghorne, Donald E. (1987). *Narrative knowing and the human sciences*. Albany: SUNY Press.

Sarbin, Theodore (ed.) (1987). *Narrative psychology: The storied nature of human conduct*. Chicago: Praeger.

Sweetser, Eve (1987). The definition of *lie*. In Dorothy Holland & Naomi Quinn (eds.), *Cultural models in language and thought*. Cambridge: Cambridge University Press, 101–127.

Verschueren, Jef (1979). What people say they do with words. Ph.D. diss., University of California, Berkeley.

Weiser, Ann (1975). How to not answer a question: Purposive devices in conversational strategy. In Robin E. Grossman, L. James San, & Timothy J. Vance (eds.), *Papers from the Eleventh Regional Meeting of the Chicago Linguistic Society*. Chicago: Chicago Linguistic Society, 649–660.

Woods, James D., & Jay H. Lucas (1993). *The corporate closet: The professional lives of gay men in America*. New York: Free Press.

Part IV

. . . .

IDENTITY
AS IMPROVISATION

. . . .

Indexing Polyphonous
Identity in the Speech of
African American Drag Queens

I n this chapter, I examine the presence and use of a "white-woman" style of speaking among African American drag queens (hereafter AADQs). I hope to demonstrate that a close examination of this language use suggests an ambivalent, sometimes critical, sometimes angry, view of whiteness that does not lend itself to a simplistic explanation of "wanting to be white." After discussing the issue of drag itself, I will discuss the ways in which AADQs create a "white-woman" linguistic style. However, this style of speaking is only one voice used by AADQs. The complete set of linguistic styles together index a multilayered identity that is sometimes strongly political with regard to issues of racism and homophobia.

Drag

Before discussing the issue of drag, it is important to distinguish drag queens from other transgender groups, such as transsexuals, transvestites, cross-dressers, and female impersonators.[1] Transsexuals are individuals who feel that their gender identity does not correspond to the sex that they were assigned at birth. Many (but not all) transsexuals undergo hormone treatment or "sex-reassignment" surgery as means of altering their physical appearance to match that typically associated with their gender identity. Transsexuality and homosexuality are independent issues, and transsexuals may be heterosexual, homosexual, bisexual, or asexual (cf. MacKenzie 1994). In contrast, drag queens do not identify themselves as having female gender (that is, they do not see themselves as women).

Unlike transsexuals, transvestites identify with the gender corresponding to their assigned sex. The terms *transvestite* and *cross-dresser* refer to anyone who wears clothing associated with the other gender. The term *transvestite* does not necessarily refer to an individual who fully crosses gender roles, and it may be used for situations such as a man wearing women's undergarments under traditional "male" clothing. Studies have suggested that between 72 and 97 percent of male transvestites are heterosexuals (Bullough & Bullough 1993). In contrast, *drag queen* refers almost exclusively to gay men (with *drag king* referring to lesbian cross-dressers).

The term *female impersonator* is very similar to *drag queen*, although (like *transvestite* and *cross-dresser*) it may be used to refer to heterosexuals. Female impersonators are professional cross-dressers who typically focus their performances on creating a highly realistic likeness of a famous woman (such as Diana Ross, Cher, Reba McEntire, or Madonna). Glamour-oriented drag queens (or "glam queens") often produce a physical representation of hyperfeminine womanhood that is quite similar to that of female impersonators. The performances of female impersonators generally build on their ability to "pass" as women, however, and drag queens usually make no pretense about the fact that they are (gay) men, even though they may present a realistic *image* of a particular type of woman (cf. Fleisher 1996:14–15). Also, female impersonators generally perform for the amusement of heterosexuals, whereas drag queens perform for lesbian and gay audiences. Although both female impersonators and drag queens may produce highly similar external conceptions of femininity, the intent and attitude behind their performances are quite different.

All the drag queens in this study are glam queens. They typically go to great lengths to produce a highly feminine image. In addition to wigs, makeup, and "tucking" (hiding one's genitals), drag queens often use duct tape to push their pectoral muscles closer together to give the impression of cleavage. Glam queens almost always wear high-heeled shoes and shave their arms, legs, chest, and (if necessary) back. The dresses worn by glam queens are quite extravagant, often covered in beads or sequins. Many dresses do not have sleeves or have high slits to make it clear that the wearer is not trying to hide masculine features under clothing. Jewelry is almost always worn, especially large earrings and bracelets. The overall goal is to produce an image of hyperfemininity that is believable—an image that could "pass" for a woman. The ideal of glam drag is to be "flawless," or to have no visual hints of masculinity that could leave one open to being "read" (insulted; see also Morgan, chapter 1, this volume).

The drag queens I studied are professional entertainers who work primarily in gay bars. In order to become a full-time professional, a drag queen must achieve a certain degree of exposure, usually by working without pay or by winning beauty pageants. Thus, to become a professional, a drag queen must prove that she is sufficiently flawless.[2] Drag queens who are not flawless may be viewed as "messy": lacking professionalism both in the image produced and in the demeanor presented in the bar. Thus, a *messy* queen is often one who is unsuccessful at presenting an image of "proper" femininity (both in speech and poise). The term *messy* may also be used for queens who cause problems by spreading gossip or getting into trouble through drugs, alcohol, theft, or prostitution. A messy queen has little chance for success as a professional performer because she is unable to convey a convincing image of femininity both on stage and during interactions in the bar.

Feminist scholars have argued that drag is inherently a misogynistic act, primarily because they feel that it represents a mockery of women or, at the very least, a highly stereotyped image of femininity and womanhood (Ackroyd 1979; Frye 1983; Lurie 1981; Raymond 1994, 1996; Williamson 1986). It has also been argued that drag is a way of reinforcing a performer's masculinity by demonstrating that he is not actually a woman but that he is able to control the qualities associated with women (Gilbert 1982; Showalter 1983). Because the goal of glam drag is to produce an outward appearance indistinguishable from that of a "real" woman, humor in the performance of glam drag is not derived from the performer's inability to "be" a woman but from the virtuoso performance itself.

The argument that drag is primarily a mockery of women relies on the stereotyped perception of drag queens displaying "big tits, fat tummies, wobbly hips and elaborate hair-dos" (Williamson 1986:48) that "draw hoots and howls in audiences of mostly men" (Raymond 1996:217). With the exception of elaborate hairstyles, this stereotyped image of drag has very little to do with the reality of the gay drag performances included in this study. The drag performers I studied do not intend to produce laughter through their appearance. As Edmund White has argued, drag (at least among gays) "is an art of impersonation, not an act of deception, still less of ridicule" (1980:240). These arguments against drag often confuse gay drag queens with the sort of transvestite shows produced by straight (usually white and wealthy) men as a sort of male bonding experience, even though the latter (often including hairy men wearing exaggerated false breasts and rear ends) are quite different in both content and intent.

More recently, commentators (Butler 1990, 1993; Feinberg 1996; Fleisher 1996; Hilbert 1995) have critiqued this perspective not only because it views all forms of transgender behavior as male homosexual activities but also because it places women at the center of male homosexuality. These scholars argue that drag is not "about" women but rather about the inversion or subversion of traditional gender roles. These scholars often praise drag queens for demonstrating that gender displays do not necessarily correlate with anatomical sex and typically see drag as a highly subversive act that deconstructs traditional assumptions concerning gender identity. Butler, for example, argues that drag exposes the imitative nature of gender, showing that gender is an "imitation without an origin" (1990:138). Rather than viewing drag as an imitation of women, queer theorists usually glorify it as a highly political deconstructive force working to undermine gender assumptions.

Drag queens themselves also adamantly reject the notion that drag mocks women. They distinguish their performances from those of heterosexual men (who, in their view, clearly *do* mock women). For example, the nationally known AADQ singer RuPaul was angry and offended when she had to copresent an MTV music award with Milton Berle, an older heterosexual comedian known for using drag in his humor. She reports in her autobiography that problems between her and Berle began when he insulted her backstage (RuPaul 1995). The problems continued onstage as well, resulting in an argument that was aired on live television. According to RuPaul, the producers of the program did not realize that there was no connection between her status as a drag queen and Berle's use of women's clothing to produce humor at women's expense. As she describes it, "They didn't get that my take on drag is all about love, saying that we are *all* drag queens. It's certainly not about putting women down. And it's not about being the butt of a bunch of cheap dick jokes" (1995:181).

In addition, drag queens sometimes see themselves as fighting against gender oppression in general, a cause that many feel should garner support rather than disdain from feminists. And despite the role of drag queens in the gay liberation movement (cf. Duberman 1993; Marcus 1992), many gay men openly express scorn for drag queens. Hapi Phace, a New York drag queen interviewed by Julian Fleisher (1996), points out, "The thing that you have to remember is that as drag queens we have a lot of the same issues as feminists in our own dealings with the gay community. To gay men, we're considered 'women.' We get to see a lot of the misogyny in gay men" (Fleisher 1996:33–34). This view sees drag performers (both kings and queens) as part of a larger set of individuals persecuted by an intolerant society for their deviance from prescribed gender norms. As Leslie Feinberg argues, "it's really only drag performance when it's transgender people who are facing the footlights . . . the essence of drag performance is not impersonation of the opposite sex. It is the cultural presentation of an oppressed gender expression" (1996:115). In other words, drag is not intended as a negative portrayal of "women" but rather is an expression of a particular gender performance (cf. Butler 1990)—a performance by those who are themselves oppressed by the forces of patriarchy.

Part of the fascination with drag is its ability to cause such diverse reactions in different contexts and with different audiences. In some instances, cross-dressing is used as a weapon of misogyny and even homophobia. In other contexts, drag may serve to question the rigidity of prescriptive gender roles, acting as a tool of liberation. One of the main functions of drag performance is to expose the disunity between perceived or performed identity and underlying "authentic" biographical identity. The "meaning" of drag is often created by audience members in their individual attempts to reconnect their physical perceptions of the performance with their personal assumptions concerning social identity and gender categories. Many drag queens argue that they are not really trying to "achieve" any great social message but are merely expressing their personal identity (which happens to involve cross-dressing).

The celebration and even glorification of drag by queer theorists such as Butler might be seen as exploiting drag-queen identity for the sake of theoretical deconstruction of gender categories. Like the feminist view of drag as inherently misogynistic, the view that drag is inherently subversive imposes a unidimensional meaning on the personal identity of a particular group. But there are certainly cases in which drag-queen performances are clearly misogynistic. As Miss Understood, another of Fleisher's interviewees, argues, "I think that men in general are pretty misogynist. Men are sexist all the time and if drag queens are men, of course there's going to be sexist things coming out of their mouths" (Fleisher 1996:32). Although drag queens may be misogynistic at times, their personal identity as drag queens does not make them *de facto* sexists. In many cases, they may be viewed as highly subversive. Thus neither the view of drag as inherently subversive nor as inherently misogynistic is "correct." Rather, drag queens are individuals whose social identity no more determines their political stance than any other aspect of their personal identities, such as gender, class, or ethnicity. Indeed, the performances by AADQs considered here generally focus on other aspects of identity (such as sexual orientation, ethnicity, and class) rather than on the issue of cross-dressing itself.

Polyphonous identity and acts of performed identity

Historically, sociolinguistic studies have tended to view identity monolithically, often assuming a one-to-one relationship between language use and membership in some identity category (usually based on class, race, or sex). Speakers were "allowed" only a single identity that was typically mapped onto a particular identity category. Those who did not fit the norms of language usage were implicitly viewed as possessing a "failed" identity, as with William Labov's (1972) *lames* or Peter Trudgill's (1983) concept of *conflicting identity*. Thus the fact that some speakers could not easily be classified into a particular identity category on the basis of their language usage was seen as a problem with the speaker rather than a problem in the research paradigm.

As Marcyliena Morgan (chapter 1, this volume) points out, Labov's focus on unemployed adolescent boys in his study of African American Vernacular English (hereafter AAVE) has contributed to stereotypes of what constitutes a "real" African American identity. Sociolinguistic research has typically perpetuated the myth that one must speak AAVE (and must usually be a heterosexual male) to qualify as a "true" African American, leaving many African Americans classified as "lames" or simply ignored. This myth of what constitutes African American identity is especially relevant to African American gay men. Because of the combined forces of racism in the white gay community (cf. Beame 1983; Boykin 1996; DeMarco 1983) and homophobia in the African American community (Boykin 1996; hooks 1989; Monteiro & Fuqua 1994), African American gay men are often pressured to "decide" between identifying with African Americans or with white gay men (Peterson 1992; Simmons 1991; Smith 1986; Tinney 1986). Due to the stereotypical view that AAVE is somehow tied exclusively to young heterosexual men and is a strong marker of masculinity (cf. Harper 1993; Walters 1996), the use of "Standard" English by African American gay men (including drag queens) contributes to the argument that they have somehow abandoned the African American community by identifying themselves as gay. Thus simplistic conceptions of the relationship between language and identity in sociolinguistic research may serve to reinforce the racism and homophobia prevalent in American society.

More recently, as studies in language and gender have moved to a practice-based approach (Eckert & McConnell-Ginet 1992), it has become clear that identities based on categories such as gender, class, and ethnicity are often enmeshed in very complex ways. Expressions of gender are simultaneously expressions of ethnicity (Bucholtz 1995; Hall 1995) and of class (Bucholtz, chapter 18, this volume; McElhinny 1995; Woolard 1995). Hence the concept of a prescriptive norm for "women's language" is often a reflection of ideology concerning not only gender but also race and class.

Given the complex relationship between linguistic form and ideologies of gender, class, race, and ethnicity, one would expect speakers to attune their linguistic performances to their personal stance toward gender and other ideologies. Speakers may heighten or diminish linguistic displays that index various aspects of their identities according to the context of an utterance and the specific goals they are trying to achieve. Thus a speaker may use the indexical value of language (cf. Ochs 1992) to "position" (Davies & Harré 1990) the self within a particular identity at a particular interactional moment. This practice implies that speakers do not have a single "identity" but rather something closer to what Paul Kroskrity (1993:206 ff.) has called a "repertoire of identity," in which any of a multiplicity of identities may be fronted at a particular moment. In addition, at any given moment speakers may also convey more than one particular "categorical" identity. For this reason I have chosen the term *polyphonous identity* rather than *repertoire* to convey the idea that linguistic displays of identity are often multivoiced or heteroglossic in the sense of Mikhail Bakhtin (1981, 1984). Thus speakers may index a polyphonous, multilayered identity by using linguistic variables with indexical associations to more than one social category. In the case of AADQs, speakers typically use language to index their identities as African Americans, as gay men, and as drag queens. Through style shifting, the linguistic variables associated with each aspect of identity may co-occur, creating a voice simultaneously associated with several identity categories (cf. Barrett 1998).

One important distinction between the language of drag-queen performances and many other forms of language is that although drag queens use language to index "female" gender, they do not generally see themselves as "women." Thus they perform an identity (as a "woman") that they may see as distinct and separate from their own biographical identity. Sociolinguistic theory has not traditionally made a distinction between a performed identity and those identities associated with the social categorization of the self. In her analysis of drag, Butler (1990) points out that, in addition to the traditional distinction made between sex and gender, drag creates the need for a third category, performance. Although gender performance often corresponds directly with gender identity, cases such as drag require an understanding that performed gender may differ from self-categorized gender identity. The majority of drag queens maintain "male" gender identity alongside "female" gender performance. Indeed, perhaps the strongest distinction between drag queens and transsexuals is the distinction between performance and identity, in that transsexuals typically maintain a gender identity that corresponds to their gender performance (but may not correspond to anatomical sex), whereas the gender performance of drag queens typically does not correspond to either gender identity or anatomical sex.

The distinction between performance and identity has not been utilized in sociolinguistic research, but it is potentially crucial, for the linguistic manifestations tied to performance are likely to be quite different from those related to personal identity. In identity performance, out-group stereotypes concerning the behavioral patterns of the group associated with the performed identity are likely to be more important than actual behavior or the group's own behavioral norms (Hall 1995). Audience assumptions and expectations may crucially help to coconstruct a performance that successfully conveys a particular identity regardless of the accuracy of the linguistic performance when compared to the behavior of "authentic" holders of the identity in question (Preston 1992). Thus the language used in a performed identity is likely to differ from the actual speech of those who categorize themselves as having that identity.

In addition to differences in linguistic form, a performed identity and a self-categorized identity are associated with different social factors. Robert Le Page and Andrée Tabouret-Keller (1985) offer four conditions that must be met if one is successfully to match the behavior of groups with which one wishes to identify: (1) identification of the groups; (2) access to the groups; (3) motivation to join them and reinforcement from group members; and (4) ability to modify one's behavior. Although these conditions may be necessary for the creation of identity based on self-categorization, they may not be required for the creation of a successful performed identity. For the sake of performance, it may be sufficient simply to identify the groups in question and to have the ability to modify one's behavior. One does not necessarily need access to the groups and one certainly does not need motivation to join the groups. In fact, in many cases performance may be used as a means to actually create distance from the group in question (as in the case of blackface). Reinforcement from the group is likely to be absent, and indeed, the performance may cause revulsion of members of the group itself (as with some feminist responses to drag). It is likely that in performing identity, reinforcement from the audience or listener will be more important than the actual behavior of the group being imitated; as with the mocking use of an ethnic dialect, performed identities may actually reflect disdain for the imitated group. Speakers in performance need only adjust their linguistic behavior to the extent necessary to index the identity in question. Such an adjustment may in fact be quite slight, possibly even consisting only of the use of specific lexical items (cf. Preston 1992).

Performances by AADQs are often judged (by audiences and other drag queens) on the basis of *realness*, or the ability to seem to be or "pass" (cf. Bucholtz 1995) as a "real" woman. In order to be "flawless," a drag queen must be "real": Her performance must plausibly lead (usually straight) outsiders to assume that she is anatomically female. Any response (whether reinforcement, rejection, or simply acknowledgment) from actual women is unimportant in the creation of a successful performance. What matters is the response of other gay men and drag queens, who base their judgment not on the actual behavior of women but rather on stereotyped assumptions concerning "feminine" behavior. The performer will also base her performance on stereotypes (and on her assumptions concerning the stereotypes held by the audience). These stereotypes may sometimes reflect the misogynist attitudes and sexist assumptions of the performer.

Traditional studies of performance have stressed the performer's responsibility to demonstrate communicative competence before an audience (cf. Bauman 1977; Briggs 1988; Hymes 1981). In drag performances, the performer must be able to produce a "real" feminine speech style or a feminine way of speaking that would sound convincing to someone who did not know that the performer was actually anatomically male. Ironically, the success of drag also depends on making the audience aware that this performance is indeed "false" in some sense (that is, the audience must be reminded that the performer is biologically male). Because a successful drag performance is one in which the audience accepts that the performer could pass as a woman, the audience must be occasionally reminded that the performer is indeed *performing* rather than claiming a female identity. Thus, although glam queens present an external image of exaggerated femininity, they also use language both to create and to undermine this surface image. For example, drag queens frequently use a stereotypically "feminine" speaking style, but a stereotypically "masculine" voice may break through during the performance, creating a polyphonous and often ambiguous performed identity.

Within the performances of AADQs in particular, a crucial aspect of communicative competence is the rhetorical device of signifyin(g) (Abrahams 1976; Gates 1988; Mitchell-Kernan 1972; Smitherman 1977). In signifying, the full intended meaning of an utterance does not rest solely on referential meaning. Rather, an utterance is valued because of its ability to index an ambiguous relationship between the signifier and the signified. Thus the signifier does not simply correspond to a particular concept but indexes a rhetorical figure or skill at verbal art. In signifying, a speaker draws attention to language itself, particularly to her or his skill at using language creatively. Specific attention to language (rather than referential content) may be created through a variety of devices, including the creation of polysemy or ambiguity, the creative use of indirection (Morgan 1991), and the contrastive use of a particular style, as in reading dialect (Morgan, chapter 1, this volume). Signifying relies on the listener's ability to connect the content of an utterance to the context in which it occurs and specifically to sort through the possible meanings and implications of an utterance and realize both the proper meaning and the skill of the speaker in creating multiple potential meanings.

Successful performances by AADQs typically include cases of signifying. A highly effective instance of signifying is sometimes picked up by other drag queens for use in their own performances. Example (1) has been used fairly widely by various AADQs in Texas:

(1)   Drag queen: Everybody say "Hey!"
      Audience: Hey!
      Drag queen: Everybody say "Ho!"
      Audience: Ho!
      Drag queen: Everybody say "Hey! Ho!"
      Audience: Hey! Ho!
      Drag queen: Hey! How y'all doin?

This example draws on the form of a call-response routine, a rhetorical trope sometimes associated with African American sermons and often used in drag performances. The example relies on the polysemy of the word *ho* as both an "empty" word frequently used in call-response routines by drag queens and as an equivalent of *whore*. After leading the audience into the chant and getting them to yell "Hey! Ho," the drag queen reinterprets the word *ho*, taking the audience's chanting of *ho* as a vocative. The polysemy is dependent on the connection between the utterance and the context. Performances of AADQs contain numerous examples of signifying, in many of which the polysemy is achieved through the juxtaposition of language styles or social dialects.

White women's language among AADQs

Marjorie Garber (1992) notes that there is a long tradition of simultaneous movement across lines of both gender and race/ethnicity. For AADQs, the move to perform female gender is often accompanied by a simultaneous movement across lines of race and class. Sometimes an AADQ will openly state that she is actually white. For example, The Lady Chablis, a Savannah drag queen made famous in John Berendt's (1994) *Midnight in the Garden of Good and Evil*, often refers to herself as a "white woman." Berendt describes one of her performances as follows: "'I am not what I may appear to be,' she will say with apparent candor, adding, 'No, child, I am a heterosexual white woman. That's right, honey. Do not be fooled by what you see. When you look at me, you are lookin' at the Junior League. You are lookin' at an uptown white woman, and a pregnant uptown white woman at that'" (Berendt 1996:14). As a "pregnant uptown white woman," The Lady Chablis moves from being a gay African American who is biologically male and from a working-class background to being upper-class, white, heterosexual, and female. In her autobiography, The Lady Chablis refers to herself and a close circle of friends as the Savannah League of Uptown White Women (or SLUWW). SLUWW was formed "to honor the belief that all of us [the league members] is entitled to spend our days sitting up under hairdryers, going to lunch, and riding around town shopping—*all at somebody else's expense*" (1996:173; original emphasis). She defines an "uptown white woman" as "the persona of a classy, extravagant, and glamorous woman—big car, big rings, etc.," adding parenthetically, *"(This term can be used for all women regardless of color)"* (1996:175; original emphasis). The term *white woman* refers primarily to a class rather than an ethnic distinction and also collapses the categories of '"real" women' and 'drag queens'. Thus each of us has the potential to become an "uptown white woman," no matter what our sexual, racial, ethnic, or gender identity may be. Instead of suggesting a category based on sex or race, *white woman* indexes a prevailing ideology of gender, class, sexuality, and ethnicity that enforces a particular view of what constitutes "femininity" in U.S. culture.

The combination of particular identity stances (white, rich, female, and heterosexual) works to produce a cultural conception of what constitutes the feminine ideal. This ideal femininity is often associated with the idea of being a "lady." As Esther Newton (1979:127) notes, "Most female impersonators aspire to act like 'ladies,' and to call a woman a 'lady' is to confer the highest honor." The "white-woman" style of speech as used by AADQs represents a stereotype of the speech of middle-class white women, of how to talk "like a lady." This stereotype is closely tied to Robin Lakoff's notion of "women's language" (WL), which also depicts a stereotype of white middle-class women's speech, a fact that Lakoff herself recognized (1975:59). Mary Bucholtz and Kira Hall (1995) have noted the pervasiveness of WL as a hegemonic notion of gender-appropriate language. Because it is such a strong symbol of ideal femininity, WL is a powerful tool for performing female identity. For example, Lillian Glass (1992) reports that she used Lakoff's (1975) *Language and Woman's Place* in speech therapy with a male-to-female transsexual to produce gender-appropriate language use. Similarly, Jennifer Anne Stevens (1990) presents many of the features of WL in her guidebook for male-to-female transgenders. In addition to discussing issues of hormones and offering tips on choosing makeup and clothing, Stevens presents details about creating a feminine voice. Many elements of Lakoff's WL are included in the features of feminine speech that Stevens suggests, including tag questions, hedges, the use of "empty" adjectives, the absence of obscenities, and the use of intensive *so*.

Because of the power of WL as a stereotype of how middle-class white women talk (or "should" talk), I will use it as a basis for discussing the "white-woman" style of AADQs' speech. Here my use of the term *white-woman style* is intended to reflect this stereotyped representation rather than the real behavior of any actual white women.

Lakoff summarizes the main characteristics of WL as follows:

1. Women have a large stock of words related to their specific interests, generally relegated to them as "woman's work": *magenta . . . dart* (in sewing), and so on.
2. "Empty" adjectives like *divine, charming, cute*.
3. Question intonation where we might expect declaratives: for instance, tag questions ("It's so hot, isn't it?") and rising intonation in statement contexts ("What's your name, dear?" "Mary Smith?").
4. The use of hedges of various kinds. Women's speech seems in general to contain more instances of "well," "y'know," "kinda," and so forth.
5. Related to this is the intensive use of "so." Again, this is more frequent in women's than men's language.
6. Hypercorrect grammar: Women are not supposed to talk rough.
7. Superpolite forms: Women don't use off-color or indelicate expressions; women are the experts at euphemism.
8. Women don't tell jokes.
9. Women speak in italics [i.e., betray the fear that little attention is being paid to what they say]. (1975:53–56)

Of these nine elements of WL, AADQs utilize only the first six. Several of these, such as the use of precise color terms and "empty" adjectives, overlap with gay male speech. However, AADQs typically distinguish between the two styles. For example, the "empty" adjectives in the gay-male style of speaking are characteristically "gay," such as *flawless, fierce, fabulous*, and so on. In the "white-woman" style, the empty adjectives are more similar to those discussed by Lakoff. For example, in (2a) an AADQ asked why I was studying "drag language." When told that I was a linguist, she responded with *Oh, really, that's cute*, where *cute* seems fairly devoid of meaning. Example (2b), also from a Texas AADQ, provides further instances of intensifiers and "empty" adjectives (*really* and *cute*). (Note also the use of intensive *so* in example (2b).)[3]

(2a) A: . . . drag language? What is . . .
      B: He's a linguist . . . linguistic.
      A: (overlap) My brain is dead.
      A: Oh really . . . that's *cute*.
(2b)   Oh, my, my . . . I lost a ring y'all and I am <u>vixed</u> [= vexed]
          <u>Really</u> vixed, because . . .
          I have no idea where it is and I just bought that little ring and it's <u>so</u> <u>cute</u>.

Example (3) is taken from an interview with RuPaul on "The Arsenio Hall Show." This example demonstrates the use of final high intonation on declarative sentences (Lakoff's second characteristic of WL):

```
(3)  L    H    L              H*            L
     You guys, I wish there was a camera so I could remember
     H*    L                  H
     all the love you're sending to me
     L   H
     and the . .
     L                        H
     the love energy from over here.
     L    H*          L
     You're absolute the best.
```

In these examples, AADQs use careful, "Standard" English phonology. In other words, they use "correct" prescriptive pronunciations as opposed to phonological features stereotypically associated with AAVE. This "white-woman" style is the most common speaking style among AADQs, and the ability to use this style is considered vital to the success of AADQs' performances. The use of this style also distinguishes AADQs from other African American gay men. Thus it functions both to index stereotypes of white femininity and to construct a unique drag-queen identity that appropriates and reworks the symbols of "ideal" femininity.

Performing polyphonous identity

Although the use of the white-woman style of speaking is closely tied to ideals of expected feminine behavior, AADQs do not use it exclusively. If such speakers actually wanted to be white, one would expect them to use white women's speech in an attempt to gain the social standing afforded to white women. Frequently, however, they use the "white-woman" style as a type of dialect opposition (Morgan, chapter 1, this volume) in which this style is contrasted with other styles of speaking, primarily AAVE, to highlight social difference. In fact, the use of white women's speech among AADQs is itself a type of signifying. It indexes not only the social status or identity of white women but also the ability of a particular AADQ to use the "white-woman" style effectively. Most of the remaining examples are cases of polysemy created through dialect opposition, reflecting the ambiguity of signifying. These examples demonstrate that although the "white-woman" style is a vital characteristic of AADQs' identity, its use does not imply an underlying desire to be white. Rather, the white-woman style is one of numerous stylistic voices related to drag-queen identity and is used to create specific personas and changing identities throughout the course of a performance. Other stylistic choices, such as AAVE or gay male speech, are used to "interrupt" the white-woman style, to point out that it reflects a performed identity that may not correspond to the assumed biographical identity of the performer.

As noted earlier, AADQs do not adopt the last three characteristics of WL (avoiding off-color expressions, not telling jokes, and speaking in italics). Although all of the features of WL are related to "acting like a lady," these three are perhaps the most important keys to "ladylike" behavior. Lakoff notes that they may indicate that women realize "that they are not being listened to" (1975:56). One major difference between the "ladylike" behavior represented by WL and the behavior of AADQs is that "ladies" do not make themselves the center of attention, whereas drag queens often do little else. AADQs sometimes flaunt the fact that they do not meet the standard of proper middle-class women's behavior by using obscenities strategically. In example (4), a drag queen points out that she is not supposed to use words like *fuck* and *shit*, accentuating the fact that she deviates from the prescribed linguistic behavior of middle-class white women:

(4)   Are you ready to see some muscles? [audience yells]. . . . Some dick?
       Excuse me I'm not supposed to say that . . .
       words like that in the microphone . . .
       Like shit, fuck, and all that, you know?
       I am a Christian woman.
       I go to church.
       I'm *always* on my knees.

The statement *I'm always on my knees* is an instance of signifying in that it conveys double meaning. In the context of the utterance, it suggests that the speaker prays all the time. Because it is spoken by a drag queen in a gay bar, however, it also insinuates that she frequently performs oral sex on other men. The failure to have an ideal "ladylike" way of speaking (the use of obscenities) is paralleled in the failure to have appropriate "ladylike" sexual behavior. Here, the white-woman style co-occurs with obscenities that suggest the "falseness" of the performed white-woman identity. By creating two contrasting voices within a single discourse, the performer plays off of the disjuncture between performed ("female") and biographical ("male") identity.

In example (5), a Texas AADQ moves from speaking fairly "Standard" English in a high-pitched voice to using an exaggerated low-pitched voice to utter the phrase *Hey what's up, home boy* to an African American audience member. This monologue occurred in a gay bar with a predominantly white clientele. The switch serves to reaffirm the fact that the AADQ is African American and biologically male while simultaneously creating a sense of solidarity with the audience member to whom it is addressed. (Note: *a butt-fucking tea* is anything that is exceptionally good.)

(5)   Please welcome to the stage, our next dancer.
       He is a butt-fucking tea, honey
       He is hot.
       Masculine, muscled, and ready to put it to ya, baby.
       Anybody in here (.) hot (.) as (.) fish (.) grease?
       That's pretty hot, idn't it?
       (Switch to low pitch) Hey what's up, home boy? (Switches back)
       I'm sorry that fucking creole always come around when I don't need it.

The speaker apologizes with *that fucking creole always come around when I don't need it,* but the word *creole* is pronounced with a vocalized /l/, and the verb *come* is spoken without the "Standard" English /+s/ inflection. Thus, in apologizing for her use of AAVE (or "creole"), she continues to include features characteristic of AAVE in her speech (just as the apology for using an obscenity in example (4) involved the continued use of obscenities). This helps shape the statement as a form of signifying by implying that what is spoken does not really convey the full meaning of the utterance. The speaker's continued use of AAVE suggests that she has no intention of actually switching totally into "Standard" English (or of totally giving in to the performed white-woman identity symbolized by that variety of English).

Unlike the previous examples, example (6) is not typical of AADQs' performances. I include it here because it deals with a complex set of issues revolving around white stereotypes of African Americans. In this example, performed in an African American gay bar, an AADQ uses the "white-woman" style in acting out an attack on a rich white woman by an African American man. Acting out the rape of any woman is a misogynistic act; yet although this misogyny should not be excused, it is important to note that the main impetus for this piece of data is anger concerning the myth of the African American rapist. As Angela Davis has pointed out (1983), fraudulent charges of rape have historically been used as excuses for the murder (by lynching) of African American men. Because it is based on the racist stereotype of African Americans as having voracious sexual appetites, the myth of the African American rapist operates under the false assumption that rape is a primarily sexual act (and not primarily an act of violence). It assumes that all African American men are desirous of white women and are willing to commit acts of violence in order to feed this desire. The fact that this assumption has no basis is especially heightened in the context of African American gay men, who may not be desirous of *any* women. Nevertheless, the patrons of the bar must continuously deal with the ramifications of the myth of the Black rapist, including unfounded white fears of violence. Lines 1 through 21 present the attack on the white woman, in which the AADQ, in interaction with a male audience member who assists in the scene, uses the "white-woman" style alternating with AAVE as she moves in and out of the persona of a white woman:

(6)   1   I'm a rich white woman in {name of wealthy white neighborhood}
        2   and you're going to try to come after me, OK?
        3   And I want you to just . . .
        4   I'm going to be running, OK?
        5   And I'm gonna fall down, OK? OK?
        6   And I'm just gonna . . look at you . . .
        7   and you don't do anything.
        8   You hold the gun . . .
        9   Goddamn- he got practice. [audience laughter] <obscured>
      10   I can tell you're experienced.
           [The audience member holds the gun, but so that it faces down, not as if he were aiming it]
      11   OK hold it.

12   You know you know how to hold it, don't play it off . . .
13   Hold that gun . . . Shit . . . Goddamn . .
14   [Female audience member]: Hold that gun!
15   That's right fish! Hold that gun! Shit!
16   OK now, y'all, I'm fish, y'all, white fish witch!
17   And I'm gonna be running cause three Black men with big dicks chasing me!
18   [Points to audience member] He's the leader, OK?
19   Now you know I gotta fall, I want y'all to say, "Fall bitch!"
20   [Audience]: Fall bitch!
     [The AADQ falls, then rises, makes gasping sounds, alternating with "bum-
     biddy-bum" imitations of the type of music used in suspense scenes in movies
     and TV shows]
21   Now show me the gun!
     [The audience member holds up the gun and the AADQ performs an exagger-
     ated faint]

It is interesting to note that the man holding the gun does not "do anything" (lines 7–
8). Despite the AADQ's insinuation that he is "experienced" (line 10), the audience
member fails to hold the gun correctly until a woman in the audience yells at him
(line 14). The "white woman" pretends that "Black men with big dicks" are chasing
her through the park (line 17) and faints on seeing the man with the gun (line 21).
Thus, the African American man is basically passive throughout the exchange and
the "white woman" reacts primarily based on fear fed by racism.
    In the remainder of the segment, the corollary to the myth of the African Ameri-
can rapist is presented, the myth of the promiscuity of the African American woman
(Davis 1983:182). In lines 22 through 26, the same scene is acted out with an "African American woman" (speaking primarily in a tough, streetwise "bangee girl" style
of AAVE) rather than a "white woman." The "African American woman," on seeing the large feet of the man with the gun (which implies he has a large penis as well),
consents to having sex with him, saying that the gun is unnecessary (lines 25–26):

22   Now this Black fish . . . . .
23   <obscured> Black men's running after her . .
24   I ain't no *boy*! Fuck y'all! Fuck y'all mother fuckers!
     [AADQ looks at the gun]
25   You don't have to use that baby, I see them size feet.
26   Come on! Come on!

To focus only on the inescapable misogyny of this example is to miss its political complexity. The performance also touches all aspects of the myth of the
African American rapist, the racist assumptions concerning both the "pure and frag-
ile nature" of white women as "standards of morality" and the "bestial nature" of
African American women and men. In this highly political performance, the drag
queen moves in and out of the personas of narrator, director, and actor in the drama
she is creating. She performs a variety of identities indexed by a variety of linguis-

tic styles to undermine a variety of stereotypes and prejudices that are all too familiar to her audience.

Conclusion

The examples discussed above suggest that the use of white women's speech by AADQs cannot be interpreted as simply reflecting a desire to be white. The femininity associated with speaking like a "white woman" simultaneously indexes a set of class, gender, and ethnic identities associated with the ideology of what constitutes "ideal" feminine behavior. Although the "white-woman" style is sometimes emblematic of status, it is also used in combination with other stylistic choices to highlight a variety of more critical attitudes toward whiteness. Thus the appropriation of aspects of dominant culture need not necessarily indicate acceptance of its dominating force. Rather, this appropriation can serve as a form of resistance (Butler 1993:137). Indeed, in some cases the appropriation of white women's language does succeed in undermining racist and homophobic assumptions associated with the dominant culture. But arguments concerning the misogyny of drag cannot be brushed aside simply because drag is sometimes subversive. Although the examples in this chapter suggest a form of resistance toward racism and homophobia, they do little to call into question the sexism in American society. The performances of AADQs should not be understood simply as "subversive" or "submissive" with regard to dominant hegemonic culture. The polyphony of stylistic voices and the identities they index serve to convey multiple meanings that may vary across contexts and speakers. A full understanding of a phenomenon such as drag requires that we follow the advice of Claudia Mitchell-Kernan and "attend to all potential meaning-carrying symbolic systems in speech events—the total universe of discourse" (1972:166).

NOTES

This chapter is dedicated to the memory of Grainger Sanders (1954–1994). Grainger inspired this research and assisted both in collecting data and in shaping my understanding of AADQs. I could never have thanked him enough. Additional thanks to Gregory Clay, Kathryn Semolic, and Keith Walters. An earlier version of this chapter (Barrett 1994) was presented at the Third Berkeley Women and Language Conference. For different but complementary analyses of some of these data, see also Barrett (1995, 1998).

1. The terms *transgenderist* and *transgender(ed) person* are often used as umbrella terms for members of these different groups. They are sometimes seen as alternatives to terms with medical connotations, such as *transvestite* and *transsexual*.

2. Following community norms for polite reference, I use *she* to refer to drag queens when they are in drag.

3. Transcription conventions are as follows:

< >   obscured material

[ ]   text-external information

{ }	segment removed from data to ensure anonymity
italics	emphasis
H	high intonation (see McLemore 1991)
L	low intonation
H*/L*	pitch accent
(.)	short pause forming separation between words
. . .	longer pause (more periods indicate greater length)
<u>underlining</u>	material under discussion

REFERENCES

Abrahams, Roger D. (1976). *Talking black*. Rowley, MA: Newbury House.

Ackroyd, Peter (1979). *Dressing up—Transvestism and drag: The history of an obsession*. New York: Simon & Schuster.

Bakhtin, Mikhail M. (1981). *The dialogic imagination*. Ed. Michael Holquist. Trans. Caryl Emerson & Michael Holquist. Austin: University of Texas Press.

——— (1984). *Problems of Dostoevsky's poetics*. Ed. & trans. Caryl Emerson. Minneapolis: University of Minneapolis Press.

Barrett, Rusty (1994). "She is NOT white woman!": The appropriation of white women's language by African American drag queens. In Mary Bucholtz, A. C. Liang, Laurel Sutton, & Caitlin Hines (eds.), *Cultural performances: Proceedings of the Third Berkeley Women and Language Conference*. Berkeley, CA: Berkeley Women and Language Group, 1–14.

——— (1995). Supermodels of the world, unite!: Political economy and the language of performance among African American drag queens. In William L. Leap (ed.), *Beyond the lavender lexicon: Authenticity, imagination and appropriation in lesbian and gay languages*. Newark: Gordon & Breach, 207–226.

——— (1998). Markedness and style switching in performances by African American drag queens. In Carol Myers-Scotton (ed.), *Linguistic choices as social messages*. New York: Oxford University Press, 139–161.

Bauman, Richard (1977). *Verbal art as performance*. Prospect Heights, IL: Waveland Press.

Beame, Thom (1983). Racism from a black perspective. In Michael J. Smith (ed.), *Black men, white men*. San Francisco: Gay Sunshine Press, 57–62.

Berendt, John (1994). *Midnight in the garden of good and evil*. New York: Random House.

——— (1996). Introduction: Chablis and me. In The Lady Chablis with Theodore Bouloukos, *Hiding my candy: The autobiography of the grand empress of Savannah*. New York: Pocket Books, 12–18.

Boykin, Keith (1996). *One more river to cross: Black and gay in America*. New York: Anchor Books.

Briggs, Charles L. (1988). *Competence in performance: The creativity of tradition in Mexicano verbal art*. Philadelphia: University of Pennsylvania Press.

Bucholtz, Mary (1995). From mulatta to mestiza: Passing and the linguistic reshaping of ethnic identity. In Kira Hall & Mary Bucholtz (eds.), *Gender articulated: Language and the socially constructed self*. New York: Routledge, 351–373.

Bucholtz, Mary, & Kira Hall (1995). Introduction: Twenty years after *Language and woman's place*. In Kira Hall & Mary Bucholtz (eds.), *Gender articulated: Language and the socially constructed self*. New York: Routledge, 1–22.

Bullough, Vern L., & Bonnie Bullough (1993). *Cross dressing, sex, and gender*. Philadelphia: University of Pennsylvania Press.

Butler, Judith (1990). *Gender trouble: Feminism and the subversion of identity.* New York: Routledge.

———— (1993). *Bodies that matter: On the discursive limits of "sex."* New York: Routledge.

Davies, Bronwyn, & Rom Harré (1990). Positioning: The discursive production of selves. *Journal for the Theory of Social Behaviour* 20(1):43–63.

Davis, Angela (1983). *Women, race and class.* New York: Random House.

DeMarco, Joe (1983). Gay racism. In Michael J. Smith (ed.), *Black men, white men.* San Francisco: Gay Sunshine Press, 109–118.

Duberman, Martin (1993). *Stonewall.* New York: Dutton.

Eckert, Penelope, & Sally McConnell-Ginet (1992). Think practically and look locally: Language and gender as community-based practice. *Annual Review of Anthropology* 21:461–490.

Feinberg, Leslie (1996). *Transgender warriors: Making history from Joan of Arc to RuPaul.* Boston: Beacon Press.

Fleisher, Julian (1996). *The drag queens of New York: An illustrated field guide.* New York: Riverhead Books.

Frye, Marilyn (1983). *The politics of reality: Essays in feminist theory.* Trumansburg, NY: Crossing Press.

Garber, Marjorie (1992). *Vested interests: Cross-dressing and cultural anxiety.* New York: Routledge.

Gates, Henry Louis, Jr. (1988). *The signifying monkey: A theory of African-American literary criticism.* Oxford: Oxford University Press.

Gilbert, Sandra M. (1982). Costumes of the mind: Transvestism as metaphor in modern literature. In Elizabeth Abel (ed.), *Writing and sexual difference.* Chicago: University of Chicago Press, 193–220.

Glass, Lillian (1992). *He says, she says: Closing the communication gap between the sexes.* New York: Putnam.

Hall, Kira (1995). Lip service on the fantasy lines. In Kira Hall & Mary Bucholtz (eds.), *Gender articulated: Language and the socially constructed self.* New York: Routledge, 183–216.

Harper, Phillip Brian (1993). Eloquence and epitaph: Black nationalism and the homophobic impulse in responses to the death of Max Robinson. In Michael Warner (ed.), *Fear of a queer planet: Queer politics and social theory.* Minneapolis: University of Minnesota Press, 239–263.

Hilbert, Jeffrey (1995). The politics of drag. In Corey K. Creekmur & Alexander Doty (eds.), *Out in culture: Gay, lesbian and queer essays on popular culture.* Durham, NC: Duke University Press, 463–469.

hooks, bell (1989). *Talking back: Thinking feminist, thinking Black.* Boston: South End Press.

Hymes, Dell (1981). *"In vain I tried to tell you": Essays in Native American ethnopoetics.* Philadelphia: University of Pennsylvania Press.

Kroskrity, Paul V. (1993). *Language, history, and identity: Ethnolinguistic studies of the Arizona Tewa.* Tucson: University of Arizona Press.

Labov, William (1972). *Language in the inner city: Studies in the Black English Vernacular.* Philadelphia: University of Pennsylvania Press.

The Lady Chablis, with Theodore Bouloukos (1996). *Hiding my candy: The autobiography of the grand empress of Savannah.* New York: Pocket Books.

Lakoff, Robin (1975). *Language and woman's place.* New York: Harper & Row.

Le Page, R. B., & Andrée Tabouret-Keller (1985). *Acts of identity: Creole-based approaches to language and ethnicity.* Cambridge: Cambridge University Press.

Lurie, Allison (1981). *The language of clothes.* New York: Random House.

MacKenzie, Gordene Olga (1994). *Transgender nation.* Bowling Green, OH: Bowling Green State University Popular Press.

Marcus, Eric (1992). *Making history: The struggle for gay and lesbian equal rights 1945–1990: An oral history.* New York: Harper & Row.

McElhinny, Bonnie S. (1995). Challenging hegemonic masculinities: Female and male police officers handling domestic violence. In Kira Hall & Mary Bucholtz (eds.), *Gender articulated: Language and the socially constructed self.* New York: Routledge, 217–243.

McLemore, Cynthia Ann (1991). The pragmatic interpretation of English intonation: Sorority speech. Ph.D. diss., University of Texas, Austin.

Mitchell-Kernan, Claudia (1972). Signifying and marking: Two Afro-American speech acts. In John J. Gumperz & Dell Hymes (eds.), *Directions in sociolinguistics.* New York: Holt, Rinehart & Winston, 161–179.

Monteiro, Kenneth P., & Vincent Fuqua (1994). African American gay youth: One form of manhood. *High School Journal* 77(1–2):20–36.

Morgan, Marcyliena (1991). Indirectness and interpretation in African American women's discourse. *Pragmatics* 1(4):421–435.

Newton, Esther (1979). *Mother camp: Female impersonation in America.* Chicago: University of Chicago Press.

Ochs, Elinor (1992). Indexing gender. In Alessandro Duranti & Charles Goodwin (eds.), *Rethinking context.* Cambridge: Cambridge University Press, 335–358.

Peterson, John L. (1992). Black men and their same-sex desires and behaviors. In Gilbert Herdt (ed.), *Gay culture in America: Essays from the field.* Boston: Beacon Press, 87–106.

Preston, Dennis (1992). Talking black and talking white: A study in variety imitation. In Joan H. Hall, Nick Doane, & Dick Ringler (eds.), *Old English and new: Studies in language and linguistics in honor of Frederic G. Cassidy.* New York: Garland, 327–354.

Raymond, Janice (1994). *The transsexual empire: The making of the she-male.* New York: Teachers College Press. (Original work published 1979)

——— (1996). The politics of transgenderism. In Richard Ekins & Dave King (eds.), *Blending genders: Social aspects of cross-dressing and sex-changing.* New York: Routledge, 215–223.

RuPaul (1995). *Lettin it all hang out: An autobiography.* New York: Hyperion.

Showalter, Elaine (1983). Critical cross-dressing: Male feminists and the woman of the year. *Raritan* 3(2):130–149.

Simmons, Ron (1991). Tongues untied: An interview with Marlon Riggs. In Essex Hemphill (ed.), *Brother to brother: New writings by Black gay men.* Boston: Alyson, 189–199.

Smith, Max C. (1986). By the year 2000. In Joseph Beam (ed.), *In the life: A Black gay anthology.* Boston: Alyson, 224–229.

Smitherman, Geneva (1977). *Talkin and testifyin: The language of black America.* Boston: Houghton Mifflin.

Stevens, Jennifer Anne (1990). *From masculine to feminine and all points in between: A practical guide for transvestites, cross-dressers, transgenderists, transsexuals, and others who choose to develop a more feminine image . . . and for the curious and concerned.* Cambridge, MA: Different Path Press.

Tinney, James S. (1986). Why a gay Black church? In Joseph Beam (ed.), *In the life: A Black gay anthology.* Boston: Alyson, 70–86.

Trudgill, Peter (1983). *On dialect: Social and geographical perspectives.* New York: New York University Press.

Walters, Keith (1996). Contesting representations of African American language. In Risako Ide, Rebecca Parker, & Yukako Sunaoshi (eds.), *SALSA III: Proceedings of the Third Annual Symposium about Language and Society—Austin (Texas Linguistics Forum* 36). Austin: University of Texas, Department of Linguistics, 137–151.

White, Edmund (1980). The political vocabulary of homosexuality. In Leonard Michaels & Christopher Ricks (eds.), *The state of the language*. Berkeley: University of California Press, 235–246.

Williamson, Judith (1986). *Consuming passions: The dynamics of popular culture*. London: Marion Boyars.

Woolard, Kathryn (1995). Gendered peer groups and the bilingual repertoire in Catalonia. In Pamela Silberman & Jonathan Loftin (eds.), *SALSA II: Proceedings of the Second Annual Symposium about Language and Society—Austin (Texas Linguistics Forum 35)*. Austin: University of Texas, Department of Linguistics, 200–220.

"She Sired Six Children"

Feminist Experiments with Linguistic Gender

> I utterly refuse to mangle English by inventing a pronoun for 'he/she'. "He" is the generic pronoun, damn it.
> —Ursula Le Guin, "Is Gender Necessary?" (1979)

> I dislike the so-called generic pronouns "he/him/his" which exclude women from discourse. . . . "They/them/their" should be restored . . . and let the pedants and pundits squeak and gibber in the streets.
> —Ursula Le Guin, "Is Gender Necessary? Redux" (1989)

A recurring theme for feminist novelists of the 1970s was the question of pronouns. Feminist theorist Elaine Morgan notes that if you use the pronoun *he* in a book about the history of man, "before you are halfway through the first chapter a mental image of this evolving creature begins to form in your mind. It will be a male image and he will be the hero of the story" (quoted in Spender 1980:151). Morgan comments that the use of *he* is "a simple matter of linguistic convenience" which, given the context, is clearly intended ironically, for the use of generic *he* is neither simple nor convenient. She goes on to remark that she longs to find a book that begins, "When the first ancestor of the human race descended from the trees, she had not yet developed the mighty brain that was to distinguish her so sharply from other species." If the feminine pronoun in Morgan's imaginary textbook produces a sense of shock, this reaction indicates that the reader has, despite the lack of overt markers of masculinity, nevertheless imagined a man. Thus the use of the generic *he* is no simple matter. Nor is it clear that linguistic convenience would cause one to choose the pronoun *he* to anaphorize *man*. This choice is more a matter of gender concord, since singular *they* is the pronoun of preference in informal speech (where convenience might be said to outweigh elegance) to anaphorize indefinite antecedents: *Everyone loves their mother.* Most theorists have rejected the substitution of the female pronoun for the male, believing that this would merely turn the problem around without solving it.[1]

In some cases the epicene (common-gender) but impossibly formal-sounding *one* is used in preference to generic *he* or "singular *they*," the latter still considered ungrammatical by purists and contemporary linguistic watchdogs.[2] Writing in French, Monique Wittig makes the epicene *on* the hero/ine of *L'Opoponax* (1964), her first novel, where, in keeping with standard spoken French, the pronoun takes the place of all three persons, both singular and plural, at different times, depending on context. Although this strategy works admirably in French, in English *one* (*on*'s nearest equivalent) sounds stuffy and scholastic. Writing of *on* and *one*, Wittig claims, "There is in French, as there is in English, a munificent pronoun . . . not marked by gender, a pronoun that you are taught in school to systematically avoid" (1986:68). She complains that the English translator Helen Weaver had absorbed the lesson on avoiding *one* so well that she "managed never to use it" in the translation of *L'Opoponax*. Wittig admits that English *one* "sounds and looks very heavy" but, she claims, "no less so in French." This is, however, simply not the case. French teachers tell their pupils not to use *on* in writing because it sounds colloquial, uneducated, marked for the spoken language. In contrast, in English *one* is often encouraged in formal writing as having a more impersonal, scholarly, and therefore more authoritative voice. With regard to register, *on* and *one* are not equivalents but opposites. Elsewhere, Wittig (1992) employs *one* as an indefinite pronoun, sometimes inclusive of, at other times in contrast to, the subject pronoun *I*:

(1) The only thing to do is to stand on one's own feet as an escapee . . .
(2) One must accept that my point of view may appear crude . . .
(3) First one must step out of the tracks . . .
(4) One might have to do without . . .

Although the use of indefinite *one* in examples (1), (3), and (4) sounds merely old-fashioned and rather aristocratic (to my British ears), the use of indefinite *one* and the deictic *my* to indicate the same referent in example (2) is incongruous because instead of forming an integral part of that body of persons encapsulated in *one*, the first person has been explicitly excluded. In French, on the other hand, the same sentence (*On doit accepter que mon point de vue paraisse grossier*) is acceptable. French *on* resists the grammatical imperative to provide gender information about the referent, but English *one*, though equally epicene, is not nearly so versatile, being restricted both by register (formal) and reference (inclusive of speaker).[3]

Writing of the century-long search for an epicene third-person pronoun, of which he gives more than eighty examples from more than 200 sources between 1850 and 1985, Dennis Baron (1986) dismisses the whole endeavor as "The Word that Failed," the heading for his tenth chapter. Indeed, he states explicitly, "the creation of a common gender pronoun to replace the generic masculine 'he' . . . stands out as the (linguistic reform) most often attempted and the one that has most often failed" (1986:190). This condemnation of failure is interesting. If success is to be measured only by the entry of one of these pronouns into everyday language, then the attempt has indeed failed, although Baron's own impressive list of contenders is testimony to the depth and longevity of concern about the issue. Yet singular *they* has shown a dogged resistance to the attempts of conservative grammarians to eradicate it, whereas the various invented pronouns such as *ne/nis/ner*, *ho/hom/hos*, and *shis/shim/shims/ shimself* exist only in the articles exhorting their use.

Baron is concerned not with literary uses of epicene pronouns but with their up-take in the language at large. This is, of course, a perfectly reasonable distinction. The carefully selected, gracefully formulated phrases of fiction bear little resemblance to spontaneous speech with its vivid lexicon and distinct syntactic structure. One cannot make valid claims about the spoken language by considering the literary texts produced by its speakers. Nevertheless, the role of literature in introducing, promoting, and popu-larizing specific words and phrases cannot be dismissed. Where would we be without the *malapropism*, so called after Mrs. Malaprop of *The Rivals*, whose every second word was *mal à propos* (not to the point)? Would the phrase *Big Brother is watching you* ever have seemed sinister without George Orwell's *1984*? As Laurel Sutton makes plain in her contribution to this volume (chapter 8), the planned language of writers can provide useful insights into language ideology (see also Inoue 1994).

Let us turn to a consideration of the work of feminist novelists who took up the challenge of the generic masculine, creating ingenious responses to the masculine pre-rogative in their own novels. In *The Kin of Ata Are Waiting for You* (1971), Dorothy Bryant proposes *kin*, unmarked for either gender or number; in *The Cook and the Car-penter* (1973), June Arnold introduces *na, nan*, and *naself*; in *Woman on the Edge of Time* (1976), Marge Piercy uses *person* as subject pronoun and *per* as object pronoun and possessive. Ursula Le Guin's science-fiction novel *The Left Hand of Darkness* (1969), which features the generic masculine *he* for the ambisexual Gethenians, caused such a storm that she was obliged to respond. (Her responses are discussed at length later.) Since three of these novels have been continuously in print for almost 20 years and all four have sold thousands of copies, they can hardly be said to have failed. Each time a reader encounters the neologisms *kin, na*, or *per*, she or he is obliged to grapple with the ideological motivation behind these terms: Why have these pronouns been invented? What is wrong with the traditional pronouns they replace? What purpose do the neologisms serve? What effect do they have? Against a 1970s backdrop of identity politics, in which gender was a crucial ingredient, what did it mean to withhold gender information? Insofar as the aim of each author was to raise these questions, the neolo-gistic pronouns work and keep working each time the books are read.

Baron uses a quotation from Mary Daly as an epigraph to his chapter on epicene neologisms: "It is a mistake to fixate on the third person singular." In the context of a chapter entitled "The Word that Failed," this quotation might mean that it is a mis-take to be obsessed with the generic *he*, since there are other, more important prob-lems to be solved in the feminist struggle. However, in the original text from which the quotation comes, Daly continues by referring to Monique Wittig's description of how the first-person singular excludes women: "'I' [*Je*] as a generic feminine sub-ject can only enter by force into a language which is foreign to it, for all that is human (masculine) is foreign to it, the human not being feminine grammatically speaking but he [*il*] or they [*ils*]" (Wittig quoted in Daly 1979:18–19). Daly's point, then, is not that it is a mistake to point out the sexism of pronouns but that the third-person singular should not be singled out for criticism.[4] It is an important point, be-cause all the writers considered in this chapter aim to highlight, each in different ways, the linguistic derogation of women and to redress the balance to some extent by the effect their fiction has on the reader. None "fixate on the third person singular."

As Le Guin recalls in the introduction to the 1976 edition of *The Left Hand of Darkness*, in the mid-1960s she was caught up in a "groundswell of feminist activity" and felt a need to define for herself the meaning of gender and sexuality. This was a period in which women were questioning all their previous assumptions about the relationship between the sexes and the role of women. Consciousness-raising groups were mushrooming, and new solutions to old problems such as childbearing, child rearing, and family life were discussed with extraordinary vigor and energy. It was in this political climate that Le Guin wrote *The Left Hand of Darkness* (1969), a novel set among the androgynous people of Gethen whose bodies, for two-thirds of each month, are ungendered. During the last third of the month they enter "kemmer," the human equivalent of being in heat. Female or male genitalia develop when they come in contact with another Gethenian in kemmer, but they never know in advance which genital formation they will exhibit. A Gethenian who has borne three children may sire two more, for example. As the quotations that head this chapter show, Gethen brought with it the thorny problem of which pronouns to use to refer to such sexless/ duosexual beings. Le Guin's initial solution was to use the masculine generic.

In the novel an Investigator from the Ekumen (an observer with both a political and an anthropological function) voices the author's views on pronouns. As in any work of fiction, author and narrator are separate entities, often with distinct or opposing worldviews and their own ethos. In the following passage, however, Le Guin's 1976 view of the role of the generic masculine (seen in Le Guin 1979 as well) may be heard in the voice of the narrator/Investigator: "You cannot think of a Gethenian as 'it'. They are not neuters. They are potentials or integrals." Instead, the Investigator asserts, "I must use 'he', for the same reasons as we used the masculine pronoun in referring to a transcendent god: it is less defined, less specific, than the neuter or the feminine" (1976:70). The Investigator remarks further that the use of the masculine generic pronoun leads her to think of Gethenians as men rather than as men-women. However, her presumption of masculinity goes beyond the ambisexual Gethenians, for when she speaks of the as-yet-unappointed envoy from the Ekumen, she again uses the masculine pronoun. She assumes the envoy will be male, predisposing readers of her dispatch to appoint a man. This problem apparently does not exist in the language of the Gethenians. We are told that they rejoice in a "human pronoun" that encodes information regarding number and animacy but not gender. In another telling passage, Le Guin shows that she is at some level aware that masculine pronouns prompt a masculine reading. In the opening scene, the envoy from the Ekumen reports on a parade and introduces an unknown member of the crowd as "the person on my left." The character is subsequently referred to as *this person*, the demonstrative *this* providing a referential link to the first mention. In the next sentence the anaphoric *his* is used to refer to the person's forehead: "Wiping sweat from his dark forehead the man—*man* I must say, having said *he* and *his* . . ." (1976:11). If the pronoun *he* had truly been generic, there would have been a choice of feminine or masculine designation, but the envoy insists that he has no choice but to call the person a man; only men may be referred to as *he*.

Le Guin was roundly criticized by feminist readers and reviewers in the late 1960s and the 1970s for her use of the generic masculine. In response to this criticism she published "Is Gender Necessary?" (1979), the article from which the quotation that opens this chapter comes. She argues that while the generic masculine is problematic, it is less restricted than either the feminine *she* or the neutral *it* and far preferable to the invention of clumsy neologisms. The story, however, did not end with this statement, and neither did feminist criticism. The groundswell of feminist activism launched itself on the language. By the mid-1970s, the French Mouvement de Libération des Femmes was grappling with the importance of semiotics and other signifying systems to the construction of the concept 'woman'. Their American cousins, having taken upon themselves the task of reassessing the world, the history of consciousness, and the individual psyche from the new feminist perspective of a woman-centered ontology, followed in the footsteps of the French and turned to an analysis of ideology and its linguistic base. In reaction, Le Guin, being part of this new period of activism, produced a piece of informed self-criticism in an essay written in 1989 (from which comes the second quotation that heads this chapter). This essay would be interesting for its structure alone—a *sous-rature* approach which preserves the original 1979 essay but adds a commentary bracketed in italics. This procedure allows the reader to see the development in Le Guin's thinking, a reminder that one had to go there to get here. The 1989 voice argues with its earlier self. The earlier voice states that pronouns were really not the issue and that had she made the female side of the Gethenians more prominent, these androgynous beings would not have struck readers as purely masculine. The later voice turns this statement around: "If I had realized how the pronoun I used shaped, directed, controlled my own thinking, I might have been cleverer" (1989:15). The 1989 voice has absorbed contemporary radical feminist and social-constructionist reworkings of the Sapir-Whorf hypothesis and applied it to her fiction.[5]

Le Guin's commentary poses the thorny question: What can a novelist do when she realizes 20 years later that she disagrees with herself, especially when her former position has been quoted "with cries of joy" (1989:7) by adverse critics? She can write a public recantation, as Le Guin did, but it was too late to revise the novel itself. It was definitely too late to revise it. However, Le Guin found an ingenious two-pronged literary solution to the problem of having one's past remain alive in one's present. Her first response was to reprint "Winter's King" ([1969] 1975), a story that was set on the planet of Gethen and that had actually predated *The Left Hand of Darkness*. This time, however, she used feminine pronouns throughout, although she was (in 1975) still adamantly opposed to invented pronouns. To refer to indefinite antecedents, Le Guin retained the use of the generic masculine.

The semantic clashes that result from the unvarying use of feminine pronouns in "Winter's King" are highly amusing, especially when juxtaposed with those caused by the use of masculine nouns and pronouns in *The Left Hand of Darkness*:

The Left Hand of Darkness (1969)	"Winter's King" (1975)
My landlady, a voluble man (38)	the young king had her back against a wall (94)
the king was pregnant[6] (73)	the ex-king of Karhide knew herself a barbarian (110)
a paranoid pregnant king and an egomaniac regent (82)	"Prince Emran is well. She is with her attendants" (99)
it certainly was difficult to imagine him as a young mother (85)	She sired six children (117)

In the novel men get pregnant; in the short story women sire children. It is hard to believe that these early exercises in gender-bending and blending, a sexual mix and match, provoked only righteous anger when their comic aspect is so apparent. The laughter produced by the clash between the generic femininity or masculinity of these examples and the biological facts and cultural identities usually restricted to the other sex points to the subversiveness of Le Guin's pronoun choice (see also Barrett, chapter 16, this volume).

The second solution Le Guin devised was to introduce invented pronouns in the 1985 screenplay of *The Left Hand of Darkness*, although she remarks that these were modeled on a British dialect and were therefore not entirely her creations (1989). The pronouns in question, *a/un/a's*, replacing *she/her/hers* or *he/him/his*, were accepted quite happily when read aloud, although some members of the audience to whom she presented this solution commented that the subject pronoun *a* sounded too like a Southern American *I*. Even here, however, Le Guin is still uneasy with the use of grammatical neologism. Although these pronouns may be acceptable in a screenplay, a guide for oral performance, they would, she hypothesizes, "drive the reader mad in print" (1989:15). This distaste for written neologisms is interesting in an author famous for her contribution to science fiction, a genre that revels in neologism. Indeed, her 1985 novel *Always Coming Home* includes a twelve-page glossary of invented vocabulary of the Kesh, an imaginary native Northern Californian culture. Le Guin's 20-year struggle to find appropriate pronominal anaphors for her anatomically unique Gethenians and her changes of heart and ideology attest to more than a commitment to feminist endeavor on the part of the novelist. The difficulty of the task itself demonstrates that, in contrast to the creation of lexical neologisms so frequent in science fiction, messing with a morphosyntactic staple such as the pronominal system brings with it problems that will affect the whole structure of the discourse.

Although Le Guin was the earliest of the writers in this chapter to grapple with questions of language and gender, by the mid-1970s several American novelists participating actively in the women's liberation movement were putting feminist ideas to work in their fiction. For example, in the language of Dorothy Bryant's (1971) Kin of Ata, *kin* is the only pronoun. Although inanimate objects are carefully divided into feminine and masculine, heterosexually paired in all arrangements from building to planting to eating, there are no pronouns for 'she' and 'he'. There are words for the concepts 'woman' and 'man', but these are seldom used, and there is only one pronoun for all human beings, which makes no distinction of gender or number. So far this is not particularly unusual for a pronoun (after all, English *you* and, as we have seen, French *on* encode neither number nor gender). Speakers use the Atan pronoun both in the second person and the vocative, however, and in the third person "they referred to one or more people by it" (1971:50). It was used "the way most people use brother" (50), except that *brother* is specifically masculine and singular. Bryant provides no examples of Atan, explaining that it has no written form.

Bryant's description of this pronoun's properties provides an insight into feminist views of the pronominal ideal. In the language of the Kin of Ata, it is possible to distinguish women from men at the lexical level, but the pronominal system distinguishes only between the animate and the inanimate. Not only are gender and number elided, but so are second and third persons (first-person reference is not mentioned). The second person is deictic—that is, the identity of the referent may be derived only from the context of utterance. The third person, in contrast, classifies the referent as a nonparticipant in the discourse (Benveniste 1966a, b). *Kin* would thus collapse two of the categories that have been perceived as fundamental to the pronominal function. How such a system might work is hard to imagine. Its promotion as an ideal of human communication is, however, instructive. A pronoun that did not change according to person, gender, or number would presuppose an extremely homogeneous community where such distinctions were mere nuances that could easily be discerned from context. The pronominal function itself would be reduced to that of a placeholder for the verb, a sign indicating "verb coming."

Aspects of *kin* are to be seen in the pronominal systems devised by other novelists. Although *kin* itself is unique to Bryant's work, ideological homogeneity, egalitarianism, and the absence of sex-role segregation were ideals dear to June Arnold and Marge Piercy. Whereas Bryant merely describes the pronoun of Ata, both Arnold and Piercy employ their epicene neologisms in their respective novels, allowing us the opportunity of a more extensive analysis. They do not, however, banish the traditional pronouns but provide a complex interplay between the two systems. The moments when the systems combine, or collide, are of great significance in each book. The epicene pronouns must be considered in terms of the whole pronominal system of each novel because they cause a redrawing of the distinctions made by all other pronominals. Whereas Le Guin opposed the introduction of grammatical neologisms because their unfamiliar forms render them so noticeable, Arnold and Piercy use this foregrounding effect to emphasize their points.

Arnold's *The Cook and the Carpenter* (1973), unlike the novels previously discussed, is set not on a science-fictional world but in a large town in Texas. The choice of setting removes ideas of gender and language from the arena of the fantastic and places them in the dust of everyday life. This move toward realism closes down, to a certain extent, the number of possible meanings of the text. Indeed, parts of Arnold's story are based closely on actual events that took place during the occupation of a disused police building at 330 East Fifth Street in New York City from January 1 to January 13, 1971, by a group of radical feminists. (The location is now a parking lot for police officers of the Ninth Precinct.)

Arnold's story begins as a woman comes to warn a group of people who have just moved to town that local residents plan to throw them out. From the opening line, Arnold introduces the pronouns *na* and *nan* without any preamble: "'You know Texas. Do you think it's true?' the cook had asked an hour ago. The carpenter's answer was forgotten in nan pursuit of truth." *Nan* slips in without explanation, leaving readers to make of it what they may. This strategy is intended to naturalize the pronouns, so that the lack of gender distinctions appears as an unproblematized status quo. As we will see further on, however, even Arnold found the neologisms unwieldy and turned to other tactics to avoid gender disclosure.

Three-quarters of the way through the novel, the group occupies a school and plans to use its ample rooms to provide health, education, and other services to the local population. Inevitably, the police come and arrest the occupiers. During the scene of the arrests, epicene pronouns prevail. In the following passage, for example, it is impossible to tell by grammatical means the gender of the deputies or Leslie: "A hand covered Leslie's nose and mouth, pushing into *nan* face; one deputy easily dragged *na* to the car; another followed by the side, whacking Leslie's body wherever *nan* stick could land" (1973:139). However, after the group has been thrown into holding cells for the night, the traditional third-person pronouns assert themselves and the neologisms are discontinued: "The sergeant pushed Three to the floor and, with *his* foot on *her* back, told the policewoman to take off *her* shoes, pull down *her* pants" (139). The questions of why the epicene pronouns are used and why traditional pronouns take over are thus planted implicitly in the text. The reader discovers that the group members are in fact all women, since all now have female pronouns assigned to them. It is by the telling phrase *with his foot on her back* that everything changes. The nongendered pronouns cannot hold out against such an onslaught; the men have won. Gender is indeed central if it means one sex has its foot on the other's back.

The epicene pronouns are backed by a battery of epicene noun phrases: *a person*, for example, is resumed as *the speaker* and *the white-haired one* (7–8), the women's liberation movement is referred to as *people who share the group's politics* (45); men as *those others* (61). Occasionally this usage sounds a little stilted: "You let that one look, now let me" (35). Instead of *that one* a pronoun would seem more natural: "You let her/him/na look, now let me." But the traditional pronoun *she* or *he* would, of course, reveal the gender of the referent, and only members of the group occupying the school use the epicene pronouns in their own speech; it is a mark of in-group status, which the narrator shares but the townsfolk do not. To use the neologisms *na* and *nan* is to place oneself inside the women's group, to declare one's identification with the feminist ideology. Because readers, in order to understand the text, are obliged to make the conceptual link between separatist practice and gender-neutral pronouns, they too are required to identify with the women's group, or at least to read from the women's position.

We later discover that the person who says, "You let that one look," insisting with prurient interest on seeing a diagram of female genital organs, is the male deputy sheriff, to whom epicene pronouns are unknown. The connection between the use of epicene pronouns and the possession of a feminist consciousness is underlined by an incident during which the status quo is overturned. It occurs early on in the novel, when the women's group is still flourishing unhindered and the epicene pronouns prevail. One day, while the children are playing, their cries become highly charged and sex-specific. At this point, instead of the epicene term *children*, they are referred to as *girls* and *boys*:

> "I am a tiger!" a boy cried.
> "I am a lion!" a second boy said. . . .
> "I'm an eagle!" a girl's voice shouted.
> "Goose!" a boy's voice threw back. (55)

This game quickly degenerates into name-calling:

> "Bitch!"
> "Bitch!" . . .
> "Pussy!"

"Pussy!"

"Cock!"

The small female voice grew weaker and shriller; the small male voices boomed like those of ordained men. (56)

Even in the women's group, sexual divisions come to the fore when the little boys begin to act like grown men. It is then not possible to refer to them as an undifferentiated group of "children." This scene makes apparent on the linguistic level conflicts that have also begun to emerge on the political level, as seen in the fraught relations between the women's group and the outside world. The women are trying to bring up nonsexist children in a nonsexist environment, of which the nongendered pronouns are an integral part. But the women cannot control all aspects of the children's lives any more than they can control the land they have occupied. The group exists within, and only with the tolerance of, a wider sexist society whose values and hierarchies also exert an influence on the children and their speech patterns. This is evidenced by the ease with which the children divide themselves into a warring group of boys versus girls and their immediate appropriation of the sexed terms *pussy* and *cock*.

But what is the metamessage of the book? Is Arnold implying that in a group composed only of women, gender is meaningless, or that police aggression forces a gender split? Because the members of the group are called by nontraditional or epicene names like *Nicky*, *Stubby*, and *Chris*, and their roles are not stereotypical for women—in the opening scene, for example, the carpenter is sanding the porch, and later in the book the cook and the carpenter become lovers—some readers may be surprised when they learn that all are in fact women. Are gendered pronouns unnecessary if sex differences are apparent from subtle cultural clues? Different readers will interpret the novel in different ways, although its frame of social realism, its setting in small-town Texas in the mid-1970s, and its feminist slogans do make a radical-feminist reading more compelling than others. The neologisms are so eye-catching and incongruous, given the realism of the rest of the text, that an obvious interpretation would be that they are intended to focus the reader's attention on what is missing, on the pronouns they replace and the reasons for grammaticalized gender distinctions.

The author's own stated purpose in using neologisms may be helpful in this regard. Arnold prefaces her novel with the following statement:

> Since the differences between men and women are so obvious to all, so impossible to confuse whether we are speaking of learned behavior or inherent characteristics . . . the author understands that it is no longer necessary to distinguish between men and women in this novel. I have therefore used one pronoun for both, trusting the reader to know which is which.

This statement would seem to provide the necessary key to the text. If the neologisms work, if readers can tell who is female and who is male without having this information grammatically coded, then one must conclude that the differences between women and men are indeed obvious and that further coding is unnecessary. If, on the other hand, readers are surprised by the return of the gendered pronouns and the sexual identities they reveal, then sexual difference may not be taken for granted.

Readers who discover only by the use of *she* and *he* two-thirds of the way through the novel that the group that occupies the school is composed of women, whereas the people who oppose them are men, demonstrate by this discovery that gender cannot be assumed. From this perspective, the preface is deliberately ironic.

Even without the preface, however, this point is made in the novel itself. The epicene speech of the women's group is utopic; it cannot sustain the onslaught of male violence to which it is subjected. The language is defeated at the same moment as its speakers. Although the book itself may end with the defeat of the women's cause, its publication points to a triumph of a different kind. *The Cook and the Carpenter* was published by one of the earliest feminist presses in the United States, Daughters Inc., a company June Arnold founded in 1972 to publish books by and for women. Arnold has in fact argued for the exclusion of men from the whole printing and publishing process: "we should wear headbands which state: My words will not be sold to 'his master's voice'" (1976:24). While Daughters Inc. flourished, she maintained a separatist preserve. From this perspective, the great pronoun war turns out to be merely a battle fought on many fronts, a strategy among others for creating and maintaining women's autonomy.

The epicene pronouns Marge Piercy created in *Woman on the Edge of Time* (1976) operate rather differently from those of Arnold. The book is an ingenious mixture of science fiction and social realism. Connie, a twentieth-century psychiatric patient, moves back and forth between her own time zone and the twenty-second century. Changes in third-person pronoun use follow this movement: The narrator and characters in the present time use traditional pronouns, whereas characters in the future time use the epicene neologisms *person* and *per*. Unlike in Arnold's novel, in which the characters' gender is not linguistically given until late in the narrative, Piercy's futuristic characters are introduced by the narrator with the pronoun appropriate for their gender.

The interchange between the time zones in Piercy's novel is much more fluid than that between Arnold's woman-only and mixed communities, and it causes frequent shifts in the pronominal system. During the sequences set in the future society of Matapoisett, the traditional and epicene pronominal systems coexist: Events described by the future-time characters feature the epicene system; those described by the narrator feature the traditional system. When a character from the future time, Erzulia, takes on the personality of another future-time character, Jackrabbit, and dances like him, the narrator recounts: "*She* danced Jackrabbit. Yes, *she* became *him*. ... Bolivar's head slowly lifted from his chest. Suddenly Erzulia-Jackrabbit danced over and drew *him* up. ... Bolivar began to dance with *him/her*. The music ended. ... Bolivar jumped back. 'But I felt *per!*' *he* cried out" (1976:316; emphasis added). The use of the traditional pronouns shows the scene from the point of view of Connie, the time traveler. Thus the gender shock of *she became him* is very apparent since the phrase itself defies the system and a new pronoun, *her/him*, must be invented. Bolivar's use of the epicene *per* shows up the world of difference between his community and Connie's. The language of the more advanced time forces changes in that of the earlier century.

Accompanying the neologistic pronouns are many epicene lexical items that refer to artifacts and concepts specific to the society of the future: *mems* (family members, although there may be no biological link among them); *kidbinder* (a person who looks after other people's children); *pillow friends* (people with whom one has a sexual relationship). This gender-neutral vocabulary causes Connie frequent difficulty since she speaks a language that encodes sex differences. She notices "people who must be women because they carried their babies on their backs" (71), guessing at gender from cultural information regarding her own time's sex roles rather than those of the future society. Because proper names are frequently epicene too, Connie manages as best she can: "The tall intense person was staring at her. Jackrabbit, Luciente had said: therefore male. He . . ." (77). Connie cannot tell Jackrabbit's sex simply from looking at him, hence the neutral *person*; she remembers that his name is Jackrabbit and is relieved to settle her dilemma with the masculine pronoun that would be appropriate to refer to a male—or "jack"—rabbit.

Another possible future is glimpsed by the reader when Connie tries to find her way to Jackrabbit and Luciente's time but gets lost in Gildina's time. Whereas the society of Matapoisett is an egalitarian utopia, Gildina's life in a futuristic New York is a nightmare dystopia. Luciente explains to Connie that in Matapoisett "we've reformed pronouns" (42), but in Gildina's version of the future people still use the traditional gendered forms, which represent the extreme pole of a sexually segregated and sexist culture.

Occasionally the characters in Matapoisett use gendered pronouns: "I have a sweet friend . . . and *her* tribe is Harlem-Black. But if you go over you won't find everybody black-skinned like *her* and me" (103).[7] There seems to be no textual reason for this; it answers no necessity of the plot. Thus one is inclined to conclude it is simply a mistake. Indeed, Piercy does seem at times unhappy with the use of epicene pronouns and often avoids them, employing other techniques such as repetition of proper names or ellipsis. This is particularly noticeable in Arthur of Ribble's memorial speech for his dead son, Jackrabbit (309–310). The passage is characterized by a high number of ellipses and proper names and by relatively little use of pronouns, although there are only two animate referents in the discourse (Arthur and Jackrabbit) and only one, Jackrabbit, who might be referred to in the third person. Because the whole episode is a eulogy to the recently dead Jackrabbit, this referent should remain active throughout the discourse, yet his proper name is given seven times, often where there is no intervening matter or where none of the intervening matter is of the type to deactivate the referent (in other words, there are no references to other characters). The continual use of Jackrabbit's name instead of a pronoun is therefore doubly marked. Connie, on the other hand, the focalizer of the story, is often referred to by a subject pronoun even where her name does not appear in the passage. In one notable episode (194–195), Connie is referred to twelve times as *she* or *her*, although her proper name is not given at all. Because she is the vehicle of the plot, the narrator may safely assume she remains active in the reader's mind throughout the novel, but Jackrabbit is just as salient in the scene of his memorial service. It seems that, like Le Guin, Piercy finds morphosyntactic neologisms cumbersome to use, even when they are her own invention.

Although the strategy of creating epicene pronouns is the same in both Arnold's and Piercy's novels, the intentions of the two authors are quite different. Piercy intends her work to reflect the egalitarian future world of Matapoisett, a world in which sex-role differentiation has been reduced to the point where fetuses are brought to term in giant "brooders," where three mothers, of either sex, volunteer to rear the baby, and where men are able to lactate just as women do. Indeed, Piercy affirms, "I use the common gender pronouns to reinforce the egalitarian nature of that society" (personal communication, December 13, 1993). In marked contrast, gender distinctions are not an issue in Arnold's short-lived women's community because, as a separatist environment, it has only one gender present. Although the children of the women's community comprise both girls and boys, they play a minor role in the novel and are distinguished by sex only in the brief episode analyzed above. It is significant that the children's genders are revealed only in a moment of explicit hostility between the girls and the boys.

With Suzette Haden Elgin we move from the 1970s to the 1980s, by which time feminist ideas about language were well established and there was already a substantial literature on the subject of language and gender. Whereas June Arnold and Marge Piercy are more interested in tackling grammatical gender and the hierarchy it creates, Elgin is concerned with lexical semantics and the expression of women's perceptions. In her science-fiction trilogy *Native Tongue* (1984), *The Judas Rose* (1987a), and *Earthsong* (1994), Láadan, the language of women's perceptions, plays a crucial role. Elgin (1987) relates her inspiration for the Láadan trilogy to the ideas she got from reviewing Cheris Kramarae's *Women and Men Speaking* for the linguistics journal *Language*. She combined the hypothesis that existing human languages are inadequate to express women's perceptions with the French feminist concept of *écriture féminine* and Gödel's theorem, as interpreted by Douglas Hofstadter (1979). In *Native Tongue*, Elgin cites two extensions of Gödel's theorem into language and culture: "For any language there are perceptions which it cannot express because they would result in its indirect self-destruction" and "For any culture, there are languages which it cannot use because they would result in its indirect self-destruction" (1984:145). Elgin's trilogy presents a society in which women are treated like children and where the specialized class of Linguist women surreptitiously creates its own language in order to cause unbearable strain on the dominant men's language. The Linguist women plan to spread their language to all women on the planet because once women have linguistic Encodings with which to express their miserable situation, the situation itself will inevitably alter. An Encoding, the Láadan Manual explains, is "the making of a name for a chunk of the world that . . . has been around for a long time but has never before impressed anyone as sufficiently important to deserve its own name" (1984:22). Elgin would appear to be taking direct issue with J. L. Austin's cozy assertion, "Our common stock of words embodies all the distinctions men have found worth drawing, and the connections they have found worth making in the lifetime of many generations" (1961:182). Or rather, Elgin's fiction points out that Austin must be using the term *men* in its masculine, nongeneric sense, for a multitude of distinctions and connections that women might wish to make are missing from the English lexicon.

Elgin remarks that the trilogy revolves around the idea that "the Sapir-Whorf hypothesis is true in its weak form, which means that language does become a mechanism for social change" (1987b:178). It is important to note that she does not say that language limits perceptions—that we are unable to think beyond the confines of our native tongue—but that the unique perceptions of women have no place in the well-trodden grooves of a patriarchal language. Because the trilogy, like Le Guin's *Left Hand of Darkness*, is a thought experiment, not scientific research, it might seem pedantic to ask which women's perceptions form the basis for Láadan: old, young, black, white, lesbian, heterosexual. Elgin's is a science-fictional world where, apparently, these differences are not as salient as in our own. The Linguist/non-Linguist distinction does have enormous importance in the novel, and Láadan is, in fact, the language of the Linguist women's perceptions. (The creation of a world in which linguists are economically and politically the most important group provides a certain gratification for those of us who feel our discipline is more often slighted than celebrated.)

The majority of the texts discussed here date from the late 1960s and the 1970s, the period when the women's liberation movement was at its height, and the goal of creating equality between women and men seemed attainable, if not overnight, then at least before the century was over. Literary experiments with gender have, in recent years, tended to take a different trajectory. With the rise of the gay liberation movement and the increased visibility of the gay community, sexual orientation has been added to the simple binary of feminine/masculine. The appearance of increasing numbers of transsexuals and their mobilization as a socially influential group have caused that binary to fragment into a multidimensional prism. Instead of creating epicene neologisms to force the reader to think in terms of persons rather than women and men, novelists such as Anne Garréta (1986), writing in French, and Jeanette Winterson (1993), writing in English, have adopted the strategy of removing all grammatical signs of gender in order to present androgynous characters who transcend sexual distinction. A tactic used in autobiographies by transsexual writers (Noël 1994; Stephens 1983) is to alternate between portrayals of themselves in the feminine and in the masculine to demonstrate the fluidity of gender. As gender has come to be seen less as a fact of individual identity and more as a homogenizing force, as a performative in the Austinian sense, the quest for gender-neutral pronouns has given way to a concept of gender as a social attribute separate from the speaker or the referent. *She sired six children* is no longer semantically incongruous, and the disapproving asterisk may be removed, for many male-to-female transsexuals have sired children as men whom they now take care of as women.

The sexual, racial, and class identities that formed the basis of many of the most important political platforms of the 1970s and 1980s have given way in the more nuanced 1990s to an acceptance of hybridity, fluidity, and performativity. The class of women, an identification so fiercely fought for in the 1970s, has been undermined from within and without. Fragmentation from within began immediately, as the concept 'woman' was exposed as both an ideological construct and a cultural performance by theorists who themselves had been trained in feminist scholarship (see for example Butler 1990 and Fuss 1989). The "woman-identified woman" began to blur ever more rapidly as male-to-female transsexuals declared that they too identified as women and challenged "women-born women" to justify the exclusion of transsexuals from all-female events (as the annual confrontations at Michigan Womyn's Music Festival bear witness; see *off our backs* and *Transsexuals News Telegraph*'s letters columns for July, August, and September 1993, 1994, and 1995). The novels discussed in this chapter could not be written with a 1990s understanding of the limitations and contradictions of a politics based on identity. The utility of an examination of these earlier feminist texts and their experimentation with pronominal gender lies in the constant slippage that is discovered even within the relatively rigid 1970s concept of identity. By eliminating gendered pronouns, these novels force the reader back on assumptions and presuppositions that may not be borne out by the text. In this way, they expose the fraught and transitory links between the pronoun and the referent and all the cultural baggage of *she* and *he*.

NOTES

I am grateful to Ursula Le Guin, Marge Piercy, and Dorothy Bryant for providing me with information, references, and opinions about their work and to Roberta Arnold for providing the same assistance with her mother's work. They are, of course, in no way responsible for the use I have made of the material they gave me. This article is an excerpt from the sixth chapter of my dissertation (Livia 1995).

1. For an overview of these discussions see, for example, Betty Lou Dubois and Isabel Crouch (1987), Fatemeh Khosroshahi (1989), and Michael Newman (1992). See also the preface to Deborah Cameron (1985:vii) for the opposite view: "Most sex-indefinite and generic referents in this book will be *she* and *her*. If there are any men reading who feel uneasy about being excluded, or not addressed, they may care to consider that women get this feeling within minutes of opening the vast majority of books, and to reflect on the effect it has."

It is interesting to note that whereas the early editions (1945–1968) of Dr. Benjamin Spock's *Child and Baby Care* systematically referred to the baby as *he*, in response to feminist criticism, pronominal reference since 1976 has alternated between the feminine and the masculine. The baby is no longer a generic boy; instead, each situation presents a specific case: "Every time you pick your baby up . . . every time you change *him*, bathe *him*, feed *him* . . . *he's* getting a feeling that *he* belongs to you" (1946:3; emphasis added), versus "Every time you pick your baby up—*let's assume it's a girl*— . . . every time you change *her*, bathe *her*, feed *her* . . . *she's* getting a feeling that *she* belongs to you" (1976:2; emphasis added).

2. Dennis Baron (1986:194) reports that singular *they* had begun to be attacked by purists as early as the eighteenth century. He quotes the example of grammarian Lindley Murray, who insisted on correcting "Can anyone, on their entrance into the world, be fully secure that they shall not be deceived?" to "Can anyone, on his entrance into the world, be fully secure that he shall not be deceived?" Baron also cites the nineteenth-century Quaker grammarian Goold Brown, who declared the sentence "No person should be censured for being careful of their reputation" incorrect because "the pronoun *their* is of the plural number, and does not correctly represent its antecedent noun *person*, which is of the third person, singular, masculine." Brown gives no reason for interpreting the noun *person* as masculine, except that he wants to justify the use of *he* to anaphorize it.

3. The systematic use of *on* as the principal pronominal vehicle of *L'Opoponax* creates other tensions at the discourse level, involving such textual features as focalization, point of view, and narrative voice, as I argue elsewhere (Livia 1995, 1998). For a discussion of other French approaches to the problem of linguistic gender (for example, in the work of Anne Garréta), see Livia (1994, 1995).

4. In languages in which gender is not coded morphosyntactically, such as Finnish, Hungarian, or American Sign Language, the question of creating gender-neutral pronouns

does not of course arise. This does not mean that these languages do not distinguish between the genders nor that the derogation of women does not occur at some other level, whether lexical, semantic, or pragmatic.

5. For feminist renderings of the Sapir-Whorf hypothesis see for example Dale Spender (1980) and Julia Penelope (1990). See also Caitlin Hines (chapter 7, this volume).

6. This quotation is so remarkable that it has made it into *Bartlett's Book of Quotations*.

7. Matapoisett might be described as a racial utopia, for the people who inhabit it are from many different racial and ethnic backgrounds, including Native American, Latino, Asian, and African, and there are no signs of interethnic or interracial hostility. However, a more fitting image than a utopia would be that of a melting pot, for the races are so blended together that little is left of their culture of origin.

REFERENCES

Arnold, June (1973). *The cook and the carpenter*. Plainfield,VT: Daughters Inc.

———— (1976). Feminist presses and feminist politics. *Quest: A Feminist Quarterly* 3(1):18–26.

Austin, J. L. (1961). A plea for excuses. In Austin, *Philosophical papers*. Oxford: Oxford University Press, 175–204.

Baron, Dennis (1986). *Grammar and gender*. New Haven, CT: Yale University Press.

Benveniste, Emile (1966a). La nature des pronoms. In Benveniste, *Problèmes de linguistique générale*. Vol. 1. Paris: Gallimard, 251–257.

———— (1966b). Structure des relations de personne dans le verbe. In Benveniste, *Problèmes de linguistique générale*. Vol. 1. Paris: Gallimard, 225–237.

Bryant, Dorothy (1971). *The kin of Ata are waiting for you*. New York: Random House.

Butler, Judith (1990). *Gender trouble: Feminism and the subversion of identity*. London: Routledge.

Cameron, Deborah (1985). *Feminism and linguistic theory*. New York: St. Martin's Press.

Daly, Mary (1979). *Gyn/ecology: The metaethics of radical feminism*. London: Women's Press.

Dubois, Betty Lou, & Isabel Crouch (1987). Linguistic disruption: He/she, s/he, he or she, he-she. In Joyce Penfield (ed.), *Women and language in transition*. New York: SUNY Press, 23–36.

Elgin, Suzette Haden (1984). *Native tongue*. London: Women's Press.

———— (1987a). *The Judas rose*. London: Women's Press.

———— (1987b). Women's language and near future science fiction: A reply. *Women's Studies Interdisciplinary Journal* 14(2):175–181.

———— (1994). *Earthsong*. New York: Daw.

Fuss, Diana (1989). *Essentially speaking: Feminism, nature and difference*. London: Routledge.

Garréta, Anne (1986). *Sphinx*. Paris: Grasset.

Hofstadter, Douglas (1979). *Gödel, Escher, Bach*. New York: Basic Books.

Inoue, Miyako (1994). Gender and linguistic modernization: Historicizing Japanese women's language. In Mary Bucholtz, A. C. Liang, Laurel Sutton, & Caitlin Hines (eds.), *Cultural performances: Proceedings of the Third Berkeley Women and Language Conference*. Berkeley: Berkeley Women and Language Group, 322–333.

Khosroshahi, Fatemeh (1989). Penguins don't care, but women do: A social identity analysis of a Whorfian problem. *Language in Society* 18(4):505–525.

Le Guin, Ursula (1969). *The left hand of darkness*. St. Albans, England: Granada.

———— (1975). Winter's king. In Le Guin, *The wind's twelve quarters*. New York: Harper & Row, 93–117. (Original work published 1969)

———— (1976). Introduction to *The left hand of darkness*. New York: Ace.

———— (1979). Is gender necessary? In Le Guin, *The language of the night: Essays on fantasy and science fiction*. New York: Putnam's, 161–171.

———— (1985). *Always coming home.* New York: Harper & Row.

———— (1989). Is gender necessary? redux. In Le Guin, *Dancing at the edge of the world: Thoughts of words, women, places.* New York: Grove, 7–16.

Livia, Anna (1994). The riddle of the Sphinx: Creating genderless characters in French. In Mary Bucholtz, A. C. Liang, Laurel Sutton, & Caitlin Hines (eds.), *Cultural performances: Proceedings of the Third Berkeley Women and Language Conference.* Berkeley: Berkeley Women and Language Group, 421–433.

———— (1995). Pronoun envy: Literary uses of linguistic gender. Ph.D. diss. University of California, Berkeley. (As Anna Livia Julian Brawn.)

———— (1998). Fear of sewers: Who sees this? Who thinks this? Who says this? In Natasha Warner, Jocelyn Ahlers, Leela Bilmes, Monica Oliver, Suzanne Wertheim, & Melinda Chen (eds.), *Gender and belief systems: Proceedings of the Fourth Berkeley Women and Language Conference*, Berkeley, CA: Berkeley Women and Language Group, 439–446.

Newman, Michael (1992). Pronominal disagreements: The stubborn problem of singular epicene antecedents. *Language in Society* 21(3):447–475.

Noël, Georgine (1994). *Appelez-moi Gina.* Paris: Lattès.

Penelope, Julia (1990). *Speaking freely: Unlearning the lies of the fathers' tongues.* Oxford: Pergamon.

Piercy, Marge (1976). *Woman on the edge of time.* New York: Fawcett Crest.

Spender, Dale (1980). *Man made language.* London: Routledge & Kegan Paul.

Spock, Benjamin (1946). *The common sense book of baby and child care.* New York: Duell, Sloan & Pearce.

———— (1976). *Baby and child care.* Rev. ed. New York: Pocket Books.

Stephens, Inge (1983). *Alain, transsexuelle.* St. Lambert, Quebec: Héritage.

Winterson, Jeanette (1993). *Written on the body.* New York: Knopf.

Wittig, Monique (1964). *L'Opoponax.* Paris: Minuit.

———— (1986). The mark of gender. In Nancy Miller (ed.), *The poetics of gender.* New York: Columbia University Press, 63–73.

———— (1992). *The straight mind and other essays.* Boston: Beacon.

· ·

Purchasing Power

The Gender and Class Imaginary on the Shopping Channel

Language and gender in popular culture

The vexed question of women's position in popular culture has been answered, broadly speaking, by two opposing schools of thought within feminism. In the predominant, text-based approach, cultural forms—newspapers, magazines, advertisements, films, televisions shows, music—are mined for patriarchal ideologies in structure and content (e.g., Modleski 1991; Mumford 1995; Winship 1980). The utility of textual analyses is confirmed by the continuing resonance of this critical work in women's lives. Nevertheless, such interpretations are brought up short when they expand their scope to include women not only as the objects of popular representation but also as the consumers of them. Given the sexism inherent in popular culture and uncovered in earlier scholarship, women's enthusiastic participation in what is widely understood as "their own oppression" is frequently viewed as deeply problematic. Explanatory theories predicated on women's "self-hate" are not uncommon (Douglas 1994), and analyses often hinge overtly or covertly on the class position of the women who are thought to engage most completely in popular culture. Such theories assume that popular culture is the transmitter of monolithic gender ideologies (see discussion in Strinati 1995) and place the feminist analyst at the opposite pole from the deluded, less-than-middle-class female consumer. In response, scholars who are critical of this outcome have issued counteroffensives from a psychoanalytic perspective that emphasizes personal, even autobiographical, pleasure (e.g., Nochimson 1992). Others have moved away from text-centered interpretation altogether, espousing instead a more ethnographic approach that takes "real" women's cultural analyses as primary (e.g., Christian-Smith 1990; Hobson 1980; Radway 1991).

Both positions, however, suffer from a limited understanding of women's identities and relations to the popular: One views the woman-as-consumer as empowered by her quest for pleasure and the other sees her as mired in oppression. Language and gender researchers have not, for the most part, entered into this debate, although they have a great deal to contribute to it. Whereas textual analysis, influenced by literary criticism, considers popular culture only as a set of "texts" or products to be read and ethnographic studies give primacy of place to the individual consumer, the methods of linguistics, and especially of discourse analysis, allow researchers to examine both aspects and thereby provide a more complete and nuanced picture of women's complex relationships to popular culture (see, e.g., Cameron 1995; Talbot 1995). The fundamental insight of discourse analysis is that "texts," or stretches of discourse, take on meaning only in interaction and that, as consumers of cultural "texts," audiences are active participants in this process of meaning making (McIlvenny 1996). In particular, as both Jennifer Coates (chapter 6) and Marjorie Orellana (chapter 3) demonstrate in this volume, women and girls do not unthinkingly consume cultural forms but construct their own meanings and identities in relation to such forms. The crucial contribution of this work is the recognition that, because identities are forged in ongoing discourse, they are not fixed for all time but fluid, often slipping beyond the theory-laden explanations of scholars (see also Goodwin, chapter 20, this volume).

Discourse analysis also calls attention to the specificities of cultural production: Viewed as a set of discourses, popular culture splinters into multiple and sometimes conflicting representations that offer similarly conflicting resources for women's identity construction. New cultural forms that blend or transcend conventional boundaries of genre or register present special challenges to analysts, for they facilitate new identity formations that may contradict traditional feminist analyses (e.g., Hall 1995) or even traditional analyses of gender itself (Barrett, chapter 16, this volume; Hall 1996). The shopping channel—a pastiche of public and private, entertainment and consumption—is an especially rich example of this discursive instability.

As a distinct form of popular culture, home shopping arose with the advent of cable television services and the concomitant expansion of channels from which viewers may select. Although there are or have been several national shopping networks concurrently on the air or in the works that target different markets, such as teenagers, upper-middle-class viewers, and so on, the network that holds the dominant market share (Fabrikant 1994) and from which I take my data is QVC—"Quality, Value, Convenience."[1] Because the network is in many ways the archetype of teleshopping, I refer to QVC generically as *the shopping channel*.

The shopping channel is, in effect, a single continuous commercial for a vast array of products. The linguistic practice that results from this genre is a complex type of public discourse that combines the intimacies of private conversation with the exigencies of the marketplace (see also Richardson 1997). Viewers—who are primarily female—are invited into a homelike setting in the television studio in which professional teleshopping hosts, through a variety of talk-based performances, display and describe merchandise for mass consumption. Models may additionally be employed to display such commodities as jewelry, clothing, and exercise equipment. Although the channel airs regularly scheduled "programs" that focus on particular products, such as "The Gold Rush" jewelry show, the network's basic format varies little throughout its 24-hour broadcasting day. Viewers participate in this economy by calling the network's toll-free telephone number to purchase products by credit card for home delivery. As the host presents and describes each commodity, the toll-free number is flashed on the screen and the discounted price is displayed while a clock in the corner counts down to the end of the product's availability. The sense of urgency created in this manner is, however, only illusory, because merchandise is made available to consumers repeatedly over the course of several days, weeks, or even longer.

If this were the extent of the shopping channel's offerings, it would be difficult to account for its impact on the cultural landscape and its billion-dollar annual revenue. However, the shopping channel differs from other recent and less successful at-home shopping forums, such as infomercials and the Internet, in its emphasis on audience participation, in which home shopping bears a certain resemblance to call-in talk shows.[2] This aspect of the shopping-channel experience is nowhere more evident than in the network's use of live, on-the-air telephone interactions between host and shopper. Occasionally, a new caller may be transferred to the host to be welcomed as a first-time teleshopper and to reveal what commodity she has purchased from the operator who took her call. But more often, frequent viewers will call up solely for the purpose of reporting their experiences with a product they purchased through the network. These telephone interactions establish a sense of community between caller and host, and by extension between all viewers and the network as a whole (see also Bucholtz forthcoming). Within this fictive community, callers and hosts discursively negotiate their own and each other's identities in relation to idealized positions of upper-middle-class authority and lower-middle-class authenticity. Callers accrue benefits in terms of both pleasure and power, but at the same time their constructed identities and those of hosts are easily destabilized and reworked within the commercial enterprise of the shopping channel.

Station identification: How to be a smart shopper

Callers frequently describe themselves with labels that link their identities to commodities: Viewers variously admit to being "a gold fanatic," "a bracelet person," "a jewelry-coholic," or simply a "QVC-ite." But such identifications should not be read as lasting elements of a caller's self-conception. These categories take on their meaning only in the context of consumption-based interaction, and within this frame the caller gains credibility as a discerning and experienced shopper. However, it is only by purchasing products offered by the shopping channel that viewers may gain access to the opportunities for discursive authority that the network may provide. Achieving the privileged position of on-the-air interlocutor with the teleshopping host requires a long-term commitment to viewing—and buying. "I've been waiting for *six* years to talk," states one waiting caller, and another reports, "I've always wanted to talk and I've *nev*—this is the first time I've *ever* been able to talk on the air." The pleasure of discussing shopping on television transcends even teleshopping itself; sentiments like "I'm just thrilled to death" or "This is so much fun!" are very common. These pleasures, of course, are profoundly gendered.

Women are the channel's target audience, as evidenced by the demographic profile of viewers and callers, by the kind of merchandise offered for sale, and by the discursive practices of the program hosts. Hosts speak directly to the camera, addressing the audience as singular *you* and gendering this virtual interlocutor as female, as shown in (1):[3]

(1)

    H   This kind of necklace reminds me of something you might <u>wear</u> to like a jazz
         concert,

The orientation to women prevails regardless of the gender of the host or the gender associations of the product being promoted for sale: Hosts often suggest husbands as potential recipients of gifts purchased from the shopping channel but rarely gender the viewer as a man who might buy an item for himself or as a gift for his wife.[4]

The primacy of women in the shopping channel offers them an opportunity for discursive power that may not be available to them in a less feminized realm.[5] This privileged status is conferred on experienced teleshoppers, who call in to share their expertise with other viewers. Such callers speak with the voice of authority, which pervades both the content and the form of their discourse, as seen in (2).

(2)

    (H = host, C = caller)
  1 C   .h I was calling about the um gold mesh watch?
  2   [I believe]=
  3 H   [Uh huh.]
  4 C   =it's: (.) twenty six eighty seven,
  5   I'm: not sure. /
  6 H   /Yeah./
  7 C   /I think that's the number.
  8   I have the <u>gold</u> one.
  9   (.)
10 H   Do you.
11 C   I have to say I get a <u>lot</u> of compliments
12   I mean these people (.)
13   l:ook at it twice you know because it's different.
14 H   Mhm.
15 C   You don't <u>see</u> that in the stores./
16 H   /R:ight.
17   [<That exquisite>]
18 C   [A:nd   ] *uh* you know I really I [really   ]=
19 H   [<piece.>]
20 C   =enjoy watching it I would tell anybody to uh (.)
21   you know to purchase it,
22   I don't think they'll be disappointed.

In this excerpt, the caller draws on numerous linguistic strategies to project her identity as a seasoned teleshopper. The caller's discourse is designed to bolster her authority by offering arguments in support of her endorsement. After establishing that she owns the item and is therefore qualified to comment on it (line 8), she notes that others covet it (lines 11–13) and that it is difficult to acquire elsewhere (line 15). She concludes with a summary statement about the pleasure she derives from the product (lines 18, 20). The testimonial speech event is characterized by this enumeration of evidence, which is either volunteered by callers or, if necessary, solicited by hosts. Evidence offered in testimonials tends to fall into several broad categories: besides the channel's bywords—quality, value, and convenience—callers attest to products' uniqueness, versatility, and ability to elicit admiration from others. Adept callers manage to incorporate all six of these categories into their testimonials.

Associated with the normative content of testimonials is a set of conventional linguistic practices used both by callers and by hosts. For callers, shopping-channel discourse introduces the everyday, private pleasures of shopping itself into a more public, formal domain in which prior shopping experiences are shared as information for the benefit of other shoppers. This specialized knowledge is imparted with an equally specialized vocabulary that lends an aura of science and seriousness to the shopping enterprise. In addition to greater formality, the register is distinguished by its large descriptive and technical lexicon. Thus *purchase* replaces *buy* in line 21 above; elsewhere callers predict *great enjoyment* for those who buy a recommended commodity or praise a product as *delicate* or *exquisite*. Such word choices also suggest refinement, a displayed appreciation for the finer things in life, which in turn is linked to the complex class relations of the shopping channel (see the following discussion).

As a result of the abundance of descriptors in the shopping-channel lexicon, tremendously dense descriptions are applied to even the most mundane items, thereby producing the heavy noun phrases that typify this register and contribute to its technical tone (example 3):

(3)

    H   It's the seven and a quarter inch Z link tennis bracelet in Diamonique and go:ld
         and you're gonna absolutely <u>love</u> it.

The register involves additional syntactic quirks that pragmatically invoke shared knowledge. Thus referring terms are often assigned definite determiners even on first mention, signaling that the referent is salient in the discourse, as illustrated in line 1 in example (2) (*the um gold mesh watch*), as well as in example (3). Because home-shopping discourse is reiterative, with the same products offered for sale again and again, the channel's entire inventory of merchandise is perpetually available for mention. Thus it is constantly susceptible to definite marking.

By virtue of this assumption of shared background, speakers may also indicate the discourse relevance of referents in other ways, such as by deleting the head noun phrase in referring expressions, as in the examples in (4):

(4a)

    C   I bought the sixteen inch Figaro necklace?
         <26 lines deleted>
    H   Well,
→   I'm <u>gl:ad</u> you got the Figaro,

(4b)

H	What are you buying tonight Lisa?
C	Well, I got the advanced order for the P-
	Pinocchio.
H	Wo:nder[ful]
C	[Film.]
	<102 lines deleted>
H	Once again,
→	advanced orders *only* for our Pinocchio,

In the most extreme invocation of shared knowledge, references to commodities are made without the use of any description at all but rather merely by reciting their catalog numbers, as in Example (5a):

(5a)

1	C	I'm ordering.
2		a graduation gift.
3		for my niece,
4		who's graduating from college,
5	H	Uh huh.
6	C	and she's a very (.)
7		<accelerated speech rate> {small blonde} pe*tite* (.)
8		young lady,
9	H	Mhm.
10	C	and so I ordered J.
11		two seven.
12		oh seven.
13		six.

The possibility—indeed, the likelihood—of successful reference using a number underscores the fact that membership in the world of the shopping channel is available only to longtime viewers. Any competent participant in the discourse must display this referential facility, a task in which hosts are aided by computer monitors, hidden from viewers, that supply important details about each item as it comes up for sale. Nevertheless, on-the-air telephone interactions can become a test of memory for both callers and hosts, whose conversation may introduce products that do not currently appear on the computer or television screen. In fact, callers who have mastered the shopping-channel discourse may prove themselves to be even more knowledgeable than the experts—that is, the network hosts—as illustrated in example (5b), which continues the exchange begun in example (5a):

(5b)

14	H	Two seven oh seven six.
15		Which one is *that.*/
16	C	/ That's the: (.)
17	H	[.h ba- the (.) <breathy> *yes*!]
18	C	[the bracelet and necklace,]
19		the three tone?

20   H   Yes.
21   The one that I have o:n.

Using a string of numbers referentially, the caller manages to stump the network host (lines 10–15). But her deft exhibition of discursive competence does not end here: in response to the host's confusion she provides a gloss of the catalog number, *the bracelet and necklace* (line 18), which, with its definite determiner in first mention, is itself part of the home-shopping register. She finally supplies another feature of the register, a headless adjectival phrase, to narrow down the item further still: *the three tone* (line 19). The caller gradually offers additional information, using increasingly specific referring expressions that are characteristic of shopping-channel discourse. In so doing, she prolongs her display of her own competent, insider identity at the expense of the host, who does not recognize the catalog number despite the fact that she is wearing the item under discussion. Such exchanges allow callers to take on interactionally authoritative roles, but this authority is sharply limited and sometimes entirely revoked. The redefinition of callers' discourse is a consequence of how class identities are constructed and projected on the shopping channel.

The shopping channel as a class act

The shopping channel's preoccupation with class positions is reflected in the frequency with which callers invoke the concept, as marked by arrows in examples (6) through (8). (Each exchange is between a different caller and host.)

(6)
    H Well,
        I'm gl:ad you got the Figaro,
        it's nice <accelerated speech rate> {to be able to} have a shorter length when
        you get into (.)
        the uh deeper necklines that come in for spring and summer.
    C Yeah. /
    H   /M[hm.]
    C   [Yeah.]
        I like the (.) the look of it. =
→   =It's real classy.

(7)
    C I wear- wore it on two job interviews,
        .h with a silver gray (.) pinstripe suit,
    H Oo:.
    C And it's just-
→   it's so cla(h)ssy.
    H Did you get the job?
    C (.) No.

(8)

    C   <u>Th:ank</u> <u>you:</u>!

    H   You're <u>wel</u>come Nancy,

        it was <u>my</u> pleasure to speak with [you.]

    C   [And-] thank QVC for the

→   <u>cl</u>ass.

      <u>a</u>ct.

Callers' approval of class arrangements on the shopping channel, however, is not echoed by the network's outside commentators. A *New York Times* article headlined "Television Shopping Is Stepping Up in Class" opens with the overt snobbery that one would expect from the highbrow *Times*: "Gone are the hallmarks of the current crop of [home shopping] shows: the cheesy sets and dowdy hosts and the hours of hard-sell pitches for budget goods like cubic zirconium rings. . . . Home shopping executives have seen the future, and it isn't the fiftyish housewives from Dubuque" (McMurray 1994).[6] This excerpt reveals the class dimension of the taste promoted by the shopping channel (cf. Bourdieu 1984), a dimension that is here linked to region, age, and, crucially, gender. However, the journalist, in charging hosts with "dowdiness," confuses the taste that the host professes to have and the class identity that she or he actually displays in self-presentation. This construction of class difference plays out in the network largely through discursive practices of displacement, a strategy for projecting class identities that Stanley Aronowitz (1992) has observed in prime-time television as well. Aronowitz notes that in many television shows working-class identity is displaced onto lower-middle-class characters—for instance, the cop is television's paradigmatic working-class male, although the occupation of police officer is not working class.[7] An analogous displacement occurs in the shopping channel, where lower-middle-class taste is mapped onto representative middle-class or even upper-middle-class bodies, those of the network hosts. The purposeful mismatch between ascribed taste and displayed identity obscures the obvious class differences between viewers and the idealized consumer typified by the host by suggesting that middle-class status is associated with—and perhaps is even achieved by—the consumption of advertised products.

But the distance between the caller and this ideal cannot be bridged so easily; notwithstanding the premise of an *L.A. Law* episode that first aired in 1994, frequent teleshoppers are not generally granted the opportunity to become telehosts. In the host, the central figure in this drama of consumption, viewers are presented with a middle-class professional who, unlike most callers, speaks Standard English with little or no trace of a regional accent, yet whose reported tastes and consumer desires are representative of the lower middle class. The anomaly of apparently middle-class speakers selling lower-middle-class goods is, moreover, an arrangement that runs counter to the findings of William Labov's (1972) groundbreaking study of speech in New York City department stores. Labov suggests that sales clerks are in lower social strata than the clientele they serve; as he comments in support of his class analysis, "C. Wright Mills points out that salesgirls in large department stores tend to borrow prestige from their customers, or at least to make an effort in that direction" (1972:45). In the discourse of the shopping channel, the opposite influence is at work: Customers strive for the prestige of the sales representatives (that is, the network hosts). This reversal is partly due to the mediated nature of the shopping channel. Hosts are not simply salespeople but television personalities, not mere facilitators of consumption but role models for consumers. Moreover, department stores and shopping malls increasingly aim at a upper-middle-class clientele, leaving lower-middle-class shoppers feeling that they and their tastes no longer belong. "As the malls have upscaled, they make it more and more uncomfortable for those of us who haven't," remarks a frequent QVC shopper interviewed by journalist Elizabeth Kaye. Kaye's rather condescending article on the network, published in the tony men's magazine *Esquire*, simultaneously reports on and reinforces this apprehension:[8] "'I wouldn't go to Worth Avenue,' says a QVC shopper for whom the most ample size sold on QVC, a size 3X—equivalent to size 24—tends to be a trifle snug. 'Salespeople don't expect me to spend money and don't rush to my side. I would feel out of place. I would feel ignored'" (Kaye 1994). Yet even while the taste of the lower middle class is celebrated on the shopping channel, its voice is displaced from the discourse, for it has been taken over by the more authoritative voice of the host, just as the model-like body of the host stands in for the unfashionably large body of the typical viewer.[9] The displacement of the lower-middle-class voice does not, however, lead to its complete disappearance, because it offers something that the shopping-channel host lacks by definition: authenticity. Viewers' class identifications beyond the shopping channel thus shape their interactional identities within it.

New and improved: Language repackaged

The language of most callers to the shopping channel indicates that they are culturally, though not necessarily economically, located in the lower middle class. That is, most callers have at least enough disposable income to make regular purchases from the network, but the taste that the channel cultivates is decidedly counter to the elite urban, bicoastal aesthetic. The class identity of shopping-channel viewers, however, cannot be read off from audience demographics, which are, in any case, closely guarded by network executives. Rather, it is a construct that emerges interactionally in shopping-channel discourse and, as already seen, in representations of the network in the wider U.S. culture.

Callers' identification with lower-middle-class "Middle America" is manifested in their regional accents and use of nonstandard forms. Examples of these are marked with arrows in (9) and (10):

(9)

    C   Um:,

→   I get a lot of gold from youse,
           and it's <u>beau</u>tiful.

(10)

    C   You know another thing I was gonna s-

→   You know them: uh—

```
              What's her name that (.) uh exercise [person]
         H                                         [Kelly ]
              [Moretti ]
→    C   [Yeah.  ] You know them: uh—
→        you know for your arms <[amz]>?
         H   Yes.
              Oh:.
         C   You know I was <u>won</u>dering . . .
```

Callers to the network construct authoritative identities for themselves on the air, but in the context of the interaction between caller and host what began as a discourse of authority becomes a discourse of authenticity. This reworking is motivated by the fact that expertise is in no short supply on the shopping channel: Hosts are of course well versed in the network register, and their descriptive presentations of merchandise are supplemented by guest appearances by vendors, exercise trainers, celebrities, and other specialists. What the shopping channel lacks, and what viewers' language offers, is authenticity. On a network that sells ersatz diamonds and look-of-leather Western wear, believability is perpetually at risk. The warmth and enthusiasm of hosts can go only so far in fostering the sense that the shopping channel is a world peopled with just plain folks who want to bring viewers quality, value, and convenience. The discourse of the callers, refracted through the lens of class relations, provides this missing element.

Because callers' language is marked for class and region, it assumes a very different value in juxtaposition to the standard, middle-class speech of network hosts. As has been shown in numerous subjective-reaction and matched-guise tests, a middle-class voice carries authority or prestige, but it may lack authenticity or trustworthiness to listeners of lower social classes (for a survey of this research, see Fasold 1984). For this reason, on-the-air telephone conversations with viewers are vital to the network's marketing success.

The following examples illustrate how the linguistic practices of the host come to participate in a discourse of authority and expertise and how the practices of the caller are relegated to a discourse of authenticity and eyewitness testimony. This role assignment is due not merely to the juxtaposition of the two interactants' language varieties but to the discursive efforts of the host.

In (11), for example, the host controls the direction of the discourse, asking the caller to frame her relation to the commodity in terms of pleasurable experiences associated with it (lines 4, 7, 11, 14, 21–26). The host reshapes these reports into a general analysis of the product's quality (lines 29–35). What is paramount in the discourse of the caller, as recast by the host, is authentic experience with commodities and the pleasurable feelings that this experience engenders. The host's discourse, conversely, is characterized by the control of numerous facts about the item.

(11)

```
         1   C   Um I have K one zero seven nine?
         2        The French white nine-piece?
         3   H   Mhm. (.)
```

```
 4        How do you like it?
 5    C   Oh I love it.
 6        I use it for everything.
 7    H   That's a nice set isn't it?
 8    C   Yes,
 9        It is.
10        (.)
11    H   And uh what is: the thing that you enjoy cooking in it
12        most?
13    C   [Uh]
14    H   [Or ] which of the pieces do you enjoy the most?
15    C   Well,
16        I I use all of them. h
17        Um.
18        I do chicken a lot and um I like using (.)
19        <low amplitude> {that for that.}/
20    H                                            /Mhm.
21        And (.)
22        do you find um (.)
23        that if you're using something if you're doing like
24        chicken on: uh an- any of the pieces like maybe the
25        the two and a half quart that oval one?
26        It- everything cooks nice and evenly in it too?
27    C   Yes.
28        And it seems like it doesn't take as long.
29    H   Right.
30        You know,
31        Corning is: has been around forever.
32        I mean if you (.)
33        have had any Corning pieces ever in your life you
34        probably still have them.
35        Because they're so durable.
```

At the end of the exchange from which this excerpt is taken, the host sums up the call for the viewing audience, casting it entirely in terms of the caller's emotional response to her ovenware: "Liz was dialing in to tell us she absolutely loves her French white ovenware set," he reports.

Although the caller in (11) seems to acquiesce in the consignment of her discourse to the realm of testimonial, in example (12) the caller actively attempts to position herself as an expert. However, her voice quality undermines this project: her hoarseness throughout the interaction detracts from the authority of her assertion that her ionizer was effective in treating her allergies. Yet the hoarseness undoubtedly lends a good deal of authenticity. The host by contrast maintains a convincing authoritative stance, immediately launching into a lengthy scientific discourse (lines 35–66) in response to a question from the caller.

(12)

1	H	Hello you're talking to us live on the air,
2		Who am I speaking with?
3	C	<raspy voice throughout> Uh my name is Joa:n [from]=
4	H	[Joa:n]
5	C	=<city deleted> California.
6	H	How you doing tonight Joan?/
7	C	/All right./
8	H	/Terrific.
9		Now have you purchased the Amcor?
10	C	Yes, I have two.
11	H	You [do?]
12	C	[As] you can tell from my voice,
13		I suffer from allergies, /
14	H	/M[hm]
15	C	[and] this is probably the
16		worst (.) time of season (.) for them,
17		and I have one in the bedroom /
18	H	/M[hm]
19	C	[and] one in the
20		family room./
21	H	/Mhm,/
22	C	/and we have about an acre behind us of (.)
23		nothing but weeds.
24	H	O:h [so]=
25	C	[So]
26	H	=you have the airborne allergies.
27	C	Yes and uh these really have kept me (.)
28		absolutely free.
29		I'm able to sleep at night,
30		to breathe at night, /
31	H	/That's wonderful.
32	C	I do have a question to ask you./
33	H	/Sure!
34	C	Why (.) is it necessary to have it away from the TV?/
35	H	/Oh because
36		of the electrostatic field that the ionizer causes in this?
37		It sometimes interferes and disturbs what's gon-
38		what it's gonna do it's gonna damage your picture tube.
39		So make sure that you have it I would say away from
40		your picture tube at least five inches away from your TV.
41	C	[I-]
42	H	[Or] anything else that's electrical like that.
43		Um: I: would not put it on the same desk as your computer?
44	C	Uh [huh.]

```
45  H      [I:  ] would not put it next to-
46         next to your radio.
47         Just make sure it's a couple feet away.
48         From- from all those (.) app[liances.      ]
49  C                                    [How about] a la:mp?
50  H   Oh if it's a touch lamp,
51         I would keep it a little bit further away
52         but a regular lamp should be just fine.
53         As long as it's a lamp with a switch
54  C   Uh huh.
55         Okay.
56         [Thanks.]
57  H   [But if   ] you have a touch lamp I wouldn't put it on
58         the same desk as a touch lamp [either.    ]
59  C                                    [Uh o:kay.]
60  H   It's primarily your uh your audiovisual equipment,
61         your television,
62         your V:CR,
63         your audiotapes,
64         um your videotapes,
65         and your computers.
66         Those are the main items you want to keep it away from.
67  C   Uh huh.
68         Well I highly recommend it for anyone who suffers from
69         allergies.
70  H   So you really have noted uh a big difference?
71  C   Oh indeed. [Yes. Uh huh. ]
72  H              [Great. Great. ]
73         Well I'm glad we could help you out with it,
74         and I hope it continues to work for you.
```

Unlike the caller in (11), who relies heavily on the host to guide her through the interaction, in (12) the caller offers a relatively long testimonial without prompting (lines 12–30). Through such a display she demonstrates her knowledge of the network's discursive conventions. But this assertion of authority does not go unchallenged by the host, who interjects a comment (*Oh: so you have the airborne allergies*; lines 24, 26) that, with its distinctive use of the definite determiner, asserts her own facility with the shopping-channel discourse while simultaneously positioning her as an expert on allergies. The host's own monologue following the caller's question continues across the caller's next bid for the floor (line 41), as well as across her acknowledgments, which are structurally sufficient to close off the sequence (lines 55–56: *Okay. Thanks*; line 59: *Uh o:kay*). The caller's final brief acknowledgment of the host's extended lecture (line 67: *Uh huh*) and her subsequent shift to her own expert discourse (line 68) suggest that she, like many of her fellow viewers, does not merely seek information from a knowledgeable source but hopes to share the spotlight with the host as coauthority. Moreover, the caller's responses to the host are information-oriented, whereas the host's acknowledgments are primarily emotional (lines 8, 31, 72). Such responses redefine the caller's own turns as personal and emotional, not public and informational.

Another example recorded on a different date also involves the ionizer (recall that the same items come up for sale repeatedly), and again the host positions the caller in the world of feelings rather than of facts. At the same time, she locates herself as an expert despite her earlier appeal to viewers to call in with testimonials, which is referred to in the initial lines of the transcript.

(13)

1	C	You wanted to know about the/
2	H	/.h /
3	C	/Amcor ionizer?
4	H	[Please.]
5	C	[I uh] <clears throat>
6		ordered one last year for my pastor.
7	H	Mhm.
8	C	He has (.)
9		so much trouble with allergies and was having so much
10		difficult speaking you know [on Sundays]=
11	H	[Sure.]
12	C	=and other times.
13		So.
14		So I kept seeing this so I decided I'd order one and
15		give it to him,
16		and he has had very little trouble with his asthma since.
17		.h And has thoroughly enjoyed having it.
18	H	Ruth you are a very very sweet person.
19		A lot of times when .h someone is having a:llergy
20		problems they go to the doctor and and they take the
21		allergy shots and the medication and everything.=
22		=A lot of doctors actually will recommend <pats machine>
23		{something like this,}
24		an ionizer air cleaner,
25		because they really do make a difference.

In this exchange the caller reports her experience as an expert (lines 1, 3: *You wanted to know about the Amcor ionizer?*), and she goes on to say at the end of the conversation that she has called in because "I just thought it might be a little bit *diff*erent than most of the calls that you get." But the host immediately recovers the authority for herself by launching into medical discourse (lines 19–25)—the network frequently dispenses medical advice that inevitably involves the purchase of advertised goods. (Note also that this move toward "scientific" discourse is again associated with the shopping-channel register's use of definite determiners: *they take the allergy shots and the medication and everything*; lines 20–21). Her positive evaluation of the caller also serves to effect this shift of authority: She praises her not for being knowledgeable but for being "sweet."

Some assembly required:
Competing constructions of identity

The ease with which hosts may reframe callers' discourse, however, does not guarantee that their own discourse is invulnerable to similar reframing. On the contrary, callers may also evaluate hosts in terms that bring their social identities to the foreground. These practices level the asymmetries between host and caller, placing both in the same discursive position as participants who may be evaluated. In my previous research on media discourse, I argued that the flexibility of mixed discourse genres such as panel discussions (or teleshopping) offers resources for participants' construction of their own and others' interactional identities (Bucholtz 1993, 1996). There I suggested that the conversational features of some public discourse genres enable participants to introduce apparently irrelevant aspects of social identity into the discourse. The earlier articles demonstrated that this strategy may be carried out in opposition to the institutional power of the media and its representatives. By contrast, in shopping-channel discourse, callers use discursive reframing to achieve solidarity with the telehosts, but, as in the panel-discussion study, they do so by eradicating interactional and social power differentials between participants (see also Tannen, chapter 11, this volume, for a discussion of the interrelationship of power and solidarity).

In offering a testimonial, callers may produce different kinds of evaluatable utterances, each of which elicits a different evaluation structure from hosts. When a caller makes a general statement about a product's virtues—usually in the present tense and with generic rather than personal pronominal forms—the evaluative response takes the form of a confirmation of truth value (such as *Right*), as in the following excerpt from example (11), which is renumbered as (14). Here the host draws out a somewhat reticent caller; after he proposes an appropriate testimonial form, the caller contributes a testimonial of her own, to which the host responds with a confirming evaluation, marked with an arrow.

(14)

26	H	It everything cooks nice and evenly in it too?
27	C	Yes.
28		And it seems like it doesn't take as <u>long</u>.
29 →	H	Right.

In positioning the caller's testimonial as evaluatable the host also positions himself as an expert who is entitled to evaluate such utterances. Likewise, in (15), the host elicits a testimonial from the caller and then provides an evaluation.

(15)

H	What do you like about the the tricolored jewelry,
	where you have the silver and the rose and the y-
	yellow gold,/
C	/<breathy> {You can wear it with anything!} /
H	/Mhm.
→	That's right.

In other instances, callers' testimonials may be cast not as general statements of truth but as personal revelations marked by first-person pronouns and simple past- or present-tense verb forms. Such statements are met with emotional responses from hosts, as exemplified in (16) through (19), which are extracted from earlier examples:

(16) = (4a)
    C   I bought the sixteen inch Figaro necklace?
         . . .
    H   Well,
→   I'm gl:ad you got the Figaro,

(17) = (4b)
    H   What are you buying tonight Lisa?
    C   Well, I got the advanced order for the P-
        Pinocchio.
→   H   Wo:nderful

(18) = (12), lines 29–31
    C   I'm able to sleep at night,
        to breathe at night, /
→   H   /That's wonderful.

(19) = (12), lines 70–74
    H   So you really have noted uh a big difference?
    C   Oh indeed. [Yes. Uh huh.]
→   H   [Great. Great.]
→   Well I'm glad we could help you out with it,
→   and I hope it continues to work for you.

Finally, hosts may evaluate callers not only on informational or emotional terms but also on the basis of their character and competence, as in line 18 of example (13) (*Ruth you are a very very sweet person*) or in (20):

(20)
    C   It was great to talk to you.
        It's the first time I got to talk!
→   H   You did a great job.

It is at this more personal level that hosts themselves become vulnerable to evaluations by callers. Such evaluations comment on hosts' communicative competence in performing their duties on the air by discursively locating them within broader social categories, such as gender and race (examples 21 and 22):

(21)
    C   <breathy> {It's a pleasure} to talk to you,
        you're my very.
        fa:vorite.

H   Thank you.
     [(I appreciate that.)]
C   [You always do   ] such a wonderful job,
     but you're always just so-
     .h pre:tty,
     and (.) always so upbeat,
H   Oh well thank you.

(22)

C   Uh I just wanted to tell before I start off with what I want-
     what I called [for   ]
H   [Mhm]
C   is that you have such a pleasant—
     I'm sure you've been told this before—
     a pleasant speaking voice,
     especially for this hour of the mor[ning h   ]
H   [Oh thank you.]
C   And you're very articulate,
     you know?
     When you present something?/
H   /Oh thank you.

In (21) the caller describes the host's appearance and behavior in gendered terms (*you're always just so- .h pre:tty, and (.) always so upbeat*), while in (22) the caller focuses on the host's linguistic abilities: his "*plea*sant speaking voice" and the fact that he is "very *arti*culate." Given that the host is one of the few African Americans on the shopping channel, the caller's evaluation conjures up a larger cultural stereotype about the speech of African Americans.[10] In praising the host's "articulate" speech the caller invokes European American assumptions of African American speech as nonstandard and "inarticulate."

Such examples demonstrate that although the hosts act as physical and linguistic exemplars of the middle class, their lower-middle-class audience feels qualified to evaluate their performance of this identity along lines of gender and race. Callers' approving comments about hosts therefore serve as a second kind of testimonial; in fact, the shopping channel explicitly encourages the commodification of those who pitch its products. When QVC shoppers phone in their orders, operators poll them about their host preferences, and hosts are awarded bonuses on the basis not of sales, as on the Home Shopping Network, but of their popularity among viewers. In light of this arrangement, callers may ultimately have greater power to evaluate the language of hosts than the reverse.

Conclusion

The complexities of language and identity on the shopping channel point up the limitations of traditional feminist approaches to popular culture. Textual analyses are likely to interpret the shopping channel as monologic and to discount the active role that shoppers assume in on-the-air telephone conversations. Feminist theories that center on pleasure, however, may fail to see that callers' construction of interactional authority is not unfettered, for callers do not control the means of linguistic production. Thus women's discourse in mass culture faces far more constraints than exist in alternative cultural forms such as zines (see Sutton, chapter 8, this volume; cf. also Cotter, chapter 19, this volume). Even feminist discourse analysis may suffer from certain blindnesses, for by taking the interaction of host and caller as the central problematic it may render the larger corporate structure invisible.

Monotonic research methods tend to yield monotonic—and sometimes monotonous—results. Having cleared the ground with numerous well-focused studies of language, gender, and identity, feminist linguists may be ready to recognize the virtues of "quick-cut camerawork"—analyses that bring multiple aspects of the social world into focus in rapid succession, cutting away before the analyst can make a final pronouncement on their meaning. Particularly in the investigation of complex discursive matrixes such as the shopping channel, such a healthy unsettling of analytic focus may bring into relief the numerous ways that facets of identity combine and recombine in late modern culture.

NOTES

I am grateful to John Bucholtz, Colleen Cotter, Kathryn Galyon, Jennifer Gurley, Kira Hall, Robin Lakoff, Anita Liang, and Laurel Sutton for their invaluable help during the researching and writing of this chapter.

1. Among these are several other QVC channels, including a health network, a channel aimed at a younger and more affluent audience (onQ), and the Fashion Channel, which evolved into Q2 and then collapsed back into QVC's main program; Penney's Shop Television Network (later bought by QVC); Montgomery Ward's Valuevision; Spiegel and Time Warner's Catalogue 1; Fingerhut's "S" The Shopping Network; Black Entertainment Television's BET Shop; Time Warner's Full Service Network; TWA's Travel Channel; Microsoft and TCI's computer channel; and shopping channels associated with MTV, Macy's, and Nordstrom. Home shopping has also gone international in recent years, mainly through joint ventures with QVC itself. Shopping networks have been proposed or have aired in Canada, England, Germany, Japan, Mexico, Norway, and Spain, among other places.

Although many similarities exist between QVC and its main competitor, the Home Shopping Network, the latter is aimed at a working-class audience and engages in hard-sell techniques. QVC, by contrast, employs more conversational and information-oriented discourse forms. As I will argue, QVC's audience appeal is largely due to its reliance on this format.

2. Another limitation of online shopping is that women, who are the primary targets of such services, are less likely than men to use computers (White 1994). Such considerations may have been an obstacle to the unveiling of QVC's computer shopping service, Q Interactive.

3. All names in transcripts are pseudonyms. Transcription conventions are as follows:

.	end of intonation unit; falling intonation
,	end of intonation unit; fall-rise intonation
?	end of intonation unit; rising intonation

!	end of intonation unit; high intonation
-	self-interruption; break in the word, sound abruptly cut off
—	self-interruption; break in the intonation unit, sound abruptly cut off
:	length
underline	emphatic stress or increased amplitude
(.)	pause of 0.5 seconds or less
h	exhalation (e.g., laughter, sigh); each token marks one pulse
.h	inhalation
< >	transcriber comment; nonvocal noise
{ }	stretch of discourse over which a transcriber comment applies
<[ ]>	phonetic transcription
[ ]	overlap beginning and end
/	latching (no pause between speaker turns)
=	no pause between intonation units
→	text under discussion

4. Despite the relative dearth of men on the shopping channel (marketing researchers estimate that no more than 30 percent of viewers are male, and the figures are even lower for callers and hosts), they play a central role in the network's discourse, as I discuss elsewhere (Bucholtz forthcoming).

5. It has been suggested to me that this authoritative discourse is particularly prized because it may be rare in viewers' lives outside of the shopping channel, but I am extremely reluctant to make this claim in the absence of any supporting evidence. Indeed, it seems likely that callers' authoritative identities emerge in shopping-channel discourse not because such identities are lacking elsewhere in their lives but because they are already developed and available for use in a new discursive realm.

6. The irony of this assertion is evident in hindsight: Following CEO Barry Diller's highly publicized expansion of QVC, profits dropped sharply. The network has since returned to its roots among middle-aged, lower-middle-class suburban women.

7. See Bonnie McElhinny (1995) for a discussion of the historical and social processes that have led to this shift in class position.

8. That an article on teleshopping would appear in such a venue may seem odd but is in fact entirely consistent with the assiduous efforts of class-conscious publications to differentiate their readership from the lower middle class. Editors of the *New York Times* in particular seem to be fascinated by QVC: In addition to dozens of news articles, the *Times* has run at least three teleshopping-related features in its Sunday magazine over the past 5 years.

9. Kaye (1994) reports that the most popular women's clothing sizes on QVC are 18 and 20.

10. On the Home Shopping Network, only three of thirty-seven hosts are African American (Hayes 1995); QVC's figures may be slightly higher.

REFERENCES

Aronowitz, Stanley (1992). *The politics of identity: Class, culture, social movements.* New York: Routledge.

Bourdieu, Pierre (1984). *Distinction: A social critique of the judgment of taste.* Cambridge, MA: Harvard University Press.

Bucholtz, Mary (1993). The mixed discourse genre as a social resource for participants. In Joshua S. Guenter, Barbara A. Kaiser, & Cheryl C. Zoll (eds.), *Proceedings of the Nineteenth Annual Meeting of the Berkeley Linguistics Society*. Berkeley, CA: Berkeley Linguistics Society, 40–51.

—— (1996). Black feminist theory and African American women's linguistic practice. In Victoria Bergvall, Janet Bing, & Alice Freed (eds.), *Language and gender research: Rethinking theory and practice*. London: Longman, 267–290.

—— (forthcoming). "Thanks for stopping by": Gender and virtual community in American shop-by-television discourse. In Mary Talbot & Maggie Morgan (eds.), *"All the world and her husband": Women in twentieth century consumer culture*. London: Cassell.

Cameron, Deborah (1995). The new Pygmalion: Verbal hygiene for women. In Cameron, *Verbal hygiene*, London: Routledge, 166–211.

Christian-Smith, Linda K. (1990). *Becoming a woman through romance*. New York: Routledge.

Douglas, Susan J. (1994). *Where the girls are: Growing up female with the mass media*. New York: Random House.

Fabrikant, Geraldine (1994). "Don't touch that dial" deal: QVC founders see future in shopping. *New York Times* (August 13):17.

Fasold, Ralph (1984). *The sociolinguistics of society*. Oxford: Blackwell.

Hall, Kira (1995). Lip service on the fantasy lines. In Kira Hall & Mary Bucholtz (eds.), *Gender articulated: Language and the socially constructed self*. New York: Routledge, 183–216.

—— (1996). Cyberfeminism. In Susan C. Herring (ed.), *Computer-mediated communication: Linguistic, social, and cross-cultural perspectives*. Amsterdam: John Benjamins, 147–170.

Hayes, Cassandra (1995). Cashing in on the home shopping boom. *Black Enterprise* (February):120.

Hobson, Dorothy (1980). Housewives and the mass media. In Stuart Hall, Dorothy Hobson, Andrew Lowe, & Paul Willis (eds.), *Culture, media, language*. London: Unwin Hyman. 105–114.

Kaye, Elizabeth (1994). The new phone sex. *Esquire* (May):76.

Labov, William (1972). The social stratification of (r) in New York City department stores. In Labov, *Sociolinguistic patterns*. Philadelphia: University of Pennsylvania Press, 43–69.

McElhinny, Bonnie (1995). Challenging hegemonic masculinities: Female and male police officers handling domestic violence. In Kira Hall & Mary Bucholtz (eds.), *Gender articulated: Language and the socially constructed self*. New York: Routledge, 217–243.

McIlvenny, Paul (1996). Heckling and Hyde Park: Verbal audience participation in popular public discourse. *Language in Society* 25(1):27–60.

McMurray, Scott (1994). Television shopping is stepping up in class. *New York Times* (March 6):5.

Modleski, Tania (1991). *Feminism without women: Culture and criticism in a "postfeminist" age*. New York: Routledge.

Mumford, Laura Stempel (1995). *Love and ideology in the afternoon: Soap opera, women, and television genre*. Bloomington: University of Indiana Press.

Nochimson, Martha (1992). *No end to her: Soap opera and the female subject*. Berkeley: University of California Press.

Radway, Janice (1991). *Reading the romance: Women, patriarchy, and popular culture*. Chapel Hill: University of North Carolina Press.

Richardson, Kay (1997). Twenty-first-century commerce: The case of QVC. *Text* 17(2):199–223.

Strinati, Dominic (1995). *An introduction to theories of popular culture*. London: Routledge.

Talbot, Mary (1995). A synthetic sisterhood: False friends in a teenage magazine. In Kira Hall &
    Mary Bucholtz (eds.), *Gender articulated: Language and the socially constructed self*. New
    York: Routledge, 143–165.

White, George (1994). On-line mice aren't stirring: Cyber shopping lacks appeal of trip to mall.
    Los Angeles Times (Dec. 15):D1.

Winship, Janice (1980). Sexuality for sale. In Stuart Hall, Dorothy Hobson, Andrew Lowe, & Paul
    Willis, (eds.), *Culture, media, language*. London: Unwin Hyman, 217–223.

· ·

From Folklore to "News at 6"

Maintaining Language and Reframing Identity through the Media

The linguistic subdisciplines of language and gender on one hand and language preservation on the other have rarely overlapped despite their shared concern with the relationship between language and identity. The traditional lack of interaction between the two fields is attributable to biases on both sides: language and gender scholars overwhelmingly study speakers of English and other thriving Western languages, and researchers of endangered languages are generally more focused on cultural and linguistic identity than on gender identity. Yet the revitalization of a minority language that is on the brink of extinction provides a rich opportunity to consider gender and other aspects of identity in a particular situation of use, and gender-based analyses may suggest promising new directions for language-maintenance programs. The approach in this chapter involves a blend of ethnographically and interactionally oriented examinations of language and culture, the language being both the Irish language and the discourse forms specific to media, and the culture being the symbolic referents of the community within Ireland, as well as the practices and norms of the discourse community of media practitioners.

From the turn-of-the-century emphasis on collecting folklore to the turn-of-the-millennium focus on integrating the Irish language in "modernizing" domains such as the news media, proponents of Irish language and identity have long appropriated textual strategies for renewing what are considered to be irreplaceable resources. In the process, women's roles in the public domain—if not entirely their voices—have expanded, so that their presence and fluency with media forms currently reflect their status as full participants in a prestige sphere. The analysis of the news data under consideration here, taken from Irish-language radio, is an attempt to illustrate that competence in the use of media-specific discourse forms accords women (and men) a functionally neutral linguistic snace in which gender identities are set aside and a primary identity as media practitioner is negotiated.

The data comprise an interview on the Bosnian situation that aired on a current-affairs program broadcast in the Dublin area in the summer of 1995. In the course of my analysis, I refer to the enfolding contexts to which the interview is linked: Irish-language radio, the larger frame of media, its operation within a preservationist paradigm, the position of language as a symbol of nationalism, and gender in relation to the participant roles that can be occupied in Irish life. This study thus filters the data through the larger issues of media language, language revitalization, and the effectively degendered forms of a high-status public discourse domain through a detailed analysis of a single speech situation.

The Irish case as a whole also provides a source of fruitful investigation across disciplinary lines and indeed argues for the necessity of interdisciplinary considerations. It allows us to consider the place of folklore genres and other conventionalized discourse forms in the construction of a national ideology and the feminist reflection on the omission of women and women's stories in this construction. It provides a counterexample to the received assumptions of the role of media in the worldwide decline of minority or lesser-used languages. It demonstrates the utility of discourse-level research on obsolescing languages. It allows a new look at women's participation in the dynamics of language maintenance. And, importantly, it reinforces the growing body of research that argues for the variable significance of gender identity, while recognizing the role of the larger social context in the articulation of gender and other parts of the self.

The Irish language in Ireland

Ireland is a mostly English-speaking country that nonetheless reveres its heritage language, Irish.[1] In Ireland, as in many once-colonized bilingual societies throughout the world, the heritage language remains a symbol of national identity but has relatively few fluent speakers (10,000 to 25,000 Irish citizens report fluency, with fewer than 3 percent speaking Irish on a daily basis, according to recent surveys; *Irish Times*, March 22, 1994, January 15, 1999; Ó Murchú 1985; Ó Riagáin 1992). Although people in principle support strengthening the use of Irish in public and in powerful contexts such as media and government, in practice no one wants to give up English. For this reason and because of historical factors deriving from past centuries of British colonial domination, the language is in serious decline; some Irish citizens declare it already dead (Hindley 1990).

The language is most robust in the Gaeltacht areas on the northern and western fringes of the country, far from Dublin. The Gaeltachts are the historical strongholds of the language and have long been the focus of preservationists. With respect to language attitudes in the late twentieth century, the ability to use the native language as spoken in the Gaeltachts is seen as highly desirable.

This modern orientation toward the language and its speakers, most of whom are bilingual, is overlaid on a past of negative attitudes and "internal colonialism" that afflicted all of Britain's "Celtic fringe" (Dorian 1981:19).[2] Negative attitudes toward the language and its rural, uneducated users persisted into this century. The speakers' low social and economic status was linked to their use of a disfavored language, making it seem only logical to eliminate the language as a first step to eliminating stigmas of other kinds. The undisputed economic advantage of knowing English has hastened the process of language loss in this century, but at the same time Irish has managed to remain strong as a symbol of Irish nationhood. In an act that linked linguistic pride with national pride, language with nationhood, Irish was named the first official language when the Republic of Ireland was formed in 1922. Language-attitude surveys conducted by the Institúid Teangeolaíochta Éireann (Linguistics Institute of Ireland) as recently as 1993 indicate that this symbolic-nationalistic link remains strong in the national consciousness. Some 73 percent in the survey agreed that "no real Irish person can be against the revival of Irish." Furthermore, attitudes toward the value of the language have improved in the last twenty years: 31 percent of respondents agreed that Irish is a dead language, down from 42 percent in 1973, and the percentage of respondents who felt that Irish could be revived for everyday use rose from 39 to 45 percent in the same 20-year period (*Irish Times*, March 22, 1994). Additionally, the results of the 1996 census, published in December 1998, reported an increase in Irish use by preschool children to 4.5 percent as compared to 3 percent of adults (*Irish Times*, January 15, 1999).

Women and language maintenance

Although scholarship on endangered languages rarely highlights the role of women in the preservation of heritage languages, numerous revitalization projects make use of women's traditional cultural roles to promote the use of the traditional language. This tendency may be an extension of women's stereotyped role as conservers of language (e.g., Labov 1990). Several projects build on women's positions as care-takers of children to foster the "mother tongue": In Hawaii, for example, parents (mostly mothers) serve as classroom aides in Hawaiian immersion programs (Hinton 1994a), and in the California-based Master-Apprentice Program led by Leanne Hinton (1994a, b), gender plays a role in how apprentices learn Native California languages and how they pass on their knowledge to younger generations. Earlier in this century, California Indian women who defended their children, their language, and their culture against the destructive forces of assimilation used their authority as mothers to speak out (Dobkins, chapter 9, this volume). And even when women step into nontraditional roles to lead efforts to preserve the heritage language, they may still be constrained by male dominance in the traditional culture (Craig 1992).

Although in these cases women assume leadership positions in their capacity as women, in the Irish situation women tend to contribute to language maintenance through the adoption of public, professional roles that do not hinge on their gender identity and that do not rely on stereotyped beliefs about women's greater linguistic conservatism. In particular, women's representative numbers on Irish-language radio and other contemporary broadcast media projects enables them to participate in a language-revitalization project that modernizes the role both of the Irish language and of Irish women in contemporary society.[3]

The use of the media to enhance the status of a language

Media language is public language, and as such it is a primary source of cultural messages. The language of media functions both as an agent and as a mediator in the construction of social identity. It reflects cultural norms and positions while at the same time offering a site for their contestation. To better understand the power that the media licenses or inhibits, it is well to examine closely the practices and assumptions that underlie the production of media language while situating these practices within their social and historical context.

The media have been blamed by linguists for their role in the recent accelerated obsolescence of languages (e.g., Krauss 1992), but in fact how they play out this role has not been explored. Moreover, there are several counterexamples to the generalization that the media contribute to language death: A number of advocates of minority languages use the mass media for their own ends, from resisting deterioration of the heritage language to contesting outright the power relations that the majority-language society imposes (Brody 1995; Jaffe 1994; Spitulnik 1994). Although the concern about the media is warranted (it is estimated that some 80 to 90 percent of the world's languages will decline in the next century), discussions about the media as a social dynamic and their role in the formation of identity have been fairly superficial. The detailed presentation of the example of Irish (see also Cotter 1996a) is intended to contribute to an expanded discussion of the media's role, positive or negative, in language maintenance and the retention of identity.

Language workers in Ireland currently use broadcast media (both radio and television) to enhance the status of the Irish language. Irish-language media give a public—and legitimating—voice to a language historically denigrated by English-speaking power-holders, and consequently the language is seen as capable of coping with the discourse needs of the modern world. In short, the status of the Irish language is "reinvented" through the media. And in the process, a new role for women is articulated.

Radio has been used explicitly for nearly 30 years as a tool for the preservation and growth of the Irish language. (Ireland's example presaged a policy of the European Union's Bureau of Lesser-Used Languages, which endorses incorporating media in any language-preservation program.) The two most prominent Irish-language stations in Ireland, which have worked to extend the language into modern contexts, are Raidió na Gaeltachta, based in the rural, formerly isolated Irish-speaking areas of the Gaeltachts, and the Dublin-based Raidió na Life.

Raidió na Gaeltachta

Raidió na Gaeltachta (RnaG) got its start in the early 1970s in the wake of now-historic protests by language activists in the Western Connemara Gaeltacht. Unhappy with Irish-language tokenism on the national radio and television stations, the activists started an unauthorized "pirate" Irish-language station in Connemara, the most populous of the Gaeltachts. The government responded by officially establishing and funding an all-Irish radio station in 1972. Declan Kiberd recounts the events leading to the formation of RnaG:

In 1969, inspired by the Civil Rights movement for black emancipation in the United States, a group of activists in the Connemara Gaeltacht launched their own campaign to revitalize the Irish-speaking areas. . . . the Cearta Sibhialta (Civil Rights) movement was in most respects remarkably successful. . . . [I]t managed to detach Irish from the purgatorial fires of the school classroom and to present it as part of a global countercultural movement constructed upon "small is beautiful" principles. (1996:567–568)

Indeed, as the only station in the world broadcasting to ethnic minorities at the time, RnaG was a "trail-blazing service in '72," according to Pádraig Ó Duibhir, manager of broadcasting services at Raidió na Gaeltachta. Now throughout the European Union there are some thirty to forty radio stations broadcasting in the minority languages of Europe. And RnaG, with its professional mix of news and current-affairs programming, has become the standard-bearer of the language and a model for quality Irish-language radio broadcast practice. Women, as well as men, are significant contributors to this practice in all areas of station work.

Raidió na Life

Aiming to fill the perceived gap left by RnaG, the programmers of Raidió na Life (RnaL), which has been on the air since September 1993, pitch their programming to the urban dweller, especially targeting young Irish speakers who do not have the benefit of a Gaeltacht to promote the linguistic solidarity and exposure that RnaG achieves. (Whereas RnaG is transmitted countrywide, RnaL's community license signal extends only 18 miles into the greater Dublin area.) The station utilizes speakers on the air whose Irish varies greatly in fluency, as well as those who speak a variety, Dublin Irish, that is low in prestige but nonetheless is spoken extensively by the bilingual natives of the urban area.

RnaL also deliberately appeals to a younger audience by using contemporary music instead of only traditional music—an equally revolutionary decision within the Irish preservation context. According to Éamonn Ó Dónaill, director of the Irish Language Centre at University College Dublin:

It is arrogant to say that young people ought to listen to the kind of music that interests us and that they are not properly Irish unless they do the same! This sort of thing puts people against the language. Irish isn't a package deal—a person should be able to be interested in the language but ignore other aspects of the culture if he or she is inclined to do that. (Ó Dónaill 1995; translation mine)

While 100 percent of the spoken word on RnaL is Irish, 80 percent of the music programming, drawn from all over the world, is in English. By offering mainstream and world music, it is RnaL's intention to attract attention to the language via popular culture and discussion of contemporary concerns. According to Ó Dónaill in a 1996 interview for this study, Irish is associated with tradition in the young person's mind: "The majority of young people think Irish is unsophisticated, and they have difficulty expressing ideas through Irish. About [the traditional Irish practice of] cutting turf they have no difficulty . . . but mass culture and TV particularly, they have great difficulty and they switch to English for that" (Ó Dónaill, personal communication).

The effects of Irish-language radio on maintenance and identity

The two stations have accomplished a great deal with regard to language revitalization. RnaG's stated goals are to use language to establish links in the Gaeltacht community and to enhance the contemporary status of Irish. A logical third goal, which is not strictly part of RnaG's ideology, would be to alleviate a historically ingrained linguistic insecurity. RnaL more explicitly addresses this issue. RnaL's goals are to evoke language change from within. Specifically, the station intends to give people an outlet for the language they learned in school and a reason to learn it; to provide a service to urban Irish speakers who would otherwise be isolated from one another, particularly those attending all-Irish schools; and to show people that the language can adjust to modern life, that one can talk about anything through the medium of Irish.

RnaG appears to have been successful in fulfilling its intentions to establish inter-Gaeltacht connections. RnaG both differentiates the dialect areas with its explicit broadcasts from the three regions and unites them through the common language and through the temporal and discourse structures of the medium. Unity among the Gaeltachts is also achieved through the content of the local broadcasts by reinforcing knowledge of community patterns, practices, and values, including artistic ones, which are held in common across the dialects since they all share a similar socioeconomic history. The result is a sense of the importance of one's own dialect and its connection to the language overall.

The structures of the broadcast genre, borrowed as they are from the English-language broadcast milieu, somewhat paradoxically reinforce a feature of the dominant English-language status quo for the purposes of linguistic continuity and vitality. This practice can be viewed as a necessary maneuver for garnering credibility, particularly when the minority language has little inherent or historical status in the public or institutional sphere, as is the case with Irish.[4] Simultaneously, the local content programming on RnaG reinforces a sense of Gaeltacht community. Radio programs cover items of Gaeltacht interest and promote traditional verbal and musical art forms (which, according to Watson [1989], the English-language media have helped to erode), as well as hybrid musical forms that rely on an interplay of traditional and contemporary resources.

The combination of Anglo discourse structure and Irish-interest content makes the language seem both normal (by using familiar structures of the dominant language community) and special (by using the referents of a once-stigmatized politically powerless community in the public, legitimizing sphere). The nature of this blend, that is to say, the negotiation of dominant ideology with the "core values" (cf. Smolicz 1992) or linguistic attributes of the minority-language community as expressed through the language of the media, remains largely unexplored. The activities of this "intertextual gap" (Brody 1995) appear to vary according to social and linguistic history, offering evidence to support various theoretical positions about language change (e.g., Thomason & Kaufman 1988) or to answer questions of social meaning posed by language-obsolescence researchers such as Kathryn Woolard (1989).

With two decades of RnaG paving the way, RnaL is able to take another direction, filling certain gaps, particularly with respect to addressing the rampant linguistic insecurity in speakers who are not from the Gaeltacht. On the local level—in the RnaL studio itself—volunteer staffers who start out with only a little School Irish speak the language with confidence a few months later. Everyone is given a job and made to feel that her or his contribution is important. This extends to the linguistic realm. In the small world of the RnaL studio, the community of speakers has managed to alleviate linguistic insecurity and make the use of Irish (and a disfavored Dublin form at that) a high-status endeavor. Because RnaL historically has been more interested in affording young speakers an opportunity for practice than in meeting traditional standards of usage, the language on the air is often marked by forms that accomplish a speaker's communicative goals at the expense of idiomatic Irish. Such disregard for the niceties of linguistic prescriptivism is unusual in the media: Indeed, in many countries the broadcast variety is synonymous with the standard (Milroy & Milroy 1991). The needs of both audience and radio workers are considered in RnaL's approach, which focuses on building an Irish-speaking speech community in an urban context not historically sympathetic to the cultivation of such a community. The distinctive feature of mass communication—the disjunction of place between community and audience—actually works in RnaL's favor. A nontraditional location, the airwaves, is used to create a nontraditional community (cf. Bucholtz, chapter 18, this volume, and Dorgan 1993 for other examples of how the media facilitate the formation of nontraditional communities). For speakers lacking access to and cultural affinity for the traditional rural strongholds of the language, RnaL creates its own place, in essence its own Gaeltacht.[5]

One of the factors that has stood in the way of a reemergence of Irish is that it has been "deprived of contemporary status," according to the Gaeltacht Authority's Pádraig Ó hAoláin (personal communication). His view is shared by both RnaG's and RnaL's personnel. A slogan of the Gaeltacht Authority, which promotes the economic, as well as the linguistic, interests of the various Gaeltachts, is "Normalise to popularise." If Irish citizens see and hear Irish being spoken on the radio and television, the reasoning goes, its prestige rises and its former "rural" taint disappears. What is normal becomes popular, no longer stigmatized. Likewise, the "modernization" of women's roles through their equal participation in the broadcast media could very well work to make such gender equity in the public sphere a normal part of Irish life. It could also help to alleviate the resistance to women's participation in the public sphere that some people have observed both historically (cf. Foley 1997) and in the modern day. Gaffney, for instance, notes that 50 percent of Irish people now believe in gender equity at home and work and suggests that "what is required is to actually begin to act, even in a small way" (1996:185).

Although it is not the explicit goal of either station to integrate women into public life, their efforts to integrate Irish into public life have offered women easier access to participation in public discourse because the media create positions that must be filled.[6] The stations' underlying methods are complementary. RnaG adopts Anglo discourse forms to give authority to Irish-language media but maintains a strict policy of Irish-only content, preserving the language as it is spoken in the Gaeltachts, the traditional repositories of Irish.[7] It thus values the prestige language forms traditionally associated with "core" Irish identity. RnaL, on the other hand, innovates with a hybrid form that challenges assumptions of the language's position in Irish life, as well as the structural form of the language itself, and meets the needs of urban speakers, creating a "Gaeltacht of the Air," as I term it. In so doing it provides opportunities for urban professional women to take up authoritative roles in the media even in the absence of fluency in standard Irish (and several announcers, female and male, have gone on to careers at RnaG and at the Irish-language television station, Teilifís na Gaeilge). Both stations facilitate Irish-language competence among interlocutors in their respective speech communities, reflecting the linguistic profiles of their target audiences. Together, they have the potential to expand the base of Irish speakers, female and male, in public and private domains, and they make a powerful statement about the social contexts of language use, their positions at either end of the preservation-growth spectrum offering a natural laboratory in which to consider the sociolinguistic and discourse parameters that characterize language and identity in flux.

Reframing roles through media language

Unlike other language-maintenance situations, traditional gender roles are not an obvious factor in current Irish-language broadcast practice. The ratio of female to male announcers and producers is similar to that anywhere else in the First World (that is, not equal but in greater numbers than in the decades before the women's movement of the 1970s; cf. Mills 1988).[8] The steering committee for the new Irish-language television station seats three women, and the "female perspective" is explicitly sought out and valued, according to Brían MacAonghusa, who oversaw the start-up of the station (personal communication). This inclusiveness suggests that in the last decade of this century, women have a chance for an equal opportunity to modulate the public voice of the media. Previously relegated to private roles in the home, women are becoming agents in the public construction of a social and cultural identity. This is not a trivial accomplishment. As historian Timothy Foley recounts, although the role of women has always been debated in Irish society—especially in the nineteenth century, of which he writes—the traditional position has always been very clear: "Rocking the cradle and ruling the world were two profoundly unconnected activities" (1997:24). Women were expected to stay within the domestic circle, to maintain the traditions and "moral health of society," and essentialist arguments, in which women's "natures" excluded them from employment and participation in the public sphere, held sway until attacks by feminists of the late nineteenth century confronted the propositions themselves.

      But this cultural shift raises other questions: To what extent does the current preservation ideology in Ireland ("Normalise to popularise," especially through the media) promote women's voices and women's place in the public sphere? When the modern preservation movement started in 1894, the collection of folklore was a focal point in the building of a new national identity, which could be articulated through narratives and other linguistic practices. Stories representative of men's genres were collected and framed as the legitimate definitions of culture, the storied equivalents of "News at 6." Genres specific to women—cradle songs, keening, fables told to children—were not (Joan Keefe, personal communication, citing Angela Bourke). Even the stories of the legendary Peig Sayers, collected alongside those of her male neighbors in the Blasket Islands, for a time in the 1960s and 1970s became an object of ridicule and cliche (cf. Bourke 1997). Women can now participate in the public discourse domain through the media (since the church still precludes any major role), but to what extent do they influence it? Is the absence of gendered media discourse a slighting or undervaluation of women's experience, a necessary accommodation to the normative paradigm (which in the Irish case follows Anglo structures for reasons having to do with the colonial past), or an underlyingly subversive act? The early folklore corpora omitted women's stories, which were not even considered for inclusion because they were "of the home," out of the public sphere (in this volume see Sawin, chapter 12, on early folklorists' devaluation of women's narrative practices and feminist folklorists' response). To what degree do modern media miss or dismiss women's stories (cf. Mills 1988)? It is important to realize that an absence of women's stories and voices is not a consequence of the Irish culture itself nor of Irish language-planning policies, overt or implied. Rather, the pattern of exclusion is much wider and more global in scope (Mills 1988); the preservation paradigm only serves to make these issues more urgent because, as most endangered languages continue to decline, time is running out for scholars interested in female speakers of such languages or in exploring the broader social context in which women participate discursively within a culture.

Wide-ranging macro-level questions such as these require a finer analysis on the micro levels of language, particularly in a bilingual context such as is found in Ireland in which identities are fashioned through more than one language. One of the claims I make here is that discourse features appear as a result of the dynamic, evolving act of talk and also serve to constitute the structure and meaning of talk and its participant relations; contrary to the assertions of some researchers (e.g., Troemel-Ploetz 1992) the gender of participants does not necessarily determine the shape of media discourse. In support of this claim I present a transcript of an extended news interview that aired on RnaL in August 1995. My goal is to show how one feature of the talk exchange, the use of English-language discourse markers, plays a part in the negotiation of turns and the position of participants in relation to each other within the situated activity frame of media language. It also demonstrates that in media discourse, gender identities may be backgrounded in favor of identities rooted in the ongoing interaction (see also Goodwin, chapter 20, this volume, on locally relevant activity-based identities in which gender is not always salient). That the markers are in English evokes the fluid identity boundaries that can be characteristic of bilingual discourse, even among speakers in a public radio broadcast.

What follows is the English translation of portions of a transcript of a live, on-air interview on RnaL's regular half-hour current-affairs program, Um Thráthnóna (in the evening). The interviewer, "Áine Uí Laoire" (designated in the transcript as

UT or "Um Thráthnóna"), is a 22-year-old Dublin native who plans a career in the broadcast media. She learned her Irish in school, graduating with a bachelor's degree in the language. She comes from a family of non-Irish speakers and is considered fluent. Her interviewee, "Maureen Cullen" (MC), was interviewed over the telephone (which accounts for some unintelligibility on the tape). Informant judgments about her Irish indicate she is a fluent Dublin Irish speaker with a great deal of prescriptively grammatical facility. Her talk thus balances what could be seen as the conflicting demands of several identities: urban dweller, woman, Irish speaker, and expert on Bosnia.[9]

(1)

UT: Welcome to Um Thráthnóna
       I'm Áine Uí Laoire with you until 6:30,
       Today, we have a special program about the situation in
       Bosnia which is getting worse every day.
       This is a complicated situation and now we have Maureen Cullen
       to explain the historical background of that country
       and the troubles there up 'til now.
[change of vocal quality]
UT: Welcome, Maureen Culllen
MC: |Thank you.

In (1), Cullen's expertise in the matter of Bosnia is assumed, by virtue of the fact that she is interviewed, but not made explicit. We do not know why she is interviewed beyond her Irish capacity and general facility with the topic. This is interesting from a media-discourse point of view, for the authority of the speaker is backgrounded; the listening audience is not bound to evaluate the discourse on anything but informational grounds. Quite possibly, she is well known for her work in relation to Bosnia, which would be part of the perceived shared knowledge of the intended audience.

Also of interest is the assumption of the opening question in (2), *Not everyone understands how the troubles started in Yugoslavia. Can you explain simply?* The question acknowledges the presence of a listening audience (for whom the program is directed and who will hear, along with Uí Laoire, the answer returned by Cullen) and its possible confusion over the complex political situation in the former Yugoslavia.

From the standpoint of media practice, it is advisable in an interview of this length to start with an "easy" question. "Easy" questions, whose answers call up information readily, serve the purpose of putting the respondent at ease—a necessity that goes beyond journalism when one or both interlocutors have limited proficiency in the language (which is often the case on RnaL, though not in this instance). Easy questions also simultaneously invoke or build a shared knowledge base for all participants, be they interviewer, interviewee, overhearers, or listening audience. The initial stages of interaction thus establish the roles of both participants in this exchange; these roles are tied entirely to the goals of the talk and have little connection to gender or other components of speakers' identities beyond this interaction. This pattern is also evident in the use of discourse markers, especially the marker *y'know*. Before considering *y'know*, however, I wish to examine the role of other English discourse markers in the interview.

Although the extensive literature on women's use of discourse markers tends not to examine their role in gaining authority, such functions are inescapable in the present data. Example (2) contains an instance (in line 2) of the speaker's use of the marker *now* in a face-saving repair.

(2)

    UT: Many people don't understand how the troubles started in Yugoslavia.
          Can you explain this simply?
    MC: Em I'll try to do that, It's em,
          as you say it's a complicated situation uh:
          as many people know Yugoslavia
          was a united country until five or six years ago.
          So that em perhaps people have heard about Marshal Tito
1   who was, uh, **y'know**, ruling the country for uh
          years since the Second World War.
          And still Yugoslavia was em six different nations-
          uh Serbia, Croatia, Bosnia, Slovenia, Montenegro,
2   an:d um: **now**.
          I can't remember what the sixth one [unintell?]
[speaks rapidly, with raised pitch and some embarrassed laughter]

Here and elsewhere in the Irish data I collected, *now* is used in its English form for discourse-level purposes that relate directly to the speaker's linguistic or discursive fluency. This function is by no means gender-specific: *I mean* was used in a similar fashion by a male interviewee in a brief telephone interview with a male interviewer that aired on RnaG. Besides its adverb status, *now* can function as a temporal marker in "discourse time," to use Deborah Schiffrin's (1987) term, while *I mean* marks speakers' evaluations of what they are producing in discourse. Understanding such gradations in discourse meaning is the first step to accounting for their presence within the bilingual domain. In the instances of their appearance in the data, *now* and *I mean* are both used specifically in repair situations. The repair itself is of a very particular kind, commensurate with the bilingual context of talk: that of restoring monolingual coherence to a turn marked by a lapse of memory (in the case of *now* under discussion) or Irish-language fluency (in the case of *I mean* in the RnaG data). In other words, in making their conversational repairs the speakers opt to use the markers of the language-of-comfort, or first language, English, rather than the markers of the language-of-discourse, Irish. Underlying this is a consciousness of the marginal position the Irish language plays within Irish public life and discourse. The interlocutors themselves know that between them and among their audience English is the dominant language. Thus English markers are a resource for discourse organization and coherence when actual or potential breakdowns occur.

Markers become pragmatically relevant to the bilingual environment of talk again in Example (3), where the use of *so* as a discourse-topicality marker is illustrated.

The interviewer's use of the marker (line 1) initiates its global possibilities: It essentially draws to a necessary close nearly four previous minutes of uninterrupted interviewee talk. Globally, it isolates a main, summarizing point (the Bosnian Serbs' quest for land as a catalyst for the existing problems), and locally it creates a logical transition for the next question, which it is the interviewer's journalistic task to produce. Here the interviewer's use of a discourse marker signals her interactional identity, and the apparent backchannels produced by MC in response (lines 2 and 3) are better seen as devices for regaining a conversational footing than as markers of collaborative speech, as found in some women's private conversations (Coates 1989).

(3)

    1 UT: <u>So</u>, the land is the thing they are trying to
             get=
             /
    2 MC: |<u>**Well**</u>, that's it=
       UT: |=are they trying for anything |else=|
    3 MC: =/<u>**yeah**</u> |<u>**yeah**</u> |
       UT: =to get |apart from the land|
    4 MC: |Well, it's: it's: |

Example (4) marks a point at which the interview becomes more interactive and departs from an idealized Q&A/speaker-hearer format which separates roles and functions. This heightened interactivity is evidenced by shorter responses by the interviewee and increased participation by the interviewer. Here, if anywhere, gender identity is most likely to emerge from the discourse. However, this is not what occurs.

(4)

       MC: It is difficult to come to a solution because:
             there are extremely strong feelings on all sides,
    1   I think / uh <u>**y'know**</u>-
       UT: /And there is the blame on one side.
    2 MC: <u>**Well**</u>:, there's: um the different groups say um:
             that there is blame on two sides
             but it is clear who started.
             em, in this case
             It is the, the Serbs, em, the Bosnian Serbs
             and originally they had support
             from Serbia itself which is sort of is a different country.
             Em, it is they who started the whole thing
             em:/
       UT: /And when did it really
             start. About? /
    3 MC: /uh about /maybe [Nineteen] ninety-one, <u>**no**</u>=
       UT: /mm
    4 MC: ninety-two. ninety-two. sorry, <u>**yeah**</u>?
             three years ago now.

uh, it's four years ago that the war started between Croatia
and Serbia.
[breath intake] And um:
5   since then they are, uh **y'know** they are not uh uh-
uh stopping until they have it all?
by the looks of it.
And even: the Muslims are trying to fight back.
But there is: uh an "international embargo,"
against giving arms,
to both sides,
to the Serbs and to the Muslims but.
it looks like the Serbs are, they were able,
em: em (.) to get arms from the East, probably from Russia?
and beforehand they had much stronger arms than the Muslims
had? [breath]=
UT: [quick intake of breath]
6   MC: =**y'know**? [reclaiming floor]
and so the Muslims weren't able to defend themselves
[breath]
UT: /[latching]

In Example (4), the increase in interaction between interviewer and interviewee does
not produce an increase in "gendered discourse." UT's questions are aimed at elicit-
ing information, and MC's apparent request for confirmation in line 6 (*y'know*) actually serves to reclaim the floor—that is, to fulfill her discourse role as interviewee.

Example (5), which continues where (4) leaves off, is the closing of the speech
event, marked by turn negotiation, floor-holding by the interviewee, overlap, and
multiple English discourse markers heretofore unused by the interviewer (line 5).
Again, these markers are used in the service not of social identities but of interactional identities as the interview winds down.

(5)

UT: And do you think the United Nations
are not doing their best about [unintell?]
MC: I think there isn't enough:,
the people there on the ground say
[deleted material]
1   they're not interested really, **y'know**?, ah:
They will make various statements
but really they don't care at all I think
[discusses the Russian, French, and U.S. attitudes]
2   **Y'know**, France and uh the United States uh
3   have made various efforts **but**,
although they could be stronger I think-
4   **Y'know** that's the trouble
[hhhh] |there.   mm:

```
5   UT:           |Oka:y, Mauree:n/  \Well,
                  thank you very much Mauree:n |Cullen|=
6   MC:                                         |yeah  |
    UT:   =for being with us on Um Thráthnóna |today              |
    MC:                                        |you're welcome |
    UT:   Thank you.
```

Unlike the other English discourse markers, which appear only once or twice in the interview and may be used by either participant, the marker *y'know* appears prominently throughout the interview (twenty-six tokens total) but is used only by the interviewee, a pattern that suggests that although the interactional tasks are distributed between participants, they are also distributed according to relative role and status. The interviewer, in the position of the ostensible controller of the discourse, is the dominant participant in terms of the communication structure of the media interview (*y'know* tends to mark the less powerful person in the discourse; Schiffrin 1987). The lack of visibility (because the interview is by phone) exacerbates the need for the respondent to engage with the interviewer (eleven tokens of *y'know* appear in sequence 2, the lengthiest sequence), for whom the customary backchannel responses of conversation are not allowed in the media discourse frame. In fact, as the interaction level increases (especially at the point of turn negotiation in example (4) but also elsewhere in example (4) and in (5)), the overall frequency of the markers increases correspondingly. Additionally, the frequency of *y'know* in the data relates to the level of response by the interviewer (the ratio is higher when the interviewer participates less). There are only two *y'know* tokens in the highly interactive example (5), which has five interviewer turns, and eleven tokens in example (2), with only one interviewer turn. Thus the interviewee's use of discourse markers does not suggest the collaborative egalitarian talk typical of some women in private interactions (Coates 1989).

English discourse markers occur in an environment in which both the careful use of Irish and attention to the multiple situated discourse needs specific to the media are cultivated. Some of the factors that condition the use of language in this public-discourse arena are news values, a conventionalized manner of organizing information, the role of the audience, and the technical limitations of the medium (cf. Cotter 1996b, in press). Discourse-marker insertion, then, as illustrated in the media data, becomes a strategy for discourse coherence and the negotiation of identity in a bilingual frame. The identity which is negotiated, however, derives from the context of use, from roles that are required by the task at hand and not by the gender of the participants.

The discourse data show us aspects of discourse structure and discourse interaction. They do not confer the possibly expected cues associated with women's communicative style (backchannel responses, hedges, and so on). What are improvised and jointly negotiated are the participants' purposes. The interviewer's purpose is to elicit information, produce well-formed discourse as a journalist and Irish speaker, convey information, and conduct her linguistic business fluently (that is, with no dead air or lapses). The interviewee's purpose is to present information, establish credibility, and ensure that she has been fully understood. Because the speakers are accomplishing a task activity, negotiation of status is minimal (see also Goodwin 1993). At the same time, the speakers improvise their Irish identities, relying on nontraditional resources (such as English discourse markers) to project fluency in the nontraditional realm of radio discourse. The fact that as women they themselves are nontraditional participants in such discourse is itself an improvisation of Irishness, though not one that is highlighted in the interaction.

It is possible, then, for speakers to degender language and wield it as a tool on behalf of their work—not simply of their profession (as, for example, radio announcer or commentator) but also of their larger goals (language maintenance) and their interactional goals (gaining the floor, closing the exchange, and so on). In noting that gender is not always salient as a theoretical category and that its effects may differ across contexts, this analysis supports Amy Shuman's (1993) and Patricia Sawin's (chapter 12, this volume) critique of the limitations of folklorist and feminist categorizations of genre, as well as the findings of Alice Freed (1996) and Alice Greenwood (1996) on the variable relevance of gender in discourse. Although it may be argued that radio discourse is a historically male-constructed form, women in mainstream media generally do not challenge the origination of the tool, and the women on RnaL are no exception, for that has not been identified as the problem to solve in this context. Instead, they are overtly challenging assumptions behind the preservation paradigm, which *has* been identified by RnaL as the central issue. In other words, neither the gendering nor the degendering of radio discourse should be seen as universal: Instead, these processes are particular to the social or ideological needs of using radio (Leitner 1980). Although women's identities as women do not play a significant role in the Irish data presented here, gender has been found to be directly relevant to the workings of radio discourse in other contexts (Bucholtz 1996; Castillo 1994). The place of gender and other aspects of identity in interaction must therefore be determined on a case-by-case basis by examining the details of discourse.

It is also important to point out with respect to women in the media in Ireland that they are occupying roles that were once unavailable to them and in so doing are breaking the boundaries of their socially assigned niches. It is possible that expanding the domain of roles, much as the revitalization movement is expanding the domain of use for language, will create different opportunities and ultimately different judgments about positions women can occupy in the public sphere. As it stands, given the current visibility of Irish-language media and their practitioners, the language is reframed as useful and viable, and women are reframed as competent in the sphere of public discourse. Additionally, this perspective on language and identity as it pertains to gender supports current cultural research into Irish life and ideology by historians and sociologists (cf. Kelleher & Murphy 1997), who see women's and men's roles as more interdependent than traditional accounts would have them.

Conclusion

The position of the media as multiply modifying, supporting, and contesting the community values and characteristics that mark social identity has been illustrated through the example of Irish-language broadcast media, which enhances the status of a language that remains a strong symbol of Irish identity. It also points to the notion of multiple marginalities—the positioning of women in Irish-language radio on the periphery of mainstream academic and political concerns. For example, Ireland tends to be overlooked in postcolonial studies (cf. Kiberd 1996), as well as in English feminism. Women's discourse forms are overlooked in traditional studies of folklore (Hollis, Pershing, & Young 1993). Radio tends to be overlooked in studies of media (Cotter 1996a; Pease & Dennis 1995), and media is not considered to the extent it could be in studies of language use (Bell 1991; Cotter 1996a; Sutton, chapter 8, this volume). Nonfluent speakers, such as those on Raidió na Life, are often disregarded in studies of identity (but see Dorian 1991 for a counterexample), and nonstandard speakers tend to be overlooked by preservationists in favor of standard speakers.

The Irish case is intended to illustrate generally a complex of points that researchers from different domains can fruitfully pursue and to consider specifically how media—through language and interaction—operate as a dynamic in the evolving process of a society's identity formation: locally, culturally, and nationally. As such, the work here is also intended to remind researchers that gender is not necessarily salient in interactions in the ways students of the subject have come to expect. The salience can be foregrounded, however, only as we consider the norms of the dominant discourse community (Cotter 1996a) in relation to communities of practice (Eckert & McConnell-Ginet 1992) within their historical context.

NOTES

1. In Ireland, the term for the language is *Irish* (or *Modern Irish*). *Gaelic* has pejorative connotations (cf. Ó Murchú 1985), suggestive of its earlier history as peripheral to Irish life and as marginal to the powerful institutions that wielded influence over citizens.

2. The concept of internal colonialism, referred to by Nancy Dorian (1981) in her groundbreaking work on the demise of a dialect of Scots Gaelic, concerns the domination of the power structures of a colonizer society over the lives of inhabitants within or near its own boundaries.

3. In fact, the increasing numbers of women working on all levels of media production was remarked on by some of my Irish-language consultants. But women's participation does not come without cost. Irish psychologist Maureen Gaffney has pointed out that women working within the public sphere wrestle with the tensions not only of breaking out of the boundaries of gendered domains particular to Irish society but also of mediating between traditional feminist orientations toward "collectivity-and-inclusivity" and the traditional male "world of hierarchies" (1996:178). She includes women working in business, trade unions, and the media in her analysis.

4. The practice also reflects a more inclusive view toward preservation that has developed in the latter half of the century after a realization that an Irish-only stance was not practical. Angela Bourke writes, "For a hundred years after the famine, Irish people behaved as though they could afford only one language; as though they had to choose between Irish and English: material poverty translated into cultural frugality" (1997:66–67).

5. Compulsory Irish in school has succeeded in making nearly every citizen familiar with the language, as Reg Hindley (1990) and others describe in detail, but has not been able to expand domains for its use.

6. Indeed, during one week in June 1997 there were nearly a half-dozen open positions in Irish-language media, from reporter to technician to desktop publishing worker.

7. Irish has no single indigenous standard; its official synthetic standard, An Caighdeán, is taught in schools and to nonnative speakers, but even the official standard does not have the prestige of the Gaeltacht varieties.

8. Because women's representation in the media is not entirely on par with men, particularly in technical areas (Majella Ní Chríocháin, personal communication), the Women on Air project was launched in 1996. The aim of the project, jointly sponsored by University College Galway, the Independent Radio and Television Commission, and Connemara Community Radio, is to promote equal opportunity for women in independent radio venues. This support is expected to come through policy development, research (a first-ever study on women's underrepresentation in broadcasting was expected to be completed in late 1997), and training, including a foundation course in radio skills and a diploma in applied communications for radio, which graduated sixteen participants in its inaugural class in May 1997.

9. Underlined words are English in the Irish text (due to considerations of length, only English translations are provided here). Brackets indicate unintelligible words or comments on manner of delivery, as well as brief stretches of content summary. Whereas in English-language discourse data, lines of talk are generally divided according to intonation unit, this is impossible to render in the present data because intonation plays a different role in Irish (Cotter 1996c). Instead, the line breaks in the data are organized roughly according to clause- or sentence-level boundaries when intonation or discourse-level "chunking" (such as self-interruption) fails to provide a reasonable alternative. Intonational features are indicated by punctuation (a period meaning falling intonation to low level and a short pause; a comma meaning falling intonation to mid level and a short pause; and a question mark meaning rising intonation). Overlaps or simultaneous speaking are indicated by |, and latching (or no gap between speakers) is indicated by / or \. Lengthened phonemes are followed by :.

REFERENCES

Bell, Allan (1991). *The language of news media.* Oxford: Blackwell.

Bourke, Angela (1997). Language, stories, healing. In Paul Brennan & Catherine de Saint Phalle (eds.), *Arguing at the crossroads: Essays on changing Ireland.* Dublin: New Island Books, 58–76.

Brody, Jill (1995). Orality, radio, and literacy in the intertextual gap. Paper presented at the annual meeting of the Linguistic Society of America, New Orleans.

Bucholtz, Mary (1996). Black feminist thought and African American women's linguistic practice. In Victoria L. Bergvall, Janet M. Bing, & Alice F. Freed (eds.), *Rethinking language and gender research: Theory and practice.* London: Longman, 267–290.

Castillo, Josefina M. (1994). Waves of change: The experience of Campesinas Unidas de Veracruz. In Mary Bucholtz, A. C. Liang, Laurel A. Sutton, & Caitlin Hines (eds.), *Cultural performances: Proceedings of the Third Berkeley Women and Language Conference.* Berkeley, CA: Berkeley Women and Language Group, 79–85.

Coates, Jennifer (1989). Gossip revisited: Language in all-female groups. In Jennifer Coates & Deborah Cameron (eds.), *Women in their speech communities.* London: Longman, 94–122.

Cotter, Colleen (1996a). Irish on the air: Media, discourse, and minority-language development. Ph.D. diss., University of California, Berkeley.

——— (1996b). Engaging the reader: The changing use of connectives in newspaper discourse. In Jennifer Arnold et al. (eds.), *Sociolinguistic variation: Data, theory, and analysis.* Stanford: Center for the Study of Language and Information, 263–278.

—— (1996c). Systems in contact: Focus in Irish and English. In Alison Henry, Martin Ball, & Margaret McAliskey (eds.), *Proceedings of the International Conference on Language in Ireland. Belfast Working Papers in Language and Linguistics* 13. Belfast: University of Ulster, 85–116.

—— (in press). Language and media: Five facts about the Fourth Estate. In Rebecca Wheeler (ed.), *The workings of language: From prescription to perspective.* Westport, CT: Praeger.

Craig, Colette G. (1992). Miss Nora, rescuer of the Rama language: A story of power and empowerment. In Kira Hall, Mary Bucholtz, & Birch Moonwomon (eds.), *Locative power: Proceedings of the Second Berkeley Women and Language Conference.* Berkeley, CA: Berkeley Women and Language Group, 80–88.

Dorgan, Howard (1993). *The airwaves of Zion: Radio and religion in Appalachia.* Knoxville: University of Tennessee Press.

Dorian, Nancy (1981). *Language death: The life cycle of a Scottish Gaelic dialect.* Philadelphia: University of Pennsylvania Press.

—— (ed.) (1989). *Investigating obsolescence: Studies in language contraction and death.* Cambridge: Cambridge University Press.

—— (1991). Surviving the broadcast media in small language communities. *Educational Media International* 28:134–137.

Eckert, Penelope, & Sally McConnell-Ginet (1992). Think practically and look locally: Language and gender as community-based practice. *Annual Review of Anthropology* 21:461–490.

Foley, Timothy P. (1997). Public sphere and domestic circle: Gender and political economy in nineteenth century Ireland. In Margaret Kelleher & James H. Murphy (eds.), *Gender perspectives in nineteenth century Ireland: Public and private spheres.* Dublin: Irish Academic Press, 21–35.

Freed, Alice (1996). Language and gender research in an experimental setting. In Victoria L. Bergvall, Janet M. Bing, & Alice F. Freed (eds.), *Rethinking language and gender research: Theory and practice.* London: Longman, 54–76.

Gaffney, Maureen (1996). *The way we live now.* Dublin: Gill/Macmillan.

Goodwin, Marjorie Harness (1993). Accomplishing social organization in girls' play: Patterns of competition and cooperation in an African American working-class girls' group. In Susan Tower Hollis, Linda Pershing, & M. Jane Young (eds.), *Feminist theory and the study of folklore.* Urbana: University of Illinois Press, 149–165.

Greenwood, Alice (1996). Floor management and power strategies in adolescent conversation. In Victoria L. Bergvall, Janet M. Bing, & Alice F. Freed (eds.), *Rethinking language and gender research: Theory and practice.* London: Longman, 77–97.

Hindley, Reg (1990). *The death of the Irish language: A qualified obituary.* London: Routledge.

Hinton, Leanne (1994a). The role of women in Native American language revival. In Mary Bucholtz, A. C. Liang, Laurel A. Sutton, & Caitlin Hines (eds.), *Cultural performances: Proceedings of the Third Berkeley Women and Language Conference.* Berkeley, CA: Berkeley Women and Language Group, 304–312.

—— (1994b). *Flutes of fire: Essays on California Indian languages.* Berkeley: Heyday Books.

Hollis, Susan Tower, Linda Pershing, & M. Jane Young (eds.) (1993). *Feminist theory and the study of folklore.* Urbana: University of Illinois Press.

Jaffe, Alexandra (1994). Media, language and identity on Corsica. Paper presented at the annual meeting of the American Anthropological Association, Atlanta.

Kelleher, Margaret, & James H. Murphy (eds.) (1997). *Gender perspectives in nineteenth century Ireland: Public and private spheres.* Dublin: Irish Academic Press.

Kiberd, Declan (1996). *Inventing Ireland.* Cambridge, MA: Harvard University Press.

Krauss, Michael (1992). The world's languages in crisis. *Language* 68(1):1–42.

Labov, William (1990). The intersection of sex and social class in the course of linguistic change. *Language Variation and Change* 2:205–254.

Leitner, Gerhard (1980). BBC English and Deutsche Rundfunksprache: A comparative and historical analysis of language on the radio. *International Journal of the Sociology of Language* 26:75–100.

Mills, Kay (1988). *A place in the news.* New York: Dodd, Mead.

Milroy, James, & Lesley Milroy (1991). *Authority in language: Investigating language standardisation and prescription.* London: Routledge.

Ó Dónaill, Éamonn (1995). Amharc Neamléanta ar staid na Gaeilge faoi láthair (An unscholarly look at the current state of the Irish language). In Seosamh Ó Murchú, Mícheál Ó Cearúil, & Antain Mag Shamhráin (eds.), *Oghma*, Vol. 7. Dublin: Foilseacháin Oghma, 57–65.

Ó Murchú, Máirtín (1985). *The Irish language.* Dublin: Department of Foreign Affairs/Bord na Gaeilge.

Ó Riagáin, Padraig (1992). *Language maintenance and language shift as strategies of social reproduction: Irish in the Corca Dhuibhne Gaeltacht: 1926–1986.* Baile Átha Cliath: Institiúid Teangeolaíochta Éireann.

Pease, Edward C., & Everette E. Dennis (eds.) (1995). *Radio: The forgotten medium.* New Brunswick, NJ: Transaction.

Schiffrin, Deborah (1987). *Discourse markers.* Cambridge: Cambridge University Press.

Shuman, Amy (1993). Gender and genre. In Susan Tower Hollis, Linda Pershing, & M. Jane Young (eds.), *Feminist theory and the study of folklore.* Urbana: University of Illinois Press, 71–88.

Smolicz, Jerzy J. (1992). Minority languages as core values of ethnic cultures: A study of maintenance and erosion of Polish, Welsh, and Chinese languages in Australia. In Willem Fase, Jaspaert Koen, & Sjaak Kroon (eds.), *Maintenance and loss of minority languages.* Amsterdam: John Benjamins, 277–306.

Spitulnik, Debra (1994). Code-mixing and ideologies of hybrid vs. "pure" language use. Paper presented at the annual meeting of the American Anthropological Association, Atlanta.

Thomason, Sarah Grey, & Terrence Kaufman (1988). *Language contact, creolization, and genetic linguistics.* Berkeley: University of California Press.

Troemel-Ploetz, Senta (1992). The construction of conversational equality by women. In Kira Hall, Mary Bucholtz, & Birch Moonwomon (eds.), *Locating power: Proceedings of the Second Berkeley Women and Language Conference.* Berkeley, CA: Berkeley Women and Language Group, 581–589.

Watson, Seosamh (1989). Scottish and Irish Gaelic: The giant's bed-fellows. In Nancy C. Dorian (ed.), *Investigating obsolescence: Studies in language contraction and death.* Cambridge: Cambridge University Press, 41–59.

Woolard, Kathryn (1989). Language convergence and language death as social processes. In Nancy C. Dorian (ed.), *Investigating obsolescence: Studies in language contraction and death.* Cambridge: Cambridge University Press, 355–367.

Constructing Opposition
within Girls' Games

S ince their beginnings in the 1970s, studies of women's language have
proliferated stereotypes, positing deficit views of female interaction patterns and supporting the notion that women's "essential nature" is
nonconfrontational and apolitical. These studies can be faulted on two
counts: First, they neglected the diversity of ways of speaking in endogenous settings where women live their lives; second, researchers assumed white middle-class
American women's speech to be the norm and found women's speech deficient with
respect to men's speech (Foster 1995; Henley 1995; Kramarae 1990; Morgan, chapter 1, this volume). Many early studies viewed women as victims forced to act in
weak, passive, irrational, ineffective ways. Looking largely at women in cross-sex
interaction rather than in same-sex groups, this model ignored the complex ways
women interact with one another, as well as the variety of codes from which they
may select.

Cultural feminists' alternative approaches celebrated the distinctiveness of
women's language and highlighted women's supportive interactional styles (for literature reviews see Bing & Bergvall 1996; Freed 1995; Freeman & McElhinny 1995).
Women's cooperative talk with its "underlying esthetic or organizing principle of
'harmony' is emphasized in this model" (Kalčik 1975:6). Women complete each
other's turns, repeat or paraphrase each other's contributions, and talk simultaneously
but not in competition for the floor, preserving equal status and maintaining social
closeness (Coates 1991; Falk 1980). According to Senta Troemel-Ploetz (1992:588),
"equality among speakers" is achieved by mitigating orders and "toning down and
camouflaging dominant speech acts." Jennifer Coates argues that women's talk in
the private sphere favors "linguistic strategies which emphasize solidarity rather than
status" (1994:79), whereas men's talk in the public sphere is more "information-

focused and adversarial in style" (1994:78). These models contrast women's cooperative talk with men's competitive conversation.

Beyond dualism and master categories

Early work viewed gender as a master category to be correlated with speech style without regard for other variables that might index social identity, such as ethnicity, social class, age, or sexuality.[1] Major problems with such an approach have been outlined by Penelope Eckert: "Gender does not have a uniform effect on linguistic behavior for the community as a whole, across variables, or for that matter for any individual. Gender, like ethnicity and class and indeed age, is a social construction and may enter into any of a variety of interactions with other social phenomena".[2] Studies of women's norms of speaking by linguistic anthropologists in Malagasy (Keenan 1974) and Gapun, New Guinea (Kulick 1992, 1993) have countered the idea that women are universally "more polite." Recent studies of the speech of women of color in the United States have shown the value of examining social class and age in conjunction with ethnicity; for example, research on the language of Latina women (Galindo 1992, 1994; Galindo & Gonzales Velásquez 1992; Mendoza-Denton 1996, chapter 14, this volume) has challenged stereotypic formulations of Latina women's speech as powerless.[3]

As studies began to "look more locally" at how speech is used within "communities of practice" (Eckert & McConnell-Ginet 1992; Lave & Wenger 1991; McElhinny 1995), a more complex view emerged. Recently, research conducted in African American speech communities has called into question the earlier focus on unemployed males' street talk as the authentic African American English speech style. And sociolinguistic studies have begun to document the rich codeswitching that takes place among African Americans (Foster 1995; Morgan 1996) and among Spanish speakers (Galindo & Gonzales Velásquez 1992; Galindo 1994; Gonzales Velásquez 1992; Urciuoli 1991; Woolard 1997; Zentella 1997) when selecting from alternative language varieties.

The relationship between language, ethnicity, and identity has been problematized as researchers seek a more contextualized understanding of how people mobilize linguistic resources for their interactive projects. Researchers who look at the relationship of ethnicity, nationalism, and language (Gumperz 1982; Jackson 1974; Le Page & Tabouret-Keller 1985) no longer assume simple one-to-one correlations between language and speech community. Rather, through language choice in multilingual situations people actively "project their view of themselves in relation to the universe in which they feel they live and the social structures it contains" (Le Page & Tabouret-Keller 1985:247). The selection of a language variety constitutes an *act of identity*—"a very overt symbolization of ourselves and of our universe" (1985:248). As John Gumperz and Jenny Cook-Gumperz (1982) argue, in addition to marking identity through language choice, speakers convey ethnicity and group membership through communicative conventions: different cultural assumptions about the presentation of self, ways of structuring information, and types of prosody and contextualization cues (1982).

This dynamic view of identity also underlies recent studies of "the anthropology of performance" (Turner 1985, 1988), which draws on Erving Goffman's dramaturgical perspective on human experience and the processual view of social relations elaborated by Sally Moore (1978).[4] Moore (1978:39) argues that social life "proceeds in a context of an ever-shifting set of persons, changing moments in time, altering situations and partially improvised interactions," in which "established rules, customs, and symbolic frameworks exist, but they operate in the presence of areas of indeterminacy, or ambiguities, inconsistencies, and often contradictions." Such a perspective informs recent gender studies as well. The notion of gender-bending or gender variance (Jacobs & Cromwell 1992) has emerged as important in studies of gender as cultural performance (Butler 1990). Examples include Sherry Turkle's (1995) vignettes of gender blurring and multiple identities on the Internet; Anna Livia's study (chapter 17, this volume) of nongendered pronoun systems in feminist fiction, and Barrett's investigation (chapter 16, this volume) of how different aspects of identity can become one's "operating culture" (Goodenough 1981) at specific moments within interaction. Repertories of identities are taken as the norm, and people play with the variety of linguistic devices through which identities are indexed. Such ideas are compatible both with Fredric Jameson's (1984) notion that, rather than being a monolithic construct, identity is situated in discrete and often self-contradicting locations and with Anthony Giddens's (1990) idea that "the self" is part of an ongoing dialogue that individuals sustain with themselves in relation to their changing experiences.

Identity and language practice

Studies of the relationships between language practices and social identity provide important commentaries on and investigations of women's position in society. As Rusty Barrett (chapter 16, this volume) argues, whereas examples of the speech of African American drag queens might "suggest a form of resistance toward racism and homophobia, they do little to call into question the sexism in American society." And Colleen Cotter's study (chapter 19, this volume) of media discourse in Irish-language radio shows that although media discourse promotes cultural identity, it does little to promote women's discourse forms, as Irish identity is filtered through "genderless" rather than female ways of speaking over broadcast media. The ways in which women's talk is manipulated for commercial gain is examined in Mary Bucholtz's study (chapter 18, this volume) of the coconstruction of a fictional community on the shopping channel.

Bucholtz's account of how shopping-channel participants build a shared social world is compatible with recent work in social constructionism (Coupland & Nussbaum 1993), a psychological perspective that views all social categories and identities as constituted through discourse (Coupland, Nussbaum, & Grossman 1993). Such a perspective within linguistics builds from work in conversation analysis, whose project is to describe "the procedures by which conversationalists produce their own behavior and understand and deal with the behavior of others" (Heritage & Atkinson 1984:1). Rather than assuming that identity can be easily correlated with social variables such as ethnicity, social class, gender, or age, conversation analysts argue that identity is shaped moment to moment through the details of how participants interact within activities.

Thus Lisa Capps (chapter 4, this volume) shows how the identity of the "irrational woman" develops within storytelling interaction. In pursuing a response from a family member who displays minimal or no responsiveness to her story, the agoraphobic woman Capps studied escalates her story of danger or helplessness, thereby amplifying her deviant status. By using the methodology of conversation analysis, Capps shows how language not only reflects social order but also constitutes it— and simultaneously constitutes a particular psychological condition.

The notion of identity developed by Capps and many other authors in this book (and in particular those included within part IV) is one that is fundamentally activity-focused, created through language choices from linguistic repertoires. As Goffman argues, it is coordinated task activity rather than conversation that organizes a great deal of conversational interaction: "A presumed common interest in effectively pursuing the activity at hand, in accordance with some sort of overall plan for doing so, is the contextual matrix which renders many utterances, especially brief ones, meaningful" (1981:143). As participants move through activities, they take on appropriate roles, which constitute *occasion-specific* identities. Such roles are located within what Goffman has called a "situated activity system": "a somewhat closed, self-compensating, self-terminating circuit of interdependent actions" (1961:96). Occasion-specific identities are those interactional practices proposed and ratified in the course of specifiable activities—for example, in the case of telephone conversations, caller and called, or in a dispute, accuser and defendant.

In addition, participants articulate their position or stance with respect to a present project through ritual *displays*, providing "evidence of the actor's alignment in the situation" (Goffman 1979:1) or *footing* (Goffman 1981)—one's stance, posture, or projected self. Indeed, for this reason Deborah Tannen (chapter 11, this volume) rejects the term *identity* altogether in favor of Goffman's concept of display, which suggests that the self is not static but created dynamically in action.[5] Participants try on and play with a host of diverse social personae as they navigate through different positions within activities.

Dualism in research on children's gendered identities

In attempting to provide global differentiations between gender groups, social scientists have often dichotomized differences between girls' and boys' interactions. Sociologists (Lever 1978) and psychologists (Borman & Frankel 1984; Borman & Kurdek 1987; Piaget [1932] 1965; Sutton-Smith 1979) have claimed that girls generally are less concerned than boys with making and arguing about rules. Sociolinguistic and psychological research on female interaction has been deeply influenced by psychologist Carol Gilligan's theory of moral development, which is based on reports told to a researcher rather than on recorded interaction and ethnography: "This [female] conception of morality as concerned with the activity of *care* centers moral development around the understanding of *responsibility* and *relationships*, just

as the conception of morality as *fairness* ties moral development to the understanding of *rights* and *rules*" (Gilligan 1982:29; original emphasis). Gilligan argues that
girls are primarily concerned with maintaining relationships within intimate social
groups. Her dualistic "different voice" argument has been echoed in the work of a
number of psychologists (e.g., Leaper 1991; Miller, Danaher, & Forbes 1986). Similarly, according to Kathryn Borman and Lawrence Kurdek (1987:248–250), girls'
games stress interpersonal understanding, whereas boys' activity is "structured, rule-
governed, competitive, and team oriented." Both they and Janet Lever (1978) cite
jump rope and hopscotch as two quintessential cooperative girls' games which, being
characterized by turn-taking, lack the elaboration of rules or differentiated social roles.
Such studies conclude that "the play activities of boys are more complex than those
of girls, resulting in sex differences in the development of social skills potentially
useful in childhood and later life" (Lever 1978:472).[6]

Studies of the actual playing of girls' games in context defy this essentialist,
deficit view of girls' interactive skills. Analyzing girls' play during hopscotch, I
found that every move within the game was fiercely scrutinized for its possible
categorization as a foul or violation. Girls seemed to delight as much in arguing,
reconstructing, and violating the rules as in actually winning. By examining the
specific linguistic resources and practices used to build turns at talk we can see
how girls actively construct themselves as agents who are responsible for monitoring the social order. These girls defy the standard, essentialized stereotypes of
Latinas as the hapless victims of a patriarchal culture (Anzaldúa 1987, 1990;
J. Moore 1991; Orenstein 1994; Sadker & Sadker 1994), for they are neither passive nor muted.[7] Like the Chicanas studied by Letticia Galindo (1994) and Norma
Mendoza-Denton (chapter 14, this volume), the girls in the present study use language creatively and without inhibition.

Fieldwork

The present data are based on a study of the interaction of bilingual Spanish- and
English-speaking girls, primarily second-generation Mexican and Central Americans,
in an elementary school located in the Pico Union/Koreatown district near down-
town Los Angeles. The school population of 828 students was predominantly Latino
(92.2%). Ninety-five percent of the children were eligible for the federal meal program under the Chapter 1 program.

Children were transitioned into English reading toward the end of the third grade;
fourth and fifth grades were taught primarily in English. The girls in this study were
in the second, third, and fifth grades and generally spoke Spanish to one another,
except when referring to hopscotch moves or numbers on the squares of the play
grid.[8] English was thus reserved for a domain-dependent lexicon; terms such as *Out!*
or *You're out* and *Sorry*, all of which meant that a player would forfeit a move, were
spoken in English. In addition, when performing a part of the game called ABC (discussed later), girls used English phonology to repeat the letters.

As a middle-aged Anglo professor and community outsider, I was obviously
different from the children I was observing, but the fact that Lori Cronyn, a colleague

at UCLA, was a teacher at this school and was well known by the children provided an extraordinary opportunity for fieldwork. My previous research on working-class African American children's interactions (Goodwin 1990) provided me with a basis for comparing speech styles; I began to see cross-cultural similarities in children's formulations of disagreement in opposition moves. Additionally, I noticed that, as in my earlier work, the identities most salient to children's interactions during hopscotch were not macrolevel categories such as gender or ethnicity but instead were locally managed identities that emerged from ongoing practices during play.

Occasion-specific identities within hopscotch

Play took place after school, during lunch break, and at two recess periods; teachers often extended recess, reasoning that outside the safety of the school grounds, children had little opportunity to play with peers. Before and during school, children often played under the supervision of a coach whose primary duties were to organize children's sports. After school, children whose parents permitted them to remain on the playground could get equipment from a playground supervisor to play billiards (played by both girls and boys, though in same-sex groups), hopscotch (primarily a girls' game in this community), or various ball games (such as dodgeball and handball) on the expansive playground, which covered two city blocks.[9] Freed from adult supervision, they could organize their own activities, a situation that provided me an excellent opportunity to observe peer interaction.

Girls and boys were in proximity to each other during after-school hours, although they tended to play in same-sex groups. During hopscotch, girls protected the boundaries of their play space from boys' intrusions, delimiting their territory through what Barrie Thorne (1993), following Fredrik Barth (1969), has called "borderwork." When Spanish-speaking boys intruded into girls' space, girls would push them away. With commands such as *Get out of the way!* girls sanctioned the boys' behavior and marked them as different by switching to English when addressing them.

Such spatial considerations are crucial in the investigation of games like hopscotch, which are locatable in a particular area of the playground. Hopscotch is a "situated activity system" (Goffman 1961) involving a physical environment (a grid with nine spaces painted on a cement schoolyard; see figure 20.1) and procedures for moving within it. The object of the game is to be the first player to advance her beanbag from the lowest to the highest square and back again by means of a series of beanbag tosses and player jumps. From behind the start line, each player in turn tosses a beanbag into a square and, without changing feet, jumps to the end of the grid and back again on one foot, avoiding squares where beanbags have been tossed. If the player falls down or steps on a line or outside the appropriate square, she must forfeit her turn. When a player performs an infraction, "Out!" is called.

Once a game has begun, girls may either welcome new players, even permitting them to advance their beanbag to the same square theirs is on, or alternatively prevent newcomers from joining. Excluded girls may either protest their denial of entry into the game and wait on the sidelines as peripheral participants commenting on the

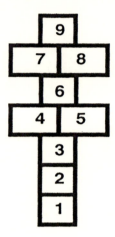

Figure 20.1. The hopscotch grid

play or they may form their own new game on an adjacent grid. Age and friendship are important factors influencing such decision making and alliance formation. In the data analyzed here, a group of fifth-grade girls who initiated the game prevented younger girls' participation as jumpers and ignored their judgment calls about plays. When the older girls went home, the younger girls initiated a new game and became outspoken critics of moves in progress.

Although it is commonplace to view a game with respect to its players, girls who observe and assess the game activity are equally relevant to the play. Onlookers are not random spectators; they have a vested interest in finding violations, for they get a chance to jump when a jumper forfeits her turn. As jumpers continually try to have their fouls overlooked, the job of girls on the sidelines is to vigilantly monitor or referee the ongoing action. However, if they are not ratified as valid participants, their judgments will be ignored.

A range of alignments to the action in progress is possible. Girls on the sidelines clap, jump up and down, and laugh loudly when other players miss. They seem to get as much pleasure from this activity as from jumping through the grid. Girls playfully tease those preparing to jump (or even in the midst of their jumps), lightly pushing them, spanking them, and trying to unnerve them—for example, pointing to their feet and shouting, "Un ratón! Un ratón!" (A mouse! A mouse!). In hopscotch, although the game is played to win, it is richly overlaid with multiple framings and textured nuances such as joking, tricking, and taunting.

Girls compete for being first in a round of hopscotch. During the course of the game girls will openly brag about their successful playing, sing-chanting, "Voy ganando, voy ganando EY::::::::::!" (I'm winning! I'm winning!) or "Qué bueno, yo voy en el último!" (How terrific, I'm going to the last square!). Although such statements are one way to claim one's relative position (which may be countered in subsequent interaction), trickery is another possibility. From the player's perspective, the most interesting part of the game is seeing what one can get away with, playfully extending possible definitions of the rules to make them fit the circumstances of the moment. Indeed, for the 20-minute session of hopscotch analyzed here, different girls selected from these alternative strategies for asserting their respective positions. One girl, a newcomer who lacked proficiency in executing some of the moves, proved quite skilled in tricking others and providing her own metacommentary on participation. Players are continuously engaged in testing the limits and boundaries of rules in this way.

Participant structure and the sequential structure of out-call sequences

In monitoring a player's activity, referees can call a foul in a number of different ways. Perhaps the most common is to yell, "Out!" and provide (1) an account for the out call (*Pisaste la raya!* 'You stepped on the line'), accompanied by (2) a demonstration of how it occurred, as in Example (1):

(1) 3:57:41
      1 Marta: *((jumps with one foot outside grid))*
      2 Roxana: ⌈Out.
      3 Carla: ⌊Out!
      4 Roxana: °Out.
      5 Marta: AY:::! *((throws up hands smiling, turning head))*
      6 Gloria: ⌈HAH HAH!
      7 Carla: ⌊Pisaste la raya! *((stepping multiple times on line where violation occurred))*
                   You stepped on the line.
      8 Gloria: *((claps hands three times excitedly while laughing))*
      9 Marta: *((throws beanbag to appropriate next square, ending her turn, and moves back to front of grid))*

Commentary on the game provides a way of displaying one's alignment toward the action in progress. During the activity of reacting to a violation, the display of affect occurs in a specific sequential position and is made relevant by practices for performing the out call. The preface is critical in constructing an opposition move, for it states quite literally a stance or footing with regard to the current action. In this example Roxana and Carla's out call and Carla's account (line 7)—*You stepped on the line!*—is followed by an animated demonstration. Carla intensifies her verbal sanctioning action by stepping several times on the line where the out occurred. Thus in multiple ways she performs the activity of evaluation.

In order for her action to count as an appropriate move in the language game of calling out, Carla's actions must be ratified by others present. The sequential organization of moves is important in that players build the game world by assessing whether their actions count as valid moves. In example (1) the referees' call is ratified not only by Gloria, another onlooker, through her laughter (line 6) and clapping (line 8) but also by the jumper Marta. Marta smiles while producing a response cry *AY:::* (line 5), closing her eyes and turning her head in a posture that displays her own humorous "take" on her foul. Through such moves she acknowledges her error and aligns herself with the positions of both onlookers; subsequently (line 9) she moves her beanbag to the next square, effectively marking that her turn has ended. The player's uptake—her response cry marking agreement with the call—contrasts with other possible displays, such as disgust or defiance (exhibited by stomping back to the start line, throwing another's beanbag across the playground, screaming, and so forth), and provides closure. The flagging of a problem leads quickly to an acknowledgment of error; the sequence thus has the character of a remedial sequence (Goffman 1971). The occasion-specific identities of *player* and *evaluator* are constructed through these actions.

If the jumper rejects an onlooker's judgment, however, the sequence will play out differently. Players frequently feign innocence and ignore out calls, especially when others who will support the player's position are present. In one instance, moments after two onlookers had called someone out, the player resumed her turn. Subsequently, when a first referee asked her coreferee "¿Verdad que sí está out, verdad?" (It's true that she's out, right?) the coreferee reversed her own prior ruling: "No sé. No me preguntas a mí" (I don't know. Don't ask me). The coreferee thereby aligned with the player's position against the other referee's call, and the player continued her turn. The identity of *friend-friend* is constructed when, as here, an onlooker sides with the player against a coevaluator's negative assessment.

The shape of out calls: Pitch contours

In children's arguments, turn shapes may display "aggravated correction" (M. Goodwin 1983). Whereas in adult forms of disagreement nonsalient intonation is preferred over expressions of disagreement (Yaeger-Dror 1986), children clearly signal opposition. In the next example an argument develops between Carla and Gloria over whose turn it is. When Carla declares, "Ya voy" (I'm going now), usurping Gloria's turn, Gloria states in response, "N'ai:::! Ya voy YO!" (No. I'm going now).

(2)   4:11:08
       Carla: Ya voy.
       Gloria: N'ai:::! Ya voy YO!

The oppositional turn vividly displays a strong emotional stance or footing, what we might gloss as outraged indignation at the first speaker's despicable behavior. How is this stance made visible? The speaker begins her oppositional turn with a preface, *N'ai*, announcing an objection to the prior move at the earliest possible opportunity. Moreover, this preface is spoken with a dramatic pitch excursion (see figure 20.2). Although the first speaker's talk is produced at a pitch between 300 and 400 Hz, the oppositional turn N'ai:::! leaps quickly and dramatically to 600 Hz. Within the single syllable of the preface, the second speaker's voice leaps from 400 to 600 Hz. The display of outrage, with its associated emotional components, is made visible as an embodied performance through the second speaker's voice and intonation. In addition, although in Spanish subject pronouns are not required, in Gloria's counter the

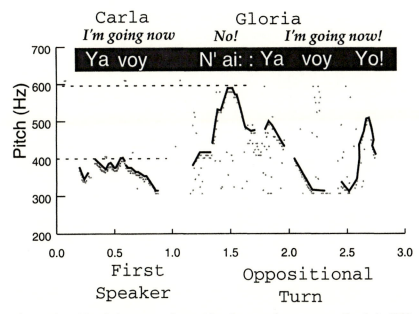

Figure 20.2. The pitch contour of oppositional turn prefaces. SOURCE: Goodwin 1998

pronoun YO! is appended to the end of the utterance and emphasized through "contrastive stress" (Ladd 1980:78); YO! is produced at 500 Hz.

Dwight Bolinger (1983) has hypothesized a relationship between higher vocal pitch and displays of increased excitement. In the present example, affective intensity is marked through vowel lengthening, singsong intonation, and raised volume. (The pitch at the beginning of example (2) is above 600 Hz; the girls' normal voice range is between 250 and 350 Hz.) However, pitch height does not function as an isolated, decontextualized display. Instead it becomes visible as a specific, meaningful event, by virtue of its embedding within a particular sequence of action.

Like the turn preface, the squeal of outrage is also indexically tied to the immediately prior action, which constitutes the point of departure for the display of opposition. The second speaker builds her moves within a field of meaning that has been brought into existence by the conditional relevance (Schegloff 1968) of the prior action. On the level of sound structure, pitch height becomes a salient action because it vividly contrasts with the preceding talk. In addition to pitch, participants may utilize posture and gesture to accuse another girl of having landed on a line while making a jump in hopscotch (M. Goodwin 1998). For example, out calls are frequently accompanied by pointing of the index finger, as shown in figure 20.3.

Turn construction in opposition moves

Sequential slots for the production of relevant responses provide participants with places where they can use a range of embodied activity to build appropriate action.

Carla: OUT! OUT!
Figure 20.3. Extended hand point in out call. SOURCE: Goodwin 1998

Polarity expressions such as *NO* (example 3), response cries (examples 4 and 5)—
terms such as *AY:!*, *EY!*, *Ou:!*, or *Ah:!*—and negative person descriptors (M. Goodwin
1990) such as *chiriona* (cheater) constitute important components of the turn, providing other ways to indicate the referee's alignment or affective stance toward a
prior action:

(3)

Gloria:	*((jumps from square 2 to square 1, changing feet))*	Problematic Move
Carla:	NO CHIRIONA!	Polarity Expression + Negative Person Descriptor
	No, cheater!	
	YA NO SE VALE ASÍ.	Explanation
	That way doesn't count anymore!	

(4)

Gloria:	*((takes a turn out of turn))*	Problematic Move
Carla:	AY: TÚ CHIRIONA!	Response Cry + Negative Person Descriptor
	Hey, you cheater!	
	EH NO PISES AQUÍ	Explanation
	Hey, don't step here.	
	PORQUE AQUÍ YO VOY!	
	Because **I'm** going here.	

(5)

| Gloria: | *((Jumps from square 3 to 2, changing feet))* | Problematic Move |
| | Carla: | EY::!! CHIRIONA! | Response Cry + Negative Person Descriptor |

Gloria: *((Jumps from square 3 to 2, changing feet))* — Problematic Move

Carla: EY::!! CHIRIONA! — Response Cry + Negative Person Descriptor
MIRA!
Hey! Cheater! Look!
TE VENISTES DE AQUÍ ASÍ! — Explanation
You came from here like this. *((demonstrating how Gloria jumped, changing feet))*

With negative person descriptors, referees argue not simply that an infraction has occurred but that the player's action is morally wrong. The term *chiriona*, derived from the English word *cheat* plus *-ona*, a Spanish agentive nominalizer or intensifier, provides an explicit characterization of the person whose move is opposed.[10] By using such a term, a judge argues not simply that an infraction has occurred but that the person who committed the foul is accountable for its occurrence. Following the opposition preface, a referee provides a reason why the move is invalid, often through a demonstration. Unlike the delayed disagreement in adult conversation (Pomerantz 1984; Sacks [1973] 1987), here the girls, through intonation and gestures (such as extended hand points), display opposition in no uncertain terms. The direct initiation of remedial sequences is consistent with other researchers' findings regarding children's practices of other-correction (Field 1994; Maynard 1986).

Breaking the rules

Some moves are deliberate violations; indeed, breaking the rules is very much a part of the game. This fact is illustrated in example (6), which occurs as Sandra, who joined the others after some 6 minutes of play, learns the rules of ABC. Looking toward the other players as she takes her third step a bit larger than permitted, the jumper herself keys her move as inappropriate through her laughter. The referees counter her move with a marker of polarity *NO::* (line 2), a response cry *AY:::* (line 3), and opposition turns containing negative person descriptors: *NO CHIRIONA!* (line 4) and *Cheater!* (line 7). Sandra persists in taking larger steps than are allowed. A referee shows her how she must place her feet precisely on the line, with each step aligning heel and toe of opposite feet, in contrast to the large steps she is taking. Her moves are countered again with *NO::* (line 9) and *AY:::!* (line 11), this time accompanied by a justification (lines 13–16): *QUE TIENES QUE METERTE EN LA RAYA DE AQUÍ LOS DOS JUNTITOS. AL OTRO PIE NIÑA!* (You have to put yourself on this line and put each foot close behind the other one, girl!). The verbal statement is accompanied by enactments of precisely how to place one's feet on the grid.

(6) 4:05:22
((Sandra has just been instructed in how to take baby steps according to ABC rules, putting the heel of one shoe against the toe of the other. Currently she is deliberately taking larger steps than permitted and laughing))

```
 1   Sandra:   A(hh) B, C (h) ((smiling))
 2   Gloria:   NO ⌈(lowers top part of body))
 3   Carla:        ⌊AY::: ((playfully giving Sandra a spank))
 4   Carla:    NO CHIRIO ⌈NA!
                           No, cheater!
 5   Sandra:               ⌊Okay.
 6   Sandra:   ⌈A
 7   Gloria:   ⌊Cheater!
 8   Sandra:   B, C.= ((taking big steps))
 9   Gloria:   NO::: ((body lowers dramatically))
10   Sandra:   ((smiles widely))
11   Carla:    AY:::!
12   Sandra:   ⌈Hih hih!
13   Carla:    ⌊QUE TIENES QUE METERTE
                You have to put yourself
14              EN LA RAYA
                on this line
                ⌈DE AQUÍ
15   Sandra:   ⌊Okay!
16   Carla:    LOS DOS JUN TITOS.
                and put each foot close
17              AL OTRO PIE NIÑA!
                behind the other one, girl!
```

The moves display various forms of opposition through their markers of polarity (*No* in lines 2, 4, 9), response cries (*Ay!*, lines 3, 11), negative person descriptors (*CHIRIONA*, line 4; *Cheater!*, line 7), and increased volume. At the same time the sequence is keyed with laughter by the jumper, Sandra. As Sandra takes a deliberately expansive step, Gloria lowers the top part of her body and produces a loud *NO* (line 2) and Carla pushes her out of the position at the start of the grid and shows her the appropriate way to take a turn. When Sandra takes even larger steps, Gloria displays her exasperation by lowering her torso as she states "No" (line 9). The interaction develops a multitextured ethos in which the judges playfully chide Sandra for her performance.

The same players who referee others' rule violations may themselves perform violations moments later. In (7), Carla, who 6 minutes earlier had critiqued the way Sandra was taking big rather than small steps, now attempts to rewrite the rules. Proposing a hypothetical version of the rules, she boasts that she is going to take four rather than three baby steps when she does ABC, arguing that the square to which she must advance (nine, the farthest square) is at some distance from her (*está más lejos*).

```
(7)  4:11:00
 1   Carla:    Ahora voy a hacer (.) cuatro ABC.
                Now I'm going to take four ABC steps.
 2   Gloria:   NO! Al cuatro no!
                No! Up to four! No!
```

3 Carla: Tiene que ser cuatro porque
            It's got to be four because
4 Carla: ya está más lejos.
            it's farther away.

Extensive negotiation and debate occurs. Far from attempting to avoid conflict, through forms of aggravated correction the girls here actively seek it out. Various keyings occur as coparticipants transform their affective alignment toward the game in different ways throughout its course.

A framework for comparison

Because many different groups play hopscotch, it provides an invaluable research tool for documenting cross-cultural variation in language use. Remarkable similarities can be observed in the way that Pico Union children and African American working-class children in rural South Carolina structure their opposition moves. As with the Pico Union children, for example, among the South Carolina children *Out* is yelled immediately after a foul (example 9):

(9) 10:47:26
     Lucianda: *((puts foot in square with token))*
     Joy: You ⌈out. *((pointing toward jumper))*
     Crystal: ⌊Out!
     Lucianda: I'm out.

Similarly, in both groups bolder, more authoritative stances occur when the judge not only proclaims the jumper out but intensifies her action through escalation of volume, physical pointing, and an explicit statement that a violation has occurred. Example (10) illustrates this pattern among the South Carolina children:

(10) 10:53:30–37
      Crystal: *((lands with foot in a square with a token on it))*
      Lucianda: YOU OUT. YOU ⌈OUT! *((pointing))*
      Crystal: ⌊Why.
      Lucianda: YOUR BO- YOUR FEET IN NUMBER **FIVE**!

Turns that begin with response cries are also similar in both groups; the African American out call in example (11) is prefaced by *Ah:* rather than the Spanish *Ay* and is followed by an out call, as well as an account:

(11) 11:15:13
      Lucianda: *((jumps stepping on lines))*
      Vanessa: Ah: ⌈Lucianda.
      Crystal: ⌊Out!
      Vanessa: Out- You step **between** the line.
                  Not **in** it.

Such authoritative stances are not unique to these two groups; I have observed similar turn shapes in arguments during hopscotch sessions among children of the fifth-grade ESL class mentioned in note 9. The population was roughly equivalent to the Pico Union school, and included children from Azerbaijan, Saudi Arabia, China, Korea, Vietnam, and Mexico.[11] By contrast, in my fieldwork among middle-class white girls from Columbia, South Carolina, children, rather than making definitive out calls, used hedges (*I think*, *sort of*, and so on) in moves such as *I think that's sort of on the line though* or *You accidentally jumped on that; but that's okay* (M. Goodwin 1998). Much more work is required to sort out the effects of ethnicity, age, and social class on norms of speaking.[12]

Although I have presented the materials here with respect to a particular context, that of Spanish-speaking children in Los Angeles, I have not demonstrated the grounds for the relevance of such categorizations in the talk of the children themselves. Many other explanations for behavior are possible, including age, gender, one's newness to the game, and friendship alliances. Similar turn structures for performing oppositional moves can be observed in the structure of interaction within other groups. Rather than focusing exclusively on the peculiarities of particular language-based groups, I prefer to be open to the possible universality of linguistic resources that children of both genders build upon to ratify or disconfirm particular visions of the self and identity (Capps & Ochs 1995).

Conclusion

Although anthropologists have documented variations on what are considered the canonical features of female speech, dichotomous views of female and male language persist, echoing Gilligan's (1982) view that girls speak in a unitary, nonconfrontational form of "different voice," one more concerned with an ethic of care than with the rules of the game. In line with such an essentialist position, the accepted wisdom on girls' play maintains that turn-taking games such as hopscotch are simple grids for the rotation of players through space, limiting girls' experience because they reputedly restrict dispute. As Lever states,

> Girls' turn-taking games progress in identical order from one situation to the next: prescriptions are minimal, dictating what must be done in order to advance. Given the structure of these games, disputes are not likely to occur. . . . Because girls play cooperatively more than competitively, they have less experience with rules per se, so we should expect them to have a lesser consciousness of rules than boys. (1978:479)

Lever's assessment of girls' activity echoes pronouncements of Jean Piaget, who argues that "the most superficial observation is sufficient to show that in the main the legal sense is far less developed in little girls than in boys" ([1932] 1965:77). According to Piaget, the game of hopscotch is "very simple and never presents the splendid codification and complicated jurisprudence of the game of marbles." He argues that few girls play marbles, and when they do they are more concerned with "achieving dexterity at the game than with the legal structure."

Such positions about girls' lack of interest in legal structure are unfounded and resemble essentialist accounts of women's language and psychology. The range of experiences encompassed in the game world of hopscotch seriously challenges characterizations of girls' play as limiting their development of social skills (Lever 1978). While playing hopscotch, girls are not simply playing *by* the rules but playing *with* the rules, and while judging the performances of their peers they are acquiring rhetorical and negotiating skills important for a range of circumstances in later life.

Close ethnographic investigation of girls' disputes during play shows that girls draw from a discourse repertoire (M. Goodwin 1990) and can incorporate cooperation and competition, legalistic language and laughter, within the interaction (Hughes 1988, 1993; Kyratzis 1992, 1994; Sheldon 1992, 1993). Footings or alignments to the action in progress shift as new positions are taken up. Stance is conveyed through body posture and affective intensity (Bradac, Mulac, & Thompson 1995) or highlighting (C. Goodwin 1994), as indicated through pitch leaps, vowel lengthening, and raised volume.

With new methods to document language use in social encounters, we no longer need to rely on a priori dualistic categories or interviews that yield information about language rather than linguistic practices. We are positioned to hear multivocality within women's and girls' speech across diverse groups and can analyze identity as shifting rather than static—"an activity or performance" rather than an attribute (McElhinny 1998:469). Arguing against a dualistic view of language and gender, Nancy Henley states that "a repeated lesson is that we must conceive of communication as socially and culturally situated action that is not universally determined by simplistically conceived gender, socialization, role, or personality" (1995:385). Through close analysis of talk in interaction we can show how individuals propose and demonstrate to each other the relevance of particular features of their identity operative on specific occasions of use.

APPENDIX: TRANSCRIPTION CONVENTIONS

Data are transcribed according to the system developed by Gail Jefferson and described in Sacks, Schegloff, & Jefferson (1974).

Cutoffs:	A dash (-) marks a sudden cutoff of the current sound.
Emphasis:	Underlining and **boldface** indicate some form of emphasis.
Overlap bracket:	A left bracket ([) marks the point at which the current talk is overlapped by other talk.
Lengthening:	Colons (::) indicate that the sound immediately preceding has been noticeably lengthened.
Intonation:	Punctuation symbols are used to mark intonation changes rather than as grammatical symbols. A period indicates a falling contour, a question mark indicates a rising contour, and a comma indicates a falling-rising contour.
Latching:	Equal signs (=) indicate latching—that is, there is no interval between the end of a prior turn and the start of a next piece of talk.

Inbreath:	An *h* preceded by an asterisk (*h) marks an inbreath.
Comments:	Double parentheses (( )) enclose material that is not part of the talk being transcribed. They frequently indicate gesture or body position.
Silence:	Numbers in parentheses (0.6) mark silences in seconds and tenths of seconds.
Increased volume:	Capitals (CAPS) indicate increased volume.

NOTES

I would like to acknowledge the following people: Salomé Santos and Carla Vale assisted in translating text; Mary Bucholtz, Patrick Gonzales, Roberta Chase-Borgatti, Alicia de Myhrer, Sally Jacoby, Pat Mason, Norma Mendoza-Denton, Marjorie Faulstich Orellana, Manny Schegloff, and Malcah Yaeger-Dror provided many useful comments; Chuck Goodwin helped in all stages of development. This research would not have been possible without Lori Cronyn, who introduced me to the teachers, principal, and children of the school where the study was conducted. I have benefited in countless ways through talks with her about children, schooling, language, and community in Pico Union.

1. On various notions of identity see Amélie Rorty and David Wong (1990). I am not using the term *identity* to refer to an aspect of one's individual nature but rather to aspects of the self that make a difference in how one conducts oneself.

2. Similarly, Ben Rampton (1995:486), countering what he terms "an absolutist view" of ethnicity, gender, and social class as "a discrete, homogeneous and fairly static cultural essence," argues that we need to look at how class, gender, or ethnicity is "activated in different ways in different contexts."

3. Marjorie Orellana (chapter 3, this volume) discusses ways in which, through "critical pedagogy," working-class Chicano children in a Los Angeles bilingual classroom learn to challenge the constraints of racism and poverty (while, however, less frequently questioning stereotypic gender roles).

4. Goffman (1971:62) defines ritual as "a perfunctory, conventionalized act through which an individual portrays his respect and regard for some object of ultimate value to that object of ultimate value or to its stand-in." He notes (1971:63) that although in contemporary society we rarely practice rituals to stand-ins for supernatural entities, we do display ritualistic behavior toward one another, "attesting to civility and good will on the performer's part and to the recipient's possession of a small patrimony of sacredness." By way of contrast, Turner (1988:75) defines ritual as "a transformative performance revealing major classifications, categories, and contradictions of cultural processes." He states that although he is concerned with "the performance of a complex sequence of symbolic acts," Goffman considers ritual "a standardized unit act, which may be secular as well as sacred."

5. The notion of stance is also developed in work on language and gender by Elinor Ochs (1992) and by Tannen (chapter 11, this volume).

6. Lever's findings are recycled in most literature on children and gender. See, for example, Evelyn Pitcher and Lynn Schultz (1983).

7. To take one example of this essentialized perspective, Peggy Orenstein, quoting the 1992 AAUW report on girls and education, states: "Latina girls report the greatest plunge in self-esteem of any girls surveyed. . . . In their teenage years, they have a more negative body image, are at greater risk of attempting suicide, and report higher levels of emotional stress— anxiety, depression, nervousness, insecurity, or exhaustion—than any other group of children, male or female, of any race or ethnicity" (1994:199).

8. In a May 1996 study of hopscotch at a comparable school in Columbia, South Carolina, with Spanish speakers from Mexico and Puerto Rico who had been in the United States for only a year, I found that children played the game almost exclusively in Spanish.

9. In other settings both girls and boys play hopscotch. In the Columbia study, I observed after-school and recess play in a magnet school. African American, Korean, Japanese, Saudi Arabian, and Mexican boys knew how to play the game. Moreover, girls and boys in a small ESL class of six students played hopscotch together.

10. Shana Poplack (1980) argues that codeswitching does not generally occur at a morpheme boundary unless one of the morphemes has been integrated phonologically into the language of the other. Norma Mendoza-Denton has pointed out to me that this example shows how the bilingual phonology of the children operates: The speaker begins with the English word *cheater* and codeswitches at a morphological boundary in the middle of the word by changing the /t/ of *cheat* to /r/. Although the vowel quality is primarily Spanish, the word has an English phonological process operating within it, with the intervocalic flapping of /t/.

11. Eighty-nine percent of the children in the magnet school received free lunches, and 10 percent were eligible for lunch at a reduced fee.

12. Working-class white children in the Baltimore community studied by Peggy Miller (1986) are socialized to be assertive when required to defend themselves. Donna Eder (1990:82) similarly argues that for the working- and lower-class white girls she studied "'toughness' is more highly valued and there is less concern about 'politeness.' " In contrast, the principal of the Columbia school where middle-class children's mitigated responses were observed actively promoted an ideology of conflict avoidance; such an ideology was consistent with the norms of the Unitarian Universalist Church, which two of the four girls in the study attended.

REFERENCES

Anzaldúa, Gloria (1987). *Borderlands / La frontera: The new mestiza*. San Francisco: Spinsters/ Aunt Lute.

——— (ed.) (1990). *Making face, making soul / Haciendo caras*. San Francisco: Aunt Lute.

Barth, Fredrik (1969). Introduction. In Fredrik Barth (ed.), *Ethnic groups and boundaries*. Boston: Little, Brown, 9–38.

Bing, Janet M., & Victoria L. Bergvall (1996). The question of questions: Beyond binary thinking. In Victoria L. Bergvall, Janet M. Bing, & Alice F. Freed (eds.), *Rethinking language and gender research: Theory and practice*. London: Longman, 1–30.

Bolinger, Dwight (1983). Intonation and gesture. *American Speech* 58:156–174.

Borman, Kathryn M., & Judith Frankel (1984). Gender inequities in childhood: Social life and adult work life. In Kathryn M. Borman, Daisy Quarm, & Sarah Gideonse (eds.), *Women in the workplace: Effects on families*. Norwood, NJ: Ablex, 113–135.

Borman, Kathryn M., & Lawrence A. Kurdek (1987). Grade and gender differences in and the stability and correlates of the structural complexity of children's playground games. *International Journal of Behavioral Development* 10(2):241–251.

Bradac, James J., Anthony Mulac, & Sandra A. Thompson (1995). Men's and women's use of intensifiers and hedges in problem-solving interaction: Molar and molecular analyses. *Research on Language in Social Interaction* 28(2):93–116.

Butler, Judith (1990). *Gender trouble: Feminism and the subversion of identity*. New York: Routledge.

Capps, Lisa, & Elinor Ochs (1995). *Constructing panic: The discourse of agoraphobia*. Cambridge, MA: Harvard University Press.

Coates, Jennifer (1991). Women's cooperative talk: A new kind of conversational duet? In Claus Uhlig & Rüdiger Zimmermann (eds.), *Proceedings of the Anglistentag 1990 Marburg.* Tübingen: Max Niemeyer Verlag, 296–311.

—— (1994). The language of the professions: Discourse and career. In Julia Evetts (ed.), *Women and career: Themes and issues in advanced industrial societies.* London: Longman, 72–86.

Coupland, Nikolas, & Jon F. Nussbaum (eds.) (1993). *Discourse and life span identity.* Newbury Park, CA: Sage.

Coupland, Nikolas, Jon F. Nussbaum, & Alan Grossman (1993). Introduction: Discourse, selfhood and the lifespan. In Nikolas Coupland & Jon F. Nussbaum (eds.), *Discourse and life span identity.* Newbury Park, CA: Sage. x-xxxviii.

Eckert, Penelope (1989). The whole woman: Sex and gender differences in variation. *Language Variation and Change* 1:245–267.

Eckert, Penelope, & Sally McConnell-Ginet (1992). Think practically and look locally: Language and gender as community-based practice. *Annual Review of Anthropology* 21:461–490.

Eder, Donna (1990). Serious and playful disputes: Variation in conflict talk among female adolescents. In Allen D. Grimshaw (ed.), *Conflict talk: Sociolinguistic investigations of arguments in conversations.* Cambridge: Cambridge University Press, 67–84.

Falk, Julia (1980). The conversational duet. In Bruce R. Caron et al. (eds.), *Proceedings of the Sixth Annual Meeting of the Berkeley Linguistics Society.* Berkeley, CA: Berkeley Linguistics Society, 507–514.

Field, Margaret (1994). On the internalization of language and its use: Some functional motivations for other-correction in children's discourse. *Pragmatics* 4(2):203–220.

Foster, Michèle (1995). "Are you with me?": Power and solidarity in the discourse of African American women. In Kira Hall & Mary Bucholtz (eds.), *Gender articulated: Language and the socially constructed self.* New York: Routledge, 329–350.

Freed, Alice (1995). Language and gender. *Annual Review of Applied Linguistics* 15:3–22.

Freeman, Rebecca, & Bonnie McElhinny (1995). Teaching language, challenging gender. In Nancy Hornberger & Sandra McKay (eds.), *Sociolinguistics and language teaching.* Cambridge: Cambridge University Press, 218–280.

Galindo, D. Letticia (1992). Dispelling the male-only myth: Chicanas and caló. *Bilingual Review* 17(1):3–35.

—— (1994). Capturing Chicana voices: An interdisciplinary approach. In Mary Bucholtz, A. C. Liang, Laurel A. Sutton, & Caitlin Hines (eds.), *Cultural performances: Proceedings of the Third Berkeley Women and Language Conference.* Berkeley, CA: Berkeley Women and Language Group, 220–231.

Galindo, D. Letticia, & María Dolores Gonzales Velásquez (1992). A sociolinguistic description of linguistic self-expression, innovation, and power among Chicanas in Texas and New Mexico. In Kira Hall, Mary Bucholtz, & Birch Moonwomon (eds.), *Locating power: Proceedings of the Second Berkeley Women and Language Conference.* Berkeley, CA: Berkeley Women and Language Group, 162–170.

Giddens, Anthony (1990). *The consequences of modernity.* Cambridge: Polity Press.

Gilligan, Carol (1982). *In a different voice: Psychological theory and women's development.* Cambridge, MA: Harvard University Press.

Goffman, Erving (1961). *Encounters: Two studies in the sociology of interaction.* Indianapolis: Bobbs-Merrill.

—— (1971). *Relations in public: Microstudies of the public order.* New York: Harper & Row.

—— (1979). *Gender advertisements.* Cambridge, MA: Harvard University Press.

—— (1981). Footing. In Goffman, *Forms of talk.* Philadelphia: University of Pennsylvania Press, 124–159.

Gonzales Velásquez, María Dolores (1992). The role of women in linguistic tradition and inno-vation in a Chicano community in New Mexico. Ph.D. diss., University of New Mexico.

Goodenough, Ward H. (1981). *Culture, language and society*. Menlo Park, CA: Benjamin/Cummings.

Goodwin, Charles (1994). Professional vision. *American Anthropologist* 96(3):606–633.

Goodwin, Marjorie Harness (1983). Aggravated correction and disagreement in children's conversations. *Journal of Pragmatics* 7:657–677.

——— (1990). *He-said-she-said: Talk as social organization among black children*. Bloomington: Indiana University Press.

——— (1998). Games of stance: Conflict and footing in hopscotch. In Susan Hoyle & Carolyn Temple Adger (eds.), *Language practices of older children*. New York: Oxford University Press, 23–46.

Gumperz, John J. (ed.) (1982). *Language and social identity*. Cambridge: Cambridge University Press.

Gumperz, John J., & Jenny Cook-Gumperz (1982). Introduction: Language and the communication of social identity. In John J. Gumperz (ed.), *Language and social identity*. Cambridge: Cambridge University Press, 1–21.

Henley, Nancy M. (1995). Ethnicity and gender issues in language. In Hope Landrine (ed.), *Bringing cultural diversity into feminist psychology: Theory, research, practice*. Washington, DC: American Psychological Association, 361–395.

Heritage, John, & J. Maxwell Atkinson (1984). Introduction. In J. Maxwell Atkinson & John Heritage (eds.), *Structures of social action*. Cambridge: Cambridge University Press, 1–16.

Hughes, Linda (1988). "But that's not really mean": Competing in a cooperative mode. *Sex Roles* 19:669–687.

——— (1993). "You have to do it with style": Girls' games and girls' gaming. In Susan Tower Hollis, Linda Pershing, & M. Jane Young (eds.), *Feminist theory and the study of folklore*. Urbana: University of Illinois Press, 130–148.

Jackson, Jean Elizabeth (1974). Language identity of the Colombian Vaupés Indians. In Richard Bauman & Joel Sherzer (eds.), *Explorations in the ethnography of speaking*. Cambridge: Cambridge University Press, 50–64.

Jacobs, Sue-Ellen, & Jason Cromwell (1992). Visions and revisions of reality: Reflections on sex, sexuality, gender and gender variance. *Journal of Homosexuality* 23:43–69.

Jameson, Fredric (1984). *Postmodernism, or, The cultural logic of late capitalism*. Durham, NC: Duke University Press.

Kalčik, Susan (1975). ". . . like Ann's gynecologist or the time I was almost raped": Personal narratives in women's rap groups. In Claire R. Farrer (ed.), *Women and folklore: Images and genres*. Austin: University of Texas Press, 3–11.

Keenan, Elinor Ochs (1974). Norm-makers, norm-breakers: Uses of speech by men and women in a Malagasy community. In Richard Bauman & Joel Sherzer (eds.), *Explorations in the ethnography of speaking*. Cambridge: Cambridge University Press, 125–143.

Kramarae, Cheris (1990). Changing the complexion of gender in language research. In Howard Giles & W. Peter Robinson (eds.), *Handbook of language and social psychology*. New York: Wiley, 346–361.

Kulick, Don (1992). Anger, gender, language shift and the politics of revelation in a Papua New Guinean village. *Pragmatics* 2(3):281–296.

——— (1993). Speaking as a woman: Structure and gender in domestic arguments in a New Guinea village. *Cultural Anthropology* 8(4):510–541.

Kyratzis, Amy (1992). Gender differences in children's persuasive justifications during pretend play. In Kira Hall, Mary Bucholtz, & Birch Moonwomon (eds.), *Locating power: Proceedings of the Second Berkeley Women and Language Conference*. Berkeley, CA: Berkeley Women and Language Group, 326–337.

———— (1994). Tactical uses of narratives in nursery school same-sex groups. In Mary Bucholtz, A. C. Liang, Laurel A. Sutton, & Caitlin Hines (eds.), *Cultural performances: Proceedings of the Third Berkeley Women and Language Conference.* Berkeley, CA: Berkeley Women and Language Group, 389–398.

Ladd, D. Robert Jr. (1980). *The structure of intonational meaning: Evidence from English.* Bloomington: Indiana University Press.

Lave, Jean, & Etienne Wenger (1991). *Situated learning: Legitimate peripheral participation.* Cambridge: Cambridge University Press.

Le Page, Robert Brock, & Andrée Tabouret-Keller (1985). *Acts of identity: Creole-based approaches to language and ethnicity.* Cambridge: Cambridge University Press.

Leaper, Campbell (1991). Influence and involvement in children's discourse: Age, gender and partner effects. *Child Development* 62:797–811.

Lever, Janet Rae (1978). Sex differences in the complexity of children's play and games. *American Sociological Review* 43:471–483.

Maynard, Douglas W. (1986). The development of argumentative skills among children. In Patricia A. Adler & Peter Adler (eds.), *Sociological studies of child development.* Vol. 1. Greenwich, CT: JAI Press, 233–258.

McElhinny, Bonnie S. (1995). Challenging hegemonic masculinities: Female and male police officers handling domestic violence. In Kira Hall & Mary Bucholtz (eds.), *Gender articulated: Language and the socially constructed self.* New York: Routledge, 217–244.

———— (1998). Strategic essentialism in sociolinguistic studies of gender. In Natasha Warner, Jocelyn Ahlers, Leela Bilmes, Monica Oliver, Suzanne Wertheim, & Melinda Chen, (eds.), *Gender and belief systems: Proceedings of the Fourth Berkeley Women and Language Conference.* Berkeley, CA: Berkeley Women and Language Group, 469–480.

Mendoza-Denton, Norma (1996). "Muy macha": Gender and ideology in gang-girls' discourse about makeup. Paper presented at the annual meeting of the American Association for Applied Linguistics, Symposium on Gendered Discourse Communities, Chicago.

Miller, Peggy (1986). Teasing as language socialization and verbal play in a white working-class community. In Bambi Schieffelin & Elinor Ochs (eds.), *Language socialization across cultures.* Cambridge: Cambridge University Press, 199–212.

Miller, P. M., D. L. Danaher, & D. Forbes (1986). Sex-related strategies for coping with interpersonal conflict in children aged five and seven. *Developmental Psychology* 22:543–548.

Moore, Joan W. (1991). *Going down in the barrio: Homeboys, homegirls in change.* Philadelphia: Temple University Press.

Moore, Sally Falk (1978). *Law as process: An anthropological approach.* London: Routledge & Kegan Paul.

Morgan, Marcyliena (1996). Women's narratives in the English-speaking African diaspora: Identity and memory. Paper presented at the annual meeting of the American Association for Applied Linguistics, Symposium on Gendered Discourse Communities, Chicago.

Ochs, Elinor (1992). Indexing gender. In Alessandro Duranti & Charles Goodwin (eds.), *Rethinking context.* Cambridge: Cambridge University Press, 335–358.

Orenstein, Peggy (1994). *Schoolgirls: Young women, self-esteem and the confidence gap.* New York: Doubleday.

Piaget, Jean (1965). *The moral judgment of the child.* New York: Free Press. (Original work published 1932)

Pitcher, Evelyn Goodenough, & Lynn Hickey Schultz (1983). *Boys and girls at play: The development of sex roles.* New York: Praeger.

Pomerantz, Anita (1984). Pursuing a response. In J. Maxwell Atkinson & John Heritage (eds.), *Structures of social action.* Cambridge: Cambridge University Press, 152–164.

Poplack, Shana (1980). "Sometimes I'll start a sentence in Spanish y termino en español": Toward a typology of code-switching. Linguistics 18:581–618.

Rampton, Ben (1995). Language crossing and the problematisation of ethnicity and socialization. *Pragmatics* 5(4):485–513.

Rorty, Amélie Oksenberg, & David Wong (1990). Aspects of identity and agency. In Owen Flanagan & Amélie Oksenberg Rorty (eds.), *Identity, character, and morality: Essays in moral psychology.* Cambridge: MIT Press, 19–36.

Sacks, Harvey (1987). On the preferences for agreement and contiguity in sequences in conversation. In Graham Button & John R. E. Lee (eds.), *Talk and social organisation.* Clevedon, England: Multilingual Matters, 54–69.

Sacks, Harvey, Emanuel A. Schegloff, & Gail Jefferson (1974). A simplest systematics for the organization of turn-taking for conversation. *Language* 50:696–735.

Sadker, Myra, & David Sadker (1994). *Failing at fairness: How America's schools cheat girls.* New York: Scribner's.

Schegloff, Emanuel A. (1968). Sequencing in conversational openings. *American Anthropologist* 70:1075–1095.

Sheldon, Amy (1992). Conflict talk: Sociolinguistic challenges to self-assertion and how young girls meet them. *Merrill Palmer Quarterly* 38:95–117.

————— (1993). Pickle fights: Gendered talk in preschool disputes. In Deborah Tannen (ed.), *Gender and conversational interaction.* Oxford: Oxford University Press, 83–109.

Sutton-Smith, Brian (1979). The play of girls. In Claire B. Kopp & Martha Kirkpatrick (eds.), *Becoming female.* New York: Plenum, 229–257.

Thorne, Barrie (1993). *Gender play: Girls and boys in school.* New Brunswick: Rutgers University Press.

Troemel-Ploetz, Senta (1992). The construction of conversational equality by women. In Kira Hall, Mary Bucholtz, & Birch Moonwomon (eds.), *Locating power: Proceedings of the Second Berkeley Women and Language Conference.* Berkeley, CA: Berkeley Women and Language Group, 581–589.

Turkle, Sherry (1995). *Life on the screen: Identity in the age of the Internet.* New York: Simon & Schuster.

Turner, Victor (1985). The anthropology of performance. In Edith Turner (ed.), *On the edge of the bush: Anthropology as experience.* Tucson: University of Arizona Press, 177–204.

————— (1988). *The anthropology of performance.* New York: PAJ.

Urciuoli, Bonnie (1991). The political topography of Spanish and English: The view from a New York Puerto Rican neighborhood. *American Ethnologist* 18:295–310.

Woolard, Kathryn A. (1997). Between friends: Gender, peer group structure and bilingualism in urban Catalonia. *Language in Society* 26(4):533–560.

Yaeger-Dror, Malcah (1986). Intonational prominence on negatives in English. *Language and Speech* 28:197–230.

Zentella, Ana Celia (1997). *Growing up bilingual.* Oxford: Blackwell.

NAME INDEX

Abelson, Robert, 47, 49, 55
Abrahams, Roger, 30, 31, 32, 33, 242, 252, 320
Abu-Lughod, Lila, 183
Ackerman, Lillian A., 196n1
Ackroyd, Peter, 315
Adams, David Wallace, 185, 189, 196, 197, 197n2
Aftel, Mandy, 308n8
Agar, Michael, 49
Allen, Barbara, 246
Alleyne, Mervyn, 31
Allport, Gordon W., 203
Althusser, Louis, 10
Amin, Qasim, 215n1
Angier, Natalie, 223
Anyon, Jean, 74, 79
Anzaldúa, Gloria, 4–5, 6, 21n2, 392
Arnold, June, 334, 338–343, 340
Aronoff, Mark, 103
Aronowitz, Stanley, 355
Arrindell, Willem A., 85
Atkins, Beryl, 105
Atkinson, J. Maxwell, 97n1, 390
Atwell, Nancie, 64
Austin, Bryn, 169
Austin, J. L., 18, 343

Bahan, Ben, 62n2
Bakalti, Souad, 215n1
Bakhtin, Mikhail M., 47, 110, 129, 243, 253, 318

Baldwin, Karen, 243, 246
Ball, Arnetha F., 31
Bankhead, Tallulah, 267
Barlow, David H., 87
Baron, Beth, 215n1
Baron, Dennis, 333, 345n2
Barrett, Rusty, 7, 9, 10, 11, 18, 65, 70, 104, 114, 164, 234, 259, 300, 308n7, 313–327, 337, 349, 390
Barth, Fredrik, 393
Barthes, Roland, 152, 156
Bascom, William, 243
Bateson, Gregory, 84, 223, 226, 308n2, 308n4
Bateson, Mary Catherine, 238n2
Bauman, Richard, 8, 50, 242, 250, 253, 319
Baumeister, Roy, 51
Beame, Thom, 317
Bean, Judith Mattson, 8
Beaver, Patricia Dunne, 245, 251, 252
Beavin, Janet, 90
Becker, A. L., 224–225
Belenky, Mary Field, 244
Bell, Allan, 178n1, 202, 384
Bell, Genevieve, 197n2
Ben Ali, Zine El Abidine, 214
Bennett, Gillian, 243–244, 255n1
Benveniste, Emile, 338

Berendt, John, 321
Bergvall, Victoria, 20, 21n1, 101, 104, 123, 388
Berle, Milton, 315–316
Berman, Laine, 245
Biber, Douglas, 176
Billson, Janet Mancini, 31
Bing, Janet M., 20, 21n1, 101, 104, 123, 388
Blake, Renee, 31
Blakeslee, Sandra, 203
Blanchard, Edward B., 87
Boas, Franz, 101, 103, 106
Bodine, Anne, 5, 101, 102, 103, 117n1
Bolinger, Dwight, 397
Bonvillain, Nancy, 103, 104
Booker, Karen, 108
Borker, Ruth A., 238, 274
Borland, Katherine, 245
Borman, Kathryn, 391, 392
Bourdieu, Pierre, 10, 201, 202–203, 355
Bourguiba, Habib, 211, 214
Bourke, Angela, 377, 384n4
Boxer, Andrew, 268, 269n1
Boykin, Keith, 317
Bradac, James J., 403
Breuer, Josef, 84
Brice, Colleen, 117n3
Briggs, Charles L., 8, 250, 319
Brody, Jill, 372, 374
Brooke, Robert E., 64

411

SUBJECT INDEX

Ideologies
of appearance, 59–60
definition of, 52
of femininity, 85, 123–141
of gender in British teenage girls'
conversations, 14, 123–141
heterosexist ideologies, 52–53, 57, 60
of homosexuality, 60
in lesbians' coming-out stories, 52–53, 55,
57, 58, 60
and letters of Native American mothers to
boarding-school officials, 15, 181–196
overview of identity as, 14–16
patriarchal ideologies, 348
in Tunisian gender and culture negotiation,
15–16, 200–215
WOMAN AS DESSERT metaphor, 14–15,
145–158
iGuide, 166
Illiteracy. *See* Education; Literacy
Implicature
gay implicature, 300–307, 308nn9–10
gender as, 295
Indecent Proposal, 153
Indians. *See* Native Americans
Instigating, 33–36, 37, 41. *See also* He-said-
she-said disputes
Interaction
among African American women and girls,
30–41
in African American children's language
play, 32–36
agoraphobic identity and family interactions,
86–97
"behind your back/in your face" dichotomy
in, 37–41
of British teenage girls, 125–141
cool social face and, 31–32, 36–37, 41
cross-sex interactions, 6, 7, 15–16, 67, 69,
206–215, 388
emergent narratives as interactional, 86
gay implicature, 300–307, 308nn9–10
he-said-she-said disputes, 33, 41
immanent reference of talk, 300
Latinas' interactional practices while playing
hopscotch, 19–20, 388–404
in lesbians' coming-out stories, 48–49
Native American women's letters to boarding
school officials, 181–196
reading dialect, 36–37
resources for and constraints on, 48–49
between shopping channel host and callers,
357–364
turn-initial *no* among Latina adolescents,
273–291

workplace interactions, 16, 229–238
See also Conversation; Discourse; Language
Internal colonialism, 370, 384n2
Internet
e-mail, 12, 51, 54–58, 308–309n11
gender blurring on, 390
online journals, 166–168, 174–178
online shopping, 350, 365n2
Intertextuality
in British teenage girls' conversations, 124,
129, 135–136
definition of, 48
resources and constraints and, 48–49
Intimacy. *See* Friendship; Love and romance
Ireland
compulsory Irish in schools in, 384n5
and Irish language generally, 370–371,
384n1, 385n7
preservation ideology in, 376–377, 384n4
women and language maintenance, 371
women's role in, 375–384, 384n3, 385n8
See also Irish-language radio
Irish language, 370–371, 374–376, 384n1. *See
also* Irish-language radio
Irish-language radio
Anglo discourse structure on, 374–375, 376
effects of, on language maintenance and
identity, 374–376
English discourse markers on, 377–382
and enhancement of status of language, 372
Raidío na Gaeltachta (RnaG), 372–376, 379
Raidío na Life (RnaL), 373–382, 384
reframing of gender roles through media
language, 376–384
and use of Irish language generally, 370–371,
375, 384n1
women's participation in, 375–384, 384n3,
385n8
Irish-language television, 376
Irrationality and agoraphobia, 13, 83–97
Islam, 15–16, 200–215
Italy, 309n13
It's a Wonderful Life, 160n8

Japan, 225, 228, 295
Japanese language, 108, 114
Java, 228
Jellybean, 177
Jews
collaborative disagreement among Jewish
Americans, 282
definition of Jewishness, 308n3
Joning, 32–33. *See also* Signifying
Journals. *See* Online journals
Judas Rose (Elgin), 343–344

Lakhota "women's language" and "men's
  language," 13–14, 101–117
languages of, in decline, 103, 105–106, 116,
  181, 371
literacy levels of, from 1916–1922, 182
Native Tongue (Elgin), 343–344
Navajo, 104
Neologisms, 334–344
New Guinea, 389
Nonstandard language
  in alternative media, 165, 168, 170–172, 176
  by shopping channel callers, 356–357
  See also African American English; African
    American Vernacular English;
    Vernacular
Novelas on Spanish television, 73, 74, 80n2
Novels. *See* Fiction

Objectification. *See* WOMAN AS DESSERT
  metaphor; WOMAN AS OBJECT metaphors
Occasion-specific identities, 391, 393–395, 396
Oklahoma, 102, 183
Online journals, 166–168, 174–178
Opoponax (Wittig), 333, 345n3
Opposition. *See* Disagreement; Resistance
Other American Dialects (OAD), 30

"Passing"
  by drag queens, 314, 319
  by female impersonators, 314
  by lesbians and gay men, 297, 305, 307
Patriarchal ideologies
  in British teenage girls' conversations, 127–
    128, 135, 136–137, 138
  popular culture and, 52–53, 163, 348
Pejoration, 150–152
Performance, anthropology of, 390
Performance frame, 50, 59
Performances of drag queens, 18, 313–327
Performed identity, 8, 307, 317–320, 323–327
Personal narratives. *See* Life stories and
  personal narratives
Phonetics, 152, 154–156
Phonology, 102–103, 209–211
Phonosemantics, 155–156
Pitch contours in hopscotch participants, 396–397
Pixxiebitch, 164, 171, 178n5
Play. *See* Games
Pleasure, 348–349, 350, 352, 363–365
Polysemy, 222, 320
Popular media
  alternative media, 15, 163–178
  computer-mediated communication (CMC),
    167–168, 174–178
  control of "mainstream" media, 165
  discourse analysis and, 349

and enhancement of status of language, 372
heterosexist ideologies portrayed by, 52–53
homosexuality portrayed in, 46, 260–261
identity and, 164
Irish-language radio, 19, 369–384
Irish-language television, 376
newspaper and magazine articles on
  teleshopping, 356, 366n8
Novelas on Spanish television, 73, 74, 80n2
online journals, 166–168, 174–178
patriarchal ideologies in, 348
retrieving gay messages from, 264, 266–267
self-publishing and, 164–178
sexism and, 52–53, 163, 348
shopping channel, 19, 348–365
soap operas, 125, 130, 267
sociolinguistics and, 163, 164–165
targeted to women, 163, 351
Tunisian television, 214–15
women's participation in, 375–384, 384n3,
  385n8
zines, 165–174, 177–178
Positioning, 224, 225
Postcolonialism, 203–215
Postfeminism, 124–125
Postmodernism, 28
Poststructuralism, 241
Poverty, 29–30, 77–78, 317
Power
  American view of, 225
  Cooperative Principle of conversation and,
    17–18, 293–307
  dominance as theory of language and gender,
    5–6
  Japanese view of, 225
  Native American women's letters to boarding
    school officials, 181–196
  politics of gender identity, 10–11
  power imbalances in cross-sex interactions, 6
  resistance and, 183
  in stories by Latina/o primary-grade students,
    77–78
  See also Status
Practice
  Butler on, 22n4
  definitions of, 22n4
  Eckert and McConnell-Ginet on, 8–9, 22n4
  identity and practice-based analysis, 8–9, 317, 389
  "marginal" members and, 8–9
Pragmatics
  Cooperative Principle of conversation and,
    17–18, 293–307
  covert meanings in lesbian and gay
    communication, 18, 300–304
  Latina teenagers' alignment and disalignment
    discourse, 17, 273–291